Revelation

"Rob Dalrymple's well-researched and well-documented (yet very readable) commentary challenges many of the misinterpretations of Revelation in vogue today. He rightly sees the last book of the Bible as a story of God's nonviolent love in Christ, and therefore a summons to hope and to sacrificial, Christlike witness. This commentary should be widely read and its interpretation taken seriously."

—**Michael J. Gorman**, chair in biblical and theological studies,
St. Mary's Seminary & University

"The Book of Revelation has long been considered to stand in irreconcilable tension with a core tenet of Christian theology, namely that God is love. Rob Dalrymple's winsomely written and accessible commentary boldly challenges this judgment. He offers a much-needed summons to readers to respond to Revelation not with speculation and fear about the future, but rather with fearless witness and work on behalf of the kingdom of our God and of his Christ in the present."

—**David A. deSilva**, distinguished professor of New Testament and Greek,
Ashland Theological Seminary

"Rob Dalrymple's Revelation commentary is mind-blowing, hope-filled, and energizing. The Bible's final word is a letter from King Jesus to his church then and now! The letter reinforces our mission as citizens of the kingdom of God and followers of Jesus. We aren't passive spectators waiting to be evacuated out of this mess. Jesus calls us into the mess as indispensable kingdom agents in God's rescue operation of the world he loves. Revelation jars us awake to the urgency of the moment. Take up and read!"

—**Carolyn Custis James**, author of *Half the Church: Recapturing God's Global Vision for Women*

Revelation

A Love Story

Rob Dalrymple

FOREWORD BY
Scot McKnight

CASCADE *Books* • Eugene, Oregon

REVELATION
A Love Story

Copyright © 2024 Rob Dalrymple. All rights reserved. Except for brief quotations in critical publications or reviews, no part of this book may be reproduced in any manner without prior written permission from the publisher. Write: Permissions, Wipf and Stock Publishers, 199 W. 8th Ave., Suite 3, Eugene, OR 97401.

Cascade Books
An Imprint of Wipf and Stock Publishers
199 W. 8th Ave., Suite 3
Eugene, OR 97401

www.wipfandstock.com

PAPERBACK ISBN: 978-1-6667-3356-3
HARDCOVER ISBN: 978-1-6667-2830-9
EBOOK ISBN: 978-1-6667-2831-6

Cataloguing-in-Publication data:

Names: Dalrymple, Rob, author. | McKnight, Scot, foreword.
Title: Revelation : a love story / Rob Dalrymple ; foreword by Scot McKnight.
Description: Eugene, OR: Cascade Books, 2024. | Includes bibliographical references and index.
Identifiers: ISBN 978-1-6667-3356-3 (paperback). | ISBN 978-1-6667-2830-9 (hardcover). | ISBN 978-1-6667-2831-6 (ebook).
Subjects: LCSH: Bible. Revelation—Commentaries.
Classification: BS2825.53 D37 2024 (print). | BS2825.53 (ebook).

VERSION NUMBER 08/01/24

This book is dedicated to our son Jason Robert Dalrymple d2004 and to all those who have lost a loved one.

The book of Revelation is a book of hope.

A hope that we will dwell in the presence of the Eternal One: where we will "see His face."

A hope that someday there will be no more death, or mourning, or crying, or pain.

A hope that someday there will be no more hunger or thirst.

A hope that we will not need to fear the onslaught of torrential rains and floods, or the fierceness of the scorching sun and drought.

A hope that we will live without fear.

A hope that we will live in peace.

And a hope that we will be reunited with loved ones for eternity.

For my wife and me, we long for that day when we will get to meet our son and be with him forever! And to share the joy with all of you as you embrace those you have lost as well; especially the ones you never met.

Contents

List of Excursi | xi
Foreword by Scot McKnight | xv
Preface | xvii
Acknowledgments | xxi

Introduction
    Chapter 1: Introduction: Revelation as a Love Story | 1
    Chapter 2: The Structure of the Book of Revelation | 3
    Chapter 3: Reading Revelation as a Narrative | 12
    Chapter 4: Understanding John's Purpose | 17
    Chapter 5: John's Use of Numbers | 21
    Chapter 6: Understanding the Message of Revelation | 28

Commentary
1:1-8 The Epilogue
    1:1-8 Epilogue | 37

1:9—3:22 The First Story/Scene
    1:9–20 John's Vision on Patmos | 57
    2:1—3:22 The Seven Messages | 74

4:1-16:21 The Second Story/Scene (The Heavenly Vision)
    4:1—5:14 John Taken to Heaven: Throne Room Scene | 95
    4:1—5:14 Throne Room Scene: Continued | 105

CONTENTS

6:1-17 The First Six Seals | 119
7:1-17 An Interlude: The 144,000 and the Great Multitude | 138
8:1—9:22 Seventh Seal and the First Six Trumpets: Introduction | 153
8:1—9:22 Seventh Seal, Introduction to the Trumpets: continued | 162
10:1—11:13 An Interlude: The Scroll and the Two Witnesses | 180
10:1—11:13 An Interlude: The Scroll and the Two Witnesses Continued | 190
11:15-19 The Seventh Trumpet | 210
12:1-18 The Woman and the Dragon | 215
13:1—14:5 The Beast, the False Prophet, and the 144,000 | 234
13:1—14:5 The Beast, the False Prophet, and the 144,000 Continued | 246
13:1—14:5 The Beast, the False Prophet, and the 144,000 Continued again | 255
14:6-20 Six "Another" Angels and One Like the Son of Man | 262
15:1—16:21 The Seven angels and the Seven Bowls | 270
15:1-8 The Seven Angels and the Overcomers | 276
16:1-21 The Seven Bowls Introduction | 281

17:1—19:10 The Third Scene: The Great Prostitute—Babylon
    17:1-17 The Great Prostitute: Introduction | 299
    17:1-17 The Great Prostitute | 307
    18:1—19:10 The Fall of Babylon and the Three Hallelujahs | 319

19:11—21:8 The Fifth "Bridge" Scene
    19:11—21:8 Transition Between the Fall of Babylon and the Descent of the New Jerusalem | 333
    19:11-16 The Returning Christ | 336
    19:17-21 Judgment of the Beast and the False Prophet | 345
    20:1-10 The Judgment of the Dragon (Satan) | 348

20:11–15 The Great White Throne judgment | 366
21:1–8 New Creation: The Introduction to the Holy City | 368

21:9—22:9 The Fourth Scene: The Bride/Holy City
21:9–27 The Bride Is the Holy City | 377
22:1–5 The Bride Is the New Eden | 390

22:6–21 Epilogue
22:6–21 Epilogue | 401

Conclusion | 411

Resources for Recommended Next Steps | 415
Bibliography | 417
Appendix: Repetition of Key Terms and Phrases | 423
Scripture Index | 439

List of Excursi

Understanding Revelation in Contrast to Popular Teachings	31–33
Revelation as an Apocalypse	38–40
The Book of Revelation and Symbols	42–44
The Authorship and Date of the Book of Revelation	45–46
Revelation as a Prophecy	46–47
Revelation as a Letter	47–48
The People of God as Kings/Queens and Priests	52
Jesus's Sword and Divine Violence	67–69
Reconciling God's Love and Wrath	80–82
John's Anti-Imperial Agenda	102–04
Hearing and Seeing	107
The Nations and Revelation's Narrative	109–11
The Scroll	114–15
Overcoming	115–16
The Seals and Jesus's Eschatological Speech (Mark 13)	122–23
Grain and the Economy of Rome	128–29
God's Delay in Bringing Justice	132–33
144,000 as Holy Warriors	142–43
Are the 144,000 Ethnic Israelites?	143–45
The Great Multitude as Holy Warriors	145–46

LIST OF EXCURSI

The Great Multitude and the Holy City/New Jerusalem	148–49
Identifying the 144,000 and the Great Multitude	150–52
John's Use of Literary Features to Advance the Narrative in the Seals, Trumpets, and Bowls	154–56
The Meaning of *Ouai*	166–67
Understanding the Seals and the Trumpets and John's Narrative Aims	171–73
Understanding the Seals in Light of John's Narrative	173–74
Understanding the Trumpets in Light of John's Narrative	175
The Role of the Fifth and Sixth Trumpets and the Prayers of the Saints	176–77
The Prayers of the Saints, the Seven Trumpets, and the Plagues in Egypt	177–79
Is the Scroll that Jesus Took from the Father's Hand (5:1–14) the Same As the Scroll in the Angel's Hand (10:1–11)?	183–87
Why Are They Measured?	196
John's Use of Various Designations of Time to Express Three and One-Half Years: "Forty-Two Months," "1,260 Days," and "A Time, Times, and Half a Time"	198–200
Who Are the Two Witnesses?	206–07
The Two Witnesses and John's Narrative	213–14
The Beast as a Parody of Christ	239–40
666	251–52
What is the Mark of the Beast	258–61
The Two Harvests, the Prayers of the Saints, and the Martyrs' Cry for Justice	267–69
Armageddon Part 1	290–92
The Roman Backdrop to John's Account of the Great Prostitute	303–05
Who/What Is the Prostitute?	309–12
John's Portrayal of Women and Patriarchy	315–18
Economic Prosperity and the Apocalypse	323–24

LIST OF EXCURSI

What Does This Mean for Western Christians Today?	328–30
John's Use of Ezekiel in the Closing Chapters of Revelation	335
The Millennium Part 1	354–56
Armageddon Part 2	356–58
The Millennium Part 2	359–60
The Demonic Hordes in the Fifth and Sixth Trumpets and the Judgment of Satan	360–63
The Millennium Part 3	363–64
The Martyrs Reign for 1,000 Years	364–65
How John's Use of "To Show" Indicates Structure within This Section	378–80
John's Use of the Number Twelve in the Account of the Holy City	383–85
John and Ezekiel's City-Temples	391–93
The Contrast Between the Bride and the Great Prostitute	396–97

Foreword

THE SUBTITLE TO ROB Dalrymple's fresh, valuable, and path-breaking study of the Book of Revelation ("A Love Story") ought to be the clue that what follows will not be boilerplate commentary as usual.

Something about Revelation has utterly captured me for more than five decades: the beginning and the ending of this most confusing, but brilliant, of New Testament books. To begin with, Revelation's opening is a more than over the top vision of Jesus Christ who then sends messages through John to seven churches. Think about this: at the time John sent this apocalypse to those seven churches there would have been only several hundred followers of Jesus in western Asia Minor. I'm guessing on the number because guessing is all we can know. Let's say at most one thousand. In other words, they are on the margin of the already marginalized in the Roman empire. If we then turn to the ending of Revelation, skipping visions and bizarre moments and battles and unearthly moments, we discover a worldwide chorus of singing and praising humans who somehow have been added to that group of maybe a thousand. That ending, even more important than the numbers, is a world at peace because injustice has been disestablished and justice has been established. That ending of peace and justice was established, not by some mighty military machine, like the one we might call Operation Rome, but by a lion-morphed-into-a-Lamb who, instead of wielding a sword in its fist, spoke sword-like words about God, about history, about justice, about creation, about evil, and about the victory of goodness.

I'm amazed, at least weekly, by the number who read Revelation for words about winning, about triumphalism, about vindication, and even about vindictiveness. Too many look for secrets for the defeat of their political and national enemies. Not so with the Lamb in the Book of Revelation. This Lamb fights the battles of love and grace and goodness and justice. Of course, this book is an apocalypse, and apocalypses gonna apocalypse, and that means there's got to be some kind of battle and some kind of defeat and some kind of victory. But the battle is cosmic, the defeat is of evil, and the victory is the Lamb's. Not Rome's. The gruesome scenes unmask the sicknesses and systemic evils of humans cooperating and collaborating with one another to aggrandize power and shove good folks off the stage. On the other side of this cosmic battle are the good people of God who long for justice, who are willing to pay the price even of martyrdom, and who work day by day in the ordinary moments of life for what God wants for all creation.

The way of Revelation is the way of love and the way of hope—for a world loved by God and in love with God and with one another. It takes a mind willing to flex and a heart ready to soar for many today to grasp the love nature of Revelation. No one is more set to help us read Revelation anew more than Rob Dalrymple, who has been teaching, preaching, and pastoring Revelation for decades. His book is courageous, careful, and compelling. What Rob provides for us is a narrative reading of Revelation—he locks us into listening to John until we hear his voice, see his face, and watch has he moves characters onto and off the stage. Instead of speculating about Who today might correspond to Who in the Book of Revelation, Rob settles it by shutting the door on speculation so we can encounter this book all over again. As if for the first time. This time, with a vision for a loving God redeeming God's people and God's creation in order to reset creation for an eternity that will go on and on with each day advancing the previous day.

Scot McKnight
Professor of New Testament
Author with Cody Matchett, *Revelation for the Rest of Us*

Preface

THERE IS MORE TO say. There is always more to say. But since I have already graciously received two extensions from the editors at Cascade Books and all good things must come to an end, I have come to the realization that I need to recognize that I have said enough and that I cannot say everything. Nor do I need to say everything. There are plenty of fine works on the book of Revelation that have already said so much.

Why the present work then? This commentary aims to contribute to our understanding of the book of Revelation by uniquely focusing on Revelation's narrative, which I contend is a love story. It is my conviction that far too many interpreters, especially, though not limited to, the popular writers, have not only failed to recognize Revelation as a narrative but, in many instances have come to embrace an understanding of the book of Revelation that at times and to varying degrees runs counter to the biblical story. In particular, the common approach to the book of Revelation, while acknowledging that God so loved the world that He gave His only Son, somehow also claims that He loves the world so much He is going to bring famine, war, and bloodshed upon its inhabitants in order to persuade those who survive to repent.

In *Revelation: A Love* Story, I contend that John's narrative begins with the assertion that with the coming of Christ—His life, death, resurrection, and ascension—God has already begun the process of bringing about both the redemption of humanity[1] and the restoration of His creation. John's narrative affirms that the means by which God continues His work of bringing about this New Creation is through the faithful, loving, and sacrificial lives of His people who, like Christ, die and

---

1. Unfortunately, the book of Revelation affirms that not all are redeemed.

are vindicated. That is, just as the process of redeeming humanity and the creation began with the life, death, resurrection, and ascension of Christ, so also it continues through His people who "follow the Lamb." Hence, the story is a love story. The story, of course, is good news and it is also news that calls for "patient endurance" on the part of the people of God who cry out, "How long, Lord?"

What then, you might ask, do we do with the plagues and devastation that Revelation is famous for? In *Revelation: A Love Story*, I argue that the Seven Seals and the Seven Trumpets, and to a lesser extent the Seven Bowls, depict the inevitable consequences that take place when humanity rules apart from the "fear of the Lord" (Prov 1:7): namely, it is human rule that brings about deception and blasphemous ideologies, that results in and promotes war, which itself brings famine and death, and the destruction of the very creation for which we were created to care. The "plagues of God's wrath," in other words, are the result of human rule, which only continues because of God's gracious delay in bringing the final judgment.

The consummation of this story occurs when Christ returns to vindicate His people, who will stand in His presence and "see His face." Christ's return marks the final judgment of the Beasts, the Dragon, Death and Hades, and all who refuse to acknowledge God's gracious love. In doing so, the throne of God and Christ descends, the earth and the heavens are made anew, death and sorrow are done away, and the Edenic restoration is made complete.

It is my conviction that in order to recognize the book of Revelation as a love story we must recognize both the structure of the Apocalypse and John's consistent use of repetition as the means by which he guides his reader/hearers. This commentary, therefore, aims to examine the text of the Apocalypse in order to point out the literary features that John has embedded in his narrative and by which the love story unfolds. I should note, of course, that because this commentary endeavors to highlight how John's love story plays out in the narrative pages of the Apocalypse, I have chosen to omit some of the introductory features that often accompany a biblical commentary: such as author, date, and place of writing. Some of these questions will be addressed in the scope of this work—though some are relegated to the footnotes.

Finally, the commentary itself is riddled with various *excursi*. These *excursi* are vital to the overall understanding of the book of Revelation and its application to the contemporary church.

PREFACE

As with any writer, there is always more to say. In fact, I said to much already. Earlier drafts of this work far exceeded the number of words in my original contract with Cascade Books. As I result, I had to delete a significant amount of the original content. I agree that the book is a better work as a result.

Rob Dalrymple

June 2023

Acknowledgments

FIRST I WANT TO thank my wife for her understanding when it came to the long hours and late nights that were needed to complete this task.

I also want to thank Ian Spencer for his input throughout this entire project. Ian is a gifted thinker and writer and his assistance throughout this project was tremendous. This book would not have been completed without his assistance. It certainly would not have been very good. I am privileged to consider Ian a friend.

In addition, I want to thank others who reviewed and commented on drafts and portions of this work: including, Jace Broadhurst, Carolyn Custis James, David Crump, Vinnie Angelo, Ian Paul, and Curtis Lillie.

I also want to thank everyone who attended my classes and seminars on the book of Revelation—especially my Wednesday night/Thursday morning Zoom Bible study (you are like a family to me). Thank you for allowing me the privilege to teach you and to speak into your life. Thank you for your feedback, questions, and critical examination of all that I taught.

Chapter 1

Introduction: Revelation as a Love Story

The Johannine story of salvation is in essence a love story.[1]

The story underlying the Apocalypse is the story of Jesus.[2]

The slain Lamb's victory through suffering love is the heart of the Revelation story.[3]

Introduction

THIS COMMENTARY CONTENDS THAT the book of Revelation is a narrative in which the redemption of the nations and the arrival of the New Creation are brought about through the faithful, loving, and sacrificial lives of God's people. Consequently, the pressing questions of, "When will His kingdom come in all its fullness?"[4] and "How are the nations redeemed?" are answered in the narrative pages of the book of Revelation with, "As soon as the faithful, loving, and sacrificial witness of God's people is finished."[5] Hence, the book of Revelation is a love story.

1. Coloe and Schneiders, *Dwelling in the Household of God*, loc. 270.
2. Barr, *Tales*, loc. 167.
3. Rossing, *Rapture Exposed*, 135.
4. This question is expressed by the souls under the altar who cry out "How long, Lord?" (6:10).
5. Bauckham has argued most persuasively that the theme of the conversion of the nations serves as "the center of the prophetic message of Revelation" (Bauckham,

That the book of Revelation is a love story should not come as a surprise—though I suspect it does. After all, the book of Revelation simply carries forward the story of Jesus.[6] And the story of Jesus is that in Him, the kingdom of God has come and it has come through love. As perhaps the most famous verse in the Bible says, "For God so loved the world, that He gave His only begotten Son" (John 3:16).[7] Paul also affirms, "God demonstrates His own love toward us, in that while we were yet sinners, Christ died for us" (Rom 5:8). This is why Paul can say, "the kindness of God leads you to repentance" (Rom 2:4).

It is my conviction that the book of Revelation continues God's grand love story and, in fact, it brings that story to its consummation.[8]

Climax, 238).

6. Richard Hays notes, "The larger point, however, is not only that placing Revelation within the New Testament canon leads to a nonviolent reading of the text, but that the book's vivid depictions of God, Christ, and the church must all be construed as part of a larger narrative whole" (Hays, *Revelation and the Politics of Apocalyptic Interpretation*, loc. 1894).

7. All citations of the biblical text outside of the book of Revelation are from the NAS. Those within the book of Revelation are the author's.

8. As N.T. Wright says, "The story Revelation tells is the same story that all four Gospels tell" (In Hays, *Revelation and the Politics of Apocalyptic Interpretation*, loc. 2760).

Chapter 2

The Structure of the Book of Revelation

A remarkable feature of the composition of Revelation is the way in which very many phrases occur two or three times in the book, often in widely separated passages, and usually in slightly varying form. These repetitions create a complex network of textual cross-reference, which helps to create and expand the meaning of any one passage by giving it specific relationships to many other passages. . . . We are dealing with . . . a skillfully deployed compositional device. One reason we can be sure of this is that such phrases almost never recur in precisely the same form. The author seems to have taken deliberate care to avoid the obviousness of precise repetition, while at the same time creating phrases which closely allude to each other.[1]

Introduction

IN ORDER TO FOLLOW the narrative flow of the book of Revelation it is vital to recognize the structure of the book. As Stephen Dempster remarks, "The structure of a literary work, particularly its beginning and ending, shapes its content. The structure provides a means of organizing the vast array of information, imparting form and contour to the material, arranging the many sub-plots into a larger pattern."[2]

Unfortunately, when it comes to recognizing the structure of the book of Revelation there has been little agreement within the scholarly

---

1. Bauckham, *Climax*, 22.
2. Dempster, *Dominion and Dynasty*, 46.

world. At times it seems as though the number of proposals forms a one-to-one correspondence with the number of scholars.[3] Although there are many reasons why scholarship has not reached a consensus when it comes to the structure of the book of Revelation, the complexity of John's presentation, and the "rhetorical skill of the author," as Schüssler Fiorenza describes it, are certainly chief among them.[4] Yet, while it is true that John has woven a complex, literary masterpiece, it is my contention that he has not left us without clues: clues that he intended for us to find.

John's Verbal Clues as Key Indicators of the Structure of the Book of Revelation

Richard Bauckham contends that the body of the book of Revelation has four major sections: 1:9–3:22; 4:1—16:22; 17:1—19:10; 21:9—22:9.[5] Bauckham defends this conclusion by claiming that John's primary tool for indicating the larger structure of the Apocalypse was verbal repetition: "For structural markers to be effective in oral performance they needed to employ such precise verbal repetition."[6] Bauckham adds, "In a text intended for oral performance the structure must be indicated by clear linguistic markers."[7]

Although I largely agree with Bauckham's assessment of the structure of the book of Revelation and John's use of repetition as a means of indicating the macro-structure of the book of Revelation, I do not believe that Bauckham's assertion that John uses verbatim repetition completely withstands scrutiny.[8] John is notorious, as we will see, for varying phrases and expressions. In addition, it is difficult to determine what constitutes "verbatim repetition." Furthermore, there are several instances in which John repeats something verbatim that does not indicate macro-structure.[9]

---

3. Barr, *Tales*, loc. 391–93. See also: Bauckham, *Climax*, 1–37; Beale, *Revelation*, 108–51; Yarbro Collins, *Combat Myth*, 5–55; Schüssler Fiorenza, "Composition," 344–66; and her, *Revelation*, 159–80; Giblin, "Structural," 487–504; Sweet, *Revelation*, 35.

4. See Schüssler Fiorenza, *Revelation*, loc. 540–41; also Bauckham, *Climax*, 1.

5. Note that Bauckham's delineation has omitted 19:11—21:8. I will address this below.

6. Bauckham, *Climax*, 23.

7. Bauckham, *Climax*, 3; emphasis original.

8. Though the point at hand may well be what does Bauckham mean by "verbatim."

9. For example, each of the seven messages repeats verbatim, "Let the one who has an ear hear what the Spirit is saying to the churches" (2:7, 11, 17, 29; 3:6, 13, 22). Also, both 21:5 and 22:6 repeat the expression, "these words are faithful and true." Yet these

Therefore, it is my contention that Bauckham's view needs an additional point of clarification. That is, John indicates major structural transitions within the book of Revelation by his use of verbal repetition and by the fact that these repetitions occur alongside significant transitions, most notably, a change of location for John himself. When it comes to minor transitions or transitions within the various scenes, John also employs verbal repetitions. This means that we can discern John's indications of macro-structure (i.e., major transitions within the book) from those of micro-structure (i.e., transitions within a larger defined section) both by the extensiveness of the verbal repetition[10] and by the presence of a change of location for John himself as he narrates his vision.

The Macro-Structure of the Book of Revelation

Prologue and Epilogue

It is widely recognized that the book of Revelation begins with a prologue (1:1–8) and ends with an epilogue (22:6–21).[11] In the prologue, John identifies himself as the recipient of the vision (1:4). He also identifies his audience as the "seven churches that are in Asia" (1:4) and as those to whom he offers "grace and peace" (1:4). The epilogue contains a closing "amen" (22:20) and a final offer of "grace" to the reader/hearers (22:21).

The prologue and the epilogue are also marked with promises of blessing (1:3; 22:7, 14). The prologue offers a blessing for the one "who reads,"[12] for those who "hear the words of the prophecy," and for those who "keep" them (1:3). The epilogue offers a blessing, which may also be understood as a warning, for, "the one who keeps the words of the prophecy of this book" (22:7).

---

verses are not an indication of macro-structure.

10. Though, contrary to Bauckham, the instances of extensive repetition are not always absolutely "verbatim" (4:1, 17:1; 21:9).

11. Though virtually all of scholarship agrees with this, many contend that the epilogue begins in 22:9. In doing so, they overlook the fact that several times in the Apocalypse John overlaps sections. Thus, 22:6–8 serves as both the conclusion of 21:9—22:9 and as the opening of the epilogue (22:6–21).

12. Note that Rev 1:3 includes a blessing to the one who reads" (singular) and "those who hear" (plural). This is singular because in the ancient world, they did not have a Bible in every pew. They would, in fact, be fortunate to have a single copy of a book. That single copy was then read aloud to everyone else who "heard" it.

Four main scenes[13]/sections and the fifth bridge section

In accordance with the proposal set forth by Bauckham and my clarification of it, I would affirm that the body of the book of Revelation (1:9—22:9) contains four main scenes or sections (1:9—3:22; 4:1—16:21; 17:1—19:10; 21:9—22:9).[14]

There is also an additional section in 19:11—21:8, which functions as a bridge between the third and fourth scenes.[15] Because this is not a "major" section in the Apocalypse, that is, this section does not include a change of location for John and thus it is not a new "scene," I am referring to it as a "fifth section" in order to distinguish it from the four major scenes—even though chronologically it is the fourth in terms of the order of the chapters within the book of Revelation.[16]

"In The Spirit" and "I Will Show You" as Indicators of the Four Main Scenes

That the four main scenes form the basic outline of the book of Revelation is supported by the fact that they all begin with John being "in the Spirit" (1:10; 4:2), or being carried, "away in the Spirit" (17:3; 21:10).[17] In addition, the final three scenes include the added phrase, "I will show you."[18]

1:9–10: "I, John, . . . was in the Spirit. . . ."

---

13. That they are "scenes" derives from the fact that John is writing a narrative and that they take place in a different location.

14. Part of the complexity of the structure of the book of Revelation is evident in the fact that John overlaps some sections. Thus, 22:6-9 serve as both the beginning of the epilogue and as the conclusion to the fourth scene. By overlapping sections, John informs his reader/hearers that there is an overall unity to the book. Bauckham notes, "To insist on assigning these verses to only one or other of these sections, as most previous scholars have done, is to misunderstand John's literary methods, among which are the overlapping and interweaving of sections of his work" (Bauckham, *Climax*, 5).

15. Bauckham labels this bridge scene "as a single section describing the transition from one to the other" (Bauckham, *Climax*, 5).

16. Recognizing this section as a distinct section within the book of Revelation is significant when it comes to the interpretation of the millennium passage (20:4–6) and questions pertaining to the Great White Throne judgment (20:11–15).

17. Which Bauckham would suggest are verbatim repetitions.

18. I will address why the first section does not contain, "I will show you" below.

THE STRUCTURE OF THE BOOK OF REVELATION

4:1–2: "After these things . . . , the first voice which I heard as a trumpet was speaking with me, saying, 'Come up here, and I will show you what must happen after these things.' Immediately I was in the Spirit. . . ."

17:1–3: "Then one of the seven angels who had the seven bowls came and spoke with me, saying, 'Come, I will show you the judgment of the great Prostitute who sits on many waters.' And he carried me away in the Spirit."

21:9–10: "And one of the seven angels who had the seven bowls full of the seven last plagues came and spoke with me, 'come, and I will show you . . . and He carried me away in the Spirit . . . ."

In accord with my proposition that the major transitions in the book of Revelation also serve to carry forth a narrative, it is important to note that each of these four scenes is marked by the fact that John is in a different location (Patmos, heaven, a wilderness, and a mountain). The first scene occurs with John "in the Spirit" on Patmos (1:9). In the second scene, he is "in the Spirit" and taken to heaven (4:1–2). In the third scene, John is "in the Spirit" and taken to a wilderness (17:3). Then, in the final scene, John is "in the Spirit" and taken to a "great and high mountain" (21:10). The change in locations (Patmos, heaven, a wilderness, and a mountain) provide natural transitions within a narrative work.[19] That these are the only occasions in the book of Revelation in which John is both "in the Spirit" and in which he changes locations serves as a justification for understanding them as indicators of major structural significance.[20]

---

19. This is similar to the way Luke structures his narrative. The Gospel of Luke indicates major changes by including a significant transition, usually consisting of a scene change with new characters and a new topic. For example, note how the narrative of Luke 15:1—17:10 is an extended section. The parables of Luke 15:3–32, which are in response to the Pharisees and scribes grumbling (15:1–2) are carried along with simple transitions: "And He told them this parable" (15:3); "And He said" (15:11). Luke 16:1 begins, "Now he was also saying to His disciples." The only transition that Luke provides us with is the fact that Jesus now turns to address His disciples. Note that in Luke 16:14, Luke introduces new dialogue partners, but not a change of scene: "Now the Pharisees, who were lovers of money, were listening" (16:14). The beginning of Luke 17 continues the previous section also. It begins with, "And He said to His disciples" (17:1). It is not until we reach 17:11–12 that Luke changes scenes by introducing new characters and a new location: "While He was on the way to Jerusalem, He was passing between Samaria and Galilee. As He entered a village, ten leprous men who stood at a distance met Him. . . ."

20. See Tenney, *Interpreting Revelation*, 33; Ladd, *Revelation*, 14; Bauckham,

The fact that in each of these four instances, John is said to have been "in the Spirit" (1:10; 4:2), or that he was "carried away in the Spirit" (17:3; 21:10), that each of the latter three instances is marked by the use of "come" (4:1; 17:1; 21:9),[21] and "I will show you" (4:1; 17:1; 21:9), and the fact that in 4:1-2, 17:3, and 21:10 John changes locations, suggests that these four scenes serve as a major indication of structure in the book of Revelation.

Finally, that the latter three scenes all have the additional expression, "and I will show you" (4:1; 17:1; 21:9), which are the only occasions in which "show" appears as a future verb in the book of Revelation, also contends that these verses serve as an indicator of structural importance. We might note that the command to "come" and the accompanying phrase "I will show you" are absent from the opening scene (1:9-10). Does this not mitigate against the suggestion that John uses "come" (4:1; 17:1; 21:9) and "I will show you" (4:1; 17:1; 21:9) as a marker of major structural transition? The answer to this observation is fairly simple. That John is not commanded to "come" in 1:9-10 derives from the fact that this scene occurs where John is already at. He does not need to "come" or to go anywhere. Instead, Jesus comes to him! Furthermore, the absence of "I will show you" from the opening scene may be accounted for on the basis that what John sees in the opening scene relates to what is before him. That is, John does not need to be shown anything, all he must do is look and see. In the latter three scenes (4:1—16:21; 17:1—19:10; 21:9—22:9), however, John is taken somewhere in order that he may see something.[22]

In light of the conclusion that the macro-structure of the book of Revelation is indicated by these four scenes, we can now begin to add some depth to our examination of the structure of the book of Revelation.

Climax, 3; Beale, *Revelation*, 111; Smith, "Structure," 384-92.

21. That John uses the adverb "come" in 17:1 and 21:9 and not the verb as in 4:1 may be accounted for more because of John's desire to connect 17:1—19:10 and 21:9—22:9 than to disconnect them from 4:1—16:21.

22. Note: one should not understand the phrase "I will show you" as though John was seeing the future. Instead, "I will show you" (4:1; 17:1; 21:9) refers to what will happen when John is obedient and "comes." This is an important distinction. John is writing a vision report. What happens "next" often refers to the order of events within the vision and not the order of events as they occur in space-time.

THE STRUCTURE OF THE BOOK OF REVELATION

Revelation's Four Major Scenes/Sections

In the opening scene or section, John is on the island of Patmos (1:9–3:22). John then sees the resurrected, glorified Jesus (1:12–20), who commands him to write what he sees and send it to the seven churches: Ephesus, Smyrna, Pergamum, Thyatira, Sardis, Philadelphia, and Laodicea (1:11). The primary content in this scene are the seven messages[23] to the seven churches (2:1—3:22).

A new scene appears in 4:1-2. This second scene, the heavenly vision, comprises the central section of the book of Revelation (4:1—16:21).[24] In this scene, John is "in the Spirit" (4:2) and taken to heaven where he sees the Father: i.e., the "One sitting on the throne" (4:2). As the scene develops, John sees that there is a Scroll in the Father's hand (5:1), which, much to John's chagrin, no one was worthy to open (5:3-4). John is then relieved when he learns that the Lamb of God who was slain is worthy to open the scroll (5:5-6).

The third (17:1—19:10) and fourth scenes (21:9—22:9) clearly parallel one another.[25] This is evident in that they begin with virtually identical introductions:

> And one of the seven angels who had the seven bowls came and spoke with me, saying, 'Come, I will show you the judgment of the great Prostitute who sits on many waters' (17:1).
>
> And one of the seven angels who had the seven bowls full of the seven last plagues came and spoke with me, saying, 'Come, I will show you the bride, the wife of the Lamb' (21:9).

---

23. Bauckham adamantly asserts that the messages to the seven churches are not letters as they are commonly referred to, but something more along the lines of "messages" (private correspondence, June 2022). That the seven messages are introduced with the common expression, "Thus says" (2:1, 8, 12, 18; 3:1, 7, 14), which in the LXX regularly introduces the message of a prophet, certainly justifies the conclusion that they are seven prophetic messages and not letters. See Smalley, *Revelation*, 60.

24. Barr divides this scene into two movements (Barr, *Tales of the End*, 11–23.). Barr's proposal, however, fails to account for the fact that John utilizes a change of scene for himself, who is carried away "in the spirit" and shown something as a means of identifying major structural transitions. What Barr presents as his third story (12–22) has no such change of scenery. And though, as I will discuss in the commentary below, Barr is correct that there is a transition that occurs in 12:1 (or 11:19), the transition is within the section and should be not considered as the beginning of a new section.

25. Bauckham asserts, "These structural markers delimiting the two parallel sections—17:1—19:10 and 21:9—22:9-are so clear that it is astonishing that so many attempts to discern the structure of Revelation have ignored them" (Bauckham, *Climax*, 4).

In addition, the endings of these two scenes parallel one another in that each closes with John falling down to worship an angel (19:10; 22:8), only to be told not to do that, but to "worship God" (19:10; 22:9):[26]

> Do not do that; I am a fellow-servant of yours and your brothers and sisters who hold the testimony of Jesus; worship God (19:10).

> Do not do that. I am a fellow servant of yours and of your brothers and sisters the prophets and of those who keep the words of this book. Worship God (22:9).[27]

Furthermore, these two scenes are thematically connected. Both describe women—the third scene narrates the account of the "Great Prostitute" (17:5) and the fourth scene tells us of the "Bride" (21:9)—which are actually two cities.

The final two scenes, therefore, are contrasting depictions of two women that are in fact cities.

The (Fifth) Bridge Scene 19:11—21:8[28]

It is my conviction that 19:11—21:8 functions as an independent section in the Apocalypse. This section is organized around the repeated phrase "And I saw," which occurs eight times in this section (19:11, 17, 19; 20:1, 4, 11, 12; 21:1).[29]

---

26. The fact that John clearly identifies the end of each of these two scenes by means of the similar endings, affirms that 19:11—21:8 functions as a bridge section between these two sections.

27. The parallel structure of the two accounts provides an explanation as to why John attempts to worship an angel for the second time. One might have thought that John learned his lesson from his first attempt and the accompanying rebuke (19:10). Why would he do so a second time? In fact, on the second occurrence, John even says, "I fell down to worship before the feet of the angel" (22:8). If, however, the repetition of his ill-warranted action serves as a structural device, then the difficulty is alleviated.

28. It is not uncommon for many to view this bridge section as a part of the narrative of the Great Prostitute. John Christopher Thomas outlines the book of Revelation in the exact same manner as I have done, except he fails to recognize this bridge section as a distinct section in the book of Revelation. See Koester, *Oxford Handbook*, 331–51.

29. Many scholars have identified the use of "And I saw" in this unit but have mistakenly asserted that it occurs seven times. How they arrive at seven, when there are indisputably eight occurrences is somewhat baffling. See Bauckham, *Climax*, 5–6.

The first "And I saw" (19:11) serves to introduce the account of the Second Coming of Jesus (19:11–16) and the eighth and final "And I saw" (21:1) marks the introduction of the new creation.

In the middle of this bridge section, the phrase "And I saw" occurs six times. These six occurrences form three pairs (19:17, 19; 20:1, 4; and 20:11, 12). The first pair forms the subunit of 19:17–21 and presents the final judgment of the Beast and the False Prophet. The second pair forms the subunit of 20:1–10 and describes the final judgment of the Dragon/Satan (20:1–10).[30] The third pair forms the subunit 20:11–15 and recounts the final judgment of everyone whose name "has not been found written in the book of life" (20:15). It should be noted that each of these three middle units concludes with enemies of Christ being cast into the Lake of Fire (19:20; 20:10; 20:14).

Although this bridge scene is clearly set apart from the accounts of the two women/cities, this does not intend to diminish the significance of this scene within the overall narrative of the book of Revelation. In particular, this bridge scene necessarily presents the coming of Christ and the final judgment of the Beasts, the Dragon/Satan, and Death/Hades, and in doing so, paves the way for the descent of the Holy City/New Jerusalem.

---

30. It cannot be overstated the importance of recognizing the structure of this section for the discussion of the "millennium" passage.

Chapter 3

Reading Revelation as a Narrative

> *It is easy to miss the most important thing for understanding the Apocalypse: it is a narrative.*[1]

It is my contention that it is necessary to read the book of Revelation narratively: that is, in light of the narrative, or narratives, that John is setting forth. In particular, the first two scenes (1:9—3:22 and 4:1—16:21) present two stories.

The First Story/Scene: John on Patmos (1:9—3:22)

The first narrative takes place with John on the island of Patmos (1:9). The story opens with John hearing a voice "like a trumpet" (1:10) which instructs him to write what he sees and to send it to the seven churches (1:10–11). In writing the seven messages to the seven churches, John carries out what he was instructed to do by the voice in 1:10–11.

At this point, we might expect the book of Revelation to conclude. After all, as David Barr points out, "In the first story John is commissioned to write to the seven churches; and he does so. And when that task is finished, the audience has no reason to suppose there's anything more to the story. But instead of ending, the story simply shifts as a door opens in the sky and John is told to ascend."[2]

---

1. Barr, *Tales*, loc. 149.
2. Barr, *Tales*, loc. 4543–51.

The story, however, does not come to an end. Instead, 4:1—16:21 presents us with a second, though intimately related, story/scene.

The Second Story/Scene: John in Heaven; the Heavenly Vision (4:1—16:21)

The second and, perhaps, central story in the narrative of the book of Revelation, begins in 4:1-2 where John is taken to heaven (4:2).

The story begins with John seeing the Father sitting on a throne (4:2).[3] As the story continues, John adds that the Father has a Scroll in His right hand that is sealed shut with seven Seals (5:1). The suspense increases when we learn that "no one was able . . . to open the book or to look at it" (5:3). John, in fact, begins to weep because no one was able to open the Scroll (5:4). His concerns, however, are allayed when He learns that Jesus, the Lamb, is able to open the Scroll (5:5-6). Jesus then takes the Scroll from the Father's hand (5:7).

This second story continues as Jesus begins to open the Scroll by breaking each of its seven Seals (6:1-17; 8:1). Although we are led to anticipate the revealing of the Scroll's contents after the breaking of the Seventh Seal, we are instead introduced to seven angels who are given Seven Trumpets (8:2).

It is not until 10:1-11 that Scroll reappears. John sees "another strong angel" (10:1), who has in his hand a Scroll which was "open" (10:2).[4] John then hears a "voice from heaven" (10:8), which tells him to take the Scroll from the angel. John subsequently asks the angel for the Scroll (10:9) and is instructed by the angel to "Take it [the Scroll] and eat it" (10:9), which he does. Then he is told, "You must prophesy again concerning many peoples and nations and tongues and kings" (10:11).[5]

As we can see, the narrative drama builds. John's reader/hearers, and even the modern reader, anxiously await the revealing of the contents of the Scroll. John has eaten the Scroll and is commanded to prophesy. This

---

3. That the One on the throne is the "Father" is warranted by the reference to the "Father's throne" in 3:21.

4. A narrative reading of the book of Revelation, as I will contend in the commentary, virtually demands that we recognize that the Scroll in 10:1-11 is the same Scroll that Jesus took from the Father's hand and subsequently broke each of its Seven Seals. After all, this scroll is opened, which is precisely what one would expect if its seven seals have been broken. See Bauckham, *Climax*, 243-57.

5. I will contend in the commentary, that John's eating of the scroll, ala Ezekiel (Ezek 2:8—3:3), is the point of his commissioning as a prophet.

is followed by the account of the measuring of the temple (11:1–2) and the Two Witnesses (11:3–13).[6] Because, as I will argue in the commentary, the account of the Two Witnesses (11:1–13) presents the contents of John's prophecy, and thereby the contents of the Scroll, it is my contention that it serves as the central narrative of the book of Revelation.

The Focus of John's Narrative

It is my contention that Revelation's narrative centers first on God as the sovereign King and Jesus as the Lamb whose death and resurrection have inaugurated God's eschatological plan for redeeming humanity and the creation—all of which is contained on the Scroll.

As the narrative proceeds we learn that God delays the final consummation in order that the nations may repent. The nations, however, continue to be ruled by those in power. Tragically, human governing brings war, bloodshed, famine, and death upon humanity (Seals 1–4) and upon the created realm (Trumpets 1–4). The nations, however, not only fail to repent (9:20–21), even though they can see that human governing only brings harm, they actually worship the demonic hordes that reside behind humanity's ruling power. Furthermore, the nations wage war against Christ and the people of God (Trumpets 5–6).[7]

The war against Christ and the people of God results in the death of God's people (11:7). It is through their death and subsequent resurrection (11:11), however, that the nations are brought to repentance.

Two Key Themes: God's Throne and the Nations[8]

The view of this commentary then is that the main narrative of the book of Revelation centers around both the throne of God and the conversion of the nations.

At the opening of the second story, the throne of God is in heaven (4:2). It is not until the fourth scene (21:9—22:9) that the throne of God descends to the New Creation (21:10). This raises the question,

---

6. I have argued that 11:1–13 forms one unified account. See my *Two Witnesses*, 40–44.

7. This is not made explicit, however, until 16:14, 16, 19:19, and 20:8.

8. In chapter 9 of *Follow the Lamb*, I present an overview of the book of Revelation as a story. In that chapter, I focus on the fact that one of the elements of the story is that God is answering the prayers of the saints.

"What is needed so that the throne of God may descend and establish the New Creation?" The answer, so it seems, is that the nations must first be redeemed.

It is important to note that the nations play an important, and albeit complex, role in the narrative of the book of Revelation. Throughout the story, they appear opposed to the work of God and His people.[9] They are, in fact, aligned with the Dragon and the Beasts. Despite the nations' opposition to the people of God and Lamb, however, the book of Revelation affirms that "The nations will walk by its [the Holy city/ New Jerusalem's] light and the kings of the earth will bring their glory into it [the Holy City/New Jerusalem]" (21:24).

This leads us to a second key question, which I will contend the narrative Revelation endeavors to answer: "How is it that the nations are brought to repentance?" It is my contention that the redemption of the nations occurs as a result of the faithful, loving, and sacrificial witness[10] of God's people.[11] Or, as Barr suggests, "John is never far from his conviction that the divine will prevails through the faithful witness rather than through the exercise of power."[12]

This implies that the reason for the delay in God's throne "coming down out of heaven" is that God is, in fact, waiting for the redemption of the nations. Now, although the book of Revelation does not state explicitly that God delays in order that the nations may have time to repent, it is my contention that it is implicit in the reply to the plea for justice by the souls under the altar in 6:10. In response to their plea, they are told that they must be patient because not all those who are to suffer for the sake of the Gospel have suffered (6:11). But if it is the suffering of the people of God that leads to the redemption of the nations, then it is reasonable to conclude that the delay in the descent of the Holy City and the throne of God also awaits the redemption of the nations. Thus, it is my contention that the storyline of the book of

---

9. Of course, the people of God are from the nations (5:9; 7:9).

10. The word "witness" will be a key to understanding the role of God's people in the book of Revelation. We must note, however, that the modern sense of "sharing our faith/testimony" is too limiting for what "witness" means in the NT and the book of Revelation in particular. As we will see from our study, the ultimate witness is in laying down one's life for the sake of the other as Jesus did. To witness, in other words, is to love and serve. See Trites, *Witness*.

11. Those familiar with the NT will note that the message of the book of Revelation is the same message as is found throughout the NT.

12. Barr, "Story John Told," 19.

Revelation asserts that the nations[13] are redeemed through the faithful, loving, and sacrificial witness of the people of God.

This is why I believe that the book of Revelation is a love story. After all, just as Jesus's love led Him to the cross, so also, it is through the loving, sacrificial deaths of the people of God that the nations are redeemed.

---

13. I do not intend to suppose that everyone from every nation is redeemed. The book of Revelation clearly depicts that some are thrown into the Lake of Fire (20:15; 21:8).

Chapter 4

Understanding John's Purpose

If we read [Revelation] to discover something about Jesus Christ, we shall be served royally! Do it for that reason alone, to reveal the riches of the person of Christ and the significance of the events of his death and resurrection for the future of the world.[1]

Writing from late-apartheid South Africa, Allan Boesak suggests that: 'Those who do not know this suffering through oppression, who do not struggle together with God's people for the sake of the gospel, and who do not feel in their own bodies the meaning of oppression and the freedom and joy of fighting against it shall have grave difficulty understanding this letter from Patmos.'[2]

The Book of Revelation Is about Jesus

IN CLAIMING THAT THE book of Revelation is a love story, I am in no way denying that it is fundamentally about Jesus.[3] It is, after all, "The Revelation of Jesus Christ" (1:1). As David Barr affirms, "The story underlying the Apocalypse is the story of Jesus."[4] In fact, I cannot stress enough that the book of Revelation places at the forefront of its story the fact that Jesus's life, death, resurrection, and ascension are the means by

---

1. Prévost, *How to Read the Apocalypse*, 1, 3. Originally cited in deSilva, *Discovering*, 102.
2. DeSilva, *Discovering*, 249–50.
3. This, in fact, is the topic of the first chapter in my book, *Follow the Lamb*, 29–37.
4. Barr, *Tales*, loc. 179.

which the kingdom of God has come. The book of Revelation begins by highlighting the significance of the Christ story.

The book of Revelation, however, also carries forward the story of Jesus by expanding Christ's work to the nations. And this is where the people of God come in. They are, by imitating Christ's sacrificial love for the nations, the means by which the story of the kingdom continues and is eventually brought to the consummation.

The book of Revelation is first and foremost about Jesus. The story begins and ends with Jesus Christ as the resurrected and glorified Lord of all creation. He is the Alpha and the Omega (22:13). He is the One who was dead and is alive (1:18). He is the One who is coming again (2:5, 16; 3:11; 16:15; 22:7, 12, 20). He is the world's true King (15:3) who is the one Who sits enthroned with the Father in heaven (3:21; 22:3). And He is also the One who has made us to be His people and to serve as kings and priests to the nations (1:6; 5:10; 20:4, 6; 22:5).

Jesus Is the Model for the People of God to Follow

The book of Revelation also centers on Jesus's message to the people of God. John, after all, wrote to the seven churches (1:4). And he didn't write to simply tell them about Jesus. He wrote to encourage them to follow Jesus and to persevere as faithful, loving, and sacrificial witnesses for Christ.[5]

The centrality of Jesus in the story continues in that Jesus serves as the model for the people of God to emulate. Jesus is the "Faithful Witness" (1:5). The implication is that the people of God are to be faithful witnesses just as Jesus was.[6] Jesus's death serves as the model for the people of God. Consequently, as we will see, the Two Witnesses are killed "where their Lord was crucified" (11:8). As a result, the people of God are to serve as kings and priests to the nations (1:6; 5:10; 20:4, 6; 22:5) in the same way that Jesus did.

Jesus Rules as the Lamb

Central to the narrative of the book of Revelation is the fact that Jesus, who rules not as the Lion but as the Lamb that was slain, becomes the

---

5. See my, *Two Witnesses*, 118–25.
6. Thus, Antipas is heralded as, "My witness, My faithful one" (2:13).

model by which the people of God are called to follow. That this is a main feature the book of Revelation's narrative should not be surprising. After all, this was fundamental to the message of Jesus to His disciples.

Jesus unequivocally contrasts the manner in which the nations exercise power and the way power was to be exercised in His kingdom: "You know that those who are recognized as rulers of the Gentiles lord it over them; and their great men exercise authority over them. But it is not this way among you, but whoever wishes to become great among you shall be your servant; and whoever wishes to be first among you shall be slave of all" (Mark 10:42–44). The nations, Jesus says, manifest power by means of violence and by the oppression of the poor and the marginalized. But, He adds, this is not the way His kingdom operates. His kingdom manifests power by loving the nations so as to die for them.

We might say then, that the story of the book of Revelation centers on the Spirit[7] empowered mission of God's people. John writes to encourage his reader/hearers to be faithful. For John, faithfulness is manifested when the people of God imitate Jesus's sacrificial love. Faithfulness, in other words, entails suffering.

Jesus Is the Source of Encouragement to the People of God

Jesus's life, death, resurrection, and ascension also serve as a means of encouragement for the people of God to persevere. Central to the person of Jesus in the book of Revelation is that He is "the Firstborn of the dead" (1:5). The clear implication is that, as Jesus was the first to rise, so also the people of God will follow. Similarly, Jesus's affirmation that "I was dead and behold I am alive forever and ever and I have the keys of Death and Hades" (1:18), serves to remind the people of God that they should not fear death because if they are killed they will rise.

Consequently, the message to the people of God rings loud and clear: "You are called to bear witness for Christ and the kingdom of God. Do not fear the nations or those in power. After all, though they may well kill you, as they killed Jesus, remember, Jesus has risen and defeated death. And He holds the keys."

Another important element of John's message to his reader/hearers is that they need to persevere to the end because the coming of Christ

---

7. It is true that the presence of the Spirit as the empowering source for the people of God is not as explicit as one might suspect.

and the day of their vindication will be only "a little while" (6:11). John does not shy away from the reality that the faithful imitation of Jesus will lead to suffering and possibly death—as it did for Jesus. This suffering, however, is not the end. The end is their resurrection and the glorious restoration of God's presence among them.

Warning Against Compromise

John also writes to warn the churches against compromise. Since faithfulness to Christ results in suffering and possibly even death, the temptation to compromise in order to alleviate suffering and the threat of death is ever-present.

As the narrative progresses, we learn that compromise manifests itself in the efforts of the Beast (13:1–8), the False Prophet (13:11–18), and the Great Prostitute (17:1—19:10). Those who fail to grant allegiance to the Beast and the False Prophet will find themselves unable to partake in the economy of the empire. Considering the fact that upwards of 90 percent of the people in the Roman empire lived hand to mouth, the enticement to compromise was real.[8] The power of Rome necessitated the people's participation. If one failed to participate, the fury of Rome was sure to follow.

John also warns of the seductive ways of the empire. The desire for food, security, community, and all that participation in the Roman system entails is represented as a Great Prostitute. Thus, an angel exclaims, "Come out from her My people" (18:4).

---

8. See Horsley, *Jesus and Empire;* and Carter, *Jesus and the Empire of God;* also, Carter, *What Does Revelation Reveal.*

Chapter 5
John's Use of Numbers

As stars guide sailors and help them negotiate the seas, so numbers help the people of God navigate the journey to the new Jerusalem. Numbers serve as danger signs to warn the exodus-people of poseurs with divine pretentions (threes, sixes, and sevens); they alert the travelers to the impending difficulties on this journey (forty-two months; three-and-a-half days); and they reinforce the presence of divine protection (time and times and half a time; one thousand two hundred and sixty days).[1]

It is part of John's meticulous literary artistry that he has worked into his work symbolic features which are not easily noticed.[2]

READING THE BOOK OF Revelation well includes discerning John's use of numbers. A careful reading of the book of Revelation confirms that John uses numbers to enhance the meaning of the text.[3] David Barr notes, "Audiences of apocalypses would expect certain images and symbols to have certain meanings. As a somewhat oversimplified beginning, we can say there are three standard categories of symbols widely used in apocalypses: numbers, animals, and colors. All of them possess fairly standard meanings."[4]

1. Resseguie, "Narrative Features," 83–84.
2. Bauckham, *Climax*, 30.
3. By "enhance" I mean that numbers do not determine the meaning. They are used by John to enhance the meaning that is already present.
4. Barr, *Tales*, loc. 327.

John's Use of Numbers in the Book of Revelation

An investigation into John's use of numbers begins with the conviction that certain numbers have well-established meanings:[5]

- Three: primarily represents a heavenly number associated with God and the Divine[6]
- Four: represent fullness or completion: especially with regards to creation and the created realm.[7]
- Seven: (four plus three) represents completion, totality, or perfection[8] and is often used for God or for evil's efforts to imitate God.[9]
- Twelve: (four times three) represents completion, totality, or perfection: especially in relation to the people of God.[10]

It should be noted that we are not just speaking of explicit numbers such as the 144,000 or "seven" when referring to the number of churches (1:20), or the number of heads on the Dragon (12:3) and the Beast (13:1), or the number of Seals, Trumpets, and Bowls—though these are important. We are also talking about the fact that certain names for God appear seven times, that the number twelve appears throughout the description of the Holy City/New Jerusalem, that there are seven blessings in the book of Revelation and dozens of other examples.

When I say that John enhances the meaning of an expression by means of its numerical frequency, I am not suggesting that there are hidden or previously unknown meanings in the text which are

---

5. In the commentary itself, I will note further derivations of numbers that play a role in the Apocalypse. For example, I will examine twenty-four (twelve plus twelve) and 144 (twelve times twelve) and ask if the numbers associated with them indicate the old and new covenant people of God.

6. Barr notes that three is a heavenly number that is associated with the divine in Plato and Pythagoras (Barr, *Tales*, loc. 339).

7. Likely based on the fact that the earth was widely believed to have four corners and four winds. See Bauckham, *Climax*, 31; Barr, *Tales*, loc. 335; Resseguie, *Revelation*, 29.

8. "This symbolic use of the number seven has an Old Testament background and signifies completion, totality, and/or perfection" (Longman, *Revelation*, 46). See also, Bauckham, *Climax*, 30; Barr, *Tales*, loc. 339.

9. Resseguie notes, "Seven, which occurs fifty-five times in Revelation out of eighty-eight occurrences in the New Testament, is a number associated with completeness, plenitude, or perfection" (Resseguie, *Revelation*, 30–31).

10. This is evident from the fact that there were twelve tribes in the OT and twelve apostles in the NT. See Resseguie, *Revelation*, 33.

manifested only after we have counted the number of times a certain word or phrase occurs. For example, we already know that God is the Almighty. The fact that the title "the Lord God Almighty" occurs precisely seven times in the book of Revelation (1:8; 4:8; 11:17; 15:3; 16:7; 19:6; 21:22) only serves to reinforce this conviction.

That John intentionally uses numbers to enhance his meaning becomes evident from the sheer volume of examples. Although space precludes me from providing too detailed a list here, I can assure you that for each example I provide in this chapter, there are ten more that could have been added.

Three

The use of three for that which is divine occurs throughout the book of Revelation. The divine title, "the Alpha and the Omega" occurs three times (1:8; 21:6; 22:13). The parallel title "the First and the Last" also occurs three times (1:17; 2:8; 22:13). These titles appear together in 22:13. In fact, in 22:13 all three titles, "the Alpha and Omega," "the Beginning and the End," and "the First and the Last" are present.

That "Jerusalem" occurs only three times (3:12; 21:2, 10) in the book of Revelation is significant. It is my suggestion that the three references to "Jerusalem" indicate that it is divine in the sense that it represents the eternal dwelling place of God (21:3).

That the divine title, the "One who is and who was and who is to come" (1:4, 8; 4:8) occurs exactly three times reinforces the conviction that John wants us to recognize God's eternality. What is intriguing, however, is the fact that the divine title, the "One who is and who was" (11:17; 16:5) occurs only twice.[11]

Four

John uses the word "four" twenty-eight times (four times seven: 4:4*, 6, 8, 10; 5:6, 8*, 14; 6:1, 6; 7:1**, 2, 4, 11; 9:14, 15; 11:16; 14:1, 3*; 15:7; 19:4*; 20:8; 21:7). Since four represents the created realm and seven is perfection or completion, the twenty-eight occurrences of "four"

---

11. See the commentary in 11:1–19 for a discussion of the significance of this abbreviated twofold title.

reinforces the conviction that John uses this number to represent the entirety of the created realm.

Interestingly, there are four references to "the Bride" (19:7; 21:2, 9; 22:17).[12] There are also four occurrences of "the Holy City" (11:2; 21:2, 10; 22:19).[13] John, as I will note in the commentary, explicitly equates the Bride and the Holy City. That each is used four times likely expresses the fullness of Holy City/New Jerusalem with regard to the New Creation.

One of the regular designations for the people of the earth is the fourfold expression, "every tribe, tongue, people, and nation" (5:9; 7:9; 10:11; 11:9; 13:7; 14:6; 17:15). This designation occurs seven times in the book of Revelation. The fourfold designation for the people of the world affirms that John has the whole world in view. That it occurs a total of seven times further strengthens the supposition that it indicates fullness or completion with regard to the people of the world. In addition, it is worth noting that the terms used in the fourfold designation never occur in the same order. In fact, on two occasions John even alters the list by omitting reference to the "tribes" in 10:11 and replacing it with "kings" and in 17:15, he replaces it with "multitudes."

There are four references to the seven spirits (or sevenfold Spirit: 1:4; 3:1; 4:5; 5:6).[14] That the seven spirits of God "have been sent into all the earth" (5:6) suggests that they play a central role in creation.

Seven

There are a number of words and phrases that occur seven, or a multiple of seven, times. As noted earlier, the divine title, "the Lord God Almighty" occurs seven times (1:8; 4:8; 11:17; 15:3; 16:7; 19:6; 21:22). This surely indicates that the Lord God is indeed the Lord of all! Bauckham notes that John employs the divine title "God the Almighty" two times (16:14; 19:15) in order to maintain the seven occurrences of the longer title:[15] "These two occurrences [God the Almighty in 16:14; 19:15] themselves perform a literary function, helping to link 16:12–16 to 19:11–21, in which the battle the former passage presages takes place,

---

12. There is a fifth occurrence of "bride" in 18:23.

13. In 21:2, 10, John explicitly identifies the Holy City with the New Jerusalem.

14. See commentary on 1:1–8 for a discussion on the identity of the seven spirits.

15. This does not intend to deny that the two occurrences of "God Almighty" (16:14; 19:15) serve no purpose besides serving as exceptions to the seven occurrences of the longer title. See commentary on 15:1—16:21.

but they also allow the number of occurrences of the full title to be the number of completeness, seven."[16]

There are, of course, "seven churches" (1:4, 20; 2:1–3:22). John introduces the seven churches by noting that he saw "seven golden lampstands ... which are the seven churches (1:20).[17] There is little doubt, and I will elaborate on this in the commentary, that the seven churches represent all of Christendom. The fact that John refers to the "seven churches" four times (1:4, 11, 20*) reinforces the conviction that they represent all the churches of the world.

Seven, not surprisingly, is used regularly with regard to Christ. Most notably, Jesus has "seven horns and seven eyes" (5:6).

The title "Christ" occurs seven times (1:1, 2, 5; 11:15; 12:10; 20:4, 6). Three of these seven occurrences of "Christ" are used with "Jesus" (1:1, 2, 5). The name "Jesus" occurs fourteen times (seven times two: 1:1, 2, 5, 9*; 12:17; 14:12; 17:6; 19:10*; 20:4; 22:16, 20, 21). Since the number of a trustworthy witness is two, the fourteen occurrences of Jesus as the "Faithful Witness" (1:5) suggest that He is the supreme faithful witness. This is clearly affirmed by the fact that the designation "witness" occurs seven times alongside the name "Jesus" (1:2, 9; 12:17; 17:6; 19:10*; 20:4).

In addition, John uses "Lamb" a total of twenty-eight times (5:6, 8, 12, 13; 6:1, 16; 7:9, 10, 14, 17; 12:11; 13:8, 11; 14:1, 4, 10; 15:3; 17:14*; 19:7, 9; 21:9, 14, 22, 23, 27; 22:1, 3)—twenty-seven of which are applied to Jesus.[18] What is significant here is that the Lamb of God is said to have "purchased for God" people from the whole world (5:9).[19] Since the number for the world is four, and the number for totality or completion is seven, John's use of "Lamb" twenty-eight times is surely intentional.

Twelve

The description of the New Jerusalem (21:9—22:9) is replete with the number twelve. In fact, there are twelve occurrences of the number twelve in the description of the Holy City/New Jerusalem.[20] Since twelve

---

16. Bauckham, *Climax*, 33.

17. See also 1:12; 2:1.

18. The only exception is that the second Beast is said to have "two horns like a lamb" (13:11).

19. The significance of John's twenty-eight uses of Lamb is heightened when one realizes that Jesus is only called the "Lion" once (5:5).

20. See discussion in the commentary on 21:9—22:9.

is the number for the people of God, and since one of the key features of the Holy City is that it represents the place where God dwells among His people, we should not be surprised that the number twelve dominates the description of the New Jerusalem.

Twelve also occurs in that there are Twenty-Four Elders (4:4, 10; 5:8; 11:16; 19:4). That there are twenty-four of them suggests that they are either the angelic representatives of the entirety of the people of God (twelve) who are faithful witnesses (times two) and/or that they are the combined representatives of the Old and New Testament people of God (twelve and twelve).

In addition, there are twelve references to the "Elders" (4:4, 10; 5:5, 6, 8, 11, 14; 7:11, 13; 11:16; 14:3; 19:4). This supports the supposition that the Elders represent the people of God. In ten of the occurrences of the "Elders," John clearly has the Twenty-Four Elders in view: five times he expressly calls them the "Twenty-Four Elders" (4:4, 10; 5:8; 11:16; 19:4) and five times they are just "the Elders" (5:6, 11, 14; 7:11; 14:30). There are two occasions in which John addresses "one of the Elders" (5:5; 7;13).

That John uses "repent" twelve times (2:5*, 16, 21*, 22; 3:3, 19; 9:20, 21; 16:9, 11) supports the conviction that the book of Revelation is a call to repentance. It is noteworthy that eight of the twelve occurrences are a call to the churches to repent in the seven messages (2:5*, 16, 21*, 22; 3:3, 19). The other four are reports that the nations did not repent (9:20, 21; 16:9, 11). This indicates that there is a greater focus on the repentance of the people of God than there is on the nations repenting.

Evil's Imitation of the Divine

There are several instances in which we might be taken aback by the fact that something evil corresponds with a number that we assume belongs to God or to what is good. For example, as noted earlier, the Dragon and the Beast each have "seven heads" (12:3; 13:1; 17:3, 7, 9). The use of such numbers with respect to evil appears to be a rhetorical strategy of John. It seems that John depicts what is evil in a manner that corresponds to what is good in order to accent its deceptive ways. That is, evil appears to be good, and John wants his reader/hearers to know that it is only a parody or a counterfeit.

For example, that the second Beast has "two horns like a lamb" (13:11) may be John's way of indicating that the Beast attempts to lure

God's people by means of deception. That is, this Beast may look like a lamb but, as John is quick to point out, it "was speaking as a dragon" (13:11).

Avoidance of Symbolic Numbers

In addition to John's use of certain words and phrases two, three, four, seven, ten, and twelve times, there are also instances in which John appears to avoid using terms and expressions in accord with these numbers.

For instance, John refers to "Babylon the Great" six times (14:8; 16:19; 17:5; 18:2, 10, 21). There are thirteen references to the "Dragon" (12:3, 4, 7*, 9, 13, 16, 17; 13:2, 4, 11; 16:13; 20:2). John uses "deceives" or "deception" eight times (2:20; 12:9; 13:14; 18:23; 19:20; 20:3, 8, 10).

Interestingly, the verbal form of "war" occurs six times. It is possible that John left the occurrences of the verb "war" at six to affirm that "war" is what the nations do. Though there is no clear-cut "symbolic" meaning to the number six, some suggest that John uses it as an indication of not attaining seven. This is likely the foundation for the meaning of 666.[21]

That John avoids significant numbers when it comes to the opponents of Christ and His people reinforces the conviction that John was very intentional in his use of words, phrases, expressions, and titles and that he was counting the number of their occurrences.

Conclusion

It is my contention that the sheer volume of examples indicates that John was quite intentional in choosing virtually every word and phrase. And recognizing this not only facilitates a better understanding of the text but should also help us see the beauty of John's work. It is indeed a literary masterpiece.

---

21. Resseguie suggests, "The heaping up of sixes, as in 666, may represent the penultimate striving to be ultimate, humanity (the beast) in the quest to be like God" (Resseguie, *Revelation*, 33). See the commentary on 13:1–18 for a more complete discussion of 666.

Chapter 6

Understanding the Message of Revelation

The slain Lamb's victory through suffering love is the heart of the Revelation story. I want to say again that this theology, this counter-understanding of victory in the Lamb, is more relevant today than ever. In the face of terrorism and the glorification of war, we need the vision of 'Lamb power' to remind us that true victory comes in our world not through military might but through self-giving love. Revelation's conquering Messiah is the slain but standing Lamb, the very opposite of Rome's victory image. In Revelation, Jesus conquers not by inflicting violence but by accepting the violence inflicted upon him in crucifixion.[1]

The Lamb really does conquer, though not by force of arms, and his followers really do share his victory, though not by violence. The combination of the Lamb and the 144,000 conveys the sense that there is a holy war to be fought, but to be fought and won by sacrificial death.[2]

The Message of the Book of Revelation

THERE IS LITTLE QUESTION that one of John's primary concerns was for his reader/hearers to remain faithful to Christ and not compromise their faith by giving in to the temptations to accommodate their faith

---

1. Rossing, *Rapture*, 135.
2. Bauckham, *Climax*, 230.

which were threatening some of the churches. John's purpose has been well captured in the subtitle of McKnight and Machett's recent book: "A Prophetic Call to Follow Jesus as a Dissident Disciple."[3]

What I intend to add to this understanding of the book of Revelation is threefold. First, I am arguing against the popular notion that God brings devastation, destruction, and death upon humanity and the creation in order to bring people to repentance. On the contrary, it is my conviction that the book of Revelation affirms that devastation, destruction, and death are what happens when humanity rules apart from the wisdom of God.[4]

Second, it is my contention that the reason why God allows devastation, destruction, and death to continue is His love for the nations. That is, God allows the nations to remain in power—even though their reigns bring devastation, destruction, and death—because He desires for the nations to come to repentance.

Third, I will contend that the book of Revelation affirms that the repentance of the nations occurs as a result of the faithful, loving, and sacrificial witness of God's people.

In saying this I do not intend to deny that John's central concern was for his reader/hearers to remain faithful in the midst of Rome's oppression and its seductive efforts to lure the people of God to compromise. I am arguing that John's concern was not simply for their sakes alone. Instead, John recognizes that the people of God must remain faithful because their faithfulness is the means by which humankind may be spared from the final judgment.

With all this being said, I find it incredulous that scholars and students of the book of Revelation approach the text as though its primary message was one of divine judgment.[5] Is it not fundamental to the New Testament that the kingdom of God comes not through power, but through

---

3. McKnight and Matchett, *Revelation*. See also, Gorman, *Reading*; and deSilva, *Unholy Allegiance*.

4. This is in accord with the biblical story beginning with Adam and Eve's expulsion and carrying forward until the return of Jesus. When humanity decides to make its own decisions of right and wrong, people like Cain kill others such as Abel.

5. This understanding is found throughout the commentaries. This sentiment is even found in two of the most respected commentaries. For example, G. K. Beale notes, "All agree that the dominant themes from 6:1 to 20:5 are, in order of importance, judgment, persecution, and salvation/reward and that these themes are intensified as the book progresses" (Beale, *Revelation*, 144). Smalley also asserts, "Controlling John's testimony is his underlying perception that God's salvation comes to his creation *through* judgment" (Smalley, *Revelation*, 10; emphasis original).

love?[6] It is remarkable to me that many Christians try to hold in tension the conviction that God is love and that He is also an angry despot who is ready and willing to inflict suffering on people as a means of driving them to repentance. I recognize that some attempt to resolve this conundrum by asserting that God's wrath is an expression of His love. I would, in fact, agree that this is true when it comes to the final judgment.

The problem, however, as David Barr contends, is that the suggestion that God uses pain and suffering in order to impose His will upon humankind makes God no different than any human ruler. Barr comments, "The . . . moral issue I face concerns the use of overwhelming power to coerce obedience. If God triumphs over evil only because God has more power than evil, then power—not love or freedom or goodness or truth—is the ultimate value of the universe."[7]

In addition to this, John makes it clear that violence done in order to bring about worship is precisely what the second Beast does. This Beast causes "whoever does not worship the image of the [first] Beast to be killed" (13:15).

---

6. Though we might say that love is the means through which God manifests his power.

7. Barr, *Tales*, loc. 4924. Barr cites C. S. Pierce who finds the violence in the book of Revelation as the act of God and then besmirches, "But little by little the bitterness increases until in the last book of the New Testament, its poor distracted author represents that all the time Christ was talking about having come to save the world, the secret design was to catch the entire human race, with the exception of a paltry 144,000, and souse them all in brimstone lake, and as the smoke of their torment went up for ever and ever, to turn and remark, 'There is no curse anymore.' Would it be an insensible smirk or a fiendish grin that should accompany such an utterance? I wish I could believe St. John did not write it" (Charles S. Peirce, "Evolutionary Love," cited in Koester, *Oxford Handbook*, 398.

Barr himself does not seem to find a suitable response: "The story John tells contains much that is deplorable. Setting aside for the moment the larger issues of theology and focusing on only the morality of the actions portrayed, we come to a harsh conclusion. This god who threatens death, and eventually enacts it on all who do not submit, is immoral. It is like an abusive marriage in which the stronger partner beats the weaker till the weaker surrenders, or else eventually dies at the hands of the one who claims to love them. I am not persuaded by the argument that it was for their own good." The best that Barr can offer is, "It could be argued that the mechanism of judgment here is not some external coercion but the inevitable result of unjust actions" (409, 11). This, I would contend is precisely the point. Barr then adds, "Much work remains to be done here" (411). It is my hope that this present work is a step towards that goal.

God Delays Judgment

It is my contention that in the narrative of the book of Revelation, God delays the final judgment. This is evident in the response to the plea of the souls of God's people under the altar who cry out for justice—"How long, Lord?" (6:10)—only to be told that they must wait until "their fellow servants and their brothers who are to be killed even as they themselves were, should be completed also" (6:11). Here we see that God not only delays justice but that the delay is directly connected to the suffering of God's people. The reason, I will argue, that God delays the final judgment, which results in the death and suffering of more of the people of God, is because the means by which the nations are brought to repentance is the faithful, loving, and sacrificial witness of God's people.[8]

Is There a Final Judgment?

Now, in saying all of this, some may want to know if I believe that there will be a final judgment for those who reject the Gospel. The answer is "Yes." The book of Revelation is clear.[9] In fact, I believe in it so much that I do not want to see anyone have to face it. Thus my conviction is that the people of God must come to recognize the message of the book of Revelation. Namely, our call is to be the people of God who reflect the image, glory, and love of God to the nations.

Unfortunately, the book of Revelation also affirms that even when God's people have finished their mission not all will believe.

Excursus: Understanding Revelation in Contrast to Popular Teachings

Unfortunately, in the past half-century, there have been too many books written, songs sung, and movies made that convey a different message.

These works often view the book of Revelation as if it were a blueprint for God's coming judgment on the world. According

---

8. The notion that God delays His final judgment until the nations repent corresponds with Peter's assertion, "The Lord is not slow about His promise, as some count slowness, but is patient toward you, not wishing for any to perish but for all to come to repentance" (2 Pet 3:9). God's patience, Peter suggests, is manifested in the delaying of His wrath. See my *Understanding*, 121–24.

9. See 20:11–15.

to this popular understanding, there must be wars, famines, plagues of locusts, and other such destructive phenomena before Jesus can return.[10] As you might suspect, I believe that these approaches represent a seriously inadequate and even highly problematic approach to the book of Revelation.[11]

In fact, I would go so far as to say that these popular approaches to the book of Revelation are dangerous for a number of reasons. For one, these views often distract the people of God from the mission to which we have been called. Tragically, instead of encouraging the people of God to faithfully, lovingly, and sacrificially maintain our witness to the nations, these popular views urge us to look for "signs" and other indications of Jesus's imminent return.

Second, these popular understandings of the book of Revelation would seemingly have us relish in wars, famines, and all sorts of calamities because these tragedies supposedly indicate that we are moving closer to the return of Jesus. There are many so-called end-times prophecy "experts" who promote an attitude of excitement over other people's misery. This, however, is the very antithesis of what Jesus meant when He said, "Blessed are those who mourn" (Matt 5:4) and "Blessed are those who hunger and thirst for righteousness" (Matt 5:6). At the very time when people need the mercy and love of God's people, these prophetic pundits cry out all the louder for the nations to repent because God's wrath is upon them.

Third, these popular readings do great harm to the church's witness. Ironically, they claim that God's wrath should be a sign for the nations to repent and turn to Christ, yet in saying this, they make a mockery of Christ and the Church. It is no wonder that people do not want to "repent and turn from their wicked ways." Who would want to repent and follow an angry, malevolent, and wrathful deity? Moreover, who would want to repent and become like the loveless Christians who are

---

10. It is also quite common for many in the camp to affirm a view of "Christian Zionism" that suggests that certain "prophesies" must be fulfilled by the Jewish people. Many who hold to such views believe that this includes the restoration of the Jewish people to the land and possibly even the rebuilding of a physical temple in Jerusalem. For a biblical theological response to Christian Zionism see my *These Brothers of Mine*.

11. For a good response to the popular "rapture" theology and the book of Revelation, see Rossing, *Rapture*.

informing them of their impending doom in the Lake of Fire? Where is the witness of God's people in all of this? Where is the love of God that we are called to make known? The lack of compassion for the poor and the oppressed is antithetical to the kingdom of God and to our calling as God's people.

Therefore, it is my conviction that these popular writings not only seriously misread the book of Revelation, but they undermine the very work to which the people of God have been called to do. This is grieving.

Significance for Us Today

If my thesis holds true, the significance of this for our understanding of the book of Revelation and our present mission as God's people cannot be overstated. There is only one King of kings (19:16) and we are called to imitate Him. As we do so, we both reign as kings/queens in His kingdom and serve as His witnesses to the nations. That is, when we—God's people—learn to imitate Jesus, love like Jesus, serve like Jesus, and lay down our lives for the sake of others like Jesus, then the nations[12] will repent. It is then that they too will walk in the light of the glory of God in the Holy City whose gates will never be shut (21:23–25).

---

12. Again, I am not saying that everyone in the nations will repent. Unfortunately, some will not.

Commentary
Revelation 1:1–8
The Prologue

Revelation 1:1–8
The Prologue

A common way to misunderstand prophecy, and especially the prophecy of the Revelation, is to suppose that it means prediction.[1]

The main themes are clear. The church and state are on a collision course of some magnitude over who runs the universe, and John fully recognizes that power and victory presently appear to belong to the state. But because of Rome's arrogance and oppression, God will bring her to ruin.[2]

The prologue serves an important role in the book of Revelation in that it sets the context for everything that is to follow.

Opening 1:1–3

Revelation of Jesus Christ 1:1

THE OPENING SENTENCE, IN particular the first five words,[3] functions primarily as the title of the work. Thus, what we commonly call, "The book of Revelation" is self-titled, "The Revelation of Jesus Christ."[4]

---

1. Peterson, *Thunder*, 20.
2. Fee, *Revelation*, xvii.
3. There are three words in the Greek text that translate into five words in English.
4. Note that the NAS and the NKJ capitalize "Revelation." This would be fitting if indeed 1:1 served as a title.

This opening title provides our first main insight into what the book of Revelation is about: it is "The Revelation of Jesus Christ" (1:1).[5] The Greek here is somewhat ambiguous—as is the English. To say it is the revelation "of" Jesus Christ could mean either: it is a revelation "about" Jesus Christ, or it is a revelation "from" Jesus. It may well be that John intended it to be ambiguous. If so, we may affirm that the book of Revelation is both about Jesus and from Jesus.

Excursus: Revelation as an Apocalypse[6]

The very first word in the Greek text of the book of Revelation is *apocalypsis* ("revelation"). This word suggests that the things which are being revealed were hidden and in need of being made known. David deSilva notes:

> The very term apokalypsis denotes, however, 'the lifting off of a veil', not the 'concealment' of meaning. As an unveiling of the larger canvas of divine and demonic activity and agendas, and as an unveiling of what the audience's lived landscape looked like against the backdrop of that canvas, Revelation might be better approached as the key that John offered to his congregations to unlock the meaning and significance of their present moment and situation.[7]

The book of Revelation is, therefore, a revealing. There is, however, a caveat: namely, the book of Revelation endeavors to reveal what was previously hidden, but only to "the one who has an ear hear" (see 2:7, 11, 17, 29; 3:6, 13, 22).

What is it that the Apocalypse is revealing? We might say that the book of Revelation makes known what is really happening. The message is simple: things are not as they appear. The book of Revelation makes clear the fact that though the kings of the world appear to be in power, and although they exercise their rule with military might in order to maintain their power, the reality is that God is the One who is seated on the throne (4:2-3) and Jesus is seated with Him (3:21; 22:1). DeSilva adds, "The Greek word means "unveiling,"

---

5. All translations of the book of Revelation are the author's unless otherwise noted. Translations of other biblical passages are from the NAS.

6. See discussion of apocalyptic in Ian Paul, "Genre," in Stewart and Bandy, *Apocalypse*, 36–50.

7. DeSilva, *Discovering*, 48.

not "cryptic encoding." Revelation was not sent to the seven churches as a mysterious text needing to be interpreted: it was sent to interpret the world of those readers."[8] As Brian Blount notes, "The ironic message is clear: looks deceive."[9]

For John, Jesus's death and resurrection reveal that true power manifests itself in lovingly laying down one's life for the sake of the other. It is, therefore, only by following the Lamb in sacrificial love for the sake of the other that we also will rise to eternal life.

One of the reasons why some modern readers struggle with the text of the book of Revelation is that they assume that it is depicting the end of the world.[10] In popular parlance, "apocalyptic" seems to suggest the "end of the world."

Apocalyptic imagery, however, is what I like to refer to as, "cosmic upheaval language." That is, apocalyptic imagery depicts the sun being darkened, the moon becoming like blood, and the stars of the sky falling (see 6:12–13)—i.e., the upheaval of the cosmos. Of course, if we take this imagery literally, as many have done, it would indicate the end of the world. But the apocalypses do not necessarily think of things this way. Instead, apocalypses use this language because they considered it a fitting way to describe God's acting in history. That is, when God acts in accord with His covenant promises, an appropriate way to describe His actions is with language that suggests the cosmos is being shaken! Of course, in one sense the cosmos is being shaken![11]

It is important to recognize that apocalyptic language is used throughout the NT. Jesus's teaching, for example, often employed apocalyptic language. In particular, Jesus's parables[12]

---

8. DeSilva, *Unholy Allegiances*, 8 (emphasis original).

9. Blount, "The Witness of Active Resistance," in Rhoads, *From Every People and Nation*, 581–82.

10. Hence the popular use of "apocalypse" in movies such as "Apocalypse Now."

11. We need to get beyond our tendency to assume everything is literal. Ironically, our own everyday speech is filled with metaphors that are not taken literally: "It was a battle out there today"; "I really put up a fight"; "This is killing me"; "I almost died when I heard the news." When we say, "This game is over now" we mean that one team has surely won. We do not mean that the game is actually over.

12. The Gospel of Mark says that parables were the primary means by which Jesus communicated to the people: See Mark 4:33–34.

were apocalyptic. This is evident in that they regularly appeal for us to "hear" or "listen" (Matt 13:18; Mark 4:3). In addition, Jesus's parables often include the command, "he who has ears, let him hear" (Matt 13:9, 43; Mark 4:9, 23), which is reminiscent of the ending of each of Revelation's seven messages, or letters as they are commonly called, in 2:1–3:22.[13]

We could list many other examples of apocalyptic imagery in the NT. For example, in Acts 2:19–20, Peter explains that the coming of the Spirit at Pentecost is the fulfillment of Joel 2:28–32 and notes:

> And I will grant wonders in the sky above
> And signs on the earth below,
> Blood, and fire, and vapor of smoke.
> The sun will be turned into darkness
> And the moon into blood,
> Before the great and glorious day of the Lord shall come.

Another critical feature of apocalyptic writings is that they often attempted to assure their recipients that God was in control and He would soon bring them relief and punish their enemies. For the recipients of the apocalypses, it certainly did not seem like God was in control. After all, they were often undergoing tremendous suffering, usually at the hands of the state. One of the primary goals of the apocalypses was to assure them that God was in control and that He will soon bring them vindication.

What Must Take Place Soon 1:1

John is told that what he is shown regards what must "soon" (*taxos*) take place. It is important to recognize that for John "soon" indicates when these things will begin, not when they will be completed. For John, in fact, "soon" refers to events that have already begun. That this is John's understanding of "soon" is evident for two reasons.

First, the lexical meaning of "soon" (*taxos*) indicates something that will occur within a "brief time subsequent to another point in time."[14] In

---

13. See 2:7, 11, 17, 29; 3:6, 13, 22.
14. BADG, 992–93. Even in English, "soon" is a relative term. It could refer to

other words, when John says, "soon," he is indicating that what he has been shown begins shortly after something else has taken place. That is, "soon" is relative to "something else" happening. The question then becomes "What is the 'something else' that takes place first?"[15] It is my conviction that the "something else" that comes first is the death and resurrection of Jesus. This is evident in that Jesus's death and resurrection are central in each of the two main stories in the book of Revelation. In the first story (1:9–3:22), Jesus's death and resurrection are central to John's description of Jesus (1:12–20) and his message to the churches (2:1–3:22). The second story (4:1—16:21) also hinges on the death and resurrection of Jesus. It is because Jesus was slain that He is worthy to open the Scroll (5:9). Consequently, the "something else" that must happen first is the death and resurrection of Jesus. Since Jesus's death and resurrection have already taken place, John's use of "soon" in 1:1 indicates things that have already begun. If this is so, then why would John use "soon," when it suggests something that is about to happen but has not yet happened? The answer to this question is likely that John employed "soon" as a means of alluding to the prophecy in Daniel.

This brings us to the second reason for understanding "soon" as something that has already begun. G. K. Beale has argued that John's use of "what must take place soon" (1:1) is an adaptation of Daniel 2.[16] In Daniel 2, the Babylonian king Nebuchadnezzar had a vision that Daniel both reveals and interprets for the king. The vision was of a statute that itself represented four kingdoms (Dan 2:36–43). As Daniel interprets the vision, he explains to King Nebuchadnezzar that the four kingdoms will ultimately be destroyed by a stone that was "cut out without hands" (Dan 2:34–35, 44). The stone, Daniel explains, will itself become "a mountain" and fill "the whole earth" (Dan 2:35). Daniel notes that in this vision God has shown the king "what will take place in the latter days" (Dan 2:28). Daniel reiterates this point and modifies his expression so that God has

---

minutes, hours, or an unknown duration. Hence, when a father is away on a business trip, and he tells his children by phone that he will be home "soon" it means something different than when he sends a text message to his spouse that he will be back from the store "soon."

15. Note: the answer to this question significantly impacts how one understands the book of Revelation.

16. See Beale for a detailed defense of this view (Beale, *Revelation*, 152–57). Beale comments, "It is the *source* of the verse, Dan. 2:28–29, 45, that provides the alert the reader with a clue to the purpose of Revelation" (Beale, *Revelation*, 153; emphasis original).

shown Nebuchadnezzar, "what will take place in the future" (Dan 2:29, 45).[17] Beale contends that John has adapted the language of Dan 2:28, 29, and 45 in order to indicate their fulfillment in Jesus. A comparison of the Greek text of Dan 2:28, 29, and 45, with Rev 1:1 and 22:6 confirms that John has Daniel 2 in view even though he slightly modifies the expressions. John's modification of Daniel 2 is evident in that Daniel says, "what will take place in the latter days" (Dan 2:28) and "what will take place in the future" (Dan 2:29, 45), and John states, "what must take place 'soon'" (1:1; 22:6). Why would John make this slight emendation? Beale notes that what was for Daniel something yet to occur, hence Daniel's "latter days" (Dan 2:28) and "the future" (Dan 2:28, 29, 45), John has come to believe indicated something that had begun with the coming of Jesus. In particular, Jesus's death and resurrection ("I was dead and behold I am alive"; 1:18) have convinced John that what God had promised Daniel has now begun. As Tremper Longman affirms, "In other words, what was in the distant future to Daniel now has a sense of immediacy to it."[18]

Made It Known 1:1

In the opening verse, John adds that the revelation of Jesus Christ has been "made known" to him (1:1). The verb *semaino* ("make known") is important for understanding the nature of the vision. In particular, this verb indicates that the means of making something known is by the use of symbols. David Barr notes, "The word I translate *signified* is *semano*, which means to show by a sign, to give signs or signals." Barr continues, "The usual English translation, 'he made it known' (RSV, NRSV, NIV, NEB, JBP), misses this sense of *how* it is made known: through signs."[19]

Excursus: The Book of Revelation and Symbols[20]

That the book of Revelation uses symbols in order to communicate its message may create a bit of consternation for some readers. After all, how are we supposed to know what

---

17. The ending of this phrase in the Greek text of Dan 2:28, 29 & 45 is actually the same: "in the last days" (my translation). That the English Bibles have "in the last days" (NAS: Dan 2:28) and "in the future" (NAS: Dan 2:29, 45) is reflective of the fact that they are translating from the Aramaic.

18. Longman, *Revelation*, 42.

19. Barr, *Tales*, 227–29.

20. For a more complete discussion of this topic see my *Follow*, 175–79.

the symbols mean if they are not literal? This is an excellent question.

I would begin by noting that just because we might be disadvantaged in that the meaning of the symbols may not be as obvious to us as it would have been to John's initial audience, this should not be used to deny the presence of such symbols. Being faithful to the text means honoring what the text was trying to say. Uncovering this is not an arbitrary exercise, however. When it comes to understanding the meaning of the text's symbols, there are several factors that make understanding the meaning easier to come by.

First, there are several instances in which John simply tells us what the symbols mean. For example, with regard to the seven-headed dragon[21] we are told, "And the great Dragon was thrown down, the serpent of old who is called the devil and Satan, who deceives the whole world" (12:9; see 20:2–3). Jesus also tells John that the seven stars in Jesus's right hand "are the angels of the seven churches" (1:20). And, He adds, "the seven lampstands are the seven churches" (1:20).

Second, there are a number of instances in which the meaning of the images is quite evident; even for us.[22] For example, in 5:5, John hears that "the Lion, the one from the tribe of Judah, the root of David, has overcome." The imagery of a lion from the tribe of Judah most certainly alludes to Gen 49:9–10 where Jacob's son Judah is depicted as a lion from whom the future Israelite king would descend. There is little doubt that John's reader/hearers would have had no trouble recognizing that the imagery of Jesus as "the Lion" who is "from the tribe of Judah" indicated that Jesus is the true King. John then notes that when he turned to look at the Lion, he saw instead "a Lamb standing, as if it had been slain" (5:6). This description of Jesus quite evidently derives from John's use of Isa 52:13–53:12. The early church's widespread conviction that Jesus is the fulfillment

---

21. See 12:3, 4, 7*, 9, 13, 16, 17; 13:2, 4, 11; 16:13; 20:2.

22. This fact seriously calls into question the notion that when John does not tell us the meaning of an image it must be taken literally. Jesus is not actually a lion. The use of "Lion" to convey that Jesus is the King is never stated by John, but it is a conclusion that easily follows from the widely recognized conviction that a lion may serve to represent kings. There is simply no need for asserting that everything else must be taken literally.

of Isaiah's Suffering Servant means that there is no need for John to interpret the symbolism for his reader/hearers.[23] Jesus is the Lamb that was slain (5:9).

Third, discerning the meaning of the various symbols in the book of Revelation is eased significantly when we recognize that most of the symbols derive from the OT.[24] As I noted with regard to John's use of Daniel 2, John understands that the promises of the OT have been fulfilled in Jesus and now he is detailing for us what this means. Therefore, once we recognize that John is employing images derived in large part from the OT and that he is viewing them in light of their fulfillment in Jesus, we are better prepared to understand the various symbols.

To His Servant John 1:1, 4

The book of Revelation identifies its author as John (1:1, 4, 9; 22:8). We have no explicit indication as to who this John was.[25] It is possible that John did not further identify himself because he was known to his initial audience.

Excursus: The Authorship and Date of the Book of Revelation

In my opinion, and one that I hold to lightly, the John who wrote this book is John the author of the Fourth Gospel. I am persuaded by the fact that the parallels between the book of Revelation, the Gospel of John, and the NT letters of John are best accounted for by suggesting common authorship. I recognize, however, that even if there is a common author to these writings, this does not prove that the apostle John was that author.

---

23. The book of Acts notes that the Ethiopian was reading Isaiah 53 (Acts 8:30–33) and Philip's explanation that the text is about Jesus (Acts 8:35) indicates that Isaiah's slaughtered lamb imagery was widely understood as fulfilled by Christ in the early church.

24. See my *Follow*, 54–63.

25. DeSilva notes, "Almost all modern scholars agree that someone named John wrote Revelation. . . . They are divided, however, on the question of which John was the author—John the apostle or an otherwise unknown Christian leader named John" (deSilva, *Discovering*, 55).

When it comes to the date for the writing of the book of Revelation, it is my belief that the book was written in the late first century. Some might argue against this position by noting that there is little evidence of any widespread persecution of Christians near the end of the first century. In response, I would contend that the book of Revelation, though it certainly indicates that the people of God will suffer, does not necessarily indicate that there was already widespread persecution underway.

Word of God and the Testimony of Jesus 1:2

Revelation 1:2 adds that John gave witness to, "the Word of God and the testimony of Jesus." This twofold expression is repeated in various forms throughout the Apocalypse,[26] and, as we will see, refers to the contents of the book of Revelation itself. It is important to observe that the phrases "the Word of God" and "the testimony of Jesus" should not be looked upon as distinct from one another. Instead, as will become evident later in the book, Jesus's testimony is "the Word of God."[27]

Blessed[28] Is the One Who Reads, Those Who Hear . . . and Keep the Things that Are Written in It 1:3

The book of Revelation is the only book in the Bible that explicitly has a blessing for those who read, hear, and do what it says. It is important to note that "the one who reads" is singular. After all, at the time, a local

---

26. The phrase occurs in several different expressions. In 1:2, 9 we see the pair "the word of God and the testimony of Jesus." This pair occurs in reverse order in 20:4: "the testimony of Jesus and the Word of God." In 6:9, we hear of those who were slain because of "the word of God and the testimony which they had." In 17:17, the "words of God" appear without any other expression. John uses "their testimony" in isolation in 11:7 and 12:11. And in 19:10, he refers to "the testimony of Jesus." And in 12:17, John combines "the commandments of God" with "the testimony of Jesus."

27. Resseguie observes, "The second step amplifies and thickens the meaning of 'the word of God'" (Resseguie, *Revelation*, loc. 259).

28. Aune translates this as "how fortunate" (Aune, *Revelation*, 1.7). He offers that it can mean "happy" or "fortunate." The problem with "happy" is that it fails to account for the sake that those who are "blessed" or "fortunate" includes those who are persecuted (see Matt 5:10). In the case of the book of Revelation those who are "blessed" or "fortunate" often face death: "Blessed are the dead, the ones who die in the Lord from now on" (14:13).

community of Christ-followers was fortunate even to have a single copy of a biblical book. That single copy was read aloud. The reference to "those who hear" (plural) includes everyone else who would be listening to the oral presentation.

Most significantly, of course, is the blessing for those who "keep[29] the things written in it" (1:3). That the book of Revelation provides a blessing for those who obey what it says presupposes that the book of Revelation was understood, or at least understandable, to its original reader/hearers. After all, how could they be blessed for doing what it says, if they have no idea what it means?

The Words of the Prophecy 1:3

In addition to the fact that the book of Revelation is in some sense an apocalypse, John now calls it a "prophecy" (1:3; 22:7, 10, 18, 19).[30]

> **Excursus: Revelation as a Prophecy**
>
> The word "prophecy" and the role of prophets is often misunderstood in contemporary, Western Christianity. Though it is popularly taught that prophets were focused on the things to come and that prophecies were about the future, the fact is that the biblical prophets were deeply concerned with the people to whom they wrote.[31] In fact, one of the central functions of the biblical prophet was to serve as the mouthpiece of God to the people. In particular, the prophets exhorted the people of God to be faithful to God's covenant promises and in doing so fulfill their role as God's "witnesses" (Isa 43:10). If they were already faithful, which was not often, the prophets exhorted them to remain so in order that God would bring about His promised blessings. If the people were unfaithful, the prophets uttered words of warning and exhortations to repent, lest they continue in disobedience and experience the consequences for violating God's covenant.
>
> In many instances, the prophets actually hoped that their predictions of impending judgment would never

---

29. The NET and NLT translate this word as "obey."
30. The word "prophecy" occurs seven times: see 1:3; 11:6; 19:10; 22:7, 10, 18, 19.
31. See: my *Follow*, 88–91 and my *Understanding*, 42–56.

happen! That is, the prophets hoped that the threat of calamity would drive the people of God to repentance and that God would relent from the proposed destruction. Thus, the book of Isaiah opens with a word to the people:

> "Wash yourselves, make yourselves clean; remove the evil of your deeds from My sight. Cease to do evil, learn to do good; seek justice, reprove the ruthless, defend the orphan, plead for the widow. Come now, and let us reason together," says the LORD, "though your sins are as scarlet, they will be as white as snow; though they are red like crimson, they will be like wool. If you consent and obey, you will eat the best of the land; But if you refuse and rebel, you will be devoured by the sword" (Isa 1:16–20).

Salutation 1:4–8

John to the Seven Churches that Are in Asia: Grace to You and Peace 1:4

The book of Revelation is an apocalypse, a prophecy, and it is also framed with features common to an ancient letter. The book opens with an identification of the author "John" (1:1, 4, 9) and its recipients, "the seven churches that are in Asia" (1:4, 11; 22:16).[32] This opening salutation is then followed by a customary offer of "grace and peace" (1:4).[33] In addition, the book of Revelation closes in a manner similar to NT letters with a final "amen" (22:21) and an offer of "grace" (22:22).

Excursus: The Book of Revelation as a Letter

The importance of recognizing that the book of Revelation is framed as a letter that was addressed to seven ancient churches is that it further establishes the fact that the meaning of the book must begin with its first-century audience. Letters were written to individuals or groups to address specific topics.

At the same time, the book of Revelation is distinct from the letters of the NT in that the NT letters are occasional

---

32. The seven churches to whom the book is addressed were in the ancient Roman province of Asia, which was located on the west coast of modern-day Turkey.

33. See Rom 1:7; 1 Cor 1:3; 2 Cor 1:2; Gal 1:3; Eph 1:2; Phil 1:2; Col 1:2; 1 Thess 1:1; 2 Thess 1:2; Phlm 3; see also, 2 Pet 2:2; 2 John 3; Jude 2.

documents that were written to a specific person or community at a specific moment in time in order to address specific situations or issues.[34] The book of Revelation, however, appears to have been written to the whole church. One may contend that the individual messages of 2:1–3:22 were first and foremost written to the churches to whom they were addressed. And though there is indeed an element of truth here, it is important to note that each of the messages closes with an address to all the churches: "Let the one who has an ear hear what the Spirit is saying to the churches" (2:7, 11, 17, 29; 3:6, 13, 22).

The book of Revelation, therefore, has features that correspond to apocalypses, prophecies, and letters. And although the book of Revelation does not fit into any of these categories perfectly, it is nonetheless, important to note that all three of these genres maintain a primary concern with the people to whom they were addressed. There is no question that the book of Revelation has an abiding significance for all readers in history, but this is no different than the Gospel of John, the book of Romans, James, or any other writing of the Old or New Testaments. The meaning of the book of Revelation, therefore, must first be grounded in its first-century context.

The Triune God 1:4–5

The offer of grace and peace are said to be from, "the One who is and who was and who is to come" (1:4, 8; 4:8)—whom we presume to be the Father[35]—and from "the seven spirits" (1:4)—which I will contend below is a designation for the Holy Spirit—and from Jesus (1:5). Taken together, the reference to the Father, the Spirit, and Jesus likely serves as a sort of trinitarian formula.[36] The order here of Father, Spirit, and Jesus, though deviating from the expected Father, Son, and Spirit, is not unusual in the NT.[37]

---

34. We call them "occasional" documents because they were written to address a particular occasion.

35. Boring comments that a similar expression was used of Zeus, "Zeus was, Zeus is and Zeus will be" (Boring, *Revelation*, 75).

36. Tabb notes, "The salutation in Revelation 1:4–5 is one of the most succinct and profound trinitarian declarations in the Scriptures" (Tabb, *All Things New*, loc. 685).

37. Most likely we expect Father, Son, and Spirit because of the familiarity with

The Father

The title, "the One who is and who was and who is to come" (1:4) is repeated in 1:8 and 4:8—though in 4:8 the past tense (who was) appears first. The use of this threefold title for God likely intends to affirm His eternality. God is at the same time the One who is, was, and is to come.

It is certainly significant that this threefold title occurs three times in the book of Revelation (1:4, 8; 4:8). Interestingly, John uses the title, "the One who is and who was" (11:17; 16:5), on two occasions. This shorter form, which omits "who is to come" occurs at points in the narrative in which the end is depicted as having come. Thus, when this latter variation of the title occurs, the reader/hearer is alerted to the fact that the end has come.

The Spirit

That John refers to "the seven spirits" in the midst of a description of God (the Father) and Jesus is a strong indication that "the seven spirits" refers to the Holy Spirit.[38] It is possible that John meant the "sevenfold" spirit,[39] which may be an allusion to Isa 11:2.

It is important to note that the Spirit is referred to as the "seven spirits" four times in the book of Revelation (1:4; 3:1; 4:5; 5:6). The fourfold reference to the "seven spirits" is appropriate because the Holy Spirit, or the "seven spirits," is described as being "sent out into all the earth" (5:6).

Jesus

Revelation 1:5 provides us with our first formal introduction to Jesus. It is not without significance that the very first title given to Jesus in the book of Revelation is, "the Faithful Witness" (1:5). In a book that is explicitly about Jesus, which exalts and magnifies Him repeatedly, in which He is described as the One clothed in magnificent splendor (1:12–16), and with exalted titles, such as "King of kings" (19:16), and as the One who

---

Matt 28:19. The NT does not have any consistent order. For examples of trinitarian formulae in the NT, see Matt 28:19; 1 Cor 12:4–5; 2 Cor 13:14; Eph 4:4–6; and 1 Pet 1:2.

38. Aune says the "seven spirits" are seven principal angels (Aune, *Revelation*, 1.33–35).

39. This is how the NLT translates it.

rides triumphantly on a white horse (19:11), this opening designation of Him as, "the Faithful Witness" appears somewhat mundane.

We might ask why, of all the accolades, titles, and attributes ascribed to Jesus, does the designation, "the Faithful Witness" appear first? I believe that the answer is found in the fact that Jesus is, in fact, "the Faithful Witness" *par excellence*! That is, Jesus is not only the resurrected, glorified Lord of all creation, who has "overcome" (5:5) but He is also the model which the people of God are called to follow.

Equally significant is the fact that the title, "the Faithful Witness" (1:5) is closely connected with His death. As we will see, what makes someone a faithful witness in the book of Revelation is persevering through death.[40] Thus, in 2:13, Antipas is identified as: "My witness, My faithful one, who was killed among you."[41] In other words, this opening title of Jesus as "the Faithful Witness" highlights Jesus's faithfulness on the cross and it serves as the model for the people of God to emulate.

Jesus is also titled "the Firstborn of the dead" (1:5). There is no question that this is meant to affirm the centrality of Jesus's resurrection. Jesus's resurrection and the fact that it was "first"—which suggests others will follow—most certainly is meant to encourage the people of God with the assurance that they too will follow Jesus in resurrection.

Finally, Jesus is "the Ruler of the kings of the earth" (1:5). As a result of His faithfulness in His death and His resurrection, Jesus has been exalted and enthroned with the Father (3:21). It is important to note that these three titles are to be viewed as a progression. That is, Jesus is "the Faithful Witness," which corresponds to His death. Jesus, however, was risen from the dead and is also "the Firstborn from the dead." As a result of His resurrection, He is now "the Ruler of the kings of the earth" and, as He will be titled later in the book, He is also the "King of kings" (19:16).

Recognizing this progression is critical for understanding not only the message of the book of Revelation but the entirety of the biblical witness. As we will see, the message to the seven churches is that, in order to reign with Christ—as the people of God are called to do—we must inherit our thrones just as Jesus did: that is, through our deaths and resurrections!

---

40. See 14:12–13.

41. I doubt that John meant to suggest that only those who are martyred for the Gospel are "faithful witnesses." After all, as far as we know, John himself was not a martyr.

The centrality of Jesus's death, resurrection, and ascension is further evident in the opening vision of Jesus and His words to John (1:12–20). John sees Jesus in His resurrected glory and notes, "When I saw Him, I fell at his feet as though I were dead" (1:17). Jesus, then, comforts John, saying, "Do not be afraid, I am the First and the Last and the One who is living, and I was dead and behold I am alive forever and ever and I have the keys of death and hades" (1:17–18).

Benediction 1:5–6

The opening description of the triune God ends with a benediction. Jesus is "the One who loves us and set us free from our sins by means of His blood . . . to Him be the glory and power forever" (1:5).

He is the One who is worthy of glory and power! In loving us so, Jesus also, "has made us a kingdom, priests to His God and Father" (1:6). The book of Revelation then reveals not merely that God sits on the throne as the world's true King, but that we, His people, are members of His kingdom. In fact, we are not merely members. After all, as we will learn, those who overcome will sit with Him on His throne (3:21). This means that, even in the present, we serve as kings/queens and priests.

In saying this, it is critical to also note that the title "servant"[42] for the people of God should remind us that this is how we become kings and queens in His eternal kingdom. That the word "servant" occurs fourteen times[43] (seven times two) indicates that as the people of God serve they become the perfect witnesses of Christ's kingdom.

---

42. See "slave" in deSilva, *Seeing*, 130n45. DeSilva notes, "it is also a traditional title of distinction, appearing frequently in early Christian literature to designate a leader (cf. Rom. 1:1; Gal. 1:0; Phil. 1:1; Titus 1:1; Jas. 1:1; 2 Pet. 1:1; Jude 1:1)" (deSilva, *Seeing*, 131).

43. See: 1:1*; 2:20; 6:15; 7:3; 10:7; 11:18; 13:16; 15:3; 19:2, 5, 18; 22:3, 6. The weakness of this suggestion is that three of the uses of "servant" indicate the nations and not the people of God (see 6:15; 13:16; and 19:18). The strength of this contention resides in the fact that John is quite intentional with his use of numbers.

That Jesus is the "Faithful Witness" (1:5), that the name "Jesus" occurs fourteen times in the book of Revelation (see 1:1, 2, 5, 9*; 12:17; 14:12; 17:6; 19:10*; 20:4; 22:16, 20, 21) and that Jesus's name occurs seven times with the designation 'witness' (1:2, 9; 12:17; 17:6; 19:10*; 20:4) lends some credence to this suggestion.

Excursus: The People of God as Kings/Queens and Priests

The idea of the people of God reigning and serving as priests is an extremely important concept in the Scriptures. It is, of course, the reason why God calls His people.

After the Lord led the Israelites out of Egypt, He told Moses to inform the Israelites that "you shall be to Me a kingdom of priests and a holy nation" (Exod 19:6). Israel's role was to be both rulers and priests to the nations. The call for God's people to rule and to serve as priests is also evident in Jesus's words to His disciples:

> The kings of the Gentiles lord it over them; and those who have authority over them are called 'Benefactors.' But it is not this way with you, but the one who is the greatest among you must become like the youngest, and the leader like the servant (Luke 22:25-26).

Notice how Jesus associates ruling with servanthood. In fact, a few verses later Jesus affirms that their call to be servants is in accord with their ruling: "just as My Father has granted Me a kingdom, I grant you" (Luke 22:29). Jesus grants His disciples a kingdom, but, He says, they are not to rule as the kings of this world do. Instead, they are to be servants.[44] That the NT people of God (and that includes us today also) are called to be kings/queens[45] as well as priests is affirmed in 1 Peter 2:9:

> But you are a chosen race, a royal priesthood, a holy nation, a people for God's own possession, so that you may proclaim the excellencies of Him who has called you out of darkness into His marvelous light.

---

44. Note the prominence of the designation "servant" to describe the people of God: 1:1*; 2:20; 6:15; 7:3; 10:7; 11:18; 13:16; 15:3; 19:2, 5, 18; 22:3, 6.

45. Since there is equality among Jew and gentile, slave and free, and male and female (Gal 3:28) there is no reason not to affirm that the NT people of God are kings and queens.

REVELATION 1:1–8

He Is Coming! 1:7–8

In 1:7, John exclaims, "He is coming with the clouds" (1:7). Our first problem here is ascertaining of whom John is speaking. In fact, both 1:7 and 1:8 present us with this difficulty.[46]

There are several indications that John has Jesus in view in 1:7. First, there is the fact that 1:7 clearly alludes to the coming of the Son of Man in Daniel 7. Daniel states, "with the clouds of heaven One like a Son of Man was coming" (Dan 7:13). Whoever this "One like a Son of Man" figure might be in Daniel,[47] we know that He is distinguished from the "Ancient of Days" because Daniel adds, "He came up to the Ancient of Days and was presented before Him" (Dan 7:13). Second, Jesus most certainly appropriates for Himself the title, "Son of Man" from Dan 7:13 in His response to the High Priest's interrogation.[48] Third, the conclusion that John has Jesus in view in 1:7 is confirmed by the fact that the, "One like a Son of Man" (14:14), who was seen "sitting on the cloud" (14:14) is most certainly Jesus.[49] This latter conclusion gains further support from the fact that "One like a Son of Man" occurs in only one other place in the Apocalypse (1:13) and there it certainly has Jesus in view.

This issue becomes more complicated in 1:8 because another speaker suddenly inserts himself into the account. The speaker identifies Himself as "the Alpha and the Omega." This title corresponds to the later couplets, "the Beginning and the End" (21:6; 22:13), and "the First and the Last" (1:17; 2:8). The meaning of these titles is clear. The speaker is the eternal One. That the speaker is eternal is highlighted by the concluding affirmation that He is the One, "who is and who was and who is to come" (1:8).

This leads to the conclusion that the speaker in 1:8 is the Father. After all, the Father was introduced in 1:4 with the same threefold designation. It is, however, conceivable that the speaker in 1:8 is also Jesus. After all, we have just concluded that the One who is coming in 1:7 is Jesus. In addition, the parallel title, "the First and the Last" is applied to Jesus in 1:17 and 2:8.[50]

46. See 22:6–7, 10–16.
47. See Longman, *Daniel*, 186–88; Lucas, *Daniel*, 183–87.
48. See Matt 26:64; Mark 14:62; Luke 21:27.
49. See commentary on 14:6–20.
50. To solve this dilemma in a unitarian way is to fail to recognize that the book of Revelation distinguishes between the persons of the Trinity. In 3:21, we are told that

Nonetheless, the conclusion that the speaker in 1:8 is the Father seems most warranted. For one, the title "the Alpha and the Omega" is used by the Father for Himself in 21:6.[51] In addition, the speaker in Rev 1:8 also says that He is the one, "who is and who was and who is to come." This title is used exclusively of God the Father throughout Revelation.[52] Finally, the speaker identifies Himself as "the Almighty" (1:8). The designation "Almighty" occurs nine times in the book of Revelation, seven of which are alongside "Lord, God," as it is here.[53] Therefore, it seems best to conclude that "the Almighty" always refers to the Father—as it certainly does in 4:8 and 21:22.

Conclusion

From the outset, the book of Revelation announces that Jesus is Lord and the world's true King. His death and resurrection have inaugurated what the Bible terms "the last days." God's people are to be encouraged and remain faithful. God, after all, is the One who is eternal and, as we will see, He sits enthroned as the world's true ruler. Therefore, just as Jesus was "the faithful witness", so shall we be!

Jesus sits on the Father's throne. In 5:7, Jesus is the Lion/Lamb who takes the scroll from the Father's hand.

51. Though one might contend (based on 3:21) that both Jesus and the Father sit on the throne, the most natural assumption throughout the book of Revelation is that the Father is the One who is seated on the throne.

52. Of course, that assumes that 1:8 is referring to the Father.

53. See 1:8; 4:8; 11:17; 15:3; 16:7, 14; 19:6, 15; 21:22.

Revelation 1:9–3:22
The First Story/Scene:
John on Patmos

Revelation 1:9–20
John's Vision on Patmos

Despite what many people today suppose, it is basic to the most elementary NT faith that Jesus is already ruling the whole world. That is one of the most important results of his resurrection[1]

John on Patmos 1:9–11

Brother 1:9

REVELATION 1:9 BEGINS THE first story (1:9—3:22). John introduces himself to his reader/hearers as their "brother." The members of the community of believers in Christ are related to one another as family. One of the revolutionary elements of Christianity was the concept that everyone, rich and poor, free and slave, male and female,[2] were equal members within the household of God. This is significantly different than how the Roman society functioned. The Roman world included both the family of the Roman Empire and the nuclear family. The Roman emperor, of course, was the head of the national family and had complete authority over it. The nuclear family was ruled by the father of the home. Slaves were included within the nuclear family but were not considered equals to the sons and daughters.

---

1. Wright, *Everyone*, 206.
2. See Gal 3:28; 1 Cor 12:12–27; Rom 8:14–17.

COMMENTARY: REVELATION 1:9–3:22

Tribulation, Kingdom, Patient endurance 1:9

We were told in the prologue that the followers of Christ are kings/queens.[3] Now John states that he also is a sharer with them in the "tribulation"[4] and "patient endurance" (1:9).[5]

Though popular theology often suggests otherwise, we should not be surprised that John associates "tribulation" with the people of God. Throughout the NT, "tribulation" refers primarily to what the people of God, as imitators of Christ, are called to endure.[6] Jesus even warned His disciples, "Then they will deliver you to tribulation, and will kill you, and you will be hated by all nations on account of My name" (Matt 24:9). Jesus also says, "In Me you may have peace. In the world you have tribulation but take courage; I have overcome the world" (John 16:33).

In the book of Acts, there are three occurrences of "tribulation" with regard to something that the people of God must undergo.[7] In Acts 11:19, Luke notes that tribulation is what the people of God endured: "So then those who were scattered because of the persecution . . . ." Then in Acts 14:22, Paul informs the churches of Lystra, Iconium, and Pisidian Antioch that they must endure many tribulations to enter the kingdom of God: "Through many tribulations we must enter the kingdom of God" (Acts 14:22). In Acts 20:23, Paul tells the Ephesian elders, "the Holy Spirit testifies to me in every city that imprisonment and afflictions await me."[8]

John's association of tribulation with "patient endurance" suggests that because the kingdom of God is one of tribulation it is also one that

---

3. See 1:6.

4. "Tribulation" occurs five times in the book of Revelation (1:9, 2:9, 10, 22: 7:14). For a discussion of "tribulation" in the NT, see my *Understanding*, 100–118.

5. The construction of the sentence in Greek links "tribulation," "kingdom," and "patient endurance" together by the use of a single article ("the"). Furthermore, they are all associated with being "in Christ." See Beale, *Revelation*, 200.

6. E.g., 2 Cor 6:4; Phil 4:14; Col 1:24; 1 Thess 1:6; 3:3; 2 Thess 1:4; Heb 10:33; Rev 1:9; 2:9, 10. The same conclusions hold true for the use of the verbal form *thlibo* (e.g., Matt 7:14; 2 Cor 4:8; 7:5; 1 Thess 3:4; 1 Tim 5:10; Heb 11:37. See: my *Understanding*, 100–118.

7. There are two other uses of tribulation in the book of Acts (7:10, 11), both of which are historical accounts: referring to either the affliction of Joseph himself or of the entire region.

8. The word for tribulation has the same meaning throughout the Greek version of the OT (LXX), where it is used consistently for the affliction of Israel and righteous individuals. The word for tribulation, *thlipsis*, in fact, occurs more than thirty times in the Greek version (LXX) of the Psalms in relation to the people of God. E.g., Ps 9:9. See Barnett, *Second Epistle to the Corinthians*, 72.

requires "patient endurance." "Patient endurance" indicates an ability to bear up under difficult circumstances. It is an active enduring. John uses "patient endurance" seven times in the book of Revelation.[9] Four of the seven occurrences of "patient endurance" are found in the seven messages (2:1–3:22).[10] The churches in Ephesus, Thyatira, and Philadelphia are commended for their patient endurance (2:2, 3, 19; 3:10).

In Revelation 13–14, John inserts a similar exhortation to the people of God. In 13:10 and 14:12, we learn that patient endurance is a necessity for God's people:

> Here is the patient endurance and the faith of the saints (13:10).

> Here is the patient endurance of the saints, the ones who are keeping the commandments of God and the faith of Jesus (14:12).

These two occurrences of "patient endurance" are helpful for our understanding of what "patient endurance" means in the book of Revelation. In 13:10, patient endurance is associated with active resistance to the Beast. In 14:12, it is directly tied to obedience to the commandment of God and faith in Jesus. For John, these two are inseparable. That is, in order to remain faithful to the commandment of God one must actively resist the Beast.

For John then, life in the kingdom of God is one of tribulation that requires patient endurance.

On the Island of Patmos 1:9

John adds that he was on the island of Patmos, "because of the word of God and the testimony of Jesus" (1:9).[11] Patmos is an island in the Aegean Sea just off the west coast of modern-day Turkey. Patmos was 37 miles from the harbor in Miletus and 65 miles from Ephesus.

When John says that he was on Patmos "because of the word of God," the most likely meaning is, "because I was proclaiming it."[12] Consequently, John appears to have been on the island of Patmos as

9. See 1:9; 2:2, 3, 19; 3:10; 13:10; 14:12.
10. See 2:2, 3, 19; 3:10.
11. See discussion of "word of God and testimony of Jesus" in 1:1–8.
12. The preposition *"dia"* never has a purposive sense—it doesn't look forward. Instead, it always looks backwards to a prior activity. This would mean that John was there not in order to preach, but because he was preaching. See deSilva, *Seeing*, 33.

a result of banishment. One of the difficulties here is that we have no knowledge that Patmos ever served as a penal colony. In fact, it is well established that Patmos was inhabited at the time of John.[13] This, of course, does not rule out the possibility that John was sent to Patmos as a political prisoner.

John Hears: Write to the Seven Churches 1:10–11

Revelation 1:10 provides us with the setting for the first story. John hears a voice and is told, "What you see write in a book and send it to the seven churches: to Ephesus, and to Smyrna, and to Pergamum, and to Thyatira, and to Sardis, and to Philadelphia, and to Laodicea" (1:11). John then turns to see who it is that was speaking to him (1:12), and when he turns he sees Jesus (1:13–16) who tells him to not be afraid (1:17) but to write[14] what he has seen (1:19).

John says that the voice he heard sounded like a trumpet. The description is reminiscent of the sound that Moses and the Israelites heard from Mt. Sinai: "there were thunder and lightning flashes and a thick cloud upon the mountain and a very loud trumpet sound, so that all the people who *were* in the camp trembled" (Exod 19:16).[15] Trumpets also bring to mind the seven trumpets that the Israelites sounded on the final day of encircling the city of Jericho (Josh 6:20). Just as the Israelites were afraid, so, apparently, was John. John is told, however, to "not be afraid" (1:17).

The Seven Lampstands and One Like a Son of Man 1:12–16

There is little doubt that John's writing of the Apocalypse builds off the prophets of the OT.[16] Longman affirms, "In 1:12–16 we read a magnificent

---

13. Aune asserts: "Patmos was certainly not a deserted island" (Aune, *Revelation*, 1.77).

14. Writing is very important: John is commanded to write 12x: 1:11, 19; 2:1, 8, 12, 18; 3:1, 7, 14; 14:13; 19:9; 21:5.

15. The association with the trumpet at Mt Sinai becomes all the more likely in light of the consistent use of Sinai and Exodus imagery throughout the book of Revelation. See Longman, *Revelation*, 59.

16. Though I will refer to the OT background for the book of Revelation throughout this commentary, I will not highlight it for a number of reasons. Most notable is the

and powerful figurative depiction of Christ, drawn from imagery describing Yahweh in both Ezekiel and Daniel."[17]

Seven Golden Lampstands 1:12[18]

After hearing the voice, John turns "to see the voice" that was speaking to him (1:12). And he sees "seven golden lampstands" (1:12). We are told in 1:20 that the seven lampstands represent the seven churches.

Lampstand has a rich significance in the Scriptures. In the OT, the lampstand was "before the Lord" and was to be tended by the priests.[19] Longman notes, "This lampstand was styled like a tree with cups shaped 'like almond flowers with buds' (Ex 25:33), clearly a tree symbol."[20] That the people of God are lampstands suggests that they are those who dwell in God's garden/temple presence.

John's use of lampstands, however, also serves to indicate the role of the people of God. That is, they are called to make Jesus, who is the lamp (21:23), known to the world. As the Gospel of Mark says, "a lamp is *coming* not to be set under a basket or under a bed, is it? Is it not *coming* to be set on the lampstand" (Mark 4:21).[21] In the book of Revelation, then, the people of God are indeed kings/queens and priests who stand in the presence of the Lord, but they do so in order to magnify the King of kings![22]

---

fact that the work has been done by others: See Longman, *Revelation*; Beale, *Revelation*. For an introduction to the OT in the book of Revelation, see my *Follow*, 54–63.

17. Longman, *Revelation*, 65.

18. "The seven churches are the menorah, and the menorah (by metonymy) is Israel. It would be hard to imagine a more direct identification between Israel and the ekklēsia." Magina, "God, Israel, and the Ecclesia in the Apocalypse," in Hays, *Revelation*, loc. 2108.

19. See Exod 27:20–21; Lev 24:4.

20. Longman, *Revelation*, 61.

21. My translation. The key here, which I have brought out in my translation is that "coming" is active in Greek—even though all the major English translations render the verb as passive, "brought." Translating the verb as a passive ("brought"), which is found in all major English translations makes sense of the fact that lamps do not come, they are brought. But if the lamp is Jesus, and the context of Mark 4 certainly supports this understanding, then Jesus is indicating that He, the lamp, is coming . . . ." To say, "The lamp is coming" accents the active verb. The point of Mark 4:21 is that Jesus [the lamp] is coming and we are not to hide him but to place Him on the lampstand.

22. See Matt 5:14–16. There is much to be said here. Certainly, making God known as His witnesses extends well beyond the spoken word. The people of God are to model

That the people of God are "golden" lampstands alludes to Zech 4:2–10. In Zechariah, the prophet sees a gold lampstand with seven lamps burning on top of it (Zech 4:2). The lamps are fed by two olive trees (Zech 4:3). Zechariah indicates that the oil signifies the Holy Spirit, who empowers the people of God. That is, the people of God are those who accomplish their work, "Not by might nor by power, but by My Spirit" (Zech 4:6). John now depicts all of God's people as lampstands.[23]

This brings to the fore the question of the role of the Holy Spirit in the book of Revelation.[24] Though the argument can be made that the Holy Spirit is not a central player in the Apocalypse, it seems best, in view of John's allusion to Zech 4:6, to conclude that the Holy Spirit is the empowering source behind the work of the people of God. Therefore, even though the Holy Spirit does not explicitly play a central role in the book of Revelation, there is an assumed prominence of the Holy Spirit in the life of God's people.[25]

One Like a "Son of Man" 1:13

In 1:13–16, John describes the appearance of Jesus. He begins by noting that he was like "a Son of Man" (1:13) We know from the Gospels that the title "Son of Man" was Jesus's favorite title for Himself.[26] The most prominent OT backdrop for the title "Son of Man" is found in the book of Ezekiel.[27] In Ezekiel, the title is often the means by which God refers to the prophet: "Then He said to me, 'Son of man, stand on your feet that I may speak with you!'" (Ezek 2:1).

Christ. They imitate Him in their suffering—which the NT associates with Jesus's silence (1 Pet 2:23; Isa 53:7). In addition, as we will see, the people of God in the book of Revelation do not compromise with the pagan world of Rome and as a result, they suffer. Those who persevere in the face of Roman threats of imprisonment and even death are the "faithful witnesses."

23. See the discussion of the Two Witnesses as lampstands in 11:1–19.

24. See Thomas, "The Spirit," in Koester, *Oxford Handbook*, loc. 331–51.

25. The diminished role of the Holy Spirit in the book of Revelation must also be understood in light of the fact that the book of Revelation is about Jesus (1:1). Even in acknowledging this, the Holy Spirit is not left out. After all, where Jesus is the Spirit is also. As 2 Cor 3:17 states, "Now the Lord is the Spirit, and where the Spirit of the Lord is, *there* is liberty."

26. The title "Son of Man" occurs 81 times in the Gospels; most of which consist of Jesus's use of the title for Himself. E.g., Matt 8:20; 12:8; 26:45; Mark 2:28; Luke 17:22; John 3:13.

27. The title occurs over 90 times in Ezekiel.

The title "Son of Man" also occurs in the book of Daniel. Its use in Dan 7:13–14 is quite likely the text John has in mind here.[28] In Daniel, the "Son of Man" is a collective noun that refers to the nation of Israel. Jesus, however, appropriates the term to refer to Himself. This leads to the conviction that Jesus viewed Himself as the representative of the people of God.

Moreover, in the Gospels, Jesus employs the title the "Son of Man" in order to identify Himself with the power and privileges that belong exclusively to God. This is most explicit in Matt 26:64, where Jesus refers to Himself as the "Son of Man" and cites both Ps 110:1 ("sitting at the right hand of power") and Dan 7:13 ("coming on the clouds of heaven"). In doing so, Jesus associates His rights and privileges as the "Son of Man" with those that belong exclusively to God.[29]

That John understands Jesus as the Son of Man in accordance with the figure in the book of Daniel is evident both from the influence of Daniel 7 in the book of Revelation[30] and in the description of Jesus that follows.

Robe and a Sash 1:13

John's description of Jesus then moves to His clothing. He notes that Jesus is "clothed in a long robe" and has a "golden sash" around His chest (1:13). This clothing corresponds to that of the High Priest.[31] Since the High Priest's role included attending to the lampstands, it may be that Jesus is depicted here as One who is intimately present in the life of God's people. Jesus's presence in the midst of the Ephesian church is surely what is meant by the opening depiction of Him in the message to Ephesus: "the One who walks among the seven golden lampstands" (2:1). John portrays Jesus, then, as the resurrected and glorified Lord who is present in the midst of God's people.

---

28. Longman, *Revelation*, 62; Beale, *Revelation*, 208.

29. That this is the best reading of Matt 26 is indicated by the High Priest's reaction: "Then the high priest tore his robes and said, 'He has blasphemed!'" (Matt 26:65).

30. See Beale, *Use of Daniel*.

31. See Exod 28:4–8.

COMMENTARY: REVELATION 1:9–3:22

Sevenfold Description of Jesus 1:14–16[32]

After the brief indication of Jesus's clothing, John then begins to describe Jesus Himself. In doing so, John includes seven features of Jesus.[33] Interestingly, many of these features correspond to attributes of the Father in the OT.[34]

Each of the seven features of Jesus in 1:14–16 highlights His role as the end times judge. Thus, on the one hand, to those who are patiently enduring the time of tribulation, Jesus is the risen Lord who has overcome and has the keys of death and Hades (1:18). Yet, on the other hand, to those who have compromised their witness, Jesus is the righteous Judge.[35] And for those who are wavering between allegiance to Jesus and allegiance to the empire, Jesus is both the One who has overcome and the righteous judge.

Consequently, the depiction of Jesus as the eschatological judge serves a twofold purpose. First, the threat of a final judgment serves as a warning to those within the people of God who have either denied their faith in Christ or are being tempted to do so. Second, it functions as a source of hope for the people of God: namely, that the day of their redemption and the end of their suffering will come.

His Head and His Hair Were White 1:14

The first description of Jesus combines two features: "His head and his hair were white like wool, like white snow" (1:14). Interestingly, the description of Jesus's head and hair echoes the description of the Father in Dan 7:9: "His vesture *was* like white snow and the hair of His head like pure wool." Longman notes, "While none of these Old Testament

---

32. That there are seven features in John's description of Jesus (see below) may be contested. In order to arrive at seven here, we must exclude His robe and His sash in 1:13 from the list that follows in 1:14–16. This appears to be justified, however, by means of the use of the particle *de* ("but" or "and") in 1:14. That is, the use of *de* in 1:14 marks the beginning of the list and it sets 1:14–16 apart from 1:13.

33. 1:14—16: His head and hair, His eyes, His feet, His voice, His right hand, His mouth, His face. Note "His" is used seven times for Jesus in 1:14–16.

34. See Longman, "The description of his clothing, body, and voice echo various descriptions of visions of Yahweh in the Old Testament" (Longman, *Revelation*, 62).

35. Note that this description highlights Jesus's role as the end-times Judge is not the same as saying that the book of about wrath. The focus of Jesus's judgment here and in the seven messages are those in the seven churches.

descriptions of the appearance of Yahweh are exactly identical to John's vision of the glorified Christ, they all echo elements of it and share similarities."[36]

Since, the context of the Ancient of Days in Dan 7:9 includes God as the righteous Judge,[37] John's association of Jesus with the Ancient of Days is another indication that Jesus is the end times judge.

Eyes Were Like a Flame of Fire 1:14

Second, John adds that "His eyes were like a flame of fire" (1:14; see 19:12). This description conforms to the portrait of the returning Christ in 19:11–16, who is certainly depicted as, among other things, the coming Judge. The presence of fire here suggests the fires of purification.[38] Paul uses a similar description when speaking of Jesus's return, he says, "being revealed from heaven with His mighty angels in flaming fire" (2 Thess 1:7). In Rev 5:6, John notes that Jesus has "seven eyes." He then adds that Jesus's seven eyes are "the seven Spirits of God, sent out into all the earth" (5:6).

That Jesus's eyes are "like a flame of fire" (1:14) and that He has "seven eyes" (5:6) suggests that He is not only the coming judge, but He is the all-seeing judge of the world and the source of true justice.

Feet Like Burnished Bronze 1:15

Third, John observes, "and His feet were like burnished bronze, as when it has been made refined in a furnace" (1:15). Fire is often used to melt away impure objects from precious metals. In 3:18, the church in Laodicea was urged to buy "gold refined by fire in order that you may become rich." Here, Jesus's feet are burnished with bronze that has been refined by fire. The purifying of the bronze in a furnace suggests moral purity. There may also be an indication of strength and stability. This derives from a contrast with the fragile feet of the statue in Daniel 2, which had feet "partly of iron and partly of clay" (Dan 2:33, 41–43).

---

36. Longman, *Revelation*, 62–63. Wilson notes, "some of the metaphorical language—white as snow, white like wool, blazing fire—is drawn from the description of the Ancient of Days in Daniel 7:9. Now John applies such language to the Living One who is the First and Last" (Wilson, "Spirit," 90).

37. Note he "took His seat" (Dan 7:9).

38. Beale suggests it "is a metaphor of judgment" (Beale, *Revelation*, 209).

COMMENTARY: REVELATION 1:9–3:22

At the very least, I would suggest that this description of Jesus characterizes Him as a person of strength and stability and as having a foundation that is morally pure. As a result, He is more than fit to serve as the coming judge.

Voice Like the Sound of Many Waters 1:15

Fourth, John says, "His voice was like the voice of many waters" (1:15). It is quite likely that the use of "many waters" here echoes Ezekiel's vision of the end-times temple, where the voice of God was also, "like the sound of many waters" (Ezek 43:2).[39]

Right Hand He Held Seven Stars 1:16

Fifth, Jesus has seven stars in His right hand (1:16). In 1:20, John tells us the meaning of the seven stars: "The mystery of the seven stars which you saw in My right hand ... is this: the seven stars are the angels of the seven churches." That the seven stars are in Jesus's right hand suggests that Jesus is the One who is in sovereign oversight and control of the churches.

Mouth: A Sharp Two-Edged Sword

Sixth, John says that "out of His mouth came a sharp[40] two-edged sword" (1:16). The most likely OT context for this imagery is that of the messianic conqueror in Isa 11:4 and 49:2.[41] In Isa 11:4, the prophet, speaking of the messianic conqueror, states:

> But with righteousness He will judge the poor,
> And decide with fairness for the afflicted of the earth;
> And He will strike the earth with the rod of His mouth,
> And with the breath of His lips He will slay the wicked.

In addition, Isa 49:2, referring to the servant, says, "He has made My mouth like a sharp sword."

---

39. See Longman, *Revelation*, 62.

40. The word for sharp (*oksis*) occurs 7x in the book of Revelation (1:16; 2:12; 14:14, 17, 18*, 19:15). Note that the first and the last occurrences depict the resurrected Christ (1:16) and the returning Christ (19:15).

41. See Weima, *Sermons*, 91.

Excursus: Jesus's Sword and Divine Violence

The presence of a sharp sword in the mouth of Christ brings into the discussion the issue of divine violence. It is commonplace among scholars of the book of Revelation to assert that Jesus's return results in violence against the nations. Longman suggests:

> The image of a lethal weapon coming from the mouth of the glorified Christ in Revelation, with its background in Isaiah 11:4, indicates that this one has the power to kill the wicked by means of his words. The description in Revelation anticipates that Jesus returns to bring violent judgment against the wicked and leads us to reject recent attempts to take the reference to the sword as having a nonviolent meaning.[42]

Beale adds, "The consensus is that this sword alludes to that of the Roman soldier, used in battle, further enhancing this idea."[43]

There are, however, a multitude of reasons to suspect that this conclusion does not necessarily follow in the book of Revelation. First, I strongly believe that to read Revelation well, and the entirety of the NT for that matter, means that we must recognize Jesus is the King of kings (17:14; 19:16). This means that it is Jesus who wields the sword and not Rome![44] At the same time, I cannot stress enough the fact that the NT clearly distinguishes the kingdom of God from the kingdoms of the world. As I noted in the introduction, the kingdoms of the world wield their power through force and military might. This is the meaning of the "sword" in the Greco-Roman world.[45] Jesus, however, uses love and sacrifice for the sake of the other. He even commands His disciples to put their swords away (John 18:11). And He healed the servant's ear which was wounded by His disciple's sword (Luke 21:51).

---

42. Longman, *Revelation*, 63.

43. Beale, *Revelation*, 212.

44. Weima affirms, "Jesus—not Rome—is the one who truly has the ultimate power over life and death" (Weima, *Sermons*, 92).

45. The *Dictionary of Biblical Imagery* notes, "The sword was the most important weapon of warfare in the ancient Near East and in the Greco-Roman world" (835).

Second, there is no question that John, along with other writers in the NT, appropriates the sword imagery and applies it to Jesus's spoken word. That the sword indicates Jesus's spoken word is supported by the statement in Heb 4:12, where the "Word of God . . . is sharper than a double-edged sword."[46] That this is the meaning in the book of Revelation is evident by the fact that the "sharp sword" comes from His mouth (1:16; 19:15, 21).

That Jesus's sword indicates His spoken word based on the parallel with Heb 4:12, however, must account for the fact that Rev 1:16 employs a different word (*romphaia*) than that which is used in Heb 4:12 (*maxaira*). A careful examination of John's use of "sword" in the book of Revelation not only accounts for why John's choice of word for the "sword" which came from Christ's mouth differs from that of Heb 4:12, but it also reinforces my contention that John's portrayal of Jesus is non-violent in contrast to the violence of Rome.

I would begin by noting that John seemingly uses *romphaia* and *maxaira* interchangeably. The two words were certainly used interchangeably in the Greek version (LXX) of the Balaam account in Num 22:23, 29, 31.[47] That John uses the two words interchangeably is indicated by the fact that John alternates between the two words in the descriptions of the Second (6:4 *maxaira*) and Fourth (6:8 *romphaia*) Seals.

At the same time, there was a distinction between the two swords in the first century. The *maxaira* was a short, dagger-like sword that, like a knife, was used for cutting. The *maxaira* was also the term used to indicate the sword of the Roman executioner. John, in fact, uses *maxaira* to refer to the Roman sword of execution in 13:10* and 14. The *romphaia*, however, was a larger sword with a two-foot-long handle and a three-foot-long blade.[48]

Although John, in accord with the LXX, uses the two words interchangeably in 6:4, 8, this does not appear to sufficiently capture his use of these two words. For, upon closer

---

46. See 13:10, 14.

47. Thanks to Mark Wilson for first pointing this out to me in a personal email: July 5, 2022.

48. See Weima, *Sermons*, 93.

examination John always uses *romphaia* to indicate Jesus's sword (see 1:16; 2:12, 16; 19:15, 21) and *maxaira* to refer to the Roman sword of execution (13:10*, 14).

It is my contention, therefore, that John both uses the two words interchangeably and he uses them with a particular referent in view. That is, he only uses *maxaira* when referring to the sword of Rome. And he only uses *romphaia* to refer to the sword that comes from Jesus's mouth. In doing so, John avoids the association of Jesus's sword with the Roman sword of death. Jesus's sword is not the same as that of the Romans.

If this is so, then we might conclude that John intentionally contrasts Jesus's sword with the sword of Rome! This would also account for why John does not use *maxaira* in accord with Heb 4:12. For John, maxaira was the sword of Rome.

Consequently, although the "two-edged sword" coming from the mouth of Jesus continues the description of Jesus as the end-times Judge, the assertion that Jesus is portrayed as a person of violence does not necessarily follow.

His Face Was Like the Sun Shining in Its Strength 1:16

Seventh, John tells us that His "appearance was like the sun shining in its power" (1:16).

Although John's description of Jesus essentially derives from the OT, it is not inconceivable that this image builds off the language of the Transfiguration of Jesus. In Matthew's account of the Transfiguration, Jesus's face "shone like the sun" and "His garments became as white as light" (Matt 17:2).[49]

There is, however, a subtle difference between Matthew's portrait of Jesus at the Transfiguration and John's description in the present account. In Matthew's account, Jesus's face (*prosopon*) "shone like the sun" (Matt 17:2).[50] In the book of Revelation, however, John says that Jesus's

---

49. The nearest OT equivalent to this description occurs in Ps 84:11: "For the Lord God is a sun and shield."

50. Mark 9:3 only refers to His garments, and Luke 9:29 says that His face became "different."

appearance (*opsis*) "shone like the sun."⁵¹ That is, for John, Jesus's entire appearance "was like the sun shining in its power."⁵²

John Reacts to Jesus's Presence 1:17–20

Fell at His Feet 1:17

After seeing the resurrected, glorified Lord ("when I saw Him" 1:17), John does what everyone should do: He "fell at His feet" (1:17). This parallels the response of Peter, James, and John at the transfiguration: they "fell face down to the ground and were terrified" (Matt 17:6), as well as the response of Ezekiel when he saw the Lord (Ezek 1:28).

John not only falls down at His feet, but he does so "as a dead man" (1:17). This is perhaps his way of expressing that he was terrified.

Do Not Be Afraid 1:17

Jesus responds to John by telling him to "not be afraid" (1:17) because the One speaking to him is none other than, "the First and the Last" (1:17). This corresponds with Daniel's vision in Dan 10:10–18. Daniel, like John, was also deeply afraid (Dan 10:10). And, like John, the messenger comforted Daniel and instructed him to not be afraid (Dan 10:12).

John's language is also reminiscent of the prophet Isaiah's reminder that the people of God should not fear because the One who called them is their Maker:

> Thus says the Lord who made you
> And formed you from the womb, who will help you,
> Do not fear, O Jacob My servant;
> And you Jeshurun whom I have chosen (Isa 44:2).

---

51. The word *opsis*, which oftentimes is synonymous with "face," has a more general reference to one's outward appearance. The NKJ uses "countenance."

52. As we proceed, we will observe that the New Jerusalem is devoid of the sun (see 21:23) which means that it will not "beat down on them" anymore (7:16). On the contrary, the nations will experience an intensification of the sun's effects so that it will "scorch people with fire" (16:9).

REVELATION 1:9–20

Living One Who Was Dead and Is Alive 1:18

Not only is Jesus the First and the Last He is also "the One who is living" and who "was dead" and now is "alive forever and ever" (1:18).

As I noted earlier, it cannot be overstated how important the death and resurrection of Jesus is for understanding the book of Revelation. It is Jesus's death and resurrection that inaugurated the eschaton. And, as we will see, it is because Jesus was dead and has come to life that He is worthy, "to take the Scroll and open its seals" (5:9). Jesus's death and resurrection also means that He has made us, "a kingdom and priests to our God" and we "will reign upon the earth" (1:6; 5:10).

Keys of Death and Hades 1:18

Jesus then declares to John that He has "the keys of death and Hades" (1:18). This signifies that Jesus is King over the realm of the dead. Gordon Fee states it well when he says: "As a great preacher in the black tradition once told it on an Easter Sunday, playing the role of Satan, he shouted to the demonic host, 'He's got away! He's got away! and He's got the keys!'"[53]

Mystery 1:20

The chapter comes to a close by revealing the "mystery" concerning the seven stars and the seven lampstands (1:20). Though the word "mystery" may suggest to the modern reader something veiled or hidden, it is important to recognize that throughout the NT the word is used consistently to indicate something that is no longer hidden but unveiled.[54] The reason why mysteries are no longer hidden is that Christ Himself, as Paul says, is "a true knowledge of God's mystery" (Col 2:2).

What is the mystery of the seven stars and the seven lampstands? "The seven stars are the angels of the seven churches, and the seven lampstands are the seven churches" (1:20). Lampstands are commonly understood as symbols of God's Spirit which was to empower Israel in the completion of the construction of the temple.[55] In Zechariah the

---

53. Fee, *Revelation*, 19.

54. See: Matt 18:11; Mark 4:11; Luke 8:10; Rom 11:25; 16:25; 1 Cor 15:51; Eph 1:9; 3:3; Col 1:26, 27; 2:2.

55. See Zech 4:6; Rev 4:5. In addition, it is worth noting that the lampstand has also long been recognized as symbolizing Israel. See Beale, *Revelation*, 208.

lampstand indicated the sufficiency of the Spirit to accomplish the rebuilding of the temple: "'Not by might nor by power, but by My Spirit,' says the Lord of hosts" (Zech 4:6).[56] This parallels the commissioning of the people of God to be His witnesses in Acts 1:8.[57] Thus, G. K. Beale concludes, "So new Israel, the church, is to draw its power from the Spirit, the divine presence, before God's throne in its drive to stand against the world's resistance. . . . Consequently, the 'lampstand' (the church) is given power by the seven lamps on it, a power primarily to witness as a light uncompromisingly to the world."[58]

Conclusion

We should not read a passage like this without stopping to ponder the magnificence of Christ. What stands out in the description of Jesus is that the dominant theme is Jesus as the end times judge. As alluded to above, it is critical to recognize the importance of the description of Jesus as the end-times judge for the communities to whom the book of Revelation was written.

Apocalypses were written in large part to encourage the people of God who were either in a crisis or about to face a crisis. For John, it was critical that his reader/hearers remain faithful and persevere as imitators of Christ. John's description of Jesus as the coming judge serves first to warn those within the seven churches who have either already compromised their faith or who are tempted to do so. After all, Jesus stands as the eschatological Judge "in the middle of the lampstands" (1:13). John also endeavors to encourage those in the seven churches to hang in there! Jesus as the coming judge serves to remind the followers of Christ that

---

56. This is an important point when it comes to the interpretation of the book of Revelation. It seems to many that the Holy Spirit does not play much of a role in the book. Though I think this is somewhat overstated, I would note both that the primary focus of the book is on Jesus as the Lamb who was slain and has defeated death and the fact that the role of the Holy Spirit is to some extent assumed.

57. The use of "lampstands" to convey the call to witnessing receives further support from the use of *lamp* in the OT and NT, the Apocrypha, and non-biblical writings. See Zech 4:2–6; Matt 5:14–16; John 5:35; Sir. 48:1; *Targ. Ps.-J.* Zech 4:7. See Beale, *Revelation*, 574, who references *Sifre* Deut 10 and *Pesitka Rabbati* 51.4. Within this literature lampstand imagery also serves as a figurative expression for the Word of God, the message of the prophets, and the presence of God.

58. Beale, *Revelation*, 207. Even more prominent than this is the association of light with witness as found in the Synoptic Gospels. See Mark 4:21–22; Matt 5:14–16; Luke 8:16–17.

they too are able to persevere in the midst of suffering. God will vindicate them. After all, what is the worst that can happen to them? Death? No problem. Jesus is "the One who is living," who "was dead," and is "alive forever and ever" (1:18). And "He's got the keys!"

Revelation 2:1–3:22
The Seven Messages[1]

John prepares the hearers for the cost of bearing witness (6:9; 17:6), but also insists that 'witness' is the path to overcoming the Satanic powers of this age (12:11). Sharing in Christ's task of bearing testimony leads to sharing in Christ's messianic reign (20:4).[2]

Complacency and compromise with an accommodating culture was at least as much a problem as conflict and opposition.[3]

Introduction to the Seven Messages

IN ORDER TO UNDERSTAND the seven messages (2:1–3:22),[4] we must first recognize that they were written to seven first-century churches (Ephesus, Smyrna, Pergamum, Thyatira, Sardis, Philadelphia, and Laodicea), which were located in the Roman province of Asia (the west coast of modern-day Turkey).[5] It is possible that John may have had some oversight of the churches in these cities and that is why he was in a position to produce these messages. It is also important to recognize that they are not strictly epistles or letters, but, as we will see, they

---

1. In consideration of the length of the present work, the discussion of the seven messages will not take the form of a "commentary" per se. Instead, I will provide an overview of 2:1—3:22 focusing on the key elements of the seven messages as it pertains to the overall thesis of the work.

2. DeSilva, *Seeing*, 71.

3. Paul, *Revelation*, 22.

4. DeSilva calls them "oracles" (deSilva, *Unholy Allegiances*, loc. 1261–70).

5. See Beale, *Revelation*, 4–27 for a detailed discussion of the dating of the book of Revelation.

function as prophetic messages to the seven churches. More importantly, they are a vital component to the rest of the Apocalypse. That is, even though I view 4:1—16:21 as a second section and distinct from the opening section of 1:9–3:22, it is important to recognize that the sections are very much interrelated.

The Genre of the Seven Messages and the Book of Revelation

It has been fairly common for interpreters to read the seven messages (2:1–3:22) in isolation from the rest of the book of Revelation. One of the primary justifications for this is that it is assumed that there is a difference in genre between the seven messages and the apocalyptic vision that comprises the rest of the Apocalypse. This conclusion is simply not accurate. It is my contention that the seven "letters" function as prophetic messages to the churches.

Epistolary

The problem with viewing the seven messages as epistolary is that they display little in common with ancient epistles. In fact, they lack most, if not all, of the common features of the NT epistles. Jeffrey Weima observes, "The almost universal identification of Rev 2–3 as 'letters,' however, is severely undermined by the fact that this material contains not even one formal feature typically found in letters of that day."[6]

Prophecy

Each of the seven messages begins with the prophetic formula, "These are the words of" (*tade legei*: 2:1, 8, 12, 18; 3:1, 7, 14). This expression is commonly used by the prophets to introduce a prophetic saying from God. This indicates that John is not serving in the role of the author of a letter but as a prophet delivering a message. The seven messages then, are prophetic revelations. This is why David deSilva refers to them as "oracles,"

---

6. Weima, *Sermons*, 2. See also, Michaels: "They are not letters, however, in any sense of the word" (Michaels, *Revelation*, 64).

The contents of these chapters, then, would be far more fittingly referred to as 'seven prophetic messages' or 'seven oracles', and they accomplish precisely what the oracles of the Hebrew prophets set out to do for their audiences: diagnosing where the hearers are going astray from God's vision for them, affirming those who are remaining loyally obedient, warning of the negative consequences of the former path, assuring those following the latter path of the good that God has in store for them."[7]

Apocalyptic

The seven messages also include apocalyptic features. This is evidenced primarily by the use of the apocalyptic catchphrase, which occurs at the conclusion of each of the seven messages, "Let the one who has an ear hear what the Spirit is saying to the churches" (2:7, 11, 17, 29; 3:6, 13, 22).[8]

This expression has roots in the OT. The prophet Ezekiel used a similar expression following a parabolic act: "But when I speak to you, I will open your mouth and you will say to them, 'Thus says the Lord God.' He who hears, let him hear; and he who refuses, let him refuse; for they are a rebellious house" (Ezek 3:27). Similarly, the prophet Jeremiah exhorted, "Now hear this, O foolish and senseless people, who have eyes but do not see; who have ears but do not hear" (Jer 5:21).

Interestingly, in the Gospels, Jesus employs the apocalyptic catchphrase, "let the one who has an ear hear," after He spoke a parable.[9] For Jesus, the expression indicates that what He was saying was not going to be understood by His listeners. Those who had "ears," however, which indicates "those who are willing to come to Jesus and to follow Him," will gain understanding. Thus, Jesus used the apocalyptic catchphrase to indicate that His parables and the message of the kingdom were for some and not for others: "To you it has been granted to know the mysteries of the kingdom of heaven, but to them it has not been granted" (Matt 13:11).[10]

---

7. DeSilva, *Discovering*, 45.
8. A similar expression occurs in 13:9.
9. See Matt 11:15; 13:9; Mark 4:9, 23; Luke 8:8; 14:35.
10. Thus, after Jesus tells the Parable of the Sower (Mark 4:3–9), Mark notes that "His followers, along with the twelve, *began* asking Him *about* the parables" (Mark 4:10). Mark explains, "With many such parables He was speaking the word to them, so

The use of the apocalyptic catchphrase in the seven messages indicates that the message of the book of Revelation is only for the "one who has an ear"—that is, for those who are willing to come to Jesus and to follow Him. This expression, therefore, indicates that there is a deeper reality to the seven messages that may only be perceived by those who are willing to follow Jesus.[11]

The Seven Messages and Their Wider Audience

It is also important to recognize that while each of the seven messages is addressed to a particular first-century church in the Roman province of Asia, each has in view the wider, and one might say universal, community of Christ-followers.

This is indicated first by the fact that each of the seven messages ends with an exhortation to all the churches, "Let the one who has an ear hear what the Spirit is saying to the churches" (2:7, 11, 17, 29; 3:6, 13, 22). Even more notable is the fact that in the very middle of the seven messages we read, "and all the churches will know that I am the One who searches the minds and hearts" (2:23).

Finally, that the seven messages have the universal church in view is suggested by the fact that there are seven churches. As noted earlier, the number seven is consistently used in the book of Revelation to refer to wholeness, completeness, and perfection.

The Structure of the Seven Messages and Their Relationship to One Another

It is also important to recognize that the seven messages should not be read simply as seven individual correspondences, but as a whole.

---

far as they were able to hear it; and He did not speak to them without a parable; but He was explaining everything privately to His own disciples" (Mark 4:33–34).

11. G. K. Beale notes that the expression "has the dual function of signifying that the symbolic revelation will be received by the elect but rejected by unbelievers" (Beale, *Revelation*, 234).

Three-Four Pattern

One of the key literary features of the seven messages is that they display a three-four structure.[12] This is evident in that in the first three messages the exhortation to "the one who has an ear" (2:7, 11, 17) precedes the promise "to the one who overcomes" (2:7, 11, 17). In the last four messages, however, this is reversed so that the promise to the one who overcomes (26; 3:5, 12, 21) precedes the exhortation to "the one who has an ear" (2:29; 3:6, 13, 22).

Chiasm and the Seven Messages

Another important feature of John's account of the seven messages is that they exhibit what I prefer to call a loose chiastic structure.[13]

The clearest indication of a chiastic arrangement in the seven messages—albeit a loose arrangement—is found in the parallels between the messages to the churches in Smyrna (second) and Philadelphia (sixth). In both of these churches, there appears to have been tensions between the community of Christ-followers and the local Jewish communities. Both of these messages refer to those who "say they are Jews" (2:9; 3:9) but are instead a "synagogue of Satan" (2:9; 3:9).[14]

Additionally, viewing the seven messages as a loose chiasm is supported by the fact that the messages to Smyrna (second) and Philadelphia (sixth) are also the only two messages that do not contain any words of censure.[15]

A loose chiastic arrangement is evident in that the messages to Ephesus (first), and Laodicea (seventh), as well as Pergamum (third) and Sardis (fifth), contain the command to "repent" (Ephesus: 2:5*; Laodicea

---

12. See Bauckham, *Climax*, 10.

13. A chiasm is a literary device that was often employed in the ancient world in which items are arranged in such a way that the first and last items correspond to one another, as do the second and second to last items, and so on (e.g., ABCDC'B'A').

14. For a discussion on whether or not John was antisemitic, see my, "Was John Antisemitic?," 128–49.

15. See the discussion below where it is noted that each of the seven messages contain both words of commendation and words of censure. The letters to Smyrna and Philadelphia stand as exceptions in that they do not contain any words of censure. It is here, however, that the evidence for a chiastic structure to the seven messages begins to break down. For example, the two messages that have no words of commendation are Sardis (fifth) and Laodicea (seventh). As such, they do not maintain the chiastic structure.

3:19; Pergamum: 2:16; Sardis: 3:3). This command then intensified in the central message to Thyatira (2:21*, 22).[16]

The significance of recognizing a chiastic structure to the seven messages, even if it is only a loose chiastic structure, is that it recognizes the centrality and therefore the prominence of the message to Thyatira (2:18–29).

The Message to Thyatira as the Center of the Apocalypse

Viewing the seven messages in light of an albeit loose chiastic arrangement heightens the importance of the message to the church in Thyatira, which forms the center of the chiasm.

The prominence of the message to the church in Thyatira is evidenced by the fact that it is the only message of the seven in which Christ is named.[17] In addition, although each of the seven messages includes an exhortation and a promise to "the one who overcomes" (2:7, 11, 17, 26; 3:5, 12, 21), the message to the church in Thyatira includes an additional phrase: "and the one who keeps my works until the end" (2:26).

The heightened importance of the message to Thyatira is evident in the extended denouncement of the prophetess[18] who is so-named "Jezebel."[19] This prophetess failed to repent even though she was granted the time to do so: "I gave her time in order that she might repent, and she is not willing to repent of her immorality" (2:21). Consequently, after noting her failure to repent, Jesus issues a stern warning: "Behold, I am throwing her on a bed [of illness], and those who commit adultery

---

16. The command to repent occurs twelves times in the book of Revelation (2:5*, 16, 21*, 22; 3:3, 19; 9:20, 21; 16:9, 11), eight of which are in the seven messages. That it occurs in the first and seventh, the third and fifth, and the central fourth messages supports the suggestion that the seven messages incorporate chiastic features.

17. Jesus is named "the Son of God" in 2:18. There are other instances in which John names something in the middle of a series. For example, in the Fourth Seal, which is the middle of the Seven Seals, John notes that the rider of the horse is named "Death" (6:8). Another example occurs in the naming of the "Son of Man" in the narrative of 14:6–20, which occurs in the middle of the six references to "another angel" (14:6, 8, 9, 15, 17, 18).

18. It is interesting to observe that John does not denounce her as false because she is a woman. One would think that if women were not allowed to teach or have authority in the churches, John would have silenced her by reiterating this fact. That John never addresses her gender as the reason why she should not be followed suggests that her gender was not an issue.

19. It is doubtful that "Jezebel" was her actual name.

with her into great tribulation, unless they repent of her works. And I will kill her children[20] with death" (2:22-23).[21] Thus, although the command to repent occurs in the messages to the churches of Ephesus (2:5*), Pergamum (2:16), Sardis (3:3), and Laodicea (3:19), it is the message to Thyatira that intensifies the command and includes a substantial threat for those who fail to do so.

The intensification of the command to repent and the extrapolation of the consequences for those who fail to do so in the message to Thyatira, which serves as the center of the seven messages, suggests that the need for the people of God to repent is at the heart of the seven messages. Recognizing that the message to the church in Thyatira functions as the center of a loose chiasm in the seven messages serves to reinforce this conviction.[22]

Excursus: Reconciling God's Love and Wrath

The words of impending judgment on "Jezebel" and "her children" appear overly harsh. This raises the question as to how we might reconcile such words with my contention that the biblical story, including the book of Revelation, is a love story.[23] In response, I would begin by noting that the concept of God as One who holds over the heads of humanity the threat of His anger—unless they repent—is fraught with difficulties.

First, the biblical story consistently indicates that God delays His just judgment in order that humanity may have

---

20. When Jesus says, "I will kill her children" (2:23), the implication is that not only will the prophetess be judged, but so will all who commit adultery with her! It is not referring to her literal children.

21. This passage appears overly harsh to our modern ears. See excursus on "Reconciling God's love and wrath" below.

22. The importance of repentance with regard to the churches is supported by the fact that the word for "repent" occurs twelve times in the book of Revelation: see 2:5*, 16, 21*, 22; 3:3, 19; 9:20, 21; 16:9, 11.

23. The consequence of Jezebel's acts of immorality is, "Behold, I will throw her on a bed [*of illness*].... And I will kill her children with death" (2:22-23). In addition, the references to "her children" are not to be understood as her actual children: as if God was striking actual kids. Instead, it refers to those who followed her ways. The act of idolatry—the following after other gods—is considered adultery throughout the OT because the people of God have entered into a covenant, which is associated with a marriage covenant, with God. Since they have broken their marriage covenant with God by following after other gods, they are guilty of sexual immorality or adultery.

time to repent.[24] Hence, a very loose paraphrase of the warning to the church in Thyatira might read, "I gave her time to repent but she did not want to. I sure hope you act more wisely and use the time I am giving you to repent" (2:21).

Second, throughout Scripture, God's wrath may be understood in terms of His giving humanity over to the very things for which they have been asking. God's wrath, in other words, is often God allowing humanity to experience the inevitable consequences of our actions. Thus, in Ezekiel 39, the prophet notes:

> The nations will know that the house of Israel went into exile for their iniquity because they acted treacherously against Me, and I hid My face from them; so I gave them into the hand of their adversaries, and all of them fell by the sword (Ezek 39:23).

The implication is that by rejecting the Lord the Israelites were expressing their desire to serve other gods. God, therefore, hid His face from them. The end result was that the Babylonians, the very ones whom the Israelites desired to serve, killed them.[25] Paul, similarly, argues this in Romans 1. He begins with the affirmation that "the wrath of God is revealed from heaven" (Rom 1:18). Then he states, "even though they knew God, they did not honor Him as God or give thanks" (Rom 1:21). Paul then states three times "God gave them over" (Rom 1:24, 26, 28).

Third, the threats of punishment for those who fail to repent should be viewed as an act of love. God is aware of what the inevitable consequences of our sins will be and He intervenes by warning us and urging us to repent. The message to the church in Laodicea affirms, "I correct and discipline those

---

24. This theme runs through the OT as well. After all, the Adam and Eve story includes the fact that they did not die the moment they ate the fruit but were only expelled from the Garden. Indeed, they died later. But the fact that they were spared from immediate death may well be evidence of God's mercy. The delay in their death provided time for repentance.

25. Now we could debate from here to eternity whether or not this is God's doing or not. Surely, if God is sovereign, then He is responsible for their fate and we might affirm that God's wrath came upon them. I do not intend to deny that here. I am arguing that we would also do well to recognize that God in His sovereignty turns humanity over to suffer the consequence of our own actions.

whom I love; be zealous, therefore, and repent" (Rev 3:19). Christ knows what is best and desires what is best for them. It is not God's desire that they suffer.

Fourth, it is critical to recognize that the threat of judgment in the seven messages is aimed at the people of God. God is not threatening wrath upon the nations in order to bring them to repentance. Instead, the judgment is directed at His covenant people.

Finally, God's concern centers on the nations. Fundamental to the biblical narrative, and the book of Revelation, is the fact that the people of God are the means through whom God wills to make Himself known to the nations. This is why God was so displeased with the people of Israel when they followed other gods. They were called to be a light to the nations.[26] This means that when the people of God sin, they not only brought destruction upon themselves, but they also fail to make God known to the nations. As the prophet Ezekiel says:

> When they came to the nations where they went, they profaned My holy name, because it was said of them, "These are the people of the Lord; yet they have come out of His land." But I had concern for My holy name, which the house of Israel had profaned among the nations where they went (Ezek 36:20–21).

As I say all of this, I do not intend to suppose that God never directly inflicts His wrath upon individuals or nations. Though a lot more could be said and perhaps should be, my point here has been to simply note that there is not an inherent inconsistency between the love of God and the wrath of God.

Other Key Features of the Seven Messages

There are two other features of the seven messages that are worthy of note.

---

26. See Isa 42:6; 49:6.

REVELATION 2:1–3:22

"I Know Your Works"

One of the more notable features of the seven messages is that five of them begin with "I know your works" (2:2, 19; 3:1, 8, 15).[27] That the word "works" appears twelve times in the seven messages,[28] highlights its importance. As the narrative of the book of Revelation continues, the responsibility of the churches to bear fruit consistently comes to the surface. Thus, in 14:13, John is exhorted, "Write, 'Blessed are those who die in the Lord from now on!' 'Yes,' says the Spirit, 'in order that they may rest from their hard work, for their works follow with them.'"

The One Who Overcomes

An important feature of the seven messages is that each contains a promise, "to the one who overcomes" (2:7, 11, 17, 26; 3:5, 12, 21).[29] The exhortation to "overcome," which occurs in each of the seven messages, may well be one of the most critical charges in the entire book of Revelation.[30]

The Source of Conflict behind the Seven Messages

It has often been proposed that the book of Revelation was written during an era of persecution.[31] The difficulty with this suggestion is that we have little to no knowledge of organized persecution against the Christ-followers in the late first century. This, of course, does not rule out the possibility that persecutions were affecting some of the churches to which John wrote.

The presence of a limited persecution is evident that in Pergamum someone named Antipas, "was killed among you" (2:13).[32] The threat of

---

27. The Greek "work" (*ergon*) occurs twenty times in the book of Revelation: 2:2, 5, 6, 19*, 22, 23, 26; 3:1, 2, 8, 15; 9:20; 14:13; 15:3; 16:11; 18:6; 20:12, 13; 22:12.

28. See 2:2, 5, 6, 19*, 22, 23, 26; 3:1, 2, 8, 15: The use of a word twelve times in a well-defined section is likely quite intentional. See the introductory chapter on numbers.

29. For a more extensive treatment of "overcome" in the book of Revelation see my, *Follow the Lamb*, 45–53.

30. For a detailed discussion of "overcome" see my, *Follow*, 45–53.

31. See Beale, *Revelation*, 12–16.

32. Antipas's death, however, was not necessarily recent but in the past as evidenced by the fact that John says, "even in the days of Antipas" (2:13). See Duff, "Synagogues" 161.

persecution also appears in the message to the church in Smyrna, "the devil is about to throw some of you into prison" (2:10). That those in Smyrna were exhorted, "Be faithful until death" (2:10) suggests that the coming persecution was to include martyrdom.

At the same time, it is important to recognize that a significant threat among the seven churches came from within. Several of the messages warn of the threat from false teachers who were encouraging the communities of Christ-followers that it was okay to compromise with the pagan gods and attend the various feasts. The temptation to do so was great because assimilation in the local culture provided the poor with the hope that they might be able to "buy and sell" (13:17).[33] The ability to buy or sell in the fragile Roman economy should not be understated.[34]

In the message to the church in Pergamum, Jesus states: "But,[35] I have a few things against you, because you have there those who are holding the teaching of Balaam, who was teaching Balak to put a stumbling block before the sons of Israel, to eat food offered to idols and to commit immorality. Thus, you also have those who also are holding to the teaching of the Nicolaitans"(2:14–15). Although it is difficult to know with any certainty the situation in Pergamum, it is quite possible that some false teachers were encouraging the people of God that it was okay to "eat foods sacrificed to idols."[36] If so, then one of John's primary concerns in writing to the churches was the fear that some were compromising with the local culture and its religious practices, as well as the growing influence of the Roman imperial cult.

Religion in Asia Minor and the Roman Imperial Cult

It is difficult for modern readers to grasp just how much religion and the imperial cult influenced Roman society. G. K. Beale notes:

> The imperial cult permeated virtually every aspect of city and often even village life in Asia Minor, so that individuals could

---

33. See discussion in 13:1–18.
34. Poverty in the Roman world was widespread. See Carter, *Roman Empire*, 10–12.
35. The word for "but" here is emphatic.
36. Stated this way, it appears that the book of Revelation conflicts with the writings of Paul (1 Cor 8:4). The contexts, however, appear to be different. Revelation is talking about eating at the pagan festivities in order to ensure economic advantages. Paul is discussing buying meat that was sacrificed to idols at the marketplace. See Beale, *Revelation*, 248.

aspire to economic prosperity and greater social standing only by participating to some degree in the Roman cult. Citizens of both upper and lower classes were required by local law to sacrifice to the emperor on various special occasions. . . . It was almost impossible to have a share in a city's public life without also having a part in some aspect of the imperial cult.[37]

The difficulty was intensified for the Christ-followers. After all, by pledging allegiance to Jesus as Lord, one was pledging allegiance to Jesus as the *only* Lord. This put them in direct conflict with the patrons of the local deities as well as the overseers of the Roman imperial religion. The problem was further exacerbated by the fact that the Romans believed that the fate of their city and even the whole of the empire was at the mercy of the gods. This meant that the failure to participate in the Roman imperial religion was viewed as being disloyal to the empire.

Participation in acts of worship included the fact that artisans were required to give honor regularly to the patron deity of their corresponding trade guild.[38] While some of these guilds may have served as social groups, others functioned as occupational associations. Participation in the various trade guilds and the regular feasts in honor of the guild's patron deity was virtually necessary in order to maintain one's business relations. In addition, many of the guilds relied on the support of the city's elite to fund their activities.[39] In a society in which food insecurity was the norm, most of the population seemingly had little choice but to participate.[40] Failure to participate in local feasts in honor of the patron deity of the trade guild meant ostracism from the guild. This would result in serious economic sanctions for an individual and his[41] family. The consequences of not participating included being banned from trade guilds, imprisonment, exile, and even death.

---

37. Beale, *Revelation*, 240–41.

38. Essentially, each guild had its own patron deity. This is, in part, the context behind the riot of Ephesus (Acts 19:23–41). Ascough notes that local guilds functioned as places of social interaction and the worship of a god or the gods (*"Religio,"* 245).

39. See Ascough, *"Religio,"* 245.

40. Most of the inhabitants of the Roman empire lived at or below the poverty line. Daily subsistence was a significant concern for most people. See Carter, *Roman Empire*, 10–12.

41. I say "his" here because the male represented the head of the Roman household and was responsible for the religion of the household (a household could include a spouse, children, an extended family, and any slaves).

We cannot overestimate the pressure for commoners to participate in the Roman civil religion. Ascough notes, "Given the social and political capital that was gained through membership and by networking in the associations, particularly at meal times, it would be difficult for Christ adherents to avoid the eating of sacrificial meat and liberal drinking that accompanied the gatherings."[42] Later he adds, "Participation in the imperial cults was not required, but significant social pressure to do so would be felt. . . . Failure to participate could be perceived by others as a lack of commitment, not only to the empire but also to the protective powers of the imperial leader."[43]

That the community of Christ-followers was a small minority within some very large urban centers,[44] made it even more difficult to resist. That they were small meant that they were unable to form any sort of community that could provide for one another. Michael Gorman observes, "The Christians in their little house churches were a tiny minority. How could they survive the pressure to 'toe the line' culturally, politically, and religiously?"[45]

One of the pressing questions within the Christian communities in the Roman province of Asia was whether or not the Christ-followers could attend the pagan feasts. There may well have been a growing number of "prophets" and "prophetesses" within the Christian communities who were advocating that participation in the worship of the pagan gods was indeed acceptable. It has been suggested that these prophets and prophetesses contended that Paul would have approved of attending such feasts since the gods did not exist.[46] Others may have argued that the Christ-followers were able to attend such feasts as long as they did not participate in the worship of the deity.

For John, however, attendance at the pagan feasts was not an option. In fact, the prophets and prophetesses, such as "Jezebel" in the church in Thyatira (2:20–23), who approved of attendance at such feasts, must repent.

---

42. Ascough, *"Religio,"* 246.

43. Ascough, *"Religio,"* 248.

44. Gorman notes that the populations of Ephesus at between 200,000 and 250,000 inhabitants, Smyrna between 75,000–100,000, Pergamum between 120,000–180,000, and Sardis at around 100,000 (Gorman, *Reading*, 91).

45. Gorman, *Reading*, 91.

46. See 1 Cor 8:4–6. For further discussion see: Tribelco, "John's Apocalypse," 259–83.

REVELATION 2:1–3:22

Roman Imperial Cult and Pergamum

That the threat of the Roman imperial religion undergirds the seven messages is evident from Jesus's opening address to the church in Pergamum: "I know where you dwell, where the throne of Satan is" (2:13).[47]

The city of Pergamum was the center of the Roman government and pagan religion in the Roman province of Asia. In addition, Pergamum was one of several cities vying for Rome's recognition for their allegiance to the imperial cult. Pergamum, in fact, had the honor of being the first city in the region to build a temple dedicated to a living ruler as a god.[48] It was also home to the cult of Asclepius—the god of healing. All of this gave the city of Pergamum great prominence in the eyes of Rome. Such prestige would readily be protected by local authorities. The reference to "the throne of Satan" (2:13), which may be a direct allusion to a large throne-like altar of Zeus which was prominent in the city,[49] confirms the pervasiveness of the imperial cult in Pergamum.

Nicolaitans

The identity of the Nicolaitans and the nature of their teachings are uncertain.[50] The problem is exacerbated by the fact that in both the messages to Ephesus (2:6) and Pergamum (2:15) they are mentioned in such a way that presupposes that John's readers knew who they were.[51]

It has been suggested that the Nicolaitans were the primary group behind each of the seven messages.[52] Trebilco contends, "As far as John is concerned, the Nicolaitans are a rival Christian group. They have at

---

47. DeSilva asks, "Does John's characterization of Pergamum as the city 'where Satan's throne is' and 'where Satan lives' (2.13) refer to some local landmark? Some have suggested that John is referring specifically to the Temple of Roma and Augustus, the seat of the provincial cult of Augustus" (deSilva, *Discovering*, 140).

48. Built for Augustus in 29 BC.

49. David deSilva notes that all seven cities to whom John wrote: "had cultic sites: six (all but Thyatira) had imperial temples; [and] five (all but Philadelphia and Laodicea) had imperial altars and subsidized priesthoods" (deSilva, *Unholy*, loc. 569–71).

50. Trebilco, "John's Apocalypse," 261.

51. There are some early traditions that the Nicolaitans derived their name from followers of Nicolas, one of the first seven deacons listed in Acts 6:5. The suspicion is that Nicolas founded a fringe movement that came alongside the early church. See Smalley, *Revelation*, 62–63.

52. Trebilco, "John's Apocalypse" 261–63.

least one teacher (Balaam) and one prophet (Jezebel), and they probably justify their teaching through prophecy."[53]

Whoever then the Nicolaitans were, it appears that they were encouraging the Christ-followers that compromise[54] with the Roman imperial cult for the sake of economic survival was acceptable. For John, Jesus's words to the churches serve as a warning and a reminder that what the false teachers were promoting was to be rejected.

Jewish Pressure on the Churches

The Jewish world in the first century faced some of the same challenges with the Roman socio-religious culture and the imperial religion as the Christ-followers. One of the ways in which the Jewish communities were able to navigate through the ever-present Roman imperial cult is that they were granted exemptions from the requirement to worship the gods of Rome and to attend religious feasts.[55]

This did not mean, however, that all was well for the Jewish communities. They often faced personal attacks and ethnic assaults by individuals who did not approve of their abstaining from the worship of the gods. Many of the Greeks in these cities resented the privileges and protections that were afforded the Jewish populations throughout the region.[56] Nonetheless, the Jewish communities enjoyed a measure of legal protection, which they naturally wanted to preserve.

An important context behind the seven messages—especially the messages to Smyrna and Philadelphia—derived from the fact that many of the early Christ-followers were ethnically Jewish.[57] Even near the end of the first century, the Christ-followers still considered themselves

---

53. Trebilco, "John's Apocalypse" 262.

54. Of course, we should suspect that they did not consider their message as a compromise.

55. Tellbe notes that the Jewish communities in the cities of Asia Minor were granted numerous privileges. He states, "These privileges included permission to assemble, permission to observe the Sabbath and Jewish festivals, permission to collect and send the temple tax, permission to observe dietary laws, exemption from military service for Jews who were Roman citizens, and exemption from participation in the imperial cult" (Tellbe, "Relationships," 219).

56. See Tellbe, "Relationships," 223–26.

57. Tellbe, "Relationships," 220.

as a sect of Judaism and benefitted from the same protections afforded other Jews.[58]

It appears, however, that some within the local synagogues, particularly in Smyrna and Philadelphia, may have been arguing before the Roman authorities that the "Christian" communities were not a sect of Judaism and, therefore, its followers should not be afforded the legal protections that Rome offered its Jewish inhabitants. If the Christian communities presented a threat to Roman customs because of their proselytizing, this may well have come down on the Jewish communities.[59] Consequently, some of the members of the local synagogues may have attempted to distance themselves from the nascent Christian movement.

Thus, as Gorman concludes:

> As for the persecution, it seems to have come in several forms: harassment for being identified as a Christian (bearing the name) at Ephesus and Philadelphia; economic and/or social deprivation, as well as slander from certain Jews, at Smyrna and Philadelphia; fear of impending arrests, suggesting investigations by provincial officials (perhaps officials of the imperial cult, and possibly based on reports from Jewish leaders) at Smyrna; and harassment, even including a violent death at Pergamum. John attributes this persecution ultimately to Satan (2:9, 13, 24; 3:9), which corresponds to his description of Satan and the Satanic beasts of Revelation 12 and 13.[60]

The Relationship of the Seven Messages to the Rest of the Book of Revelation

Although it is easy for modern readers to divorce the seven messages (2:1–3:22) from the rest of the book of Revelation, a careful examination

---

58. According to J. J. O'Rourke, "After the first Jewish revolt (A.D. 66–73) a change began to take place in the legal status of Christians. Due to the harsh measures taken against the Jews, particularly under Domitian, Christians and Jews disassociated themselves to a greater degree than before so that Christianity no longer appeared in Roman eyes as part of Judaism. Since it was illegal to form new religions, Christianity as a new religion separate from Judaism gradually ceased to be tolerated" (O'Rourke, "Roman Law and the Early Church," 179).

59. See Schnabel, Eckhard J, "Jewish Opposition to Christians in Asia Minor in the First Century," 233–70.

60. Gorman, *Reading*, 91.

affirms that they provide a critical foundation for understanding the rest of the book of Revelation.

The clearest indication that the seven messages are intimately connected with the rest of the Apocalypse is found in the link between the close of the last of the seven messages—the first scene—and the opening of the heavenly vision in 4:1-2—the second scene. The heavenly vision (4:1—16:22) begins with John noting, "Immediately I was in the Spirit; and behold, a throne was standing in heaven, and One sitting on the throne" (4:2). The reference to the Father[61] sitting on the throne certainly reminds the reader/hearers that just three verses earlier, the message to the church in Laodicea was brought to a close with an exhortation that those in Laodicea who "overcome" will "sit down with Me on My throne" (3:21). John, therefore, clearly links the seven messages with the opening of the heavenly vision.

In addition, the connection between the first two scenes (1:9-3:22; 4:1—16:21) is also made explicit in that the heavenly vision opens with the affirmation that "the first voice which I heard like a trumpet was speaking with me" (4:1). This "first voice," which was "like a trumpet," certainly refers to the trumpet-like voice that John heard in the opening of the first section (1:10).

Furthermore, that the seven messages are integral to the rest of the book of Revelation is evident in that many of the promises of blessings to those in the seven churches who overcome are realized later in the book of Revelation. For example, the promise to the church in Ephesus that "the one who overcomes" will "eat from the tree of life" (2:7) finds its fulfillment in the account of the Holy City/New Jerusalem (22:2). Also, the promise to the church in Smyrna that the "one who overcomes will not be hurt by the second death" (2:11) anticipates the exemption from the second death as mentioned in 20:6. The promise to Philadelphia that they will become "a pillar in the temple of My God" (3:12) looks forward to the descent of the Holy City/New Jerusalem (21:9—22:9) and the incorporation of the people of God into it.[62]

---

61. That the One sitting on the throne is the Father derives from the fact that He is clearly distinguished from the Lamb in 5:5-7, and from the fact that Jesus has just promised those in Laodicea that they would "sit down with Me on My throne, just as I overcame and sat down with My Father on His throne" (3:21). That 4:2-3 introduce a throne and One sitting on it immediately after the promise of 3:21 indeed affirms that the Father is the One sitting on the throne.

62. Longman notes that in the OT temple, there were two pillars (1 Kgs 7:15-22). He notes, "These pillars, a temple innovation compared to the tabernacle which did

Finally, those who overcome in Philadelphia are promised that God will write on them "the name of the city of My God, the New Jerusalem, which comes down out of heaven from my God" (3:12). This promise clearly anticipates the descent of the New Jerusalem which is "coming down out of heaven from God" (21:2; see 21:10).

Conclusion

The seven messages are an integral part of the Apocalypse and they cannot be read in isolation from the rest of the book. In them, we get a glimpse of what will become a central theme in the book of Revelation: namely, that the people of God are called to be the means through which Christ is made known. As we will learn, making Him known will come at a great cost.[63] As Loren Johns affirms, "So the one who conquers is the one who bears faithful witness to the end, who maintains that witness until one's death. Thus, conquering—both for Jesus and for the followers of the lamb—is closely related to the death of a faithful witness."[64] Warren Carter summarizes well John's primary exhortation in the seven messages: "The central issue concerns how believers should live in their urban contexts."[65]

---

not have pillars, reinforced the idea that God had established his people in the land after the defeat of their internal enemies through the leadership of David, the conquest completer." Then he adds, "to be a pillar in the temple means that these faithful Philadelphians would live forever in God's presence: 'never again will they leave it'" (Longman, *Revelation*, 97).

63. See 20:4.
64. Johns, "Jesus," loc. 6640.
65. Carter, *Reveal*, 29.

Revelation 4:1—16:21
The Second Story/Scene
(The Heavenly Vision)

Revelation 4:1—5:14
John Taken to Heaven:
Throne Room Scene

> *Symbols, most of which had established meaning in Jewish or pagan contexts, communicate the glory of God. A throne (symbol of sovereignty), surrounded by a rainbow (reminder of God's covenant with Noah), emits flashes of lightning and peals of thunder (echoes of Sinai). In front of the throne are seven flaming torches. Also in front of the throne is a sea of glass, just as the temple of Solomon once features a massive 'molten sea' water basin (1 Kings 7:23–26). . . . Four winged creatures, perhaps representative of all living things, serve as worship leaders for the whole of creation. Such winged beasts commonly appear in portrayal of divine scenes in the ancient world.*[1]

The One on the Throne Receives Worship 4:1–11

IN ORDER TO TRULY grasp the narrative that John is about to set forth, we must begin with a proper foundation. For John, that foundation begins with the fact that it is God who is the One on the throne! He is the Sovereign Lord of creation and the One who is worthy of worship! Therefore, even though, as I will argue in the pages to come, God is not the cause of the suffering in the accounts of the Seals, Trumpets, and Bowls, He is nonetheless sovereign. That is, although the powers of this world, whose rule brings devastation and destruction upon humanity and upon creation, continue to rule, their rule is nonetheless subordinate to the rule of God.

---

1. Kraybill, *Allegiance*, 83–84.

After these things 4:1

Revelation 4:1-2 marks the beginning of our second story, John's heavenly vision, which extends from 4:1—16:21. This second story opens with, "After these things" (4:1).[2] Since the book of Revelation is primarily a narrative, we must understand the meaning of "After these things" in light of John's narratival concerns. That is, John is not using "After these things" in order to say, "The next thing that will happen is. . . ." Instead, John is indicating, "The next thing that happened in the vision which I saw. . . ."[3] John then, is presenting the order of things within the vision that he is narrating. "After these things" (4:1), therefore, should be understood along the lines of, "After I saw this, then I saw that." Or, as David Barr puts it, John refers to "story time" and not "chronological time."[4]

The One on Throne 4:2-3

John begins by asserting that he was taken to heaven where he saw God sitting on a throne (4:2). In doing so, John affirms that it is God the Father who sits on the throne and is therefore the world's rightful ruler.[5] Craig Koester refers to John's account of God on the throne as, "Revelation's theological center." He then adds, "The throne identifies God as the rightful ruler of all things and shows that all things must be understood in

---

2. There is, however, much debate over how "after these things" is to be understood. See Beale, *Revelation*, 152-70. The expression "after these things," which occurs nine times in the book of Revelation (1:19; 4:1*; 7:9; 9:12; 15:5; 18:1; 19:1; 20:3) indicates a transition within the vision (see esp 7:9; 18:1; 19:1): i.e., it marks a literary development. That it does not serve as an indicator of major structural importance is evident from its occurrence in 9:12, where it introduces the Sixth Trumpet, which is most certainly not the beginning of a major section in the book of Revelation. Furthermore, there are two occurrences of "after these things" (4:1b; 20:3) that are not introductory phrases, but instead mark a somewhat parenthetical phrase at the end of a statement and, thereby, indicate something that must occur at a later time: e.g., in reference to the binding of Satan, John closes with, "after these things it is necessary for him to be released for a little time" (20:3). Similarly, in 4:1, John continues by noting, ". . . and the first voice which I heard like a trumpet was speaking with me, saying, 'Come up here, and I will show you what must happen after these things.'"

3. This does not necessarily have to be understood as though John had an actual vision. Ian Paul argues that John simply used a genre known as "vision report" (Paul, *Revelation*, 22-25),

4. Barr, *Tales*, loc. 2500.

5. Schüssler Fiorenza calls this the "central theological query" (*Vision*, 120).

relationship to God."[6] Resseguie affirms, "This setting captures the major plot conflicts of the story: "Who sits on the throne?" "Who rules?"[7] Thus, at the beginning of the second story, John establishes that the "One sitting on the throne" (4:2) is the One who is worthy of worship (4:8–11).

At the same time, it is important to observe that John's account of the One on the throne depicts the majesty and splendor that surround the throne more than it provides us with a description of God. In fact, at this point in the narrative, God cannot be seen, He can only be described. By the end of the narrative, however, those who reside in the Holy City/New Jerusalem will not only be in the presence of God, but "they will see His face" (22:4).[8]

John begins by noting that the Father was like "a stone of jasper" (4:3). Most scholars suggest that jasper was opaque reddish brown in color.[9] John then adds that the Father's appearance was also like "carnelian" (4:3).[10] The carnelian was also reddish in color. Taken together, the jasper and carnelian stones suggest a fiery appearance that corresponds to the opening description of God in Ezekiel:[11]

> In the midst of the living beings, there was something that looked like burning coals of fire, like torches darting back and forth among the living beings. The fire was bright, and lightning was flashing from the fire. . . . Then I noticed from the appearance of His loins and upward something like glowing metal that looked like fire all around within it, and from the appearance of His loins and downward I saw something like fire; and *there was* a radiance around Him (Ezek 1:13, 27).

John adds that "a rainbow was around the throne with an appearance like an emerald" (4:3). Here again John alludes to the opening description of God in Ezekiel: "and *there was* a radiance around Him. As

---

6. Koester, "Revelation's Visionary Challenge," 12.

7. Resseguie, *Revelation*, 40.

8. John's reader/hearers, let alone modern readers, were not to lose sight of this fact.

9. Smalley, however, proposes that it may have been translucent. See Smalley, *Revelation*, 115.

10. The NAS and NKJ use "sardius" here.

11. Ezekiel 1:1—3:11 and Daniel 7:9–28 provide an important background for Rev 4–10. Tabb observes, "John's vision in Rev 4 recalls the Old Testament prophets' depictions of God seated on his heavenly throne, surrounded by his heavenly attendants (cf. 1 Kgs 22:19; Isa. 6:1–4; Ezek. 1:26–28; 10:1; Dan. 7:9)" (Tabb, *All Things New*, Loc 840). G. K. Beale argues that Rev 4–5 follow the order and structure of Daniel 7 (Beale, *Use of Daniel*, 181–82).

the appearance of the rainbow in the clouds on a rainy day, so *was* the appearance of the surrounding radiance" (Ezek 1:27–28).

The reference to a jasper, carnelian, and emerald-like rainbow serve to intensify the light and glory that surrounds the One on the throne.

Around the Throne 4:4–8

John continues his description by noting the presence of various beings around the throne in an ever-widening series of concentric circles (4:4–8). These beings recall the Old Testament prophets' descriptions of the heavenly attendants that surround God and His heavenly throne.[12]

That God made humanity to be his representative rulers can be seen from the first pages of the biblical text (Gen 1:26–27). This, I believe, is part of the significance of John's description of the Twenty-Four Elders. They are representatives of the people of God who rule alongside the Father. It is quite likely that John's description of the Twenty-Four Elders serves to remind and encourage the seven churches to persevere in light of the promise that they too will reign with Christ.

Twenty-Four Elders 4:4

First, John observes that "around the throne were twenty-four thrones, and upon them "I saw Twenty-Four Elders" (4:4). There is little doubt in my estimation that the use of "twenty-four" derives from the addition of twelve and twelve[13] and, therefore, the Twenty-Four Elders are the combined representatives of the twelve tribes and the twelve apostles.[14] Or, in other words, they are heavenly representatives of the totality of the people of God. That the word "elder" occurs twelve times in the book of Revelation[15] further supports the conclusion that the "Elders" represent the people of God.[16]

---

12. See 1 Kgs 22:19; Isa 6:1–4; Ezek 1:26–28; 10:1; Dan 7:9.

13. Beale, *Revelation*, 325.

14. Note that it was so important for the early church to maintain the number of apostles at twelve that they determined that it was essential to replace Judas who was not worthy of being a representative of the people of God (Acts 1:15–26).

15. See 4:4, 10; 5:5, 6, 8, 11, 14; 7:11, 13; 11:16; 14:3; 19:4. Note that on two occasions (5:5; 7:13) only one of the Elders is mentioned.

16. See Beale, *Revelation*, 323.

That the Elders are wearing "white garments" (4:4) also reinforces the conclusion that they are representatives of the people of God. White garments, after all, are what the overcomers in Sardis were promised (3:5), and what those in Laodicea were exhorted to buy (3:18).

In addition, the Twenty-Four Elders are also enthroned (4:4), which suggests that they rule alongside God. The depiction of the Elders as enthroned as kings/queens ruling alongside God, corresponds to the explicit declaration in the prologue that "He has made us a kingdom" (1:6).[17] This too reinforces the conclusion that the Twenty-Four Elders are representatives of the people of God.

The Twenty-Four Elders also have "golden crowns" (4:4) on their heads. The presence of crowns on the heads of the Twenty-Four Elders closely associates them with Christ and His kingship. In fact, the only other occurrence of a "golden crown" is the one on the head of Christ in 14:14.

Seven Lamps 4:5

John then sees seven lamps of fire, which he says are, "the seven spirits of God" (4:5). John certainly has the account in Zechariah 4 in mind here.[18] Interestingly, deSilva contends that the "seven spirits" do not represent the Holy Spirit. He notes, "John's use of the singular pneuma throughout Revelation to refer to the Holy Spirit (2.7, 11, 17, 29; 3.6, 13, 22; 14.13; 22.17) suggests that he intends a different referent for the plural pneumata here and elsewhere."[19]

I would contend, however, that "the seven spirits of God" is indeed a reference to the Holy Spirit. First, I have argued that in light of the fact that the "seven spirits" (plural) in 1:4 are introduced in the midst of a description of the Father and Christ (1:4–5), John surely has the Holy Spirit in view there. Second, John's description of the spirits as "seven" (4:5) likely serves to indicate the fullness or totality of the spirits and not necessarily that it/they is/are actually plural in essence. As Longman notes, "The use of symbolic numbers like seven is particularly common in apocalyptic literature. Symbolic numbers should not be pressed literally in a quantitative

---

17. See also 5:10; 22:5.
18. See Zech 4:2, 3, 6, 10.
19. DeSilva, *Discovering*, 150.

sense."[20] Third, I would contend that John's use of seven here derives from the "seven lamps" in Zech 4:2–6. In Zechariah, the continuous burning of the lamps was a sign of Yahweh's presence among His people, which corresponds to the description here. In fact, a case can be made that in Zechariah the lampstand and its seven lamps represent the Holy Spirit. After all, Zechariah concludes, "Not by might nor by power, but by My Spirit,' says the Lord of hosts" (Zech 4:6).

Sea of Glass 4:6a

John then adds that "before the throne was as it were a sea of glass, like crystal" (4:6).[21] John again alludes to the opening description of God in the vision of Ezekiel: "Now over the heads of the living beings *there was something like an expanse, like the awesome gleam of crystal, spread out over their heads*" (Ezek 1:22).

The opening description of God and His throne in Ezekiel suggests that the sea of glass represents the waters above the sky. Longman, however, suggests that "the mention of a sea before the throne of God resonates with the fact that the temple had a huge laver of water (holding 11,000 gallons) in front, which was named 'the Sea' (1 Ki 7:23–26)."[22] He then suggests, "a calm, 'glassy' sea before the throne of God would represent his subduing of the powers of chaos."[23] This conclusion certainly corresponds to the fact that John's account of the One on the throne includes the fact that He is worthy of worship because "You created all things, and on account of Your will they existed, and were created" (4:11).

Four Living Creatures 4:6b–8

John also saw "Four Living Creatures" (4:6-8) before the throne. John describes the creatures as, "each one of them having six wings, were full of eyes around and within" (4:8; see also 4:6).[24] At the same time, the Four Living Creatures have features that distinguish them from one

---

20. Longman, *Revelation*, 47.
21. The uncertainty is due in part to the fact that the word "sea" is used in a variety of ways in the book of Revelation. See discussion in 21:1.
22. Longman, *Revelation*, 112.
23. Longman, *Revelation*, 112.
24. See Ezek 10:12.

another: the First Creature was "like a lion" (4:7). The Second Creature was "like an ox" (4:7). The Third Creature "had a face as of a human" (4:7). And the Fourth Creature was "like a flying eagle" (4:7).

It is my conviction that the Four Living Creatures are heavenly beings that represent wild and domesticated land animals, humankind, and the birds of the air.[25] As such, they represent the totality of the created animals.[26] This follows from the fact that the lion and the ox represent the strongest of the wild (lion) and domesticated animals (ox). The Third Living Creature represents humanity. Finally, the eagle, which was widely acknowledged as the fastest bird, represents the flying creatures.[27]

That the Four Living Creatures are heavenly representatives of the totality of the created animals also gains support from the fact that there are four of them. As I have argued, John consistently uses "four" to represent the created realm.

That the Four Living Creatures are heavenly beings derives support from their relationship with both the Cherubim in Ezekiel[28] and the Seraphim in Isaiah.[29] There are some subtle differences between John's account and that of Ezekiel. Most notable is the fact that in Ezekiel each of the four living creatures had four faces (not one): "each had the face of a man; all four had the face of a lion on the right and the face of a bull on the left, and all four had the face of an eagle" (Ezek 1:10). Ezekiel's creatures also have four wings (not six).[30] In addition, in Revelation, the Four Living Creatures sing; whereas, in Ezekiel they are silent. Nonetheless, the similarities between John's account and that of Isaiah 6 and Ezekiel 1 are significant. Since the Cherubim of Ezekiel and the Seraphim of Isaiah are considered heavenly beings, then it follows that the Four Living Creatures in Revelation are as well.[31]

---

25. See Smalley, *Revelation*, 120. The notable absence of marine life may be accounted for by the fact the sea, as noted above, is regularly associated with judgment and the abode of the Beast (see 13:1).

26. Longman notes, "Elder is never used of angels elsewhere, but their closeness to God indicates to some that they must be spiritual, not human" (Longman, *Revelation*, 110).

27. See Tabb, *All Things New*, 901.

28. See Ezek 1:5–21; 10:12–15, 20–22.

29. See Isa 6:2–3.

30. See Ezek 1:6.

31. It is important to recognize that John's description of God's throne and its attendants in 4:1–11 correspond quite closely to the OT prophets. Richard Bauckham concludes, "There is nothing in . . . [Rev 4] which could not have been written by a

It is also important to note that the Four Living Creatures are closely connected with the Twenty-Four Elders. In fact, in every account but one in which the Twenty-Four Elders are present, the Four Living Creatures appear alongside them.[32] Moreover, the Twenty-Four Elders and the Four Living Creatures are paired together a total of seven times in the book of Revelation (5:6, 8, 11, 14; 7:11; 14:3; 19:4).

The Four Living Creatures are also closely connected with the Twenty-Four Elders in that both are described as participating in the worship of God. There are four instances in which the Elders and the Living Creatures are said to have "worshiped" together (4:10; 5:14; 11:16; 19:4). There are also two additional instances in which both the Twenty-Four Elders and the Four Living Creatures fall down together and worship (5:8; 19:4).

Together then the Twenty-Four Elders and the Four Living Creatures are angelic representatives of the people of God and all created beings and they are central figures in the worship of God in the book of Revelation.

The Father Is Worshiped (4:8–11)

The worshiping of the Father is an essential feature of the opening throne room scene (4:1–11). In this unit, John notes that the Four Living Creatures continuously worship: "they have no rest day or night saying, 'Holy, holy, holy is the Lord God, the Almighty, the One who was and who is and who is to come'" (4:8). The Twenty-Four Elders also participate in the worship of the Father by falling down and casting their crowns before the throne (4:10). In addition, while the Four Living Creatures give, "glory and honor and thanks to the One who is sitting on the throne" (4:9), the Twenty-Four Elders give, "glory and honor and power" (4:10). Finally, the Father is worthy of worship, we are told, both because He is holy (4:8) and He is the creator of all things (4:11).

Excursus: John's Anti-Imperial Agenda

Greg Carey contends, "Revelation is the most explicitly counter-imperial book in the New Testament."[33]

---

non-Christian Jew" (Bauckham, *Theology*, 32).

32. The only exception is 11:15–19.
33. Carey, "Revelation as Counter-Imperial," loc. 2050.

As we read through the narrative of John's heavenly vision (the second story; 4:1—16:22) and the whole of the book of Revelation for that matter, it is critical to recognize that one of John's pressing concerns is to remind his reader/hearers, "Who it is that rules"?[34] For John, it is God the Father and, as we will see later, the Lamb who sit on the throne. This is why the throne room scene (4:1-11) begins with an affirmation of the absolute sovereignty of the One who is sitting on the throne (God the Father)[35] and why it is vital to understanding the narrative of the book of Revelation. It is my conviction that these affirmations must be viewed against the backdrop of the Roman imperial cult.

John's political intentions are evident in the declaration of the Four Living Creatures that God is, "the Lord God, the Almighty" (4:8). Karrer notes, "Suetonius uses the phrase *dominus et deus noster* [our lord and our god] for his criticism of Domitian, corresponding exactly to the Greek text of 'our Lord and God' in Rev 4:11."[36] The direct implication of John's vision of God sitting on the throne is that God, not Caesar, rules.[37]

In addition, John's observation of the words of praise from the Twenty-Four Elders, "Worthy are You, our Lord and our God" (4:11), most certainly intends to undermine the claims of Rome. Karrer adds, "At the time of Revelation's composition, the Roman writer Cornutus makes a word play in his compendium on the Greek gods using the name and the preposition dia: 'We call him Dia (Zeus) since through (dia) him everything comes into being and is preserved.'"[38]

Furthermore, John's description of the Twenty-Four Elders as crowned with "golden crowns" (4:4) also undermines Rome's claim to rule. Carey contends that the "crowns relate

---

34. Schüssler Fiorenza calls this the "central theological query" (Schüssler Fiorenza, *Vision*, 120).

35. That this is God the Father becomes clear in 5:1 where the One on the throne is clearly distinguished from Jesus (see 5:1-6).

36. Karrer, "God," 289. See also, Smalley, *Revelation*, 125.

37. Aune argues that the divine throne room scene here is a deliberate parody of Rome's imperial court ceremony: God is the antithesis of the emperor (Aune, "Influence," 5-26).

38. Karrer, "God," 288-89.

to honor and power in the imperial society."[39] He then adds, "Crown imagery also belongs to the counter-imperial script of Revelation, since crowns were prominent in the Roman imperial cult."[40]

At the same time, it is critical to recognize that God's rule does not go unchallenged. After all, we have already been told that Satan has a throne in Pergamum (2:13). And, as we proceed, we will learn that the Beast also has a throne (13:2), which was given to him by Satan (13:2).

The throne of the Beast and the throne of Satan, of course, stand in marked contrast to the throne of God. After all, from God's throne light emanates (21:23). By way of contrast, "the throne of the Beast" becomes "covered with darkness" (16:10). In addition, God's throne is where "the One who lives forever and ever" (4:9) resides. The Beast and Satan, by way of contrast, are those who will be "thrown alive into the Lake of Fire" (19:20; 20:10), "which is the second death" (21:8).

Since God's rule from the throne in heaven must be viewed in opposition to Rome's claim to rule, then, it stands to reason that the rule of God's people is also in opposition to the rule of Rome. This accentuates the necessity for those in Smyrna to "be faithful until death" so that God will "give you the crown of life" (2:10). The promise of a crown indicates that those who rule faithfully now will have their rule extend into eternity.

Conclusion

As I noted in the opening, one of the keys to understanding Revelation's narrative is to observe the fact that although God's throne is presently in heaven, by the time the story reaches its climax (Rev 21:9—22:9), the throne of God comes down to the New Creation.

---

39. Carey, "Revelation as Counter-Imperial," loc. 2268–69.
40. Carey, "Revelation as Counter-Imperial," loc. 2269–70.

Revelation 4:1—5:14
Throne Room Scene Continued

> *The key point to be noticed is that, in contrast between what is said to John (5:5) and what he sees (5:6), he first evokes the idea of the Messiah as the Jewish nationalistic military conqueror and then reinterprets it by means of the notion of sacrificial death for the redemption of people from all nations (cf. 5:9-10). The juxtaposition of the contrasting images of the Lion and the Lamb expresses John's Jewish Christian reinterpretation of current Jewish eschatological hopes.*[1]

The Scroll 5:1–4

JOHN'S DESCRIPTION OF THE throne room scene (4:1—5:14) continues with, "And I saw in the right hand of the One sitting upon the throne a Scroll" (5:1). The presence of the Scroll in the Father's hand (5:1) marks a clear transition from the description of the Father (the One on the throne)—or the glory that emanates from the Father—and the beings who surround the throne and their worship of the Father (4:1-11).

John then notes that a "strong angel" inquires, "Who is worthy to open the Scroll and to break its seals?" (5:2). John seemingly knows that the Scroll is important and that opening it is critical. The problem is that "no one was able . . . to open the Scroll or to look at it" (5:3). Once John learns that no one was able to open it, he says, "I began to weep much, because no one was found worthy to open the Scroll or to look into it" (5:4).

---

1. Bauckham, *Climax*, 214.

A Lion and a Slain Lamb 5:5–6

One of the Elders then says to John, "Do not weep" (5:5). After all, the Elder explains, there is no need for weeping because, "the Lion, the one from the tribe of Judah, the root of David, has overcome so that He can open the Scroll and its seven Seals" (5:5).

The reference to a Lion from "the tribe of Judah" (5:5) certainly derives from Gen 49:9–10 where Jacob describes his son Judah as a "lion." The implication in the Genesis account is that Judah has been set apart as the kingly tribe. This understanding continued through Judaism until the time of John. Loren Johns explains, "In late Second Temple Judaism, the lion became the prime symbol of the messiah (see esp. 2 Esdras 12:31–32)."[2] The Elder then adds that Jesus is also "the root of David." This title, which surely alludes to Isa 11:1, 10, further establishes Jesus's kingship.[3] Taken together, the "Lion of Judah" and the "root of David" are two ways of signifying Jesus as the true king of Israel.

John then looks, presumably to see the Lion, but instead of seeing a Lion he sees "a Lamb" (5:6). One might suspect a measure of surprise on the part of the reader/hearers. After all, John heard that the Lion "has overcome" (5:5), but when he looks, he does not see a lion. Instead, he sees a Lamb (5:6).

Of course, the contrast between a lion and a lamb could not be greater. The imagery of a lion suggests ferocity and strength.[4] The imagery of a lamb, however, suggests weakness. Yet, John consistently depicts Jesus as the Lamb. In fact, John refers to Jesus as the Lion only here in 5:5. Yet, John employs "Lamb" in relation to Jesus twenty-seven times in the Apocalypse. The importance of this cannot be overstated. Caird, in fact, declares:

> It is almost as if John were saying to us at one point after another: "Wherever the Old Testament says 'Lion', read 'Lamb.'" Wherever the Old Testament speaks of the victory of the Messiah or the overthrow of the enemies of God, we are to remember that the gospel recognizes no other way of achieving these ends than the way of the Cross."[5]

---

2. Johns, "Jesus," 314.
3. Both Gen 49:9–10 and Isa 11:1–10 were central to Jewish Messianic hopes.
4. See Amos 3:8.
5. Caird, *Revelation*, 75.

Excursus: Hearing and Seeing

There are several instances in the book of Revelation in which John hears one thing but when he looks he sees something else. John's use of "hearing" and "seeing" is a rhetorical tool by which he aims to capture the reader/hearers' imagination. Smalley suggests, "It is more accurate to say that the author of Revelation uses what is seen to interpret what is heard."[6] James Resseguie goes so far as to declare, "The alternation between seeing and hearing is a hermeneutical key in the Apocalypse."[7] John, in other words, contrasts two things that appear to be substantially different but are, in fact, the same. G. B. Caird observes the contrast between the Lion and the Lamb and proclaims that with "one stroke of brilliant artistry John has given us the key to all his use of the Old Testament."[8] Moyise, after noting Caird's assertion, concludes, "What John hears is the Old Testament view of a conquering Messiah but what he is now enabled to see is the Christian view of victory through suffering."[9] Bauckham affirms its impact on how we are to understand the OT narrative: "The juxtaposition of the contrasting images of the Lion and the Lamb expresses John's Jewish Christian reinterpretation of current Jewish eschatological hopes."[10]

The imagery becomes even more provocative when we learn that the Lamb which he saw was "standing, as if it had been slain" (5:6).[11] Although we might suspect that John was taken by surprise, the fact that the imagery of a slain Lamb[12] was well known in the early Christian community, as it is today, as a symbol of the crucified Jesus, mitigates any measure of surprise.[13]

---

6. Smalley, *Revelation*, 131.

7. Resseguie, *Revelation*, 152.

8. Caird, *Revelation*, 74; emphasis original.

9. Moyise, "Models" in Hays, *Revelation and the Politics of Apocalyptic Interpretation*, loc. 806; emphasis original.

10. Bauckham, *Climax*, 214.

11. That the Lamb is described "as if" slain because it actually was slain but is now alive—as evidenced by the fact that it was "standing" (5:6). For further discussion on "as if slain," see commentary on 13:2.

12. Loren Johns aptly notes that "Jesus is not 'sacrificed' in Revelation. Rather, he is executed, or murdered" (Johns, "Jesus," 317).

13. The primary OT text behind the imagery of a Lamb is Isaiah 53 (esp. 53:7; Acts

Lamb Has Seven Horns and Seven Eyes 5:6b

As John continues his description of Jesus as the slain Lamb we learn that he has "seven horns" (5:6). The horn was a common symbol in the ancient world for power or strength.[14] That Jesus has seven horns indicates that He is all-powerful. He also has "seven eyes" (5:6), "which" John adds, "are the seven Spirits of God that have been sent into all the earth" (5:6; see 4:5). As noted earlier, it is my conviction that the "seven spirits of God" refer to the Holy Spirit. That they "have been sent out into all the earth" (5:6) suggests that the work of Christ is being made known through the power of the Spirit throughout the world.

The Lamb Takes the Scroll and Is Worshiped 5:7–9

The Lamb then takes the Scroll from the Father's hand (5:7). Once He does so the Four Living Creatures and the Twenty-Four Elders "fell down before the Lamb" (5:8).[15] The Elders, John notes, have "golden bowls full of incense" (5:8), which, we are told, represents "the prayers of the saints." At this point in the narrative, we have no idea what John might mean by "the prayers of the saints." As we proceed, we will learn that these prayers are a central component to the narrative.[16]

The Four Living Creatures and the Twenty-Four Elders then sing "a new song" (5:9). Throughout the biblical text, a "new song" represents a song sung after a military victory over one's enemies.[17] The Israelites sang such a song after God brought them safely through the

---

8:25–40).

14. See: 1 Kgs 22:11; Ps 18:2; Zech 1:18–21 (Deut 33:17; 1 Kgs 22:11; Ps 89:17; Dan 7:7—8:24).

15. This statement is quite significant for our understanding of NT Christology. The Scriptures are clear that God alone is to be worshiped. Yet here, in the divine throne room itself, the very creatures that are responsible for the endless worship of God (4:8) now turn their devotion to Christ, the slain Lamb.

16. The "prayers of the saints" serve as another key theme in the Apocalypse. For further discussion see the commentary on 8:2–4. The term "saints" is used thirteen times in the Apocalypse for the people of God (5:8; 8:3, 4; 11:18; 13:7, 10; 14:12; 16:6; 17:6; 18:20, 24; 19:8; 20:9).

17. See 14:3; see Exod 15:1–18; Ps 96:1–3; 33:3. Longman notes, "'New song' is used in the book of Psalms (33:3; 40:3; 96:1; 98:1; 144:9; 149:1) and Isaiah (42:10) in the context of warfare as well as here in Revelation (as well as in 14:3). A new song is a hymn of victory sung after God has made all things new by his defeat of the forces of evil" (Longman, *Revelation*, 129).

Red Sea.[18] The "new song" sung by the Four Living Creatures and the Twenty-Four Elders exults Christ, the Lamb, because He is "worthy . . . to take the Scroll and open its Seals because you were slain and you purchased for God by means of your blood people from every tribe and tongue and people and nation (5:9).

It is critical for our understanding of the book of Revelation that we recognize that Jesus has "overcome" and is "worthy" because He was slain. As the Four Living Creatures and the Twenty-Four Elders declare, "worthy are you to take the Scroll and open its seals because You were slain" (5:9). David Barr notes, "This inappropriate pairing of power and weakness should cause the reader to reevaluate the meaning of power."[19] Craig Keener adds, "Here the central paradox of Revelation and of the Christian faith in general comes to the fore: Jesus conquered not by force but by death, not by violence but by martyrdom."[20] Farmer adds, "By means of this imagery John asserts that suffering, redemptive, persuasive love is the most powerful force in the universe, an expression of the perfect wisdom of God."[21]

Excursus: The Nations and Revelation's Narrative

I noted in the introductory chapter on numbers that John uses a fourfold reference to the nations seven times.[22] In light of John's consistent use of "four" to indicate fullness with regard to the created realm, there is little doubt that John intends the fourfold designation for the nations to represent all humanity.

Interestingly, the first two occurrences of the fourfold designation for humanity both indicate that the people of God come from every nation. In the present passage, the Four Living Creatures and the Twenty-Four Elders affirm that those who were purchased for God are "from every tribe and tongue and people and nation" (5:9). Then in 7:9, the fourfold designation is used to denote the origin of the Great Multitude: "and behold a Great Multitude that no one could count from

---

18. See Exod 15:1–18.
19. Barr, *Tales*, loc. 2274–75.
20. Keener, *Revelation*, 186.
21. Farmer, *Reading*, 115.

22. 5:9; 7:9; 10:11; 11:9; 13:7; 14:6; 17:15. As I noted in the introductory chapter on numbers, the fourfold designation for the nations never occurs in the same order.

every nation, tribes, peoples, and tongues standing before the throne and before the Lamb."[23]

At the same time, it is important to note that as the narrative progresses the people of God are distinguished from the nations. For example, in 13:7, we are told that the Beast wages war against "the saints" and he is given "authority over every tribe and people and tongue and nation." In this instance, the fourfold designation for the nations depicts those over whom the Beast has authority and they appear to be distinguished from "the saints." That the people of God in 13:7 are, in fact, distinguished from the nations becomes clearer from the very next verse. In 13:8, John refers to "those who inhabit the Earth." The designation "those who inhabit the earth" occurs ten times in the book of Revelation and in each of its occurrences it excludes the people of God.[24] That this designation excludes the people of God in 13:8 is evident from the fact that John declares that they "will worship him [the Beast]."[25]

What is significant at this point is to recognize that John often uses the fourfold designation for the nations interchangeably with the expression, "those who inhabit the Earth." Thus, in 11:9, John declares that those from the "peoples, tribes, tongues, and nations" refuse to permit the Two Witnesses to be buried.[26] Then, in the very next verse, he adds that "those who inhabit the earth" will "rejoice" over the death of the Two Witnesses (11:10).

23. I will address the significance of this in the commentary on 7:1–17. The point that I will make there is that the fact that the people of God are *from* all the nations is in accord with the fulfillment of the promise to Abraham that "in you all the families of the earth will be blessed" (Gen 12:3).

24. See 3:10; 6:10; 8:13; 11:10*; 13:8; 13:14*; 17:2; 17:8. An examination of all ten occurrences affirms that John reserves this designation to distinguish the nations from the people of God. That John reserves "those who inhabit the earth" to distinguish the nations from the people of God is clearly evident in 17:2 and 17:8 where those who inhabit the earth "were made drunk from the wine of her [the Prostitute's] immorality" (17:2) and they are those "whose name has not been written in the Book of Life" (17:8). In 13:6, the people of God are deemed, in contrast to "those who inhabit the earth," to be "those who dwell in heaven" (13:6).

25. We must be reminded that John is writing the churches. His warning to them is that those who worship the Beast cannot also be considered part of God's people. For John, then, this distinction was critical.

26. I will argue below that the Two Witnesses represent all of the people of God (i.e., all Christians). See my *Two Witnesses*, 2011.

The fourfold designation for the nations in the three other occurrences also appears to exclude the people of God; though the use of the designation in 10:11 is ambiguous.

It is uncertain if the fourfold designation for the nations in 10:11 includes the people of God or not. The command for John to "prophesy" to "many peoples and nations and tongues and kings" suggests that his prophetic activity is directed at the unbelieving world. That the account of the Two Witnesses (11:1–13) immediately follows the command to prophesy bolsters this conclusion. After all, the prophetic witness of the Two Witnesses certainly appears to be directed at the unbelieving nations. In addition, the case may also be made that the fourfold designation for the nations in 14:6 does not include the people of God since they are warned to "fear God and give to Him glory, because the hour of His judgment has come" (14:7).[27] Finally, the fourfold reference to "peoples, multitudes, nations, tongues" in 17:15 certainly excludes the people of God since they are those upon whom "the Prostitute is seated."

It certainly appears to be the case then, that John's use of the fourfold designation for the nations along with the title "those who dwell on the Earth" has in view all the people of the world who are not, at least as of yet, a part of the people of God.

This makes the first two occurrences of the fourfold expression (5:9; 7:9), in which John describes the people of God as those who have come from the nations, even more significant. I have proposed that one of the narrative goals in the book of Revelation is to discern how it is that the nations are redeemed. In 5:9, we learn that the Lamb, "purchased for God . . . people from every tribe and tongue and people and nation" (5:9). Then, in 7:9, John sees "a Great Multitude that no one could count from every nation, tribes, peoples, and tongues standing before the throne and before the Lamb clothed in white robes" (7:9).

Consequently, John appears to depict the nations as opposed to Christ and the people of God and at the same time the place from which the people of God have come.

---

27. See commentary on 14:6–11.

COMMENTARY: REVELATION 4:1—16:21

Worship of the Lamb Continues 5:10–14

The worship of the Lamb continues with the affirmation that Jesus has also, "made them [those whom He purchased] a kingdom and priests for our God" (5:10). The song of praise to the Lamb concludes with the added assertion that the people of God, "reign upon the earth" (5:10).[28] The language that the people of God are kings/queens and priests in 5:10, as in 1:6, derives from Exod 19:4–6, which is one of the key covenantal declarations:

> You yourselves have seen what I did to the Egyptians, and how I bore you on eagles' wings, and brought you to Myself. Now then, if you will indeed obey My voice and keep My covenant, then you shall be My own possession among all the peoples, for all the earth is Mine; and you shall be to Me a kingdom of priests and a holy nation.' These are the words that you shall speak to the sons of Israel.

John then asserts that in the same way that the Israelites were rescued from Egypt and the Red Sea and were made to be a kingdom of priests, so too, through the victory of the Lamb, the people of God today are

---

28. Though all the major English translations render the verb here with the future—"they will reign"—the manuscript evidence is unclear. There are two significant manuscripts when it comes to the book of Revelation (Sinaiticus and Alexandrinus). Unfortunately, they differ in the reading here. When faced with such uncertainty due to the discrepancies among the manuscripts, scholars endeavor to discern which reading is more difficult. The idea is that it makes more sense to suppose that a scribe found a "difficult" reading and altered the text accordingly than it is to suppose that the scribe altered an easier reading and presented us with a more difficult reading. Brian Tabb notes, "Many commentators prefer the future tense *basileusousin* in 5:10 (they shall reign on the earth), a strong case can be made for the present tense *basileuousin* (they are reigning on the earth). The manuscript evidence is evenly divided, with Sinaiticus supporting the future tense and Alexandrinus the present. The present tense *basileuousin* in 5:10 is the more difficult reading, which scribes may have changed to conform to the future tense in 20:4 [sic; 20:6] and 22:5" (Tabb, *All Things*, 1729). I have opted for the present "they reign" for two reasons. First, as Tabb notes, it is the more difficult reading. That is, it is easier to account for why a scribe would change the reading from the present to the future than it is to account for why a scribe would change the future to the present. Second, although the future, "they will reign," can fit with the narrative flow of the text, it is my conviction that the present corresponds better with the overall narrative flow of the text. John has just affirmed that the people of God have been purchased. Now, he notes the result of that purchasing is that they reign. Therefore, in light of the fact that the death and resurrection of Jesus are foundational for John's narrative, it simply makes more sense to conclude that Jesus's death and resurrection have brought about the present reign of God's people.

becoming a kingdom of priests.[29] Bauckham notes the significance of John's application of Exod 19:5–6 to the people of God, "In Revelation this statement is applied to the church as the eschatological people of God, the people of the new Exodus, who have been redeemed by the blood of Christ, the eschatological Passover Lamb."[30]

After the song of the Four Living Creatures and the Twenty-Four Elders, John looks and hears the voice of an innumerable host of angels joining in the worship: "And I saw and I heard the voice of many angels around the throne and the Living Creatures and the Elders" (5:11). He notes that the number of angels was, "ten thousands of ten thousands[31] and thousands of thousands" (5:11). They were crying out, "Worthy is the Lamb that was slain to receive power and riches and wisdom and strength and honor and glory and blessing" (5:12). The innumerable angels thus expand the threefold ascription of "glory, honor, and power" given to the Father (4:11) into a sevenfold ascription to Jesus, by adding, "riches and wisdom and strength . . . and blessing."

John then states that he heard, "every creature"—which includes those "in heaven and upon the earth and under the earth and upon the sea and all the things that are in them" (5:13)—worshiping the Father and the Lamb by ascribing to them "blessing, honor, glory, and power" (5:13).[32]

---

29. The depiction of the people of God as a kingdom also occurs in Dan 7:18.

30. Bauckham, *Climax*, 327.

31. The Greek here says, "*myriads of myriads.*" The NET, NIV, and NKJ all use "ten thousand times ten thousand." The problem is that the Greek is plural—as reflected in my translation. The NAS, ESV, and NRS read, "myriads of myriads." The use of *myriads* is not a translation but a transliteration. The word "*myriads*" in Greek is technically the word for ten thousand. The difficulty here is that *myriads* is plural. This means it should be rendered in English as "ten thousands" (hence, the NLT "millions" is suitable). What makes translating the text here so difficult is that the text reads "*myriads of myriads,*" which might be rendered "ten thousands of ten thousands" or "ten thousands times ten thousands." Since "ten thousands" (plural) is not a definable number, it is impossible to multiply the two numbers and thereby derive any definable number. This appears to be John's point. There were "countless" angels around the throne.

32. It is likely that the threefold ascription of worship to the Father (4:11) corresponds with God as the eternal one ("who was and who is and who is to come"; 4:8). The sevenfold ascription of worship to the Lamb that was slain (5:12) likely corresponds to Christ with regard to perfection and the totality of the fulfillment. The fourfold ascription of worship to the Father and Christ (5:13) likely indicates the fullness of the worship in relation to creation. That the worship comes from "every created thing" (5:13), which occupy four distinct places within the creation, supports this conclusion.

The throne room scene (4:1—5:14) then concludes with the Four Living Creatures and Twenty-Four Elders falling down and worshiping (5:14). Though John does not specify who they worshiped, the context suggests that they worship both the Father and the Lamb. If so, the narrative movement within the throne room scene is such that what began with the revealing of the One on the throne (i.e., the Father; 4:2-3), then moved to the worship of the One on the throne (i.e., the Father; 4:8-11), to the revealing of the Lamb (i.e., Jesus; 5:5-6), to the worship of Jesus (5:8-12), and then the scene finally comes to a close with the worship of both the Father and Jesus (5:13-14).

Excursus: The Scroll

It is my conviction that as the narrative proceeds, the Scroll and its contents, and secondarily "the prayer of the saints," take center stage. That is, Revelation's second story, the heavenly vision of 4:1—16:21, focuses on the Scroll at least through 11:13, and the significance of this for understand the narrative, and the interpretive questions that arise, cannot be overstated.

The preeminence of the Scroll is evident from John's consternation when he first learns that no one was able to open it (5:3-4). The fact that John weeps because "no one was able . . . to open the Scroll or to look at it" (5:4) suggests that he knows the weightiness of the Scroll and its contents. In addition, the fact that Jesus is the One who is worthy "to take the Scroll and open its seals" (5:9) surely highlights its significance. Furthermore, the fact that Jesus is worthy to take the Scroll and to open it "because you were slain" (5:9) further heightens the significance of the Scroll.

What, then, does the Scroll represent, and what is on it?[33] Surely the narrative to follow will tell us. As Richard Bauckham

---

33. Caird lists four common understandings of the Scroll: "The first identifies it with the Lamb's book of life." Second, "the scroll contains the revelation of those coming events which John has been charged to communicate." Third, "the scroll is the Old Testament." And fourth, "the content of the scroll is God's redemptive plan" (Caird, *Revelation*, 70-72; emphasis original).

David deSilva notes, "What is this scroll at the centre of so much to-do? Early church fathers tended to connect it with the Scriptures, and the opening of the scroll to the interpretation of Scripture. Primasius regarded the writing on the outside of the scroll as representing the Jewish Scriptures or Old Testament, and the writing on the inside the writings of the New Testament, for the New Testament 'lay hidden within the Old.' Similarly, Victorinus reads this scene as an affirmation that the meaning of the

affirms, "It would be intolerable if John left it unclear what the content of the scroll is."[34]

It is my contention, which is widely affirmed among commentators, that the Scroll contains God's will. In particular, I would add that the Scroll contains God's plan for how He will redeem humanity and restore His creation. This is what I believe Bauckham intimates when he says, "It is a reasonable conclusion, then, that the content of the scroll which the One who sits on the throne holds in his right hand is his secret purpose for establishing his kingdom on earth."[35] Resseguie, likewise, asserts, "Since the scroll is in the right hand—the hand of deliverance and judgment—it appears to be related to God's plan of salvation and justice."[36] Farmer adds, "Commentators generally agree that this sealed scroll represents the redemptive plan by which God's purpose will be achieved."[37]

Excursus: Overcoming

One cannot overstate the significance of 5:5–6 for our understanding of the book of Revelation. The heavenly vision of 4:1—16:21 (the second story) opened by affirming that God is the One who is enthroned. He is the world's true king. Now, in 5:5–6, John adds that Jesus is also the world's true king. John declares, however, that the means by which Jesus has become the King (the Lion) is by being the Lamb that was slain.

We have already observed the importance of the exhortation to "overcome" in the seven messages.[38] What had not been stated to this point in the narrative is what it means to "overcome." With the introduction of Jesus as the One who "has overcome" (5:5), John provides us with, as we will see, the first of several critical insights as to what it means to "overcome." The first insight is that Jesus overcame by becoming

---

Old Testament remains sealed up unless it is read in the light of the Lamb, that is, in the light of the life, death and resurrection of Jesus, for only in Christ is the veil removed from the reading of the Old Testament" (deSilva, *Discovering*, 153–54).

34. Bauckham, *Climax*, 249.
35. Bauckham, *Climax*, 249.
36. Resseguie, *Revelation*, loc. 2470–71.
37. Barr, *Reading*, 114.
38. See 2:7, 11, 17, 26; 3:5, 12, 21.

the Lamb that was slain! The preeminence of Christ as the Lamb that was slain is evident in that the Elders and the Living Creatures affirm that Christ is worthy "because you were slain" (5:9). Their affirmation is followed by an uncountable multitude of angels who also cry out, "Worthy is the Lamb that was slain" (5:12).

This, of course, corresponds well with the rest of the NT. As G. B. Caird affirms, "Wherever the OT speaks of the victory of the Messiah or the overthrow of the enemies of God, we are to remember that the gospel recognizes no other way of achieving these ends than the way of the cross."[39]

Conclusion to the Throne Room Scene (4:1—5:14)

The second story (the heavenly vision of 4:1—16:21) opens with John being taken into heaven where he saw a throne. The throne affirms God's sovereignty. The One who sits on the throne is the world's true sovereign, king, and judge. As the scene progresses, we learn that God's sovereign plan will unfold precisely because the Lamb was slain.

For John and his reader/hearers, of course, the fact that God is on the throne had far greater implications. Namely, they are not to be afraid of, nor to compromise with the imperial powers because, although it may appear as if Caesar rules, the reality is that God is the One on the throne. As Brian Tabb concludes:

> First, the Apocalypse clarifies for readers that the Creator God—not Caesar—has ultimate authority and thus deserves ultimate allegiance. Second, John's prophecy challenges readers to resist and repent of spiritual complacency, worldly compromise and false teaching, while holding fast to the sure promises of God. Third, Revelation comforts afflicted believers with assurances that the supreme Judge will hold their oppressors accountable, will vindicate his people and will secure a glorious future for those who conquer 'by the blood of the Lamb and by the word of their testimony.'"[40]

DeSilva adds:

---

39. Caird, *Revelation*, 75.
40. Tabb, *All Things New*.

Augustus had claimed his power to be legitimate on the basis of being granted primacy 'by universal consent' (*Res Gestae* 34). The scene with which John closes this vision of heavenly worship, however, shows a far more genuinely universal consent upholding the reign of the God of Israel and this God's Messiah, and on the basis of far more fundamental benefits."[41]

For modern Western readers, we might say that, though it appears as if power, wealth, sex, and military[42] might are on the throne, the book of Revelation assures us that it is God and the Lamb who are enthroned.[43] Michael Gorman captures the significance of this for us today:

> Human beings, even apparently faithful Christians, too often want an almighty deity who will rule the universe with power, preferably on their terms, and with force when necessary. Such a concept of God and of sovereignty induces its adherents to side with this kind of God in the execution of (allegedly) divine might in the quest for (allegedly) divine justice. Understanding the reality of the Lamb as Lord—and thus of Lamb power—terminates, or should terminate, all such perceptions of divine power and justice, and of their erroneous human corollaries."[44]

There is another critical element to the story of the book of Revelation, which I will develop as we proceed, though it deserves mentioning here: namely, that, as the prologue affirms, "He has made us a kingdom" (1:6). Jesus's rule, in other words, has opened the door by which the people of God now also rule. This, I will argue as the narrative proceeds, is fulfilled in the account of the Two Witnesses.

What this means for John's reader/hearers and, by extension, for the people of God today cannot be overstated. Namely, the people of God are called to imitate Christ as His kings/queens and to rule the same way that He does. That is, we rule by sacrificially loving the other. Thus, as Resseguie asserts, "This counterintuitive battle—victory through suffering and apparent defeat—is a main theme of the Apocalypse and a pattern that

---

41. DeSilva, *Discovering*, 160.

42. Or, perhaps we might say, "although it appears that multinational corporations and the military industrial complex are on the throne...."

43. There are many scholars who believe that John is using a literary style of "vision casting" in order to write His narrative. That is, John did not actually have a vision *per se*, but is using the literary style of a vision in order to write what was revealed to him.

44. Gorman, *Reading*, 111.

faithful Christians are to follow."[45] Or, as Farmer puts it, "Jesus's sacrificial death may have enabled God to inaugurate the divine purpose, but the continued implementation of God's purpose depends upon the follower of Jesus making his lifestyle their lifestyle."[46]

The implication is clear: for the people of God to become kings/queens alongside Jesus, we too must overcome by being lambs that are slain just as Christ! The love story, in other words, is not just about Jesus laying down His life for the world. It is also about the people of God continuing to love the world so much that they too, like Jesus, lay down their lives for the nations.

---

45. Resseguie, *Revelation*, 2507–8.
46. Farmer, *Reading*, ed Barr, "Undercurrents" 117.

Revelation 6:1–17
The First Six Seals

God's judgment, already taking place, is less about angry thunderbolts than it is about a permissive stance toward the world. God allows Rome to experience the consequences of its own rule. It seems justice, rather than revenge, is operative.[1]

People with money can always buy food; famine affects only the poor.[2]

Introduction

I HAVE PROPOSED THAT the book of Revelation must be read from the perspective that John is advancing a narrative. In doing so, John utilizes apocalyptic imagery in order to provide his reader/hearers with a portrait of what is really happening in the world.

John began the second story, or the heavenly vision (4:1—16:21) narrative with an opening throne room scene (4:1—5:14). In this opening scene, John, in true apocalyptic fashion, revealed to His reader/hearers that although it may seem as if Rome rules the world, in reality, it is God who is enthroned. As the narrative progresses, we are anticipating that John will make known to us the contents of the Scroll. In order to read the Scroll, of course, the Seals with which it is closed must be broken.

---

1. Carter, *Roman Empire*, 125.
2. Sider, *Rich Christians*, 12.

Understanding the Seven Seals

Unfortunately, popular eschatological readings of the book of Revelation have led to some seriously mistaken understandings of the Seven Seals. In order to understand the meaning of the Scroll and the Seven Seals within the narrative, we must recognize the following.

First, I begin by noting that the breaking of the Seals does not incrementally reveal the contents of the Scroll. After all, the contents of an ancient scroll would not have been accessible until all the Seals have been broken.[3] As Warren Carter affirms:

> Ancient readers familiar with sealed scrolls would not suppose that the events which occur when the Lamb opens each of the seals are intended to represent the content of the scroll. These events simply accompany the opening of the scroll. The progressive opening of the scroll is a literary device which John has created in order to narrate material which prepares us and is presupposed by the content of the scroll itself"[4]

Second, although it is commonplace among some popular writers to propose that the breaking of the Seven Seals represents the first in a series of judgments that God inflicts upon the nations of the world in the "last days," it is my contention that the effects that follow the opening of the Seven Seals, or more specifically the first four Seals, are not divine judgments. Instead, the effects that follow the breaking of the Seals should be understood as a depiction of the inevitable consequences of humanity's rule apart from God. In other words, the Seals relate what happens when God allows humanity to continue to rule apart from God's wisdom. Kraybill affirms, "The first four sufferings of this cycle seem, at least in part, to issue from human greed and violence."[5]

The Seals, therefore, affirm that the tragic result of human rule is deception, violence, famine, death, and destruction. That is, they describe the consequences of what happens when, as Paul says, "God gave them over" (Rom 1:24, 26) to our own desires.[6] Barr agrees stating that the first four

---

3. The contents of the scroll, as we will see, are revealed only after John eats the scroll (10:10) and prophesies (10:11). I will contend that the contents of his prophecy are captured in the account of the Two Witnesses in 11:1–13.

4. Bauckham, *Climax*, 250.

5. Kraybill, *Allegiance*, 102.

6. See also Rom 1:18–32.

Seals, "form a logical and consistent series that has often been acted out in history: first a conqueror appears, followed by war, famine, and death."[7]

Third, those who suffer the most from the destructive behaviors unleashed by human rulers and their lust for power are the poor and marginalized. Carter asserts:

> The violent destruction does not come about because God intervenes. Conquest, war, economic exploitation, and famine are expressions and consequences of empire.[8]

Justo Gonzalez adds:

> The geopolitical order is not just a matter of world politics, of empires and kingdoms; it is also a matter of people going hungry, of families not being able to sustain themselves, and of the rich and the powerful making sure that the system continues working for the benefit of those in power, even if it means hunger and starvation for others.[9]

Of course, in describing the tragic consequences of humanity's rule, John is not denying that God is sovereignly in control of all things. John's narrative, in fact, should be read in a manner similar to the prophets and their declarations that God brought about the destruction of Jerusalem, when in fact it was the doing of Babylon.

Fourth, those who mistakenly assert that the effects described at the breaking of the Seals depict God as the source of the nations' suffering often wrongly assume that the people of God are excluded from the suffering. On the contrary, the suffering of the people of God is a central component of the first four Seals.[10] After all, from what we can ascertain, most of the early Christ followers to whom John wrote were members of the poor and the marginalized. There is, therefore, little doubt that the people of God suffer as a result of humanity's rule.

---

7. Barr, *Tales*, 2622–23.
8. Carter, *Roman Empire*, 125.
9. Gonzalez, "Revelation," loc. 914–16.
10. Again, this is not to say that others do not suffer as a result of the Seals. Certainly, economic hardships will affect all of the poor—whether they are followers of Christ or not. I am simply contending that the focus of the Seals includes the present suffering of God's people.

Excursus: The Seals and Jesus's Eschatological Speech (Mark 13)[11]

Another key factor that illuminates the meaning of the Seven Seals and their role in the narrative of the book of Revelation is the relationship between John's narrative of the Seven Seals and Jesus's eschatological (i.e., end-times) discourse in Mark 13:5–13.

The account in Mark 13 begins with Jesus's prediction of the destruction of the temple in Jerusalem: "Do you see these great buildings? Not one stone will be left upon another which will not be torn down" (Mark 13:2). This is followed by disciples inquiry, "When will these things be?" (Mark 13:4).

Jesus begins His response by noting, "Many will come in My name, saying, 'I am He!' and will mislead many" (Mark 13:6). The coming of false teachers corresponds to the First Seal (6:1–2).[12] Then, paralleling the Second Seal, Jesus continues, "When you hear of wars and rumors of wars, do not be frightened; those things must take place; but that is not yet the end. For nation will rise up against nation, and kingdom against kingdom" (Mark 13:7–8). Jesus's next statement corresponds to John's description of the effects that follow the opening of the Third Seal: "there will also be famines" (Mark 13:8).[13] Of course, it must be noted that, at this point in His response, Jesus is not necessarily providing the disciples with any indication as to "when" these things will take place as the disciples had asked. After all, wars, famines, and earthquakes are characteristics of every age. Jesus, in fact, appears to be indicating that life will continue as it has for a time.

As we continue through the opening verses of Jesus's words to the disciples in Mark 13, we see further indications of the parallels with John's account of the Seven Seals. Jesus states, "But be on your guard; for they will deliver you to the courts, and you will be flogged in the synagogues, and you will stand

---

11. See Mark 13:6–13; Matt 24:1–14 and Luke 21:9–19. For an extended discussion of Mark 13, see my *Understanding*, 136–54.

12. Mark 13:22 adds, "For false Christs and false prophets will arise." See also Matt 24:24.

13. Note Luke 21:11 adds "plagues and famines," which even more closely parallels the Third and Fourth Seals. Mark's addition that there will be "earthquakes" (Mark 13:8) corresponds to the Sixth Seal.

before governors and kings for My sake, as a testimony to them. The gospel must first be preached to all the nations" (Mark 13:9–10). In saying this, Jesus indicates that in the midst of false teachers, wars, and famines, the disciples will experience suffering and possibly even death (Mark 13:12). This corresponds to the Fourth Seal, which as I will note below, appears to serve as a summary of the first Three Seals and to note that the end result of humanity's rule is death (6:8).

Jesus then informs His disciples, "but the one who endures to the end, he will be saved" (Mark 13:13). Similarly, John narrates that after the Fifth Seal is opened, the souls of the people of God cry out, "How long?" (6:10). Why are the people of God crying out? As we will see, it is because the present is a time of suffering for many, including the people of God. Thus, they rightly ask, "How long?" (6:10).

The parallels between John's narrative of the Seven Seals (i.e., the first four and perhaps the first five in particular) and Jesus's words to His disciples in Mark 13 are quite apparent and, in my opinion, instructive for our understanding the Seals narrative (6:1–17; 8:1, 5). Reading the two passages alongside one another leads to the supposition that as long as the powers of the world remain in control, the world, including the people of God, suffer.

This leads to my conclusion that the Seven Seals inform the people of God that the nations will remain in power and continue to wreak devastation upon the earth for a time. As a result, the people of God must persevere. After all, the people of God are sharers with John "in the tribulation, kingdom, and patient endurance in Jesus" (1:9).

Literary Design in the Seals Narrative

In order to best understand John's account of the Seven Seals, it is important to recognize that the first four Seals are set apart from the final three. The obvious distinction between the first four Seals and the last three is that following the breaking of each of the first four Seals, one of the Four Living Creatures says, "Come!" (6:1, 3, 5, 7). John then looks and sees[14] a

---

14. Technically, he only states "And I saw" after the breaking of the First (6:2), Third

rider on a horse (6:2, 4, 5, 8). After the breaking of the Fifth Seal, however, instead of *hearing* he *sees* ("I saw"; 6:9). In addition, the breaking of the Fifth Seal is not accompanied by any disastrous effects on humanity.

First Four Seals 6:1–8

First Seal: The Rider on the White Horse 6:1–2

John begins, "I saw when the Lamb opened one of the Seven Seals" (6:1).[15] He then notes that he heard one of the Four Living Creatures saying, "Come!" (6:1). He adds that the voice of the Living Creature was like a "voice of thunder" (6:1).[16] John then says, "And I saw, and behold a white horse" (6:2).[17]

Identifying the rider on the white horse has been a matter of debate among commentators. There are three basic positions.

The first two views both contend that the rider on the white horse represents Christ. Those who affirm this position do so by appealing to John's description of Jesus's return in 19:11–16, where Jesus is described as riding on a "white horse" (19:11).[18] In both accounts, we read: "behold a white horse and one/One sitting on it" (6:2; 19:11).

The difference between these first two views—and it is a significant distinction—has to do with whether the rider on the first horse represents Christ at His first coming—that is, the coming of Christ as marked out in the Gospels[19]—or if it is a depiction of Christ coming

---

(6:5), and Fourth (6:8) Seals.

15. John begins the First and Sixth Seals the same. In both, he says, "And I saw, when the Lamb/He opened" (6:1, 12). This indicates the presence of an inclusio marking the beginning and the end of a unit.

16. There are two other occasions in which John hears a voice of thunder and, in both instances, it is the voice of the people of God: see 14:2; 19:6. A voice of thunder often represents the presence, or the voice, of God (see especially Ps 29:3–4; also, 1 Sam 7:10; Job 37:2–5).

17. John introduced the First (6:2), Third (6:5), and Fourth (6:8) Seals with "And I saw, and behold."

18. The fact that John uses "white horse" only three times (6:2; 19:11, 14), two of which are in the account of Christ's return (one describing the horse that Jesus is riding and one describing the horses that the people of God are riding), further links the two accounts. See the discussion below and in 19:11–16.

19. See: Hendriksen, *Conquerors*, 96. Although I agree with Hendriksen's assessment of the present work of Christ, I strongly disagree, as I will explain below, with the conclusion that the rider on the white horse is Christ.

in the future. Those who believe that the rider on the first horse is a depiction of a future coming of Christ often contend that the opening of the First Seal represents the coming of Christ in order to rapture[20] the people of God and to inaugurate the events that follow.

The third view, to which I subscribe, suggests that the rider on the white horse represents false Christs and false prophets. As noted above, this understanding accords well with Jesus's speech in Mark 13, which begins with Jesus's warning to His disciples that false teachers will continue to peddle their false beliefs.[21]

If this rider does not represent Jesus, how might I account for the fact that the introductions to the rider of the white horse (6:2) and Jesus as a rider on a white horse (19:11) are identical? My response is that John wants us to see the rider on the white horse in light of his blasphemous claims. The very fact that this rider is depicted in a manner that leads us to even speculate as to whether or not this is Jesus is precisely what John intends. As the narrative unfolds, John will regularly depict Satan and his minions as making every effort to imitate God and disguise themselves as agents of good. For example, John describes the Beast as having a head that was, "as if it had been slain" (13:3). This language of "as if it had been slain" is identical to that used to introduce Jesus as the Lamb in 5:6. Yet, we know that the Beast is evil. It is my conviction that John expects his reader/hearers to recognize that this rider on a white horse is nothing more than one of Satan's agents endeavoring to imitate Jesus. As Paul says, "such men are false apostles, deceitful workers, disguising themselves as apostles of Christ. No wonder, for even Satan disguises himself as an angel of light" (2 Cor 11:13–14).

That John expects his reader/hearers to recognize that the rider on the white horse is a false Christ is evident from a number of features. One of the first clues that the rider on the white horse is not Jesus is that

---

20. This view, which has become marketed in the popular world of Christian theology through the *Left Behind* series presents the idea that God "raptures" (or "seizes up") all Christians for a period of three-and-one-half, or seven, years before the second coming. This rider represents Christ coming "for" His saints either three-and-one-half or seven years before the final descent of Christ. Needless to say, I find this understanding to be a seriously erroneous and even potentially dangerous misreading of the book of Revelation.

For more discussion on the issue of the rapture and the book of Revelation, see Rossing, *Rapture Exposed*.

For a fuller discussion of the Second Coming and the idea of a rapture, see my *Understanding*, 116–17.

21. See Mark 13:6.

the rider has a bow (6:2). Jesus, of course, has a sword (1:16; 2:12, 16; see also, 19:15, 21). This may not seem like much, but the difference is enormous. Christ's sword, which comes out of His mouth, indicates that the means by which He wages war is through His spoken word. Jesus, as I have already argued, and will continue to expound, does not wage war with violence, but instead suffers violence. The rider on the white horse's bow, however, symbolizes military power.[22] In addition, this rider has a "crown" (6:2). Jesus, however, has "many diadems" (19:12).[23] John also notes that the rider's crown "was given" to him (6:2). Throughout the book of Revelation the passive verb "was given"[24] consistently refers to something given by God to an evil agent.[25]

The rider on a white horse, therefore, represents false prophets who not merely condone the behavior of human rulers it and their use of force to maintain their power, but also provide an ideological justification for it and attempt to entice the people of God to comply. This rider may appear to be Christ, but John's reader/hearers are well served to recognize its deceptive ways.

Second Seal: The Rider on the Red Horse 6:3–4

After Jesus breaks the Second Seal, John sees a rider on a red horse (6:4). To this rider John says, "it was given to him to take peace from the earth and that people might slay one another" (6:4). John also notes that the rider on the red horse was given "a great sword" (6:4). The sword given to this rider is not the same as the sword that proceeds from the mouth of Christ. As noted earlier,[26] the word for *sword* here is used three other times in the book of Revelation and each time it appears in a context that suggests the emperor's sword, which was used for capital punishment.[27]

---

22. See Ps 46:9; Isa 21:15; Jer 50:42; Hos 2:18.

23. John does employ a completely different word for Jesus's "diadems." Interestingly, the Dragon (12:3) and the Beast (13:1) are also wearing "diadems." See note at 19:12 for further discussion.

24. It is one word in Greek (*edothe*). See 6:2, 4*, 8, 11; 7:2; 8:2, 3; 9:1, 3, 5; 11:1, 2; 13:5*, 7*, 14, 15; 16:8; 19:8; 20:4.

25. "Was given" is what is often termed a "divine passive": meaning that God is the one who gives. This is not to be understood as God causing or encouraging evil to do its work, but as God allowing evil to do so.

26. See excursus: "Jesus's sword and divine violence and the book of Revelation" in commentary on 1:9–20.

27. See 13:10*, 14.

That those who are killed by this rider include the people of God gains support from John's use of "slay" in 6:4.[28] John uses the verb "to slay" eight times. In addition to the present account (6:4), John uses the verb "to slay" four times to identify Jesus as the Lamb that was "slain" (5:6, 9, 12; 13:8). A sixth occurrence of "to slay" appears in the account of the Fifth Seal where John depicts the souls under the altar as those: "who had been slain because of the word of God, and because of the testimony which they had" (6:9). The seventh use of "to slay" appears in the account of the judgment of Babylon as the place where one finds "the blood of prophets and of saints and of all who have been slain on the earth" (18:24). Here again, the verb "to slay" describes the killing of the people of God. There is, however, an eight occurrence of the verb "to slay" in 13:3. In this instance, the verb is not applied to Christ or the people of God. John notes, in the description of the Beast that he saw "one of his [the Beast's] heads as if it had been slain" (13:3). As I noted above, the fact that one of the heads of the Beast was "as if it had been slain" (13:3) is an ironic use of the verb designed to highlight the Beast's blasphemous efforts to imitate Christ. This suggests, therefore, that those who are slain by the rider on the red horse include the people of God.

Third Seal: Rider on the Black Horse[29] 6:5–6

After Jesus breaks the Third Seal, John sees a rider on a black horse with a pair of scales in his hand (6:5). The use of scales here indicates the weighing out of food for sale or purchase. John then hears that the price of grain has been seriously inflated: "a quart of wheat for a denarius and three quarts of barley for a denarius" (6:6).[30] Since a quart of wheat represents enough food to feed one person for a day, "a quart of wheat for a denarius grain" indicates that grain was being sold at twelve times the usual rate. And since three quarts of barley was enough food to feed one family for a day, it is estimated that barley was being sold at eight

---

28. See: 5:6, 9, 12; 6:4, 9; 13:3, 8; 18:24.

29. Unfortunately, it is not uncommon to hear these days alarmists claiming that Covid-19 is the third horseman of the Apocalypse. See my blog post "Are the Seven Seals of the Book of Revelation Unfolding Today," https://www.patheos.com/blogs/determinetruth/2020/03/are-the-seven-Seals-of-the-book-of-revelation-unfolding-today/.

30. The denarius was the equivalent of a day's pay.

times the usual rate. At such rates, a poor family would have no surplus funds to meet any other need.[31]

This high rate of inflation on staple foods like wheat and barley, which would have been disastrous to the poor, is a common effect of war. What the third rider depicts, in other words, is the natural result of the war and bloodshed brought about by the second rider.

John also hears, "and do not damage the oil and the wine" (6:6). Since "the oil and the wine" represent some of the comforts of life, the implication may well be that the goods of the wealthy were not negatively impacted in the same way as those of the poor.[32] Sure the wealthy would have had to pay higher rates for grain, but they could afford it.

The Third Seal then, depicts a world of inflation in which the poor were disproportionately affected in adverse ways.[33] Given the fact that many of the Christ followers in the first century would have been included among the poor, the Third Seal, like the first two, represents factors that would also have negatively impacted many of the first century Christ followers.[34]

Excursus: Grain and the Economy of Rome

In order to grasp the full scope of the effects of the Third Seal it is important to understand the socioeconomic context of the Roman world.

At the time of the first century, the city of Rome was home to a small but powerful group of wealthy individuals. In order for the few elites in Rome to live in extreme opulence, there was a tremendous need for large numbers of slaves and day laborers. Although slaves were not hard to come by—as a result of Rome's many conquests, the city of Rome had an abundance of slaves. There remained, however, a tremendous demand for laborers who would help supply Rome with the requisite supply of goods the powerful elite needed to retain their lavish lifestyle.

---

31. Lev 26:26; 2 Kgs 7:1; Ezek 4:10, 16.

32. Joel 1:10–11.

33. See deSilva: "Revelation 6:5–6 reflects a situation in which the prices of staples are grossly inflated, while production of oil and wine proceeds unabated" (deSilva, *Unholy Allegiances*, 991–92).

34. This does not mean that others are not suffering or that God is not concerned with their suffering.

In hopes of attracting such laborers, Rome decided to offer all of its residents an incentive: free grain.[35] Since grain was an important staple in the Roman diet, the offer of free grain was a great encouragement for many to come and settle in Rome. Providing every resident in Rome with its needed supply of grain, however, put a tremendous strain on the rest of the empire.

The strain was caused in part by the fact that Rome fixed the price it was willing to pay for its grain. That is, instead of the growers setting the price of grain based on supply and demand, Rome paid them a fixed fee. This created havoc in the grain markets throughout the empire. As a result, many landowners decided that it was more profitable to produce oil and wine, and other higher-end crops! After all, there would always be a demand for such items, especially among the wealthy. In addition, it was quickly realized that the wealthy were always willing to pay full price for wine and oil. Unfortunately, the transference of many landowners from the production of grain to the production of oil and wine only intensified the plight of the poor because it meant even less grain was available and less grain meant higher prices.

There were numerous adverse effects from all of this upon the poor. For one thing, the combined effect of Rome always receiving its quota of grain at a fixed price and of landowners refusing to grow grain meant that there was a consistent lack of grain for much of the empire. As a result, the price of grain rose significantly! In addition, in the event of famine (and with an empire the size of Rome, such occurrences were not infrequent) there was an even greater strain on the supply of grain. The greater the shortage of grain, the higher the prices. Of course, the residents of Rome were rarely impacted. The constant supply of free grain remained steady. Instead, those who were most affected by the increasing prices of grain throughout the empire were, of course, the poor.

This context sheds even more light on how John's reader/hearers would likely have understood the account of the Third Seal.

---

35. Kraybill, *Imperial Cult*, 107.

Fourth Seal: Rider on Pale Horse—Death 6:7–8

After Jesus breaks the Fourth Seal, John sees a rider on a pale[36] horse. The rider is named "Death" and Hades was following closely (6:8).[37] John adds, "authority was given to them over a fourth of the earth to kill by means of the sword, by means of famine, by means of death, and by wild beasts of the earth" (6:8).

As I alluded to above, the effects accompanying the rider of the fourth horse appear to represent a summary of the effects brought about in the previous three Seals. This is especially evident in that this rider brings death by means of "the sword" and "famine"[38] (6:8). In addition to summarizing the effects that occur after the breaking of the first three Seals, the account of the rider on the fourth horse adds that the end result is death. Included in the means by which people die are the "wild beasts of the earth" (6:8).

Summary of the First Four Seals

The breaking of the first Four Seals then, must be understood in terms of John's effort to remind his reader/hearers that false prophets will arise who will attempt to lure them to compromise their witness. They must be faithful, however. For, in the present, God will continue to allow the rulers of the world to remain even though they bring injustice, devastation, and death.

---

36. This color can mean green; but when applied to persons it indicates sickliness and death in contrast to a person's normal color.

37. One may surmise that Death is the state of the dead and Hades is the place of the dead. See 20:13–14.

38. Although "famine" was not used in the account of the Third Seal, there is little doubt that this is what John had in mind.

REVELATION 6:1–17

Fifth and Sixth Seals 6:9–17

Fifth Seal: The Souls Under the Altar 6:9–11

After Jesus opened the Fifth Seal, John notes that he "saw underneath the altar the souls of the ones who had been slain because of the Word of God,[39] and because of the testimony[40] which they had" (6:9).

A significant change occurs in John's introduction of the Fifth Seal. As noted above, after the opening of each of the first four Seals, John says "I heard" (6:1, 3, 5, 7). With the opening of the Fifth Seal, however, he states "I saw" (6:9). The significance of the change from "I heard" to "I saw" might be overlooked by a modern reader. For the ancient reader/hearers, who were much more skilled at listening, the variation would have been striking. The change is further evidenced by the fact that the account of the Fifth Seal does not include a reference to one of the Four Living Creatures, a command to "Come," or the description of a rider on a varied colored horse. The literary changes from the first four Seals to the Fifth clearly mark the first four Seals as a distinct set. They also serve to draw increased attention to the Fifth Seal.

The narrative of the Fifth Seal explicitly introduces us to the people of God, who, as I have asserted, are among those impacted by the first four Seals. If the people of God are indeed among those who suffer from the effects of the first four Seals, then the prophetic cry of the people of God, "How long?" (6:10),[41] functions as a plea for relief from their present suffering.

Of course, the prophetic cry of the people of God is not a vindictive plea for vengeance, but a petition to God for justice.[42] Their plea expresses the desire for God to manifest His righteousness on earth. Thus, the people of God are in effect asking, "When will you bring your kingdom in fullness?"

John then notes that in response to their plea, they were each given a "white robe" (6:11).[43] That the people of God are clothed in white

---

39. See also 1:2, 9.

40. See also 1:2, 9; 11:7; 12:11, 17; 19:10*; 20:4. See discussion on the word of God and the testimony of Jesus in 1:2.

41. See Ps 13:1–2; 74:10; 79:5.

42. The difference between vengeance and justice is that vengeance is taking it into one's own hands.

43. White clothing occurs seven times; though the word for clothing varies: 3:5, 18; 4:4; 6:11; 7:9, 14; 19:14. See Zech 3:1–5.

indicates that they have been redeemed and purified. This is made explicit in the account of the Great Multitude (7:9–17), where we learn that the clothing of the people of God is white because it has been washed in the blood of the Lamb (7:14).

The souls under the altar were told that "they should rest for a little while longer" (6:11). But "how long?" They are told that they must wait, "until both their fellow servants and their brethren who were to be killed even as they themselves were, should be completed also" (6:11). The reason they are given for God's delay in replying to their request for justice, in other words, is because the number of those who are to be killed has not yet been "completed" (6:11). This might come as a surprise to the people of God. Their crying for justice is delayed. Why?

Excursus: God's Delay in Bringing Justice

It is my conviction, which I will believe will become more evident as the story progresses, that God's delay is a result of his love for the nations. That is, if God were to bring His kingdom in fullness now, in accordance with the plea of those who have been slain, then the nations would have to undergo the final judgment. As G. B. Caird notes, "The martyrs have been condemned in a human court of law, and that decision stands against them unless it is reversed in a higher court. But the heavenly judge cannot declare them to be in the right without at the same time declaring their persecutors to be in the wrong and passing sentence against them."[44]

It is also important to note here that the reason for the delay in justice is explicitly in order that the number of servants and brothers who are to be killed should be "completed also" (6:11).[45] We might also say that the answer, which I believe that the narrative will set forth, is that since the nations have not yet been redeemed in totality, the souls under the altar have to wait. Of course, these two are not mutually

---

44. Caird, *Revelation*, 85.

45. It is worth noting that the delay may not be for only martyrs. The text may be read: "until the number of their 'fellow servants' and 'their brothers', 'those who are about to be killed'" (6:11). In this reading, there are two groups within the people of God. The first is the "fellow servants" (6:10). There may be no indication that this group will suffer martyrdom. The second group would then be "their brothers" who are "about to be killed."

exclusive. In fact, they are highly interrelated. After all, if, and I believe John will make it clear in the account of the Two Witnesses, it is by means of the deaths of the people of God that the nations will be redeemed, then, once that number is complete, their cry for justice be fulfilled!

Sixth Seal: The Nations and the Final Judgment 6:12–17

In the same way that the narrative of the breaking of the Fifth Seal introduced us to the people of God and their cry for justice, the narrative of the breaking of the Sixth Seal introduces us to the nations and their cry.[46]

John notes that "when He opened the Sixth Seal, there was a great earthquake, and the sun became black like sackcloth made of hair, and the whole moon became like blood, and the stars of heaven fell to the earth . . . and the heaven was split apart like a scroll when it is rolled up and every mountain and island were moved from their places" (6:12–14). There is little doubt that the effects of the opening of the Sixth Seal correspond to that of the final judgment. In fact, this is made explicit when the nations cry out, "the great day of their wrath has come and who is able to stand?" (6:17).[47]

The imagery of earthquakes and signs in the sun, the moon, and the stars is common apocalyptic imagery.[48] Though it might appear to the modern reader as if John's description was a portrayal of the end of space and time as we know it, this would not likely have been in John's purview. Biblical authors often utilized apocalyptic imagery, which I prefer to designate as "cosmic upheaval" language, to describe the actions of God within His creation. Perhaps the best way to understand such language is to note that when God invades creation and acts in accordance with, or better yet, in fulfillment of, His covenant promises, the prophetic voices that announce God's actions have no better means with which to describe His acts except by employing "cosmic upheaval" language.[49]

---

46. The sevenfold people groups in 6:15 surely indicate the nations and is not meant to include the people of God. That the sevenfold people groups do not include the people of God is evident from the fact that they cry out because of the wrath of God that is coming on them.

47. See Mal 3:2.

48. See Isa 34:4 LXX; Isa 13:10–13; 24:1–6, 17–23; Ezek 32:6–8; Hos 10:8; Joel 2:10, 30–31; 3:15–16; Hab 3:6–11; Mark 13:24–26; Acts 2:19–20.

49. This may or may not mean that we have reached the end of time as we know it.

This language has a rich history in the Scriptures. For example, in Isaiah 13 we read:

> For the stars of heaven and their constellations
> Will not flash forth their light;
> The sun will be dark when it rises
> And the moon will not shed its light. . . .
> Therefore I will make the heavens tremble,
> And the earth will be shaken from its place
> At the fury of the Lord of hosts
> In the day of His burning anger (Isa 13:10, 13)."[50]

The prophecy in Isaiah 13, which seemingly depicts the dissolution of the universe, refers to the destruction of Babylon which occurred in 539 BC. The destruction of Babylon, of course, did not result in the end of the cosmos. Instead, the prophet chose to describe the destruction of Babylon in terms that seemingly depict the end of the cosmos.[51] N. T. Wright notes, "There is virtually no evidence that Jews were expecting the end of the space-time universe. There is abundant evidence that they, like Jeremiah and others before them, knew a good metaphor when they saw one, and used cosmic imagery to bring out the full theological significance of cataclysmic socio-political events."[52] Such language was chosen by the author because it represents the most appropriate language to depict God's acts of covenant faithfulness.

As for the imagery in 6:12–14, we know that one of the many uses of "earthquakes" in apocalyptic literature was as a symbol for the destruction of rebellious nations.[53] In addition, earthquakes signified the presence of God.[54] For example, God's presence at Mount Sinai resulted in an earthquake: "Now Mount Sinai was all in smoke because the Lord

---

Only the context of the passage can ascertain if the author conceived of an event as the end of history as we know it. The biblical writers appear to utilize this language because they considered it the most appropriate means of depicting God's actions in history.

50. See Isa 24:1–6, 19–23; 34:4, 12; Ezek 32:6–8; Joel 2:10, 30–31; 3:15–16; Hab 3:6–11; Matt 24:29; Mark 13:24–25; Acts 2:19–20; and we might include: Amos 8:8–9; Jer 4:23–28; Ps 68:7–8.

51. Similar language occurs throughout the prophets: e.g., Isa 24:21–23; 34:4–5; Jer 4:23–28.

52. Wright, *People of God*, 333.

53. See 16:19.

54. See Exod 19:18; Isa 24:18–20; 29:6; Joel 2:10; 3:16.

descended upon it in fire; and its smoke ascended like the smoke of a furnace, and the whole mountain quaked violently" (Exod 19:18).

John then adds, "and every mountain and island were moved from their places" (6:14). The reference to mountains recurs in 6:16. There John notes that the nations were "saying to the mountains and the rocks, 'Fall on us.'" It is best to understand John's use of "mountain" in accordance with its meaning in prophetic and apocalyptic texts. Within these texts, mountains and islands represent stability in the creation.[55] Thus, the removal of them was a sign of divine judgment. In addition, mountains often signify kings and kingdoms. This is evident in 17:9: "The seven heads are seven mountains on which the woman sits, and they are seven kings." If this is the meaning of "mountain" in 6:14, then the account of the Sixth Seal depicts judgment on the kings and kingdoms of the world. The tragedy, of course, is that the nations do not cry out to God in repentance. Instead, they cry out to the mountains: that is, the nations cry out to alternative kings and kingdoms.

That the opening of the Sixth Seal represents the final judgment gains support from the closing description of it as, "the great day of their wrath" (6:17). The use of the definite article ("the") suggests that this "great day" was a known day. In addition, if the effects following the opening of this Seal constitute as an answer to the prayer in 6:9–11, then it must be the final judgment.

It is also relevant to note that there are seven categories of people who come under the judgment of God: namely, "the kings of the earth and the great men and the commanders and the rich and the strong and every slave and free person" (6:15). That there are seven people groups surely indicates that they represent all the people of the Earth.

Of course, there is no reason to suppose that this sevenfold group includes the people of God. After all, the narrative of the Fifth Seal refers to the people of God and the Sixth Seal refers to the nations. Furthermore, they call to the mountains and the rocks to hide them from "the face of the One who is sitting on the throne, and from the wrath of the Lamb" (6:16). This cannot include the people of God. After all, seeing God's face is the end result of those who follow the Lamb (see 22:4).

The account of the Sixth Seal, then, presents us with the first description of the final judgment.[56] The description of the final judgment

---

55. See: Ps 18:7; Isa 54:10; Jer 4:23–26; Ezek 26:18; Mic 1:4; Hab 3:6; Zeph 2:11; Zech 14:4.

56. The final judgment occurs in several places in the narrative of Revelation: see

in the narrative of the Sixth Seal literally serves as the fitting response to the prayers of the saints in the account of the Fifth Seal. We already know from the account of the Fifth Seal that the end does not occur immediately.

The opening of the Sixth Seal, then, is a forward-looking event that functions as a reminder that even though there may be a delay, the nations that bring about injustices against the people of God will face judgment. That the judgment of the Sixth Seal looks forward towards the final judgment is also reinforced by the link between 6:15–17 and the final judgment scene in 19:17–19. In the judgment scene of 19:17–19, the birds are summoned: "Come, gather together for the great supper of God" (19:17).[57] The meal, we are told, is "the flesh of kings, the flesh of commanders, the flesh of the strong, the flesh of horses and those who sit upon them, and the flesh of all: of the free and, also, of the slaves and the small and the great" (19:18). Since both 6:15 and 19:18 include a list of seven people groups and six of the seven people groups appear in both lists, there are strong rhetorical reasons to view these accounts in light of one another.[58] Since the judgment of 19:17–19 is directly tied to the Second Coming of Christ (19:11–16), it only stands to reason that the judgment in 6:15–17 also depicts the final judgment that occurs at the return of Jesus.[59]

It is also worth noting that the judgment in 6:17 is titled, "The great day of their wrath." That is, it is the wrath of both God—the One who sits on the throne—and the Lamb. Of course, there is a great irony in the nations' cry to be saved from "the wrath of the Lamb" (6:16). Lambs, of course, are not typically considered agents of wrath.

The account of the Sixth Seal presents the cry of the nations[60] in a manner that contrasts the cry of the people of God in the Fifth Seal. Whereas, in the account of the Fifth Seal the people of God's cry for justice: "How long?" (6:10), now in the account of the Sixth Seal the nations' cry out to the mountains and the rocks, 'Fall on us and hide us

---

6:12–17; 11:15–19; 14:14–20; 16:1–21; 18:1–24; 19:20–21; 20:11–15.

57. See Ezek 39:4, 17–20.

58. That the lists are not identical is not of great significance. After all, John regularly varies his lists.

59. See 16:14; 1 Cor 5:5; 1 Thess 5:2; 2 Thess 2:2–3; 2 Pet 3:10; and, the "day of Christ" in Phil 1:10; 2:16.

60. The sevenfold people groups in 6:15 surely indicate the nations.

from the face of the One who sits on the throne and from the wrath of the Lamb'" (6:16).

From a literary perspective, the judgment of the nations in the account of the Sixth Seal functions as a direct response to the people of God's cry for justice in 6:10.

Conclusion

What then does all this mean? In the narrative of the book of Revelation, Jesus has taken the Scroll in order to unveil the will of God. As Jesus opens the first four Seals, we learn that life will proceed as it always has. There will be false prophets and false Christs. There will also be wars and famines and death. The accounts of the first four Seals, then, convey that life will continue as normal and that this period will be marked by the suffering of God's people.

As I have noted throughout, it is critical to understanding the narrative that we recognize that the effects of the opening of the first four Seals are also experienced by the people of God.

The account of the Fifth Seal introduced us to the people of God who were crying out, "How long, Lord . . . until you avenge our blood?" (6:10). The account of the Sixth Seal, by way of contrast, introduces us to the nations and it serves as a response to the cries for justice from the people of God in the narrative of the Fifth Seal.

Revelation 7:1–17
An Interlude:
The 144,000 and the Great Multitude

> *The countless multitude from every nation, tribe, peoples, and language is the new Israel, the perfectly complete number represented by the twelve thousand from each of the twelve historic tribes. John's vision, as usual, reinterprets the biblical tradition. What had first been the forming of an ethnically pure tribal confederation from out of Egypt and within Israel now is revealed to be a multinational, multicultural, multilinguistic multitude.*[1]

> *The beautiful vision of 'a great multitude that no one could count, from every nation, from all tribes and peoples and languages, standing before the throne and before the Lamb, robed in white, with palm branches in their hands' (Rev 7:9) is—or should be—at the heart of the church's self-understanding. This is what God is up to in the world.*[2]

Introduction

I have argued that beginning in 5:1 the Scroll has occupied center stage in the narrative of the heavenly vision (the second story). As a result, John's reader/hearers have anticipated the moment when the Scroll is opened and its contents are revealed. Naturally, then, after the breaking of the Sixth Seal (6:12–17), the reader/hearers are surely expecting that Jesus will next break the Seventh Seal and reveal the contents of the Scroll.

---

1. Howard-Brook and Gwyther, *Unveiling Empire*, loc. 5280.
2. Gorman, *Reading*, 133.

Yet, much to our surprise, 7:1 does not introduce us to the breaking of the Seventh Seal. Instead, 7:1–17 presents us with a pause, which is often deemed an "interlude" or an "embedded narrative."[3] Resseguie notes the rhetorical significance of 7:1–17: "John uses embedded narratives to slow down the narrative pace and to focus the reader's/hearer's attention on what is important. An embedded narrative, also called an interlude or intercalation, retards the frantic, rapid-fire pace, interrupts the seemingly relentless progression to the end, and draws attention to what is significant."[4]

The interlude of 7:1–17[5] divides into two seemingly distinct accounts. First, John describes 144,000 Israelites who are divinely protected by being sealed, or marked, by God (7:1–8). This is followed by an account of a Great Multitude who are from every nation and have been brought through the Great Tribulation and to the throne of God (7:9–17).

A close examination of these two accounts, however, confirms that these two seemingly disparate groups form a single portrait of the people of God prior to and after the time of tribulation that awaits God's people.

144,000 Are Sealed 7:1–8

Four Angels and the Four Winds 7:1–2

The account of the 144,000 opens with "four angels standing at the four corners of the earth, holding back the four winds of the earth" (7:1). The repetition of "four" with regard to the number of angels, the number of the corners of the earth, and the number of winds sets this opening scene

---

3. Resseguie, *Revelation,* loc. 850. Bauckham also uses "intercalation" and "parenthesis" to refer to the role of 7:1–17. See Bauckham, *Climax,* 11, 55.

4. Resseguie, *Revelation,* loc. 850.

5. It is important to observe that the present interlude occurs after the Sixth Seal (6:12–17) and before the Seventh Seal (8:1). John will similarly insert an interlude in the account of the Seven Trumpets (10:1—11:13). And, in a manner similar to the present account, the interlude of 10:1—11:13 occurs after the Sixth Trumpet and before the Seventh. These two interludes are also parallel in that they both depict the people of God. In the present interlude (7:1–17), John introduces us to two seemingly diverse groups: a 144,000 (7:4–8) and a Great Multitude (7:9–17). In the interlude of 10:1—11:13, he introduces us to the account of the Two Witnesses (11:1–13). For a thematic comparison of the 144,000 and the Great Multitude with the Two Witnesses, see my, *Two Witnesses,* 86–97.

within a global perspective.⁶ John then adds that the four angels are holding back the four winds "so that no wind could blow" (7:1), which suggests that the four winds represent destruction. Suddenly, another angel appears having "the Seal of the living God" (7:2). This angel "cries out with a great voice" (7:2) to the four angels "saying, 'Do not harm the earth, nor the sea, nor the trees until we have sealed the servants of our God on their foreheads'" (7:3). The command not to harm confirms the suspicion that the four angels are about to bring disaster to the earth.

It is quite likely that the "harm" that the four winds are about to unleash relates back to the account of the first six Seals in 6:1–17.⁷ If so, then the present scene is a movement backward in narrative or story time.

That the unleashing of the four winds corresponds with the first four Seals in 6:1–8 reinforces this conviction. That this is the case gains support from the fact that Zechariah 6 serves as the primary OT backdrop for both the four winds and the first six Seals. In Zech 6:1–8, the prophet had a vision of four chariots. Zechariah notes that each of the four chariots, in a manner that parallels the four horses of the first four Seals (6:1–8), was a different color (Zech 6:2–3). Zechariah then asks the angel who was revealing these things to him, "What are these, my lord?" (Zech 6:4). The angel responds, "These are the four spirits of heaven, going forth after standing before the Lord of all the earth" (Zech 6:5). It is important to note that *"ruach,"* which is Hebrew for "spirits" in Zech 6:5, may be rendered in English as, "spirit, breath, or wind." The Greek translation (LXX) of Zech 6:5, however, does not employ the expected *"pneuma,"* which is regularly used when translating *"ruach."* Instead, the LXX of Zech 6:5 has *"anemoi,"* which is the plural for "winds." John, then, appears to be reading the LXX of Zech 6:5. If this is so, then the first four Seals (6:1–8) and the four winds (7:1) correspond with "the four spirits" (or "winds") of Zech 6:5. Consequently, narratively speaking, the crying out of the angel with the seal of God to not bring harm (7:2–3), occurs prior to the breaking of the first four Seals.⁸

The interlude of 7:1–17, therefore, serves to assure the people of God that although they will face tribulation that results from the continued allowance of human rulers to remain in power, they have been sealed in order that they may endure (7:3).

---

6. See Jer 49:36; Dan 8:8; 11:4; Matt 24:31.

7. It is worth reiterating that only the first four Seals bring "harm."

8. Again, this must be understood in light of John's story. That is, John is telling a story that may or may not relate to specific events in space and time.

Seal of the Living God 7:3

The sealing of the people of God has a background in both the OT and NT.

The OT context is found in the "marking" of the people of God in Ezekiel 9.[9] In Ezekiel, the prophet is told to "put a mark on the foreheads of the men who sigh and groan over all the abominations which are being committed in its midst" (Ezek 9:4). Ezekiel then adds that everyone in the city who does not have this mark is to be killed (Ezek 9:5–6). For Ezekiel, the "mark" serves to provide the people of God with the assurance that despite the devastation that is about to occur God will preserve a remnant.[10]

In the New Testament, Paul refers to the Seal of God and applies it to the presence of the Holy Spirit within the people of God. This is evident in 2 Cor 1:21–22 where he says, "Now He who establishes us with you in Christ and anointed us is God, who also sealed us and gave *us* the Spirit in our hearts as a pledge." Paul similarly writes to the Ephesians, "In Him, you also, after listening to the message of truth, the gospel of your salvation—having also believed, you were sealed in Him with the Holy Spirit of promise, who is given as a pledge of our inheritance, with a view to the redemption of *God's own* possession, to the praise of His glory" (Eph 1:13, 14).

In light of Ezekiel and Paul, we may confidently assert that the sealing of the people of God in 7:3–8 represents the presence of the Holy Spirit in the life of God's people and it serves to assure them that God will protect and provide for them in the midst of suffering.[11] That is, although deception, wars, bloodshed, and famine will continue (Seals 1–4), the people of God are to be encouraged by the awareness

---

9. See Beale, *Revelation*, 409–10; Bauckham, *Climax*, 216.

10. The promise is made explicit in Ezek 6:8, where God states unequivocally, "I will leave a remnant."

11. That the sealing of the people of God entails that they are divinely protected by God is supported by an appeal to the account of the Fifth Trumpet (9:1–12). Bauckham contends that those who are sealed are "marked out for martyrdom" (Bauckham, *Theology*, 79). Although one might suggest that being marked out for martyrdom contradicts the notion that the sealing represents divine protection. I suspect, however, that John's first reader/hearers would not have considered the sealing and martyrdom as incongruous. After all, we know from the Second Seal (6:3–4) that some of God's people will suffer death at the hands of the second horseman.

that they have been sealed so that they will be able to endure in their salvation despite any suffering that they might incur.[12]

The 144,000 7:4–8

John introduces us to the 144,000 by noting that he "heard the number of those who were sealed, 144,000" (7:4). He then adds that they were "from every tribe of the sons of Israel" (7:4).

Though a first reading of 7:1–8 might lead to the conclusion that the 144,000 are ethnic Israelites, there are numerous textual indicators that suggest that John has all of God's people in view. Consequently, it is my conviction that John's account of the 144,000 depicts the people of God as holy warriors who are divinely protected so that they may endure the effects of the first four Seals.

> **Excursus: 144,000 as Holy Warriors**
>
> In discerning the identity of the 144,000 it is important to recognize that the numbering of them (144,000) has the earmarks of a census. In the Ancient Near Eastern (ANE) world, a census would be conducted in order to determine the military strength of the nation.[13] In the book of Numbers, for example, we are told that only men of military age were to be counted: "Take a census of all the congregation of the sons of Israel from twenty years old and upward, by their fathers' households, whoever is able to go out to war in Israel" (Num 26:2).
>
> Consequently, the numbering of them as 144,000 serves to identify them as an army prepared for holy war.[14]

---

12. I hesitate to suggest that they are "spiritually" protected while they are "physically" subjected to harm. Such language too often reflects a modernist dualistic worldview that is foreign to the biblical world. Perhaps, we might say that the sealing of God's people serves to ensure that they will be able to endure in their salvation despite the suffering that they might incur. See Beale, *Revelation*, 410–12.

13. Bauckham, *Climax*, 217; deSilva, *Discovering*, 177. We must note, of course, that while the people of God are presented as an army, their only weapon is their words and the means by which they wage war is through sacrificial love.

14. Interestingly, there is only one prior occurrence in the Bible in which God approved of a census. After all, there was no need for the Israelites to count their military strength, since, when Israel was called into battle, Yahweh was to go before them. See Num 1:3, 18, 20; 26:1–65; 1 Chr 27:23; 2 Sam 24:1–9.

That the 144,000 are depicted as soldiers prepared for holy war gains further support from the fact that they reappear in 14:1–5 where they are clearly depicted as an army of holy warriors. Thus, in 14:3, they sing a "new song." A "new song," as was noted in the commentary on 5:9, is a song sung after a military victory. The 144,000 are also described in 14:4 as those, "who have not been defiled with women, for they are pure" (14:4). This statement, which understandably has been quite controversial, suggests that the 144,000 are men who have remained sexually pure. The description of the 144,000 as those who "have not been defiled with women, for they are pure" (14:4) does not intend to suggest that they are only men, but instead, corresponds with the biblical requirement of sexual purity when engaged in holy war.[15] Since only men engaged in war in the ANE world, the 144,000 are said to be men. That they are sexually pure confirms that they are holy warriors.

Excursus: Are the 144,000 Ethnic Israelites?

John's explicit affirmation that the 144,000 are "from every tribe of the sons of Israel" (7:4) suggests that they are ethnic Israelites.[16] This conclusion is quite understandable. A close examination of the description of the account of the 144,000, as well as a comparison of them with the Great Multitude (7:9–17) confirms that both the 144,000 and the Great Multitude represent the totality of the people of God.

The first indication that the 144,000 are not restricted to ethnic Israelites arises from an examination of the list of the tribes from which they come (7:5–8). The problem with identifying the 144,000 of 7:5–8 as ethnic Israelites is that these are not the twelve tribes. The fact is, as Richard Bauckham has thoroughly demonstrated, John's list of the twelve tribes

---

15. It appears from the OT narrative that soldiers were required to be pure before engaging in war (see Josh 3:5). Since Moses apparently included abstaining from sexual relations as a part of the process of gaining purity (Exod 19:14–15), it was the practice to not have sexual relations during wartime. This appears to provide the context for the story of David and Uriah in 2 Sam 11. This suggests, as I will argue below, that the 144,00 may not be restricted to men, but that they are depicted as such in order to portray them in accord with the biblical imagery of holy warriors.

16. This view has been very commonly asserted by those who aim to take the text "literally." See Thomas, *Revelation*, 473–82; Walvoord, *Revelation*, 140–41.

in 7:5–8 does not correspond to any extant list of the twelve tribes.[17] John's list omits the tribes of Dan and Ephraim and replaces them with Levi (7:7) and Joseph (7:8). Although Levi and Joseph were two of the twelves sons of Jacob, they were not members of the twelve tribes who were allotted land as the Israelites entered the Promised Land.[18] John's unique listing of the twelve tribes likely serves as an indication that He has something more than just ethnic Israelites in view.

In addition, as I have noted, the use of "twelve" in the book of Revelation is well-established as a means of identifying the people of God.[19] In the case of the number 144,000, the math is straightforward: 144,000 is the product of twelve times twelve times 1000 (or 10 x 10 x 10). The most reasonable conclusion then, is that, in the same way that "twenty-four," which was used with regard to the number of Elders,[20] suggests that the Elders represent the OT tribes and the NT apostles, so here the 144,000 represents the OT people of God and the NT people of God as a result of multiplying twelve and twelve.

The fact that John multiplies 144 by 1000 may serve to indicate that the 144,000 are a vast but "countable" number.[21] David Barr affirms:

> The number is based on 12 and 10, the first squared [12x12] the second cubed [10x10x10]. The meanings of the root numbers have to do with being God's people and with totality; the effect of squaring and cubing is only to enhance the root meaning. So its significance is not quantitative but qualitative: all God's people."[22]

---

17. Bauckham, *Climax*, 220. While it is true that there are variations within the listing of the twelve tribes even in the OT (See Longman, *Revelation*, 167), John's list does not correspond with any of them nor any listing of the tribes in any extant Jewish literature of the Second Temple period.

18. Instead, Joseph was given a double portion, the portion of the firstborn, and his two sons Ephraim and Manasseh were each allotted a portion. The tribe of Levi was not allotted any land because they were to serve as priests and dwell among all of the tribes.

19. This will be very evident in John's description of the Holy City/New Jerusalem in 21:9—22:9.

20. See: 4:4, 10; 5:8; 11:16; 19:4

21. John uses 1,000 for a vast but countable number, and 10,000—which is always in the plural (5:11*; 9:16)—to indicate an uncountable number.

22. Barr, *Tales*, loc. 2762-64.

Beale adds, "12 is the number of God's people, which is squared to indicate completeness and multiplied by one thousand to connote vastness."[23]

The 144,000, therefore, are not exclusively ethnic Israelites.[24] Instead, as deSilva notes, "In the world of Revelation, one has either God's seal or the beast's mark, so the seal, and hence the roster of 7.4–8, most probably pertains to all believers."[25] At the same time, the 144,000, though they are not limited to 144,000, are not an innumerable lot either.

The Ones Who Have Come Out of the Great Tribulation 7:9–17

The Great Multitude 7:9–10

The account of the Great Multitude begins with, "After these things I looked" (7:9). As John looks, he announces, "and behold a Great Multitude that no one could count from every nation, tribes, peoples, and tongues standing before the throne and before the Lamb clothed in white robes and palm branches were in their hands" (7:9).

A first reading of 7:9 might well suggest that the Great Multitude stand in marked contrast to the 144,000. After all, in contradistinction to the 144,000, the Great Multitude both transcend ethnic Israelites and are innumerable.[26]

Excursus: The Great Multitude as Holy Warriors

The Great Multitude, in parallel with the 144,000, are also depicted as holy warriors. That they are holy warriors is suggested by the fact that the Great Multitude were holding "palm branches in their hands" (7:9), which identifies them

---

23. Beale, *Revelation*, 61.

24. Beale lists two other reasons to believe that the 144,000 represent all of God's people. He notes, "all redeemed believers are included when *douloi* ("servants") is used. He also notes that Ezekiel 9 "knows of no distinction between major groups of the faithful" (Beale, *Revelation*, 413).

25. DeSilva, *Discovering*, 177.

26. It is important to note here that the use of the fourfold formula serves to link them with the redeemed in 5:9.

as holy warriors celebrating a military victory.[27] Furthermore, the Great Multitude were also crying out, "Salvation to our God who sits on the throne and to the Lamb" (7:10), which reflects a proclamation of victory after a return from war.[28] In addition, that the Great Multitude are those who have "washed their robes" (7:14) indicates that they are participating in ritual purity that accompanies those who are returning from war after shedding blood.[29]

Angels Sing 7:11–12

After the introductory description of the Great Multitude, John then sees "all the angels" (7:11) worshiping God, "saying, 'Amen, blessing and glory and wisdom and thanks and honor and power and strength to our God'" (7:12). The angelic worship corresponds to the worship of the Lamb by the innumerable number of angels in 5:11-12. That the worship of God here in 7:11-12 parallels the worship of the Lamb in 5:11-12 is apparent in that both scenes ascribe seven terms of adoration in their worship.[30] A comparison of the two lists of terms reveals that six of the seven words of adoration appear in both lists—though as expected John varies the order of words.[31] The only difference between the two lists of sevenfold praise is that 7:12 omits "riches" from the list of 5:12 and replaces it with "thanksgiving."[32]

---

27. DeSilva, *Discovering*, 177. Also, note: 1 Macc 13:51; 2 Macc 10:7.

28. Cf. 5:9; 14:3. The shout of praises also associates the Great Multitude with the redeemed in 5:9.

29. See Num 31:19-20, 24.

30. That the angels ascribe virtually identical worship to the Lamb and the Father testifies to the high Christology of the book of Revelation.

31. That each list has one word that is unique and that the order of the terms varies is the result of John's normal stylistic pattern.

32. The use of "riches" was appropriate in 5:12 because the Lamb had "purchased" (5:9) everyone with His blood. The use of "thanksgiving" in the present account is also appropriate because, as we will note below, having been brought through the "Great Tribulation" (7:14) is certainly a reason for thanksgiving.

It is also worth noting that the angels in 5:12 ascribed worship to the "Lamb," whereas, in 7:11, they "fell before the throne upon their faces and worshiped God."

REVELATION 7:1–17

Great Multitude Have Come Through the Great Tribulation 7:13–14a

John then notes, "And one of the Elders asked me, 'These who are clothed in white robes, who are they and from where have they come?'" (7:13). The question might initially appear to be surprising—after all, we should expect John to be the one asking questions. It is not uncommon, however, in prophetic literature for a prophet to be asked a question to which he does not know the answer only then to be told the answer.[33] John naturally replies, "My lord, you know" (7:14). The Elder then answers, "These are the ones who have come out of the Great Tribulation" (7:14).[34]

Washed Their Robes 7:14b

The Great Multitude are also said to have "washed their robes and made them white by means of the blood of the Lamb" (7:14).[35] As noted above, the washing of garments was part of the ritual purity of returning from war after shedding blood. As Beale affirms, "They have been 'clothed in white robes' to signify their redemptive purity."[36]

It is significant to note that the white robes of the Great Multitude associate them with the souls under the altar who were crying out and were given white robes and told "to rest for a little time" (6:11). This connection gains strength from the fact that 6:11 and 7:14 represent the only two uses of "white robes" in the book of Revelation.

33. See Jer 1:11–12; Ezek 40–48; Dan 7–12; Zech 1–6.

34. The concept of a "tribulation," unfortunately, has been the object of great misunderstanding. What is often missing from modern discussions of the Tribulation is that in the Scriptures "tribulation" is what the people of God endure. In fact, we may well conclude that in the NT "tribulation" always results from being a faithful witness of Christ. Another misconception regarding the use of "tribulation" is the suggestion that it is something future. Whereas, in the NT, "tribulation" refers to a present reality. E.g., Rev 1:9; 2:9–10, 22; John 16:33; Acts 14:22; Rom 5:3; 8:35–36; 2 Tim 3:12. In fact, 21 of Paul's 23 uses of 'tribulation' relate to a present reality. For a more complete discussion of the Tribulation and the use of "Great Tribulation" see my *Understanding*, 100–18. The primary OT background for "tribulation" is Dan 12:1, 10; and 11:30–39, 44.

35. Howard-Brook and Gwyther note that this imagery, "reverses the logic of Israel's tradition of holy war, in which persons who killed during war were required to wash their robes to remove the blood of their enemies in order to be purified (e.g., Num. 31:19–20). In Revelation, it is not the enemy's blood that must be removed to achieve purity, but a sharing in the Lamb's blood itself which generates purity" (Howard-Brook and Gwyther, *Unveiling Empire*, loc. 5291).

36. Beale, *Revelation*, 436.

It is, therefore, my conviction that the Great Multitude represent a proleptic account of the souls under the altar at the final consummation.

The Great Multitude before the Throne 7:15–17

The interlude of 7:1–17 closes with a description of the Great Multitude dwelling in the glorious presence of God. John notes that they are "before the throne of God" and that they will "serve Him day and night in His Temple" (7:15). John continues by noting that they will "hunger no more, nor thirst anymore, nor will the sun beat down on them, nor any heat" (7:16).

This description of the Great Multitude corresponds closely with the promise in Ezek 37:26–28:

> I will make a covenant of peace with them; it will be an everlasting covenant with them. And I will place them and multiply them, and will set My sanctuary in their midst forever. My dwelling place also will be with them; and I will be their God, and they will be My people. And the nations will know that I am the Lord who sanctifies Israel, when My sanctuary is in their midst forever.[37]

John continues by affirming that the Lamb who is "in the center of the Throne[38]... will shepherd them[39] and lead them to springs of the water of life" (7:17).[40] He closes by adding that "God will wipe every tear from their eyes" (7:17).

Excursus: The Great Multitude and the Holy City/New Jerusalem

It is my conviction that the depiction of the Great Multitude is a proleptic look at the glorious rewards that await the people of God at the final consummation. As such, the account of the

---

37. It also serves to contrast with the enemies of God's people who will face the scorching of the sun (16:9).

38. We learned earlier that Jesus shares the throne with the Father (3:21: see also 21:22–23; 22:1, 3).

39. The OT imagery of God as the Shepherd of Israel is found in Ezek 34:11–16; as well as the famed Psalm 23. It was an appropriate image for the people; many of whom made their living with such animals.

40. This is also reminiscent of Jesus's words to the woman at the well: "If you knew the gift of God, and who it is who says to you, 'Give Me a drink,' you would have asked Him, and He would have given you living water" (John 4:10). In the Gospel of John, the living water that Jesus promised was the Holy Spirit (John 7:37–39).

Great Multitude serves to provide encouragement to John's reader/hearers by reminding them of the hope that is before them and the rewards for those who endure.

That this account is best understood as a proleptic look at the people of God and their dwelling in God's eternal presence at the descent of the Holy City/New Jerusalem (21:9—22:9), is evident from the closing promises in 7:15-17. Most notable is the fact that the Great Multitude are those who will dwell in the presence of God (7:15) which, is one of the primary characteristics of the New Jerusalem.[41] In addition, the indication that the Great Multitude will "hunger no more, nor thirst anymore; nor will the sun beat down on them, nor any heat" (7:16) alludes to the same features in the account of the New Jerusalem (see 21:6; 22:1, 17). Also, the assurance that the "Lamb in the center of the throne will shepherd them" (7:17) finds its fulfillment in the account of the New Jerusalem (see 21:22-23; 22:1, 3). The indication that the Lamb will "lead them to springs of the water of life" (7:17) corresponds to the promise in the New Jerusalem (22:1). The promise that neither "will the sun beat down on them, nor any heat" (7:17) finds its fulfillment in the description of the New Jerusalem where there is no sun (21:23; 22:5). John's concluding assurance that "God will wipe every tear from their eyes" (7:17), surely looks forward to the final descent of the New Jerusalem when "He will wipe away every tear from their eyes; and there will no longer be any death; there will no longer be any mourning, or crying, or pain; the first things have passed away" (21:4).

That the account of the Great Multitude looks forward to the people of God dwelling in the eternal presence of God finds further confirmation in the clothing of the Great Multitude. That their "robes" have been made "white by means of the blood of the Lamb" (7:14) corresponds with those who "wash their robes, so that they will have the right to the Tree of Life and may enter through the gates into the city" in 22:14. That the "robes" of 22:14 are linked with the clothing of the Great Multitude is supported by the fact that 22:14 and 7:14 are the only two occurrences of "robes" that were "washed."

---

41. See 21:6; 22:1, 17; Isa 49:10; John 6:35.

Excursus: Identifying the 144,000 and the Great Multitude

As noted earlier, a first reading of 7:1–17 understandably leads the reader/hearers to suspect that the 144,000 and the Great Multitude are two distinct groups. After all, the 144,000 are numbered (7:4) and the Great Multitude are innumerable (7:9). In addition, the 144,000 are identified as coming from "every tribe of the sons of Israel" (7:4), and the Great Multitude are "from every nation, tribes, peoples, and tongues" (7:9).

It is my contention, however, that just as Jesus is presented as the Lion and the Lamb (5:5–6), so also the 144,000 Israelites and the innumerable Multitude from every nation represent the totality of the people of God. As G. K. Beale concludes, the 144,000 and the Great Multitude represent "the totality of God's people throughout the ages, viewed as true Israelites."[42]

That the two groups are to be identified is supported by several literary clues. For one, the two accounts are linked by John's use of hearing and seeing.[43] In 7:4, John "heard the number of those who were sealed." Then, in 7:9, he says, "I looked, and behold a Great Multitude." This suggests that, just as the Lion and the Lamb were two means of depicting Christ, so also the two seemingly disparate descriptions of the 144,000 and the Great Multitude are one. Other literary links include the fact that both accounts open with "a great voice" (7:2, 10). Also, both accounts appear to answer to the nations' query at the close of chapter 6: "who is able to stand?" (6:17). The account of the 144,000 begins with four angels who are "standing" (7:1) and the account of the Great Multitude depicts them as those who are "standing" before the throne" (7:9).

The two accounts are also interrelated thematically. This is most evident in that both the 144,000 and the Great Multitude are depicted in terms of holy warriors. Thus, on the one hand, the 144,000 are sealed and protected in order that they may endure the Holy War. The Great Multitude, on the other hand, are described as those who have been victorious in Holy War.

Richard Bauckham has also presented a significant argument that these two apparently diverse groups both refer to

---

42. Beale, *Revelation*, 733.
43. See Bauckham, *Climax*, 215.

the totality of the people of God. Bauckham contends that the 144,000 and the Great Multitude should be viewed in light of the fulfillment of God's promise to Abraham that "in you all the families of the earth will be blessed" (Gen 12:3). In Bauckham's evaluation, the 144,000 represent God's promise to Abram (Abraham) that He will make him "a great nation" (Gen 12:2). The promise to Abraham in Genesis 12 is reiterated in Genesis 15 where he learns that his descendants will someday be innumerable: "'Now look toward the heavens, and count the stars, if you are able to count them.' And He said to him, 'So shall your descendants be'" (Gen 15:5).[44] Then, in Genesis 17, the promise is reiterated again to Abraham. This time the promise is made explicit that he will be the "father of a multitude of nations" (Gen 17:5).[45] Bauckham contends that the 144,000 represent the people of the promise. He then argues that the Great Multitude represent the fulfillment of God's promise that through Abraham, "all the families of the earth will be blessed" (Gen 12:3). The Great Multitude, in other words, are the fulfillment of God's promises to Abraham of an uncountable number of persons from every nation coming from Abraham's seed.

Bauckham's thesis also explains why the description of the 144,000 has indications that they represent more than just ethnic Israelites. That they are depicted as being from the twelve tribes indicates their origin. The fact, however, that John's listing of the tribes does not correspond to any extant list of the twelve tribes suggests that John has something beyond just the twelve tribes in view. That they are 144,000, which is the product of twelve and twelve and a thousand also suggests that they transcend the twelve tribes and incorporate both the OT (twelve) and the NT (times twelve) people of God.[46]

---

44. See Gen 13:16; 16:6; 26:4. This promise is reiterated throughout the OT: see Exod 32:13; Deut 1:10; 10:22; 28:62; 2 Sam 17:11; 1 Kgs 3:8; 4:20; Neh 9:23; Isa 10:22; 48:19; 51:2; Hos 1:10.

45. Hence, his name is changed to "Abraham" (Gen 17:5). See also: Gen 22:17–18; 26:4. One may argue that the fulfillment of these promises to Abraham was realized in the Exodus (see Deut 10:22) and the conquest (Josh 21:45). Nonetheless, the book of Revelation indicates that the inclusion of the nations into the people of God leads to a grander fulfillment.

46. The multiplying of twelve and twelve by a thousand simply indicates that they are not yet an innumerable entity.

Consequently, both the 144,000 and the Great Multitude depict the totality of the people of God. As such, they represent the fulfillment of God's promises to Abraham. As Magina says, "The finite has become the virtually infinite."[47]

The interlude of 7:1–17, therefore, should be read as a whole in which, although the people of God began as a countable number of Israelites, they have become an uncountable multitude "from every nation, tribes, peoples, and tongues" (7:9). David Barr affirms this reading when he concludes, "The worshiping community is at the same time 'gathered from every nation' and 'God's true Israel,' just as they are at the same time innumerable and 144,000."[48]

In terms of John's narrative, the 144,000 represent the people of God in the present. This is why they are in need of being sealed—they are the ones who are presently experiencing persecution and suffering. The Great Multitude, however, represents the people of God in eternity, after they "have come out of the Great Tribulation" (7:14).[49]

Conclusion

Revelation 7:1–17 presents a pause, or an interlude, in the narrative of the heavenly vision (the second story). John's objective in presenting this pause is in order that he might bring comfort and encouragement (and possibly an exhortation) to his reader/hearers. John does so by providing them with the awareness that, although they (the 144,000) presently suffer, they have been sealed by God (7:3–8) and are under His divine protection and, by implication, those who persevere will be brought "out of the Great Tribulation" (7:14) and are "before the throne of God" (7:15) where they will "hunger no more, nor thirst anymore" (7:16).

---

47. Magina, "God," loc. 2221.
48. Barr, *Tales,* loc. 2417–18.
49. This understanding corresponds to the pattern set forth in Deuteronomy. There we learn that the Israelites went down to Egypt as a countable number ("seventy persons"; Deut 10:22), but returned to the land "as numerous as the stars of heaven" (Deut 10:22).

Revelation 8:1—9:21
Seventh Seal and
the First Six Trumpets:
Introduction

A series of horrible plagues that appears in the middle chapters of Revelation is unquestionably the most difficult aspect of the book.[1]

To punish people for their deeds is to assume that they are responsible for their deeds, that they have chosen them, that they have free will. But if violence is used to coerce behavior, free will disappears. If you put a gun in someone's back and demand their wallet, you cannot later claim that they gave it of their own free will. The choice between dying and giving up your wallet is not a real choice.[2]

The trumpets and bowls do not lay out a playbook for the end times but narrate the systematic deconstruction of Caesar's world—and the order allegedly upheld by Caesar's gods—as the one true God makes room for God's kingdom.[3]

Introduction

I NOTED IN THE opening discussion on 7:1–17, that after the Sixth Seal has been broken (6:12–17), the reader/hearers are expecting that the Seventh Seal will be broken and the contents of the Scroll will be revealed.

---

1. Rossing, *Rapture*, 123.
2. Barr, "Violence," 404.
3. DeSilva, *Revelation*, 184.

Instead, in 7:1–17, John inserts an interlude. In the interlude, John affirms that the people of God are divinely sealed in order that they might persevere (the 144,000; 7:3–8) and they are also those who ultimately will come through the Great Tribulation and into the glorious presence of God (the Great Multitude: 7:9–17). It is not until 8:1 that the narrative resumes and the Seventh Seal is broken. Surprisingly, however, even after the Seventh Seal is broken (8:1), the contents of the Scroll are still not revealed.[4] Instead, John presents another series of sevens known as the Seven Trumpets (8:2, 6—9:21; 11:14–19).[5]

Though the account of the Seven Trumpets has traditionally been understood as a depiction of God's wrath upon the creation, it is my contention that this traditional understanding fails to identify the literary features in the account of the Seven Trumpets which provide an indication of John's narrative aims. Furthermore, as I noted in the introduction, the supposition that God is the direct agent of the Seven Trumpets (as with the Seven Seals) raises serious, complex moral questions related to the person and nature of God.[6]

Excursus: John's Use of Literary Features to Advance the Narrative in the Seals, Trumpets, and Bowls

In order to understand the role of the Seven Trumpets in John's narrative it is important to keep in mind the fact that John is advancing a narrative. That he is doing so is evidenced by the literary progression that occurs in the accounts of the Seals, Trumpets, and Bowls. This progression is apparent in that following the breaking of the Seven Seals[7] an effect occurs that impacts one-fourth of humanity.[8] Then, after the sounding of each of the Seven Trumpets,[9] an effect occurs that results in

---

4. I will argue that the Scroll and its contents are revealed in the interlude of 10:1—11:13.

5. The first series of seven is the Seven Seals (6:1–17; 8:1, 5). A third series, the Seven Bowls occurs in 16:1–21.

6. This is not to say that there is a final judgment in which those who fail to repent experience God's justice. My point here is that God does not use wrath as a means of soliciting repentance.

7. Technically only the first four Seals are in view here.

8. See 6:8.

9. Technically only the first four Trumpets are in view here.

the devastation of one-third of the creation.[10] Finally, after the pouring out of the Seven Bowls, the devastation that follows affects the whole of creation.[11]

Additionally, the narrative movement is evidenced in that the seventh occurrence in each of the three septets brings us, as Richard Bauckham affirms, "towards the final judgment in the seventh of each series."[12] Perhaps the best way to state things is that the seventh in the series of Seals and Trumpets certainly leads us to suspect that the end has arrived. The fact, however, that only one-fourth and one-third are effected by the Seals and the Trumpets should cause us to recognize that the end is still to be anticipated. Therefore, in the analysis of Resseguie, only the "announcement that the days of the end have come."[13]

That the three series of sevens serve to advance John's narrative is also evidenced by the presence of the theophanic manifestations that mark the close of each of the series of seven. The first occurrence of the theophanic manifestations appears in the throne room scene (4:1—5:14) in which John notes that emanating from the throne, "came flashes of lightning and sounds and peals of thunder" (4:5).[14] The second occurrence marks the close of the account of the Seven Seals: "there were peals of thunder and sounds and flashes of lightning and an earthquake" (8:5). It is critical to note that this occurrence of the theophanic manifestations essentially repeats what was stated in 4:5, and adds, "and an earthquake" (8:5) to the formula.[15] The third occurrence of the theophanic manifestations marks the close of the account of the Seven Trumpets: "and there were flashes of lightning and sounds and peals of thunder and an earthquake and great hail"

---

10. See 8:7*, 8, 9*, 10*, 11, 12***; 9:15, 18.

11. See 16:2, 3, 4, 8, 10, 12, 20. It is conceivable to conclude that the Seven Thunders (10:3–4) would have continued the progression and affected one-half, but this is purely conjecture.

12. Bauckham, *Climax*, 10.

13. Resseguie, *Revelation*, 66.

14. It is worth noting note that since the first occurrence of the theophanic manifestations occurs in the throne room scene (4:1–5:14), each subsequent occurrence serves to link the series of sevens back to the throne room.

15. Note: John rarely repeats a list such as this verbatim.

(11:19). Again it is critical to observe that John essentially repeats the earlier expressions, including the earthquake in 8:5, and again adds to the list, this time including, "and great hail" (11:19). Finally, the account of the Seven Bowls repeats and expands the theophanic manifestations to the extent that the expression encompasses five verses (16:17–21), so that the earthquake becomes, "such as there has not been since man was upon the earth" (16:18), and the hail becomes, "great hail the weight of a talent" (16:21).

The fact that each recurrence of the theophanic manifestations expands on the previous one indicates that the narrative is moving forward. As James Resseguie asserts, "The expanding literary expression is placed at key junctures in the story—at the initial throne vision and at the conclusion of the seals, trumpets, and bowls—to warn of a final dénouement in which all restraint vanishes."[16] In addition, the theophanic manifestations link the three series of septets (the Seals, Trumpets, and Bowls) to the divine throne room. This does not intend to suggest that God is the direct agent behind each series. It does, of course, indicate that God is sovereign over all of history and the story is moving towards the conclusion. Consequently, though human rulers continue to reign and bring devastation upon humanity and, as we will learn in the account of the Seven Trumpets, upon the creation, God remains sovereignly in control and will bring history to a just end.

Literary Features Indicating the Relationship between the Seals and the Trumpets

Another key to understanding the role of the account of the Seven Trumpets is to recognize the interrelationship between the accounts of the Seven Seals and the Seven Trumpets.

Overlapping of the Seven Seals and the Trumpets

One of the more important literary features present in the account of the Seven Trumpets is that John overlaps the beginning of the account

---

16. Resseguie, *Revelation*, 964–65.

of the Seven Trumpets (8:2, 6) with the ending of the account of the Seven Seals (8:1, 5).

In 8:1, John resumes the narrative of the Seven Seals with the breaking of the Seventh Seal. Then, in 8:2, he introduces, "the seven angels" to whom "Seven Trumpets were given." At this point, the reader/hearers is expecting that the Seven Seals narrative has been completed and that the narrative of the Seven Trumpets has now begun. In 8:5b, however, John returns to the narrative of the Seven Seals by inserting the theophanic manifestations, which, as I noted above, mark the close of each of the three septets. In 8:6, John then resumes the narrative of the Seven Trumpets.

In constructing his narrative this way, John intentionally overlaps the close of the account of the Seven Seals (8:1, 5b) with the beginning of the account of the Seven Trumpets (8:2, 6). By overlapping the end of the Seals narrative with the beginning of the Trumpets narrative, John alerts his reader/hearers that the narratives of the Seals and the Trumpets are interrelated.

The Four-Three Design Pattern in the Seven Trumpets

John's use of the four-three pattern provides another link between the accounts of Seven Seals and the Seven Trumpets. That the Seven Seals display a four-three pattern is evident in that after the breaking of each of the first four Seals a rider on a various colored horse is unleashed (6:2, 4, 5, 8). In addition, the first four Seals are also marked by the fact that after the breaking of each of the first four Seals, John "heard" one of the Four Living Creatures say, "Come" (6:1, 3, 5, 7). In the account of the Fifth Seal, however, John neither hears one of the Four Living Creatures say, "Come,"—instead, the Fifth Seal opens with, "And . . . I saw" (6:9)—nor does a rider on a various colored horse appear.

The account of the Seven Trumpets similarly utilizes a four-three pattern. This is evident in that after narrating the first four Trumpets, John interjects the voice of "an eagle" who introduces the last three Trumpets with, "Woe, woe, woe to those who inhabit on the earth, at the remaining sounds of the Trumpet of the three angels who are about to blow" (8:13). The Fifth and the Sixth Trumpets, in fact, are brought to a close with, "The first woe has passed" (9:12), and "The second woe has passed" (11:14) respectively.

In addition, the accounts of the last three Trumpets are distinguished from the first four Trumpets is indicated by their relative length. In John's presentation of each of the first four Trumpets, they appear in fairly rapid succession. In fact, each of the first four Trumpets comprises only one or two verses (8:7; 8:8–9; 8:10–11; 8:12). The accounts of the Fifth, Sixth, and Seventh Trumpets, however, are significantly longer. The account of the Fifth Trumpet extends to eleven verses (9:1–11), the Sixth comprises nine verses (9:13–21), and, although the account of the Seventh is only six verses (11:14–19), it is still considerably longer than any of the first four Trumpets.

Finally, the effects that follow the sounding of the first four Trumpets directly affect the four divisions of creation[17]—the earth, the sea, the rivers and springs (freshwater), and the sun, moon, and stars[18]—while following the sounding of the Fifth and Sixth Trumpets are depictions of demonic beings waging warfare, clearly distinguishing the first four Trumpets from the last three.

Interludes

Another link between the accounts of the Seven Seals and the Seven Trumpets is that John includes an interlude in the midst of each series. In fact, in both the Seals and the Trumpets narratives, the interlude occurs after the account of the Sixth and before the Seventh item in each corresponding series. Thus, the interlude depicting the 144,000 (7:1–8) and the Great Multitude (7:9–17) occurs between the accounts of the Sixth and the Seventh Seals. Similarly, the interlude depicting John's prophetic commissioning (10:1–11) and the story of the Two Witnesses (11:1–13) occurs between the accounts of the Sixth and the Seventh Trumpets.

The Relationship Between the Fifth and Sixth Trumpets

It is also critical for understanding the account of the Seven Trumpets to recognize that following the sounding of the Fifth and the Sixth Trumpets demonic entities unleash torment (9:5–6) and death (9:18) upon

---

17. I do not intend to deny that there are, of course, implied, and even stated effects on humanity as a result of the first four Trumpets.

18. The Second, Third, and Fourth Bowls similarly affect the sea (16:3), the rivers and springs (16:4), and the sun (16:8–9).

humanity.[19] The relationship between the accounts of the Fifth and Sixth Trumpets is also evident by John's use of hearing and seeing. Whereas, in the account of the Fifth Trumpet, John *sees* (9:1) a demonic horde, in the account of the Sixth Trumpet, he *hears* (9:13) of a demonic horde.

Other Literary Features in the Series of the Seven Trumpets

There are embedded in the narrative of the Seven Trumpets several other literary features which are of great significance.

Prayers of the Saints

Another literary feature that deserves our attention is that references to "the prayers of the saints" (8:3, 4)[20] are sandwiched between the account of the breaking of the Seventh Seal (8:1) and the theophanic manifestation that marks the conclusion of the Seals narrative (8:5). The references to "the prayers of the saints" is also sandwiched between the introduction to the seven angels with the Seven Trumpets (8:2) and the seven angels as "prepared to sound them" (8:6).

This means that in 8:3–4—which is in the middle of the overlapping section that both concludes the account of the Seven Seals (8:1, 5) and inaugurates the account of the Seven Trumpets (8:2, 6)—John includes a scene with "the prayers of the saints." This interjection of "the prayers of the saints" (8:3, 4) suggests that both the Seals and the Trumpets are in some way an answer to "the prayers of the saints."[21]

It is also important to note that John's use of "the prayers of the saints" in 8:3, 4 links with "the prayers of the saints" (5:8) in the throne room scene.[22] The fact that "prayer" occurs only three times in the

---

19. I will argue later that the war (9:7, 9) that these demonic agents prepare for is linked to the famed "battle of Armageddon," which is nothing more than the war which the Dragon wages against Christ and His people throughout history. See the excursus, "Armageddon Part 2" in the discussion in 20:1–10.

20. I am using 8:3, 4 and not 8:3–4 because it is important to note that the expression "the prayers of the saints" is repeated in both 8:3 and 8:4. This is true also for John's use of "incense" in 8:3, 4.

21. See my *Follow*, 124–33.

22. That the article ("the") is used with "*the* prayers of the saints" in 8:3, 4 may well serve as another link with "the prayers of the saints" in 5:8. In both 8:3, 4, the

entire Apocalypse and that these three occurrences are in 5:8 and 8:3, 4 reinforces this conviction that "the prayers of the saints" are connected with the narratives of the Seven Seals and the Seven Trumpets. In addition, the reference to "incense" in 8:3, 4 also links the accounts of the Seven Seals and the Seven Trumpets with the use of "incense" (5:8) in the throne room scene. That fact that "incense" occurs only four times (5:8; 8:3, 4; 18:13) in the Apocalypse provides another strong link between "the prayers of the saints" and the accounts of the Seven Seals and the Seven Trumpets."[23]

The Trumpets and Decreation

It is also worth noting at this point that the devastation of creation that follows the sounding of the first four Trumpets is presented as a sort of decreation—that is, a reversal or undoing of God's original creation.

The presence of the theme of decreation is evident, for example, in the devastation of the vegetation that follows the sounding of the First Trumpet (8:7), which indicates a reversal of God's creation of vegetation on the third day of creation (Gen 1:11–12). The theme of decreation also appears after the sounding of the Second Trumpet. John's indication of the destruction of, "a third of the creatures that were in the sea" (8:9), reads as a reversal of the creation of the sea life which God formed on the fifth day (Gen 1:20–23). In addition, the death of many humans, which results "from the waters because they were made bitter" (8:11), after the sounding of the Third Trumpet presents a reversal of the formation of human life on the sixth day in the creation account (Gen 1:26–27). Finally, after the sounding of the Fourth Trumpet, it is revealed that "one-third of the sun was struck, and a third of the moon, and a third of the stars" (8:12), bringing darkness to one-third of the day and one-third of the night. This presents a reversal of God's formation of the Sun, the moon, and the stars on the fourth day of creation.

---

article may be an "article of previous reference." If so, then the prayers most certainly refer back to the only prior occurrence of "the prayers of the saints" in 5:8. Of greater importance, is the presence of the article in 5:8. Since this was the first occurrence of "the prayers of the saints," the article there cannot refer to a prior occurrence. This would suggest "the prayers of the saints" is something known to John's reader/hearers and it is central to the narrative.

23. That "incense" also occurs in 18:13 does not mitigate against this conclusion for, as we will see in the commentary on 17:1—19:10, there are several indications that 18:13 also connects with the throne room scene in 5:8.

REVELATION 8:1—9:21

God Destroys Those Who Destroy the Earth

What is often overlooked in discussions of the Seven Trumpets is that words of praise to the Lord that follow the sounding of the Seventh Trumpet includes a decree "to destroy those who destroy the earth" (11:18). This presents a significant problem for those who contend that God is the agent of destruction. The implication is that God will bring justice upon those who brought the devastation. If God is the agent of destruction, then He would be announcing judgment upon Himself.

Revelation 8:1—9:21
The Seventh Seal and the First Six Trumpets: Continued

The Seventh Seal, The Introduction to the Seven Trumpets, and the Prayers of the Saints 8:1–6

The Seventh Seal 8:1

THE BREAKING OF THE Seventh Seal reveals silence for half an hour (8:1). Silence is a common result of judgment in the biblical text as seen in 1 Sam 2:9: "He keeps the feet of His godly ones, but the wicked ones are silenced in darkness."[1] This leads to the conclusion that the Sixth Seal describes the destruction of the nations (6:12–17) and the Seventh Seal presents their judgment before God.[2]

The Seven Angels with Seven Trumpets 8:2, 6

John then sees "the" seven angels who have Seven Trumpets (8:2). The use of the article ("the") may indicate that these seven angels are known—though we are not left with any certainty as to whom they might be.[3]

---

1. See also Isa 47:5; Ezek 27:32; Amos 8:2–3; Lam 2:10–11; Zeph 1:7, 11; Zech 2:13—3:2. For further discussion see Beale, *Revelation*, 446-54.

2. This will be the fate of the Great Prostitute, Babylon: See 18:22–23.

3. Possible candidates include the seven angels of the seven churches. See 1:20; 2:1, 8, 12, 18; 3:1, 5, 7, 14.

REVELATION 8:1—9:21

Another Angel: Prayers of the Saints 8:3–5a

Before continuing on with the narrating of the Seven Trumpets, as the reader/hearers might expect, John tells us that "another angel came and stood[4] at the altar" (8:3). This angel has a "golden censer" and is given "much incense... in order that he might add it with the prayers of all the saints on the golden altar that was before the throne. And the smoke of the incense went up, with the prayers of the saints, from the angel's hand before God" (8:3–4). The significance of the fact that John sandwiches "the prayers of the saints" in the midst of the conclusion of the account of the Seven Seals and the introduction to the account of the Seven Trumpets, will be the focus on the excursus at the end of this chapter.

The First Four Trumpets 8:7–12

The sounding of trumpets in the ancient world was a common means of heralding an announcement. Such an announcement could be a declaration of war, an announcement of impending judgment, or a warning to repent.[5] In the present case, perhaps, all of these are applicable.

As I noted above, the first four Trumpets are clearly distinct from the last three and they parallel the first four Seals—although the Trumpets affect the creation and not directly the people.

The First Trumpet 8:7

After the First Trumpet sounds, John says that "hail and fire, mixed with blood" were thrown to the earth, and "a third of the earth was burned up, and a third of the trees were burned up, and all the green grass was burned" (8:7).[6]

---

4. I noted the significance of standing in the last chapter, where the Sixth Seal ended with the cry, "who is able to stand?" (6:17). It may well be that this angel, who "stood," is but one answer to the question: "who can stand?"

5. See Josh 6; Judg 7:16–22; Jer 4:5–21; 6:1, 17; Joel 2:1, 15. Trumpets may precede the enthronement of a King (1 Kgs 1:34, 39; 2 Kgs 9:13); represent end-time judgment or salvation; the gathering of God's people; or, a summons of people to battle (Judg 3:27–29; Neh 4:20). In the NT, trumpets summon the people of God (Matt 24:31); they announce the return of Christ (1 Thess 4:16); and, they awaken dead for resurrection (1 Cor 15:51–52). See Leland et al., *Dictionary of Biblical Imagery*, 900.

6. Note that each of the first three Trumpets has an element of fire (see Jer 51:25–26, 63–64). Fire is used often to symbolize judgment.

The Second Trumpet 8:8–9

After the Second Trumpet sounds, John notes that "something like a great mountain burning with fire was thrown into the sea" (8:8). The result is that one-third of the sea becomes blood, one-third of the sea life dies, and one-third of the ships are destroyed (8:8–9).

There are good reasons to suppose that John intends for us to see a prelude to the fall of the kingdoms of the earth. This follows from the fact that mountains, as I noted in the discussion of the Sixth Seal,[7] were commonly associated with kingdoms throughout the prophetic literature.[8] The fact that the Great Prostitute, of whom we will learn about in 17:1—19:10, sits on a seven-headed Beast (17:3; compare 13:1), and that the seven heads, "are seven mountains " and "they are seven kings" (17:9) reinforces this conclusion.

In addition, the fact that the great mountain, "was thrown into the sea" indicates that the effects following the sounding of the Second Trumpet also impact the Roman economy and the economic well-being of those who profited from Rome's excessive prosperity. In light of the fact that ships were one of the primary means of transporting wealth to Rome, it may well be that the Second Trumpet is a description of the destruction of the Great Prostitute. Hence, among those who lament the destruction of the Great Prostitute in 18:9–19, are, "all who had ships at sea became rich by her wealth" (18:19). That John intends to link these passages gains support from the fact that 8:9 and 18:19 are the only two occurrences of "ships" in the Apocalypse.

It is reasonable then, that the effects that follow the sounding of the Second Trumpet serve as a prelude to the coming destruction of Rome and its economy.[9]

---

7. See comments on 6:14–16.

8. See especially 17:9; also 16:20; 21:10; and arguably 14:1. This may also be the meaning in 6:14, 15, and 16. If so, then every occurrence of "mountain" outside the present passage has kingdom(s) as its referent; see also 6:16; 8:8; Isa 41:1; 45:16; 49:1, 22; 51:5; 60:9; Jer 38:10; 51:25; Ezek 26:18; Dan 2:35, 45.

9. See 17:1—19:10; Rossing notes that the turning of the sea to blood in 8:9 is a critique of sea trade and commerce (Rossing, *Two Cities*, 146).

The Third Trumpet 8:10–11

The Third Trumpet sounds and then John sees, "a great star fell from heaven, burning like a lamp, and it fell on a third of the rivers and on the springs of waters" (8:10). The result of this star's fall is that one-third of the fresh waters became bitter and many died (8:11). John then adds that the name of the star is "Wormwood" (8:11)—which designates a bitter herb.[10] When wormwood occurs in the OT, it often represents the punishment that comes upon the nations that have been polluted by idolatry.[11] Tabb notes, "'wormwood' is consistently used metaphorically for the bitterness of suffering (Lam 3:15, 19), the effects of sin (Deut 29:19; Prov 5:4) and retributive judgment (Jer 9:15; 23:15)."[12]

The Fourth Trumpet 8:12

The Fourth Trumpet sounds and John says that "a third of the sun was struck, and a third of the moon, and a third of the stars" (8:12). The result is that one-third of the heavenly sources of light for both day and night are missing. The darkness that this Trumpet brings may be another indication of the approaching judgment. That the heavenly bodies are struck looks forward to a coming judgment on heavenly beings.[13]

Interjection: An Eagle Warns, "Woe, Woe, Woe" 8:13

An eagle interrupts the account of the Seven Trumpets by crying out, "Woe, woe, woe [Gk *ouai*] to those who inhabit on the earth, at the remaining sounds of the Trumpet of the three angels who are about to blow!" (8:13).[14]

---

10. See Smalley, *Revelation*, 222. When water is contaminated by this herb, the water can become "poisonous if drunk over a long period of time" (Beale, *Revelation*, 479).

11. Deut 29:18; Jer 9:15; 23:15.

12. Tabb, *All Things*, loc. 2705.

13. Thanks to Ian Spencer for bringing this point to my attention.

14. I noted earlier that this title refers to the inhabitants of the earth excluding the people of God. See 3:10; 6:10; 13:8, 12, 14; 14:6–11; 17:2, 8.

Excursus: The Meaning of *Ouai*

Although it is commonly asserted that *ouai*[15] indicates a divine decree along the lines of "I'm warning you, it is about to get really bad,"[16] there are some difficulties with this reading. First, the common reading is based on an incomplete understanding of *ouai*. Although *ouai* may indicate a warning of the impending devastation,[17] it is also used to indicate a lament. In fact, *ouai* has the connotation of lament in at least six of its fourteen occurrences in Revelation (see 18:10*, 16*, 19*).[18] Second, although *ouai* may indicate a warning with regard to impending destruction, this meaning, as I will contend below, does not fit well within the context of the account of the Seven Trumpets. Third, it is difficult to suppose that the Fifth and Sixth Trumpets are even judgments at all. This is especially evident in that the account of the Sixth Trumpet parallels the account of the Sixth Bowl and the famed war of "Armageddon"[19] (16:13–17). If this relation holds up, then, as I will contend later in the commentary, the agent behind the demonic hordes in the account of the Fifth and Sixth Trumpets, is Satan. If so, then the notion that God is about to inflict three "woes" upon the land and the people becomes problematic.

What then is the meaning of *ouai* in 8:13? It is my contention that Barbara Rossing correctly identifies the role of *ouai* in this passage. She notes:

> 'Woe' is not really a helpful translation for the Greek word. Its sense is rather one of lament—like a mourner keening in grief, wailing out repeated cries of 'Oh, oh, oh' at the death of a loved one. Spanish Bibles simply translate the sound as 'Ay, ay, ay.' I would translate the word as, 'Alas.' The meaning of the Greek word *ouai* is first of all a cry of pain, like the word 'ouch' in English. It can mean 'woe,' but it can also

---

15. All major English translations use the thrice-repeated "woe" here except the NLT, which employs, "terror, terror, terror."

16. The NLT explicitly suggests this when it translates *ouai* as, "Terror, terror, terror to all who belong to this world...."

17. "Woe" has the connotation of a warning of impending devastation in 12:12.

18. Note that the ESV, NKJ, and NRS all translate *ouia* as "alas" in 18:10, 16, 19.

19. See commentary on 16:16 for a discussion of the use of "Armageddon." As I will note there, the Greek likely reads, "Harmagedon."

express deep lamentation or mourning, as in the laments of the merchants and kings over Rome in chapter 18, 'Alas, Alas, Alas, for the great city!'—the same Greek word *ouai*. It is as if God is crying 'ouch' or 'alas' on behalf of the suffering world: 'Alas for the inhabitants of the earth.' It is a subtle but significant shift in direction because 'Alas' conveys God's sympathy in a way that 'woe' does not.[20]

In support of Rossing's claims is the fact that her understanding of *ouai* makes the most sense of the eagle's interjection in 8:13. That is, the eagle's interjection is not a warning of the severity of the following judgments, but both a lament over the state of affairs and an urging for the nations to repent—which, unfortunately, as John reveals in 9:20–21, they do not do.

The Fifth and Sixth Trumpets 9:1–19

The Fifth Trumpet 9:1–12

After the sounding of the Fifth Trumpet, locusts come out from the Abyss (9:1–2).[21]

It is my contention that the locusts represent a demonic horde. That they come from the Abyss supports this assertion. After all, the Abyss was often used as a synonym for torment or hell and considered a place of detention for evil spirits.[22] That "smoke went up out of the pit, like the smoke of a great furnace" (9:2) suggests that it is a hellish location. David deSilva affirms, "Given the emergence of these locust-like scourges from the abyss, however, John's audiences might justifiably regard these beings not as creaturely aberrations but as demonic hordes, restrained from ravaging humankind until this moment (9.1–3, 11)."[23]

That the locusts are a demonic horde is also evidenced by the fact that John notes that they have the power to torment like that of a scorpion (9:5, 9). The scorpion-like nature of the demonic horde is reiterated at the close of the account of the Sixth Trumpet: "And they have tails like

---

20. Rossing, *Rapture*, 129; see also, Rossing, "Healing," Loc 2654.
21. The "Abyss" occurs seven times in the book Revelation: 9:1, 2, 11; 11:7; 17:8; 20:1, 3.
22. Beale, *Revelation*, 493.
23. See deSilva, *Discovering*, 183:

scorpions" (9:10). That the locusts are a demonic horde derives further support from Jesus's association of scorpions with Satan and his minions:

> I was watching Satan fall from heaven like lightning. Behold, I have given you authority to tread on serpents and scorpions, and over all the power of the enemy, and nothing will injure you. Nevertheless do not rejoice in this, that the spirits are subject to you, but rejoice that your names are recorded in heaven (Luke 10:18–20).

Furthermore, that they are a demonic horde is also indicated by the fact that the locusts have as their king, "the angel of the Abyss; his name in Hebrew is Abaddon, and in Greek, he has the name Apollyon" (9:11),[24] which means "destroyer."[25]

Sixth Trumpet 9:13–19

The Sixth Trumpet sounds and John then hears, "a voice, one from the four horns of the golden altar which is before God" (9:13). We are not told whose voice this was.[26] We are only told that the voice comes from the "four horns of the golden altar" (9:3).[27] The voice then commands the angel with the Trumpet, "Release the four angels who have been bound at the great river Euphrates" (9:14). John notes that the four angels were released, "in order that they might kill a third of humanity" (9:15). He then adds, "And the number of the mounted troops was two ten thousands times ten thousands" (9:16).

John's description of the armies and the horses certainly indicates that they also represent a demonic horde.[28] The fact that they are "angels who have been bound" (9:14) implies that they are demonic. In

---

24. John's use of both Hebrew and Greek will be important to recall as we proceed.

25. Locusts by nature have no leader (Prov 30:27).

26. Unfortunately, this voice does not match the voice of any being elsewhere in the book of Revelation. The nearest we come is the voice from the altar itself in 16:7. Even there, we are not told whose voice it is.

27. The reference to the "golden altar" likely links this with the "golden altar" in 8:3. The fact that these are only two occurrences of the "golden altar" in the book of Revelation and John's propensity to link passages by means of common terms and expressions strengthens this conclusion.

28. As John begins his description of this army, he states, "This is how I saw in the vision" (9:17). This is the only place John describes a "vision"; which further suggests the symbolic nature of what he sees.

addition, the fact that "out of their mouths"[29] come fire and smoke and sulfur" (9:17) also reinforces the conclusion that they are demonic. In light of the fact that the mouth is the source of one's words and since they are a demonic horde, it is likely that the fire which proceeds out of their mouths (9:17) indicates that they are agents of deception. This is reinforced by the association of the demonic horde with the serpent in Eden.[30] Finally, that they have tails that "are like serpents" (9:19) confirms the demonic nature of the beings.[31]

That these demonic hordes are agents of deception also explains why they have heads, "like the heads of lions" (9:17). That this demonic horde has heads like those of lions suggests that they represent a ruling authority that claims the authority that belongs to Christ—who is the true Lion from Judah (5:5).[32] That they represent human rulers likely serves as a prelude to John's account of the Beast in 13:1–8. That the Beast in 13:1–8 also has a mouth which "was as the mouth of a lion" (13:2) supports this connection. If so, then John is already giving us an insight into the demonic nature of the Beast.[33]

The Rest Did Not Repent 9:20–21

John does not follow the closing the Sixth Trumpet with the Seventh Trumpet. Instead, he first inserts a parenthetical note about the "rest."

---

29. Note that it is what comes out of their mouths that kills one-third of mankind (9:18).

30. See Gen 3:1–5. Beginning in 12:1, the book of Revelation makes a strong contrast between the truth that is in Jesus—He who is the one who is "true" (3:7)—and the deception of the Dragon and his minions. Satan, after all, is explicitly identified as the one "who deceives the whole world" (12:9). As we will learn in 12:3–4 and 9, the book of Revelation depicts Satan as the serpent, and John's description of Satan as the serpent in 12:3–4, 9 is directly tied to his role as the deceiver: "the serpent of old who is called the devil and Satan, who deceives the whole world" (12:9). As we will see, deception is the primary weapon of both of the beasts in Revelation 13.

31. See excursus "*The demonic hordes in the Fifth and Sixth Trumpets and the judgment of Satan*" in the commentary on 20:1–15, where I argue that the demonic horde of the Sixth Trumpet corresponds with Satan and his army that wage war against the people of God in 16:13–16, 19:19, and 20:8.

32. Note again that John only uses "Lion" once for Jesus in the entire book of Revelation. John's reservation of "lion" for those who falsely claim to be the true rulers serves to accent his stress on the means by which the kings of the earth rule (violence and power) and the means by which Jesus rules (as a Lamb, who suffers violence).

33. In the description of the Beast in 13:2, John explicitly states, "And the Dragon gave to him [the Beast] its power and its throne and great authority."

The Rest Did Not Repent

In 9:20–21, John adds, "And the rest of humanity, those who were not killed by these plagues, did not repent of the works of their hands, in order that they might not stop worshiping demons" (9:20).[34] DeSilva affirms the deep and tragic irony: "This would introduce the irony that the earth-dwellers refuse to cease worshipping the very forces that seek to harm rather than bless them."[35] Unfortunately, at this point in the narrative, God's delay has not led to the hoped for repentance.[36]

Conclusion

That the Scroll and its contents were not revealed immediately following the breaking of the Seventh Seal serves as an indication that the account of the Seven Trumpets also represents a delay in the final judgment. Sadly, the delay represented in the account of the Seven Trumpets adds to the narrative of the heavenly vision (4:1—16:21) by revealing that God's allowing the nations to continue their rule also has adverse effects on the creation. The insertion of the eagle's lament after the Fourth Trumpet (8:13) affirms that God's desire is for humanity to see the ruin and devastation upon the creation that results from humankind's continued rule and to be driven to repentance.

Tragically, those in power continue to deceive the nations. And, as the parenthetical note at the close of the account of the Sixth Trumpet reveals, the nations not only fail to repent but they are further deceived by the very demonic influences that undergird the nations' rule.[37] Even more so, they also use the delay in God's coming judgment to wage war on God's people.[38] But, as we will learn in the very next unit

---

34. The failure of persons to repent is reiterated at the close of the Fourth (16:9) and Fifth (16:11) Bowls as well.

35. DeSilva, *Discovering*, 183.

36. The association of idolatry with the worship of demons has a long history in the prophetic tradition. Jer 7:5–11; Hos 3:1—4:2; 2 Kgs 9:22; Isa 47:9–10; 48:5; Mic 5:12—6:8; Nah 1:14; 3:1–4; Acts 15:20; Rom 1:24–29; Gal 5:20; Eph 5:5; Col 3:5. For an excellent treatment of this topic see Wright, *Here Are Your Gods*.

37. That the nations' rule is undergirded by demonic entities will become clearer as we proceed in the narrative.

38. That it is God's people upon whom they wage war will become increasingly clear as the narrative proceeds.

(10:1—11:13), it is the killing of the people of God that leads to the repentance of the nations!

Excursus: Understanding the Seals and the Trumpets and John's Narrative Aims

I began this commentary by contending that one of the central features of John's narrative is that power in the kingdom of God is manifested through love. Hence, John's emphasis on Jesus as the Lamb (twenty-seven times) and not the Lion (one time). For John, and one may argue the rest of the NT,[39] if not the whole of the biblical text,[40] the kingdom of God represents an alternative way of exercising power. God does not operate the way the world's rulers do. Instead, He demonstrates His power through love. Jesus is the Lamb that was slain (5:6). As we examine the accounts of 10:1–11 and 11:1–19, I will contend that this is precisely where the narrative of the book of Revelation leads us. Namely, the contents of the Scroll reveal that it is through the faithful, loving, and sacrificial witness of God's people that the nations are redeemed.

This may sound all well and good, but the question remains, "What do we do with the accounts of the Seven Seals and the Seven Trumpets?" That is, in order to make the case that the book of Revelation presents love as the means by which God manifests His power, it is necessary to address the moral dilemma that arises from the common understanding of the Seals and Trumpets.

Consequently, at this point in our study, it seems best to reflect on the accounts of the Seven Seals and the Seven Trumpets and how my thesis that the book of Revelation is a love story corresponds to what we see in these accounts.

The most common reading of the Seven Trumpets, even among much of the scholarly community, is that they represent God's wrath on the creation as a result of human sin.[41] The

---

39. See Mark 10:42–45. Further discussion on this point would necessitate a multi-volume work and is well beyond the scope of the present study.

40. This, of course, which is also well beyond the scope of the present study, is much more difficult to defend.

41. For example, Beale concedes, "If the trumpets are modeled only literarily on the exodus plagues, then it is possible to view their ultimate aim as admonitory. But if the

perception is that the Trumpets represent God's wrath, though not in fullness, upon the creation both as an act of justice and as a warning for humanity to repent.[42]

One of the theses of this commentary, however, is that readings like this fail to recognize John's narrative trajectory. As a result, such readings radically undermine John's message. In addition, the belief that God is the final source behind the plagues revealed in both the series of Seven Seals and the Seven Trumpets[43] controverts the way of the cross, which is central to the narrative of the book of Revelation.

In saying this, as I have noted earlier, I am not denying that there is a final judgment for those who refuse to repent and acknowledge that Jesus is the world's true Lord. The question is to whether or not God precedes the final judgment with various plagues. More specifically, the question relates to whether or not in John's narrative God uses wrath as the means by which He brings the nations to repentance.[44]

There is an additional question that arises with the conception that God is the source behind the Seven Trumpets. David Barr claims that the belief that God is the source of the Seven Trumpets and that He sends them upon the creation in order to bring justice to the earth and to allow those who

---

theology of the exodus plagues has been formative for the composition of the trumpets, then the trumpets must ultimately be understood as punishments that further harden the majority of people" (Beale, *Revelation*, 467).

I do not intend to deny that such a reading makes sense of the text from the perspective of a first reading. My conviction, however, is that a closer examination reveals that this reading conflicts with John's narrative. If, indeed, John's portrayal, let alone that of the entire NT, of Christ lays the stress on the fact that Jesus rules like a Lamb and not a Lion, and that it is the nations who rule by violence, then we are hard-pressed to reassess the text. As Barr says, "It is my experience that understanding grows in stages. First you read and understand a little, then you learn to ask new questions about your understanding, and then you read more and find that your earlier understanding either grows or changes dramatically" (Barr, *Tales*, 4773).

42. Not all scholars affirm the latter point. Beale, for example, rejects the notion that the Trumpet plagues aim to bring humanity to repentance (Beale, *Revelation*, 467).

43. I recognize that I have only addressed the first six Trumpets at this point in the commentary. The Seventh Trumpet, which like the Seventh Seal and the Seventh Bowl, represents the final judgment, will be discussed in the commentary on 11:1–19. And, although the Seven Bowls could be part of the present discussion, I will reserve comment on them until our study of 16:1–21.

44. I do not intend this statement to be an absolute either/or. Sure, He could use both.

are spared the opportunity to repent raises questions as to whether or not God is a moral monster on a par with Caesar and other human rulers:

> This is the first moral issue the story raises for me: how can a story that glorifies war and violence be considered moral? . . . The second moral issue I face concerns the use of overwhelming power to coerce obedience. If God triumphs over evil only because God has more power than evil, then power—not love or freedom or goodness or truth—is the ultimate value of the universe. . . . And this leads to a third moral dilemma. Let's assume for a moment that there is a force in the universe capable of exacting universal obedience and that the result of such coercion will be universal peace and justice. Why delay?[45]

Barr summarizes his concerns: "In short, if Revelation is read as a story about some future event when God and/or Jesus will dramatically intervene in human affairs and coerce obedience, it raises complex moral issues. These moral issues are never faced by the popular readings of Revelation."[46]

At this point, some may assert that the sounding of the Trumpets and the unleashing of wrath that follows is meant to affirm God's sovereignty. In response, I would note two things. First, the question is not whether God is sovereign. Instead, the question is what kind of God is He. Second, I agree that the Seven Trumpets affirm God's sovereignty, but this does not necessarily entail that He is the immediate cause of the devastation. Instead, John's portrayal of God as sovereign is meant to reassure his reader/hearers that God is in control and that He will not allow evil to operate without restraints.

Excursus: Understanding the Seals in Light of John's Narrative

In examining the series of Seals and Trumpets, I have made the case that the destruction and devastation of creation which is depicted in the account of the Trumpets—particularly the first four Trumpets (8:7–12)—is not the work of God but is the

---

45. Barr, *Tales*, 4926.
46. Barr, *Tales*, 4934.

result of humanity's continued rule. This corresponds to what I argued in our look at the Seven Seals (6:1–17; 8:1, 5).

In the account of the Seven Seals, I argued that the effects that follow the opening of the first four Seals (6:1–8) depict what happens when humanity remains in power: namely, that human governing brings deception (First Seal: 6:1–2), war (Second Seal: 6:3–4), famine (Third Seal: 6:5–6), and death (Fourth Seal: 6:7–8). I also argued that the effects of humanity's reign especially impact the poor and the marginalized. And, I added, in light of the fact that many of the early Christians were among the poor, the suffering must have impacted those within the Christian community also.

I then noted that the account of the Fifth Seal presents the cries of God's people (6:9–11). The martyrs' cry, "How long, Lord?" (6:10), affirms my conviction that the people of God also suffer from the effects that follow the opening of the first four Seals. In response to the plea for justice, we learn that justice will not come to them until all of God's people, who are going to be martyred, have been martyred.

If the Fifth Seal presents the cry of the people of God, the Sixth Seal (6:12–17) contrasts it by presenting the nations' outcry. That the nations cry out in response to the presence of "the great day of their [God and the Lamb's] wrath" (6:17) does not mitigate my theses that God is not the final source of the plagues and that the account of the first four Seals represents a delay in the final judgment. The Sixth and the Seventh Seals are after all a proleptic glance at the final destruction of the nations and their judgment.

I am arguing then, that God delays the final judgment because of His love for the nations and that during that delay the nations remain in power. Unfortunately, by allowing them to remain in power, their continued rule brings devastation upon humanity—especially the poor and the marginalized.

In sum, the account of the Seven Seals indicates that God delays the final judgment and that in doing so the nations are permitted to remain in power. Unfortunately, those who remain in power continue to use that power to bring devastation to humanity. I also noted that the devastation that results from humanity's abuse of power affects the people of God also.

Excursus: Understanding the Trumpets in Light of John's Narrative

The question then becomes how the account of the Seven Trumpets fits within my understanding. In order to understand the Seven Trumpets and their role in John's narrative, it is first critical to recognize, as I noted in the commentary, that the first four Trumpets, in a manner parallel to the first four Seals, are set apart from the final three Trumpets. I then argued that the first four Trumpets depict the devastating effects of humanity's continued rule upon the creation. Pablo Richard affirms my understanding when he contends, "the plagues of the trumpets and bowls in Revelation refer not to 'natural' disasters, but to the agonies of history that the empire itself causes."[47] That is, whereas the first four Seals depict the devastating effects upon humanity's rule upon itself—especially the poor and the marginalized—the first four Trumpets extend the devastating effects of humanity's rule to the creation.

That the devastation wrought by the first four Trumpets is the doing of humanity and not God finds support in the fact that in the description of the Seventh Trumpet (11:14–19), the Twenty-Four Elders announce that God will, "destroy those who destroy the earth" (11:18). This serves as an explicit affirmation that the destroying of the earth, which most certainly refers back to the events in the account of the first four Trumpets, is not the work of God.

It is worth noting here the tragic irony inherent in the understanding of the Seven Trumpets as found in the work of many commentators of the book of Revelation. Too many perceive the account of the Seven Trumpets as a depiction of God's somewhat reserved judgment on the created order.[48] The problem is that, as the Seventh Trumpet reveals, God's judgment comes on those who destroy the earth (11:18). The reality is that God does not plan to destroy the earth, as we will learn in the account of the descent of the Holy City/New Jerusalem (21:9—22:9), but to restore it.

---

47. Richard, *Apocalypse*, 86.

48. I say "somewhat reserved" because the Seven Trumpets repeatedly only affect one-third of the creation.

Excursus: The Role of the Fifth and Sixth Trumpets and the Prayers of the Saints

It is my contention that the accounts of the Fifth and Sixth Trumpets assume the furtherance of the delay in the final judgment, but in doing so they underscore two vital elements in John's narrative. Before setting forth these two elements it is necessary to recall the relationship between the account of the Seven Trumpets and the prayers of the saints.

I noted that John introduces the seven angels with the Seven Trumpets in 8:2. Yet the account of the Seven Trumpets does not begin until 8:6. In 8:3 and 8:4, the narrative of the Seven Trumpets is interrupted with reference to "the prayers of (all) the saints."[49] The significance of "the prayers of the saints" at this juncture is underscored by the fact that both 8:3 and 8:4 include the phrase "the prayers of (all) the saints" and that this phrase alludes to "the prayers of the saints" which was first mentioned in the throne room scene (5:8).[50] Beale notes that 8:3-5, which he calls a parenthesis, "functions in a dual manner: it primarily continues the description of the last judgment of the seventh seal as a divine response to the saints' prayer of 6:9-11, but secondarily it likewise shows that the entire following series of trumpets is also a divine response to the saints' petition."[51]

The question then arises, "In what sense does the Trumpets' narrative provide us with an answer to the prayers of the saints?" I believe that John has two narratival goals with respect to the prayers of the saints.

It is my contention that John's first objective in narrating the account of the Seven Trumpets and associating them with the prayers of the saints is to reiterate that there will be a delay. That there will be a delay is implicit in the fact that the Scroll and its contents are not immediately revealed after the breaking of the Seventh Seal. That is, just as we learned in the account of

---

49. Note that 8:3 includes "all," whereas, 8:4 omits it.

50. The importance of the allusion to 5:8 and the throne room scene is that the throne room scene serves as the initial setting for the entire narrative of the heavenly vision (4:1—16:21).

51. Beale, *Revelation*, 462-63.

the Fifth Seal, that there will be "a little time" (6:11), so also the Seven Trumpets indicate that there will be a delay.

At the same time, the account of the Seven Trumpets does not simply reiterate that there will be a delay. Instead, the account of the Seven Trumpets indicates that the delay in the final judgment is in order that the nations may have time to be brought to repentance. Though admittedly this is not explicitly stated as the reason for the delay, it is nonetheless implied in the parenthetical remark at the close of the Sixth Trumpet: "the rest of humanity, those who were not killed by these plagues, did not repent" (9:20).[52] The tragic irony is that the nations not only fail to repent but they actually worship the very demonic entities that are bringing about the devastation (9:20–21).

John's second narratival goal in presenting the account of the Seven Trumpets and the delay in the final judgment is to specify that the delay indeed results in the death of the people of God. This is evident from the accounts of the Fifth and Sixth Trumpets which reveal the demonic origins of the war that the nations will wage against the people of God. That this is what the narrative of the Fifth and Sixth Seal depict is admittedly not yet clear. It will not, in fact, become clear until we reach the description of the Sixth Bowl and the "war of Armageddon," as it is popularly called.

Excursus: The Prayers of the Saints, the Seven Trumpets, and the Plagues in Egypt

As I noted earlier, there is little question that the ten plagues on Egypt certainly provide the narrative background for the account of the Seven Trumpets.[53] Though virtually all commentators recognize the connections between the Exodus account and the series of Trumpets in the book of Revelation,

---

52. If we were to look at this practically speaking, we might note, "Why should it bring about their repentance?" That is, one of the leading causes of the destruction of creation is industry and humanity's insatiable lust for more. Since those in power are the ones who often profit from the destruction of creation and they are the ones who have the power to bring about the changes needed to eliminate, or at least, limit the destruction of creation, there is little incentive for them to bring about the necessary changes.

53. The parallels between the plagues in Egypt are also apparent in the account of the Seven Bowls.

it is my contention that many fail to recognize John's intent in making this connection. It is often assumed that the literary connections between the account of the Seven Trumpets and the plagues on Egypt suggest that just as God brought about the plagues in Egypt, so also He will bring about the events in the account of the Seven Trumpets. Pablo Richard asserts, "What is the overall meaning of the plagues that John sees...?"[54] Richard, who, as cited above, seemingly affirms my thesis that the Trumpets are the result of humankind's rule, nonetheless continues, "we find the meaning in the Exodus tradition: God hears the cry of his people, decides to liberate them, and to do so sends plagues and unleashes divine fury on Pharaoh and the Egyptians."[55]

I, however, believe that this connection misses an important element in the Exodus account. It is my contention that John employs the imagery of the Exodus plagues because the plagues on Egypt were a direct response to the cries of distress among the people of God:

> And the sons of Israel sighed because of the bondage, and they cried out; and their cry for help because of their bondage rose up to God. So God heard their groaning; and God remembered His covenant with Abraham, Isaac, and Jacob. God saw the sons of Israel, and God took notice of them" (Exod 2:23–25).

John uses similar language in the introduction to the Seven Trumpets. He states that the prayers of the people of God "went up" to God (8:4). In doing so, John employs the same term used as in the LXX of Exod 2:23, where the cry for help of the people of Israel "rose up." This, I believe, is one of the primary reasons why John uses the imagery of the Exodus in the narrative of the Seven Trumpets. Namely, that both the Seven Trumpets and the Seven Bowls represent God's response to the cry of His people.

With this being said, it is critical to observe that in the Exodus account the plagues on Egypt do not immediately

---

54. Richard, *Apocalypse*, 85.
55. Richard, *Apocalypse*, 85–86.

follow the cry of the Israelites.⁵⁶ Instead, God first sends Moses to Pharaoh in order to summon him to repent and release the Israelites. This, as we will see in the interlude of 10:1—11:13, is precisely where John takes his story.

What does all of this mean? It is my contention that the destruction of the creation, which is relayed in the account of the first four Trumpets, is the result of humanity's continued rule and not the result of divine wrath. Barbara Rossing summarizes the present crisis that the world faces as a result of human abuse of the world and its resources: "We are told that one billion people in our world lack access to clean drinking water, while at the same time 'a legacy of factory farming, flood irrigation, the construction of massive dams, toxic dumping, wetlands and forest destruction, and urban and industrial pollution has damaged the Earth's surface water so badly that we are now mining the underground water reserves far faster than nature can replenish them.'"⁵⁷

It is time, therefore, for God to send a new Moses onto the scene!

---

56. The plagues in the Exodus account do not begin until Exod 7:14.
57. Rossing, "Healing," loc. 2839-42.

Revelation 10:1—11:13
An Interlude:
The Scroll and the Two Witnesses

The point here is that the pattern of allusion to Ezekiel's prophetic commissioning in Ezekiel 2:8–3:3 shows that John intends Revelation 5 and 10 to tell a single story of his own reception of a prophetic revelation which is symbolized by the scroll. . . . [Revelation] Chapter 5 therefore leads us to expect that the revelation of the content of the scroll will be of major importance to John's prophecy. It would be intolerable if John left it unclear what the content of the scroll is.[1]

Introduction

AT THIS POINT IN the narrative, John's reader/hearers are expecting him to announce that the second woe has passed and to affirm that "the seventh angel sounded his Trumpet." After all, from 8:7—9:21, John announced in succession each of the first six Trumpets: "and the (First, Second, etc.) angel sounded his Trumpet."[2] Instead, 10:1-2 announce, "And I saw another strong angel . . . and he had in his hand a Scroll, which was open" (10:1).

A careful examination of 10:1—11:14 indicates that John has inserted another interlude into the narrative. In the same way that 7:1-17, and the accounts of the 144,000 (7:1-8) and the Great Multitude (7:9-17), interrupted the narrative of the Seven Seals, so also 10:1—11:13, and the

---

1. Bauckham, *Climax*, 247, 249.

2. See 8:2, 6, 7, 8, 10, 12; 9:1, 13, 14. Note that "angel" is omitted in the description of the First Trumpet.

accounts of the angel with the scroll (10:1–11) and the Two Witnesses (11:1–13), interrupt the narrative of the Seven Trumpets.[3]

That 10:1—11:13 functions as an interlude gains further support by a comparison with 7:1-17. For one, both interludes occur after the sixth item in their corresponding series of seven. That is, the interlude of 7:1-17 occurred between the Sixth and the Seventh Seal. In the same way, the present interlude of 10:1—11:13 occurs between the Sixth and the Seventh Trumpets. In addition, both interludes focus on the people of God. As we have seen, the interlude of 7:1-17 introduced us to the 144,000 and the Great Multitude. Similarly, the present interlude introduces us to the Two Witnesses (11:1–13).

The Interlude (10:1—11:13) and the Prayers of the Saints (5:8; 8:3, 4)

As I noted in the discussion of 8:1—9:21, the introduction to the Seven Trumpets is linked with the "prayers of the saints" (8:3, 4; See 5:8), which itself appears to be tied to the martyrs' cry for justice, "How long, Lord?" (6:10). The account of the Seven Trumpets seemingly responds to their prayers by reiterating that there will be a delay. The interlude of 10:1—11:13, however, provides the long-awaited answer to the martyrs' cry. This is evidenced by the angel's affirmation, "there will no longer be time" (*chronos*; or "delay"; 10:6).

Another Strong Angel 10:1–2

In 10:1, John introduces "another strong angel." Though we may wonder what John means by "*another*," the key is that this angel is called a "strong angel."[4] At this point in the narrative the only prior appearance of a "strong angel" has been the angel in 5:2 who was "proclaiming in a great voice 'who is worthy to open the Scroll and to break its seals?'"

---

3. Note that the end of the Sixth Trumpet occurs in 11:14 and the sounding of the Seventh Trumpet follows in 11:15.

4. John refers to "another angel" a total of ten times, see: 7:2; 8:3; 10:1; 14:6, 8, 9, 15, 17, 18; 18:1. In five of the occurrences of "another angel" (7:2, 8:3, 10:1, 14:6, 18:1) it serves to mark a transition within a scene. The other five occurrences all cluster in the transitional scene beginning in 14:6 (14:8, 9, 15, 17, 18). They are not exceptions, per se, since they serve to continue the scene begun in 14:6.

That John intends for his reader/hearers to link the "strong angel" of 10:1 with the "strong angel" of 5:2 is evidenced by several factors. There is, of course, the obvious recurrence of the "strong angel." John's use of a "strong angel," though occurring seven times,[5] is restricted to only three passages: 5:1–14; 10:1–11; and 18:21–24. There is little doubt, which I will defend in more detail in the discussion of 17:1—19:10, that the recurrence of a "strong angel" in 18:21 serves to link each of these passages. In addition, there is the obvious link between the present account and the throne room scene in 5:1–14 in that in both accounts there is a Scroll and that Scroll is in someone's hand (5:1; 10:2).

The Identity of the Strong Angel 10:1

The identity of the "strong angel" in 10:1 is somewhat intriguing. What is most puzzling is that this angel has attributes that unmistakably correspond to the Father and Jesus, yet, the being is clearly called an "angel" (10:1).

That the angel has attributes that correspond to the Father is evident in John's description of the angel as having a "rainbow ... upon his head" (10:1). This correlates to John's account in the throne room scene, where he notes that "a rainbow was around the throne" (4:3). In addition, John says that the angel's, "feet were like pillars of fire" (10:1). This echoes OT descriptions of God in the wilderness with the Israelites.[6]

At the same time, the angel also has attributes that correspond to Jesus. For instance, the angel's, "face was like the sun" (10:1). This is reminiscent of the description of Jesus in 1:16.[7] In addition, the angel is, "wearing a cloud" (10:1). And, although a cloud often indicates the presence of God in the OT,[8] in the book of Revelation it is Jesus who is either "coming with the clouds" (1:7) or "sitting on the cloud" (14:14).[9]

---

5. See: 5:2; 10:1, 5, 8, 9, 10; 18:21.

6. See Exod 14:24; 16:10; 40:36–38; Lev 16:2; Num 11:25; 12:5; 14:14; Deut 31:15; Neh 9:12, 19; Ps 78:14; Ezra 1:4.

7. There is a slight difference in that 1:16 uses *opsis* ("outward appearance") and 10:1 uses *prosopon* ("face": see 4:7; 7:11; 9:7*; 10:1; 11:16; 22:4).

8. See Exod 13:20–22; 14:20, 24; 16:10; 19:9, 16; 24:15–16, 18; 40:34–37; Num 14:14; Deut 1:33; 4:11; 5:2; Neh 9:12, 19; Ps 78:14; 105:39; Isa 4:5; Ezek 1:4.

9. John uses "cloud" seven times (1:7; 10:1; 11:12; 14:14*, 15, 16). In five of these instances, it is Christ that is either sitting on the cloud (14:14*, 15, 16) or "coming with the clouds" (1:7).

Also, the voice of the angel is said to be "like a lion" (10:3), which alludes to the opening description of Jesus (5:5). Perhaps the most significant argument that the angel may be Jesus, however, is that in 10:2 the angel has, "in his hand a Scroll, which was open" (10:2). The fact that the last time we saw this Scroll it was in Jesus's hand and that Jesus had subsequently broken each of the Seven Seals with which it was closed suggests that this angel might actually be Jesus.[10]

Whether or not the "strong angel" of 10:1 is Jesus is certainly not critical to the narrative of the book of Revelation. What is critical is the fact that the Scroll has reappeared in the narrative. In fact, the Scroll is "open" (10:2), which surely indicates that we are about to find out about the contents of the Scroll.

> **Excursus: Is the Scroll that Jesus Took from the Father's Hand (5:1–14) the Same As the Scroll in the Angel's Hand (10:1–11)?**
>
> There are numerous factors that affirm the Scroll which was in the Father's hand in 5:1 is indeed the same Scroll that is "open" in the hand of the angel in 10:1–2. Richard Bauckham goes so far as to contend, "A major key to the correct interpretation of Revelation has been missed by almost all scholars. It is that the scroll which John sees, sealed with the seven seals, in the hand of God in 5:1 is the same as the scroll which he sees open in the hands of an angel in 10:2."[11]
>
> Perhaps, the most important argument for identifying the Scroll is that John's narrative essentially begs us to recognize that it is the same Scroll. After all, since the Scroll was first introduced in 5:1, we have been anticipating the moment when its contents will be revealed. This point cannot be overstated. The introduction of the Scroll in 5:1–14 led us to expect that the Scroll would be opened and its contents disclosed. When reading the book of Revelation as a narrative, it should not come as a surprise to find the Scroll lying open in the hands of an angel (10:2).[12] This is what the narrative has led us to

---

10. It is certainly plausible that Jesus has given the Scroll to the angel who brings it down from heaven to the earth.

11. Bauckham, *Climax*, 243.

12. We might be surprised that it is in the hands of an angel and not Jesus. There are two major options to understanding this. First, the "strong angel" in 10:1 is Jesus. Second, Jesus has given the Scroll to the angel who now gives it to John. The latter, of

anticipate. Therefore, those who contend that the Scroll that Jesus took from the Father's hand (5:7) is distinct from the Scroll that is open in the hand of the angel (10:2) must provide a reasonable explanation as to what happened to the first scroll and what was on it. As Bauckham affirms, "recognizing that the scroll of chapter 10 is the scroll of chapter 5 solves the otherwise insoluble problem of the nature and content of the scroll of chapter 5."[13]

Once again, John has not left us without clues. There are several literary connections between the Scroll in the Father's hand in Revelation 5 and the one in the angel's hand in Revelation 10.

As I noted above, there is the obvious connection that both passages have a "Scroll" which is in someone's hand (5:1; 10:2). And there is the fact that both passages refer to a "strong angel" (5:2; 10:1)[14] who cries out with a "great voice" (5:2; 10:3).[15]

Even more significantly, however, are the obvious parallels between John's Scroll and that of Ezek 2:8–3:3. The relationship between the Scroll in 10:1–11 and the scroll in Ezek 2:8–3:3 is virtually unquestionable.[16] That the Scroll in the Father's hand (5:1) builds off the Ezekiel narrative is evident in that both the Scroll in 5:1 and the scroll in Ezek 2:8–3:3 have writing on both sides (5:1; Ezek 2:10). In both 10:1–11 and Ezek 2:8–3:3, John and Ezekiel are told to eat their scrolls (10:9; Ezek 3:1). After John eats the Scroll, he reports, it "was in my mouth as sweet as honey" (10:10). Ezekiel similarly eats his scroll and affirms, "it was sweet as honey in my mouth"

---

course, is not stated in the narrative.

13. Bauckham, *Climax*, 248.

14. Bauckham affirms that since 5:2 is the only prior occurrence of a "mighty angel" (his translation), then it functions as a "close literary connection." (Bauckham, *Climax*, 245).

15. Since a "great voice" occurs multiple times in the book of Revelation and is uttered by various beings (see 1:10; 5:2; 5:12; 6:10; 7:2, 10; 8:13; 10:3; 11:12, 15; 12:10; 14:7, 9, 15, 18; 16:1, 17; 19:1, 17; 21:3) this argument is not as persuasive. Nonetheless, since the strong angel of 5:2 speaks with a "great voice," it should come as no surprise that the strong angel in 10:3 does as well.

16. Smalley, *Revelation*, 258–59.

(Ezek 3:3). Then, after consuming their scrolls, both John and Ezekiel are called to prophesy (10:11; Ezek 3:4).

The fact that the Scroll in 5:1–14 and the Scroll in 10:1–11 both parallel the scroll of Ezek 2:8–3:3 leaves little doubt that the Scroll in 10:1–11 is the same Scroll as that which Jesus took from the Father's hand in 5:1–14.

This raises the question as to why so many scholars suggest that the two scrolls are different.[17] The primary argument that these scrolls are not the same is that John employs two different forms for the word "Scroll" in 5:1–14 and 10:1–11.[18] The argument is that in 5:1–14, John uses the form "biblion" ("scroll"; 5:1, 2, 3, 4, 5, 8, 9), whereas, in 10:1–11, he uses "biblaridion" (which many translate as "little scroll" (10:2, 9, 10).[19]

First, it is simply not correct to claim that John is using two different **forms** of the same word. Instead, John uses two different **ways** of writing the same **form** of the same word. That is, "biblaridion" and "biblion" are both diminutive forms of the word for "scroll." That is, they represent two different ways of writing the same word. Thus, if we were to claim that we should translate "biblaridion" as "little scroll," then we should also translate "biblion" as "little scroll." The fact that John uses the regular form of the word ("biblos") in 13:8 to refer to the Book (or scroll) or Life confirms that he is aware of the regular form.

Second, John uses both "biblaridion" (10:2, 9, 10) and "biblion" (10:8) interchangeably to refer to the Scroll in the angel's hand which John is commanded to eat. If the two

---

17. E.g., see Caird, *Revelation*, 126, Mounce, *Revelation*, 202. Mounce, in fact, suggests that *biblaridion* is a diminutive of *biblion* (Mounce, *Revelation*, 202n12); Beale makes a similar argument (Beale, *Revelation*, 526).

18. By two different "forms" of the same word it is meant that one form is the "regular" and one is the diminutive" (A diminutive indicates something that is "smaller" or lesser"; it may help to think of "small" and "smaller"). Even Smalley, who affirms that the two scrolls "should be interpreted in light of the same symbol" (*Revelation*, 259) concludes that the two different forms mean that the scrolls "are not absolutely identical" (*Revelation*, 259; see 258–59).

19. See NAS, ESV, NET, NIV, NKJ, and NRS all read "little scroll." The NLT reads "small scroll." Longman suggests, "The other indicator that casts doubt on the connection between the two scroll references is that the second scroll is described as 'little.' In Revelation 5, the Greek has simply 'scroll' (*biblion*), while in Revelation 10, the Greek has the diminutive 'little scroll' (*biblaridion*)" (Longman, *Revelation*, 213).

different **ways** of writing the same word somehow establish that the Scroll in 5:1–14 is not the Scroll of 10:1–11, are we somehow supposed to conclude that the scroll which the angel instructed John to take was not the same scroll that the angel had in his hand—despite the fact that the entire scene has focused on only one Scroll and that the command was for John to "take the Scroll which is open in the hand of the angel" (10:8)? This suggestion would require us to further believe that John subsequently approached the angel and asked for the wrong scroll (10:9) and that the angel then gave him the wrong scroll, which he ate (10:10).

Third, John also uses the regular form ("biblos") and the diminutive form ("biblion") interchangeably when referring to the "Book of Life."[20] This shows that John uses the diminutive and the regular forms interchangeably.

Finally, it is widely acknowledged that the diminutive form had lost its force by the time John wrote.[21] That John uses "biblos" and "biblion" interchangeably attests to this. Bauckham goes so far as to contend that none of the diminutives in the book of Revelation retain their force.[22]

Therefore, in light of the strong indications that the Scroll of 5:1–14 and 10:1–11 are the same, and the fact that the primary reason for not recognizing them as the same fails, we have every reason to believe that the Scroll in the angel's hand in 10:2 is the Scroll which Christ took from the Father and subsequently broke each of the Seals with which it was closed. David deSilva affirms, "It seems highly likely that the open scroll that John sees in Revelation 10—also written on both sides—represents the same scroll that the Lamb had been

---

20. John refers to the "Book of Life" six times in the book of Revelation. On two occasions he uses the regular form *biblos* for "book" (3:5; 20:15) and on four occasions he uses the diminutive *biblion* for "book" (13:8; 17:8; 20:12; 21:27).

21. For a complete discussion see Aune, *Revelation*, 2.558.

22. See Bauckham, *Theology*, 80–84; and, *Climax*, 243–55. There is some evidence that these two words were used interchangeably at the time John penned the book of Revelation. The Shepherd of Hermas, which contains the only other known use of "biblaridion," uses both forms interchangeably. Note Hermas was written at or near the same time as Revelation—assuming a date for Revelation in the AD 90s. See Bauckham, *Climax*, 244.

opening throughout Revelation 6."[23] Beale, in his comments on 10:2, likewise, affirms, "this open scroll is difficult to identify unless it is linked with the scroll of ch. 5."[24] Beale later affirms, "The similarities are so striking that a close connection between the two scrolls is probable."[25]

Seven Thunders 10:3–4

John reports that "when he [the strong angel] cried out the Seven Thunders spoke their voices" (10:3). The introduction of the Seven Thunders suggests that they represent another septet. If they are another set of sevens, alongside the Seals, Trumpets, and Bowls, then we might suppose that, in accordance with John's literary pattern of the Seals (one-fourth) and the Trumpets (one-third), this series of seven would affect one-half.[26]

This, however, is something that we will never know! John says that, as he was about to write, he heard "a voice from heaven" instructing him, "Seal up the things that the Seven Thunders have spoken and do not write them" (10:4). This voice, which speaks twice in this passage (10:4, 8), is never identified.

The command to "seal up" (10:4) the contents of the Seven Thunders is somewhat ironic. After all, sealing up is precisely the opposite of what occurs in the book of Revelation. The book of Revelation began with the indication that its intent was "to show . . . what must happen soon" (1:1). And at this point in the narrative, Christ has broken each of the Seven Seals that enclosed the Scroll suggesting that its contents are about to be revealed.

There Will No Longer Be Time 10:5–7

The reason for the sealing up of the Seven Thunders is precisely because, as the angel announces, "there will no longer be time" (10:6). As I noted above, the announcement that "there will no longer be time" seemingly refers back to the announcement of delay given to the saints

---

23. DeSilva, *Discovering*, 154.
24. Beale, *Revelation*, 527.
25. Beale, *Revelation*, 527.
26. That the Bowls affect the whole supports this deduction: see 16:1–21.

under the altar (6:11). If so, then the likely indication here is that the prayers of the saints are about to be answered.

If the prayers of the saints are about to be answered, then surely this suggests that we are about to learn the contents of the Scroll! This supposition gains credibility from the fact that the angel continues, "in the days of the voice of the seventh angel, when he is about to sound the Trumpet, then the mystery of God will be finished" (10:7).

John's Commissioning 10:8–11

As noted above, the account of the prophetic commissioning of Ezekiel (Ezek 2:8—3:3) provides an important background for understanding the narrative of 10:1–11. The book of Ezekiel opens with the prophet[27] receiving a vision of God on His throne (Ezek 1:22-28). Ezekiel is then called to be a prophetic voice to the people of Israel: "I am sending you to the sons of Israel" (2:3). His commissioning begins with the command to take a scroll and eat it (2:9-10). The scroll, like the one in the Father's hand in Revelation 5:1, had writing "on the front and back" (Ezek 2:10). God then gives the prophet the scroll and commands him to eat it (Ezek 2:8—3:1). Upon eating the scroll, Ezekiel notes, "it was as sweet as honey in my mouth" (Ezek 3:3). Ezekiel, then receives his prophetic commissioning (Ezek 3:4).

Based on the obvious connections between Ezek 2:8–3:3 and Revelation 10:8-11, we may surmise that in 10:1—11:13 John, like Ezekiel, is being commissioned as a prophet. After all, John too is commanded to take the book and eat it (10:9). Eating a scroll is clearly a symbolic act signifying that God is placing a message in the prophet's mouth so that they might consume it and speak accordingly.

John, after eating the scroll (10:10), affirms, like Ezekiel, "it was in my mouth as sweet as honey" (10:10). He then adds, "when I ate it, my stomach was made bitter" (10:11). We are not told why it was sweet in his mouth and bitter in his stomach. It has been suggested that it was sweet because God is about to bring to a climax the fulfillment of His promises.[28] That is, God's will is about to be revealed! But why would it make

---

27. Ezekiel was of priestly stock (Ezek 1:3). Since, however, he was in exile in Babylon, and since the temple was destroyed a few years later, there was no ability for him to function as a priest in the Jerusalem temple. Hence, God calls him to function prophetically.

28. See Resseguie, *Revelation*, 206.

his stomach turn sour? Perhaps, as the narrative of the Two Witnesses (11:1–13) confirms, it was also a message of great tribulation for the people of God. Resseguie affirms, "The message is sweet because there will be no more delay in the fulfillment of God's plan (10:6), but it is sour because the church faces intense persecution."[29]

John's commissioning closes with, "And they were saying to me, 'It is necessary for you to prophesy again concerning many peoples and nations and tongues and kings'" (10:11).[30] Again, the fourfold designation of persons, has consistently been John's means of referring to all persons of the earth—though this designation excludes the people of God.

Conclusion

The narrative of the book of Revelation virtually demands that the Scroll, which is open in the hands of the angel in 10:2, is the same Scroll that Jesus was "worthy" to take from the Father's hand because He was slain (5:9). Now that the Seals by which the Scroll was sealed closed have been broken, John is commanded to take the book and eat it (10:8), which he does (10:9–10). In doing so, John is commissioned as a prophet. He is then commanded to "prophesy" (10:11), which surely indicates that he is to reveal the contents of the Scroll.

The narrative of Revelation's heavenly vision (4:1—16:21: the second story) appears to be reaching its climax. After all, as the NAS reads, "there will be delay no longer" (10:6). It is my contention that the climax in John's narrative will be reached in the account of the Two Witnesses which follows (11:1–13). It is there that we will learn that the means by which God brings redemption to humanity is through the faithful, loving, and sacrificial witness of God's people.

---

29. Resseguie, *Revelation*, 206.

30. Bauckham suggests that it is primarily positive (Bauckham, *Climax*, 264). Beale contends that it is primarily negative (Beale, *Revelation*, 554).

Revelation 10:1—11:13
An Interlude:
The Scroll and The Two Witnesses Continued

Whether Revelation envisages the conversion of the nations of the world to the worship of the one true God is a question on which commentators disagree. This in itself is rather surprising.... [T]he question of the conversion of the nations—not only whether or not it will take place but also how it will take place—is at the centre of the prophetic message of Revelation.[1]

The Lamb's conquest, which had the initial effect of redeeming the church from all the nations, has the aim of bringing all the nations to repentance and the worship of God. It achieves this aim as the followers of the Lamb participate in his victory by their suffering witness. This is what the scroll reveals.[2]

Introduction

REVELATION 10 CLOSED WITH John's prophetic commissioning and the exhortation, "It is necessary for you to prophesy again" (10:11). In 11:1–13 the narrative continues with John carrying out his assignment.

In this account, John is "given a measuring rod" (11:1) and told to "rise and measure the temple of God, and the altar, and those who are worshiping in it" (11:1). The measuring of the temple (11:1–2) is

---

1. Bauckham, *Climax*, 238.
2. Bauckham, *Climax*, 258.

then followed by a description of the ministry of the Two Witnesses (11:3-4).³ It is my contention that the measuring of the temple in 11:1-2 is deeply intertwined with the account of the Two Witnesses in 11:3-13. In fact, I will argue that the measuring of the temple signifies the divine protection of the people of God which is then carried forth in the narrative as the Two Witnesses are to prophesy without harm for the duration of their ministry.

As we turn to 11:1-13, it is important to be reminded that the larger unit of 10:1—11:13 forms an interlude in the midst of the account of the Seven Trumpets. In fact, this interlude, similar to the interlude in 7:1-17, occurs between the accounts of the Sixth and Seventh Trumpets. And, like the interlude in 7:1-17, it also addresses the people of God.

Measure the Temple of God, the Altar, and the Worshipers 11:1

In 11:1-2, John begins the prophetic ministry to which he was commissioned. He is commanded to measure, "the temple of God, and the altar, and those who are worshiping in it" (11:1).

The command to measure, "those who are worshiping in it" appears somewhat strange on a first reading. After all, the notion of measuring a temple and an altar makes sense. But how does one measure people?[4] It is my conviction, as I will argue below, that the temple, the altar, and the worshipers all represent the people of God. If this is so, the question then becomes not how do you measure people, but what does measuring people mean?

The act of measuring was not uncommon among the prophets.[5] The most notable example is found in Ezekiel 40-48 where the prophet

---

3. For a complete discussion of the Two Witnesses and the people of God in the book of Revelation, see my *Two Witnesses*.

4. The NIV attempts to address this dilemma by translating the last phrase with, "and *count* the worshippers there." The idea of "counting" is also suggested by Michaels, *Revelation*, 137; and, Thomas, *Revelation*, 94. A difficulty with this view is that the word "count" is not present in Greek. The sentence has only one verb, which is translated as "measure." The notion of "counting" requires us to translate the singular occurrence of the verb with two different English verbs.

5. See Ezek 9, 40-48; Zech 2:1-5.

had a vision of a temple/city[6] which was then measured.[7] The prophet Zechariah also had a vision in which he saw Jerusalem being measured.[8] In both of these instances, the act of measuring signified the divine protection of that which was measured. This suggests that the act of measuring in our present passage (11:1) signifies the divine protection of the temple, the altar, and the worshipers.[9]

Identity of the Temple, the Altar, and the Worshipers

There are a number of indications that the temple, the altar, and the worshipers represent the people of God and, therefore, the measuring of them represents the divine protection of the people of God.

First, the command to measure the temple, the altar, and the worshipers (11:1) follows the account of John eating the Scroll and being instructed, "to prophesy again concerning many peoples, and nations, and tongues, and kings" (10:11). That John begins his prophesying concerning "many peoples" by measuring the temple, the altar, and the worshipers suggests that the measuring of the temple, the altar, and the worshipers relates back to command to prophesy to "many peoples. . . ."

Second, the phrase "the temple of God" occurs a total of ten times in the NT[10] and in each instance, it applies to either the body of Jesus Himself,[11] the people of God as the temple,[12] or God's heavenly temple.[13] That the temple, or a portion of it, in 11:1-2, is also referred to as the "Holy City" provides a further indication that the temple in 11:1-2 represents the people of God. This derives from the fact that the designation, "the Holy City" appears only four times in the book of Revelation: once

---

6. Ezekiel 40-48 is very important for our study of the book of Revelation. The context of Ezekiel displays several parallels with Revelation 11. Harrington, *Apocalypse*, 151.

7. See Ezek 40:5, 6, 8, 9, 11, 13, 19, 20, 23, 24, 27, 28, 32, 35, 47, 48; 41:1, 2, 3, 4, 5, 13, 15; 42:15, 16, 17, 18, 19, 20; 43:10; 45:3; 47:3, 4, 5, 18.

8. Zech 2:2.

9. See Beale, *Revelation*, 558-59, 570-71; Caird, *Revelation*, 131-32; Mounce, *Revelation*, 219; see also, my "These Are The Ones . . . (Rev 7)," 396-406.

10. See Matt 26:61; 1 Cor 3:16, 17*; 2 Cor 6:16*; 2 Thess 2:4; Rev 3:12; 11:1, 19.

11. See Matt 26:61. See note below.

12. See 1 Cor 3:16, 17*; 2 Cor 6:16*; 2 Thess 2:4; 11:1. See note below on 2 Thess 2:4.

13. See 3:12; 11:19. I have argued extensively that Jesus is the fulfillment of all that the temple was pointing to in both *Understanding*, 57-78; and *These Brothers of Mine*, 31-44.

in the present account (11:2), and three times with reference to the Holy City/New Jerusalem (21:2, 10, 19).[14] But, as I will argue in detail in the description of the Holy City/New Jerusalem, the Holy City/New Jerusalem is not actually a city but the Bride: that is, the people of God.[15]

Furthermore, the fact that John applies temple imagery to the people of God should not be surprising since he has already done so. In the message to the church in Philadelphia, we are told that the one who overcomes, "I will make them a pillar in the temple of My God" (3:12).

Moreover, John's depiction of the people of God as a temple corresponds with the NT's affirmation that the people of God are the "temple of God." Paul, in fact, uses the title, "temple of God" and applies it to the church in Corinth: "Do you not know that you are a temple of God?" (1 Cor 3:16; see also 1 Cor 3:17; 2 Cor 6:16).[16] For Paul, the fact that the people of God are filled with the Holy Spirit serves as the primary justification for identifying the people of God as the temple of God. In fact, in 1 Cor 3:16, Paul continues, "Do you not know that you are a temple of God and *that* the Spirit of God dwells in you."

Third, from a narrative perspective, the measuring of the temple, the altar, and the worshipers is parallel with the sealing of the 144,000. This is evident in that both the sealing of the 144,000 and the measuring of the temple occur in the midst of an interlude. In addition, in both instances, the interludes occur after the Sixth and before the Seventh in their corresponding septets (the Seven Seals and the Seven Trumpets). Since the sealing of the 144,000 conveyed the divine protection of the people of God, it stands to reason that the parallel account of the measuring of the temple also represents the divine protection of the people of God. That the sealing and the measuring both indicate the divine protection of the people of God as a result of the indwelling presence of the Holy Spirit provides further justification for understanding the measuring of the temple in 11:1–2 as signifying the divine protection of the people of God.

Fourth, the narrative flow of 11:1–13 suggests that the account of the Two Witnesses constitutes John's carrying out of the "measuring" of the temple, the altar, and the worshipers. This follows from the fact that

---

14. The "Holy City" is identified as the "New Jerusalem" in 21:2 and simply as "Jerusalem" in 21:10.

15. See commentary on 21:9—22:9 for further discussion.

16. Temple imagery is also applied to the people of God in Eph 2:19–22 and 1 Pet 2:4–10. For a more complete discussion of the people of God as the temple, see my *These Brothers of Mine*, 39–41.

John is commanded to measure in 11:1–2, but he never seems to actually measure anything. Instead, he immediately describes the Two Witnesses (11:3–13). This suggests that the account of the Two Witnesses constitutes John's carrying out of the command to measure. After all, if the account of the Two Witnesses does not depict John's carrying out of the command to measure, then we must conclude that John never actually measures the temple, the altar, or the worshipers as he was instructed.[17]

Finally, John has provided several literary links between the command to "measure" in 11:1 and the account of the Holy City/New Jerusalem. For one, as noted above, the designation the "Holy City" occurs only four times in the book of Revelation. The first is in the present account of the measuring of the temple (11:2). Each of the other three occurrences is in the description of the New Jerusalem (21:2, 10; 22:19). In addition, the command to measure the temple in 11:1–2 also links with the description of the Holy City/New Jerusalem. The verb "measure" occurs only five times in the book of Revelation and all five occurrences are with reference to the command to measure the temple, the altar, and the worshipers in 11:1, and the negative command not to measure the outer court in 11:2, as well as in the measuring of the Holy City/New Jerusalem in (21:15, 16, 17). In fact, the only time anything is actually measured in the book of Revelation is in the account of the Holy City when the city and its wall are measured (21:16, 17).

The Holy City/New Jerusalem, however, as I will defend in detail in the commentary on 21:9—22:9, is not actually a city. Instead, it is a description of the Bride—i.e., the people of God—eternally dwelling in the presence of God. In fact, as I will contend in 21:9—22:9, John's description of God's dwelling among His people takes the form of a city that is also a temple![18] In light of this, the measuring of the temple/city in 11:1 is a prelude to the measuring of the Holy City in 21:9—22:9. The fact that the Holy City is described as a temple and, yet, it depicts the people of God eternally dwelling in the presence of God only reinforces this conclusion.

Therefore, the measuring of the temple, the altar, and the worshipers serves to indicate the divine protection of the people of God in such a way that it foreshadows the Holy City/New Jerusalem.[19]

---

17. Note: I will argue below that John has provided literary clues that serve to link 11:1–2 and 11:3–13.

18. See commentary on 21:9—22:9 for further discussion.

19. As I will contend in Rev 21:9—22:5, the Holy City and the temple are one.

The above discussion raises the question as to why John is told to measure, "the altar and those who are worshiping in it" (11:1). I have argued elsewhere that one could translate 11:1 as, "Rise and measure the temple of God, *both* the altar and those who are worshiping in it."[20] This translation helps us to recognize that the inclusion of "the altar and those who are worshiping in it" serves to clarify specifically what it is that John is commanded to measure. That is, the command to measure the temple means that he is to measure both "the altar" and "the worshipers" (11:1).[21]

What, then, does it mean that John is to measure the altar? We know from the account of the Fifth Seal that the martyrs are located "under the altar" (6:9). If John intends for us to connect "the altar" here with the altar in 6:9-11,[22] then perhaps we are to understand that the measuring of "the altar" refers to those among the people of God who are about to be martyred.[23]

The voice also instructs John to measure, "those who are worshiping in it" (11:1). Of course, those who worship in the temple are priests. We have already noted, however, that in the book of Revelation all of God's people are priests.[24] If, therefore, there is a distinction to be made between "the altar" and "those who are worshiping in it" it may well be that the former are specifically those about to be martyred and the latter represent the rest of God's people.

That is, in the end, there is no distinction between the city and the temple because the temple encompasses the entire city. After all, the presence of God and Christ will envelop the entire city! The parallel with Ezekiel 40-48 is very important here. In both Ezekiel and the book of Revelation, the people of God are described in terms of a city that is a temple.

20. See my, "Use of καὶ in Revelation 11,1," 387-94.

21. This translation fits very well with the understanding that the temple of God refers to the people of God. See below.

22. John seemingly links the various uses of "the altar." See 6:9; 8:3*, 5; 9:13; 11:1; 14:18; 16:7. Note that in 6:9 and 16:7 there is a voice that is "saying" connected with the altar. Also, 8:3 and 9:13 are connected in that the altar is "golden." The altar in 8:5 is connected to the altar in 14:18 by the use of "fire." And the use of "altar" in 6:9 and 8:3 are connected via 5:8 and the reference to the prayers of the saints. This leaves the altar in 11:1 with no textual links to any of the other uses of "altar" in the book. To suppose, however, that it is a different altar would need some significant support. Unfortunately, the text offers none. I, therefore, conclude that the altar here is the same altar that appeared earlier in 6:9, 8:3-5, and 9:13.

23. There would be no reason to "measure" those who have already died.

24. See 1:6; 5:10; and 20:6.

Excursus: Why Are They Measured?

The measuring of God's people signifies their divine protection in order that they might persevere in their faith in the midst of suffering. As I noted in the discussion of the sealing of God's people, the divine protection of the people of God does not imply that they will not suffer or even be killed. In fact, the account of the Two Witnesses explicitly affirms they will be killed (11:7). The meaning of the measuring then is to signify that the people of God's status as God's people is under God's protection. This does not mean, however, that they cannot and will not suffer. It merely assures them of the eternal reward for those who persevere. This is why the connection with the Holy City/New Jerusalem is critical for understanding the present account.

Leave Out the Court Outside the Temple and Do Not Measure It 11:2

After being commanded to measure the temple in 11:1, John is then commanded, "leave out [lit.: cast it outside][25] the court which is outside the temple and do not measure it, because it has been given to the nations and they will trample the Holy City for forty-two months" (11:2). This seems somewhat surprising. After all, if measuring indicates God's sovereign protection, why would John be told to not measure something? In order to answer this question and to discern its place in the narrative of the book of Revelation, we need to ascertain what it is that John is commanded not to measure.

It is my contention that "the court which is outside the temple" (11:2) also represents persons. This follows from the fact that the temple, including the altar and the worshipers, represents persons. There is no reason to suppose that the narrative has suddenly shifted away from the people of God. Consequently, if John is to measure people (11:1), then it stands to reason that it is people who are not measured in 11:2.[26] John is not only commanded to not measure this court, but

---

25. The Greek word *ekbalo* ("leave out") may be translated as "cast out." Compare Luke 4:29. The parallel with Luke 4:29 is evident in that the people of Nazareth attempt to "drive out" Jesus from the city.

26. Bauckham has argued that the use of "leave out" in 11:2, most likely has a

he is to "cast [it] out" (11:2). The expression "cast out" is regularly used throughout the NT with regard to people.[27]

This means that not measuring "the court which is outside the temple" (11:2) indicates that there is an aspect in which the people of God are not measured—that is, in which they are not protected. That this divine protection does not extend to an exemption from physical harm makes the most sense of the text and the narrative of the Two Witnesses that follows. Resseguie affirms:

> The measured temple with its unmeasured court outside represents the paradox of the church in the in-between times (11:1, 2). The church is at once protected (thus the measuring) yet vulnerable to persecution (thus the unmeasured court that is trampled). The character of the church is safe space though vulnerable space.[28]

They Will Trample the Holy City 11:2

In 11:2, John indicates why it is that the outer court is not measured. The command to not measure the outer court is "because it has been given to the nations and they will trample the Holy City for forty-two months" (11:2).[29]

It is important to recognize that "the Holy City" is a moniker for the people of God in the book of Revelation.[30] That "the Holy City" is a title for the people of God is clear from its occurrence in the opening description of the Holy City/New Jerusalem, "And I saw the Holy City, New Jerusalem, coming down of heaven from God, prepared as a bride" (21:2). Here "the Holy City, New Jerusalem" is depicted as a

---

real-world reference to people because of the impracticality of casting out a temple court (Bauckham, *Climax*, 270).

27. Cp. Luke 4:29; Acts 7:58; John 9:34–35; 12:31. See Aune, *Revelation*, 2:607.

28. Resseguie, *Revelation*, 37–38.

29. The title "Holy City" occurs four times in the book of Revelation. See 11:2; 21:2, 10; 22:19. The title is used in the OT and the NT for the literal city of Jerusalem (Neh 11:1, 18; Isa 48:2; 52:1; Dan 9:24; Matt 4:5; 27:53). Revelation, however, clearly employs imagery throughout and in the case of the "Holy City" never uses it literally. Thus, the use of this designation in Revelation itself must be determinative for its application here. See Beale, *Revelation*, 568.

30. Though some may attempt to understand "the Holy City" as an indication of the physical city of Jerusalem, this reading does not fit with the narrative of Revelation. See Thompson, *Revelation*, 125.

bride. Then, in the account of the Bride (21:9—22:9), John notes that the Holy City is not merely "prepared as a bride" (21:2) but it is the Bride: "one of the seven angels ... spoke with me saying, 'Come, and I will show you the Bride, the wife of the Lamb.' And he carried me away in the Spirit to a great and high mountain and he showed me the Holy City, Jerusalem" (21:9–10).[31]

It is my conviction that the trampling of the Holy City indicates that the people of God will also suffer at the hands of the nations. That this is the meaning of the trampling in 11:2 is supported by the fact that John uses "trample" only three times. The other two occurrences are in 14:20 and 19:15, and in both instances, "trampling" occurs in the context of judgment on the nations. The implication, as I will argue in the commentary on 14:20, is that the nations will be "trampled" (14:20) because they have trampled on the people of God.[32]

> **Excursus: John's Use of Various Designations of Time to Express Three and One-Half Years: "Forty-Two Months," "1,260 Days," and "A Time, Times, and Half a Time"**
>
> In 11:2, John also notes that the nations' trampling of the Holy City lasts, "for forty-two months." Then in 11:3, John observes that the Two Witnesses "will prophesy for 1,260 days." In 12:14, we come upon a third time designation: "a time, times, and half a time." It appears that each of these designations of time is interchangeable and indicates a period of three and one-half years.
>
> In 11:2, John states that the nations "will trample the Holy City for forty-two months." It is important to note that the designation of "forty-two months" occurs only twice in the book of Revelation. The other occurrence is in 13:5, where it indicates the duration of the Beast's authority: "And it was given to him authority to act for forty-two months." Since John regularly links passages by repeating unique terms or expressions, it appears reasonable to conclude that the trampling of the Holy City for "forty-two months" (11:2)

---

31. Contra Seiss: "We understand it by what the Scriptures always mean by the phrase, and interpret it with confidence of *Jerusalem*" (Seiss, *Apocalypse*, 205–6).

32. This functions in accord with the principle of *lex talionis* (the law of retaliation; or "an eye for an eye").

corresponds to the "forty-two months" (13:5) in which the Beast wields his power.

In 11:3, John then uses the designation "1,260 days" to indicate the period of time in which the Two Witnesses minister. The designation "1,260 days" also occurs in 12:6 where it specifies the period of time in which the Woman finds refuge in the wilderness and is "nourished" by God. Since these are the only two occurrences of "1,260 days" in the book of Revelation, it is reasonable to conclude that John intentionally links these two accounts so that the time in which the Two Witnesses minister (11:3) corresponds to the time in which the Woman finds refuge and is nourished by God in the wilderness (12:6).[33]

In the account of the Woman and the Dragon (12:1–18), John employs a third expression of time when he states that the Woman, "was nourished for a time, times, and half a time away from the Serpent's face" (12:14). Although 12:14 is the only place John uses the expression, "a time, times, and half a time," the fact that the verb "nourish" occurs only in 12:6 and 12:14 serves as a link between the two verses. That this conclusion is warranted finds support from the fact that both verses refer to the Woman being "nourished" in the wilderness.[34] This suggests that the time designation of "1,260 days" in 12:6 and the "a time, times, and half a time" in 12:14 are also interchangeable.

Therefore, the designations of "forty-two months," "1,260 days," and "a time, times, and half a time" are interchangeable and refer to the same period of time. This conclusion gains support from the fact that both "forty-two months" (11:2; 13:5) and "1,260 days" (11:3; 12:6) equate to three and one-half years—based on a thirty-days-per-month calendar. That John's use of "a time, times, and half a time" (12:14) derives from the book of Daniel,[35] and this expression has also been understood to connote a period of three and one-half years

---

33. I will discuss the identity of the Woman in the commentary on 12:1–18.

34. John uses wilderness three times: 12:6, 14; 17:3. This raises a very interesting question as to how the "wilderness" in 17:3 connects back to the "wilderness" in 12:6, 14.

35. See Dan 7:25; 12:7.

reinforces the conviction that these three expressions of time are interchangeable and that they represent a three and one-half year period of time.[36]

This naturally raises the question, "What does this period of time signify?" We begin by noting that Daniel's designation of "a time, times, and half a time," appears throughout the Second Temple literature to refer to a period of tribulation. In particular, the Second Temple writings apply Daniel's time frame to refer to either a general era of trial[37] or a time of suffering for the nation of Israel.[38]

In light of this, it is my conviction that John uses the various means of expressing a period of three and one-half years in order to refer to the era in which the people of God minister (the Two Witnesses), and are afforded divine protection, and in which they suffer.

Introduction to the Two Witnesses 11:3–13

It is my conviction that the account of the Two Witnesses serves as the focus of John's prophesying and, therefore, constitutes the contents of the Scroll. That the ministry of the Two Witnesses functions within the narrative as the focus of John's prophetic commissioning, as I alluded to above, is indicated by, among other things, the narrative flow of the book of Revelation. In 10:11, John was commanded to "prophesy." That the account of the measuring of the temple (11:1–2) and the ministry of the Two Witnesses (11:3–13) immediately follows this commissioning suggests that these constitute the fulfillment of John's prophesying. In addition, that the verb "to prophesy" only occurs twice (10:11; 11:3) further justifies this conclusion.

God's Witnesses 11:3–6

The account of the Two Witnesses opens with the affirmation that they serve as God's witnesses (11:3). The use of *two* with regard to the number of witnesses derives its primary import from the OT law of legal

---

36. See Dan 7:25; 12:7. See my *Two Witnesses*, 16n47.
37. E.g., Midr. Ps. 10:1.
38. E.g., B. Sanhedrin 97b–98a.

witness.[39] This serves as confirmation that a leading feature of the Two Witnesses is that they bear valid legal testimony.

John's opening description of them as "Witnesses" (11:3) uses a form of the noun *"martus."* John concludes his description of the ministry of the Two Witnesses in 11:7 by using the cognate *marturian* ("testimony"): "when they have finished their testimony. . . ." The use of *martus* ("witness") in 11:3 and the cognate *marturian* ("testimony") in 11:7 function as an inclusio, or frame, for the central depiction of the Two Witnesses. That is, they are God's witnesses who testify. Thus, as Bauckham observes, "The church was not redeemed from all nations merely for its own sake but to witness to all nations. Martyrdom is not simply the church's deliverance from the world, but the culmination of the church's effective witness to the world."[40]

Clothed in Sackcloth 11:3

The prophetic call of the Two Witnesses is further supported by the fact that they are "clothed in sackcloth" (11:3). The wearing of sackcloth indicates a ministry associated with repentance and/or mourning.[41] Sackcloth is also associated with the attire of the prophets.[42]

Two Olive Trees and the Two Lampstands 11:4

John then identifies the Two Witnesses as "the two olive trees and the two lampstands who stand before the Lord of the earth" (11:4).

The use of "lampstands" (11:4) associates the Two Witnesses with the seven churches, which were depicted as "seven golden lampstands" (1:12;

---

39. Deut 17:6; 19:15. See Johnson, *Triumph*, 170; Morris, *Revelation*, 143; Seiss, *Apocalypse*, 175.

40. Bauckham, *Climax*, 258.

41. See 2 Kgs 1:8; Jon 3:4–10; Matt 11:21; Mark 1:6; Luke 4:13. See Bauckham, *Climax*, 277. Beale notes that twenty-seven of forty-two occurrences of sackcloth in the OT are associated with mourning alone, while an additional thirteen include repentance (Beale, *Revelation*, 576).

42. Cp. Isa 20:2; 2 Kgs 1:8; Mark 1:6. See Beale, *Revelation*, 576.

1:13, 20; 2:1, 5).[43] That they are also the "two olive trees" (11:4)[44] along with "lampstands" surely alludes to the prophecy of Zechariah 4.[45] In Zech 4:2–3, the prophet says, "I see, and behold, a lampstand all of gold with its bowl on the top of it, and its seven lamps on it with seven spouts belonging to each of the lamps which are on the top of it; also two olive trees by it, one on the right side of the bowl and the other on its left side."[46] Zechariah then identifies the two olive trees as, "the two anointed ones" (Zech 4:14). Most commentators affirm that the two anointed ones represent the king (Zerubbabel) and the high priest (Joshua).[47]

If John's imagery of the lampstands and the olive trees derive from Zechariah, then his depiction of the Two Witnesses suggests that they also are kings/queens and priests. This corresponds with John's opening description of the people of God: "He has made us a kingdom, priests to His God and Father" (1:6).

The question arises at this juncture as to why John envisions two lampstands when Zechariah has only one. It is my suggestion that John's primary concern was to demonstrate the legal validity and trustworthiness of the Two Witnesses' testimony. The fact that there are two lampstands highlights the theme of witnessing and it emphasizes the legitimacy of their testimony.[48]

---

43. Beale affirms, "Despite resistance, the Christian community's successful establishment as God's temple throughout the church age is assured by means of the Spirit's empowerment of the church's faithful prophetic witness" (Beale, *Revelation*, 578).

44. This receives further support by means of the use of the anaphoric article "the" which is best accounted for in terms of referencing the lampstand and olive trees of Zechariah. Smalley observes, "Both images, olive trees and lampstands, appear in verse 3 with the definite article; . . . and this suggests that the metaphors and their significance would be well known to John's audience" Smalley, *Revelation*, 277. Aune affirms that it is articular, "because it is an allusion to the well-known menorah of Zech 4:2–3, 11" Aune, *Revelation*, 2.612.

45. DeSilva, in fact, asserts, "John assumes the hearers' familiarity with Zechariah 4:1–14, referring to the two witnesses in a way that forces intertextual conversation" (deSilva, *Seeing Things*, 154).

46. The notable distinction between Revelation 11 and Zechariah 4 is that Zechariah has only one lampstand. Nonetheless, it is beyond question that John's imagery derives from this OT passage. See Bauckham, *Climax*, 162–66; Beale, *Revelation*, 576–79.

47. Smith goes so far as to suggest that this passage provides evidence for a diarchic structure between the king and priest in Israel at this time (Smith, *Micah-Malachi*, 207). See Caird, *Revelation*, 134; Keener, *Revelation*, 290; Mounce, *Revelation*, 217n80.

48. See introductory chapter on numbers.

Fire Proceeds from Their Mouth 11:5

That the Two Witnesses suffer at the hands of their opponents is suggested in the conditional clause, "If anyone wishes to harm them" (11:5). At the same time, the Two Witnesses have the ability to defend themselves by having, "fire [come] out of their mouth" (11:5).[49] This fire, in fact, "consumes their enemies" (11:5). The likely OT background for the imagery of fire proceeding out of their mouths is Jer 5:14: "Because you have spoken this word, Behold, I am making My words in your mouth fire and this people wood, and it will consume them" (Jer 5:14).[50]

The ability to spew fire from their mouths likely contrasts with the demonic hordes in 9:17, 18.[51] As we will see, the references to the mouths of demonic, or demonically empowered entities (13:5), and the reiteration of the deceptive aims of these beings (13:14), form a stark contrast to the testimony of the Two Witnesses.

Of course, it goes without saying that the means by which the Two Witnesses defend themselves is by affirmation of the truth. Not only, then, must we wrestle with the fact that the description of the people of God is non-violent, but we must also recognize that their proclamation of truth will often fall on deaf ears: especially when that truth directly impacts the power and wealth of those in power.

These Have Authority 11:6

The depiction of the Two Witnesses as prophetic figures continues in 11:6 where John affirms, "These have authority." It is here that we begin to recognize the Two Witnesses as prophets in accordance with the prophetic ministries of Moses and Elijah.[52] Thus, like Elijah, the Two Witnesses have the authority, "to shut heaven, in order that it might not rain" (11:6).[53] And, like Moses, they have authority, "over the waters to turn them into blood" (11:6).[54] They, also like Moses, are able, "to strike the earth with every plague whenever they wish" (11:6). The connection with Moses and Elijah suggests that their ministry is in accord with that

---

49. Note the word "mouth" is singular in the Greek. See below for more discussion.
50. See also, Isa 11:4; 1:16; 2:12, 16; 19:15, 21.
51. The same phrase "fire came out of their mouths" occurs in 9:17, 18.
52. See Bauckham, *Climax*, 276–77; Beale, *Revelation*, 573.
53. 1 Kgs 17:1.
54. Exod 7:14–25.

of the OT people of God. Moses stands as the representative of the Law, while Elijah represents the Prophets.⁵⁵

There is another connection with Moses that may or may not have been in John's purview. Namely that the cry of the people of God for justice in Exod 2:23–25 got the attention of YHWH: "God saw the sons of Israel, and God took notice *of them*" (Exod 2:25). The Lord's immediate response, however, was not to issue the series of ten plagues. Instead, the Lord's first response was to summon Moses (Exod 3–4). This strikes me as similar to the narrative of John's Apocalypse.

At center stage in the narrative of the book of Revelation is the martyrs' cry for justice (5:8; 6:10; 8:3, 4). Once again, contrary to many readings of the book of Revelation, God does not respond with plagues, but with the summoning of His people—His people who are like Moses and Elijah.

The Beast Makes War, Overcomes, and Kills the Two Witnesses 11:7

The account of the ministry of the Two Witnesses takes a dramatic turn in 11:7. After John's description of the prophetic ministry of the Two Witnesses, John says, "the Beast who comes up from the Abyss will make war with them and overcome them and kill them" (11:7). DeSilva observes the paradox: "There is a certain temporal paradox here, since enduring persecution is both the 'necessary result of the conquest of Satan' and 'the means to his defeat' in the earthly realm."⁵⁶

At the same time, the suddenness with which the war against the Two Witnesses occurs (11:7) leaves the reader somewhat startled. This is likely John's rhetorical intent.

What is striking is that the Beast will, "overcome them" (11:7): this fact is reiterated in the depiction of the Beast in 13:7, where it says, "It was given to it to make war with the saints and to overcome them."⁵⁷ This is remarkable because up until this point in the narrative, the people of God have repeatedly been exhorted to "overcome."

---

55. Luke 24:27; Matt 5:17; 7:12; 22:40; Acts 13:15; 24:14; Rom 3:21.

56. DeSilva, *Discovering*, 222n4.

57. The parallels between 11:7 and 13:7 support the contention here that the Two Witnesses are all of God's people. After all, the fact that both 11:7 and 13:7 depict a "war" against the people of God and the fact that the war in 11:7 is against the "Two Witnesses," and the war in 13:7 is against the "saints" affirms this.

Now, suddenly, we learn that they themselves are overcome, and it is the Beast who overcomes them.

John is clear, however, the Two Witnesses will not suffer death until "they have finished their testimony" (11:7). There appears to be an implicit measure of encouragement in this pronouncement. For the war of the Beast will not result in the death of God's people until their ministry is complete!

They Will Refuse Them Burial 11:8–10

Their Body Will Lie In the Street of the Great City 11:8

John then notes that after they have been killed "their body[58] will lie in the street of the Great City which is figuratively called Sodom and Egypt" (11:8). Howard-Brook and Gwyther note, "Empire is allowed not only to murder God's witnesses but also to dishonor them by leaving their dead bodies in the city's main street and not allow them to be buried."[59]

The naming of "Sodom and Egypt," two identifications that appear incongruous,[60] likely indicates places where the people of God have suffered at the hands of their enemies. Egypt, of course, regularly earns the epitaph as the paradigmatic nation that mistreats God's people.[61] Sodom also was well known for its ill-treatment of the people of God.[62] Trites suggests, "This city is called 'Sodom' because it is devoted to evil and destined to destruction. . . . It is termed 'Egypt' because in it the people of God are persecuted and oppressed."[63] In doing so, John associates the suffering of the Two Witnesses with the suffering of the great prophets.

The connection of the Great City with places where the people of God have suffered is further heightened by the indication that the Great City is, "where also their Lord was crucified" (11:8). In saying this, John links the suffering of the Two Witnesses with the suffering of Christ.

---

58. The Greek here is singular. All of the major translations use the plural. The significance of the singular is evidence that John did not view them as two individuals but as a collective.

59. Howard-Brook and Gwyther, *Unveiling Empire*, loc. 3945.

60. After all, one is a city and the other a nation.

61. See Joel 3:19.

62. See Gen 19:1–29; Deut 32:32.

63. Trites, *Witness*, 168. Beale also affirms that the description of 'Sodom and Egypt' suggests, "places where the saints lived as aliens under persecution" (Beale, *Revelation*, 591).

This is critical for our understanding of Revelation's narrative. We know already that the death and resurrection of Christ are the means by which Christ has brought redemption: *"because* you were slain and you purchased for God by means of your blood people from every tribe and tongue and people and nation and you have made them a kingdom and priests for our God, and they will reign upon the earth" (5:9-10). If redemption was brought through the death of Christ, then it makes sense to conclude that the death of the people of God, in imitation of Christ, is the means by which God continues to bring redemption to the nations. This, as I will note below, is precisely where the narrative of the book of Revelation leads.

Excursus: Who Are the Two Witnesses?[64]

One of the key questions pertaining to the account of the Two Witnesses is the question, "Who are they?" Though some have suggested that they are two literal individuals who will walk on the Earth during the "last days," such as Enoch and Elijah[65] or Moses and Elijah,[66] it is my conviction that the Two Witnesses are corporate representatives of the entirety of the people of God: i.e., they are all of God's people.

That the Two Witnesses are the entirety of the people of God is evidenced by the fact that they are specifically designated as, "the two lampstands" (11:4). The description of them as "lampstands" surely relates them to the seven churches in 1:9-3:22 and it suggests that they are a corporate entity. After all, if "lampstands" represented a corporate entity in the seven messages, then surely it does in the account of the Two Witnesses as well.[67]

Of course, some may naturally conclude that the Two Witnesses represent only a part of the people of God and not the totality of the people of God. After all, it is reasoned, they are only two lampstands, which suggests that perhaps they

---

64. See my *Two Witnesses*, 34-46 for a detailed discussion of their identity as well as an interaction with the plethora of views.

65. Enoch and Elijah were virtually the unanimous picks of early church after Irenaeus and Tertullian. See Lang, *Revelation*, 185; Seiss, *Apocalypse*, 242-68.

66. Moses and Elijah: Charles, *Revelation*, 1.281; Hal Lindsay, *New World*, 149-50.

67. The burden of proof that they are not a corporate entity in the present account would reside on the one making such a claim.

represent only two of the seven lampstands. Though this line of reasoning is sound, I would contend that they are "two" because John's primary concern was to indicate that their testimony is trustworthy and true. This derives from the OT law of legal witness,[68] which required two or three witnesses to verify the trustworthiness of a claim. Bauckham affirms:

> John is nothing if not consistent in his very precise use of imagery. If the seven lampstands are churches, so must be the two lampstands. But it would be better to say that, if the seven lampstands are representative of the whole church, since seven is the number of completeness, the two lampstands stand for the church in its role of witness.[69]

Another indication that the Two Witnesses are corporate representatives for the entirety of the people of God is the fact that the Beast makes "war" against them (11:7). It does not make any sense to describe the Beast's war against two individuals as a "war." After all, one hardly makes war against only two persons.

Finally, that the Two Witnesses are corporate representatives of the people of God is supported by the fact that they are always described in terms of their unity. In fact, they are never described as anything but a unity. John regularly uses singular nouns, such as "mouth" (11:5) and "body" (11:8, 9), in his description of them.

Three and a Half Days (11:9, 11)

John then says that the body[70] of the Two Witnesses remains unburied, "for three and one-half days" (11:9, 11). A first reading of "three and one-half" may strike the reader/hearers as something odd. After all, if John wanted to associate the Two Witnesses with the death and resurrection of Jesus, which he certainly does, then we might have expected him to use "three days."

---

68. See Deut 17:6; 19:5.
69. Bauckham, *Climax*, 274.
70. Note that again the Greek is singular.

The use of "three and one-half days," however, continues John's preference for the prophetic tradition of three and one-half. Bauckham concludes:

> John has converted the 'third day' of the Gospel tradition into 'three and a half days,' just as the tradition he followed with regard to Elijah's drought converted the 'third year' of 1 Kings 18:1 into 'three and a half years'. The fate of the witnesses is given an apocalyptic period appropriate to the allusion to Daniel 7:21 in 11:7, but the Danielic allusion is interpreted by reference to the history of Jesus which provides the model for his faithful followers.[71]

Resurrected and Ascend into Heaven in a Cloud 11:11–12

The parallels with Jesus continue in the account of the Two Witnesses in that just as Jesus "was dead" and "behold I am alive forever and ever" (1:18), so now the Two Witnesses rise and ascend to heaven (11:11–12). John adds that there was "a great voice from heaven" (11:12) saying, "Come up here" (11:12). They ascend into heaven, John notes, in the presence of their enemies (11:11).

The resurrection and ascension of the Two Witnesses serve to confirm the promises to the people of God that the one who overcomes will be vindicated.[72] Just as those in Smyrna were promised a reward if they were, "faithful until death" (2:10), so also the Two Witnesses are resurrected. Thus, Beale concludes:

> It seemed that God had deserted the witnesses by leaving them in a subdued condition.... But he vindicates them by delivering them and demonstrating that he is their covenantal protector.... At the least, the ascent of the witnesses figuratively affirms a final, decisive deliverance and vindication of God's people at the end of time.[73]

---

71. Bauckham, *Climax*, 280.

72. Ladd affirms that it serves as a "sign to those whom they had been witnesses that they were truly prophets" (Ladd, *Revelation*, 159).

73. Beale, *Revelation*, 597.

The Rest Became Terrified and Gave Glory to God 11:13

John then notes, "in that hour there was a great earthquake" (11:13). As a result of the earthquake, "a tenth of the city fell and 7,000 people were killed" (11:13). The use of 7,000 is reminiscent of the number of those who remained faithful at the time of Elijah.[74] John's description may indicate a reversal of the OT remnant imagery where a tenth is spared. Now, only a tenth is destroyed.

It is not until after the death, resurrection, and ascension of the Two Witnesses that "the rest became terrified and gave glory to the God of heaven" (11:14). The content of the Scroll has been revealed. The means by which the nations are brought to repentance is through the faithful, loving, sacrificial witness of God's people. DeSilva affirms, "What visitations of judgment, however spectacular, cannot achieve is accomplished through obedient and empowered witness."[75] Resseguie adds, "The church accomplishes what judgments alone were unable to accomplish."[76]

At this point, the narrative has reached the climactic moment. We have been asking since the throne room scene (4:1—5:13), "What is it that leads to the repentance of the nations? And how is it that the nations 'will walk by' (21:24) the light of the New Jerusalem?" I have noted that God's delay has granted the nations time to repent. We have continued to see that the delay, which allowed the nations to maintain their destructive rule, has yet to lead them to repentance.

The death, resurrection, and ascension of the people of God do what nothing else could: it results in the repentance of the nations. Thus, in accord with the thesis of this commentary, it is the faithful, loving, and sacrificial witness of God's people that results in the redemption of the nations. It is indeed, as Paul affirms, "the kindness of God leads you to repentance" (Rom 2:4).

---

74. See 7,000: 1 Kgs 19:14–18; or a tenth: Amos 5:3; Isa 6:13.
75. DeSilva, *Discovering*, 146.
76. Resseguie, *Revelation*, loc. 3581.

Revelation 11:15–19
The Seventh Trumpet

Second Woe Has Passed 11:14

THE INTERLUDE (10:1—11:13) HAS been completed and John returns to the narrative of the Seven Trumpets. John announces, "The second woe has passed" (11:14). It is the repentance of the nations (11:13) that signals the end of the second woe and the Sixth Trumpet (11:14).

Seventh Trumpet 11:15–19

The sounding of the Seventh Trumpet results in, "great voices in heaven" (11:15). These voices declare, "The kingdom of the world has become the kingdom of our Lord and of His Christ; and He will reign forever and ever" (11:15). The Seventh Trumpet, as with the Seventh Seal, brings us to the end—at least an announcement of the end.[1] Of course, we have been expecting the end since we were told, "But in the days of the voice of the seventh angel, when he is about to sound the trumpet, then the mystery of God will be fulfilled" (10:7).

To further emphasize that the narrative has reached the end, the worship of God includes the amended title: He is "the One who is and who was" (11:17). No longer is the affirmation of God as "the One who is about to come" (compare 1:4, 8; 4:8) necessary.

---

1. See Resseguie, *Revelation*, 66.

The Twenty-Four Elders Worship 11:16

John then states, "And the Twenty-Four Elders, who are sitting upon their thrones before God, fell upon their faces and began to worship God" (11:16). The worship of the Twenty-Four Elders before the throne presents an oddity in that they are mentioned here without reference to the Four Living Creatures.[2]

I noted earlier that in the opening section of the second story (4:1–16:21), the worship of the Twenty-Four Elders was expressed as if it were something future by means of four future tense verbs.[3] In addition, the four verbs all occur first in their clauses, which, though not uncommon, suggests a point of stress. In the present account, however, the verbs are placed at a more natural location in their clauses.[4] This indicates that as far as the narrative is concerned, the anticipation of worship in the throne room scene has given way to the actual worship: they "began to worship God" (11:16). The worship of the Twenty-Four Elders in the account of the Seventh Trumpet, then, serves as the fulfillment of their worship as it was anticipated in 4:10. The exclusion of the Four Living Creatures from the present account is likely explained by the fact that the focus of the worship of the Father here is on the fulfillment of the worship that the account of the Twenty-Four Elders looked forward to.

The Time Came 11:18

John then declares, "the nations were enraged" (11:18). Of course they are enraged. Their reign has come to an end. John, in fact, adds that "the time" has come (11:18). He then lists three things for which the time has come. First, it is time for "the dead to be judged" (11:18). The dead here are those from among the nations who have not repented. Second, the time has come "to give the reward to your servants" (11:18). This indicates the faithful people of God. Finally, the time has come "to destroy those who destroy the earth" (11:18). This refers to those who

---

2. In every other mention of the Twenty-Four Elders, the Four Living Creatures are mentioned alongside them. See 4:4, 10; 5:8; 11:16; 19:4.

3. See note on 4:9–10. The verbs "give," "fall," "worship," and "throw" are all in the future (4:9–10)—suggesting something the Twenty-Four Elders will do.

4. Greek has the ability to vary word order much more than English. The natural word order (just over 50 percent) in Greek is still subject-verb-object.

brought about the destruction of the creation indicated in the accounts of the first four Trumpets.

Temple of God Is Opened 11:19

Suddenly, John declares, "And the temple of God which is in heaven was opened and the ark of His covenant appeared in His temple, and there were flashes of lightning and sounds and peals of thunder and an earthquake and a great hailstorm" (11:19). As I noted earlier, the presence of the theophanic manifestations marks the close of each of the septets.

The recurrence of theophanic manifestations also, as I noted earlier, serves as one of John's literary means of advancing the narrative. John accomplishes this by adding to the descriptive formula in each subsequent occurrence. Thus, at the close of the account of the Seven Trumpets, he repeats the formula but adds, "and a great hailstorm" (11:19). The repetition of the theophanic manifestations also functions as a literary tool to connect the series of Seals, Trumpets, and Bowls to the throne room. As such, it serves as a reminder that God is in control.

There is no question, then, that 11:19 marks the end of the account of the Seven Trumpets. At the same time, just as the close of the account of the Seven Seals and the opening of the account of the Seven Trumpets overlapped, so also 11:19 serves as both the conclusion to the account of the Seven Trumpets and the beginning of the narrative that follows.

The relationship between the account of the Seven Trumpets (8:2, 5—11:19) and the section that follows (12:1—16:21) is indicated by the fact that the only two times the temple is referred as being "opened" are in 11:19 and 15:5. In terms of the narrative, then, this means that, although we have reached the "end," John has more to reveal.

What is there to reveal? The section that follows (12:1—16:21) will offer insights that will help us understand this second story. In particular, 12:1—13:18 provide details regarding the "Beast" and the "war" (11:7) that the Beast wages against the people of God. This is followed by the final septet, the Seven Bowls. With the advent of the Seven Bowls, the opportunity for repentance has passed.

Conclusion

John is clear: the suffering, martyrdom, and resurrection of the people of God serve as the means by which the nations are redeemed. God's delay in justice was not simply to buy time for more of the people of God to suffer and die (compare 6:11). God's delay was an act of love in that through the suffering and death of the people of God the nations might come to repentance. DeSilva summarizes Revelation's narrative:

> Faithful witness in the power of God, leading ultimately to being slain by the powers of the kingdom of this world, is "the way in which the nations will be brought to repentance and faith, and the sovereignty over them transferred from the beast to the kingdom of God" following the example of the Lamb who also attained victory "by his faithful witness, death and vindication." In this way, the followers of the Lamb will share in his victory and "give the victory universal effect."[5]

Excursus: The Two Witnesses and John's Narrative

The importance of 11:1–13 for the narrative of Revelation cannot be overstated. The second story began in 4:1–11 with the worship of the Father. We were then introduced to a Scroll in the Father's hand which was sealed shut (5:1). The Lamb, however, was worthy "to take the Scroll and open its seals" (5:9). Jesus breaks the seals (6:1–17; 8:1). The scroll then lies open in the hand of an angel (10:1). In anticipation of the end, the angel declares, "there will be no more delay" (10:6). John then takes the scroll and eats it (10:10), and is commissioned to prophesy (10:11).

The story of the Two Witnesses (11:3–13) serves as the content of the Scroll. As such, it is the central account in the book of Revelation. It is here that we finally learn that the nations are redeemed through the faithful, loving, and sacrificial witness of the Two Witnesses.

That the redemption of the nations occurs as a result of the Two Witnesses being killed, raised, and taken to heaven corresponds with John's presentation of the gospel. It was the Lamb's death and resurrection that brought about the

---

5. DeSilva, *Discovering*, 191.

redemption of the nations (5:9). It follows then, that the totality of the nations' redemption results from the faithful, loving, and sacrificial witness of God's people. David Barr summarizes the book of Revelation's narrative flow:

> The sequence of kernels then is: the divine liturgy; the dilemma of the sealed scroll; the revelation of the lion/lamb worthy to open the scroll; the unsealing of the scroll; the trumpets signal; the proclamation of God's reign; the resumption of the divine liturgy. This is a plot of order, disruption, reestablishment of order—probably the most common plot in literature. It is also the plot of the basic Christian story: God created the world good; humans forsook this goodness and turned away from the divine plan; God redeems the world through Jesus.[6]

The establishment of God's kingdom, "on earth as it is in heaven" (Matt 6:10), has been one of the goals of Revelation's narrative. When is God going to establish His rule over the entire creation? The angel with the Scroll had said that it would happen, "in the days of the voice of the seventh angel" (10:7). The seventh angel, however, was not about to sound immediately after the sixth. It is not until after the Two Witnesses "have finished their testimony" (11:7) and are killed, resurrected, and ascended into heaven, that the nations "give glory to God" (11:13). DeSilva affirms, "What visitations of judgement, however spectacular, cannot achieve is accomplished through obedient and empowered witness."[7] Now the seventh angel may sound the final Trumpet! Bauckham concludes, "Thus God's kingdom will come, not simply by the deliverance of the church and the judgement of the nations, but primarily by the repentance of the nations as a result of the church's witness."[8]

---

6. Barr, *Tales*, loc. 2467–72.
7. DeSilva, *Discovering*, 191.
8. Bauckham, *Climax*, 258.

Revelation 12:1–18
The Woman and the Dragon

What chapters 12–14 add to the account in 11:1–13 is primarily a much fuller exposition of the conflict between the forces of evil and the witnessing church to which 11:7 briefly alludes.[1]

Introduction

THE STORY OF JESUS in the Gospels begins with the devil as the adversary.[2] As the Gospel stories progress, Jesus claims that He has entered Satan's domain and bound him so that He might bring redemption.[3] Jesus then tells a parable explaining that those who continue to oppose Him are unable to receive His word because the devil has blinded them.[4] In fact, those who continue to oppose Jesus do so in accord with the work of the devil.[5]

Revelation 12 similarly places the story of the people of God in the context of the cosmic struggle between Satan and God. Here, the devil is a Dragon who stands opposed to the people of God.

David Barr has argued that 12:1—16:21 provides us with a third narrative in the book of Revelation. Though I believe that Barr's observations in general are correct, I would nuance his conclusion for a few reasons. First, 12:1 does not begin a new (third) story because it does not contain

---

1. Bauckham, *Climax*, 285.
2. See Mark 1:12–13; Matt 4:1–11;
3. Mark 3:27
4. See Mark 4:4, 14; Matt 13; This accords with Paul's words in 2 Cor 4:4.
5. See Mark 3:23–30; John 8:44; 13:2, 27.

the structural indicators that John has embedded in his narrative. In accord with the thesis first set out by Richard Bauckham, I have contended that the book of Revelation marks the beginning of each of its four key stories by noting that John was "in the spirit." The last three stories also include a change of location.[6] Thus, in the first story/scene, John was "in the spirit" and on Patmos (1:9). The second story/scene (the heavenly vision) begins in 4:1-2 where John was again "in the spirit" and is taken to heaven. The third story/scene begins in 17:1-3 where John again was "in the spirit." This time he is taken to a wilderness where he sees a Woman/city (the Great Prostitute; 17:3). The final story/scene is similarly marked in 21:9-10 where John is again "in the spirit." In this scene, he is taken to "a great mountain" where he sees a Woman/city (the Bride; 21:10). If this assessment is correct, and I believe that it is, then 12:1—16:21 does not present another story as Barr suggests.

At the same time, there is no question that 12:1 marks a significant transition in the narrative. We know that 11:19 concludes the account of the Seventh Trumpet. In addition, the main storyline of the second story has reached its climax. This is evident in that the Scroll has been opened and its contents have been revealed. In addition, the people of God's cry "How long" (6:10) has been answered: "there will no longer be time" (10:6). And the fact that the nations have repented (11:13) suggests that we have reached the end of the narrative. We might, in fact, expect the Seven Bowls to immediately follow. After all, as we will learn, the Seven Bowls are complete in their effect—as opposed to the Seals and Trumpets which only affected one-fourth and one-third of the creation.

What, then, is the role of 12:1—14:20? It is my conviction that 12:1—14:20[7] pauses the narrative—which is resumed in 15:1. This pause continues the second story by providing details as to the nature of the "war" (11:7) that the Beast wages against the people of God. As such, 12:1—14:20 goes "back in time"—so to speak. Richard Bauckham recognizes a similar function for this section, though he includes chapters 12-15, when he notes, "The main function of chapters 12-15 is to deal much more fully with the subject that was adumbrated in the two

---

6. Note: 4:1-3 John is taken to heaven; 17:1-3 John is taken to a wilderness; and 21:9-10 John is taken to a mountain. See the opening chapter on the structure of Revelation.

7. Though it might be more accurate to say 12:1—14:5.

intercalations (7:1–17; 10:1—11:13): the people of God in their conflict with the forces opposed to God."[8]

It is my conviction that the second story continues in 12:1—14:20 in order to provide answers to two key questions: "Who is the Beast?" and, "What is the nature of this war that he instigates against the people of God?"

The Woman 12:1–2

The narrative begins with the introduction, "And a great sign appeared in heaven" (12:1).[9] The great sign is of, "a Woman who was clothed with the sun, and had the moon under her feet, and a crown of twelve stars on her head" (12:1). It is my conviction that the Woman represents the people of God throughout history. At the beginning of the narrative, the Woman appears to represent the people of God prior to Christ. By the end of the narrative, she seemingly represents the people of God after Christ.[10]

The imagery of the Woman has much in common with the story of Joseph's dream in Genesis 37: "Now he had still another dream, and related it to his brothers, and said, 'Lo, I have had still another dream; and behold, the sun and the moon and eleven stars were bowing down to me'" (Gen 37:9).[11] This suggests that the twelve stars on the Woman's head represent the twelve tribes of Israel.

John then adds that this Woman was "pregnant" (12:2). The identity of the child becomes apparent when John says, "And she gave birth to a son, a male, who is going to rule all the nations with an iron rod" (12:5). The reference to an "iron rod" is most certainly an allusion to Psalm 2:7, 9. Since the imagery from Psalm 2 is applied to Jesus in 19:15, as well as in several passages of the NT,[12] there is little doubt that the child is Jesus. This has led some to suggest that the Woman is Mary.[13]

---

8. Bauckham, *Climax*, 17.

9. This is the first of seven occurrences of the noun "sign": see 12:1, 3; 13:13, 14; 15:1; 16:14; 19:20.

10. DeSilva notes that Victorinus regarded the Woman as the people of God throughout history (deSilva, *Discovering*, 200).

11. That Gen 37:9 has only eleven stars and Rev 12:1 has twelve is easily explained in light of the fact that Joseph himself is the twelfth star.

12. Psalm 2 is applied to Jesus in Mark 1:11; 9:7; Matt 3:17; ; Luke 3:22; Acts 4:25-27; 13:33; Heb 1:5.

13. It is not uncommon for Catholic scholars to propose that the Woman was Mary. Beale notes, "Catholic commentators have written an immense amount of literature

A Great Dragon 12:3–4

John then says that "another sign appeared in heaven" (12:3). This sign is of "a great red Dragon" (12:3).

It is important to observe that John's introduction of the Woman and the Dragon have several things in common: most notably is the fact that both include the use of "sign," "appeared," "in heaven," and "great" (12:1, 3). That the Woman and Dragon stand in contrast to one another is evident in that John has embedded a subtle distinction in John's opening description of each: John introduces the woman with, "And a great sign appeared in heaven" (12:1); whereas, the Dragon is not a great sign but, "a great Dragon" (12:3).

The use of Dragon imagery, in most cultures of the ancient world, represents an untamable, sea-going creature.[14] Dragon imagery has a long history in the ancient world. Longman notes, "Multiheaded dragons represent forces of evil and chaos against whom God fights. The imagery goes back to the picture of Lothan, the seven-headed sea monster against whom the god Baal fought, according to Canaanite mythology."[15] A. Y. Collins adds, "The parallels between the myth of Leto, Apollo and Typhon, on the one hand, and the story of Revelation 12 are immediately clear."[16]

The image of a great Dragon who represents the nations and opposes God's people plays a role in the OT narrative as well. In Ezekiel, Pharaoh, who is the archetypal enemy of God's people, is a serpent:

> Speak and say, 'Thus says the Lord God,
> "Behold, I am against you, Pharaoh king of Egypt,

---

arguing that the heavenly women symbolize Mary, the mother of Jesus. Though the mother of Jesus may be secondarily in mind, the primary focus here is not on an individual but on the community of faith within which the messianic line ultimately yielded a kingly offspring" (Beale, *Revelation*, 628). This is certainly a viable option. The problem with this view is that it does not account well for the latter part of this narrative (12:13–17). At the same time, the idea of a single image representing a collective is common in biblical literature. See the "Bride" in 19:7; 21:2, 9; 22:17—in 21:9 she is called "the Bride, the wife of the lamb"; 21:9—22:9 the "Bride" is a collective for all of the people of God.

14. This is the *tannin* of the biblical world. See Heiser, *Unseen Realm*. Of course, in Job 41:1–34 God is able to tame this creature (Job 26:12–13).

15. Longman, *Revelation*, 259.

16. Yarbro, *Combat*, 72.

The great monster that lies in the midst of his rivers (Ezek 29:3).[17]

As the narrative proceeds, John leaves his reader/hearers with no doubt as to the identity of the Dragon: "And the great Dragon was thrown down, the ancient serpent, the one who is called the Devil and Satan, the one who deceives the whole world" (12:9). That the Dragon represents a demonic power that opposes God and His people finds further justification by the fact that it is red. The only other occurrence of red in the book of Revelation depicts the second horse in the opening Seals—which represented war.[18]

The presence of the Dragon's tail (12:4) further accents his demonic origin. Throughout the book of Revelation tails only appear on the Dragon and the demonic hordes in the Fifth and Sixth Trumpets.[19] In the account of the Fifth Trumpet, the locusts have tails that have the power to hurt people for five months (9:10). Similarly, the demonic hordes in the account of the Sixth Trumpet have serpent-like heads and tails which is the source of their power to kill and do harm (9:19).

At the same time, it is critical to recognize that this Dragon also appears partly in the guise of one who is good. John states that the Dragon has, "seven heads and ten horns, and seven diadems on his heads" (12:3).[20] In light of the consistent application of the number seven to represent perfection or completion, the Dragon's "seven diadems" likely indicate its claims to sovereignty over all the earthly kingdoms. Nonetheless, it is a bit surprising to see John use the number seven for something that is not God or from God. This, however, will not be the last time that a creature who opposes Christ and the people of God will be portrayed with characteristics resembling one who is good. The application of the number seven to the Dragon likely illustrates his efforts to parody God. The Dragon, in other words, makes every effort to deceive by appearing to be good. This is why it is critical to recall that the book of Revelation was written to the churches. As an apocalypse, John is revealing things for what they truly are. His reader/hearers may think

17. See also Ezek 32:2–3; Hab 3:8–15; Ps 74:13, 14; 89:10; Isa 30:7; 51:9.
18. See 6:4; note "scarlet" is used only of the Harlot: 17:3, 4; 18:12, 16.
19. See 9:10*, 19*; 12:4.
20. As we will see more clearly in the depiction of the Beast in 13:1–8, the seven heads and ten horns are likely a direct allusion to Dan 7:1–8. The difference is that in Daniel, there are four beasts who have a combined total of seven heads. This assumes that three of the beasts have only one head. The third beast is said to have four (Dan 7:6).

of the Dragon as the embodiment of royal power, but John wants them to understand that it is a dragon and nothing more than the primordial enemy of the people of God.

John adds that the Dragon's tail, "swept down a third of the stars of heaven and he threw them to the earth" (12:4).[21] It is commonly asserted that this represents one-third of the angels that fell along with Satan.[22] This finds justification in that stars represent angels in the Apocalypse (1:20).[23] In addition, in 12:7, John adds that the Dragon has "angels" who wage war with him.[24]

After sweeping the stars to the earth, the Dragon, "stood before the Woman who was about to give birth, so that when she gave birth he might devour her child" (12:4). Since the child is most certainly Christ, there is justification for finding a specific application to Herod's decree to kill the children in Bethlehem or in the account of those in Nazareth attempting to throw Jesus off the cliff.[25]

Birth and Ascension of the Child 12:5

Despite the efforts of the Dragon, the Child was born: "And she gave birth to a Son, a male, who is going to rule all the nations with an iron rod" (12:5). John then adds that the Child was "taken away to God and to His throne" (12:5). Somewhat surprisingly John glosses over Jesus's life, death, and resurrection. This is surprising because the death and resurrection of Jesus play key roles in the narrative of Revelation. We recall that Jesus was worthy to open the Scroll "because You were slain" (5:9). John's opening vision of Jesus (1:13–18) also heralded Jesus's death and His resurrection: "I was dead and behold I am alive forever and ever" (1:18). And it is the resurrected Jesus who has overcome that promises those in Laodicea, "The one who overcomes I will give to that

21. See Dan 8:10.

22. Beale rejects this supposition. He states, "In light of the Daniel 8 background, the falling of starts in Rev 12:4 does not portray a fall of Satan or of his angels in the distant past or at some primordial time" (Beale, *Revelation*, 636).

23. We might also suppose that the "star" in 8:10 was demonic. See Isa 14:12.

24. Although this conviction may well be true, a measure of caution is warranted. After all, the text, unfortunately, provides no clear indication as to the significance of one-third of the stars being thrown down to the earth.

25. See Matt 2:16; Luke 4:28–30. The difficulty with these propositions is that the text is not explicit enough. In addition, it seems out of character for the book of Revelation to have such a specific application.

person to sit down with Me on My throne, just as I overcame and sat down with My Father on His throne" (3:21).

For John, however, neither Jesus's death nor His resurrection is central to the present narrative. Instead, John's concern is to provide a background for understanding that the opposition to the people of God is the work of the Dragon.

Women Flees into the Wilderness 12:6

Immediately after the child is caught up to God's throne, John says, "The Woman fled into the wilderness" (12:6).

The "wilderness" plays an important role in Scripture.[26] On one hand, the wilderness functions as a place of trial and temptation.[27] Life in the wilderness is arduous.[28] In fact, the wilderness was the place where the Israelites failed.[29] On the other hand, the wilderness was also a place of God's protection and provision for His people. As such, the wilderness was a sanctuary in times of trouble.[30] For example, it was into the wilderness that Moses fled from Egypt and found refuge.[31] The wilderness is also where the Israelites later fled.[32] And the wilderness is where God sovereignly provided for and nourished His people.[33] In the wilderness, the Israelites lacked nothing.[34] In the same way, many years later, Elijah retreated into the wilderness for safety.[35] The prophet Ezekiel adds that the wilderness represents a place of security.[36]

---

26. Smalley notes, "The 'wilderness' is an important motif in the literature of Judaism (as in 1QM 1.1–3, where a retreat to the desert is a prelude to the final eschatological conflict between the sons of light and the children of darkness)" (Smalley, *Revelation*, 321). Barr adds, "Israel's pursuit into the desert where she is kept safe by God is an essential element of the Exodus story (e.g., Ezek 29:3, Deut 1:30f)" (Barr, *Tales*, loc. 3836–37).

27. Beale, *Revelation*, 645.

28. Deut 8:14–16.

29. Exod 17:7; Ps 95:8–11; compare Heb 3:8–11.

30. See Ps 136:16; 1 Kgs 17:2–3; 19:3–4. See Mounce, *Revelation*, 234; Caird, *Revelation*, 151.

31. See Exod 2:15.

32. See Exod 15:22.

33. See Exod 16:4–35; Deut 8:3; 32:10; 1 Kgs 17:2–6; 19:3–8; Hos 2:14.

34. See Deut 8:3.

35. See 1 Kgs 17; 19:3–8.

36. See Ezek 34:25.

The wilderness also conjures up positive images. The wilderness, after all, was the place of God's presence among the Israelites.[37] The Lord's presence was with the people as a flame of fire by night and a cloud by day.[38] Nehemiah affirms, "Indeed, forty years You provided for them in the wilderness *and* they were not in want; their clothes did not wear out, nor did their feet swell" (Neh 9:21).[39] Jeremiah affirms that the people, "found grace in the wilderness" (Jer 31:2). The wilderness experience was a defining moment for the Israelites. Consequently, they were to be continuously reminded of God:

> Who brought you out from the land of Egypt, out of the house of slavery. He led you through the great and terrible wilderness, *with its* fiery serpents and scorpions and thirsty ground where there was no water; He brought water for you out of the rock of flint. In the wilderness He fed you manna which your fathers did not know, that He might humble you and that He might test you, to do good for you in the end (Deut 8:14-16).

The NT continues to employ the wilderness theme in a similar manner.[40] The Gospel of Mark opens with John the Baptist in the wilderness announcing the beginning of the eschatological fulfillment of Isaiah's prophecy: "The voice of one crying in the wilderness, 'Make ready the way of the Lord, make His paths straight'" (Mark 1:3).[41] In Matthew's account, Jesus has an Exodus-like experience in the wilderness.[42] Later, Jesus is baptized and anointed by the Spirit in the wilderness.[43] And it was in the wilderness that He was tempted by the Devil.[44] The author of Hebrews builds on this understanding and contends that the people of God presently dwell in the wilderness.[45]

---

37. "A place of spiritual refuge" (Mounce, *Revelation*, 234). See Deut 2:7.

38. See Exod 13:21-22.

39. See Neh 9:19-21; Deut 8:3.

40. See Heb 3:7—4:7; compare Rom 5-8; see also: 1 Cor 10:1-13; Acts 7:39-43; Heb 11:38.

41. See Isa 40:3. See also Matt 3:3; Luke 3:4. Of course, Mark's citation is a combination of Isa 40:3; Exod 23:20; and Mal 3:1.

42. See Matt 2:15. This passage is quite controversial in terms of identifying if it refers to Jesus's leaving Egypt, or if it refers to His leaving Judea—with Herod acting as another Pharaoh who kills the Israelite children.

43. Matt 4:1.

44. Mark 1:12-13; Matt 4:1-11; Luke 4:1-13.

45. See Heb 3:7—4:7.

John adds that the Woman fled into the wilderness because "she had a place there which had been prepared by God" (12:6).[46] The word for "place" (*topos*) has a rich history in Scripture and Jewish writings.[47] Among its primary meaning is that of a sacred place: i.e., a temple.[48] In addition, place (*topos*) also indicates the location of suffering.[49] This becomes evident when John says that the Dragon "pursues/persecutes the woman" (12:13) and that he "spewed water like a river out of his mouth after the woman, in order that he might sweep her away with a flood" (12:15). The Serpent's pursuit of the Woman into the wilderness, the very place where God carried her, accords with what we saw in the description of the measuring and trampling of the temple in 11:1–2. That is, the people of God are in one sense divinely protected and in another sense they suffer.

War in Heaven 12:7–9

After the Woman's flight into the wilderness, John states, "And there was war in heaven" (12:7).

The description of a war in heaven might be somewhat surprising. The idea, however, has a rich history in apocalyptic literature where angels and demons, who often represent Israel and evil kingdoms, wage war. Although the war here is a heavenly battle, we should not restrict it to the heavens. After all, the nature of apocalypses is to indicate that what happens on the earth is to some extent a playing out of what has happened in heaven. Thus, this war in heaven precipitates the war against the people of God. We have already been introduced to this

---

46. Interestingly, the only other instance in the entire NT where both "prepare" and "place" are used together is John 14:3, "If I go and prepare a place for you, I will come again and receive you to Myself, that where I am, *there* you may be also." There are several reasons for connecting the words of Jesus in John 14 and the narrative of Rev 12. Among them includes the fact that in both passages the "place" which has been "prepared" for them suggests a place of protection and also a place of struggle.

47. An important background for John's use of "place" is found in Daniel 8:13. For a detailed discussion of Dan 8 in the book of Revelation see my *Two Witnesses*, 132–36; see Bauckham, *Climax*, 267–73.

48. See Dan 8:11–13. Beale, *Revelation*, 635–36.

49. Note that Matt 24:15, 15–22; Mark 13:14–20; Luke 21:20–24; and Dan 8:11 locates the abomination that makes desolation in the holy place (*topos*). The use of "place" in Rev 12:6 likely derives from Dan 8:11–13. For a detailed discussion of Dan 8 in the book of Revelation see my *Two Witnesses*, 132–36. See also Bauckham, *Climax*, 267–73.

war in the account of the Two Witnesses (11:7). And the account of the Beast, which follows, will continue to expand upon the notion of a war against the people of God (13:7).

John adds that the war is between "Michael and his angels" and "the Dragon and his angels" (12:7). In the end, "he [the Dragon] was not strong enough ... and he was thrown down" (12:8-9). The Dragon is not the only one expelled from heaven: "his angels were thrown down with him" (12:9). As a result of the Dragon's defeat, "there was no longer a place found for them in heaven" (12:8).[50] Surely, the contrast is intentional: the Woman has a "place prepared by God" (12:6), but for the Dragon and his angels, "there was no longer a place found for them" (12:8).

The Dragon 12:9

John now makes the identity of the Dragon clear. He is the "great Dragon" (12:9; see 12:3) and "the ancient serpent" (12:9).[51] John adds that the Dragon is called by two names. First, he is the Devil (*diabolos*), which means "slanderous; or the slanderer." Secondly, he is called "the Satan," which means "the adversary" or "the accuser." In 12:10, a heavenly voice rejoices "because the accuser of our brothers and sisters has been thrown down." The heavenly voice iterates that the Dragon is "the one who accuses them day and night before our God" (12:10). Thus, the Dragon functions as the adversary of God and His people ("the Satan") and as the slanderer of God and his people ("the Devil"). It is critical to note that one of the Dragon's chief characteristics is that he, "deceives the whole world" (12:9).[52] In fact, in 20:10, the Dragon is again titled, "the one who deceives."

The prominence of deception as the weapon of the Dragon and his minions is foundational to the narrative of the book of Revelation. This is why Jezebel was such a threat to the people of God in Thyatira (2:20). And it also lends support to the conclusion that the demonic hordes in the accounts of the Fifth and Sixth Trumpets are agents of deception.[53] Deception, as we will continue to see, is the weapon of the devil.

50. See Isa 8:14; 14:12-21; 28:16; Luke 20:17-18.
51. See Gen 3:1-5; see also, Rom 16:20; 2 Cor 11:3, 14.
52. Note that the binding of Satan, as I will address in 20:1-3 is "so that he would not deceive the nations any longer" (20:3; see 20:8, 10).
53. That is why their "mouths" were so central to the descriptions: "The power of the horses is in their mouths and in their tails; for their tails are like serpents and have

A Great Voice Proclaims 12:10–12

John then hears a great voice (12:10). The proclamation of the voice (12:10–12) corresponds to a three-part hymn.

First Proclamation: The Kingdom of God Has Come

The first part is the proclamation that as a result of the expulsion of the Dragon from heaven, "the salvation and the power and the kingdom of our God and the authority of His Christ have come" (12:10). The narrative suggests that this is something that in real-time has already occurred.

Second Proclamation: They Overcame Him

The second part of the hymn describes how the battle was won: "And they themselves overcame him" (12:11). Now, John adds to our understanding of what it means to overcome. The presence of "overcome" here is one of the most significant uses of the word in the book of Revelation. Thus far, we have observed that overcoming included imitating Christ's overcoming (3:21). We have also learned that Christ overcame by being the Lamb that was slain (5:5). His note that, "they themselves overcame him" (12:11) clearly identifies the Dragon/Satan as the one who must be overcome. John adds a threefold[54] description of what overcoming the Dragon entails: first, they overcame, "by the blood of the Lamb"; second, they overcame, "by the word of their testimony"; and finally, they overcame because, "they did not love their life until death" (12:11). This, however, raises the question as to who is the "they" that overcame him.

By the Blood of the Lamb

John begins by affirming that the people of God overcame the Dragon, "by the blood of the Lamb" (12:11). I have argued throughout this study that the death of Christ is the key event for the inauguration of the kingdom of God. In the present account, we see that Christ's death and resurrection also result in the defeat of the Dragon.

---

heads, and with them they do harm" (9:19).

54. Though, as I will note below, the grammar may well indicate that it is only twofold.

The defeat of the Dragon corresponds with Jesus's declaration in the Gospel of Luke: "I was watching Satan fall from heaven like lightning" (Luke 10:18). Though we may read Luke 10:18 as an indication of a past event (i.e., Satan has already fallen), it is quite probable that it is a proleptic (i.e., a forward-looking) description of the fall of Satan (i.e., the Dragon). If Jesus's words are a forward-looking description of Satan's fall, we still need not look any further than Jesus's impending crucifixion and resurrection as the moment of Satan's fall. Thus, in John 12:31, Jesus affirms, "Now judgment is upon this world; now the ruler of this world will be cast out." That this declaration is indeed in connection with the crucifixion of Jesus is confirmed by the very next verse: "And I, if I am lifted up from the earth, will draw all men to Myself" (John 12:32). If, however, the fall of Satan in Luke 10:18 is a description of a past event, then we would be best served to link the fall of Satan with the coming of Christ—most notably the anointing of Christ at His baptism.[55] Either way, as far as the narrative of the Apocalypse is concerned, Satan has already fallen.

This accords with the rest of the NT, which also affirms that Satan is a defeated foe. The book of Hebrews states, "that through death He might render powerless him who had the power of death, that is, the devil" (Heb 2:14). Similarly, 1 John 3:8 declares, "The Son of God appeared for this purpose, to destroy the works of the devil." Consequently, John's narrative affirms that the Dragon, the accuser of the people of God, has been cast out.

John's narrative of the Woman and the Dragon (12:1–18) suggests that Satan was kicked out of heaven following the ascension of the Child (12:5) and contemporaneously with the Woman's fleeing in the wilderness (12:6). Although we must be cautious when making such determinations within the Apocalypse, this conclusion appears justified for several reasons.

First, if the account of the Woman and the Dragon (12:1–18) functions as the backstory for the "war" against the Two Witnesses (11:7), then it makes the most sense of the text to conclude that the present narrative indicates what took place prior to the Beast's war against the Two Witnesses.

Second, there is a sense in which this is most the natural reading of this passage. That is, according to the narrative, Satan stood before

---

55. See Mark 1:9–11; Matt 3:13–17; Luke 3:21–22; John 1:24–29.

the Woman to devour her child (12:4); the child (Christ) was born and brought to heaven (12:5); the Woman fled into the wilderness (12:6); Satan wars with Michael and is kicked out of heaven (12:7–9); heaven rejoices because the kingdom of God has come (12:10–12); Satan pursues the Woman and her offspring (12:13–17).

Third, John's note in 12:11 declares that the victory over the Dragon was in part, "by the blood of the Lamb." This too suggests that Jesus's death and resurrection resulted in the Dragon's expulsion. Resseguie affirms, "With the defeat of Satan by Christ's death on the cross, the longed-for victory of God's sovereign rule has arrived."[56]

Fourth, as I have noted throughout, the entire narrative of the book of Revelation centers around the finished work of Christ. Everything has been set in motion because of the cross and the resurrection. Because Jesus is the Lamb that was slain, He has rightfully taken His place on the throne (3:21). And because He was slain, He is also worthy to open the Scroll (5:9). It stands to reason then, that because He was slain that the Dragon has also been kicked out of heaven.

By the Word of Their Testimony

The people of God also overcame the Dragon by, "the word of their testimony" (12:11). This recalls the souls under the altar, "who had been slain because of the word of God, and because of the testimony which they had maintained" (6:9). It appears then that the "they" who overcame are the souls under the altar in 6:9–11. This reading is further supported by the fact that 6:9 and 12:11 are connected by reference to "the word" and to "their testimony."

And They Did Not Love Their Life Even When Faced With Death

Finally, John adds that they overcame the Dragon because "they did not love their life even when faced with death." That the preposition "by" (*dia*) is not repeated before this third clause suggests that the final two clauses ("by the word of their testimony" and "they did not love their life even when faced with death") are closely related. If so, then it might be best to conclude that they "overcame" the Dragon by two things: the blood of the lamb; and the word of their testimony and the fact that

56. Resseguie, *Revelation*, 3795–96.

they lived faithfully to death. If this is correct, and I believe that it is, then we should note the close relationship between the "testimony" of the people of God and their "death." This reading leads to the conclusion that the faithful, loving, and sacrificial witness of the people of God inevitably result in their deaths.

Third Proclamation: Rejoice

The third part of the hymn is a cry for heaven to rejoice: "For this reason, rejoice, O heavens and you who dwell in them" (12:12). The command to rejoice parallels the command in 18:20: "Rejoice over her, heaven, and you saints and apostles and prophets, because God has brought the judgment for you upon her [the Great Prostitute/Babylon]."

At the same time that heaven rejoices, John adds a strong warning to the rest of creation, "Woe to the earth and the sea, because the devil has come down to you, having great wrath, knowing that he has a little time" (12:12). The reason for the concern is that the Dragon, who formerly was in heaven, now operates on "the earth and the sea" (12:12). Even though he was defeated in heaven, he has not yet been destroyed. Instead, as a result of his expulsion, he is full of rage. And he knows, "he has only a little time" (12:12).

John now specifies that the warning goes out to "the earth and the sea" (12:12). The narrative, however, seemingly indicates that this warning is also for the people of God. After all, it appears that one of John's objectives in 12:1—14:20 is to warn the people of God that they too must be prepared to overcome because they have an enemy (the Dragon). This enemy, who is none other than the devil himself, having been expelled from heaven, is full of rage. As Peter says, "Your enemy, the devil, prowls around like a roaring lion, seeking someone to devour" (1 Pet 5:8).

Jesus's victory means the defeat of the Dragon. At this point in the narrative, however, the victory has only been realized in heaven. The result is that the people of God must be prepared to join John as, "a sharer in the tribulation, kingdom, and patient endurance in Jesus" (1:9).

REVELATION 12:1–18

Dragon Pursues the Woman in the Wilderness 12:13–17(18)[57]

In 12:13–18, the narrative returns its attention to the Woman and the "war" (12:7) that was in heaven now moves to the earth (12:17).

Dragon Pursues the Woman 12:13

The Dragon, recognizing that he has been cast down, "pursues/persecutes" the Woman (12:13).[58] The pursuit of the Woman by the Dragon is reminiscent of the pursuit of the Israelites by Pharaoh.[59]

That the pursuer is the Dragon—Satan—is important. After all, it is the nature of the Apocalypse to provide the reader/hearers with insight as to what is really happening. Although history tells us that Egypt, Assyria, Babylon, and now Rome are the ones who oppress the people of God, John indicates that it is the Dragon that is pursuing the Woman. That the Dragon empowers the rulers of the world to do this is precisely what the narrative of 13:1–18 will affirm.[60]

Two Wings of an Eagle 12:14

John adds that the Woman's escape into the wilderness was by means of, "the two wings of the great eagle" (12:14). John's reference to the rescuing eagle provide a certain allusion to the exodus narrative. In Exodus, we are told, "You yourselves have seen what I did to the Egyptians, and *how* I bore you on eagles' wings, and brought you to Myself" (Exod

---

57. Note the Greek text has 12:18. Whereas, English Bibles place, "and he stood on the sand of the sea" as the opening line in 13:1. There is an interesting question that results from what appears to be a minor difference in versification. Namely, is it the Dragon who "stands on the sand of the sea" or is it the Beast?

58. The Greek here can certainly be translated as "persecutes" (NAU, NKJ), but in light of the narratival nature of the passage "pursues" (ESV, NIV, NLT, NRS) seems to fit the context better. I have chosen to use both words, separated only with the slash because although pursues better fits the context, the use of "persecutes" adds the extra element of clarity confirming the Dragon's purpose in pursuing the Woman.

59. See Exod 14:8–10. Throughout the OT, Pharaoh is like a Dragon (see Ps 74:13–14; Isa 51:9–10; Ezek 29:3).

60. See 13:2.

19:4).⁶¹ The "two wings of the great eagle" (12:14) most certainly refer to the work of God in rescuing His people.

Away from the Serpent 12:14–16

The Woman was brought to the wilderness and, "away from the presence of the serpent" (12:14). Interestingly, in the very next verse, we learn that the Woman is not out of the serpent's reach. John continues, "And the serpent spewed water like a river out of his mouth after the Woman, in order that he might sweep her away with a flood" (12:15). That the Dragon spews water "out of his mouth," likely indicates the Dragon "pursues" the Woman through deception.⁶² This accords with the account of the First Seal. Namely, that deception precedes war. Or, shall we say, the Dragon wages war by means of deception?

That the Dragon has a river coming out of His mouth contrasts with Christ who has a sword coming from His mouth (1:16; 19:15). Christ is also, "The One who is holy, the One who is true" (3:7), and He is "the Amen, the Faithful and True Witness" (3:14). The Dragon, on the other hand, is "the ancient serpent, the one who is called the devil and Satan, the one who deceives the whole world" (12:9).

John then adds, in accordance with the use of Exodus imagery, that the Woman is preserved because, "the earth helped the Woman and the earth opened its mouth and swallowed the river" (12:16).⁶³

Dragon Wages War 12:17

That the earth helped the Woman only further angers the Dragon. As John says, "The Dragon was enraged at the Woman and went to make war with the rest of her offspring" (12:17). This brings us to the climactic moment in the narrative of the Woman and the Dragon (12:1–18). The Dragon, who stood opposed to the Woman even before Christ was born (12:4), and who attempted to "devour" Christ once He was born

---

61. God is often depicted as an eagle protecting Israel; see Deut 32:10–12; Isa 40:3, 31. David uses the imagery of God's wings protecting him: Ps 17:8; 36:7–8; 63:1–2, 7; 91:4, 11–13.

62. See 9:17, 18, 19; 16:13; see also 1:16; 2:16; 3:16; 10:9, 10; 11:15; 12:15, 16; 13:2, 5, 6; 14:5; 19:15, 21.

63. See, "the earth swallowed them"—the Egyptians (Exod 15:12).

(12:4), has been thrown down to the earth (12:9, 13) and is endeavoring to "make war" with the offspring of the Woman (12:17).

Woman's Offspring 12:17

The Woman's offspring are then defined. They are, "the ones who keep the commandments of God and have the testimony of Jesus" (12:17). John's description of the Woman's offspring parallels those under the altar who were slain "because of the word of God, and because of the testimony which they had" (6:9). This parallel does not necessitate an identity between them, but it does affirm a continuity within John's depictions of the people of God. This is supported by the fact that in 19:10, John attempts to offer worship to the angel who identifies himself as a, "fellow servant of yours and your brothers and sisters who hold to the testimony of Jesus" (19:10). Similarly, in 20:4, we learn of, "the souls of those who had been beheaded because of the testimony of Jesus and because of the word of God" (20:4). The likelihood, then, is that the offspring of the Woman are the people of God in their entirety—or at least the people of God living on the earth at any one time.

The Dragon Stood on the Sand of the Sea 12:18 [13:1][64]

In many ways, this verse serves as the introduction to the account of the two Beasts in 13:1–18. As such, John begins the account of the two Beasts with an ominous note: "And he [the Dragon] stood on the sand of the sea" (12:18). This short statement cannot be overlooked. The narrative of the two Beasts begins with the Dragon on the seashore. The Dragon then is well situated for the arrival of the two Beasts—the first coming from the sea (13:1) and the second coming from the land (13:11). Smalley states, "The satanic dragon stands on the seashore (12.18), ready to call

---

64. In the Greek text, this sentence is marked as 12:18. The NET, NLT, and NRS list it as 12:18. The NAS and NIV, place it in 13:1; The ESV includes it with 12:17. The NKJ includes it as part of 13:1, but favors a manuscript tradition in which the verb is first person and not third person: "Then I stood. . . ." This is a very peculiar decision for two reasons. First, John's location is well situated in heaven (4:1–2). I have noted, in accordance with Bauckham's analysis, that when John changes locations it serves as a major structural indicator. That the present narrative carries forth the account of the Woman and the Dragon affirms that 12:18 [13:1] does not present a major structural break in the narrative. Second, as Beale notes, the manuscript evidence in favor of the third person is "superior" (Beale, *Revelation*, 681).

up his bestial acolytes from the troubled waters in front of him (13.1–10) and from the earth behind (13.11–18)."[65]

The Dragon's efforts to pursue/persecute the Woman takes on a different strategy.

Conclusion

John's closing remark (12:17) This conclusion helps us affirm the identity of the Woman. According to the narrative, the Woman exists prior to and after the ascension of Jesus (12:1–18). There is little question that the Woman's offspring are followers of Jesus. Thus, it is my contention that the Woman herself represents the people of God throughout the entirety of the OT and NT eras.[66]

In accordance with its role in the larger narrative begun in 4:1, the account of the Woman and the Dragon (12:1–18) provides us with the backstory regarding the "war" against the Two Witnesses (11:7). The account of the Woman and the Dragon begins by asserting that "the war" that is being waged against God's people is the work of the Dragon. John makes it clear that the "war" against the people of God is none other than the war which the Dragon has been waging against the people of God since the beginning. After all, the Dragon stood before the Woman prior to Christ (12:4). The Dragon also attempted to destroy Christ at His birth (12:4). And the Dragon remains opposed to the Woman after the birth of Christ (12:15). In fact, the Dragon continues to wage war against, "the rest of her offspring" (12:17).

It is critical to recognize that John places this war in the context of the finished work of Christ. Because Christ has been "victorious" (i.e., He "overcame") on the cross and has ascended (12:5), the Dragon has been completely defeated. And the Dragon knows it. He has been kicked out of heaven and he knows that he has only a short time left. So he is enraged! And he is coming after you—after all of us!

John's message to his reader/hearers, and to us as well, runs clear: beware, the Dragon is still pursuing the people of God and, in fact, he is even more enraged (12:13) because he knows that he has been defeated!

65. Smalley, *Revelation*, 335.

66. In 12:1–2 the Woman represents the people of God from whom Christ came. Now, in 12:5–17 the Woman and her offspring represent the people of God after Christ. Thus, we conclude that the Woman represents the people of God. The Woman, then, is not Israel, Mary, or the Church. The Woman is all of the above.

At this point, we might do well to skip forward to John's exhortation in 14:12—13:

> Here is the patient endurance of the saints, the ones who keep the commandments of God and the faith of Jesus. And I heard a voice from heaven saying, "Write, 'Blessed are those who die in the Lord from now on!' 'Yes,' says the Spirit, 'in order that they may rest from their hard work, for their works follow with them.'"

Revelation 13:1—14:5
The Beasts and the 144,000

The first beast, described in 13:1–10, represents the Roman Empire and particularly its emperor, depicted in ways that recall the emperor Nero (54-68 C.E.), who is regarded as the epitome of evil.[1]

The beast is not merely 'Rome'. . . It is the inhuman, anti-human arrogance of empire which has come to expression in Rome—but not only there. . . . All who support the cultural religion, in or out of the church, however, Lamb-like they may appear, are agents of the beast. All propaganda that entices humanity to idolize human empire is an expression of this beastly power that wants to appear Lamb-like.[2]

Like Rome, the image of the beast looks good and appealing to us. We may benefit from it greatly, as many people benefited from the Roman Empire in the first century. In so doing, however, it blinds us to the corrupt and destructive reality of the thing and prevents us from seeing the idolatrous allegiance we have given to it.[3]

Introduction

REVELATION 13:1—14:5 IS ONE of the more famous and yet complex passages in the book of Revelation. Unfortunately, our understanding of this text has been clouded by the plethora of popular interpretations

---

1. Carter, *What Does Revelation Reveal?*, 90.
2. Boring, 156–57.
3. Westhelle, "Between" in Rhoads. *From Every People and Nation*, loc. 3153–55.

that have often "discovered" contemporary political events as the fulfillment of John's prophecy.[4]

It is my conviction that the present account continues the narrative by introducing us to two Beasts (a Beast from the Sea, 13:1–8; and a Beast from the land, 13:11–18). As such, the present narrative serves to expand on the account of the Woman and the Dragon by providing even more insight into the nature of the Dragon's campaign against the people of God. In particular, we learn that the Dragon empowers the two Beasts to carry out his "war" against the people of God. Or, as Beale titles this section of his commentary, "The Devil Authorizes the State as His Agent to Persecute the Church and to Deceive the Ungodly."[5]

The Beast Coming Out of the Sea 13:1–2

In 13:1, John introduces us to the first Beast, "And I saw a Beast coming up out of the sea." In the account of the Two Witnesses, John had described the Beast as one who, "comes up out of the Abyss" (11:7). Now we are told that the Beast arises from the sea (13:1). There is little doubt that the sea (13:1) and the Abyss (11:7) are synonymous.

The image of the "sea" is rich in biblical and apocalyptic works. Beale notes, "Without exception the imagery of the sea monster is used throughout the OT to represent evil kingdoms who persecute God's people."[6] The sea was widely believed to be a place of chaos and destruction.[7] It also symbolized forces that are hostile to God. As noted in the discussion of the Dragon in 12:3–4, the sea is the home of Leviathan (Lothan), or as John prefers to call it, the "Dragon."[8] Longman, thus, asserts, "Even without further description we know that this beast represents evil because of its origins from the sea."[9]

---

4. Carey affirms, "Over the centuries interpreters have tried to map out these symbols in one-to-one correspondences of the Beasts with particular historical figures or institutions. This 'Dick Tracy Apocalyptic Decoder Ring' approach has not served us well" (Carey, "Counter-Imperial," loc. 2153–54).

5. Beale, *Revelation*, 681.

6. Beale, *Revelation*, 683.

7. See Gen 1:2.

8. Beale tempers the use of the Leviathan tradition for the Beast. He contends that the primary background for John's portrait of the Beast is Daniel 7 (Beale, *Revelation*, 683).

9. Longman, *Revelation*, 280.

At the same time, John's reader/hearers may well have understood the fact that the Beast comes from the sea as an indication that it embodies imperial power. After all, what comes from the sea, from John's perspective, surely indicates that its ultimate origin is Rome. The Beast, therefore, represents Roman imperial power[10] and the Dragon is the source of his power and authority.[11]

The Beast Has Ten Horns and Seven Heads 13:1

John begins his description of the Beast by noting that it, "has ten horns and seven heads and upon its horns were ten diadems and on its heads were blasphemous name(s)" (13:1).[12] It is important to be reminded that the Dragon also has seven heads and ten horns (12:3). The Beast's seven heads confirm that it and the Dragon are closely allied. Perhaps we might even suggest that the Beast is dragon-like. Barr contends that the Beast's, "seven heads represent perfect or complete authority."[13] Of course, its claims to complete authority are in fact "blasphemous."

In order to recognize the nature of the Beast it is important to recognize John's use of Daniel 7. There is little doubt that John's depiction of the Beast from the sea (13:1–8) has the four beasts of Daniel 7 in view.[14] In Daniel's account, the four beasts have a combined total of seven heads.[15] Consequently, the seven heads of John's one Beast (13:1) correspond to the seven heads of Daniel's four beasts. In addition, the "ten horns" (13:1) which is a common symbol of power,[16] of John's Beast correspond with

---

10. We must be careful as modern readers not to limit John's description of the Beast to something ancient. Sure, for John, Rome was the embodiment of the Beast. But, we must ask ourselves, "what does the Beast look like today?" The failure to ask such questions becomes a failure to read Revelation well. See Howard-Brook and Gwyther, *Unveiling Empire*; Gorman, *Reading Revelation Responsibly*; McKnight and Matchett, *Revelation for the Rest of Us*; deSilva, *Unholy Allegiances*.

11. Beale, *Revelation*, 683.

12. It is uncertain here whether or not the Greek text should read "names" or "name." Does each head have a blasphemous name, thus "names?" Or is it the same name on each head, thus, rendering it "a blasphemous name on its heads"?

13. Barr, *Tales*, loc. 292.

14. See Hieke, "Reception."

15. See Dan 7:4–7. The third beast is said to have four heads (Dan 7:6). Since it is presumed that the other three beasts each have one head, the total number of heads of the four beasts is seven.

16. See Deut 33:17; 1 Kgs 22:11; Ps 89:17; Rev 5:6; 1 En. 90:6–16.

the ten horns of the Beasts in Daniel. In particular, the Beast's ten horns correlate with the "ten horns" of Daniel's fourth beast (Dan 7:7).

The presence of *diadems* on the horns of the Beast, and the fact that they are ten in number, confirm the Beast's blasphemous claims of royalty. The presence of ten *diadems* corresponds closely to the Dragon who has "seven diadems" (12:3). Interestingly, the only other use of *diadem* in the book of Revelation is of Christ (19:12). Whereas Christ's *diadems* are not numbered—they are simply "many" (19:12)—the Beast and the Dragon's *diadems* are limited in number (ten and seven; 12:3; 13:1).

The Beast Has Blasphemous Names 13:1

John then adds that the Beast also has, "blasphemous name(s)" on its heads (13:1).[17] Resseguie contends that the Beast's blasphemous names indicate its "self-deifying intention to displace God."[18] Blasphemy is a key trait of rebellious characters in the Apocalypse. As we will see, those who refuse to repent in the midst of the Seven Bowls, "blaspheme His name" (16:9, 11, 21).

The Dragon Empowers the Beast 13:2

Lest there be any doubt in the minds of John's readers, the Beast's Satanic authority is made explicit: "And the Dragon gave to him [the Beast] his power and his throne and great authority" (13:2).

This becomes one of the keys to the present narrative. Namely, that, in 13:1–8, we learn that the means by which Satan wages his "war" against the people of God is by empowering the Beast to do his work for him. As deSilva notes, "John's polemical perspective becomes much clearer. The imperial house is now aligned with the character who plays the role of Python—Satan, the Dragon-Snake who is the power behind and doppelgänger of the Principate."[19]

Consequently, As Hieke notes, "Revelation 13 proclaims exactly what Daniel 7–8 insinuates: the community's daily experience of

---

17. See 17:3.
18. Resseguie, *Revelation*, 239.
19. DeSilva, *Discovering*, 152–53.

persecution and oppression is a reflection of a cosmic battle."[20] John's rhetorical aims are clear: to side with the Beast is to side with Satan.

The Beast Was Like a Leopard, a Bear, and a Lion 13:3

As he continues, John reveals that the Beast is a hybrid creature: "And the beast which I saw was like a leopard, and its feet were as a bear, and its mouth was as the mouth of a lion" (13:2). In Scripture, hybrid creatures often represent evil.

The description of John's Beast, however, is more than just a hybrid. John's Beast combines attributes from the first three beasts of Daniel 7.[21] There is little question that Daniel 7 not only provides the background for understanding the Beast from the sea, but, in light of the fact that John's Beast has seven heads and ten horns, it is a composite of all four of Daniel's beasts. Of course, the four beasts in Daniel 7 are explicitly identified as representing earthly kings/kingdoms: "These great beasts, which are four *in number*, are four kings *who* will arise from the earth" (Dan 7:17).

The parallels between John's Beast and the four beasts of Dan 7:1–8 affirm that John's Beast also represents empire and its blasphemous claims. In fact, since John's Beast combines the features of all four of Daniel's beasts into one, it is reasonable to conclude that John's Beast represents all empires. As Resseguie affirms, "By combining Daniel's four beasts into one hybrid, John suggests that the beast is representative of all historical manifestations of evil empires."[22]

One of the Beast's Heads Was as If It Had Been Slain to Death 13:3

John continues his description of the Beast by noting, "one of his heads was as if it had been slain to death, and the plague of its death had been healed" (13:3). Though the translation of the verse may give the appearance that one of the heads merely looked like it was slain,[23] there are several indications that John considers that this head really was slain.

---

20. Hieke, "Reception," loc. 1200.
21. See Dan 7:4–6.
22. Resseguie, *Revelation*, loc. 3977–78.
23. See NAS: "as if it had been slain." The ESV reads, "seemed to have a mortal

For one, the narrative makes it clear that the Beast's head was actually slain. The next clause in 13:3, in fact, mentions, "the plague of his death" (13:3).[24] This is further supported by the declaration that the Beast is said to be the one who had the wound of the sword and "came to life" (13:14).[25]

In addition, the language that one of the heads of the Beast was, "as if it had been slain" (13:3) is intended as a parody of the Lamb. In John's introduction to the Lamb, he noted that the Lamb appeared, "as if it had been slain" (5:6). John used this expression because when he looked to see the Lamb it appeared to have been killed, yet it was "standing" (5:6). There is no question that John's reader/hearers would have understood that the Lamb actually was slain. The Four Living Creatures and the Twenty-Four Elders, in fact, affirm, "Worthy are you [the Lamb] to take the Book and open its seals because You were slain" (5:9). Bauckham contends, the "use in the same phrase in 13:3 cannot mean that the beast's head only appeared to be mortally wounded."[26]

Excursus: The Beast as a Parody of Christ

That one of the heads of the Beast was, "as if it had been slain" (13:3) reinforces John's conviction that the Beast is a blasphemous imitator of Christ. As Bauckham asserts, "It is clearly intended to create a parallel between Christ's death and resurrection, on the one hand, and the beast's mortal wound and its healing, on the other."[27]

That the Beast is a parody of Christ is subtle, and, yet, at the same time explicit. Beale notes, "Indeed, there are so many parallels between the description of the beast in ch. 13 and that of Christ elsewhere in the Apocalypse that it is clear that John intends to identify the beast with the grand

---

wound." The NET says, "appeared to have been killed." The NIV says, "seemed to have had a fatal wound." The NJK reads, "as if it had been mortally wounded." The NLT says, "seemed wounded beyond recovery." And the NRS says, "seemed to have received a death blow."

24. Note: this is repeated in 13:12; see also 13:14.

25. Note: the expression "the wound of the sword" is figurative for death by capital punishment.

26. Bauckham, *Climax*, 432.

27. Bauckham, *Climax*, 432.

nemesis himself rather than with just one emperor or even one historical empire."²⁸

That the Beast also has horns (13:1) provides another indication that the Beast is a blasphemous imitation of Jesus who has seven horns (5:6). Additionally, the fact that the Beast is given "authority over every tribe and people and tongue and nation" (13:7) parodies Christ, who purchased people, "from every tribe and tongue and people and nation" (5:9). Furthermore, as we proceed, we will learn that both the followers of the Lamb and the followers of the Beast have their corresponding names written on their foreheads (14:1; 13:16-17). As Resseguie concludes, "The beast mimics good, making it difficult to distinguish the genuine from the fraudulent, which accounts for evil's extraordinary appeal."²⁹

The Blasphemy of the Beast 13:4–6

John adds that the nations cry out, "'Who is like the Beast and who is able to wage war with him?'" (13:4).³⁰ The question itself is blasphemous because it is a distortion of a biblical expression used throughout the OT to affirm God's incomparability in relation to the false gods: "To whom then will you liken God? Or what likeness will you compare with Him?" (Isa 40:18).³¹

John continues, however, by noting, "And it was given to him a mouth speaking great things and blasphemies" (13:5). For John, the Beast's blasphemies (13:5, 6) constitute its false claims to deity and its demand for worship.³² John adds that the Beast, "opened his mouth in blasphemies against God" (13:6).

John then specifies that the Beast blasphemes, "His [God's] name and His dwelling place" (13:6). This is followed by what is best understood as a clarifying clause, "that is, those who are dwelling in heaven" (13:6).³³ The structure of the Greek in 13:6 suggests that this clause is the

28. Beale, *Revelation*, 690-91.
29. Resseguie, *Revelation*, loc. 4001-2.
30. See Dan 8:11, 25; 11:36-37
31. See Exod 8:10; 15:11; Isa 40:25; 44:7; 46:5; Ps 35:10; 71:19.
32. See 13:11-18; also, Dan 7:6, 8, 11, 20, 25; 11:36.
33. Note that the NAS, ESV, NET, NLT, and NRS all insert "that is" as I have done. The NIV and the NJK instead add the word "and."

focal point of the Beast's blasphemies. The fact that the Beast blasphemes "those who are dwelling in heaven" (13:6) indicates that it is the people of God who are the focus of the Beast's blasphemies. Consequently, by directing his blasphemy at the people of God, the Beast blasphemes both God's "name and His dwelling place" (13:6). This statement reflects a rich theology of the people of God. On the one hand, the people of God are the representatives—or one might say, "the image bearers"—of God. This means that to blaspheme the people of God is to blaspheme God, whose image they bear. On the other hand, the people of God also represent the place of God's presence on the earth. As such, they are His temple or His "dwelling place." Consequently, to blaspheme them is also to blaspheme God's "dwelling place."

It is important to recognize that the aim of the Beast's blasphemies is the people of God. DeSilva affirms this when he notes, "the Greek word *blasphēmia* covers a wider range of abusive speech and denunciation than the English 'blasphemy'. It is less likely that the speech of this group is directed against God and far more likely that it pertains to the Christian congregation."[34] Of course, the Beast does far more than direct his blasphemy at the people of God: he wages "war" against them (13:7).

By designating the people of God as "those who dwell in heaven," John indicates not their physical location but the location of the one to whom they give allegiance. The designation of the people of God as, "those who dwell in heaven" (13:6) also serves to distinguish them from the nations, whom John commonly refers to as, "those who inhabit the earth" (13:8, 14).[35]

Beast Acts for Forty-Two Months 13:5

John continues his account of the Beast from the sea by noting, "And it was given to him authority to act for forty-two months" (13:5). The time frame reminds John's reader/hearers that, although the Beast has authority to act, it is a limited authority.

The designation of "forty-two months," as I noted earlier, corresponds to the "1,260 days" during which the Two Witnesses minister (11:3) and in which the Woman flees into the wilderness (12:6). The forty-two month reign of the Beast is also the same time frame that the

---

34. DeSilva, *Discovering*, 126.
35. See 3:10; 6:10; 8:13; 11:10*; 13:8; 13:14*; 17:2, 8.

nations trample on the Holy City (11:2). This suggests that the Beast's rule is contemporaneous with the ministering of the Two Witnesses and the Woman's refuge in the wilderness.

Authority to Make War with the Saints 13:7–8

John next informs us, "And it was given to him to make war with the saints and to overcome them" (13:7).[36] As noted above, the Beast not only blasphemes God and His people, but he wages war against them. In fact, John adds that the Beast not only wages war against the people of God but is able to "overcome" them. This statement would be truly shocking if it were not for the fact that John already made virtually the same statement in 11:7. That 13:7 closely parallels the language of 11:7 reinforces the conviction that the present account of the Beast serves to elaborate on the "war" against the Two Witnesses (11:7).[37]

Tragically, despite the blasphemous and boastful ways of the Beast, "all who dwell on the earth will worship him" (13:8).

Call for Perseverance and Faith 13:9–10

If Anyone Has Ears 13:9

Revelation 13:9 pauses to exhort the reader/hearers: "If anyone has an ear, let him hear." The depiction of the Beast and his waging war against the people of God is intended to be understood by those who have ears to hear. The exhortation, "If anyone has an ear, let him hear," of course, reminds the reader that reality is deeper than what is normally perceived.[38]

---

36. The NAS reads, "It was also given to him." Similarly, the ESV and NRS add "also." The problem with the addition of "also" is that 13:7 is clarifying what the Beasts authority looks like. It is not adding to the Beast's abilities but further defines the abilities that he already has.

37. Note in both 11:7 and 13:7, John refers to a "Beast" who "makes war" and "conquers" the people of God.

38. Beale notes that the phrase "occurs in connection with symbolic or parabolic revelation." Beale, *Revelation*, 236.

If Anyone Is to Go Into Captivity or Be Killed 13:10

John adds, "If anyone is to go into captivity, into captivity they go; if anyone is to be killed by the sword, by the sword they will be killed" (13:10). John's declaration appears somewhat matter-of-fact. The result of the Beast's work is that those who are to be arrested and killed will be arrested and killed.

Here Is the Patient Endurance and the Faith 13:10

John concludes, "Here is the patient endurance and the faith of the saints" (13:10).[39] The exhortation to "patient endurance" reminds us of John's self-identification to his reader/hearers: "I, John, your brother and sharer in the . . . patient endurance" (1:9). God's people must endure. After all, the Dragon is pursuing them (12:13) and he has empowered the Beast to do his work for Him!

Of course, we know that the death of the people of God is not the end of their story. After all, Jesus has the keys of death and Hades (1:18). In fact, as we will learn, "And the souls of those who had been beheaded because of the testimony of Jesus and because of the word of God . . . they came to life and they reigned with Christ" (20:4–5).

Conclusion

By depicting pagan rulers as the Beast, John draws an ironic portrait of human rulers. Instead of humanity fulfilling its role as divine image bearers and ruling over the beasts,[40] John depicts human rulers as beasts. As Resseguie affirms, "The monster represents what happens when humanity claims the loyalty and obedience that belongs to God alone: it ceases 'to be human and becomes bestial.'"[41] That the Beast signifies imperial rule is evident in John's account of the Beast (13:1–8). John's consistent use of four to refer to totality with regard to the creation suggests that by combining the four beasts of Daniel 7, which are explicitly said to be "kings" (Dan 7:17), into one the Beast is the embodiment of all empires in history.

---

39. See 14:13.
40. See Gen 1:26, 28.
41. Resseguie, *Revelation*, loc. 3984–85; citing Caird, *Revelation*, 162.

John, of course, wants his reader/hearers to recognize that, despite the fact that the Beast's external appearance may be perceived—at least by those who fail to be discerning (see 13:18)—as good, and for some, even Christlike, the Beast is actually empowered by the Dragon and his claims to royalty are false. Unfortunately, many will believe that his claims to royalty are legitimate. The result is that the whole earth, "worshiped the dragon because he gave his authority to the beast, and they worshiped the beast" (13:4). The followers of the Beast, in fact, not only worship him, but they also worship the Dragon (13:4).

In addition, as we proceed, John's portrait of the Beast intends to assure his reader/hearers that Rome's rule is only temporary. As Carey explains, "Roman imperialism may be powerful and glorious, but it lives on domination and exploitation. To participate in the imperial order is to defile oneself. Moreover, Roman power is temporary and illusory. The Beast may conquer the Lamb's followers for a period (13:7), but in the end the Beast goes down in judgment while the Lamb illuminates the new city."[42]

What does all this mean? Carey notes, "Revelation stands in a tradition of Jewish visions about imperial rule." The significance of this cannot be overstated. Carey adds, "These comparisons provide Revelation's basic counter-imperial script. It works at two levels, the moral and the pragmatic. Roman imperialism may be powerful and glorious, but it lives on domination and exploitation."[43] Resseguie adds, "Two perspectives thus emerge at this point in the narrative. From the perspective of those who follow the beast, it is a godlike being, exercising worldwide power and unrestrained authority. From John's and the reader's point of view, however, the beast is a counterfeit deity subject to God's inscrutable plan and divine sanction."[44]

John, in true apocalyptic style, writes to inform his reader/hearers so that they may see things the way they really are. Although it may appear that the Beast rules, in reality, the Father and the Lamb are on the throne. In saying this, however, we cannot look past the fact that John must have been concerned. After all, some within the seven churches had already compromised with the Beast and others were being tempted to do so.

---

42. Carey, "Counter-Imperial," loc. 2223–24.
43. Carey, "Counter-Imperial," loc. 2222.
44. Resseguie, *Revelation*, loc. 4018–20.

We, too, should not look past the Beast's deceptive aims. After all, the Beast's Christlike appearance is directed at deceiving even the people of God.

Revelation 13:1—14:5
The Beast, the False Prophet, and the 144,000 Continued

If the first beast is the Roman Empire, the second beast is some entity that induces people of the world to give loyalty to the empire and its emperors.[1]

Worshipping the beast and its image, hence receiving the beast's stamp of approval, provides access to participation in the Roman economy and the enjoyment of physical security. Refusal of such worship would bring the opposite.[2]

The beast that comes up from the abyss [who] will make war on them and conquer them and kill them" (11:7). This deadly opponent, apparently the same figure as the king of the war-locusts (9:11), will be the focus of 13:11–18, where his imperial role as propagandist for the emperor is revealed. In that role, the two prophetic witnesses must be destroyed so that the imperial message cannot be unveiled as the diabolic lie that it is.[3]

Although it seems likely that John meant 666 to refer to Nero, we should not limit the meaning of the number of the beast or the symbol of the beast to one demented ruler. Structural evil is bigger than the reign of Nero; any human entity that usurps allegiance that belongs to God is beastly. It is possible that the number six, used three times, simply was an abstract symbol for John.[4]

---

1. Kraybill, *Allegiance*, 53.
2. DeSilva, *Discovering*, 207–8.
3. Howard-Brook and Gwyther, *Unveiling Empire*, loc. 3945.
4. Kraybill, *Allegiance*, 67.

REVELATION 13:1—14:5

The Beast from the Land 13:11–12a

IN 13:11, JOHN INTRODUCES us to "another Beast." If the first Beast corresponds to the nation(s)—i.e., empire—then this second Beast, who is later identified as "the False Prophet,"[5] corresponds to the religious elements within the empire.[6]

False Prophet Has Two Horns Like a Lamb 13:11

John states that the False Prophet, "had two horns like a lamb and was speaking as a dragon" (13:11). That the False Prophet has a lamb-like appearance but spoke as a dragon continues John's stress on the deceptive nature of the Dragon and the Beasts. As with the first Beast, his deceptive aims are concealed by his Christ-like appearance. Resseguie observes that the False Prophet has, "a deceptive trait that makes it difficult to distinguish good from evil."[7]

The False Prophet's role as a deceiver is made explicit by John: "it deceives those who inhabit the earth" (13:14). Beale summarizes the two Beasts: "Whereas the first Beast speaks loudly and defiantly against God and His people, the second beast makes the first Beast's claims sound plausible and persuasive."[8]

The False Prophet Exercises the Authority of the Beast 13:12a

John adds that the False Prophet "exercises all the authority of the first Beast" (13:12). Of course, the authority of the first Beast came from the Dragon (13:2). Consequently, the False Prophet's authority and even its ability to perform miracles must also derive from the Dragon. That the Dragon, the Beast, and the False Prophet appear together in 16:13

---

5. See 16:13; 19:20; 20:10. In light of the fact that John identifies the second Beast as the False Prophet, it might be easier for our sakes to refer to the first Beast as "the Beast" and the second Beast as "the False Prophet."

6. Of course, the problem with this designation is that making a strict distinction between the political and the religious is to impose a modern understanding on an ancient text. We must recall that there was no separation of church and state in the ancient world. Furthermore, the socio-political-economic spheres were highly intertwined.

7. Resseguie, *Revelation*, loc. 4509. The significance of this cannot be overstated.

8. Beale, *Revelation* 708.

bolsters the connection between the False Prophet and Satan. In fact, 16:14 states that the "signs," which presumably are those that the False Prophet performs, "are the spirits of demons" (16:14). This too further establishes the connection between the Beast and the Dragon.

False Prophet Uses Miraculous Abilities to Deceive 13:12b–15a

The intent of the False Prophet's exercising of the Beast's authority is that "the earth and those who inhabit it to worship the first Beast" (13:12). In order to facilitate the worship of the first Beast, the False Prophet, "performs great signs, so that it even makes fire come down out of heaven to the earth in the presence of people" (13:13). On account of these signs, the False Prophet, "deceives those who inhabit the Earth because of the signs which it was given to it to do" (13:14).[9]

The False Prophet not only performs signs, but it tells, "those who inhabit the earth to make an image to the Beast who has the plague of the sword and came to life" (13:14). Certainly one of the grander signs that the False Prophet performs is that it has the ability, "to give breath to the image of the Beast, so that the image of the Beast might speak" (13:15). The False Prophet's ability "to give breath to the image of the beast" (13:15) corresponds to the "breath of life from God" (11:11) that was granted to the Two Witnesses.

> Excursus: The False Prophet and the Two Witnesses
>
> There is, therefore, a sense in which the False Prophet assumes a role similar to the Two Witnesses. Thus, the False Prophet like the Two Witnesses, has "authority" (13:12; 11:6*).[10] And the authority of the False Prophet and the Two Witnesses is linked with the ability to do miracles (13:13–15; 11:6). Of course, the contrast could not be greater. Whereas the Two

---

9. John's description of the False Prophet serves to remind the reader/hearer of the words of Jesus when He warned, "For false Christs and false prophets will arise and will show great signs and wonders, so as to mislead, if possible, even the elect" (Matt 24:24). In a much more difficult passage, Paul alludes to the coming of a lawless one who will deceive by means of "all power and signs and false wonders" (2 Thess 2:9).

10. Only the NRS uses "authority" in 11:6. All other major English translations use "power."

Witnesses are "two" because their testimony is true, the False Prophet is, as the moniker states, a "false" prophet.

At the same time, the False Prophet is associated with the person of the Holy Spirit so that the Dragon, the Beast, and the False Prophet comprise a counterfeit, Satanic trinity. The role of the Dragon and the Beasts in imitating God, Christ, and the Holy Spirit, as well as the people of God, should not be overlooked. Satan's weapon with which he wages war is deception. His deception is not so blatant and obvious that everyone will say: "Hey, look at that dragon. Let's stay away from him!" Instead, the Dragon and the Beasts appear to be good! What they profess appears to be the truth. And, I might add, even though False Prophet's lies are clearly evil, they appeal to our pride, and our desire for security, wealth, comfort, and peace. And in doing so, they may quite easily cause us to look past their obviously evil nature so that we too follow.

Consequently, the False Prophet is depicted as the imitator of the Holy Spirit and as one who performs works that correspond to the work of the people of God. The major differences, of course, are that the source of the False Prophet's authority is the Dragon and that the False Prophet lures humanity to worship the Beast and not Christ. Furthermore, we should note, the False Prophet coerces obedience, as we shall see, by means of the threat of economic ostracization and death. The Two Witnesses, however, suffer economic ostracization and death.

False Prophet Ensures Compliance 13:15b–17

The depiction of the False Prophet includes two primary motivations by which the False Prophet secures compliance.

First, the False Prophet ensures that "whoever does not worship the image of the Beast should be killed" (13:15). The threat of suffering, especially death is a common means by which empires secure allegiance. Second, the False Prophet also secures conformity to the ways of the empire by forcing, "all, the small and the great, and the rich and the poor, and the free and the slaves, so that a Mark is given to them on their right hand or on their forehead" (13:16). John then adds, "no one will be able to buy or to sell, except the one who has the Mark" (13:17). Consequently, the False Prophet secures compliance by restricting dissenters ability to participate in the empire's economic system.

Consequently, those who inhabit the earth are compelled to worship the Beast not merely to avoid death (13:15), but also so that they may participate in the economic system upon which most in the Roman world were dependent for daily survival (13:17). And those among the people of God are similarly tempted to conform to the ways of the empire so that they too may partake of the imperial system and eat.

There is a deep irony running throughout the depiction of the two Beasts which John's reader/hearers are surely intended to recognize. Namely, that humanity, which was made in God's image and called both to worship Him alone and to rule the beasts, is portrayed as rejecting the very purposes for which they were created and instead as worshiping the beasts. Human rulers, therefore, not only fail to rule over the beasts, they have become them.

Here Is Wisdom 13:18

John concludes his description of the False Prophet by exhorting them, "Here is the wisdom. Let the one having a mind calculate the number" (13:18).[11]

The exhortation itself presumes that John's reader/hearer were able to discern what the number of the Beast was—which affirms that its meaning was not buried in a secret code only to be unearthed by some twentieth or twenty-first-century prophetic pundit. With regard to John's use of "mind and wisdom," Dixon affirms, "In both Daniel and Revelation the combinations of these terms is used to exhort the faithful to exercise spiritual insight in order to understand correctly the eschatological tribulation and persecution brought about by an evil king who practices deceit and false authority."[12]

What is it that they were to figure out? John continues by adding that they were to "calculate the number of the Beast" (13:18), which, John says, "is of a person and his number is 666" (13:18).[13]

11. See the parallel statement in 17:9. See also, Dan 12:10; Mark 13:14.

12. Dixon, *Exalted*, 120.

13. The number 666 has a prehistory in the OT. 1 Kgs 10:14 notes that Solomon received 666 talents of gold yearly (See 2 Chr 9:13; Ezra 2:13). Reading the passage in context suggests that this was not a good thing! After all, kings were not supposed to

Excursus: 666

When it comes to discerning the number of the Beast and the meaning of 666, there is a general consensus within the scholarly world today that John had in view the ancient practice of gematria.[14] The practice of gematria ascribes numerical values to the letters of the alphabet. By using gematria, individuals were able to embed or hide the reference to something else by using the numerical value of the word.[15]

John says that the Mark represents either, "the name of the Beast or the number of his name" (13:17). We know that the numerical equivalent of the word "beast" (Greek *therion*), when transliterated[16] into Hebrew has the numerical equivalent of 666. This may account for the first part of the statement: it is "the name of the Beast" (13:17).

The larger question is what does John mean when he says that it is also, "the number of his name" (13:17)? The most widely held conviction is that it refers to Nero.[17] There is, however, one oddity in the supposition that the "number of his name" refers to Nero. Namely, one must use the Greek

---

acquire too much wealth (See Deut 17:14-17).

14. See especially Bauckham, *Climax*, 384-407. Bauckham adds to his discussion of John's use of numbers with relation to Nero and 666 by commenting on the legends of Nero's return that circulated around the empire in the late first century (Bauckham, *Climax*, 407-31). See also, Beale, *Revelation*, 718-20; Smalley, *Revelation*, 351-52.

15. There was graffiti discovered in the ruins of Pompey that read, "I love the girl whose number is 545."

16. To "transliterate" means to provide a letter for letter correspondence. In other words, the Greek word for "beast" is *therion*. *Therion* is a transliteration, or letter-for-letter equivalent, of the Greek word for "beast." The English word "beast" is a translation of the Greek word *therion*; i.e., this is what *therion* means.

One might be suspicious of using *gematria* because one has to first transliterate *therion* in Hebrew and then find its numerical value. Some have suggested that this may have been an extra layer of protection for the Christian community. Regardless, the fact that John has no qualms about using Hebrew letters or words is evident in the account of the Fifth Trumpet, "They have as king over them, the angel of the Abyss; his name in Hebrew is Abaddon, and in Greek, he has the name Apollyon" (9:11). John also uses Hebrew in the famed "Armageddon" passage: "they gathered them to the place that is called in Hebrew is called, 'Harmagedon'" (16:16)—see commentary in 16:16 for further discussion.

17. Bauckham notes that "few of the many other solutions by gematria that have been proposed offer a *name*, which the phrase 'the number of his name' (Rev 13:17; 15:2) requires, and of those few which do this seems eminently the most preferable" (Bauckham, *Climax*, 387; emphasis original).

version of Nero's Latin name (Neron) and then transliterate it into Hebrew. While the Greek version of Nero is "Nero," the Latin version is "Neron"—with the additional "n." The final "n" is needed in order to arrive at 666. Without this "n," Nero's name equals to 616.

That Nero's name in Greek is 616 further supports the proposition that the number 666 indicates Nero. There are, in fact, a few manuscripts that read in 13:18, "616."[18] The presence of 616 in these manuscripts may be accounted for by the fact that scribes were convinced that the number referred to Nero, but they knew that Nero's name in Greek only equaled 616.[19] Thus, perhaps thinking that they were correcting a mistake in the manuscript, they altered the text to 616 in order to conform to their conviction that the Beast was Nero.

Conclusion 13:11–18

To understand well John's depiction of the False Prophet we must bear in mind that the economic and religious aims of the empire were deeply intertwined. In order for someone to partake in the empire's economic system and to receive the provisions it provided,[20] one must also participate in Rome's socio-political-religious system. From John's perspective, to do so was to participate in the worship of the Dragon/Satan.

Although John's Beast was embodied by Rome, and, perhaps, Nero in particular, we should be cautious about concluding that the meaning of the Beast relates only to the past. DeSilva notes:

> John uses Nero as a kind of symbol to characterize the Principate: he invites his hearers to see in Nero the true character of the Principates.[21]

DeSilva concludes:

18. Beale states that "Almost all manuscripts support, 'six hundred sixty-six,' which is the probable reading" (Beale, *Revelation*, 719n298).

19. Beale notes that 616 could be accounted for by an effort to associate Caligula with the Beast (Beale, *Revelation*, 719n298).

20. Empire does not necessarily ensure anyone anything. Over 90 percent of the population in the Roman Empire lived day by day. The uncertainty of food and daily survival, however, makes participation in the economic system of Rome a virtual necessity. See Carter, *Roman Empire*, 10–11.

21. DeSilva, *Discovering*, 160.

When John uses images from Daniel representing world empires to speak of a "beast" (Rev 13:1-2; see Dan 7:3-7), fatally wounded but healed (Rev 13:3), worshiped by 'the inhabitants of the earth' in a manner involving a cult image (Rev 13:4, 8, 14), and exercising authority over a multi-ethnic, multi-lingual, multi-national empire (Rev 13:7), the Roman emperors were immediately available to John's hearers as plausible referents, whose cult was practiced in every one of their cities and whose rule and divinity were everywhere proclaimed.[22]

Excursus: the Beasts today

In order to understand John's account of the Beasts (13:1-18) we would do well to recall John's intended contrast between the Lamb's means of exercising power and the Beast's means of exercising power. For John, the Lamb manifests power in sacrificial love for the sake of the other. And, although we know that this is true power, it is not the way the world does power. In fact, we may even say that the Lamb's power will not get you very far in this world.

Throughout history, societies may be defined by the ever-present struggle for power. Those in power strive first and foremost to remain in power. Such efforts to hold onto power are almost always at the expense of the poor and the marginalized. In the ancient world, and perhaps even in much of the world today, the poor and the marginalized are far more concerned with daily survival than with trying to "get ahead."[23]

By the end of the first century, subsistence in the Roman world was due in large part to one's participation in the Roman imperial system and the cult of the emperor. This system served as a reminder for the common person that they were dependent upon those in power for their survival. The belief was that the gods had granted the emperor and those in power the responsibility to maintain stability and "peace" throughout the Roman world.

John writes to contrast the power of empire (Rome) with the power of the Lamb. In doing so, he alerts the people of God that Roman power was beastly and Satanic. As Carey notes,

---

22. DeSilva, *Unholy Allegiances*, loc. 677–681.
23. See Carter, *Roman Empire*, 10–13.

"The inhabitants of the earth may voice their submission to the Beast, but John's audience knows its nature from the beginning. The Beast is, well, Beast-ly. It rules by Dragon power. It devours the saints. While Revelation eventually reveals that the Beast has been condemned by God, it provides the basic reasons for resisting the Beast right from the beginning."[24]

We must be careful, then, in reading the book of Revelation and concluding that "that was then and this is now." As Boring notes:

> The beast is not merely 'Rome' . . . it is the inhuman, antihuman arrogance of empire which has come to expression in Rome—but not only there. . . . All who support the cultural religion, in or out of the church, however Lamb-like they may appear, are agents of the beast. All propaganda that entices humanity to idolize human empire is an expression of this beastly power that wants to appear Lamb-like.[25]

Koester adds, "The contrasts are made starkly not because the alternatives were obvious to his readers, but because the alternatives were not obvious."[26] Resseguie warns, "Some within the Christian community were willing to merge Jerusalem and Babylon, to follow the way of the Lamb and the way of the beast, and to assimilate to the norms, values, and beliefs of the dominant culture."[27] This, I fear, is as true today in many Western Christian churches as it was then.

---

24. Carey, "Counter-Imperial," loc. 2197–99.
25. Boring, *Revelation*, 156–57.
26. Koester, *Revelation*, 136.
27. Resseguie, *Revelation*, loc. 4293–95.

Revelation 14:1–5
The Beast, the False Prophet, and the 144,000

REVELATION 14:1–5 OPENS WITH Christ and the 144,000 on Mount Zion (14:1). This account has certainly led to a variety of interpretations. The primary questions relate to "when" this scene takes place in history and "where" the scene actually occurs.[1] In my opinion, such questions have their place, but they tend to obscure or overlook the more important narrative concerns: namely, that the 144,000, who have the Seal of God, stand in contrast with those who inhabit the earth and have received the Mark of the Beast.

The Lamb and the 144,000 on Mount Zion 14:1

John begins with, "And I saw, and behold the Lamb standing on Mount Zion and with Him the 144,000" (14:1).

In Scripture, "Zion" often becomes synonymous with Jerusalem. Zion, in fact, is considered to be the true city of God. It was on Zion's mountain that God had His dwelling.[2] Zion is also a place of justice and peace. As a result, those who dwell in Zion are said to have security.

---

1. For some, it refers to a heavenly location (Mounce, *Revelation*, 265). Others place it on the earth (Ladd, *Revelation*, 188–90). Walvoord sees this as a reigning of Christ from Jerusalem during the millennium (*Revelation*, 214–15).

2. Ps 2:6. Mount Zion is central to Psalm 2, which was widely acknowledged as a Messianic Psalm. It has already been applied to Christ several times in the book of Revelation. Caird contends that the book of Revelation should be understood as a Christian reflection of Psalm 2 (*Revelation*, 178).

John's seeing "the Lamb standing on Mount Zion" (14:1) indicates that the Lamb is indeed the promised King.[3] That Jesus is the world's true King stands in marked contrast with the blasphemous claims of the Beast (13:1–8)! Standing with Jesus are the 144,000. They are described as those who had, "His name and the name of His Father having been written on their foreheads" (14:1). There is little doubt that the 144,000 serve to contrast those who have the Mark of the Beast.

John Hears a Voice 14:2–3a

In 14:2, John hears, "a voice from heaven like the voice of many waters and like the voice of great thunder and the voice which I heard was like the voice of harpists playing on their harps" (14:2).

Upon reading this, our initial suspicion may well be that this is the voice of Jesus. After all, in the opening of the first story, John observes that Jesus's "voice was like the voice of many waters" (1:15). As John continues His description, however, we quickly realize that it is not Jesus's voice but the voice of the 144,000.[4] This becomes apparent as John continues. John adds, "And they sang a new song" (14:3). The use of "they" affirms that it is the voice of a group. John makes it explicit that the voice is that of the 144,000 when he states, "and no one was able to learn the song except the one hundred and forty-four thousand" (14:3).

Although it might be initially surprising that the depiction of the voice of the 144,000 accords with the voice of Jesus, we would do well to be reminded that John regularly describes the people of God in terms that identify them with Christ. John did this when he states that the Two Witnesses were killed, "where their Lord was crucified" (11:8). The people of God, in other words, are not just those who follow the Lamb (14:4), they are those who represent the Lamb. And, perhaps we could add, they are those who imitate the Lamb.

They Have Been Purchased 14:3b–4

John continues his description of the 144,000 by noting that they "have been purchased from the earth" (14:3). In 14:4, he adds, "These have

---

3. See Ps 2:6.

4. In 19:6, it is the voice of the Great Multitude. See discussion in the commentary on 19:1–6.

been purchased from humankind as first fruits to God and to the Lamb." John's description of the people of God as those who "have been purchased" (14:3, 4) serves as an exhortation for his reader/hearers that there is no need to give in to the threats of the Beast. For, although the Beast prohibited those without the mark to be "able to buy or sell" (13:17), they are those who "have been purchased" (14:3).

They Have Not Been Defiled With Women 14:4

John adds to the description of the 144,000, "These are the ones who have not been defiled with women, for they are pure" (14:4).[5] Though this statement admittedly has a bit of a cringe factor for modern readers.[6] Resseguie, however, captures the significance of the language, "If porn-words are metaphors for religious infidelity, then 'virgin' and virginity represent the opposite. The 144,000 'virgins' remain unentangled with the norms, values, and beliefs of the dominant culture."[7]

For John, however, it was simply another means of depicting the 144,000 as holy warriors. This conclusion derives from the fact that only men of military age and who were sexually pure were allowed to engage in battle.[8]

These Are the Ones Who Follow the Lamb 14:4b

Perhaps John's most significant description of the 144,000 occurs when he says, "these are the ones who are following the Lamb wherever He goes" (14:4). The indication that they are "following the Lamb wherever He goes" (14:4) may be understood in one of two ways.

First, it could be understood in terms of the people of God following Christ into heaven. This reading gains support from the fact that 14:1–5 seemingly functions as an *inclusio* with the throne room scene in 4:1—5:14. If so, the scene begins in the heavenly throne room (4:1—5:14) and concludes in the heavenly throne room (14:1–5). The

---

5. They were not required to be "virgins" as the ESV, NET, NLT, NKJ, and NRS read. They were to be abstinent during the time of said war. Hence, the translation here (and in the NIV) of "pure" (the NAS uses "chaste").

6. Kraybill refers to it as an "unfortunate metaphor" (Kraybill, *Allegiance*, 117).

7. Resseguie, *Revelation*, 22.

8. Purity was required because Israelite soldiers were fighting in a holy war. See Deut 23:9—14; 1 Sam 21:5; 2 Sam 11:9–13.

parallels between the account of the Lamb and the 144,000 in 14:1–5 and the throne room scene of 4:1—5:14 include the fact that the 144,000 sing "a new song" (14:3), which parallels the "new song" in 5:9. Also, in both accounts, the Lamb is standing (14:1; 5:6). Also, each account incorporates the sound of thunder (14:2; 4:5). Additionally, both include the presence of harps (14:2; 5:8), the four Living Creatures (14:3; 4:6), and the Elders (14:3; 4:4). Finally, both passages include a reference to those who were "purchased" (14:4; 5:9).

Second, the 144,000 may be understood as following the Lamb in the present. This understanding gains support from the fact that one of John's primary emphases is to contrast the people of God with the followers of the Beast. Thus, Resseguie affirms, "The 144,000 are the spiritually faithful who remain unentangled with the norms, values, and beliefs of the dominant culture."[9] This suggestion, however, does not eliminate the possibility that John's vision of the 144,000 standing with Christ on Mount Zion is also a proleptic look at the future blessedness of the people of God. After all, a preview of the people of God following the Lamb in the eternal city would also serve as an encouragement for them to persevere.

Perhaps, it is best to conclude that the 144,000 represent the faithful people of God who follow the way of Christ in the present, and, as a result, they are also the ones who will stand with the Lamb on Mount Zion.

They Are Blameless 14:5

John closes his description of the people of God on Mount Zion by noting, "in their mouth[10] there was not found a lie, they are blameless" (14:5). That they are "blameless" corresponds with the fact that they are pure (14:4) and is probably best understood in terms of their fitness or purity as holy warriors.

Excursus: What Is the Mark of the Beast?

John refers to the "Mark" seven times in the book of Revelation[11] and in each occurrence, it denotes loyalty to the Beast.

---

9. Resseguie, *Revelation*, loc. 4318–19.

10. Note the Greek for "mouth" is singular. This is another example of how the people of God are viewed as a collective: i.e., a singularity that represents a plurality.

11. See 13:16, 17; 14:9, 11; 16:2; 19:20; 20:4.

That the Mark may be located on the forehead most certainly serves to indicate one's ownership and loyalty. As noted above, the Mark provides its recipient with the ability to participate in the empire's economic system in return for one's loyalty to the empire. The fact that the Mark may also be placed on the right hand suggests that the means by which the Beast gains loyalty is by offering an economic incentive.

Though our modern Bibles place a chapter break between 13:18 and 14:1, there was no such break in the ancient texts. This means that the reintroduction of the 144,000 (14:1–5), who have the Seal of God, follows immediately after the description of the False Prophet and his forcing all the inhabitants of the earth to receive the Mark. In order then to fully grasp John's intent with the Mark, we must note the evident contrasts that John includes between the Mark of the Beast and the Seal of God.

There is little doubt that the Mark on the followers of the Beast mimics the Seal of God on the 144,000.[12] That the Mark of the Beast stands in contrast to the Seal of God is evident from the fact that John immediately follows the account of the Mark of the Beast with an account of the 144,000 who have been sealed: "having His name and the name of His Father written on their foreheads" (14:1).[13] That the Mark and the Seal are on the foreheads likely connotes a sign of ownership: whereas the Mark of the Beast indicates that they are owned by the Beast, the Seal of God indicates that they are owned by the Lamb. Moreover, that both the Mark and the Seal represent the name, either the name of the Beast or the name of Christ or the Father, furthers the contrast between the two. In addition, both the Mark and the Seal entail economic implications. Those who have the Mark are able to purchase and sell (13:17); whereas, the followers of the Lamb are those who "have been purchased" (14:3, 4). Therefore, in the words of Resseguie, "The tattoo is a travesty of the seal that is imprinted on the saints' foreheads."[14]

12. See 7:3, 4*, 5, 8; 9:4.

13. Since the Seal of God does not carry with it any economic benefits, there is no need for it to be on their right hand.

14. Resseguie, *Revelation*, loc. 4091.

In light of the fact that the Mark of the Beast contrasts with the Seal of God, we may say emphatically that the Mark of the Beast is not a literal mark. After all, the Seal of God is not "literally" branded on the foreheads of the people of God. Instead, the Seal of God represents the divine presence of the Holy Spirit within the people of God.

It is somewhat grieving that these questions are so relevant today. Unfortunately, there are many in our modern churches who contend that the Mark of the Beast is a literal mark. By doing so, however, they fail to appreciate what John is telling the churches. One of John's ambitions was to exhort his reader/hearers to "Watch out! Beware! Stay awake!" The belief that it is a literal mark minimizes the need to, "watch out, beware, or stay awake." After all, if the Mark is a literal mark, it will be pretty easy to spot. Furthermore, many who suggest that the Mark is a literal mark suggest that it is not something that Christians can receive. If a Christian cannot receive such a mark, and if it will be obvious to all, then there is little need to "watch out, beware, or stay awake."

John's descriptions of the Beast and the False Prophet were directed at the churches to whom he wrote. John was concerned that they may be deceived and even compelled to compromise with the Beast and its idolatrous system so that they might either gain economically or avoid suffering and death (13:10).

John's concerns were similar to Jesus's admonition, "You cannot serve God and wealth" (Matt 6:24). Understanding that the Mark can be found anytime we compromise our faith in order to ensure financial security, power, and pleasure, or anytime we compromise our commitment to Christ in order to escape persecution and suffering heightens the importance of the book of Revelation's warning. To propose that it is a literal mark undermines John's concerns and suggests that we may take solace as long as we have not received such a mark.

Third, the notion that this is a literal Mark is somewhat silly. After all, how will anyone be deceived? Sure, it is possible that some who have no knowledge or regard for the Bible will gladly accept it. But if we literalize the accounts of the Beasts, then will it not be obvious when you see a seven-headed and ten-horned leopard/bear/lion-like creature followed by a two-horned lamb-like creature that speaks as a dragon, calls fire down from heaven, and demands that we worship the talking statue that he/she erected? Oh, and by the way, if you see such creatures, you should probably avoid getting the stamp with his name or image on your foreheads or your right hands.

Revelation 14:6–20
Six "Another" Angels and
One like the Son of Man

Introduction

THE SECTION OF 14:6–20 serves to prepare the reader/hearers for the final judgment, which follows in the account of the Seven Bowls in 15:1—16:20. In 14:6–20, John presents a distinct section the forms around seven beings: six angels and "One like the Son of Man" (14:14).

That 14:6–20 forms a distinct section within the second story (the heavenly vision: 4:1—16:21) is evident from the fact that six times, in two sets of triads, John refers to "another angel" (14:6, 8, 9, 15, 17, 18).[1] In the first triad, the angels are even counted: "And I saw another angel" (14:6); "and another angel, a second one, followed saying . . ." (14:8); "and another angel, a third one, followed them saying . . ." (14:9). The first triad of angels are also linked with one another by the fact that each of the angels makes a pronouncement: "saying" (14:7, 8, 9).[2] The second triad of angels, though not numbered, are linked with one another by the fact that each of the angels either, "came out of the temple" (14:15, 17), or "came out from the altar" (14:18), which is within the temple. In

---

1. Calling the first angel "another angel" seems to suggest that there was one prior. What angel might John be referring to? The most recent angel was the "angel" who stood on the land and the sea with the scroll in his hand (10:1). The problem is that there are no other indications that John is linking the angel of 14:6 with the angel of 10:1. It is more likely that John uses "another angel" in 14:6 to establish the link with the two uses of "another angel" that follow (14:8, 9).

2. Note that the first and third angels frame the first triad with "saying with a loud voice" (14:7, 9); whereas the second angel is merely, "saying" (14:8).

addition, the angels of the second triad are also linked in that each either has, "a sharp sickle" (14:17), or commands those who have such a sickle to, "Send your sickle (14:15, 17).[3]

This means that there are two distinct units within this section. The first unit, 14:6–11, contains the first triad of angels, and consists of the proclamations of the first three occurrences of "another angel." The second unit, 14:14–20, contains the second triad of angels. This unit, however, is introduced by the appearance of "One like a Son of Man" (14:14)." The inclusion of the "One like a Son of Man" makes a total of seven beings in this section.

In the middle of this section, John inserts a parenthetical exhortation to the reader/hearers encouraging them to persevere (14:13).

Warnings of the First Triad of Angels 14:6–11

Each of the angels in the first triad is introduced as "saying" (14:7, 8, 9) something. The content of their sayings includes either a prophetic call to repent or a warning of impending judgment.

The First Angel Says 14:6–7

The first "another angel" has "an eternal gospel to proclaim to those who are sitting on the earth and to every nation and tribe and tongue and people" (14:6). The angel exhorts them, "Fear God and give to Him glory, because the hour of His judgment has come" (14:7). The exhortation of this first angel (14:7) recalls the "great fear" (11:11) that came upon those "who were watching them" (11:11).

The Second Angel Says 14:8

The second "another angel" follows, saying, "Fallen, fallen is Babylon the Great" (14:8). The proclamation that "Babylon the Great" has fallen comes as somewhat of a surprise. Although John makes reference to "Babylon" six times in the book of Revelation (14:8; 16:19; 17:5; 18:2, 10, 21), this is its first occurrence.[4] That John refers to Babylon as "fallen"

---

3. John mentions a "sickle" seven times between the introduction to the "One like a Son of Man" in 14:14 and the close of the account in 14:19. See 14:14, 15, 16, 17, 18*, 19.

4. John does refer to the "Great City" in 11:8, which refers to Babylon in each of its

without any prior introduction as to who/what Babylon is suggests that his reader/hearers may have known who/what Babylon was. That "Babylon" was well-known in the first century as an epithet for Rome[5] reinforces this supposition.

The second angel's exclamation regarding the fall of Babylon adds to the first angel's cry to, "Fear God and give to Him glory" (14:7). After all, not only is it true that "the hour" of God's judgment has come (14:7), but now we learn that Babylon offers no hope (14:8).

The Third Angel Says 14:9–11

The third "another angel" follows, saying, "If anyone worships the Beast and his image and receives the Mark on their forehead or on their hand, they themselves will drink from the wine of the wrath of God" (14:9–10).

This angel's warning certainly references back to the account of the second Beast in 13:11–18. As such, the angel's proclamation serves as an exhortation to the reader/hearers not to compromise. Although the lure to receive the Mark in order to participate in the Roman economy, which for most in the empire was about ensuring one's daily food as much as it was anything else, was strong, this angel puts allegiance to Rome in an eternal context. Those who worship the Beast and his image will experience the wrath of God.[6]

Exhortation to the People of God 14:12–13

After the first triad of angels, John inserts an exhortation to his reader/hearers: "Here is the patient endurance of the saints, the ones who are keeping the commandments of God and the faith of Jesus" (14:12). It is important to note that John identifies the people of God as "the saints" (14:12; see 13:10) and as "the ones who are keeping the commandments of God and the faith of Jesus" (14:12). These exhortations serve to remind the reader/hearers that what they have read/heard calls

---

eight occurrences: see 11:8; 16:19; 17:18; 18:10, 16, 18, 19, 21.

5. Peter used "Babylon" to indicate Rome in 1 Pet 5:13. Tabb states, "Babylon is not simply a cipher for Rome but is a rich biblical-theological symbol for the world's idolatrous, seductive political economy—the archetypal godless city" (Tabb, *All Things New*, loc. 2939)

6. This is the first of seven occurrences of "the wrath of God" (14:10, 19; 15:1, 7; 16:1, 19; 19:15).

for "perseverance" (14:12). The exhortation to persevere heightens the intensity of the message.

John then includes the second of seven blessings in the book of Revelation: "And I heard a voice from heaven saying, 'Write, "Blessed are those who die in the Lord from now on!"' 'Yes,' says the Spirit, 'in order that they may rest from their hard work, for their *deeds* follow with them'" (14:13). There is little doubt that a connection exists between the exhortation to endure in 14:12 and the promised blessing of rest for "those who die in the Lord" in 14:13. The implication is clear: faithfully following the Lamb means difficulties in the present from which those who remain faithful will find, "rest from their hard work."

The Son of Man and the Two Harvests (14:14–20)

The second unit (14:14–20) within this section (14:6–20) centers on four beings.

The unit begins with the introduction of "One like a Son of Man" who is "sitting on the cloud" (14:14).[7] There is, then, a second triad of angels who are each identified as "another angel" (14:15, 17, 18)—though this time they are not numbered.[8]

This unit focuses on two distinct harvests.[9] In the first harvest (14:14–16), the "One like a Son of Man" is commanded to "*reap*" (14:15), which indicates the harvesting of grain. In the second harvest (14:17–20), an angel[10] is commanded to "gather the clusters from the vine of the earth" (14:18), which certainly indicates the harvesting of grapes. The distinction between the two harvests is significant. Most notably, the harvesting of grain requires only reaping and is, therefore, associated with the harvesting of the righteous.[11] That the second harvest includes both

---

7. Surely the "One like a Son of Man"—which occurs here and in 1:13 only—is building off Dan 7:13 and indicates Christ as the true human in contrast to the Beasts.

8. This unit also adheres around the seven uses of "sickle" (14:14, 15, 16, 17, 18*, 19).

9. Bauckham provides the most exhaustive case for seeing the harvest of 14:14–16 and 14:17–20 as distinct: See Bauckham, *Revelation*, 290–96. That they are distinct harvests is debated by some: see Beale, *Revelation*, 777–78.

10. Bauckham contends that although John does not identify this angel in the present passage, he does identify it as Jesus in 19:11—16: *Climax*, 294.

11. See Bauckham, *Climax*, 293–94. Harvesting alone is commonly viewed positively (Mark 4:29; John 4:35–38); Matthew affirms that God is the 'Lord of the Harvest' (Matt 9:37–38). When harvesting is an act of judgment upon the unrighteous, either

the gathering of the grapes and the trampling of the wine press (14:19)[12] suggests that it is a harvesting of the unrepentant for judgment.

The Grain Harvest 14:14–16

John introduces the harvesting of the grain by saying, "And I saw a white cloud, and sitting on the cloud was One like a Son of Man" (14:14). It is important to recognize that throughout the Scriptures God is the One who rides the clouds.[13] Wilson affirms, "referring to a cloud as a symbol of theophanic presence is ubiquitous in Jewish Scripture and texts."[14] That the One on the cloud in 14:14, however, is identified as "One like a Son of Man" (14:14)[15] most certainly indicates that it is Jesus.[16]

The "sharp sickle," which the One like a Son of Man (14:14) and the fifth angel (14:17) hold, indicates an instrument of judgment. Christ is then exhorted, "Send your sickle and reap, because the hour to reap has come, because the harvest of the earth is ripe" (14:15).[17] The command to "reap" indicates that it is a harvest of grain. Thus, this harvest is for the people of God.[18]

The Grape Harvest 14:17–20

The second harvest is distinguished from the previous one in that the angel with the sickle is told, "Send your sharp sickle" and "gather the

---

threshing is specified (Jer 51:33; Mic 4:12–13; Matt 3:12; Luke 3:17), or the wicked are associated with the chaff (Ps 1:4; Dan 2:35; Matt 3:12; Luke 3:17).

12. See Joel 3:13.

13. Longman notes, "Interestingly, this passage is the only one which pictures the cloud that God or Jesus rides as white, since the imagery comes ultimately from ancient Near Eastern storm god imagery where the clouds would be dark" (Longman, *Revelation*, 308). See also Dan 7:13; Matt 24:30; 26:64; Mark 13:26; Luke 21:27; Rev 1:7.

14. Wilson, "Spirit in Revelation," 91.

15. Note: the only other mention of "One like a Son of Man" is in 1:13, where it surely refers to Jesus.

16. Bauckham affirms, "The figure who reaps the grain harvest is certainly Jesus Christ." (Bauckham, *Theology*, 97; Bauckham, *Climax*, 294).

17. There is no problem with an angel "commanding" Jesus. What transpires is the will of God and of Christ. The angel is simply requesting Christ to do what is right and just: i.e., what His nature demands.

18. See Bauckham, *Climax*, 290–96.

clusters from the vine of the earth, because her grapes are ripe" (14:18). This harvest is explicitly stated to be a harvest of grapes.

That the grape harvest is a judgment upon the nations is supported in that the second angel in the first triad declares, "Fallen, fallen is Babylon the great" (14:8). The angel then informs us that Babylon has, "made all the nations drink of the wine of the passion of her immorality" (14:8). That the third angel of the first triad then follows with an affirmation, "If anyone worships the beast and his image and receives the Mark on their forehead or on their hand, they themselves will drink from the wine of the wrath of God," further established the links the grape harvest (14:17–20) and the first triad of angels.

John then notes that as a result of the trampling of the grapes, blood proceeds, "from the wine press up to the horses' bridles, for 1,600 *stadia*" (14:20).[19] The fact that "1600" is the product of ten squared and four squared suggests the comprehensiveness of the judgment.

Excursus: The Two Harvests, the Prayers of the Saints, and the Martyrs' Cry for Justice

It is my conviction that John links both of the harvests to "the prayers of the saints" (5:8; 8:3, 4) and the martyrs' cry for justice (6:10).[20] That the grain harvest (14:14–16) is a harvest of the people of God suggests that it is a response to the martyrs' cry for justice. After all, the plea of the martyrs was "How long, Lord?" (6:10). The grain harvest presents the answer as "Now." At the same time, the martyrs' cry was specifically a cry for justice. Thus, they exclaimed, "How long, Lord, the One who is holy and true, until you judge and avenge our blood on those who inhabit the earth?"

That John intends for us to view the grape harvest in light of the answer to the prayers of the saints gain support from the locations from which the second triad of angels come. John introduces both the fourth "another angel" and the fifth "another angel" as having come "out of the temple" (14:15, 17). The sixth "another angel," however, came from the altar" (14:18). That

---

19. The Greek is "1,600 stadia"—as reflected here and in the ESV and NIV.
20. Bauckham, in much greater depth, makes the argument that I present here (Bauckham, *Climax*, 290–96). He does not, however, connect the two harvests to the prayers of the saints as I do below. Beale's objections to Bauckham's arguments fall short in light of the additional arguments that I present below (Beale, *Revelation*, 776–78).

these angels came either from the temple or the altar, which itself was in the temple, suggests that the grape harvest is a response to "the prayers of the saints" (5:8; 8:3, 4).[21]

For one, that the sixth angel "came out from the altar" (14:18), links this passage with the martyrs' cry for justice (6:9) in that the altar was the very place from which the martyrs were crying out.

Also, that John adds to his description of the sixth angel by noting that it is, "the one who has authority over fire" (14:18), links this angel with the angel in 8:3–5 who had the "prayers of the saints" (8:3, 4) and who "took the censer and filled it from the fire of the altar, and threw it to the earth" (8:5). This suggests that the sixth angel who cries out, "Send your sharp sickle and gather the clusters from the vine of the earth, because her grapes are ripe" (14:18), is the angel who one who has "the prayers of the saints" before the altar in (8:3, 4). Since, as I argued earlier, "the prayers of the saints" in 5:8 and 8:3, 4 are linked with the martyrs' cry for justice in 6:10, it stands to reason that the harvest of the grapes and the command to "gather the clusters" (14:18) is a command to avenge the blood of the saints. The martyrs' cry for justice is being answered.

A third indication that the grape harvest is a direct response to the saints' cry for justice occurs in the description of the grape harvest. John first notes that after the grapes are harvested by the angel, they were thrown "into the wine press" (14:19). Then he adds, "the wine press was trampled outside the city" (14:20).[22] The use of "trampled"[23] links the description of the grape harvest with the account of the Two Witnesses. In the opening of the account of the Two Witnesses, John was commanded, "Leave out the court which is outside the temple and do not measure it, because it has been given to the nations; and they will trample the Holy City for forty-two months" (11:2).

---

21. In the commentary I argued that the "prayers of the saints" are closely linked to the martyrs' cry for justice in 6:10. If the harvests of 14:14–20 are a response to the "prayers of the saints," then it stands to reason that are also a response to the martyrs' plea.

22. Italics added for stress.

23. Greek is *pateo*. John uses the verb for "trampled" three times: 11:2; 14:20; 19:15. The latter two are in the context of the grape harvest and the final judgment.

The repetition of the verb "trample"[24] in 11:2 and 14:20 most certainly links the trampling of 11:2 and 14:20.

If, as I argued in the commentary on 11:1–2, the trampling of the Holy City refers to the suffering of the people of God, then it stands to reason that the trampling in 14:20 conveys the righteous judgment of the nations for their treatment of the people of God.[25] This conclusion also gains support from John's closing remark that "the wine press was trampled outside the city" (14:20). Throughout the book of Revelation, John's use of "city" refers to either the "Holy City"[26]—which is identified as the "New Jerusalem" in 21:2—or the "Great City"[27]—which is identified as "Babylon" in 18:10, 21. Although we cannot be certain which of the two cities, if either, John has in view here, it is my conviction that the trampling takes place outside the Holy City. This conclusion is based on the link between the trampling of the winepress (14:20) and the trampling of the outer court of the Holy City (11:2).[28]

---

24. See also Luke 10:19; 21:24; Rev 11:2; 14:20; 19:15; compare Dan 8:13.

25. This is the principle of *lex talionis*—the law of retaliation—which is also known as "an eye for an eye" (Exod 21:24). Our study of the fall of Babylon in 17:1—19:10 will reinforce the connection between the trampling of the righteous in 11:2 and the just trampling of the wine press in 14:20.

26. See 3:12; 11:2; 20:9; 21:2, 10, 14, 15, 16*, 18, 19, 21, 23; 22:14, 19.

27. See 11:8, 13; 16:19*; 17:18; 18:10*, 16, 18, 19, 21.

28. There is another possible link between 11:2 and 14:20 as a result of John's use of the adverb "outside." This adverb occurs five times in the book of Revelation. It occurs twice in the shorter form *"exo"* (3:12; 22:15). In both instances, it refers to the Holy City. The adverb is also found three times in the longer form *"exothen"* (11:2*; 14:20). That the longer form *"exothen"* only occurs in the present account (14:20) and the account of the Two Witnesses (11:2*) supports the conclusion that the trampling of the grapes is in response to the trampling of the Holy City.

Revelation 15:1—16:21
The Seven Angels and the Seven Bowls

> *A brief look at the sequence of bowl plagues shows how each one corresponds to a specific 'sin' of empire. This should not be understood as a 'punishment' initiated by God, as modern fundamentalists have interpreted the link between homosexuality and AIDS or between a 'permissive' society and natural disasters, but as the apocalyptic perspective on the actual effects of empire's sins.*[1]

> *Thus, despite the intervention of chapters 12-14, the whole sequence of bowls is clearly marked as a development of the seventh trumpet.*[2]

Introduction

I HAVE ARGUED THAT the narrative of the second story (4:1—16:21), which I have also referred to as the heavenly vision, climaxed in the account of the Two Witnesses (11:1-13) and the Seventh Trumpet (11:14-19). In particular, in accord with Bauckham's thesis, I have argued that John depicts the nations as fearing the Lord (11:13) because of the faithful, loving, and sacrificial lives of the people of God (the Two Witnesses).

I then argued that 12:1—14:20 continues the narrative, but not by moving it forward. Instead, 12:1—14:20 provides further details as to the nature of the "war" (11:7) that the Beast wages against the Two Witnesses. First, we learn that the "war" is one that the Dragon has been waging against the people of God since the beginning (12:1-17). We then learn

---

1. Howard-Brook and Gwyther, *Unveiling Empire*, loc. 4075.
2. Bauckham, *Climax*, 9.

that the Dragon empowers two Beasts to wage war for him (13:1—14:5; esp. 13:7). Finally, in 14:6-20, we see the consequences that await those who participate with the Beast in the war against the people of God.

In the present account (15:1—16:21), John resumes the main narrative that he paused at the end of the Seventh Trumpet (11:19). And, in doing so, he brings the story to its consummation.

Literary Links in John's Account of the Seven Bowls

I have noted throughout that there are a number of literary links that John embeds in his narrative. Recognizing them is critical for understanding the role of the Seven Bowls.

John's Use of Interruption

Once again, John's does not provide us with a neat, systematic outline. He begins the account of the Seven Bowls (15:1—16:21) with an introduction of the seven angels to whom the Seven Bowls are given, "And I saw another sign in heaven seven angels having seven last plagues, because in them the wrath of God is complete" (15:1).[3] Instead of continuing with the account of the seven angels and the Seven Bowls, however, John interrupts the scene and introduces us to the victorious people of God: "And I saw ... the ones who had overcome the Beast and his image and the number of his name" (15:2). John depicts the victorious people of God as, "standing on the sea of glass having harps of God and they were singing the song of Moses the servant of God and the song of the Lamb" (15:2-3). Then, after they have sung their song (15:3-4), John returns to the description of the seven angels and the Seven Bowls (15:5-8).

It is incumbent upon us, therefore, to ascertain the significance of this interruption with regard to the narrative of the Seven Bowls. I will contend that John's interruption of the opening of the narrative of the Seven Trumpets with an account of those "who had overcome" and who were, "standing on the sea of glass having harps of God and they were singing the song of Moses the servant of God and the song of the Lamb"

---

3. This is similar to what John did in his introduction of the Seven Trumpets (8:1-6). There John both overlapped the ending of the Seven Seals (8:1, 5) with the introduction to the Seven Trumpets (8:2, 6); and he inserted in the middle of both the ending of the Seven Seals and the introduction to the Seven Trumpets the description of the angel who had the prayers of the saints (8:3, 4).

(15:2–3) serves to reinforce one of John's primary goals: namely, as their song (15:3–4) reveals, it is through the faithful, loving, and sacrificial witness of God's people that the nations are redeemed.[4]

John's Use of Inclusio

Another important feature of John's presentation of the Seven Bowls is his use of *inclusio*. In 15:5, John notes, "the temple of the tabernacle of testimony in heaven was opened" (15:5).[5] This statement forms an *inclusio* with the closing statement in the account of the seventh Trumpet, "And the temple of God which is in heaven was opened" (11:19). It is my conviction that this *inclusio* indicates that the account of the Seven Bowls resumes the narrative of the heavenly vision that climaxed in the resurrection and ascension of the Two Witnesses and the accompanying repentance of the nations (11:11–13).

Seven Bowls, the Throne Room Scene, and the Prayers of the Saints

Another important feature of the account of the Seven Bowls is the relationship of the Seven Bowls with the throne room scene (4:1—5:14) and the prayers of the saints (5:8; 8:3, 4)—which, as I have argued, are themselves deeply correlated with the martyrs' cry for justice (6:10).

That the account of the Seven Bowls is linked with the throne room scene is evident in that John's opening description of those who had overcome includes the fact that they are "standing on the sea of glass" (15:2). That the "sea of glass" (15:2) relates to the throne room scene derives from the fact that the only other occurrence of the "sea of glass" is the one that appears before the throne in 4:6.[6]

Equally significant is that at the center of the account of the Seven Bowls (15:1—16:21) are the seven angels who are given "seven golden

---

4. Or, as Bauckham contends, it is through the vindication of the people of God that the nations are redeemed. Bauckham makes the argument in far greater depth than I will present below. For more details, see Bauckham, *Climax*, 296–307.

5. The Greek places "opened" at the beginning of the clause: "and opened was the temple . . ." (15:5).

6. Note that "sea of glass" occurs three times (4:6; 15:2*) in the book of Revelation and two of these are in 15:2.

bowls" (15:7).[7] These "golden bowls" most certainly relate back to the "golden bowls" of the Four Living Creatures and the Twenty-Four Elders in 5:8.

That John intends for us to link the "golden bowls" of the Four Living Creatures and the Twenty-Four Elders (5:8) with the "golden bowls" given to the seven angels in the present account (15:7) is indicated by several literary links. First, the "golden bowls" in 5:8 and 15:7 represent the only two occurrences of "golden bowls" in the entire book of Revelation. It has been an unmistakable practice of John to link passages by means of the repetition of keywords or phrases. The strength of this argument increases when the said words or phrases occur only in the two or three passages under discussion. Second, the "golden bowls" in 5:8 is the only other mention of "bowls" in the entire book of Revelation that does not refer to either the Seven Bowls as a whole or to one of the Seven Bowls in particular.[8] Third, that "one of the Four Living Creatures" gives the "golden bowls" to the seven angels in 15:7 most certainly links the account of the seven angels with the Seven Bowls to the golden bowls in the throne room scene since it was the Four Living Creatures, along with the Twenty-Four Elders, that had the "golden bowls" in 5:8. It is my conviction, therefore, that the seven "golden bowls" that are given to the seven angels are unquestionably linked with the "golden bowls" that the Four Living Creatures and the Twenty-Four Elders had in 5:8.[9]

The significance of this link is that the "golden bowls" in 5:8 were "full of incense, which are the prayers of the saints." That means that when the seven angels "pour out" the Seven Bowls, they are "pouring out" the prayers of the saints.[10]

---

7. In the OT, bowls were associated with the priestly service at the altar in the Temple. See Exod 25:29; 37:16; also 24:6; 27:3; 38:3.

8. That is, 5:8 is the only reference to a "bowl" that does not indicate either the Seven Bowls as a whole or one of the Seven Bowls: see 5:8; 15:7; 16:1, 2, 3, 4, 8, 10, 12, 17; 17:1; 21:9.

9. One may contend that they are the same bowls. That is, one of the Four Living Creatures gives to the seven angels seven of the very same bowls that the Four Living Creatures and the Twenty-Four Elders had in 5:8. This may be true. But it seems to me that it is pressing the text too far. From a literary perspective, all that is necessary here, for my argument to stand, is that the bowls of 15:7 are linked literarily with the bowls of 5:8. That this is so appears to be unquestionable.

10. Nine times in this account the angels are said to have "poured out" the Bowls: 16:1, 2, 3, 4, 6, 8, 10, 12, 17. These, of course, are the only occurrences of "poured out" in the book of Revelation.

Now, one may argue that the Seven Bowls in 15:1—16:21 are "full of the wrath of God" (15:7) and therefore they represent God's divine wrath.[11] Longman, in fact, contends, "The four living creatures, the ones closest to the throne of God (see note at 4:6–8), now give bowls to the seven angels whose contents they will pour out over humanity to bring divine judgment upon them.[12] Longman adds to his analysis, "Attempts to minimize or remove God's active involvement in this description of violent judgment ring hollow."[13]

In response to Longman's analysis, I would note that this is precisely the point. The Bowls are full of the wrath of God. But they are also full of the prayers of the saints. And the fact that the Bowls, which most certainly correspond to the bowls in 5:8 are being "poured out" indicates that God's wrath, or perhaps we might say His justice, constitutes His response to the prayers of the saints.

In order to put this into the context of the narrative flow of the book of Revelation we need to reflect on how the three series of sevens (Seals, Trumpets, and Bowls) relate to the prayers of the saints. Without repeating all that I have said previously, I would reiterate that the Seven Seals and the Seven Trumpets both functioned, in part, as responses to the prayers of the saints and the cry of the martyrs. In both of the Seven Seals and the Seven Trumpets, however, the response to the prayers of the saints was that there would be a delay—although with the coming of the Seventh Trumpet, "there will be no more time" (10:7; 11:15–19). Conversely, with the Seven Bowls, the saints' cry for justice is now being answered. This is most evident in John's indication that each of the Seven Bowls is "poured out" (16:1, 2, 3, 4, 8, 10, 12, 17).[14] That the "pouring out" of each of the Bowls represents Divine retribution is affirmed by the angel of the waters who cries out "Righteous are you, ... because they poured out the blood of the holy ones and of the prophets" (16:6).[15] That the account of the Seven Bowls begins with "a

---

11. See Longman, *Revelation*, 324.

12. Longman, *Revelation*, 325.

13. Longman, *Revelation*, 325.

14. Note that the prophets use "pour out" in relation to God's wrath: see Ezek 14:19; Jer 10:25; Ps 69:24; Zeph 3:8.

15. In order for an English reader to see that the "pouring out" of the Seven Bowls is a direct response to the "pouring out" of the blood of the saints and prophets, it is essential for our English translations to render the Greek verb *ekcheo* consistently. The result is that the same verb which is used to describe the "pouring out" of the Seven Bowls (16:1, 2, 3, 4, 8, 10, 12, 17) is also used in the angel's explanation of God's justice:

great voice from the temple" (16:1) also indicates that the prayers of the saints are about to be answered. For it is from God's temple, specifically under the altar, that the martyrs cry out.

I have also argued that the delay in God's response to the prayers of the saints was intimately connected to both the suffering of the people of God and the redemption of the nations. Both of these, however, were depicted in the account of the Two Witnesses (11:1–13). Consequently, in terms of the narrative, it is time for the prayers of the saints to be answered.

Thus, I will argue below that the interruption in the opening of the narrative of the Seven Bowls (see 15:2–4), reiterates this very point. The nations have been redeemed, as the song of the victors exclaims: "Because all the nations will come and worship before You" (15:4). This means that God's justice has come. The time to answer the prayers of the saints and to "avenge" their blood has arrived.

---

it is because they have "poured out" (16:6) the blood of God's people.

Revelation 15:1–8
The Seven Angels and the Overcomers

Seven Angels 15:1

JOHN BEGINS WITH, "AND I saw another sign in heaven," which was "great and marvelous" (15:1). The introduction of "another sign" instead of "another angel" (14:15, 17, 18)[1] marks a clear transition from the account of the seven beings in 14:6–20. John then adds that the sign that he saw in heaven was of "seven angels having seven last plagues" (15:1).[2] These seven angels are "last," we are told, "because in them the wrath of God is complete" (15:1). This provides explicit confirmation that the account of the Seven Bowls brings us to the end of the narrative.

It is possible that these seven angels are linked with the seven angels who stand before God in the account of the Seven Trumpets (8:2). The fact that every occurrence of "the seven angels" (8:2, 6; 15:1, 6, 7, 8; 16:1; 17:1; 21:9) occurs exclusively in relation to either the seven angels of the Seven Trumpets or the seven angels of the Seven Bowls supports this assertion.[3]

---

1. Instead of using "another angel," which was repeated in the close of the previous account (see 14:15, 17, 18), John marks the transition here with, "another sign."

2. The "seven angels" who have "seven last plagues" appear seven times in the book of Revelation (15:1, 6, 7, 8; 16:1; 17:1; 21:9).

3. Note the only other uses of "the seven angels" are in 17:1 and 21:9. Both of these occurrences, however, relate back to the seven angels of the Seven Bowls.

The Song of the Overcomers 15:2–4

After introducing us to the seven angels (15:1), John interrupts by introducing us to the victorious people of God: "the ones who had overcome" (15:2–4).

John again says, "And I saw" (15:2). This time he sees, "the ones who had overcome the Beast and his image and the number of his name standing on the sea of glass" (15:2).[4] That the people of God are "the ones who had overcome" (15:2) and that they are "on the sea of glass" (15:2) suggests that they have successfully come through the judgment. That they are "standing" also suggests not only that they are victorious but that they are prepared for the final judgment.[5]

Previously, the sea of glass was "like crystal" (4:6). In the present scene, it is "mixed with fire" (15:2). The presence of "fire" furthers the association with judgment.[6] Thus, the sea of glass is "mixed with fire" because the final judgment is approaching.

John then adds that the Overcomers, "had harps of God" and were "singing the song of Moses . . . and the song of the Lamb" (15:3). The presence of harps and singing serves to link the Overcomers with the 144,000 who were with Christ on Mount Zion and had harps and were singing (14:2–3). That the Overcomers are singing "the song of Moses" (15:3) recalls the song that the Israelites sang after walking victoriously through the Red Sea.[7] Consequently, the Overcomers are presented as victors over the Beast in terms of a new Exodus.

Interestingly, none of the words of their song (15:3–4) correspond with the song of Moses in Exodus 15. Bauckham notes that this is not unheard of. He cites an example from *Pseudo-Philo* in which the song of Deborah (Judg 5:1) is introduced but the words of the song do not match any of the words of the song of Deborah in Judg 5:2–31.

---

4. Beale notes that the portrait of the people of God *on* the sea, "is in contrast to Israel of old, who could only stand by the sea" (Beale, *Revelation*, 791).

5. Their "standing" reminds us of the cry of the nations in the Sixth Seal who exclaim, "the great day of their wrath has come" and then they asked, "and who is able to stand?" (6:17).

6. "Fire" occurs twenty-five times in the book of Revelation: see 1:14; 2:18; 3:18; 4:5; 8:5, 7, 8; 9:17, 18; 10:1; 11:5; 13:13; 14:10, 18; 15:2; 16:8; 17:16; 18:8; 19:12, 20; 20:9, 10, 14, 15; 21:8. Beale argues that throughout the book of Revelation fire is used as a symbol of judgment (Beale, *Revelation*, 792). I would note that of twenty-five occurrences of fire, twenty-four are in the context of judgment: 3:18 is the lone exception.

7. The song of Moses is found in Exod 15:1–17 and Deut 31:30–31:43. Note that Isa 12:1–6 predicts that Israel will sing the song of Moses after the new Exodus.

Bauckham then claims that the words in *Pseudo-Philo* are "the author's own, ... by which he expresses his own interpretation of the great deliverance of the Israelites from the army of Sisera."[8] For Bauckham, the son of Deborah in *Pseudo-Philo* represents, "a new version of the song of Deborah" that is able to, "provide a fresh interpretation of the significance of that deliverance."[9]

In Bauckham's assessment, John is doing the same thing. That is, John interprets the song of Moses from Exodus 15 in light of Jesus. The fact that John specifies that the song of the Overcomers is not just the song of Moses but it is also "the song of the Lamb" (15:3), suggests that indeed John is reinterpreting the song of Moses in light of the Jesus event.

One of the key features of John's version of the song is its universalizing nature:

> Righteous and true are Your ways,
> King of the ages . . .
> Because all the nations will come
> and worship before You (15:3–4)

John's universalizing of the song is nothing strange to the world of OT interpretation. Tellbe notes, "The song of Moses and the image of the new exodus in 15:2–4 should also be interpreted in line with the most universalistic strains of the Old Testament hope: all the nations will come to acknowledge the God of Israel and to worship him."[10]

Bauckham also notes that John's placement of this song in the middle of the introduction to the account of the Seven Bowls strongly suggests that John wants us to view the Seven Bowls as an announcement of God's victory over the nations:

> The vindication of the martyrs is the victory of God celebrated in the song of the Lamb, corresponding to the wondrous deeds done by Yahweh at the Red Sea. Just as the latter led to the awed recognition of his deity by the nations who heard of them (Exod 15:14–16), so the former leads to the repentance and worship of all the nations (Rev 15:4).[11]

---

8. Bauckham, *Climax*, 298. Bauckham notes that the words of the song in Rev 15:3–4 derive from Exod 15:11; Jer 10:6–7a; Ps 86:8–10, 98:1–2 (Bauckham, *Climax*, 302–3).

9. Bauckham, *Climax*, 298.

10. Tellbe, "Relationship," 232.

11. Bauckham, *Climax*, 306.

This is precisely, as I argued earlier, what the account of the Two Witnesses affirms. Namely, God summons the people of God to heaven (11:12) and the nations "became terrified and gave glory to the God of heaven" (11:13).

Thus, by John's use of interruption, he indicates that the redemption of the nations occurs as a result of the victory of God's people and their vindication by God. As a result, the final judgment may come.

15:5–8 Temple Is Opened

John then says, "After these things[12] I saw, and the temple of the tabernacle of testimony in heaven was opened" (15:5). The seven angels with the seven last plagues then "came out of the temple" (15:6).[13] That the seven angels come out of the temple conveys, as it did in the account of the two harvests in 14:17–20, that the final judgment is coming in accord with the answer to the prayers of the saints.

John then describes the angels. They were clothed in "clean, bright linen and wrapped around their chests were golden sashes" (15:6). That they had "golden sashes" (15:6) corresponds to the opening description of Christ in the first story (1:13). In fact, these are the only two occurrences of "sashes" in the book of Revelation. At the same time, their clothes are "clean, bright" (15:6), which anticipates the clothing of the Bride in 19:8.

John then says, "And the temple was filled with smoke from the glory of God and from His power" (15:8). Throughout the OT smoke is a regular symbol of the presence of God.[14] As Isaiah announced, "The whole earth is full of His glory. And the foundations of the thresholds trembled at the voice of him who called out, while the temple was filling with smoke" (Isa 6:3–4).

John concludes the introduction to the seven angels who had the Seven Bowls by noting, "no one was able to enter into the temple until the seven plagues of the seven angels were finished" (15:8).

In light of the fact that the present scene is an introduction to the final judgment in which God responds to the prayers of the saints, the observation that "no one was able to enter into the temple" (15:8)

---

12. See note on 4:1. "After these things" does not refer to the order of events in history.

13. Two of the angels in the account of 14:14–20 are also described as "coming out of the temple" (14:15, 17).

14. See Exod 19:16–18; 40:34–35; Ps 18:7–9; 104:32; Isa 6:1–6.

suggests that in narrative time the opportunity for intercession has passed. There is no more need to offer prayers asking for divine justice because God is about to act.

Revelation 16:1-21
The Seven Bowls
Introduction

Introduction

THE SONG OF THE Overcomers asserts that the ways of God are "righteous and true" (15:3). This affirmation confirms the links between the song of the Overcomers and the narrative of the Seven Bowls that follows. For in the midst of the account of the Seven Bowls, a voice cries out from the altar, "Yes, Lord God, the Almighty, true and righteous are Your judgments" (16:7).

The Relationship between 15:1-8 and 16:1-21

As we proceed into the account of the Seven Bowls, it is evident that 16:1-21 is a continuation of the temple scene begun in 15:5-8. The relationship between the account of the Seven Bowls and the preceding temple scene (15:1-8) is also indicated by John's use of *hearing* and *seeing*. The temple scene depicts what John "saw" (15:5). The account of the Seven Bowls then opens with "and I heard" (16:1).[1]

The distinction between the two units is that the temple scene (15:1-8) and the account of the Seven Bowls (16:1-21) present contrasting depictions of the people of God with those who follow the

---

1. There are also a number of literary connections between the temple scene of 15:5-8 and the account of the Seven Bowls. In both sections, God is addressed as "O Lord God, the Almighty" (15:3; 16:7). In addition, both sections affirm that "Your ways" or "Your judgments" are "righteous and true" (15:3; 16:7).

Beast. The contrast is most apparent in that the people of God are introduced as, "the ones who overcame the Beast and his image and the number of his name," and as those who "were singing the song of Moses . . . and the song of the Lamb" (15:2–3). Whereas those who had the Mark of the Beast, "blasphemed the name of God . . . and . . . did not repent to give Him glory (16:9).

The Seven Bowls and the Wrath of God

The question arises as to whether or not the Seven Bowls depict God's end times wrath upon the nations. I argued that the Seven Seals and Seven Trumpets do not depict divine wrath, but instead, they reveal the consequences that come upon humanity (the first four Seals) and upon the creation (the first four Trumpets) as a result of humanity's own rule. I further argued that God allows humanity to continue to rule, despite the prayers of the saints for justice, because of His love for the nations. That is, God's delay provides the nations with the opportunity to repent. I also contended that the suggestion that the Seals and Trumpets relay God's wrath undermines the nature of God. That is, the conception that God inflicts suffering on some in order to coerce those who survive into obedience makes God no different than human rulers.

The same question arises when it comes to the Seven Bowls. It is my contention, however, that the Seven Bowls play a different role in the narrative. Namely, as I have noted, 16:21 clearly marks the end of the second story (the heavenly vision) which began in 4:1. This leads to the conclusion that the Seven Bowls are a depiction of the consummation of all things. If so, then the Seven Bowls represent the eschatological wrath of God. As such, this eliminates the moral dilemma in that the Bowls do not represent God's wrath upon some so that those who are spared might repent. Instead, they depict the final destruction that befalls those who do not repent. The interjection of God's justness (16:5–7), affirms this conclusion.

At the same time, there are clues within the narrative of the Seven Bowls that they represent that both humanity and the creation will suffer the inevitable consequences that their rule ultimately brings. For example, the unleashing of a demonically inspired war against the people of God, depicted in the account of the Sixth Bowl, surely mitigates the view that God is the direct agent of every aspect of the Seven Bowls.

Thus, it is my conviction that the account of the Bowls, in accordance with what I have argued for the Seals and the Trumpets, indicates that the devastation that arises upon the nations is the result of the nations' own actions. The account of the Bowls depicts the inevitable end for those who worship the Beast and his image. At the same time, they are also presented as the divine retribution for the nations' treatment of the people of God.

In order to reconcile these two apparently conflicting positions I would assert that the Seven Bowls represent God's wrath upon the nations who have failed to repent for what they have done to the people of God. The nations have "poured out the blood of the holy ones and of the prophets and You gave them blood to drink, they are worthy of it" (16:6). The means by which God does such is to accelerate the processes of destruction that humanity has put into place through their own destructive actions. That is, the Seven Trumpets confirm that humanity's rule has begun to turn the waters into blood (8:8–11). Now, in the account of the Seven Bowls, we learn that the total devastation of the creation has come. Did this happen because God brought about his wrath upon the creation, or because humanity has brought about the demise of God's creation? It is my proposal that John would have simply answered, "Yes."

As I previously noted in the discussion of the Seals and the Trumpets, God as the one true sovereign is a major theme of the book of Revelation. The narrative began with an explicit affirmation that God is the One on the throne and not Caesar. Consequently, the portrayal of God as the source of the plagues derives from a biblical conception of God's sovereignty. Reading the book of Revelation from a narrative perspective, however, confirms that God displays His sovereignty by allowing the nations to suffer the consequences of their own rule. The account of the Seven Bowls brings us the inevitable end result of humanity's rule: namely, the complete devastation of humanity and creation.

The Structure of the Seven Bowls

The account of the Seven Bowls parallels the accounts of the Seven Seals and the Seven Trumpets. This is evident in that the account of the Seven Bowls also displays a four-three structure. The four-three pattern is most evident in that the first four Bowls, which, in direct parallel to the first four Trumpets, affect the elements of nature (the earth: 16:2; the sea: 16:3; the rivers and springs of waters: 16:4, and the sun: 16:8).

At the same time, however, and perhaps even more prominently, as I noted in the discussion on the seven messages, the Seven Bowls employ a three-four structure that parallels the messages to the seven churches (2:1–3:22).[2] The three-four structure of the Seven Bowls is evident from the interjections of "the angel of the waters" (16:5) and "the altar" (16:7) that occur after the Third Bowl. The three-four structure is also evident in that the first three Bowls are poured "into" something (16:2, 3, 4), while the last four Bowls are poured "upon" something (16:8, 10, 12, 17). Furthermore, only within the accounts of the first three Bowls do we read that something "became" (16:2, 3, 4).

What is the significance of the use of a three-four structure in the account of the Seven Bowls? It is my conviction that the divergence in the Seven Bowls from the four-three structure of the Seven Seals and the Seven Trumpets to a three-four structure further signals that the account of the Seven Bowls presents us with the end of the story. This supposition gains merit when we recognize that the three-four structure in the account of the Seven Bowls corresponds with the three-four structure of the seven messages. That the structure of the Seven Bowls parallels the structure of the seven messages links the end of the first story (John's vision on Patmos: 1:9–3:22) with the end of the second story (the heavenly vision: 4:1—16:21).

The Seven Angels Prepare 16:1

The account of the Seven Bowls begins with, "a great voice from the temple" who issues a command authorizing the seven angels to pour out their Bowls (16:1). That the voice comes out of the temple serves as a link between the account of the Seven Bowls and both the temple scene (15:6) and the account of the two harvests (14:15, 17, 18; 15:6).

The First Bowl 16:2

The first *angel*[3] went and "poured out" his Bowl "into the earth" (16:2). After the pouring out his Bowl, we are told that, "it became a bad and

---

2. Contra Bauckham, *Climax*, 10.
3. "Angel" is not in the text in the description of any of the Seven Bowls. The text

evil sore upon the people who have the mark of the Beast and who are worshiping his image" (16:2). There is a measure of ambiguity in the text in that it is not clear what "it" is that "became a bad and evil sore." It is my contention that the "it" refers to the Mark of the Beast itself. That is, they have received the Mark of the Beast and the result is that the Mark itself becomes the source of their pain.

The Second Bowl 16:3

The Second Bowl is "poured out" by the second *angel* "into the sea" (16:3). The result is that after the Second Bowl is poured into the sea, the sea, "became blood as of the dead" and "every living thing in the sea died" (16:3). The effects that follow the pouring out of the Second Bowl describe the inevitable result of humanity's economic exploitation of the sea. Beale suggests, "the sea being turned into 'blood' in 16:3 is figurative, at least in part, for the demise of the ungodly world's economic life-support system."[4] Beale's supposition gains merit from the account of the judgment of the Great Prostitute that follows (17:1—19:10).

The Third Bowl 16:4

The Third Bowl is "poured out" by the third *angel* "into the rivers and springs of water" (16:4). The result is that after the Third Bowl is poured into rivers and springs, "it became blood" (16:4). The effects that follow the pouring out of the Third Bowl, like the effects that follow the pouring out of the Second Bowl, also appear to entail the destruction of the world's economic systems. This conviction gains strength from the apparent allusion to the striking of the Nile,[5] which was a major source of prosperity for Egypt.

That both the account of the Second and the Third Bowls depict the destruction of the world's economic systems is supported by the pronouncement of Babylon's destruction in the account that follows. 17:1—19:10.[6]

---

simply reads, "And the first. . . ." This implies, however, that it is the "first angel." After all, the seven angels are the ones who have the Seven Bowls.

4. Beale, *Revelation*, 815.
5. See Exod 7:14-21.
6. See 18:2, 9-19.

Angelic Interjections 16:5–7

Instead of narrating the pouring out of the Fourth Bowl, John notes that he "hears" (16:5, 7) "the angel of the waters" (16:5) and "the altar" (16:7). Thus, as noted above, John inserts two interjections (16:5–6, 7) between the pouring out of the Third and Fourth Bowls. These interjections offer a response to the unspoken but assumed, question of God's justice.

First, "The angel of the waters" was "saying, 'Righteous are you, the One who is and who was, the Holy One, because you judged these things, because they poured out the blood of the holy ones and of the prophets and You gave them blood to drink, they are worthy of it'" (16:5–6). Then, "the altar was saying, 'Yes, Lord God the Almighty, true and righteous are Your judgments'" (16:7).

The Fourth Bowl 16:8–9

The Fourth Bowl is "poured out" by the *angel* "upon the sun" (16:8). The result is that "it was given to it to scorch people with fire and the people were scorched by great heat" (16:8–9). Unfortunately, those who suffer after the Fourth Bowl is poured out chose to "blaspheme the name of God" and "not repent to give Him glory" (16:9).

As noted earlier, the account of the Fourth Bowl directly contrasts the fate of the people of God and the fate of those who fail to repent—which likely entails those who have the Mark of the Beast. The contrast is evident: in the present account, those who fail to repent suffer from the sun and its heat; whereas, for those who have come out of the Great Tribulation" (7:14), it is said, "the sun will not beat down on them, nor any heat" (7:16). That these are the only two occurrences of "heat" in the book of Revelation underscores the intended contrast.

The Fifth Bowl 16:10–11

The Fifth Bowl is "poured out" by the fifth *angel* "upon the throne of the Beast" (16:10), after which "his kingdom became covered with darkness" (16:10). Unfortunately, as a result of the Fifth Bowl, as with the Fourth, humanity, "blasphemed the God of Heaven" and "they did not repent of their works" (16:11).[7]

---

7. The failure to repent as a response to the affliction after the pouring out of the

The effects that follow the pouring out of the Fifth Bowl surely affect the realm of the Beast's power. This, too, stands in marked contrast with the promises to the people of God. Whereas Babylon is assured, "the light of a lamp will certainly not shine in you any longer" (18:23), the people of God are assured that they will walk in the light of the Holy City/New Jerusalem where, "the city does not have need of the sun nor of the moon to give it light, for the glory of God gives it light and its lamp is the Lamb" (21:23).

The Sixth Bowl 16:12–14

The Sixth Bowl is "poured out" by the *angel* "upon the great river Euphrates . . . in order that the way might be prepared for the kings of the East" (16:12). The indication that the waters of the Euphrates "dry up" (16:12), reminds the reader/hearers of the exodus story and the Red Sea.[8] John's allusion, however, serves as a contrast to the exodus narrative. After all, the drying up of the waters of the Red Sea enabled the people of God to pass through. In the account of the Sixth Bowl, the waters of the Euphrates dry up to prepare the way "for the kings of the east."

For John, however, the more significant link appears in the parallels between the account of the Sixth Trumpet and that of the Sixth Bowl (16:12–16). In both the Sixth Trumpet and the Sixth Bowl, we have an army crossing the "Euphrates" (9:14; 16:12). That these are only two references in the book of Revelation to the "Euphrates" reinforces the link between the two passages.

John continues his description of the account of the Sixth Bowl by noting that he saw coming, "from the mouth of Dragon and from the mouth of the Beast and from the mouth of the False Prophet three unclean spirits like frogs" (16:13).[9] In case we were uncertain as to the nature of the frog-like beings, John adds, "they are the spirits of demons doing signs" (16:14).

Fifth Bowl contrasts with the response to the ministry of the Two Witnesses. When the Two Witnesses had ascended into heaven, John notes, "the rest became terrified and gave glory to the God of heaven" (11:13). The relationship between the response of the nations to the Two Witnesses in 11:13 and their response as a result of the Fifth Bowl in 16:11 is heightened by the fact that they are the only two places where the title "the God of Heaven" occurs.

8. See Exod 14:13–25.
9. See Exod 8:1–15.

As I noted in the discussion of the False Prophet, the ability to perform signs was one of its primary features (13:13–14). That the frog-like beings in the account of the Sixth Bowl which proceed from the mouth of the Dragon, the Beast, and the False Prophet "are the spirits of demons doing signs" (16:14) links the account of the Sixth Bowl and the description of the False Prophet (13:11–18). This is evident in that every instance in which both "doing" and "signs" occur together it refers to the False Prophet (13:13, 14; 19:20).

In the account of the False Prophet, the signs that he performed were the means by which he "deceives" the nations (13:14). In the account of the Sixth Bowl, the signs are given to "the kings of the inhabited world in order to gather them for the war" (16:14). By linking the present account with that of the False Prophet, the implication is that the False Prophet deceives the nations (13:14) and at some point it does so, "in order to gather them for the war" (16:14).

The gathering of the kings of the inhabited world for the war (16:14), therefore, refers to the war that the Dragon wages by means of the Beast against the people of God. That, as I argued in the discussion of 13:1–8, the Beast embodies the kingdoms of the world reinforces this conclusion.

Parenthetical Exhortation to the People of God 16:15

John interrupts the account of the Sixth Bowl in order to exhort the people of God.[10] In what may be the words of Jesus, we learn: "Behold, I am coming like a thief" (16:15).[11] The exhortation to the people of God continues, "Blessed is the one who stays awake and keeps their garments, in order that they may not walk naked and people see their shame" (16:15).[12] These words strongly echo the message to the church in Sardis: "if you will not wake up, I will come as a thief" (3:3).[13] The reference to "garments" in the message to the church in Sardis (3:4, 5) corresponds

---

10. In many translations, 16:15 is viewed as a parenthetical insertion—and rightly so.

11. Matt 24:43; Luke 12:39–40; 1 Thess 5:2, 4; 2 Pet 3:10.

12. I have opted for the generic plural ("their," "they," and "their") here. The Greek is singular.

13. The relationship between 3:3 and 16:15 is supported by the fact that these are the only two occurrences of "thief" in the book of Revelation. In addition, the warning to Sardis and the exhortation here both refer to "clothes" and "walk" (3:3, 4, 5; 16:15).

to the use of "garments" in 16:15. In addition, both the message to Sardis and the parenthetical exhortation to the people of God in 16:15 employ the verb "walk" (3:4; 16:15). Clearly, then, the parenthetical exhortation in 16:15 is directed at the people of God.

This raises the question as to why John inserts a parenthetical exhortation which is directed to the people of God in the midst of the description of the war that follows the pouring out of the Sixth Bowl. Why issue a promise of blessing to the people of God alongside a reminder that they need to stay awake (16:15)? The only reasonable answer is that the war directly pertains to them.

Sixth Bowl: Armageddon/Harmagedon 16:16

In 16:16, John returns to the account of "the war." After stating that the waters of the Euphrates were dried up, "in order to gather them for the war" (16:14), John now adds that the place to which they were "gathered"[14] is "called in Hebrew, 'Harmagedon'" (16:16).

One of the difficulties with regard to the interpretation of this passage is determining what the original text of 16:16 read. There are two primary readings found in the manuscripts. The first is "Har Magedon"—meaning "Mount of Megiddo." The second is the more popular reading, "Armageddon"[15]—meaning "battle of Megiddo." Though the difference in the Greek is slight,[16] the result is not.

In my opinion, the more likely reading is "Har Magedon": that is, "Mount of Megiddo." The difficulty with this reading is that there is no such mountain.[17] As David Barr notes, "In spite of much scholarly

---

14. The repetition of "gathered" is important. See discussion in the second excursus on Armageddon in 20:1–10.

15. The major English translations evidence the discrepancy: "Harmagedon," (NAS; NRS—though the NRS reads, "Harmagedon"); "Armageddon" (ESV; NET; NIV; NKJ; NLT).

16. The difference has to do with accenting (rough [acute] or smooth [brave]). The best manuscripts favor the acute accent so that the proper reading should be "Harmagedon."

17. Megiddo is in the valley of Jezreel: See Beale, *Revelation*, 839; Fee, *Revelation*, 224–25; Mounce, Revelation, 301; Smalley, Revelation, 412. Note: not only was there no 'Mount Megiddo" but there is also no reference to such in the entire OT nor any ancient Jewish literature. The apocalyptic indications of a final battle are in Zech 12:11 (the only apocalyptic reference to "Megiddo"—though there it is the plain of Megiddo) and Ezekiel 38–39 (where the final battle in history takes place on the "mountains of Israel")—see Beale and Carson, *NT Use of OT*, 1136.

ingenuity, Harmagedon has never appeared on any map of the known world; it is a fictional place."[18]

Why would John refer to the "mount of Megiddo" when there is no such mountain? It is my conviction, that John uses mountain in terms of kingdom. That is, the famed war of "Armageddon" is actually the war of the kingdoms of the world against the kingdom of God.

Excursus: Armageddon Part 1[19]

The noun "war" occurs nine times in the book of Revelation (9:7, 9; 11:7; 12:7, 17; 13:7; 16:14; 19:19; 20:8). The first two occurrences (9:7, 9) are in the description of the demonic horde that arises in the fifth Trumpet, though neither of these occurrences makes reference to an actual war. Instead, they depict the demonic hordes as prepared for war. These two occurrences, however, are nonetheless linked to the war of "Armageddon:", though I will reserve discussion on them for the excursus on Armageddon in the commentary on 20:1–10.

There are then, seven references to a "war" (11:7; 12:7, 17; 13:7; 16:14; 19:19; 20:8). As I have stressed on multiple occasions, each of the occurrences depict a war that is led by the Dragon and/or his agents (the Beast and the False Prophet) against the people of God, Christ, Michael and the angelic beings, or against Christ and the people of God.[20]

As for the verb "to make war," it occurs six times in the book of Revelation (2:16; 12:7*; 13:4; 17:14; 19:11). The first and the last occurrences (2:16; 19:11) refer to Christ as One who makes war.[21] The verb "to make war" occurs twice in 12:7 and in both cases, it refers to the war between the Dragon and his angels against Michael and his angels. In 13:4, the Beast is set forth as one who is unable to be opposed by war. Thus, they were saying, "Who is like the Beast and who is able to wage war with him?" The final occurrence of the verb "to make war"

---

18. Barr, *Tales*, loc. 3638–39.

19. See my *Understanding*, 155–65.

20. Though "the armies that are in heaven" (19:14; see also 19:19) may also include angelic beings.

21. We would do well to remember that, as 2:16 specifies, Christ wages war with the "sword of My mouth."

is in 17:14 where we learn that "these [the ten horns and the Beast] will make war with the Lamb."

There is, therefore, not even a hint in the book of Revelation of the popular notion of a literal war that takes place in the plains of Israel which is waged by the nations of the world against the modern, or even a future, state of Israel.

Shall we say then, that "the war" in the book of Revelation is merely symbolic? I prefer not to use the word "symbolic" to describe "the war" because symbolic too easily connotes something that does not actually take place in the physical realm. There is no question that "the war" in the book of Revelation is real. In fact, I would contend that this war happens every day. All we must do to verify this is to ask our brothers and sisters in Nigeria, Indonesia, N. Korea, and China, just to name a few. The Dragon is not only waging war against the people of God every day, but he will continue to do so until the day Christ returns. This, I would contend, is John's whole point.

That is why, in the middle of the description of the so-called "war of Armageddon," John inserts a parenthetical exhortation to the people of God, "Blessed is the one who stays awake" (16:15).

The "war of Armageddon" then, is none other than the war which the Dragon has been waging against the people of God throughout history. The notion that we are to watch our nightly news or our Twitter feed to discern if some impending battle is about to take place in the plains of modern-day Israel is part of the insidious plan of the Dragon. Instead, of the people of God being prepared each day to wage war against the Dragon and his minions, the Dragon has us sitting back, watching, and maybe even hoping for news that war has broken out in the Middle East. The idea that some Christians are excited to learn of an impending war in the Middle East is deeply grieving. When we, the people of God, the ones who are called "blessed" when we pursue peace (Matt 5:9), spend our time looking for signs of war in the Middle East, and when we rejoice at the prospects of such a war, we do more damage to the kingdom of God than we can imagine. Such an outlook distracts us from our call to follow the Lamb and to love the nations. Can we not see that to love the nations means that we hope that war does not break out among them? And too often, while we are sitting back watching for the alleged "signs of the times," we are neglecting our call to follow the Lamb as faithful witnesses by loving our neighbors and laying down our life for them.

In the second excursus on Armageddon in the commentary on 20:1–10, I will note that the language of 16:14, 19:19, and 20:8 is such that John clearly links "the war" in these three passages. If this is so, and I believe that it is, then we cannot read "the war" in 16:14, 16 in isolation from "the war" of 19:19 and 20:8. In the latter two passages, however, it is clear that "the war" is none other than that which the Dragon wages against Christ and His people.

The war of "Armageddon," therefore, is simply John's name for the grand war that Satan has been waging throughout all of history against Christ and the people of God. Therefore, "Blessed is the one who stays awake and keeps their garments in order that they may not walk naked and people see their shame" (16:15).

The Seventh Bowl 16:17–21

After the seventh *angel* "poured out" its Bowl "upon the air" (16:17), John heard, "a loud voice came out from the temple from the throne saying, 'It is done'" (16:17). The Seventh Bowl brings the narrative of the second story, or the heavenly vision (4:1—16:21), to an end. Following the pronouncement, there is a recurrence of the theophanic manifestations: "And there was lightning, and sounds, and thunder, and a great earthquake, . . . and great hail" (16:18, 21).[22]

As we have observed, the repetition of the theophanic manifestations in each series of sevens links the three septets to the first occurrence of the theophanic manifestations in the divine throne room (4:5).[23] In addition, each of the occurrences of the theophanic manifestations expands on the previous occurrence. This indicates that the theophanic

---

22. The presence of a "loud voice" links the Seventh Bowl to the vision of God on the throne. The first occurrence of a "loud voice" came from the "strong angel" who was before the throne in 5:2. See also: 5:12; 6:10; 7:2, 10; 8:13; 10:3; 11:12, 15; 12:10; 14:7, 9, 15, 18; 16:17; 19:1, 17; 21:3.

23. See also 8:5; 11:14–19.

manifestations also serve as a literary device carrying the narrative forward. As each expression of the theophanic manifestations intensifies, the narrative brings us closer to the divine presence.

The theophanic manifestations in the Seventh Bowl significantly expands the previous occurrences. Interestingly, the Seventh Bowl does not add an item to the expression. Instead, this occurrence intensifies the phenomena. Consequently, there is not merely an earthquake (as there was in 8:5 and 11:19), but it was "a great earthquake, such as has not happened since humanity has been on the earth so great an earthquake was it" (16:18). And there is not only hail (as there was in 11:19), but the hail was "great" and weighed "as a talent"[24] (16:21).[25]

Earthquakes often herald the coming of God in justice.[26] The fact that an "earthquake" occurs seven times in the book of Revelation (see 6:12; 8:5; 11:13*, 19; 16:18*) and that the earthquake here in the account of the Seventh Bowl (16:18) is the last of these seven occurrences, adds to the conviction that the Seventh Bowl has taken us to the end of the story. As a result of the earthquake, John notes that "the Great City was split into three parts and the cities of the nations fell" (16:19).

What is the Great City?[27] John used this designation earlier in the description of the death of the Two Witnesses (11:8). There the Great City, "is figuratively called Sodom and Egypt, also, where their Lord was crucified." This has naturally led some to conclude that the Great City is Jerusalem. It is my conviction that John uses this designation exclusively for Rome. As I will argue in the account of the Great Prostitute (17:1—19:10), John's message to his reader/hearers is that Rome, by means of its deceptive and seductive lures, is attempting to lead the people of God to follow after the Beast. John's indication here that, "the Great City was split into

---

24. A talent was a Roman unit of measure. The weight of one talent varied so we are not able to discern with any certainty what it weighed. Of course, John was hardly concerned with what it actually weighed! John's concern was that they were huge hailstones! Barr affirms, "a talent weight, a measure of 125 Roman pounds (12 ounces each), thus roughly 90 pounds by our measure. But the expression is best understood to mean they were impossibly big. In our idiom, we might say they weighed a ton." Barr, *Tales*, 4118–19.

25. As noted with the account of the Sixth Bowl, there is a strong association with the closing prophecy in Ezekiel. See Ezek 38:19–22.

26. See Heb 12:26–27.

27. See the discussion in the account of the Great Prostitute in 17:1—19:10 where it likely indicates Rome. See 17:18, 18:10, 16, 18, 19, and 21.

three parts and the cities of the nations' fell" (16:19) serves to inform us that the Beast and the Prostitute represent defeated foes.

John also adds, "every island fled and the mountains were not found" (16:20). The association of mountains with kingdoms reinforces the conclusion that Seventh Bowl depicts the destruction of the imperial powers.[28]

Finally, John notes, "the people blasphemed God" (16:21). Tragically, even though the present account opened with the affirmation, "all the nations will come and worship before You" (15:3), John does not intend for us to understand that every person without exception was worshiping God.

Conclusion

On the one hand, the Seven Bowls reflect both the inevitable consequence of humanity's continued rule over the earth. David Barr concludes, "If our waters are polluted it is not because God is exercising some tyrannical power over us; it is because we foul our own streams. It requires no divine, coercive power to bring about the 'destroying those who destroy the earth' (Rev 11:18)."[29] Barr later adds, "For crooked walls fall as an evitable result of their crookedness (see Amos 7:1–9)."[30]

This is most apparent in the account of the Sixth Bowl. The nations are deceived by the demonic agents (16:14) that come from the mouth of the Dragon, the Beast, and the False Prophet (16:13). These agents deceive the nations in order to gather them [the kings of the inhabited world] for the war" (16:14).

At the same time, the Seven Bowls are also the work of God's divine intervention in bringing about justice. The angels' affirmations, "because You judged these things" (16:5) and "Yes, Lord God, the Almighty, true and righteous are Your judgments" (16:7) affirm that God is directly involved in the effects that follow the pouring out of the Bowls.

Therefore, it is my conviction that the account of the Seven Bowls reveals the inevitable end that follows when humanity fails to repent but instead serves the Beast and its voracious appetite for wealth, power, and

---

28. The only other occurrence of islands (plural) occurs in the description of the Sixth Seal (6:14). This serves to bolster the argument that the Sixth Seal is also the depiction of the end.

29. Barr, *Tales*, loc. 4943.

30. Barr, *Tales*, loc. 4954.

pleasure. The result is the total devastation and destruction of the creation. At the same time, the Seven Bowls also reflect God's divine justice.

With the completion of the account of the Seventh Bowl, the heavenly vision (4:1—16:21; i.e., the second story) has come to an end. Of course, there is more for John to reveal. After all, he has yet to depict the grand restoration of God's Edenic-like city/temple. This is what follows. But first John details the judgment of those who stand opposed to Christ's rule.

Revelation 17:1—19:10
The Third Scene:
The Great Prostitute—Babylon

Revelation 17:1–17
The Great Prostitute
Introduction

While John saw Rome as an embodiment of Babylon, the ideological significance of Babylon extends far beyond the historical capital of the Roman Empire. Rather, Babylon exists wherever sociopolitical power coalesces into an entity that stands against the worship of YHWH alone. Babylon expresses God's judgment on all human attempts to displace God from the center of reality in favor of human power arrangements.[1]

Rev 17 depicts the worldly and idolatrous, oppressive powers as a rich and self-indulgent prostitute, enthroned on a beast which ultimately turns on her and brings about her destruction.[2]

Introduction

As I noted throughout, 17:1 marks the beginning of the third story/scene in the narrative of the book of Revelation. In the first scene, which I presented as the first story (1:9–3:22), John was on the island of Patmos when he saw the resurrected and glorified Jesus who commissioned him to write to the seven churches. In the second scene, which I presented as the second story, or the heavenly vision (4:1—16:22), John was taken to heaven where he saw the Father sitting on the throne and where he learned of the Scroll and its contents. Now, in this third story (17:1—19:10), John is told that he is going to be shown "the judgment of the Great Prostitute

---

1. Howard-Brook and Gwyther, *Unveiling Empire*, loc. 4191.
2. Smalley, *Revelation*, 424.

who sits on many waters" (17:1). He is then taken into a wilderness (17:3) where he sees a woman sitting on the Beast (17:3).

Although we have a new story/scene in the narrative of the Apocalypse, it is important to recognize that this story is not independent of what preceded it. John makes this explicit when he opens the third story by connecting it to the Seven Bowls, "One of the seven angels who had the Seven Bowls" (17:1). Perhaps more importantly, this third story depicts the judgment of the Great Prostitute which links to the second story in that it is a direct response to the martyrs' cry for justice. Furthermore, this judgment was announced by the second angel in 14:8, "Fallen, fallen is Babylon the great, who from the wine of the passion of her immorality gave drink to all the nations."

The Great Prostitute and the Bride

As I noted in the opening discussion on the structure of the book of Revelation, in order to understand John's objectives in the depiction of the Great Prostitute and her judgment (17:1—19:10) it is critical to recognize that this third story/scene (17:1—19:10) parallels the account of the Bride in the fourth and final story/scene (21:9—22:9).

The parallel is clearly evident in that these two scenes have virtually identical openings:

> And one of the seven angels who had the seven bowls came and spoke with me, saying, 'Come, I will show you the judgment of the great Prostitute who sits on many waters'" (17:1).

> And one of the seven angels who had the seven bowls full of the seven last plagues came and spoke with me, saying, 'Come, I will show you the bride, the wife of the Lamb'" (21:9).

In addition, the two scenes are linked thematically in that they depict contrasting visions of two women. In the present story/scene, John learns of the "Great Prostitute" (17:5); whereas, in the fourth story/scene, he is shown the "Bride" (21:9). In addition, the two women are actually cities: The Great Prostitute is "the Great City that rules over the kings of the earth" (17:18);[3] and the Bride is "the Holy City, Jerusalem" (21:10).[4]

---

3. See Isa 23:16–17; Nah 3:4.

4. For a list of contrasts between the Great Prostitute and the Bride, see Howard-Brook and Gwyther, *Unveiling Empire,* loc. 4239–61.

Finally, the closing of each scene is similarly indicated in that each contains an account of John falling down in an attempt to worship an angel (19:10; 22:8), only to be told not to do that but to "worship God" (19:10; 22:9).

The parallels between the two women/cities are also evident in the marked contrasts between the two women/cities. Perhaps the most obvious contrast between them is that one is a "Prostitute" (17:1–5), while the other is "the Bride, the wife of the Lamb" (21:9). The clothing of the two women/cities is also contrastive. Thus, while the Great Prostitute is "clothed in purple[5] and scarlet" (17:4)[6] the Bride is "clothed in bright, pure, fine linen" (19:8). The description of each of the cities furthers the contrast between them. The Great Prostitute is identified as Babylon (17:5) and is said to be, "a home of demons and a prison of every unclean spirit and a prison of every unclean bird" (18:2). The Bride, however, is the Holy City/New Jerusalem into which, "nothing unclean will enter" (21:27). In addition, the accounts of the two women/cities contrast with one another in the descriptions of their eternal destinies. In the case of Babylon, John learns that "the Great City will certainly not be found any longer" (18:21). The account of the Bride, however, describes the city as the eternal dwelling place of God among his people (21:3; 22:3) and adds, "they will reign forever and ever" (22:5). Finally, contrasting exhortations are given to the people of God concerning each of the two women/cities. With regard to the Great Prostitute, Babylon, a voice says, "Come out of her, My people" (18:4). But with respect to the Bride, it is affirmed, "Blessed are the ones . . . who enter into the city" (22:14). DeSilva concludes, "The two ways of ordering human community, like the feminine images John sets before our eyes, could not be more different, and John will make clear that one cannot both cavort with Babylon, profiting from her favours, and be welcomed by—and as a part of—the bride of the Lamb."[7]

---

5. Rossing notes, "Purple garments and gold and jewels were favorite motifs of the evil-woman *topos*" (Rossing, *Two Cities*, 78).

6. The abundance of self-indulgence is seen in her dress. As Tabb notes, "the 'great city' embodies civilization that prizes human ambition, lust, wealth and power" (Tabb, *All Things New*, loc. 3288).

7. DeSilva, *Discovering*, 225.

COMMENTARY: REVELATION 17:1—19:10

The Divine Lawcourt

In order to understand John's account of the Great Prostitute it is also important to recognize John's use of the Divine law court motif.[8]

The entire third story/scene (17:1—19:10) is framed as a courtroom scene in which judgment will be pronounced on the Great Prostitute. In this courtroom, the people of God ("you saints and apostles and prophets": 18:20) function as the plaintiffs. The defendant, of course, is the Great Prostitute. God, who is explicitly identified as, "the One sitting on the throne" (19:4), serves as the judge.[9] The charge against the Prostitute is murder: "in her was found the blood of prophets and of saints and of all who have been slain on the earth" (18:24).[10] The case before the judge is the martyrs' cry for justice.

As the courtroom scene climaxes, the angel announces to the people of God, "God has brought the judgment[11] for you upon her" (18:20). The verdict has been rendered. Babylon, the Great Prostitute, is guilty:[12] "I heard another voice from heaven saying, 'God has remembered her crimes.'" (18:4). Consequently, the Great Multitude exclaims, "Hallelujah! Salvation and glory and power to our God, because true and just are His judgments; because He judged the Great Prostitute who corrupted the earth by means of her immorality and He avenged the blood of His servants from her hand" (19:2). The punishment will be meted out: "Give to her even as she herself has given and repay her double according to her deeds, in the cup which she mixed mix double for her'" (18:4, 6).[13]

---

8. See Bandy, "Prophetic Lawsuit." Schüssler Fiorenza suggests that Revelation does not depict war against Babylon but uses a courtroom/lawsuit motif and a shipwreck or commercial-destruction model (Ezek 26-28; Jer 50-51): See Schüssler Fiorenza, *Justice and Judgment*, 7.

9. The phrase, "the One who sits upon the throne," occurs seven times: 4:9; 5:1, 7, 13; 6:16; 7:15; 21:5. References to the Father's throne occur thirty-nine times: 1:4; 3:21*; 4:2*, 3, 4, 5*, 6*, 9, 10*; 5:1, 6, 7, 11*,13; 6:16; 7:9, 10, 11, 15*, 17; 8:3; 12:5; 14:3; 16:17; 19:4, 5; 20:11, 12; 21:3, 5; 22:1, 3.

10. Kraybill notes, "Christians were only a small minority among countless victims of the great imperial beast" (Kraybill, *Imperial Cult and Commerce in John's Apocalypse*, 200).

11. The Greek rather woodenly reads, "God judged the judgment."

12. It is somewhat ironic that a skeptic might contend that God is unreasonable and evil for bringing such destruction. Yet, we so often hear that God is unjust because He allows evil and corruption to persist.

13. Recall the brief interjection between the pouring out of the third and the fourth Bowls, where John hears the cry of the "angel of the waters" who was "saying, 'Righteous are you, the One who is and who was, the Holy One, because you judged these

Excursus: The Roman Backdrop to John's Account of the Great Prostitute

Historians suggest that as much as 90 percent of the population in the Roman empire constituted what is rightly deemed "the poor."[14] Of the top 10 percent, only 3 percent of them were the wealthy members of the ruling classes.[15] The other 7 percent of the population may have been living above the poverty line, but they were by no means what we would consider "the middle class." There is little question that in the Roman world, the wealthy (the 3 percent) ruled at the expense of the poor and the marginalized (the 90 percent). Rome flourished on the backs of millions of slaves and countless others who struggled daily just to survive.

Not only did Rome rule at the expense of the poor and the marginalized, but it was also established on the backs of the oppressed. As deSilva notes, "But even the Roman historian Tacitus, a privileged member of the dominant culture, knows how Roman domination looks from the margins: 'Robbery, savagery, and rape they call "government"; they make a desert and call it "peace."'"[16] Howard-Brook and Gwyther add:

> The Roman Empire employed various forms of execution both as means of eliminating those perceived as threatening the empire and as threats to keep people in line. This is why mass crucifixions occurred along public thoroughfares and on the tops of hills and why people were thrown to the wild animals in the arenas. The mere fact that public executions took place would have been an effective deterrent to many who were dissatisfied with Rome. Where seduction and the threat of force failed, the use of violence inevitably followed. Revelation clearly portrays Babylon as a place where murder is a method of social control.[17]

As I have noted throughout our study, the book of Revelation must be viewed through the lens of contrasting kingdoms.

---

things, because they poured out the blood of the holy ones and of the prophets and You have given to them blood to drink, they are worthy of it'" (16:5–6).

14. Carter, *Roman Empire*, 3–9.
15. Carter, *Roman Empire*, 3.
16. DeSilva, *Discovering*, 244.
17. Howard-Brook and Gwyther, *Unveiling Empire*, loc. 4469.

The contrast is most apparent in how they rule: the kingdom of God does not rule the way the nations do. The nations rule through the use of force and brutality for the benefit of the wealthy and the elite, and at the expense of the masses. For John, Rome was the present embodiment of empire. In 13:1–18 and 17:1—19:10, John describes a system whereby Rome maintained its power structure and the oppression of the people by creating a state in which the masses were dependent on the Roman system for survival. This system incorporated religious ideology as a means of justifying their positions. The refrain in the Roman world was that the gods placed the emperor in power and recognizing his rule was an essential component of one's religious duties. In fact, appeasing the gods was critical to maintaining order and peace within the empire. For the masses, this meant that one's civil and religious duties were a necessary component for ensuring the status quo, the "Pax Romana" (The Peace of Rome). Participating in the system meant securing one's own economic survival. After all, upsetting the status quo might jeopardize one's viability.[18] For the poor and the marginalized, whose viability was a daily concern, the incentive to compromise with the state was high.

For John, the kingdom of God, by way of contrast, rules through love. God's kingdom, as exemplified by Jesus, manifests love by denying one's own interests and even sacrificing self for the sake of the other. Jesus is the Lamb! Ironically, then, the cross was the ultimate embodiment of love and power. The cross was both the very means by which God demonstrated His love and the means by which Rome displayed its power.[19]

This serves as the basis for John's contrasting descriptions of the two women/cities. The kingdoms of the world—which for John was personified by Rome—are a seductive, self-indulging prostitute (17:1—19:10).[20] The people of God, by way of contrast, are the faithful, loving bride (21:9—22:9).

---

18. The Roman world, of course, was not a homogenous society. Some areas enjoyed greater freedom than others.

19. The irony is great. Jesus's exercising of power through love led Him to the cross. Rome's exercise of power was to utilize crosses to oppress the masses and maintain order.

20. It may well be that John's reader/hearers already had a conception of Rome as

This background is critical for understanding the depiction of the Great Prostitute and the account of her judgment. As Bauckham contends, "The judgments of chapters 16–19 are primarily aimed at destroying the systems—political, economic and religious—which oppose God and his righteousness and which are symbolized by the beast, the false prophet, Babylon, and the kings of the earth."[21] God's judgment is indeed just!

The OT Background for the Great Prostitute

The use of female imagery to depict people and nations was commonplace in the ancient world.

Throughout the OT, the relationship between YHWH and the people of God was viewed in terms of a marriage covenant with God as the groom and the people of God as His bride.[22] It is against this backdrop that the OT prophets consistently likened Israel's idolatry to adultery and prostitution.[23] The prophets often seized upon this imagery by categorizing the unfaithful people of God as, "playing the prostitute" (Ezek 6:9).[24] The prophets then use the analogy of the marriage

---

the city of over-indulgence that oppresses the poor. Carey notes that "Jewish and Christian texts used Babylon as a cipher for Rome (1 Pet. 5:13; 2 Bar; 4 Ezra; Sib. 5.143, 159)" (Carey, *Shadow of Empire*, loc. 2177).

21. Bauckham, *Theology*, 102.

22. Smalley notes, "The imagery of harlotry was commonly used by the prophets of the Old Testament to denote religious apostasy (cf. Isa 1.21; Jer. 2.20–28; 13.27; Ezek.16:15–41; Hos. 2.5)" (Smalley, *Revelation*, 426).

23. That the OT people of God are regularly depicted as a prostitute or as prostituting themselves to other gods, provides the basis for some modern scholars to suggest that the Great Prostitute in the book of Revelation is the Jewish people who have remained in Judaism and failed to acknowledge Christ (see Isa 23:16–17). Others suggest that the Prostitute is the apostatizing members of the early Christian communities. The former option is a bit anachronistic in that there does not appear to have been a clean break between Judaism and the early Christian movement. That notion that apostatizing members of the Christian community are the Prostitute has more merit. After all, John is taken to the wilderness (17:3) to see her, which is where the Woman (i.e. the people of God) fled in 12:6, 14. The difficulty, however, with both of these options is that the text is quite explicit: "The women whom you saw is the Great City that rules over the kings of the earth" (17:18). There is no question, however, that some in the early Christian community were falling to the temptations and snares of Babylon. Hence, John's exhortation: "Come out from her my people" (18:4). For an exposition of the view that Jerusalem is Babylon, see Chilton, *Days of Vengeance*.

24. See also: Hos 4:17–18.

covenant and conclude that God's people have forsaken their husband and gone after another:

> Surely, as a woman treacherously departs from her lover,
> So you have dealt treacherously with Me,
> O house of Israel," declares the Lord (Jer 3:20).

The prophet Ezekiel frequently employed such imagery in his condemnation of the people of God.[25] For Ezekiel, the people of Jerusalem were like an unfaithful wife who accommodated with the surrounding culture. The people, "played the harlot" (Ezek 16:15). They "took some of your clothes, made for yourself high places of various colors and played the harlot on them" (Ezek 16:16). They "also took your beautiful jewels *made* of My gold and of My silver, which I had given you, and made for yourself male images that you might play the harlot with them" (Ezek 16:17).

The account of the judgment of the Great Prostitute (Rev 17:1—19:10), therefore, is deeply rooted in the prophetic critique of the people of God who broke their covenant with YHWH and followed other gods.

---

25. See: Ezek 16:15–52. See also, Ezek 26–28; Isa 23–24, 27; Jer 50–51.

Revelation 17:1–17
The Great Prostitute

John Carried Away in the Spirit
to the Wilderness 17:1–3a

THE ACCOUNT OF THE Great Prostitute opens with John being told by an angel, "Come, I will show you the judgment of the Great Prostitute" (17:1). This Great Prostitute is identified as, "the one who is sitting upon many waters" (17:1).[1] She is also the one, "with whom the kings of the earth committed acts of immorality and those who inhabit the earth were made drunk from the wine of her immorality" (17:2). John is then carried "away in the Spirit" and taken into the wilderness (17:3).

John Sees a Woman on a Beast 17:3–7

In the wilderness, he sees a woman sitting, not upon many waters, but upon a Beast (17:3). This Beast, who has "seven heads and ten horns" (17:3, 7, 9, 12, 16), is most certainly the Beast from the Abyss who killed the Two Witnesses (11:7) and whom John introduced in 13:1–8. John adds that the woman was "clothed in purple and scarlet and adorned with gold and precious stones and pearls" (17:4).[2]

---

1. Later in the passage, John makes matters simple for us noting, "The waters which you saw where the harlot sits, are peoples and multitudes and nations and tongues" (17:15). See Jer 51:13.

2. Unfortunately, contemporary artwork often presents a caricature of her as a bejeweled prostitute more akin to a woman in a brothel, than as a queen (18:7). This is why contemporary readers might do well to not search for images of Revelation's characters despite the fact that there are many such images available. One of the

It is important to recognize that although we, the omniscient reader, know that the woman is a "Great Prostitute," John's portrait of her suggests that she is attractive and seductive. Bauckham affirms, "At first glance, she might seem to be the goddess Roma, in all her glory, a stunning personification of the civilization of Rome, as she was worshipped in many a temple in the cities of Asia. But as John sees her, she is a Roman prostitute, a seductive whore and a scheming witch, and her wealth and splendour represent the profits of her disreputable trade."[3]

Gold Cup in Her Hand 17:4

Perhaps the most startling feature of John's portrait of the woman pertains to what she is holding. He says, she had "a golden cup in her hand full of detestable things and the unclean things of her immorality" (17:4). Moreover, her cup was full of the blood of God's people, "And I saw that the woman was drunk from the blood of the saints and from the blood of the witnesses of Jesus" (17:6). For John, "This image of Babylon holding the cup of blood is a powerful indictment of empire."[4] As Ian Paul notes, she may be "clothed in scarlet but drenched in the blood of the innocent."[5]

---

problems with such illustrations is that they often portray the Dragon and the Beasts, as demonic, mutant, evil, and the Prostitute as a despicable whore. The problem is that the weaponry of Satan is deception. Illustrations that depict the Dragon, the Beast, and the Prostitute as blatantly evil undermine the very essence of the Apocalypse. John is telling his readers, "This is what they really are." The fact is, however, that this is not what they look like. For John's reader/hearers, and for us as well, the Prostitute appears as something attractive. To them, the power of the Beast was enticing—especially the security that he offers for those whose very survival is a daily struggle. The False Prophet performed miraculous signs to deceive them. The book of Revelation is deeply concerned to inform them that what the Beast, the False Prophet, and the Great Prostitute look like to John's reader/hearers is not what they actually are. Modern readers of the book of Revelation would do well to see them first for how John's reader/hearers would have seen them. Only then are we able to recognize how John's message might manifest itself in our world.

3. Bauckham, *Theology*, 17–18.
4. Howard-Brook and Gwyther, *Unveiling Empire*, loc. 4558.
5. Paul, *Revelation*, 303.

Name: "Mystery, Babylon the Great"

John then identifies the Great Prostitute as "Babylon" (17:5). In fact, he says, she has "upon her forehead a name, 'Mystery, Babylon the Great, the mother of immorality and of the abominations of the earth'" (17:5).[6] There is little question that John used the epitaph "Babylon" as a cipher from Rome. DeSilva notes, "Authors who are near-contemporary with John frequently use the label 'Babylon' to designate Rome. This is especially the case after Rome reprises Babylon's historic destruction of Jerusalem and its Temple (Sib. Or. 4.158–61; 5.143, 159; 2 Baruch; 4 Ezra; 1 Pet. 5.13)."[7] Aune acknowledged that Babylon is "a symbolic name for Rome.... Babylon and Rome are comparable because both were centers for world empires and both captured Jerusalem and destroyed the temple."[8]

John interjects, "I was amazed after seeing her: greatly amazed" (17:6). John's sense of amazement may be understood in one of two ways. He may have been amazed because although he was told that he would be shown the judgment of the Great Prostitute, at this point in the narrative, she has not only not been judged, but she appears triumphant. It is also possible, and, in fact, more likely that John was amazed in that he had a sense of awe and wonder at the woman. That the latter is the case follows from the fact that the only prior occurrence of "amazed" was in 13:3, where "the whole earth was amazed" when they saw the Beast (13:3). That this is the case also makes the most sense of the angel's response, "Why are you amazed?" (17:7). After all, the angel makes it clear, being amazed is what the nations do when they see the Beast: "those who inhabit the earth will be amazed" (17:8).

The angel then informs John, "I will explain to you the mystery of the woman and of the beast which is carrying her" (17:7).

Excursus: Who/What Is the Prostitute?

As we continue reading in the account of the Great Prostitute, John begins to reveal, albeit quite cryptically, the woman's

---

6. That she has a name on her forehead corresponds to the 144,000 who are described as "having His name and the name of His Father having been written on their foreheads" (14:1).

Note that throughout the book of Revelation the "forehead" represent the place of a name (see 7:3; 9:4; 13:16; 14:1, 9; 17:5; 20:4; 22:4). Christ, however, has the name, "King of kings and Lord of Lords" written "upon his garments and upon His thigh" (19:16).

7. DeSilva, *Discovering*, 227.

8. Aune, *Revelation*, 2.829–31.

identity: "And the woman, whom you saw, is the Great City that rules over the kings of the earth" (17:18).[9]

John's opening description of the Great Prostitute as sitting on the Beast (17:3) likely serves as an ironic portrayal of the woman's blasphemous claims: she "says in her heart, 'I sit as a queen'" (18:7).[10] Yet, we have known since the opening throne room scene that God is the One who is seated on the throne (4:1-2).

The fact that John sees the woman sitting atop the Beast (17:3, 7) also indicates her interrelationship with the Beast.[11] This may have presented a measure of confusion for the modern reader. If, as I have argued, the Beast represents Rome, how then can the Great Prostitute, who is identified as "Babylon the Great" (14:8; 16:19; 17:5; 18:2, 21),[12] also represent Rome? Perhaps the clearest way to distinguish between the Beast and the Great Prostitute is to recognize that the Great Prostitute represents the material and economic side of the Roman Empire.

Of course, it is important to understand that in the ancient world, the lines between politics, religion, culture, and economics were quite blurred. Therefore, although we might want to draw lines of demarcation that distinguish the Beast as the empire, the False Prophet as the imperial religion that fostered the worship of the empire and the emperor, and the Great Prostitute as the material and economic side of the Roman economy, the reality is that in the Roman world, the

---

9. This corresponds with the reference to the "Great City" in the account of the Two Witnesses where John states that the city "is figuratively called Sodom and Egypt, also, where their Lord was crucified" (11:8). Though some understandably have attempted to identify the city as Jerusalem (see Thomas, *Revelation*, 94), after all, it is, "where their Lord was crucified," the narrative, as we will see, makes it clear that the Great Prostitute is Rome. Caird, in fact, asserts, "The city is Rome. Yet, even this cannot e said without qualification. For this city has a longer history than Rome.... Rome is simply the latest embodiment of something that is a recurrent feature of human history. The great city is the spiritual home of those John dubs inhabitants of the earth; it is the tower of Babel, the city of this world, Vanity Fair" (Caird, *Revelation*, 138).

10. Rossing notes that "Riding on the beast of Rome, the woman is transformed from an evil-woman seductress figure into a thorough political figure" (Rossing, *Two Cities*, 81).

11. It is, therefore, ironic that the Beast ultimately hates her (17:16).

12. The only variation is 18:10: where it is called "the Great City, Babylon, the strong city."

political, religious, social, and economic spheres were highly intertwined.[13] Tabb notes, "'The beast' likely signifies the state's political and military might that commands total allegiance and even worship, while 'Babylon the great' is its cultural and economic system that seductively promises affluence."[14] Smalley adds, "'Babylon' in the Apocalypse represents the allurement offered by demonic forces in drawing people away from Christian values.... The beast, in contrast, is that part of the ungodly world which is prepared to submit to the superficial attraction of satanic institution (Babylon/Rome), with their unrighteous religious, economic and social aspects."[15]

The Beast, the False Prophet, and the Great Prostitute constitute the formidable enemies of God's people. The empire, embodied by the Beast, rules. The False Prophet provides the imperial propaganda that demanded the worship of the Beast (13:12). As noted earlier, the propaganda certainly included the proposition that the well-being of the empire ("Rome"; i.e., the Beast) was in the hands of the gods. The imperial religion (i.e., the False Prophet) aimed to ensure that the gods were placated.[16]

In the present account, we now learn of Babylon, the Great Prostitute, which represents the material and economic side of life in the empire. For John, the material prosperity within the Roman culture is nothing more than a drunken prostitute.

---

13. Warren Carter notes, "We often think of religion and politics as separate and distinct. Religion is personal, individual, private. Politics is societal, communal, public. Of course, just how separated religion and politics really are is debatable (think of the "political" slogan, "God bless America," or of those who seek martyrdom in the name of Islam). But in the first-century Roman world, no one pretended religion and politics were separate. Rome claimed its empire was ordained by the gods" (Carter, *Roman Empire*, 2).

14. Tabb, *All Things New*, loc 2343.

15. Smalley, *Revelation*, 429.

16. It is in this sense that we might consider participation in the imperial religion as mandatory for the people within the Roman empire. Hence, the False Prophet makes, "the earth and those who inhabit it to worship the first Beast" (13:12). For those who resisted the ideology, the imperial religion imposed economic and material consequences. Hence, "whoever does not worship the image of the Beast should be killed" (13:15). Those who fail to oblige will then be cut off from the Beast's economic system. Thus, only those who have received the Mark of the Beast are "able to buy or sell" (13:17).

For John then, it is imperative that his reader/hearers recognize the Great Prostitute for what she really is. Most notably, just as the Beast had established "peace" by deception and war, so also the Great Prostitute's wealth was brought about through deception, slavery, and murder. John affirms, "And I saw that the woman was drunk from the blood of the saints and from the blood of the witnesses of Jesus" (17:6). In fact, "in her was found the blood of prophets and of saints and of all those who have been slain upon the earth" (18:24).

Finally, it is critical to recognize that the Great Prostitute, like the Beast and False Prophet, receives her power from the Dragon: "by means of your sorcery all the nations were deceived" (18:23).

17:8–13 The One Having Wisdom: The Beast and Its Seven Heads and Ten Horns

As the account of the Great Prostitute continues, the angel further delineates the nature of the Beast upon which the Great Prostitute was sitting.

John is told that the Beast "was and is not and is about to come up from the Abyss and is going to destruction" (17:8). John exhorts his reader/hearers: "Here is the mind, the one having wisdom" (17:9). The exhortation for the reader/hearers to have wisdom is quite similar to the exhortation issued in 13:18. There John specified, "Here is the wisdom. Let the one having a mind calculate the number of the Beast" (13:18). In the same way, the exhortation in 17:9 serves to inform John's reader/hearers that they need wisdom in order to discern the meaning of the Beast's seven heads and ten horns.[17] After all, if the Beast "is about to come up from the Abyss" (17:8), this is not good news for the people of God. We know, of course, that he comes from the Abyss to "make war with them and overcome them and kill them" (11:7).

The angel continues: "The seven heads are seven mountains on which the woman sits, and they are seven kings" (17:9). That the seven

---

17. The implication is that they were capable of determining the meaning of the number. The need for having wisdom in 17:9 remains an enigma for us. After all, if John's audience was able to discern the number of the Beast (666), what further need was there for "having wisdom" in discerning the meaning of the seven heads and the ten horns? The best solution, as I will note below, is that the heads and horns simply represent all empires.

heads of the Beast represent both "mountains" and "kings" adds to the complexity of the passage. John's use of "mountains" and "kings" (17:9) is likely pleonastic. As I noted earlier, "mountains" are closely related to both kingdoms and temples. The reason for specifying the heads are both "mountains" and "kings" may be to further the identification—as if such were needed—of the Beast with the city of Rome. Rome, after all, was the city of seven hills (i.e., "mountains").

As for the fact that the seven heads are also seven kings, the angel further explains, "five have fallen, one is, the other has not yet come" (17:10). Then it adds, "And the Beast that was and is not is himself also an eighth and is one of the seven and is going to destruction" (17:11). The angel also notes that the "ten horns are ten kings" (17:12).

Though the meaning of the seven heads and the ten horns may have been evident for John's reader/hearers—though I doubt that it was—it has certainly eluded modern interpreters. Perhaps, the best insight is that offered by David Barr:

> Series of seven events no longer need to be read as a literal sequence, for we know that seven represents completion. Thus, any sequence of any length will be a sequence of seven in John's system. If John says there are ten rulers, we don't need to try to count them or identify them. There will always be ten whenever John talks about the imperial powers of this age.[18]

If Barr's assessment is correct, then John does not intend for us to associate the ten kings with any kings in particular. Instead, we are to recognize that they represent all the kings and kingdoms of the world. Smalley agrees, "Just as 'Babylon' (17.1) represents the idolatrous forces of the state in any period of world history, so the satanic beast symbolizes *any* incarnation of the worldly misuse of power."[19] This conclusion gains support from John's description of the war that follows.

They Will Make War against the Lamb 17:14

John continues by adding, "These will make war with the Lamb" (17:14). It is not merely the Lamb with whom they wage war. John adds, "and those who are with Him [the Lamb] are called, chosen, and faithful"

---

18. Barr, *Tales*, loc. 362.
19. Smalley, *Revelation*, 437.

(17:14). The implication is that the war is also waged against those who are with Him.

As I noted throughout our study, in the book of Revelation "the war" corresponds to that which is waged against Christ and the people of God. Of course, technically, "the war" is waged against the people of God. After all, Christ has ascended and is seated on the throne with the Father (3:21). Since, however, the people of God are the representatives of Christ, to wage war against the people of God is to wage war against Christ; and vice versa, to wage war against Christ one must wage war against His people.

That the ten horns, which are ten kings, do not specify ten particular kings but instead represent all kings and kingdoms in history gains support from the comparison of the war in 17:14 and the war in 16:14. In 16:14, we learn, "the kings of the inhabited world" gather for war. In the present account, we learn that it is the ten kings who wage the war. The implication, therefore, is that the ten kings do not represent ten particular kings but all the kings of the earth.

The mention of the war against Christ concludes with the affirmation that Christ is the One who is victorious. John affirms, "the Lamb will overcome them because He is the Lord of Lords and King of kings" (17:14).

The Prostitute Is Destroyed 17:15–18

Although this third section/story opened with one of the seven angels exhorting John, "Come! I will show you the judgment of the Great Prostitute" (17:1), John has yet to learn of Babylon's judgment. It is not until 17:16 that John even begins to hear of her demise.

Interestingly, John notes that the Great Prostitute is destroyed by the combined forces of the ten horns and the Beast. He states, "these will hate the prostitute and will make her desolate and naked and they will eat her flesh and burn her up in the fire" (17:16). John adds, "For God has placed it into their hearts to do His purpose" (17:17). Although this may seem at first glance to be a bit surprising, it reflects the nature of empires. Empires are often destroyed by forces from within. Those who were once allied become enemies and the means by which one another is destroyed. DeSilva adds, "The scene of the great prostitute stripped, naked, devoured by her allies, and burned up (17:16–17) is John's final answer to Rome's self-glorifying propaganda."[20]

This accords with the supposition set forth throughout this commentary that while God sovereignly rules, His actions include His divine intervention and they are mediated. In the present account, the systems of the world are also the agents of destruction.

Excursus: John's Portrayal of Women and Patriarchy

Tina Pippin presents a sharp critique of the book of Revelation. Pippin expresses disdain for the book of Revelation, and in particular its portrait of the Great Prostitute, on the basis that it reflects misogyny and patriarchy. She states, "When I looked into the face of Babylon, I saw a woman."[21] With regard to Rev 17:16, which says, "these will hate the prostitute and will make her desolate and naked and they will eat her flesh and burn her up in the fire," Pippin alleges that the story depicts, "the sexual exploitation of a prostitute and ultimately a voyeuristic episode of the torture and murder of a woman." In fact, in her estimation, Rev 17:16 is, "the most vividly misogynistic passage in the New Testament."[22] Howard-Brook and Gwyther assent to this criticism, "One of the challenges for us in interpreting the images of Babylon and New Jerusalem is the blatant gender stereotyping of the apocalyptic cities as 'evil' or 'good' women."[23]

Although I believe that Pippin's accusations are the result of a misreading of the text, I do not intend to deny nor dismiss the fact that the biblical writers were immersed in patriarchal cultures. And although I would argue that the biblical writers present an ethic of women that radically elevates the dignity of women in the ancient world, it is not unfair to say that we would have liked them to go further. Howard-Brook and Gwyther affirm:

> We hear Tina Pippin's experience of the text as degrading, violent, and hateful of women. We offer no excuses for

---

20. DeSilva, *Unholy Allegiances*, loc. 1034–35.
21. Pippin, *Death and Desire*, 80.
22. Pippin, *Death and Desire*, 58.
23. Howard-Brook and Gwyther, *Unveiling Empire*, loc. 4261.

John's language. It is small solace to suggest that if we were choosing how to express a vision of empire and its alternative, we would find other images than those of women's bodies. It is with acknowledgment of our participation in the privileges of patriarchy and our solidarity with women's cry for justice in the church and in the world that we take on the task of interpreting these difficult images. In case there is doubt, however, let us be clear at the outset. The images of women used by Revelation were not intended to, nor should they ever, legitimate violence against women of any kind.[24]

David deSilva agrees: "One must also consider how the objectification and stereotyping of women over the millennia preceding John nurtured the entire tradition of using females as symbols in these particular ways—a tradition in which John stands (and not for misogynistic ends!), but a tradition that John also fails to question and critique along the way."[25]

In response to Pippin's criticisms of the book of Revelation, I have seven[26] points for consideration. First, Pippin's critique fails to recognize that the book of Revelation's imagery is not meant to suppose that Babylon is actually a female prostitute. John, in fact, explicitly says that "And the woman, whom you saw, is the Great City" (17:18). Barbara Rossing affirms, "Rome was an empire, not a woman."[27] DeSilva offers the following assessment:

> Babylon is not a woman. "She" is a city. "She" is not an individual with a face who has been shaped by male fantasies and uses these, in turn, to her profit. "She" is the powerful center of a political and economic system of domination, enforced by generally irresistible military might and legitimated by such heady propaganda as makes self-critique impossible. When we look into the face of that "woman" we see a politico-economic context established on a slave economy, on military and "legal" violence when the complex is threatened (or even questioned), on the redirection of local populations' goods, services, and even longings

---

24. Howard-Brook and Gwyther, *Unveiling Empire*, loc. 4289.
25. DeSilva, *Discovering*, 235.
26. Do I need to explain why I have "seven" points?
27. Rossing, *Rapture*, 133.

from the interest of their native lands to the interests of the seat of empire."[28]

Second, John's choice to depict Babylon as a prostitute must also be viewed against the imperial portrait of the goddess Roma as the official symbol of the city. John's rendering of Rome as Babylon, in other words, represents a critique of an imperial symbol. For John, Rome was not a goddess but a drunken Prostitute responsible for the death of millions.[29] John's voice, in other words, represents a voice from the margins crying out against the empire on behalf of the millions who were exploited so that Rome might prosper.

Third, the book of Revelation also portrays the people of God as the Bride. In other words, not all of the women in Revelation are evil and seductive mistresses. Some women are the faithful Bride of God Himself. In fact, the Bride represents the totality of all who are redeemed. That is, the Bride is composed of men and women.

Fourth, the imagery of the Prostitute and the Bride must be read in light of the biblical depiction of Lady Wisdom and Lady Folly in Proverbs 1–9.[30] Rossing observes, "Revelation is tapping into a two-women tradition that had strong evocative power in the first century."[31] In other words, such imagery was common in the ancient world. This, of course, does not make it acceptable. At the same time, we must be careful about overly criticizing an ancient society based on modern standards.

Fifth, the use of feminine pronouns to describe cities derives from the fact that the Greek word for "city" was a feminine noun that required a feminine pronoun. Rossing notes, "In the ancient world it was conventional to personify

---

28. DeSilva, *Seeing Things*, 325–26.

29. DeSilva notes, "John presents the city of Rome (itself already a symbol of the massive web of domination systems that constitute Roman imperialism) using the symbol of a kind of woman in large measure because he is responding directly to the official and ubiquitous presentation of the city of Rome in female guise, namely as the goddess Roma" (*Discovering*, 234).

30. Rossing, *Two Cities*, 77. See also, Isa 1:21; 23:16–17; Jer 3:6–10; Ezek 16:15–22; 23:1–49; Hos 4:12–13; 5:3; Nah 3:4.

31. Rossing, *Two Cities*, 58–59.

cities as feminine figures, but this reflects only grammatical gender—not literal gender."[32]

Sixth, John was not writing from a position of power. John, himself, was one of the oppressed. The criticism that John is misogynistic and reflective of patriarchy does not do justice to the historical setting that gave rise to the book of Revelation. Regardless of which "John" wrote the book of Revelation, the text itself indicates that he was a political exile of Rome. DeSilva, referring to John's denouncing of the prophetess Jezebel in 2:20–23, notes, "First, both John and Jezebel stand on a level and equal playing field (indeed if anyone is disadvantaged it is John, who speaks from exile). John does not have the power to exclude or silence Jezebel. He has only the power to persuade people in the congregations that Jezebel's accommodationist teachings, if heeded, will lead them to betray the witness and obedience to which Christ has called them."[33]

Seventh, in response to Pippin's criticism that Rev 17:16 depicts rape, Rossing responds by noting that the imagery of making naked, devouring flesh, and burning with fire are all associated with siege warfare. Thus, she concludes, "This is a threat of economic and spiritual reversal and not sexual exposure."[34]

---

32. Rossing, *Rapture*, 133.
33. DeSilva, *Discovering*, 136.
34. Rossing *Two Cities*, 97.

Revelation 18:1—19:10
The Fall of Babylon and the Three Hallelujahs

People usually do not enter rationally and deliberately into a situation of evil; rather, they are seduced into it. Why is empire able to enlist so many into its service? Why do so many good people cheer for empire and give their lives for it? Why do those willing to seek peace, justice, and community always seem so few? The answer resides in the seductive character of Babylon.[1]

John condemns the imperial order of Rome, not only because Rome persecutes Christians and Rome blasphemes against God, but also because Rome has become rich by exploiting the peoples of the earth.[2]

Continued partnership with and profiting from Roman imperialism means continued participation in its systemic injustices, both towards human beings who are exploited, excluded or victimized and against God whose unique claim on human allegiance is denied. Thus, continued partnership exposes one to the same judgment that hangs over Rome. The angel's summons calls 'those who could share in her profits to side with her victims and become victims themselves.'[3]

There comes a time in every oppression when the amount of coercion needed to maintain a system will itself destroy the system, as we ourselves have seen in the Soviet Union and South Africa.

---

1. Howard-Brook and Gwyther, *Unveiling Empire*, loc. 4387.
2. Gonzales, *Every People*, loc. 898–99.
3. DeSilva, *Discovering*, 247.

COMMENTARY: REVELATION 17:1—19:10

So the great whore has become drunk with the blood of the saints (17:6); Rome's very act of killing becomes her own death.[4]

Introduction

AS I NOTED AT the close of the last chapter, John was told in 17:1 that he would see the destruction of the Great Prostitute but it was not until 17:16 that he even mentions her demise. It is here in 18:1–24 that John provides an extensive description of Babylon's fall.

The judgment of the Great Prostitute is explicitly attributed to the work of God. The Great Multitude affirm, "He judged the Great Prostitute who corrupted the earth by means of her immorality" (19:2). At the same time, however, the Prostitute's judgment includes drinking from her own cup: "in the cup which she mixed, mix double for her" (18:6). The judgment of the Great Prostitute and her destruction then, is both the work of God and the result of humanity's systems bringing about their own demise. The political, religious, and economic systems of humanity are predicated upon power and greed and, in the end, it is their lust that results in the implosion of that very system. As David Barr says, "Those who seek to dominate others will be devoured in the process."[5]

Throughout this account, there is also a reiteration of the justness of God's judgment of the Great Prostitute. God is just because what the Great Prostitute receives corresponds with what she has done. She is reaping the consequences of what she has sown. The opening cry of the angel affirms: "Give to her even as she herself has given" (18:6). In addition, it is because, "in her was *found* the blood of prophets and of saints and of all those who have been slain upon the earth" (18:24) that "Babylon, the Great City, will certainly not be *found* any longer" (18:21).[6] Thus, because the Great Prostitute has a cup that is full of "blood" (17:6), she must now drink: "in the cup which she mixed mix double for her" (18:6).

In terms of John's narrative, the judgment of the Great Prostitute represents the climax with regard to the prayers of the saints.

---

4. Barr, *Tales*, loc. 4955–58.
5. Barr, "Doing Violence," 104.
6. Emphasis added in 18:6 and 18:24.

REVELATION 18:1—19:10

Announcement of the Fall of Babylon 18:1-8

John begins his description of the Great Prostitute's destruction with the expression, "After these things" (18:1), which simply indicates a transition in the Apocalypse. John then states, "I saw another angel coming down from heaven" (18:1). It is my suspicion that John's labeling of "another angel" in 18:1 intends for us to link this occurrence to the "another angel" in 14:8. After all, in both 14:8 and 18:1-3, we have "another angel" crying out, "Fallen, fallen is Babylon the great" (14:8; 18:2). That John intends for us to link the introduction of "another angel" in 18:1 with the "another angel" in 14:8 gains further support from the fact that both 14:8 and 18:1-3 also include references to "all the nations" and to "the wine of the passion of her immortality" (14:8; 18:3).

The reference to "another angel" in 18:1 also links the present account with "the prayers of the saints" in 8:3, 4. In the introduction to the prayers of the saints in 8:3, 4, John says that "another angel" came and "much incense" was given to him "in order that he might give it with the prayers of all the saints on the golden altar that was before the throne" (8:3). That "incense" occurs in only four places in the book of Revelation, three of which refer to the "prayers of the saints" (5:8; 8:3, 4), and the fourth is in the description of the goods that flowed through Rome (18:13), reinforces the link between the judgment of the Great Prostitute and the prayers of the saints.

Because God is bringing judgment on the Great Prostitute, John exhorts the people of God, "I heard another voice from heaven saying, 'Come out from her My people'" (18:4).[7]

Three Laments over the Destruction of Babylon 18:9-19

In 18:9-19, John records the laments of three groups who mourn the destruction of Babylon. First, in 18:9-10, "And the kings of the earth" will "weep and wail over her" (18:9). Then in 18:11-17a, "And the merchants of the earth" will "weep and mourn over her" (18:11; also 18:15). Finally, in 18:17b-19, "And every shipmaster and all who travel by ship

---

7. The exhortation to "come out" alludes to a similar exhortation in Isaiah, "Go out from Babylon, flee from Chaldea" (Isa 48:20; 52:11). Jeremiah also expressed a similar imperative: "Flee from Babylon, and go out of the land of the Chaldeans" (Jer 50:8; 51:6, 45). For more insights into John's use of the OT in Rev 18:1-24, see Howard-Brook and Gwyther, *Unveiling Empire*, loc. 4495-24.

and sailors and as many as make their living on the sea" (18:17) will "weep and mourn" (18:19).

The three laments have much in common. For one thing, each includes the double "alas" (18:10, 16, 19). Also, each of the three laments is directed at Babylon, whom they deem "the Great City" (18:10, 16, 19; see also 18:18). In addition, each of the groups is said to "mourn" (18:11, 15, 19).[8] Finally, each of the three groups is standing, "far away" (18:10, 15, 17).

It is important to note that each of the laments is not because of sorrow over the destruction of Babylon herself *per se*, but because of what the destruction of Babylon means for their own security and economic well-being.

Kings Lament 18:9–10

Thus, the kings of the earth lament because Babylon was "the strong city" (18:10) whose strength provided them with security. Because of this protection, they were not likely to leave her. Hence, the Great Prostitute boasts that she is "not a widow" (18:7). Ironically, she is indeed not a widow, but her demise leaves those who were allied with her as widows.

Merchants Lament 18:11–17a

Similarly, the merchants of the earth, "who became rich from her" (18:15), lament because with her destruction, "no one buys their cargoes any longer" (18:11). Babylon's excessive wealth brought work for the merchants. Her destruction means that their economic security is gone.

Those Who Make Their Living by the Sea Lament 18:17b–19

Finally, John notes, "all who had ships at sea" and who, "became rich by her wealth" (18:19) lament because "in one hour she has been made desolate" (18:19). As with the kings and the merchants, those who sail the sea and make their living from it lament because the source of their wealth has disappeared with her.

---

8. These are the only three occurrences of "mourn" in the book of Revelation.

Excursus: Economic Prosperity and the Apocalypse

In the midst of the lament of the "merchants of the earth" (18:11–17a), John provides a list of goods that accented Rome's excessive wealth (18:12–13). As deSilva notes, "From the viewpoint of the imperial markets and the houses of the elite families in the capital, however, the availability of (literally) a world of goods was seen as a sign of Rome's unparalleled achievements."[9] The question arises, however, as to what John thought of such extravagance.

Bauckham argues that the list must be important. Why else, he queries, would John waste his time listing each of the items?[10] Bauckham adds that the significance of the list is evident in that there are twenty-eight items listed, which he understands as representing seven times four. This list, therefore, embodies the totality of the wealth in the empire.[11]

Howard-Brook and Gwyther assert, "The list depicts Babylon as appropriating everything from the entire earth. In the Hebrew scripture texts from which Revelation's list is drawn, there is an implicit critique of an exploitative imperial economy. Revelation's list similarly critiques Rome's exploitation of the world's wealth."[12]

David deSilva contends that the list highlights Rome's extravagance:

> In a speech praising Rome, Aelius Aristides, a near-contemporary of John, describes the scene in Rome thus: . . . Anyone who wants to behold all these products must either journey through the whole world to see them or else come to this city . . . One can see so many cargoes from India or if you wish from Arabia.[13]

DeSilva concludes:

---

9. DeSilva, *Discovering*, 88.

10. Bauckham, *Climax*, 350.

11. Bauckham contends that there are twenty-eight items in the list of 18:12–13 (Bauckham, Climax, 370). Beale, however, states that there are twenty-nine items in the list (Beale, *Revelation*, 909). The difference in counting has to do with the end of the list. Namely, are we to read "bodies and souls of people" as indicating one item or two?

12. Howard-Brook and Gwyther, *Unveiling Empire*, loc. 4540.

13. DeSilva, *Unholy Allegiances*, loc. 499–505.

The wealth to be enjoyed by participating in the larger global economy was, as far as John was concerned, a dangerous lure toward sharing in the violence and political injustice that undergirded such an economy, as well as sharing in the economic injustice that allowed the resources and produce of the provinces to be siphoned off to satisfy the immoderate cravings of Rome's inhabitants and worldwide elite.[14]

The length of this unit (18:9–19) raises the question, "Why, did John think it necessary to elaborate so fully on the destruction of Babylon, the Great Prostitute?" It is my contention that the significance of this unit corresponds to the extent of Rome's prosperity and thereby indicates both the severity of Rome's oppression and the seductiveness with which Rome aimed to seduce the nations.

As a result, I cannot impress upon the modern reader enough the significance of John's critique of Rome's wealth and power. The extreme wealth enjoyed by the rare few in Rome was simply unfathomable. More significant, however, is the fact that such wealth was obtained at the expense of the overwhelming majority of its people. The elite in Rome bathed in luxury while the rest wallowed in the blood of her victims: "the blood of prophets and of saints and of all those who have been slain upon the earth" (18:24).

Of course, as we have seen—especially in the account of the Seven Trumpets—the raping of the world in order to satisfy the lust of Rome's elite came at a cost to the earth as well. As Barbara Rossing notes, "Distant lands and forests were being stripped bare in order to provide for Rome's insatiable appetites."[15] As we are coming to realize more and more in the twenty-first century, the world cannot sustain such exploitation.

This reinforces the prominence of the exhortation, "Come out from her My people" (18:4).[16]

---

14. DeSilva, *Unholy Allegiances*, loc. 1013–19.
15. Rossing, "Ecology," loc. 2813–14.
16. We should not be naïve and assume that what was true for "empire" in the first century is no longer true today. Certainly, the nature of empire has changed. But the threat of the Great Prostitute upon the people of God is just as much a problem for the Church today as it was in John's day.

Faithful Rejoice Over Her Destruction 18:20

While some lament the destruction of the Great Prostitute, the people of God, who are addressed as "the saints and the apostles and the prophets" (18:20), are summoned to "rejoice" (18:20). After all, "God has brought the judgment for you upon her" (18:20). Babylon's destruction means that their oppression has ended. Ironically, the people of God "rejoice" at the fall of Babylon, just as the earth-dwellers had "rejoiced" at the death of the Two Witnesses (11:10).

Babylon's Destruction 18:21–24

John announces the final destruction of Babylon by noting the appearance of "a strong angel" (18:21). The strong angel hurls a "great millstone . . . into the sea" (18:21) and then declares, "Babylon, the Great City, will be thrown down with violence, and will certainly not be found any longer" (18:21).

This is the seventh and final occurrence of "a strong angel" in the Apocalypse.[17] That there are seven occurrences of "a strong angel" is most certainly intentional. As I noted in the discussion of 10:1–11, the fact that the seven occurrences are limited to three passages (5:1–14; 8:3–5a; 18:21—19:10) serves as an indication that these three passages are interrelated. It is my contention, as I will argue below, that the recurrence of "a strong angel" in these three passages indicates that the destruction of Babylon is most certainly God's answer to the prayers of the saints.

The destruction of Babylon results in more than just the devastation of the world's economic systems. It also entails the end of all those who labored in order to both satisfy her cravings and secure their own well-being. Therefore, the angel adds that Babylon will not only not be found any longer, neither will her cultural celebrations, nor a vast array of her artisans (18:22–23).

---

17. See 5:2; 10:1, 5, 8, 9, 10; 18:21. As with the recurrence of the "another angel," the question is not whether this "strong angel" is the same being as the "strong angel" in 10:1, 5, 8, 9, 10 and 18:21 (in fact, it is most certainly not the same being, since the strong angel in 10:1–11 has the Scroll and we know that since 5:7 Jesus, who appears to be distinct from the strong angel in 5:1–14, has the scroll).

Great Multitude: Three Hallelujahs 19:1–6

John now hears the voice of the Great Multitude[18] who express praise to God for His judgment of Babylon by crying out three times, "Hallelujah" (19:1, 3, 6).[19] Their response of praise certainly contrasts the three groups who lamented the fall of the Great Prostitute by crying out, "Alas, alas" (18:10, 16, 19).

In our first introduction to the Great Multitude in 7:9–17, they cried out, "with a great voice saying, 'Salvation to our God'" (7:10). In 19:1, John again hears the Great Multitude. This time they are crying out with, "a great voice" and ascribing, "salvation and glory and power to our God" (19:1). They also affirm that God is worthy of such praise, "because true and just are His judgments" (19:2).[20] The Great Multitude also note that God is worthy of praise because "He avenged the blood of His servants" (19:2).

That the judgment of the Great Prostitute functions as the answer to the prayers of the saints is evidenced by the Great Multitudes' affirmation that God has "avenged" the blood of His servants. This clearly is a response to the martyrs' cry, "How long . . . until you avenge our blood?" (6:10). The link to the martyr's cry in 6:10 gains credibility from the fact that "avenge" occurs only in these two verses in the entire book of Revelation (6:10; 19:2). Therefore, they had cried out to have their blood avenged (6:10) and now God has "avenged" their blood (19:2).

Further confirmation that the judgment of the Great Prostitute serves as the answer to the prayer of the saints derives from the Great Multitudes' second "Hallelujah" (19:3). Here they exclaim that "her smoke went up forever and ever" (19:3). The reference to smoke further links the judgment of the Great Prostitute with the prayers of the saints. After all, in the description of the prayers of the saints before the altar in 8:3, 4, John notes, "the smoke of the incense went up" in accord "with the prayers of the saints" (8:4). Now, in the present account, we

---

18. There is no reason to suppose that the Great Multitude are not the same group we met in 7:9–17. That the "Great Multitude" only occurs three times (7:9; 19:1, 6) and only in two passages suggests that the two accounts are meant to be read in light of one another.

19. There are four hallelujah's here because the Twenty-Four Elders and the Four Living Creatures interject a "hallelujah" (19:4).

20. The assertion that God's actions are "true and just" corresponds to the voices of those who overcame the Beast (15:3) as well as the voice from the altar (16:7).

are told, "her [the Great Prostitute's] smoke went up" (19:3) as a result of her judgment.[21]

The Marriage Feast of the Lamb 19:7–9a

The Great Multitude's third "Hallelujah" acknowledges that "the Lord reigns" (19:6). As a result of His reign, "the wedding of the Lamb has come" (19:6).[22] For this wedding, the Bride "has prepared herself" (19:7). Her preparation includes her clothing: it was "given to her to be clothed in bright, pure, fine linen" (19:8).[23] To make certain that his reader/hearers understand the significance of the Bride's clothing, John notes that "the fine linen is the righteous deeds of the saints" (19:8).[24]

The clothing of the Bride, of course, serves as a stark contrast with the Great Prostitute's nakedness: "these will hate the prostitute and will make her desolate and naked and they will eat her flesh and burn her up in the fire" (17:16).

John is again commanded to write, "Blessed are the ones who have been invited to the feast of the wedding of the Lamb" (19:9). With this announcement, the eternal dwelling of the people of God is described in terms of a wedding feast. The depiction of a heavenly feast brings to mind the eschatological banquet of Isaiah 25:

> Now the Lord of armies will prepare a lavish banquet for all peoples on this mountain; a banquet of aged wine, choice pieces with marrow, *and* refined, aged wine. And on this mountain He will destroy the covering which is over all peoples, the veil which is stretched over all nations. He will swallow up death for all time, and the Lord God will wipe tears away from all faces, and He will remove the disgrace of His people from all the earth; for the Lord has spoken. And it will be said on that day, "Behold, this is our God for whom we have waited that He might save us. This is the Lord for whom we have waited; Let's rejoice and be glad in His salvation" (Isa 25:6–9).

---

21. Note the parallel with the "smoke of their torment" that rises "forever and ever" (14:11). This too provides a link between the present passage and the "another angel" of 14:6–20.

22. The idea of Israel as the wife of God is common in Scripture. See Isa 49:18; 54:5–6; 62:5; Jer 2:2; Ezek 16:15–63; Hos 2:14–23.

23. The Great Multitude were dressed in white (7:13–15).

24. See Isa 61:10–62:5; Hos 2:14–20; 2 Cor 11:2.

John Attempts to Worship the Angel 19:9b–10

The angel then assures John, "These are the true words of God" (19:9). John then falls down in an attempt to worship the angel (19:10). The angel, of course, forbids him from doing so. After all, the angel acknowledges, he too is "a fellow-servant" (19:10). John is instead exhorted to "worship God" (19:10).

The third major scene/story in the book of Revelation (17:1—19:10) comes to a close with the affirmation, "the testimony of Jesus is the Spirit of prophecy" (19:10). Although there is some debate over the meaning of this phrase, it is my contention that Tabb summarizes the text well: "19:10 establishes that the Apocalypse is true Christian prophecy that communicates the witness of the exalted Christ, and the church must heed and hold fast to this testimony as Jesus' witnesses in the world."[25]

Conclusion

Rome's insatiable desire for wealth and comfort leads to her own destruction. As a result, the exhortation goes out to the people of God: "Come out of her My people" (18:4). After all, while those who profited from her will lament, the people of God are to rejoice. In terms of John's narrative, the destruction of Babylon represents the answer to the prayers of the saints. God "has avenged the blood of His bond-servants on her" (19:2).

Excursus: What Does This Mean for Western Christians Today?

It is my conviction that the exhortation, "Come out of her My people" (18:4) remains just as relevant a command for the people of God today as it was for John's reader/hearers!

John is clear: Rome is a seductive and dangerous prostitute, an evil economy, and an unjust empire. And it is the desire for wealth, comfort, and pleasure that entices us into bed with the Great Prostitute. Michael Gorman asserts:

> Revelation 18 raises questions about how we spend the money we have earned. Like the economy judged in Revelation 18, many contemporary economies are based on lust (material and sexual), dominion, and exploitation, even human trafficking.... We may live in just such an economy,

---

25. Tabb, *All Things New*, loc. 1574.

where more is always better and sex consistently sells, and we may inadvertently support other economies, where the poor are exploited and even traded.[26]

The problem that Western Christianity must face is the serious incongruity between the gospel's radical call to cross-bearing love and its concomitant denial of self, with the abundance of wealth that pervades our society and even our churches. The fact that many Christians in the West do not even consider the possibility that the Great Prostitute is a present concern underscores her powers of seduction. Of course, one of the problems is that we do not perceive ourselves as idol worshipers.[27] Nor do we consider the possibility that our wealth is ill-gotten gain. Surely it is nothing more than the proper reward for our hard work. Should we not, however, ask ourselves, "Have we been seduced by the world's lust for power and called it wisdom?"

In addition, we in the Western church must also do a better job of considering how our excess might be used to further the work of the global church. The fact is that Christians throughout the world are laboring to serve Christ but lack the very resources that we have all too readily available. The Western Church is replete with teachers, books, and other resources that the pastors and churches in most of the world need access to in order that they might know the Word more deeply and, consequently, minister more effectively. The Western Church also has expertise in leadership and professional training that would enable churches in other parts of the world to be better leaders. And we have the financial resources that could allow pastors and church leaders to get the training (preferably local training) they need to be more effective in their ministries. We also have skilled laborers, engineers, and entrepreneurs that could help grow exponentially the work of the global church. More than anything, we have the financial resources to assist the global church so that

---

26. Gorman, *Reading*, 149.

27. We certainly do. It is just that our idols of material goods, trust funds, homes, families, and pride do not have the appearance of gods in terms of images that reside on our mantels. They are, however, just as much an idol as those in the ancient world and we would do well to recognize them.

they may be a blessing to their communities and do the work of the kingdom more effectively. Rossing concludes, "The audience is called to make a choice. The Babylon and New Jerusalem visions aim to persuade the audience to 'come out' of Babylon (Rev 18:4) so that they will be able to participate in the New Jerusalem (Rev 3:12; 22:14, 19)."[28]

---

28. Rossing, *Two Cities*, 59.

Revelation 19:11—21:8
The Fifth "Bridge" Scene

Revelation 19:11—21:8
Transition between the Fall of Babylon and the Descent of the New Jerusalem

I take it as absolutely fundamental to the Apocalypse that the violence through Jesus is said to conquer evil is the violence done to him. The character of Jesus, his ethos, is the Lamb slain. What truly shocks me is how few readers actually believe John: they insist that the lion remain a lion. Now this may be partly John's fault. . . . John's choice of the Holy War paradigm to structure the last segment of his vision may have been a mistake; the paradigm is so strong and so violent that readers may have trouble remembering that John reverses even these symbols.[1]

God's creation reaches its eschatological fulfilment when it becomes the scene of God's immediate presence. This, in the last resort, is what is 'new' about the new creation. It is the old creation filled with God's presence.[2]

Introduction

As I SET FORTH in the opening discussion of the structure of the book of Revelation, there are four clearly marked sections in the Apocalypse.[3] These four sections, however, do not account for the present section (19:11—21:8). It is my conviction that this present section functions as a "bridge" between the accounts of the two women: the Great Prostitute

---

1. Barr, "Lamb," 209.
2. Bauckham, *Theology*, 140.
3. See 1:9—3:22; 4:1—16:21; 17:1—19:20; 21:9—22:9.

(17:1—19:10) and the Bride (21:9—22:9). Consequently, I have labeled it as a "fifth bridge section"—even though chronologically it is the fourth section in the Apocalypse.[4]

Recognizing the structure within this bridge section is critical to understanding some of the major interpretive concerns, such as the millennium, as well as understanding the overall narrative that John has set forth. This bridge section is comprised of five units. The first unit (19:11-16) sets forth the descent of Christ as the eschatological judge. The middle three units (19:17-21; 20:1-10; 20:11-15) present the final judgment for the enemies of Christ and for those who choose not to repent. The final unit (21:1-8) presents an introduction to the descent of the New Jerusalem. Therefore, just as heaven was opened at the beginning of the second scene so that John might ascend into it, so now heaven has opened once again; only this time, it is opened so that what is in it may come down.

The question becomes: what is the role of this bridge section? (19:11—21:8). I have argued that one of the keys to understanding the story of the book of Revelation is that the throne of God begins in heaven (4:1-3) but, by the end of the story, it comes down to the new creation (21:10). I have also noted John's stress on the redemption of the nations. It is my conviction that before the Holy City/New Jerusalem can descend, Christ must descend and bring judgment on the enemies of God. That is what this bridge section depicts. Consequently, the significance of this bridge section with regard to John's narrative cannot be overstated.

John's Use of "And I Saw" in 19:11—21:8

John opens with, "And I saw" (19:11). Contrary to some proposals, as I noted in the opening discussion on the structure of Revelation, the phrase, "And I saw," which recurs throughout the Apocalypse and often in the midst of clearly marked sections, indicates a point of transition within a section.

The structure of this bridge section, however, revolves around eight occurrences of "And I saw."[5] These eight uses of "And I saw" form

---

4. Although I do not want to diminish the importance of this "bridge" section, I have designated it as a "fifth" section—even though it fits in the book in terms of the order of the narrative as the fourth—in order to highlight the centrality of the four main scenes/stories. I am using "section" here because it is a complete and distinct literary unit and not a part of any of the other sections.

5. See 19:11, 17, 19; 20:1, 4, 11, 12; 21:1. Though it has been asserted that there are

five units. The first (19:11) and last occurrences of "And I saw" (21:1) mark the opening (19:11–16) and closing (21:1–8) units within the section. These two units frame the section by introducing the descent of Christ (19:11–16) and the introduction to the descent of the new heavens and new earth (21:1–8).[6]

The three middle units, each of which is marked by the two uses of, "And I saw,"[7] set forth the judgment of the enemies of Christ in the reverse order in which they were introduced in the narrative. Thus, in 19:17–21, John narrates the judgment of the Beast and the False Prophet, who first appeared in 13:1–9 and 13:10–18. Then, in 20:1–10, which is in the very middle of the entire section, John sets forth the judgment of the Dragon, who first appeared in 12:1–17. Finally, in 20:11–15, John presents the final destruction of Death and Hades, who first appeared in 6:8. It should be noted that in each account of the judgment of the enemies of Christ the final result is that they are thrown in the Lake of Fire (Beast and the False Prophet: 19:20; Satan: 20:10; and Death and Hades: 20:14).

It should also be noted here that the account of the judgment of Satan in the middle unit (20:1–10) is interrupted with a description of the victorious people of God (20:4–6). Recognizing this is critical to understanding John's reference to the thousand years as well as to the understanding of "the war" in 19:19 and 20:8.

> **Excursus: John's Use of Ezekiel in the Closing Chapters of Revelation**
>
> It is worth commenting here, though only in brief, that an important background for both the bridge section (19:11—21:8) and the account of the Bride that follows (21:9—22:9) is found in Ezekiel 37–48.
>
> The parallels between Revelation and Ezekiel in this section are more than evident.[8] Both Revelation and Ezekiel depict birds gorging on the flesh of God's enemies (19:17–19; Ezek 39:17–20). Both also describe the enemies of the people of God as "Gog and Magog" (20:8; Ezek 38:2, 3, 14, 16, 18; 39:1, 6, 11). And, both include fire coming down from Heaven and destroying Gog and his followers (20:9; Ezek 39:6).

---

seven occurrences of "And I saw" in this section, a closer reading of this unit notes that it occurs eight times.

6. Of course, 21:9—22:9 provides the details of the Holy City/New Jerusalem.

7. "And I saw" occurs in the first couplet in 19:17 and 19; in the second couplet it occurs in 20:1 and 4; and in the third couplet it occurs in 20:11 and 12.

8. See Longman, *Revelation,* 393–401.

Revelation 19:11–16
The Returning Christ

In the opening unit of this section, John begins with, "And I saw heaven opened" (19:11). The opening of heaven, of course, serves as the necessary precursor for the descent of what is in heaven. And what comes down first is Christ Himself (19:11–16). Christ returns as the just King and Judge who brings about the just judgment of the enemies of the people of God.

Rider on a White Horse 19:11–16

John's description of Jesus begins with, "and behold a white horse and One sitting on it" (19:11). The description of Christ sitting astride "a white horse" (19:11) surely intends to depict Him as a divine warrior.[1]

It is critical to bear in mind, as I have argued throughout, that Jesus does not wage war the way the nations do. After all, Jesus's only weapon is the sword that proceeds from His mouth (19:15). David Barr affirms:

> Visions of the Lamb bracket that of the warrior (14:1; 19:11; 21:9, 22); and even the warrior conquers by what comes from his mouth, not his arm (19:21). Surely this story is built on the mythology of holy war (and that itself may be ethically problematical). Just as surely, John consistently demythologizes the war—or perhaps more accurately, remythologizes it. For the warrior now appears in the image of the suffering savior so

---

1. See Longman, "Divine Warrior," 290–307.

that the death of the warrior and not some later battle is the crucial event of the war.[2]

That John's description of Jesus intends to contrast Jesus's rule with the nations gains support from the fact that a "white horse" occurs only twice in the book of Revelation: here in 19:11 and after the breaking of the First Seal (6:2).[3] I argued in the discussion of the First Seal, that the rider on the white horse represented false Christs. Consequently, the description of Jesus on a white horse surely functions as a contrast to the rule of others.

Faithful and True 19:11

John continues by noting that the rider on the horse is "the One who is called 'Faithful and True'" (19:11). This corresponds to Jesus's title, "the Faithful and True Witness" (3:14) in the message to the Laodiceans. The title is likely reiterated here because of John's concern to portray Jesus as the righteous judge who is coming to bring justice. That Jesus is called "the One who is Faithful and True" further supports my conviction that one of John's aims is to contrast Jesus's rule with the nations. They represent false Christs, but Jesus is "the One who is Faithful and True."

Eyes Are Like a Flame of Fire and He Has Many Diadems 19:12

John continues by observing, His "eyes are like a flame of fire" (12). This corresponds with John's description of Jesus whom he saw while on Patmos (1:14).[4] That His "eyes are like a flame of fire" surely connotes the presence of God and His authority as judge.

Jesus also has "many diadems" (19:12). Interestingly, "diadems" appear only three times in the Apocalypse.[5] Its first occurrence is in the description of the Dragon, who has seven diadems (12:3). The other use of "diadems" appears in the account of the Beast, who has ten diadems (13:1). Jesus, however, is said to have "many diadems" (19:12). There

---

2. Barr, *Tales*, loc. 4926–46.

3. There is a third occurrence of "white horse" in 19:14, where it is plural and refers to the horses of those who are following Christ.

4. See 1:14; 2:18, 23.

5. See 12:3; 13:1; 19:12.

is little doubt that John's description of Jesus having "many diadems" serves to contrast Him with the Dragon and the Beasts in order to expose their illegitimate claims.

Jesus's "many diadems" provide another indication of John's effort to contrast Jesus from the rule of the nations.

A Name Which No One Knows 19:12

Jesus also has, "a name written on Him that no one knows except Himself" (19:12). This also serves to juxtapose Jesus with the Beast, who is "full of blasphemous names" (17:3). In the biblical world, it was widely believed that to know one's name, or to place a name on another, indicated ownership or authority over the other.[6] Since Jesus is not owned, nor does He pledge allegiance to anyone other than Himself, His name is not known to anyone "except Himself" (19:12).

Garment Dipped in Blood 19:13

John then adds, Jesus "is wearing a garment that has been dipped in blood" (19:13). Commentators are often divided over the identification of the blood on His garment.[7] The primary question pertains as to whether it is His own blood or the blood of His enemies.

It is my conviction that the blood on Jesus's clothing is His own. For one thing, that it is His own blood corresponds with John's overall portrayal of Jesus in the book of Revelation. Jesus is the Lamb of God, of whom it is said, "you were slain and you purchased for God by means of your blood . . ." (5:9). In light of the fact that Jesus is consistently pictured as the One who was victorious through His own suffering, it stands to reason that the blood on His garment is His own. Dana Harris affirms, "on balance, the latter view [that it is His own blood] coheres better with the rest of Revelation, since it continues the centrality of the lamb and his

---

6. In Mark 1:24, a demon attempts to usurp authority over Jesus by invoking His name, "What business do we have with each other, Jesus of Nazareth? Have You come to destroy us? I know who You are—the Holy One of God!" Elsewhere, Jesus demands to know the name of the demonic entities, "What is your name?" (Mark 5:9).

7. See Beale, *Revelation*, 957–63; Hays, "Faithful Witness," loc. 1894; Longman, *Revelation*, 387; Caird, *Revelation*, 243.

blood as the means by which evil is conquered."[8] Hays go so far as to say He, "must be wearing a garment drenched with his own blood."[9]

Some commentators, however, contend that the blood on Jesus's garments is that of His enemies.[10] Those who support this view appeal to the triumphant warrior in Isa 63:3.

In Isaiah, the warrior's clothing is blood-stained because he is returning from the defeat of his enemies, and, "their lifeblood is sprinkled on My garments" (Isa 63:3). If this text serves as the background for John's imagery in 19:13, then the blood on Jesus's clothes would indeed be that of His enemies. Longman, who favors this view, suggests, "The description derives from the picture of Yahweh the divine warrior found in Isaiah."

That it is the blood of His enemies gains further support from the fact that John adds that Jesus, "tramples the wine press of the wrath of God" (19:15). Since "trampled" occurs only three times in the book of Revelation (11:2; 14:20; 19:15), it is likely that John intends for us to link these passages. This argument is strengthened by the fact that John's use of trampling in 14:20 surely alludes to Isa 63:3.

Although the argument that the blood on Jesus's garments is that of His enemies is sound, it is my conviction that it fails to give sufficient weight to the fact that in John's narrative, Jesus does not rule like the nations. Furthermore, although the appeal to Isa 63:3 is warranted, the argument does not account for the fact that John often reads his OT sources in light of Christ.[11] John, therefore, is not afraid to read an OT source about God's trampling of the wine press so that it becomes Jesus Himself who is the one who suffers that others might have life.

Thus, as I have stressed throughout this study, John, while acknowledging that Jesus is the Lion (5:5), places far more stress on the fact that Jesus is the slain Lamb. In fact, as I have noted, John only uses "lion" once with reference to Christ. Yet, he refers to Jesus as the Lamb twenty-seven times. This surely confirms that John intends to portray Jesus's rule as distinct from the nations. In addition, the notion that Jesus is coming back

---

8. Harris, "John and Punishment," 81.

9. See Hays, "Faithful Witness," loc. 1894.

10. Beale, *Revelation*, 957–63.

11. Ian Spencer reminded me of this point. He noted, "John often gives his own spin on the OT backgrounds/imagery he draws on, so taking a passage where God is returning from judgment with his enemies' blood on him and turning that into Jesus going off to battle with his own blood on him is in keeping with the rest of the book both in theme and how he uses his sources" (private message, 3-5-23).

to wage war, which is certainly in accord with the imagery of Jesus as the divine warrior, must be understood through the lens of the manner in which Jesus wages war in the Apocalypse; namely, through suffering violence and not inflicting it. And while it is true that John alludes to Isa 63:3 in 19:15, the description of blood on His garment is in 19:13.

In saying this, I do not intend to deny that He is coming back as the eschatological judge who will avenge the blood of the martyrs. This is certainly John's point in the verses that follow. The question simply is, "When He comes back in what way does He wage war?" I see no reason to answer this question than to say, "The same way He has always done so."[12]

Another difficulty with the argument that the blood on Jesus's garments is that of His enemies is that the present description of Jesus presents Him as coming to the battle and not coming from the battle. Thus, Caird asserts, "The picture of the vintager carefully dipping his garment in grape-juice as a sign of his trade before beginning to treat the winepress is too ridiculous to be entertained."[13]

Word of God 19:13

That the returning Jesus's name is the "Word of God" should not be a surprise to readers of the NT. After all, it certainly resonates with the opening of the prologue in the Gospel of John (1:1–3). In the book of Revelation, however, although John uses "Word of God" seven times (1:2, 9; 6:9; 17:17; 19:9, 13; 20:4), this is the only occurrence of the title as a name for Jesus.

Armies in Heaven were Following Him 19:14

John continues his description of the returning Christ by noting, "the armies that are in heaven were following Him" (19:14). The identity of

---

12. I am sure that some will respond to this by asserting that God has waged war with violence through the biblical story. It is my conviction that Jesus's death and resurrection demonstrate how He does power. And it is through love. Does this mean that perhaps we need to reread the OT? Perhaps.

Now, in saying this, I do not, as I have noted already, deny that God will destroy His enemies and those who shed the blood of the martyrs. I am just not convinced that He does so with violence.

13. Caird, *Revelation*, 243. Caird, of course, believes that the blood on Jesus's garments is that of His followers.

the "armies" here is somewhat obscure. Throughout the Scriptures, the "armies of heaven" refer to angels, the people of God, or both.[14]

It is my conviction that the armies of heaven in 19:14 at least include the people of God. The fact that the armies of heaven are "wearing white, pure fine linen" (19:14) supports the identification of them as the people of God in that their clothing corresponds to the clothing of the people of God elsewhere in the book of Revelation. For example, although the Great Multitude were wearing "robes" and not the "fine linen" of the armies of heaven, their clothing was also described as "white" (7:13, 14). A stronger parallel with the clothing of the armies of heaven is found with the "fine linen, bright and pure" promised to those who are invited to the wedding feast of the Lamb (19:8). Resseguie affirms the relationship with the clothing of the armies of heaven and earlier descriptions of the people of God: "Their clothing recalls the bride's 'fine linen, bright and pure' (19:8), whose spotless and pure dress symbolizes her spiritual and moral purity. The armies of heaven are clothed with the same pure, linen garments as the bride, although their robes are 'white,' not 'bright.' White is the color of the multitude's garments (7:9, 13, 14), the clothing of the subaltern martyrs (6:11), and the dress of the victors at Sardis and Laodicea (3:5, 18), in contrast to the soiled garments of some at Sardis and the apparel of the whore."[15]

Sharp Sword 19:15

That Jesus has a "sharp sword" that comes from His mouth corresponds to the description of Jesus in the opening vision on Patmos (1:16). That the sword comes from His mouth surely indicates that it is His spoken word. Consequently, when John says, "And the rest were killed by means of the sword of the One who sat upon the horse, which came out of His mouth" (19:21), it surely indicates Jesus's spoken word. This also seems to rule out the use of violence as His mode of operation.[16]

---

14. Amos 3:13; Dan 7:10; Zech 14:5; Matt 13:40–42; 25:31–32; Mark 8:38; 1 Thess 4:16–17; 2 Thess 1:7; Jude 14–15; See Aune, *Revelation*, 3:1059; Beale, *Revelation*, 960.

15. Resseguie, *Revelation*, loc. 5313–17.

16. It is relevant to reiterate here that the Dragon's method of waging war is deception. Thus, the frog-like demonic entities come out of the mouth of the Satanic triumvirate (16:13). Of course, the Dragon and his minions do use violence against those who are not willing to conform to their ideology.

Rod of Iron 19:15

John then affirms, "He Himself will shepherd them with the rod of iron" (19:15). As I noted in the discussion of 12:1–18, the fact that Jesus will "shepherd all the nations with a rod of iron" (12:5; 19:15) most certainly alludes to Ps 2:9 and Isa 11:4.[17] Although this imagery is widely believed to depict Christ as "ruling with stern judgment,"[18] I am not convinced that it does.

To begin with, John's use of "shepherd" here is noteworthy. His choice conforms to the LXX rendering of Ps 2:9. Beale comments, "John, the LXX translator, or both may have seen in the unpointed Hebrew text an irony whereby the 'staff of iron' was a symbol of destruction to the ungodly nations but a sign of protection to Israel."[19]

It may also be that John employs "shepherd" because he has "ruling" or "shepherding" of the people of God in view. John uses "shepherd" four times in the book of Revelation (2:27; 7:17; 12:5; 19:15) and in three of these passages there is an allusion to the "rod of iron" from Ps 2:9 (2:27; 12:5; 19:15). In 7:17, John is told that "The Lamb in the center of the Throne will shepherd them." The "them" in 7:17 refers to the ones who have come out of the Great Tribulation (7:14). Just as importantly, the Lamb's shepherding activity in 7:17 connotes an ongoing activity of care. Mounce notes that the image of Christ as the shepherd in 7:17, "builds on the OT picture of God as the shepherd of Israel."[20] He then proposes, however, that "Elsewhere in Revelation, the shepherding activity of the Lamb is of a radically different sort."[21] But is it?

Before I offer a possible reading of 19:15, it is worth noting that the first allusion to Ps 2:9 in the book of Revelation occurred in the promise to those who overcome in the church at Thyatira (2:27). The parallel with 2:27 is instructive in that, whereas Christ is the shepherd in 19:15, in 2:27 the imagery is applied to those who overcome: "I will give to them authority over the nations; and they shall shepherd them with a rod of iron." This likely conveys the notion that the victorious people of

---

17. See Beale, *Revelation*, 961–63.
18. See Smalley, *Revelation*, 494.
19. See Beale, *Revelation*, 962
20. Mounce, *Revelation*, 166. Most notable is Ezekiel 34. Jesus adapts the imagery of God as Israel's shepherd and applies it to Himself in John 10:1–30.
21. Mounce, *Revelation*, 166.

God in Thyatira will rule either alongside Christ or in His place.[22] There is, however, no indication in the book of Revelation that the people of God use violence even though they are often depicted as holy warriors. There is little question that the holy warfare imagery in the book of Revelation has clearly been appropriated by John so that the people of God wage war in the same way that Jesus does: namely, as I argued in the account of the Two Witnesses, they suffer violence.

In addition, if Christ's only weapon is His spoken word, through which He executes justice, then it follows that this is how His people rule. This, of course, corresponds with the description of the Two Witnesses in 11:1–13. The Two Witnesses have "fire" that comes "out of their mouth and consumes their enemies" (11:5).

If my supposition is correct, then the indication that Jesus will, "Shepherd them with a rod of iron" (19:15) is not of a "radically different sort"—as Mounce suggests—from the shepherding activity of Christ throughout the whole of the NT.

Treads Wine Press 19:15

That Jesus tramples the wine press (19:15), as noted above, corresponds to the image of trampling the wine press in 14:20. This imagery certainly conveys that Jesus is the righteous judge who is coming to bring lasting justice.

God, the Almighty 19:15

The wine press is said to be that of "God, the Almighty" (19:15). I noted in the discussion of numbers that John uses the title, "Lord God, Almighty seven times" (1:8; 4:8; 11:17; 15:3; 16:7; 19:6; 21:22). Bauckham has argued that John uses the abbreviated title "God, the Almighty" on two occasions (16:14; 19:15) so as to keep the number of occurrences of "Lord God, the Almighty" at seven.[23] What is important for our concerns, however, is that the two occurrences of the alternative title, "God, the Almighty" (16:14

---

22. That the people of God rule in Christ's place corresponds with the creation narrative in which humanity was made in God's image so that they might "rule" (Gen 1:26–28).

23. Bauckham, *Climax*, 33.

and 19:15) serve to link the present account of Jesus's descent with the account of the Sixth Bowl and the war of Armageddon.

King of Kings and Lord of Lords 19:16

John's final description of Jesus affirms, "He has on His garment and on His thigh a name written: 'King of kings and Lord of lords'" (19:16).[24] The title, "King of kings and Lord of lords" intensifies the stress on John's description of Jesus as the world's true King.

---

24. This is a title for God alone: Deut 10:17; 1 Tim 6:15.

Revelation 19:17–21
Judgment of the Beast and the False Prophet

Introduction

THE NEXT TWO OCCURRENCES of "And I saw" (19:17, 19) form a couplet and mark the second unit in this section. This unit describes the judgment of the Beast and the False Prophet who are cast into the Lake of Fire.[1]

The Great Feast of God 19:17–18

John begins, "And I saw an angel standing in the sun," who is crying out to the birds, "Come, gather together for the great feast of God" (19:17).[2] That John uses "feast" only twice (19:9, 17) provides a clear link between the present feast and the wedding feast in 19:9.

There are two elements of "the great feast of God" that are noteworthy. First, "the great feast of God" stands in marked contrast to "the feast of the wedding of the Lamb" (19:7, 9). One of the key differences relates to the guests who are doing the eating. Whereas, at the wedding feast of the Lamb, the people of God dine with Christ, at "the great feast of God," it is the birds who are dining (19:18).[3] Second, the food itself

---

1. Bauckham, affirms, "the judgment they anticipate in 6:17 is at last described in 19:11–21" (Bauckham, *Climax*, 19).

2. The likely background for the "great feast of God" is the prophetic warning in Ezekiel 39.

3. The list of persons upon whom the birds dine is very similar to the list in the

marks a grand distinction between the two meals. Although the food for the wedding of the Lamb is not stated, it does not take much to conclude that it is radically distinct from the food at the great feast of God which is comprised of the flesh of Christ's enemies (19:17–18).

It is also worth noting that the summoning of the birds to eat such flesh appears out of place. After all, how could there be flesh to eat when there has yet to be a battle? It appears that John simply provides us with the outcome of the war without any mention of the war itself. In fact, the outcome is given even before the kings are said to even assemble to wage war on Christ and His army, which occurs in the following verse (19:19).[4]

The Judgment of the Beast and the False Prophet 19:19–21

John then depicts the final judgment of the Beast and the False Prophet. He notes, "And I saw the Beast and the kings of the earth and their armies having been gathered to make war with the One sitting upon the horse and with His army" (19:19). It is important to observe that the war is waged against both, "the One sitting upon the horse" and "His army" (19:19).[5]

When it comes to the war itself, however, it is critical to recognize that aside from the war in which the Beast kills the Two Witnesses, and the "war" in heaven (12:7) John never describes a war as actually taking place. In the present passage, he simply notes that the participants have gathered to make war (19:19). Then, in a somewhat anticlimactic and matter-of-fact way, he states, "and the Beast was captured" (19:20). Again, no description of a battle is provided.[6]

Sixth Seal (6:15).

4. Note again that the "war" in the book of Revelation is that which is waged against Christ and His people. In this passage, it is waged by the Beast and the kings of the earth and their armies (19:19).

5. Of the nine occurrences of the noun "war" in the book of Revelation, seven of them depict the enemies of Christ waging war against either the people of God (11:7; 12:17; 13:7; 16:14; 20:8), angelic beings (12:7), or Christ and the people of God (19:19; note, it is possible that the war in 19:19 is also against angelic beings. After all, "the armies of heaven" who "were following Him" [19:14] may well have included angelic beings.) The only exceptions are the two uses of "war" in 9:7, 9.

6. As I noted in the excursus "Armageddon: part 1," the book of Revelation displays little interest in providing details of an actual battle taking place in the fields of Megiddo.

Not only is the Beast captured, but "with him the False Prophet" (19:20), who is further identified as "the one who deceived" (19:20). This added detail identifying the False Prophet appears unnecessary. After all, John has already provided plenty of insights into the False Prophet's deceptive efforts, "it deceives those who inhabit the Earth because of the signs which it was given to it to do" (13:14). John's reiteration that the False Prophet is "the one who deceived" highlights the fact that deception is the chief weapon of the enemy and that the False Prophet functions as its lead commander.[7]

The judgment of the Beast and the False Prophet is then made complete: "these two were thrown alive into the Lake of Fire that burns with sulfur" (19:20).[8] In terms of the narrative, the Beast and the False Prophet are the first to be thrown into the Lake of Fire. They will be followed by "the devil" (20:10), then "Death and Hades" (20:14), and, finally, "those who are cowardly and unbelieving and detestable and murderers and sexually immoral and sorcerers and idolaters and all liars their part will be in the Lake that burns with fire and sulfur, which is the second death" (21:8).[9]

John concludes his description of the judgment of the Beast and the False Prophet by observing that the armies of the Beast are also destroyed: "And the rest were killed by means of the sword of the One who sat upon the horse, which came out of His mouth, and all the birds gorged themselves on their flesh" (19:21).

---

7. See 2:20; 12:9; 13:14; 18:23; 19:20; 20:3, 8, 10.

8. This is the first of six references to the Lake of Fire (19:20; 20:10, 14*, 15; 21:8). Here it is "the Lake of Fire that burns with sulfur." In 20:10, it is simply "the Lake of Fire and sulfur." In 21:8, it is "the Lake that burns with fire and sulfur." On three other occasions, it is deemed "the Lake of Fire" (20:14*, 15).

9. What, then, is the Lake of Fire? In 20:14, John equates it with "the second death." A significant problem with ascertaining the meaning of the Lake of Fire is that all six occurrences are in the book of Revelation—in fact, they occur only in this bridge section.

Revelation 20:1–10
The Judgment of the Dragon (Satan)

Careful reading will show that at every point where John introduces images of violence and conquest, he undermines the symbols with images of suffering and suffering testimony. This is why there can be no final battle or final victory in this Apocalypse; or to be more accurate why there are five final battles none of which ever involves a battle scene.[1]

Introduction

THE PRESENCE OF "AND I saw" in 20:1, marks the next transition within the bridge section. This unit (20:1-10) continues the description of the enemies of Christ and His kingdom by presenting the final judgment of Satan.

The account of Satan's judgment, and the reference to the thousand years in 20:4-6, in particular, has been the subject of significant debate.[2] It is my conviction that recognizing the structure of the bridge section as a whole (19:11—21:8), and of this unit (20:1-10) in particular, provides critical insights into John's narrative goals and potentially illuminates our understanding of the binding and loosing of Satan and the role of the millennium in the larger narrative.

With this in mind, it is critical to observe that the judgment of Satan is interrupted with a depiction of the victorious people of God. That is, the unit begins with a description of Satan being bound and thrown into the Abyss for "a thousand years" (20:1-3). In 20:3, John indicates that after the

1. Barr, "Lamb," 210.
2. See Clouse, *Meaning*.

thousand years, "it is necessary for him [Satan] to be released for a little time" (20:3). In 20:7, he resumes the narrative of Satan's judgment and informs us that after Satan is freed, he gathers an army and attempts to wage war against Christ and the people of God (20:8–9). John concludes this unit by nothing that Satan's efforts are in vain and that he also will be thrown into "the Lake of Fire and sulfur" (20:10).

The importance of the interruption addressing the victorious martyrs is evident by the fact that the account not only functions as an interruption in the middle of the depiction of the judgment of Satan, but it also resides in the very middle of the entire section.

Satan Is Bound for a Thousand Years 20:1–3

John begins the account of the judgment of Satan with, "And I saw an angel coming down out of heaven having the key of the Abyss and a great chain in his hand" (20:1). He then adds that the angel "seized the Dragon" (20:2) and "bound him for a thousand years and threw him into the Abyss" (20:2–3).

John then identifies the Dragon by adding that he is, "the ancient serpent, who is the Devil and Satan" (20:2). This identification of the Dragon is somewhat odd. After all, we have known since 12:9 that the Dragon is the devil and Satan. This raises the question as to why John thought it necessary to expand on the Dragon's identity. It may be that John reiterates the fact that Satan is "the ancient serpent" and "the Devil" in order to lay stress upon his role as the "deceiver." After all, in 12:9, which is the only other instance where Satan is given all three titles (the Dragon, the Devil, and Satan), the Dragon was, "the one who deceives the whole world." That John's intent was to highlight Satan's role as the deceiver finds affirmation in his assertion that he was bound and thrown into the Abyss, "in order that he might not deceive the nations any longer" (20:3).[3]

---

3. In my opinion, it is critical to note that Satan is bound, "in order that he might not deceive the nations any longer." This suggests that the binding of Satan is limited to his acts of deception. This conclusion gains credibility in that, upon his release, Satan "will come out to deceive the nations" (20:8).

Throne and Souls 20:4–6

The second "And I saw" (20:4) does not continue the narrative with regard to the final judgment of Satan as we might have expected. Instead, John, in a somewhat parenthetical manner, introduces us to the victorious people of God. As suggested above, this raises the question, "Why does John interrupt the account of the judgment of Satan in order to introduce us to a group that is not only not judged, but has "the authority to judge" (20:4)? I will address this question more fully in the excursi below.

I Saw Thrones and Souls 20:4a

John notes, "And I saw thrones and they sat upon them and the authority to judge was given to them" (20:4). Then he adds, "And I saw . . . the souls of those who have been beheaded because of the testimony of Jesus and because of the word of God" (20:4).

That the souls in 20:4 correspond with the souls in 6:9 makes sense in light of John's narrative. We first met the "souls" in 6:9–11, where they were under the altar and crying out for justice (6:10). In 19:2, we learned that God finally "avenged" their blood. Now we find out that "the authority to judge" was given to them and that "they came to life and they reigned with Christ" (20:4).[4]

That the victorious martyrs in the present account (20:4–6) correspond with the martyrs under the altar (6:9–11) also gains support from the fact that both have suffered death at the hands of the Roman authorities.[5] In 6:9, John says that the souls of the martyrs' were "slain." That those who were "slain" (6:9) are victims of Rome's brutal savagery is made certain in 18:24, where John attributes the murder "of all those who have been slain upon the earth" to the Great Prostitute. In the present account, John notes that they have been "beheaded" (20:4). There is little question that "beheaded" indicates death by capital punishment.[6]

Furthermore, that the accounts of the souls under the altar in 6:9–11 and the martyred souls in 20:4–6 are to be both read in light of one another

---

4. Not all commentators recognize the relationship between the souls under the altar in 6:9–11 and those in 20:4–6. See comments below.

5. It is quite likely that the people of God in 12:11 also suffered death at the hands of the Romans. That they are linked with the martyrs in 6:9–11 and 20:4–6, as noted above, supports this conclusion.

6. See Smalley, *Revelation*, 507.

is evidenced by the verbal links within the two accounts. In both accounts, John refers to them as those who have suffered death on account "of the testimony" and "the word of God" (6:9; 20:4). In the book of Revelation, John pairs the "testimony of Jesus" and "the word of God" five times.[7] The first occurrence of this expression (1:2) appeared in the prologue where it served to introduce the expression and its central role in the Apocalypse. The second occurrence was in 1:9, where John identifies himself as their "brother and sharer in the... kingdom" who was on the island of Patmos, "because of the word of God and the testimony of Jesus." The final three instances in which "the testimony" and "the word of God" are paired (6:9; 12:11; 20:4) and are applied to the people of God. It is quite likely then, that John intends to link these three texts.

In addition, John's identification of the people of God in these three passages as "souls" (6:9, 12:11, and 20:4) further establishes the link between the martyrs under the altar and the victorious people of God in the present account. Though it is true that John uses "souls" seven times in the book of Revelation (6:9; 8:9; 12:11; 16:3; 18:13, 14; 20:4), it is worth noting that 6:9, 12:11, and 20:4 are the only three places in which the term is applied to the people of God.

They Had Not Worshiped the Beast; They Came to Life and Reigned with Christ 20:4c

John continues his description of the people of God by adding that they were "those who had not worshiped the Beast or his image and they did not receive the Mark upon their forehead and upon their hand" (20:4).[8]

I noted in the account of the 144,000, in 14:1–5, that the Seal of God stands in contrast with the Mark of the Beast. I also argued that both the Seal and the Mark signify an attribution of allegiance. As a result, it is my contention that in the present account, John aims to encourage his reader/hearers by informing them that those who are faithful to the word of God and the testimony of Jesus, in contrast to "The rest of the dead" (20:5), will be rewarded. Hence, "they came to life and they reigned with Christ" (20:4).

---

7. See also 1:2, 9; 6:9.

8. The "Mark of the Beast" (16:2; 19:20) is also deemed "the Mark of his name" in 14:11.

Second Death 20:5

John then, somewhat parenthetically, interjects, "The rest of the dead did not come to life until the thousand years were finished" (20:5).[9]

First Resurrection 20:6

John closes the parenthetical insertion pertaining to the victorious martyrs with a blessing: "Blessed and holy is the one who has a part in the first resurrection; over them the second death has no authority, but they will be priests of God and of Christ and they will reign with Him a thousand years" (20:6). The assurance that those who partake of the first resurrection will reign with Christ corresponds to the opening affirmation: "He [Christ] has made us a kingdom, priests to His God and Father" (1:6)[10] The reference to the first resurrection raises two questions: namely, "What is the first resurrection"; and "When does it occur?"

Unfortunately, John does not provide us with much help in answering these questions. Since, there are only two occurrences of "the first resurrection" in the book of Revelation and since they both occur in the present account (20:5, 6), examining John's use of "first resurrection" throughout the Apocalypse does not offer us any assistance. All we really know is that "the first resurrection" is the reward for the people of God who overcome. It may well have been the case that John's reader/hearers knew what he meant and, therefore, no further clarification was necessary.[11]

It appears that the coming to life of "The rest of the dead" (20:5) is equated with "the second death" (20:6). This, of course, raises the question as to what is the second death. In each of the next two occurrences of "the second death" it is equated with "the Lake of Fire" (20:14; 21:8).[12] This suggests that "the second death" is the result of the final judgment. Consequently, "The rest of the dead" will come to life only to experience

---

9. The "rest of the dead" refers back to 19:21 where "the rest" were killed.

10. See 5:10.

11. I base this conclusion on the fact that the reference to "the first resurrection" (20:5, 6) appears without an explanation. This suggests that John may have assumed that his initial reader/hearers understood what he was talking about.

12. The "second death" also occurs in the message to Smyrna (2:11), but it offers no help for our understanding.

"the second death"; i.e., "the Lake of Fire." This most likely is depicted in the judgment of Death and Hades that follows this unit in 20:11–15.

Final Judgment of the Dragon (Satan) 20:7–10

In 20:7–10, John returns to the description of the final judgment of Satan. In 20:3, John had ended the opening description of the judgment of Satan by noting, "after these things, it is necessary for him to be released for a little time" (20:3). Now, in 20:7, he resumes the account of the judgment of Satan by reiterating, "when the thousand years are finished, Satan will be released from his prison" (20:7).

Naturally, upon his release, Satan does the only thing he knows how to do: "he will come out to deceive the nations" (20:8). John adds that Satan's purpose in deceiving the nations is "to gather them for the war" (20:8). That the nations whom Satan deceives are "in the four corners of the earth" (20:8) surely indicates that they represent all of the nations. That John further identifies them as "Gog and Magog" (20:8) supports this conclusion.[13] For, although "Gog and Magog" have been taken to refer to two distinct entities, it is more likely that "Gog and Magog" stand in apposition to "the nations. That is, "Gog and Magog" do not designate particular nations, but instead "Gog and Magog" is a representative designation for all nations.[14]

John's use of "Gog and Magog" (20:8) serves to provide an undeniable link between Satan's war against Christ and the people of God (16:14, 16; 19:19; 20:8–9) with the gathering of forces against the people of God in Ezekiel 38–39.[15] In Ezekiel, "Gog and Magog," or more likely, "Gog of the land of Magog," appears as the eschatological enemy army that battles against the people of God.

In the present passage, John says that Satan and his army, "surrounded the camp of the saints and the beloved city" (20:9).[16] Since this is the only occurrence of "the beloved city" it is difficult to determine

---

13. See Ezek 38:2; 39:1, 6. For a discussion of the role of Ezekiel in the book of Revelation, see Longman, *Revelation*, 394–400. See also, Robinson, *Temple of Presence*.

14. The difficulty with any attempt to identify "Gog and Magog" with particular nations is that in the book of Ezekiel "Gog is a person and Magog is a place" (Longman, *Revelation*, 398).

15. Smalley, *Revelation*, 410.

16. The reference to the "camp of the saints" reminds the reader/hearers of the Exodus wanderings (Exod 14:19–20; 16:13; Josh 1:11).

what city John has in view. It is my conviction that John's designation of the city as "the camp of the saints" (20:9) indicates that this war takes place wherever the people of God dwell. That is, John does not specify a particular city because until the Holy City/New Jerusalem descends there is no one city where the people of God dwell.[17]

Satan Is Thrown into the Lake of Fire 20:10

One of the benefits of a narratival reading is that it helps to accent the suspense that is inherent within the narrative. In the present account, we have seen that Satan is released (20:7). This might cause a bit of consternation among the reader/hearers. Perhaps, we might consider, "Why would the Lord allow that?" We then learn that Satan prepares for the war by gathering an army (20:8). The tension mounts. In 20:8, the suspense reaches a point of climax when we learn that Satan and his army surround the camp of the saints. Then, in what may only be described as the epitome of an anticlimax, John says, "And fire came down from heaven and consumed them" (20:9).[18] Again, as with the previous references to "the war," no battle is actually described.

John concludes the account of the judgment of Satan by noting, "and the Devil, the one who deceives them, was thrown into the Lake of Fire and sulfur where also the Beast and the False Prophet are" (20:10).

Excursus: The Millennium Part 1

The meaning of the millennium (the "thousand years") has been one of the more disputed issues related to the study of the end times. Since my primary concern has been to discern the significance of the text with regard to how it relates to John's narrative, I will weigh into the debate only so far as to suggest what I perceive to be the manner in which this passage relates to the larger narrative of the Apocalypse.

When it comes to the millennium in popular discourse, one of the central questions relates to "When the millennium occurs." Some argue that the order of events in 19:11—20:10

---

17. Although John has already used the designation "Holy City" (11:2) to refer the people of God. The difference is that in 11:2 the Two Witnesses are the "Holy City." In the present account, John is describing the place *where* they are located.

18. The irony here is that fire coming down from heaven was one of the signs that the False Prophet used to induce worship (13:13–14).

indicates that the millennium follows the return of Jesus.[19] After all, the reasoning is, John narrates the return of Jesus (19:11–16), then the final war that results in the defeat of the Beast and the False Prophet (19:17–20), and, then, the binding of Satan for a thousand years (20:1–3). Therefore, it is asserted, the millennium follows the return of Christ.

It is my conviction, however, that this line of argumentation fails to recognize the nature of the Apocalypse. For one thing, it assumes that John's vision is relaying actual "events" that transpire in history. And although I have no hesitation in affirming that the Second Coming of Jesus (19:11–16) refers to an actual (future) event, not everything in the book of Revelation is intended to correspond with an actual event(s) in history. For example, are we to suppose that the Father actually had a scroll in His right hand, which Jesus actually took, and then began to actually break each of the seven seals with which the scroll was closed? And, does John intend for us to suppose that he was actually brought into heaven to witness such "events" transpire?[20] When it comes to the issue of the millennium then, we should inquire as to whether or not John intends for us to believe that Satan was/is actually thrown into the Abyss for a specified amount of time—whether it be a literal or figurative thousand years.

A narratival approach to the book of Revelation suggests that John's primary concerns do not lie with depicting events in the order and manner in which they transpire in real-time. Instead, John's concerns center on his efforts to inform his reader/hearers regarding the world as it really is.

Furthermore, even if we are to suppose that John is describing actual historical events when he speaks of the casting of Satan into the Abyss, it is difficult to maintain the argument that the book of Revelation describes such events in the order in which they occur. The argument for a chronological reading of the book of Revelation, in fact, becomes a double-edged

---

19. See Mounce, *Revelation*, 360—though Mounce is admittedly not overly committed to this view. For further discussion of the views see Smalley, *Revelation*, 502–4; Clouse, *Meaning*.

20. Note: saying that it happened in a vision is not the same as saying that it happened as an actual "event."

sword. After all, as I will argue below, "the war" which Satan wages upon His release from the Abyss (20:8), most certainly corresponds to the war in 16:12-16 and 19:17-21. If this is so, then the demand for a chronological reading faces a conundrum. Does "the war" occurs before the millennium as it does in 16:12-16 and 19:17-21? Or does it occurs after the millennium as it does in 20:7-10?

Excursus: Armageddon Part 2

There is little doubt that John provides clear literary links in his descriptions of "the war" in 16:12-16; 19:17-21; and 20:7-10 so as it indicate that each account has the same war in view. We know that John has consistently linked passages by repeating keywords or phrases. In light of this, the following evidences provide a formidable argument that "the war" in 16:12-16, 19:17-20, and 20:7-10 is indeed the same war.

First, that these three passages recount the same war is evident from the repetition of the phrase, "to gather them together for the war" (16:14; 19:19; 20:8). This phrase, in fact, which first occurs in 16:14, is repeated verbatim in 20:8, and with only a slight modification in 19:19.[21]

Second, that the verb "gather" occurs only five times in the book of Revelation (16:14, 16; 19:17, 19; 20:8) and that all five occurrences appear only in these three accounts provides another strong indication that John intended for us to view "the war" in these passages in light of one another.

Third, that "the war" which Satan wages upon his release is waged by "the nations" who are "in the four corners of the earth" (20:8) clearly links with the description of "the war" in 16:14 and 19:19. In 16:14, John says that "the war" is waged by, "the kings of the inhabited world." And, in 19:19, he says that "the war" is waged by, "the kings of the earth and their armies."[22]

---

21. 19:19 John simply alters the form of the verb and adds the infinitive "to make." The difference is insignificant.

22. Beale affirms, "The battle imagery in 19:17-18, 21 and 20:8-9 is from the same eschatological battle in Ezekiel 39 (Ezek 39:4, 17-20 and 1, 6 respectively). In this light, it is very plausible that the scene in 20:8-10 supplements the scene in 19:17-21, if John is using this OT passage with the original context in mind" (Beale, *Revelation*, 132).

Fourth, each of the accounts of "the war" is linked by the explicit indication that the enemies of Christ and the people of God are the Dragon (Satan), the Beast, and/or the False Prophet. In the account of Armageddon in 16:14, 16 all three are mentioned as instigators of "the war" (16:13). In 19:17–21, the Beast and the False Prophet wage war against Christ and His armies (19:19). Lastly, in 20:7–10, the Dragon/Satan and the nations are explicitly mentioned as those who wage war against Christ and the people of God.

These literary links surely indicate the three accounts of "the war" (16:12–16; 19:17–20; 20:7–10) all refer to the same war. This, of course, raises the question as to what is the role of "the war" in each of the accounts.

From a narrative perspective, the famed Armageddon passage (16:12–16) serves as the preliminary account of what may be described as the final phase of the eschatological war.[23] In this account, we learn that "the war" is the work of the Dragon, the Beast, and the False Prophet who deceive the nations ("the kings of the inhabited world" 16:14) so that they wage war. And although it is not stated in this account against whom the war is waged, the parenthetical warning for the people of God to stay "awake" (16:15) certainly functions as an implicit indication that the war is indeed against the people of God.

In 19:17–21, John attributes "the war" to the work of the Beast and the False Prophet (Satan is not mentioned). As was the case in the Armageddon passage, the Beast and False Prophet wage war by deceiving the nations ("the kings of the earth and their armies"). This time John states explicitly that "the war" is waged against Christ and the people of God ("with the One sitting upon the horse and with His army"; 19:19). This account presents the ultimate outcome of the Beast and the False Prophet: "these two [the Beast and the False Prophet] were thrown alive into the Lake of Fire that burns with sulfur" (19:20).

In 20:7–10, John attributes "the war" to the work of the Dragon (Satan). Thus, this account depicts Satan's destruction

---

23. We must bear in mind that Satan has been waging this "war" against the people of God since the beginning.

and his being tossed into the Lake of Fire (20:10). As with the previous accounts, John reiterates that Satan's means of waging war is deception (20:7). In addition, this account places an emphasis on the fact that "the war" is waged against the people of God wherever they may be.

Thus, as David Barr concludes, "At least three times the same pattern holds: the forces of evil gather for battle against God's forces and are utterly defeated and destroyed (16:14; 19:19; 20:8). They seem more like three ways of telling the story rather than three stages of the same war."[24] Beale, likewise, affirms, that these three passages, "have in common not only the same language from the gathering together of forces for war, but also the idea that the gathered forces have been deceived into participating. This enforces the impression that Satan's deception of the nations in 20:8 . . . is the same event as the deception of the nations in 16:12–16 and 19:19."[25]

From a literary standpoint, the repeated descriptions of the war clearly build off one another. The first account (16:13–16) lays the foundation for understanding "the war." Note that in this account there is no explicit mention as to whom the war is waged against, nor of the outcome of the war. The second (19:17–21) and third (20:7–10) accounts explicitly declare that the war is waged against Christ and the people of God. These latter two accounts also set forth the outcome of the war. Even here, however, John's literary concerns are first and foremost. This is evident in that the second account emphasizes that the war is waged against Christ and His army and that the Beast and the False Prophet are destroyed in the Lake of Fire. The third account then details for us that the war is waged against the people of God wherever they may be located and that the devil, that is, the Dragon/Satan, is destroyed in the Lake of Fire.

With all this in view, we now return to the discussion of the millennium.

---

24. Barr, *Tales*, loc. 3696–99.
25. Beale, *Revelation*, 980.

Excursus: Millennium Part 2

I have argued that we must begin our reading of the book of Revelation by trying to discern John's narratival goals. When we approach the millennium passage from the perspective of John's narratival goals, it becomes critical to recognize the literary clues that John has embedded in his narrative.

We begin by noting that John "interrupts" the account of the destruction of Satan (20:1–3, 7–10) with the account of the victorious people of God (20:4–6). That 20:7 resumes the narrative that was left off in 20:3 is evident, as noted above, in that 20:3 ends with the affirmation Satan is not able to "deceive the nations any longer, until the thousand years were finished." John then resumes the narrative in 20:7 by reiterating, "And when the thousand years were finished."[26] John also links the account of the victorious martyrs (20:4–6) and the account of the binding and release of Satan (20:1–3, 7–10) by means of the repeated use of a "thousand" (20:2, 3, 4, 5, 6, 7). That these six occurrences of "a thousand" are the only instances in which the word "thousand" is applied to the number of years strengthens this link.

What is the significance of these links? That the account of the victorious martyrs (20:4–6) interrupts the description of the binding of Satan (20:1–3) and his subsequent destruction in the Lake of Fire (20:7–10) suggests that these two accounts are to be read in light of one another. That is, John's interruption of the account of the binding of Satan in order to provide a description of the victorious people of God, "who had not worshipped the Beast or his image and . . . did not receive the Mark upon their forehead and upon their hand" (20:4), only makes sense if the suffering of the people of God corresponds to the present activity of Satan.[27] This leads to the conclusion that the binding of Satan represents a present reality.

---

26. Note: 20:3 and 5 both have the added conjunction "until" preceding the phrase "the thousand years were finished." In 20:7, John precedes the expression with the adverbial conjunction, "when."

27. As for the number one thousand, it is highly unlikely that John intended for it to be understood as a designation for a literal period of time. David Barr suggests that one thousand is, "Derived from 10, thus signaling complete time." Barr, *Tales*, loc. 4373.

I suppose that some might respond to this proposition by contending that the binding of Satan indicates that he is inactive during the time in which he is bound. I would question, however, if this is what the binding of Satan means. In fact, the binding of Satan in the Gospels is instructive at this point.

Revelation's depiction of the binding of Satan corresponds with Mark's account of the "binding of the strong man" in Mark 3:20–30. In Mark 3:27, Jesus indicates that He is carrying out His work because He has first, "bound the strong man"—which most assuredly refers to Satan. That Satan, however, remained actively opposed to the work of Christ, even though Jesus has already bound him, is evident in that in the very next chapter of the Gospel of Mark, Jesus presents the Parable of the Sower (Mark 4:3–9). In this parable, Jesus explains that the seed which fell on the roadside represents those who, "when they hear, immediately Satan comes and takes away the word which has been sown in them" (Mark 4:15). This warning makes no sense if Satan has been bound and is out of the picture. In addition, Satan's continued active resistance to the work of Christ is evident from Jesus's rebuke to Peter in Mark 8:33, "Get behind Me, Satan." The Gospels of Luke and John also note Satan's continued opposition to Jesus when they declare that "Satan entered Judas" (Luke 22:3; John 13:27). It is clear from the Gospels that Satan can be both bound and yet active.

Excursus: The Demonic Hordes in the Fifth and Sixth Trumpets and the Judgment of Satan

An important, and often overlooked, element in the description of the judgment of Satan (20:1–3, 7–10) is the relationship between the demonic hordes in the accounts of the Fifth and Sixth Trumpets (9:1–11, 13–19) and the judgment of Satan (20:1–10).

That John links the account of the demonic hordes in the Fifth Trumpet (9:1–10) with the account of the judgment of Satan (20:1–3, 7–10) is indicated in that both accounts begin with the descent of a heavenly being who has a key to the Abyss

(9:1; 20:1). That John uses "key(s)" only four times (1:18; 3:7; 9:1; 20:1) seemingly links these two passages.[28]

Furthermore, the link between the Fifth Trumpet and the judgment of Satan is also indicated in that the demonic hordes in the accounts of the Fifth and Sixth Trumpets are linked with the three accounts of "the war" (16:12–16; 19:17–21; 20:7–10)—the third of which is the final judgment of Satan.

First, that the demonic hordes in the accounts of the Fifth and Sixth Trumpets are linked with the three accounts of "the war" (16:12–16; 19:17–21; 20:7–10) gains credibility from the apparent links with the Sixth Trumpet and the famed war of Armageddon in the Sixth Bowl (16:12–16). That the demonic hordes in the account of the Sixth Trumpet, who are "prepared . . . in order that they might kill a third of humanity" (9:15) link with "the war" of Armageddon in 16:12–16 is evidenced by the reference to "the great river Euphrates" in 9:14. The fact the "Euphrates" occurs only twice—once in the account of the Sixth Trumpet (9:14) and once in the Armageddon passage of the Sixth Bowl (16:12)—surely indicates that the demonic horde in 9:14 is released in order to engage in the war of Armageddon (16:12–16).

Second, in the account of the Sixth Trumpet (9:11–19), John states that the demonic horde's power, "is in their mouths and in their tails" (9:19). This links with the account of the Sixth Bowl where we learn that demonic frog-like beings come, "from the mouth of Dragon and from the mouth of the Beast and from the mouth of the False Prophet" (16:13).

Third, there are two uses of "war" (9:7, 9) in the account of the demonic horde in the Fifth Trumpet. As I noted in the previous excursus on Armageddon (part 1) that the term "war" appears nine times in the book of Revelation (9:7, 9; 11:7; 12:7, 17; 13:7; 16:14; 19:19; 20:8). In the excursus "Armageddon part 2," I argued that the last seven occurrences of "war" depict "the war" that is waged by the Dragon and/or his minions against Christ, Michael and his angels, and/or against

---

28. John's first two uses of "key" both refer to Christ as the One who has "the keys of Death and Hades" (1:18) and "the One who has the key of David" (3:8). These two uses are linked with one another and serve, if anything, as a contrast to the key of the heavenly beings in 9:1 and 20:1.

the people of God. It only makes sense of the narrative to link John's use of "war" in 9:7, 9 with the other seven uses of "war." After all, if the other seven instances of "war" all refer to the same war, then it would be surprising and almost unexplainable if the two uses of "war" in the account of the Fifth Trumpet did not pertain to the same war. The fact that throughout the entire narrative of the book of Revelation there is only one war mentioned virtually demands that the "war" that the demonic horde are preparing for is the same war.

In addition, there are also clear links with the demonic hordes in the accounts of the Fifth and Sixth Trumpets and the description of the final judgment of Satan (20:1–3, 7–10). First, there is John's seemingly unnecessary reiteration that the Dragon is, "the ancient serpent, who is the Devil and Satan" (20:2). The reiteration that the Dragon is the ancient serpent, however, serves as a means by which John further links the account of the binding and loosing of Satan with the demonic horde of the Sixth Trumpet whose, "tails are like serpents and have heads" (9:19). The link gains further strength from the fact that John only uses "serpent" five times in the book of Revelation (9:19; 12:9, 14, 15; 20:2). Three of the uses of "serpent" appear in the account of the Dragon and the Woman (12:1–17), which served to introduce the Dragon. This means that 9:19 and 20:2 are the only two occasions in which "serpent" occurs outside the introductory description of Satan as the Dragon.

At this point, some may wish to contend that the Fifth and Sixth Trumpets do not correspond to the account of Satan's final judgment because of the differences within the accounts. In particular, the heavenly being[29] with the key to the Abyss in the account of the Fifth Trumpet is said to have "fallen out of heaven" (9:1); whereas, in the present account the angel was

---

29. Of course, 9:1 says it was a "star," which we assume is an angel since John has identified angels as stars already (1:20)—though not all "stars" are angels; such as, when "star" is associated with the sun and the moon, as it is in 6:13 and 8:12, or in 12:1, where it is used as a symbol for the people of Israel (see Gen 37:4). Beale concludes that the star in 9:1 is demonic since it "fell." He contends that the language of a falling star "is uniquely reserved for evil angels in the OT, Jewish writings, and the NT." Beale, *Revelation*, 492.

"coming down out of heaven" (20:1).[30] I would respond that from a literary perspective, it is irrelevant if the heavenly beings are the same being or not.[31] What matters is whether or not John provides the literary links in order that his reader/hearers might connect the two scenes. The fact that the account of the Fifth Trumpet and the account of the judgment of Satan both depict "angels" who are coming from "heaven" certainly appears to establish a strong link between the two accounts.

In addition, some may contend that these passages should not be read in light of one another because the angel opens the Abyss in 9:2 and the angel in 20:3 "shut it." This argument, however, fails to persuade because it overlooks the narratival nature of the Apocalypse. After all, the opening and closing of the Abyss suggest movement within the story.

Excursus: Millennium Part 3

The opening and closing of the Abyss may be accounted for in one of two ways. First, it may be that the Abyss is opened in 9:2 and then it is closed in 20:3. This, of course, would make sense from a chronological reading. We know, however, that the narrative is not always to be read chronologically—the narrative of Woman and the Dragon (12:1–17) surely confirms this. Thus, it may be that in terms of the narrative the account of the throwing of Satan into the Abyss (20:1–3) may well take place prior to the release of the demonic horde (9:1–3).

This reading gains support from the fact that the Gospel narratives indicate that the binding of Satan has already occurred. If this understanding was already in the mindset of John's reader/hearers, then it would have been evident to them that the account of the binding of Satan in 20:1–3 refers to something that has already happened. Such an understanding would have been assumed.

---

30. This difference might be accounted for in light of John's use of variation. John rarely repeats things verbatim. Furthermore, there is doubt as to whether ancient hearers would have considered this to be a significant enough difference to mitigate connecting the two scenes.

31. Similarly, it makes no difference from a literary perspective if the "strong angel" in chapters 5, 10, and 18 are the same angels or not. John's use of "strong angel" is simply a rhetorical device with which he aims to draw the reader/hearer's attention to the potential links between the various passages.

Furthermore, we know that "the war" that Satan wages upon his release (20:8) occurs prior to the account of Jesus's return in 19:11–16. Thus, the whole account of Satan's being bound and being released depicts "events" that are not strictly chronological.

Therefore, from a narrative reading, the account of Satan being thrown into the Abyss (20:3), which is shut and sealed, takes place prior to the angel opening the Abyss (9:2) in order to release the demonic hordes—which presumably includes Satan. That the demonic hordes are "prepared for war" (9:7), as I have noted above, associates this scene with the eschatological war that Satan—along with the Beast and the False Prophet—wages against the people of God (20:8).

The narrative of the final judgment of Satan, therefore, in 20:1–10, begins by taking us backward in terms of time to include his binding and releasing. This was a necessary step for John because his reader/hearers would have wondered how Satan could partake of a war predicated on deception when he was in the Abyss and unable to deceive the nations.

Excursus: The Martyrs Reign for 1,000 Years

This brings us back to the question as to why John interrupted the account of the binding and loosing of Satan in order to highlight the victorious people of God (20:4–6). The interruption suggests that the activity of the victorious people of God corresponds to the binding of Satan.

That this is so makes sense of the narrative in that Satan's binding, "in order that he might not deceive the nations any longer" (20:3) is what enables the people of God to partake in an effective witness to the world. Since one of John's primary descriptions of the people of God is that they are to be effective witnesses for Christ,[32] the binding of Satan becomes a critical assumption for the narrative. That is, if Satan were not already bound, then, we may surmise, the nations would remain under his deception. This would render the mission of God's people to the nations (Matt 28:18–20) ineffective. Consequently, the missional role of the people of God to the

---

32. See my *Two Witnesses*.

nations ensues because Satan has already been bound. Again, I would contend that this was assumed by John's reader/hearers. They understood quite well what John was saying here.

At the same time, as I noted above, the binding of Satan does not mean, nor would it have been understood to mean, that he is unable to do anything. John's description of the binding of Satan specifically states that Satan is bound, "in order that he might not deceive the nations any longer" (20:3). This suggests that Satan is still active—as he was in the Gospel story as well as the rest of the NT—opposing the work of the people of God and persecuting them.

John's insertion of the victorious people of God in the middle of the account of the judgment of Satan serves to encourage the reader/hearers to persevere in light of the glorious outcome that awaits them. That is, those who have already been slain are the ones who "came to life and they reigned with Christ" (20:4).

Revelation 20:11–15
The Great White Throne Judgment

Introduction

IN 20:11–15, JOHN PRESENTS the final account of the judgment of the enemies of Christ by narrating the destruction of Death and Hades. As with the previous two units, the present unit is marked by two uses of, "And I saw" (20:11, 12). The unit beings with, "And I saw a Great White Throne" (20:11). Then, John adds, "And I saw the dead. . . ." (20:12).

Great White Throne 20:11–15

There is little question that the Great White Throne belongs to the Father and that it is the same throne that was first introduced in the temple scene in 4:2. After all, every one of the thirty-nine occurrences of "throne" in the singular and without qualification in the book of Revelation has referred to the throne of the Father.[1] That the throne here is "white" does not conflict with the throne room scene because the throne itself was never described.

---

1. John uses the word "throne" forty-six times in the book of Revelation (1:4; 3:21*; 4:2*, 3, 4, 5*, 6*, 9, 10*; 5:1, 6, 7, 11*,13; 6:16; 7:9, 10, 11, 15*, 17; 8:3; 12:5; 14:3; 16:17; 19:4, 5; 20:11, 12; 21:3, 5; 22:1, 3) and in thirty-nine of these occurrences it has indicated the throne of the Father. The only exceptions have been a single reference to Satan's throne (2:13), a reference to Jesus's throne (3:21), three references to the thrones of the Twenty-Four Elders (4:4*; 11:16—all plural), two references to the throne of the Beast (13:2; 16:10), and a single reference to the thrones of the people of God (20:4; plural). Thus, the "throne," in the singular, and without qualification, always indicates the throne of the Father.

John then says, "And I saw the dead, the great and the small standing before the throne" (20:12). There is some debate as to whether "the dead" who are "standing before the throne" includes the people of God. It is my unequivocal conviction that this is the final judgment of the nations and that it does not include the people of God.

That the "dead" represent the unbelieving and unrepentant makes sense in light of the overall purpose of this bridge section (19:11—21:8), which has been to narrate the final judgment of the enemies of God. In addition, the fact that John has just described the people of God as sitting on thrones and having been given "the authority to judge" (20:4-6) strongly suggests that they are not included in those who are "standing before the throne" (20:12) and about to face judgment.

John then adds that "the dead were judged by the things that were written in the books, according to their works" (20:12). Sadly, as with the Beast and the False Prophet in 19:17-21, and Satan in 21:1-10, "Death and Hades," as well as, "the rest" whose names have "not been found written in the Book of Life," were "thrown into the Lake of Fire" (20:14-15).

Revelation 21:1–8
New Creation:
The Introduction to the Holy City

Introduction

In 21:1–8, which is the final unit within the bridge section of 19:11—21:8, John presents an introductory description of the new heavens and new earth (21:1).

A New Heaven and a New Earth 21:1–2

As with the previous units within this section, John begins with, "And I saw (21:1). What John saw was "a new heaven and a new earth" (21:1). John, somewhat parenthetically, adds, "there was no longer any sea" (21:1). The reason for singling out the sea likely derives from the fact that within the book of Revelation,[1] the sea has been connected with that which is opposed to God.[2] For instance, the sea is where the Drag-

---

1. The "sea" was widely used throughout the biblical text as the antithesis to the divine or creation. It is the place of seafaring monsters—which likely serves as the background for the depiction of Satan as a Dragon (12:3–4)..

2. These are not the only instances of the sea in the Apocalypse. The "sea" occurs twenty-six times in the book of Revelation. See 4:6; 5:13; 7:1, 2, 3; 8:8*, 9; 10:2, 5, 6, 8; 12:12, 18; 13:1; 14:7; 15:2*; 16:3*; 18:17, 19, 21; 20:8, 13; 21:1. See Heiser, *Unseen*, 382. Mark Wilson notes that "the sea" in the book of Revelation has a wide spectrum of meanings: "For John, sea is a metaphor for heavenly splendour (4:6; 15:2), the realm of God's creation (5:13; 10:6), a place for judgment (7:1–3; 8:8–9), the abode of the first beast (13:1), a domain of commerce (18:17, 19), the holding place for souls (20:13), and a lacuna in the new heaven and earth (21:1)" (Wilson, "Water of Life," 3).

on stood (12:18) and it is the place from which the Beast arose (13:1). In addition, the Great Prostitute was said to sit upon "many waters (17:1), which John informs us, represent the nations (17:15).[3] And, in 20:13, the sea was the place of the dead, which was emptied so that its occupants might be brought for judgment before the Great White Throne (20:13).[4] Resseguie affirms, "The sea represents threat. It is a place of chaos where terrifying monsters of the deep lurk, such as Leviathan and Rahab (Job 9:13; Ps. 74:13–14; 89:10; Isa. 27:1). The sea is a metonym 'for everything that is recalcitrant to the will of God.'"[5] In light of this, it stands to reason that in order for there to be "a new heaven and a new earth" there must be no more sea.[6]

Instead of describing the new heaven and the new earth, however, John limits his focus to the Holy City: "And I saw[7] the Holy City, the New Jerusalem[8] coming down out of heaven" (21:2). At this point, we might suppose that the Holy City comprises the entirety of the new creation. After all, it does not appear as if John saw two things: that is, "a new heaven and a new earth" (21:1), and "the Holy City" (21:2), as if the latter was only a component of the former. Instead, what he saw was "the Holy City," which itself appears to constitute the totality of the new heaven and the new earth.

John then adds that the Holy City was, "like a bride adorned for her husband" (21:2).[9] Of course, as we will see in 21:9—22:9, this is because the Holy City is the Bride!

---

3. This may represent John's universalizing tendency. For, in the Greco-Roman world, the sea represented Rome. See Barr, *Tales*, loc. 4410.

4. Rossing notes, "Revelation portrays the sea politically and economically—as well as mythologically—as a location of evil (Rev 13:1) and a place where commercial ships sail . . . the eschatological end to the sea in Rev 21:1 must be read as more economic than mythological, hailing the end of Rome's cargo ships and trade" (Rossing, *Two Cities*, 146).

5. Resseguie, *Revelation*, 35.

6. The "sea" has a long history in the OT and the ANE world. It represents the place of chaos monsters and that which is opposed to God and creation. See Ps 29:3, 10; 74:12; 77:16–19; 104:28; Prov 8:29; Isa 27:1; Nah 1:4. Thanks to Jace Broadhurst for helping supply these verses.

7. The Greek of 21:2 places the verb "I saw" in the middle of the sentence so that the sentence does not begin with "And I saw." It is the nature of English grammar to render it as "And I saw. . . ."

8. Note: the city is called "the New Jerusalem" in 3:12 and 21:2, and it is called "Jerusalem" in 21:10.

9. In the OT, Israel is depicted as a bride finely adorned (Ezek 16:8–14) and as a mother (Hos 4:5; Isa 50:1).

Dwelling of God Is with People 21:3–4

What John *sees* in 21:1–2 is followed by what he *hears* (21:3). I have noted throughout our study that what John *sees* and what he *hears* often interpret one another. If this is the case here, then what John hears (21:3–8) provides even more insights into the nature of the Holy City.

John hears "a loud voice from the throne" (21:3). This is the third time we have heard a voice from the throne.[10] Though we might suspect that it is the voice of the Father, the fact that the voice refers to God in the third person ("He") suggests that it is the voice of another being. The voice declares, "Behold the dwelling place of God is with mankind, and He will dwell with them, and they themselves will be His people, and God Himself will be with them" (21:3). In saying this, the voice iterates the great covenantal promise of Scripture as found in Leviticus, "Moreover, I will make My dwelling among you, and My soul will not reject you. I will also walk among you and be your God, and you shall be My people (Lev 26:11–12). The promise was then reiterated by the prophet Ezekiel: "And I will place them and multiply them, and will set My sanctuary in their midst forever. My dwelling place also will be with them; and I will be their God, and they will be My people (Ezek 37:26–27).[11]

Further reference to the great covenantal promise occurs in 21:7, when the One seated on the throne says, "I will be God to him and he himself will be my son." This is not the first occurrence of the covenantal promise in the book of Revelation. The promise was first affirmed to those who have come out of the Great Tribulation: "and the One who sits on the throne will dwell among them" (7:15). The covenantal promise appears again in 22:3, where John adds, "the throne of God and of the Lamb will be in it."

The voice from the throne also states that God will, "wipe away every tear from their eyes; and there will no longer be *any* death; there will no longer be *any* mourning, or crying, or pain" (21:4).[12] This reflects the promises to those who had come out of the Great Tribulation in the interlude of 7:14–17.

---

10. See 16:17; 19:5.

11. See Wright, *Mission of God*.

12. See: Isa 25:8; 49:10; 43:18–19. Note the contrast with Babylon which is "found no more" (18:21–23). See Rossing, *Two Cities*, 146.

REVELATION 21:1–8

The One on the Throne Speaks 21:5–8

In 21:5, we hear for only the second time in the entire Apocalypse the voice of the Father:[13] "And the One sitting on the throne said, 'Behold, I am making all things new'" (21:5). The Father then commands John, "Write, because these words are faithful and they are true" (21:5). In 21:6, the Father addresses John personally: "And He said to me, 'It is done'" (21:6).

The affirmation, "It is done," reiterates what was spoken by the great voice that came from the throne after the Seventh Bowl was poured out (16:17). The distinction between the two affirmations of "It is done" resides in the fact that in 16:17, the affirmation, "It is done" indicated that the time for the final judgment has come. In the present verse, it signals that the time to reward the people of God has arrived.

The Father then further identifies Himself, "I am the Alpha and the Omega, the Beginning and the End" (21:6).[14] As noted earlier, each pair of titles expresses the timelessness of God.

The Father also states that for anyone who thirsts, "I myself will give freely from the spring of the water of life" (21:6). This promise echoes the promise given to those who have come out of the Great Tribulation in 7:16. It also harkens back to the Gospel of John and Jesus's words to the woman at the well, "whoever drinks of the water that I will give him shall never thirst" (John 4:14).

That the gift is the "water of life" (22:17), of course, indicates abundance and prosperity. Water is vital to life. In many parts of the world even today, fresh water remains a matter of critical concern.[15] Mark Wilson, perhaps the leading contemporary biblical scholar related to the seven ancient churches of Asia, states:

> Water was particularly important for life in the cities of the Greek East, especially of Roman Asia. Three of the seven churches—Ephesus, Smyrna, and Pergamum (via nearby Elaia)—were ports on the Aegean; the other four were on or near rivers—Thyatira (Lycus), Sardis (Hermus), Philadelphia

---

13. The Father speaks in 1:8 and 21:5. There are voices from the throne in 16:7 and 19:5, but it is not certain that either is the voice of the Father. Though the voice in 16:7, as in 21:6, also says, "it is done."

14. An abbreviated form of this title is applied to Jesus in the message to Laodicea: "the beginning of the creation of God" (3:14).

15. It came as a great surprise, and with much grief when I learned how many people die from the lack of access to clean water. And this does not even begin to assess the health issues that accompany the lack of clean water.

(Cogamus), and Laodicea (Lycus/Meander). Most had fresh water delivered via aqueducts or siphon systems. Water therefore provided various benefits—economic (commerce), aesthetic (fountains), sanitary (baths and sewer systems), and domestic (potability)—to these cities.[16]

That the water is "free" (22:17) demonstrates the contrast between the new creation and the economy of Babylon. As Barbara Rossing asserts, "God's gift of water 'without payment' flows freely through this paradisiacal landscape. . . . The water given without money becomes a pointed critique of Babylon/Rome's exploitive economy."[17] Howard-Brook and Gwyther agree, "Water freely given contrasts the economy of God with the economy of empire."[18]

The Bride, therefore, is the antithesis of the Prostitute. In addition, that it is a "free gift" (21:6; 22:17)[19] indicates that the blessings of the Holy City are available to everyone. Rossing continues, "Why so much attention to the gift of the water of life 'without money'? Because the author of Revelation knew that poor people lack the money to buy even the essentials of life."[20]

This final unit within the bridge section of 19:11—21:8 concludes by delineating between the people of God and the enemies of Christ. The people of God are reminded that "The one who overcomes will inherit these things" (21:7).[21] John then concludes the section with a list of those who do not "inherit these things" (i.e., the new creation). The list sets forth eight groups of people who are identified by their negative characteristics: "those who are cowardly and unbelieving and detestable and murderers and sexually immoral and sorcerers and idolaters and all liars" (21:8).[22] DeSilva notes, "John's lists (Rev 21:8, 27; 22:15) are notable

---

16. Wilson, "Water of Life," 3.
17. Rossing, *Two Cities*, 151–52.
18. Howard-Brook and Gwyther, *Unveiling Empire*, loc. 4882.
19. 21:6 and 22:17 are the only two occurrences of the adverb "freely."
20. Rossing, "Healing," loc. 2834–35.
21. Throughout the OT the promise of inheritance was tied to the land as a central tenet of the OT covenant. The Father's assurance that for the one who overcomes, "I will be God to him and he himself will be My son" (21:7) is a central affirmation of this covenant and affirms the covenantal significance of the promise. This suggests that the promise of inheritance is here understood in accordance with the OT covenant promises to Israel.
22. This is not the only list of those who are excluded from the new creation. An abbreviated list occurs in 21:27, and a list of six items appears in 22:15. One item that especially stands out in each of the lists is the presence of "liars" (21:8, 27; 22:15). Also,

insofar as they involve not ritual pollution but moral failure, particularly the failure to take a courageous and loyal stand by God and God's Christ. In this manner, they align with the broadening of the scope of God's salvation to members of every nation (John does not exclude "the uncircumcised" as such, as do Isaiah and Ezekiel)."[23]

Conclusion

The final unit in this bridge section has prepared us for John's description of the Bride/Holy City. In light of the fact that 21:1-2 relate what John *sees* and 21:3-4 what he *hears* it appears then that the totality of the new heavens and the new earth, of which the Holy City, which is named as the "New Jerusalem" (21:2), constitutes the entirety of, is actually the restored presence of God among His people. That is, as we will see in 21:9—22:9, John will describe the Bride/Holy City, which, in one sense is not a city, but the magnificent restoration of God's presence among His people.

Although this bridge section may not be one of the four main narrative sections of the Apocalypse, its significance should not be underestimated. While the narrative expectation at the end of the judgment of the Great Prostitute (17:1—19:10) might lead us to believe that "the feast of the wedding of the Lamb" (19:9) will follow immediately, we now realize that John had much to conclude before he depicts the Bride.

While the second story/section began with John seeing "a door opened" (4:1), the bridge scene begins with "heaven opened" (19:11). This time, instead of John going up as he did in 4:2, Christ is depicted as coming down (19:11-16). Christ's return depicts Him both in terms of the victorious warrior and as the righteous judge. The judgment of Christ's opponents, or shall we say, the opponents of the people of God, are then judged and thrown into the Lake of Fire. Once the enemies of the kingdom have been judged, John sees, "a new heaven and a new earth" (21:1).

The fourth and final main section in the body of the book of Revelation follows (21:9—22:9), and in it, the consummation finally arrives.

---

in each instance, "liars" or "lying" occurs last. There is little doubt that John means to contrast "liars" with the followers of the Lamb, of whom John says, "no lie was found in their mouths" (14:5). For John, adherence to the truth and following the One who is called "Faithful and True" (19:11) was a prerequisite for entering the New Jerusalem.

23. DeSilva, *Unholy Allegiances*, loc. 1896.

Revelation 21:9—22:9
The Fourth Scene:
The Bride: Holy City

Revelation 21:9—22:9
The Bride Is the Holy City

Eden is where the idea of the kingdom of God begins. And it's no coincidence that the Bible ends with the vision of a new Edenic Earth.[1]

My thesis is that the Old Testament tabernacle and temples were symbolically designed to point to the cosmic eschatological reality that God's tabernacling presence, formerly limited to the holy of holies, was to be extended throughout the whole earth.[2]

Empire's economic exploitation is reversed in New Jerusalem. Rather than stealing wealth and resources from the world, people and nations will freely bring their glory to the Holy City. The traditional image of nations bringing tribute to Zion is democratized to express people's universal sharing of God's gifts with one another.[3]

Both the Whore and the Bride represent cities, Babylon and the New Jerusalem. Babylon is defined by her promiscuity; she merely rides the Beast. Yet the Bride is adorned for her marriage to the Lamb. While Babylon wears luxurious garments, the Bride is adorned in modest wedding attire. Babylon does commerce in all sorts of luxury items, while the Bride provides water from the River of Life and a Tree of Life that bears a different fruit every month (22:1-2). Babylon may wear gold and jewels and pearls, but the New Jerusalem is made of pure, clear gold, decorated with "every precious stone" (21:18-19), and

---

1. Heiser, *Unseen*, 51.
2. Beale, *Temple*, 25.
3. Howard-Brook and Gwyther, *Unveiling Empire*, loc. 4911.

guarded by gates of pearl (21:21). Whatever Babylon's glory, the New Jerusalem surpasses it by far.[4]

Introduction

THE FOURTH MAJOR STORY/SCENE in the book of Revelation (21:9—22:9) presents the consummation of John's narrative, and one might say the entire biblical story. As we learned in the close of the previous unit (21:1–8), the new creation represents the dwelling of God among His people: "Behold the dwelling place of God is with men, and He will dwell with them, and they themselves will be His people, and God Himself with be with them" (21:3).

In this final section, John now provides the details of this new creation. In contrast to the Great Prostitute, John portrays, "the Bride, the wife of the Lamb" (21:9). John's description of the new creation, however, is of a garden-like, city-temple. In fact, upon closer examination, the only part of the garden-like, city-temple that John depicts is that which corresponds to the Holy of Holies.

Excursus: How John's Use of "To Show" Indicates Structure within This Section.

I noted in the opening chapters on the structure of the book of Revelation that John begins the fourth and final section of the Apocalypse (21:9—22:9) in a manner similar to the opening of the second (4:1—16:21) and third (17:1—19:10) stories/sections, by being exhorted, "Come, and I will show you" (21:9).[5] This is followed by, as was the case in the second and third major stories/sections, "And he carried me away in the Spirit" (21:10).[6] In the second story/section (the heavenly vision), John was then taken to heaven (4:2). In the third story/section (the Great Prostitute), John was brought into the wilderness (17:3). Now, in the present story/scene, (the Bride) he will be taken to "a great and high mountain" (21:10). The verb "to show" occurs in the opening verses of

---

4. Carey, "Revelation as Counter-Imperial," 2218–22.
5. Compare 4:1; 17:1.
6. Compare 17:3. In 4:2, John was "in the Spirit."

the second (4:1—16:21), third (17:1—21:8), and the fourth (21:9—22:9) major stories/sections of the book of Revelation. The verb "to show" also occurs in the opening verses of the prologue (1:1-8) and the epilogue (22:6-21).[7] I also noted in the opening chapter on John's use of numbers, that John uses the verb "to show" a total of seven times in the book of Revelation.[8] If, in five of the uses of "to show," the verb has structural significance, this raises the question as to what this means for the other two uses of the verb.

Interestingly, those other two uses of "to show" both occur within the present account of the Bride. After introducing the account of the Bride in 21:9-10a, John begins his description of the Bride with, "And he showed me" (21:10). The final occurrence of the verb occurs in 22:1, where John again says, "And he showed me."[9] In light of the fact that John has been so careful with his choice of words, it seems odd that he would randomly use one of the key verbs, which has consistently had structural significance, within the midst of a section without it also having some measure of structural importance. It is, therefore, my conviction that John employs, "And he showed me" in both 21:10 and 22:1 to indicate the structure within the account of the Bride.

---

7. The only major sections of the book in which the verb "to show" does not occur in the opening verse of the section are 1:9 and 19:11. The absence of "I will show you" in 1:9 (which marks the beginning of the first scene/story in the book of Revelation) is accounted for by the fact that John is not shown anything in 1:9—3:22; instead, he turns and sees (1:12). In addition, since the first scene occurs on Patmos, John is not taken or "shown" anything. The absence of "I will show you" in 19:11 is accounted for by the fact that 19:11—21:8 does not function as a major section within the book of Revelation. Instead, as I have argued, it is a bridge section between the accounts of the two women/cities.

8. See 1:1; 4:1; 17:1; 21:9, 10; 22:1, 6.

9. The various forms of this verb also support the understanding of John's structure as set forth in this commentary. Of the seven occurrences of this verb, the first and the last occurrences (1:1; 22:6) are both aorist active infinitives ("to show"). This supports the conviction that 1:1 and 22:6 serve as the beginning of the prologue and the epilogue. The next three occurrences of the verb (4:1; 17:1, 21:9) are all first-person singular future active indicatives ("I will show"). This supports the contention that 4:1, 17:1, and 21:9 help to identify the major sections within the Apocalypse—aside from the opening section. The final two occurrences of this verb (21:10; 22:1) are in the midst of the present section depicting the Bride/Holy City. In both of these occurrences the verb "to show" occurs as a third-person singular aorist active indicative ("he showed me").

If this is so, then John's description of the Bride contains an introduction (21:9-10a), two central units (21:10b-27; 22:1-5), and a conclusion (22:6-9).[10] Each of these two central units in the section emphasizes key features of the Bride. In the first of the two central units (21:10b-27), John highlights the fact that a fundamental feature of the Bride, which is depicted as the Holy City, is that it represents the presence of God among the totality of the redeemed people of God. In doing so, John stresses both the Bride/Holy City is the consummation of the OT and the NT people of God and their dwelling in the presence of God. And he presents the Bride/Holy City as the place where the nations dwell in the presence of God. That is, in the first unit, the Bride is the Holy City. In the second of the two central units (22:1-5), John both reinforces the identification of the Bride/Holy City as the eternal dwelling place of God's presence among His people and he relates it to the image of a restored Eden.[11] That is, in the second unit, the Bride is the new Eden.

John Carried Away in the Spirit to a Mountain 21:9-10a

John begins again with being told, "Come, and I will show you" (21:9).[12] And again John is carried "away in the Spirit" (21:10).[13] This time he is taken "to a great and high mountain" (21:10).

Mountains, as I noted earlier,[14] have great significance throughout Scripture. They often symbolized kings and kingdoms.[15] Of course, at the center of ancient kingdoms was the temple, which was customarily located on the highest part of the mountain. As a result, mountains

---

10. As I noted in the opening chapters on structure, 22:6-9 are both a part of the conclusion to the account of the Bride (21:9—22:9) and the opening of the epilogue (22:6-21).

11. Beale, *Temple,* 351. Prophets describe the restoration in terms of Eden Isa 51:3; Ezek 36:35; 47:1-7.

12. See 4:1; 17:1. Recall that John is not told to "come" in 1:9-10 because the vision occurs on Patmos where he already was.

13. See 1:10; 4:2; 17:3.

14. See discussion in 17:9-10.

15. Note that in the temptations of Jesus, when Satan shows him, "all the kingdoms of the world" (Matt 4:8), he does so after bringing Jesus to a "very high mountain" (Matt 4:8).

also indicate the place of the temple. Mountains also represent places of revelation. It was, of course, on a mountain that Moses met the Lord[16] and later received the law.[17]

The mountain that John is carried to is "great and high" (21:10). This language parallels the vision of Ezekiel: "In the visions of God He brought me into the land of Israel and set me on a very high mountain, and on it to the south *there was* a structure like a city" (Ezek 40:2).[18] It also echoes Isaiah's throne-room vision: "I saw the Lord sitting on a throne, lofty and exalted" (Isa 6:1).[19] John, in other words, is taken to the presence of God.

The Bride Is the Holy City 21:10b

Though John is told that he is to come so that he may be shown, "the Bride, the wife of the Lamb" (21:9), he says instead that the angel "showed me the Holy City, Jerusalem, coming down out of heaven from God" (21:10). Again, we have another instance of John's use of *hearing* and *seeing*. John's use of *hearing* and *seeing* has regularly served to identify two things that might appear to be distinct, but are in fact the same. In this instance, John is told (*hears*) that he is going to be shown, "the Bride" (21:9), but what he *sees* is, "the Holy City" (21:10). Bauckham affirms what we have seen throughout our study of Revelation, "The juxtaposition of more than one image with a single referent is a characteristic of John's visions"[20] Consequently, the Bride is the Holy City or, perhaps, we should say, the Holy City is the Bride.[21]

---

16. See Exod 3:1—4:17; Ezek 40:2; Exod 19:3-23; Deut 34:1-4; Matt 5:1; Mark 9:2-9.

17. See Exod 19-20.

18. See Exod 19:3-23; Deut 34:1-4; It was on a mountain that the sermon of Matthew 5-7 is set (See Matt 5:1). It was on a mountain that Jesus was transfigured (Mark 9:2-8).

19. The word for "lofty" in the LXX of Isa 6:1 is the same word John uses here for "high" (see also LXX of Isa 52:13 where the verbal form is used so that the servant will be "high and lifted up and greatly exalted."

20. Bauckham, *Climax*, 179.

21. This raises the question as to whether or not the Holy City is actually a city with streets of gold. I suspect that this is not what John was trying to convey. Instead, John's concern appears to have been to describe the restoration of God's presence among His creation and His people. And John does so by describing a city in which the glory of God dwells that has no need of the sun or the moon, and in which the nations enter in order that they might be healed and no longer experience any curse.

Glory of God 21:11a

John begins his description of the Bride/Holy City by repeating virtually verbatim from the introduction to the Holy City in 21:2. In both 21:2 and 21:11, John makes reference to "the Holy City, Jerusalem." Both verses also describe the Holy City as "coming down out of heaven from God." The differences in the two descriptions are slight, though not insignificant.

First, in 21:2, John includes the use of "New" in the title "New Jerusalem," which is omitted in 21:11. Second, whereas in 21:2, the Holy City was "prepared like a bride adorned for her husband," in 21:11, John says that Holy City had, "the glory of God" (21:11).[22] The significance of the affirmation that the Holy City had, "the glory of God" resides in the fact that the "glory of God" (21:11) was a vital component of the temple complex.[23] Beale notes, "But in the new creation God's presence will not be limited to a temple structure, with the people outside the structure, but the people themselves will be both the city and the temple in which God's presence resides."[24]

Therefore, although in 21:1–8, John describes the Holy City as a Bride, in 21:9—22:9, he introduces us to the Bride in terms of the Holy City, but it is not the Holy City but the temple within the Holy City. In fact, as will become evident as we proceed, John's description of the temple corresponds solely to the inner sanctum of the temple (i.e., the Holy of Holies).[25]

Brilliance of the City 21:11b

John continues his description of the glory of the Bride/Holy City/temple, "Her brilliance was like a precious stone, as a stone of crystal-clear jasper" (21:11). It is important to note that "jasper" occurs only four times in the book of Revelation (4:3; 21:11, 18, 19). Three of these occurrences are in

---

22. Beale, *Revelation*, 1066.

23. Resseguie observes, "The major trait of the new Jerusalem is that it reflects the glory of God." (Resseguie, *Revelation*, loc. 5654–55). See Exod 40:35; 1 Kgs 8:10; Isa 40–66; 58:8; 60:1–2, 19.

24. Beale, *Revelation*, 1066.

25. The Holy of Holies represented the place of God's presence or the "portal" to His presence (after all, God "does not dwell in *houses* made by *human* hands"; Acts 7:48.) Hence, the cherubim are the defenders who protect mankind from entering the presence of God; Gen 3:24.

the present account of the Bride/Holy City/temple. The only other occurrence was in the opening throne room scene (4:1–11) where it served as the only term used in the description of God: "And the One who was sitting had an appearance like a stone of jasper" (4:3).

That "jasper" describes God in 4:3, and that it is the featured stone in his description of the Holy City confirms that the Bride/Holy City/temple is not so much a place as it is the glorious description of the presence of God among His people of God. This is Eden.

Great and High Wall 21:12–14

John continues by noting that it had "a great and high wall" (21:12). In the ancient world, walled cities provided safety and protection for their inhabitants. The irony is that this city has no need for protection. After all, "the kings of the earth will bring their glory into it" (21:24).[26] And, in fact, "its gates will never be shut" (21:25).[27]

> **Excursus: John's Use of the Number Twelve in the Account of the Holy City**
>
> That John depicts the Holy City as the people of God (Bride) is evident from the abundant use of "twelve." John, in fact, not only employs the number twelve in his description of the Holy City, but he does so twelve times.[28]
>
> Ten of the twelve occurrences of "twelve" are explicit. The word "twelve" appears three times in 21:12, where we are told that the city has "twelve gates" with "twelve angels" and on the gates are "the names of the twelve tribes of the sons of Israel." "Twelve" appears three more times in 12:14, where the wall of the city has "twelve foundation stones" and on them are the "twelve names of the twelve apostles of the lamb." The seventh occurrence is in 21:16, where we are told that the city's length, width, and height measures, "12,000 stadia."[29] The eighth and

---

26. See Isa 60:5, 11. In Isaiah, it is the "wealth" of the nations that is brought.

27. One might ask, "If there is no need for protection from the outside, why then does this city have a wall?" It is likely that this city has a wall because all ancient capital cities had walls. If so, it is not the wall that is important, but the gates. That is, with the New Jerusalem the gates will never be closed (21:25).

28. See Bauckham, *Climax*, 36.

29. As I have noted, it is critical to be aware of the number in the Greek text and not

ninth occurrences of "twelve" appear in 21:21, where John says, "the twelve gates are twelve pearls." The tenth occurrence is in 22:2, where we learn that the Tree of Life has "twelve fruits."

In addition to these ten explicit uses of twelve, the number twelve occurs implicitly twice in the measurement of the city's walls[30] which are "144 cubits" thick (21:17). The fact that "144" is comprised of twelve times twelve places the number of occurrences of "twelve" in the description of the Holy City at twelve.

John's depiction of the people of God in terms of the Holy City, however, also reflects the unity of the people of God.[31] That is, the Holy City represents the totality of the OT and NT people of God. This is evident in that while the twelve gates have, "the names of the twelves tribes of the sons of Israel" (21:12), the twelve foundation stones of the city wall have, "the twelve names of the twelve apostles of the lamb" (21:14). In addition, that the walls are "144" cubits (21:17) further establishes that the Holy City represents the combined OT and NT people of God.

In addition, that the Holy City represents the combined presence of the Old and New Testament people of God is evident in that in the description of the Holy City, John alludes to both the 144,000 (7:3–8; 14:1–5) and the Great Multitude (7:9–17; 19:1–6).

I have already noted that John's description of the Great Multitude in 7:15–17 was a proleptic description the Holy City. The allusion to the 144,000 is evident in his reiteration of the "twelve tribes" (21:12). John uses "tribe(s)" twenty-one times. John uses "tribes" once to refer to, "all the tribes of the earth" (1:7). It is used to refer to Jesus as the One who comes "from the tribe of Judah" (5:5). John uses "tribes" five times in the fourfold designation for the nations (5:9; 7:9; 11:9; 13:7; 14:6). Interestingly, as I noted in the opening chapter on numbers, the fourfold designation for the nations occurs seven times.

---

rely on English translations.

30. Compare the measuring of the Holy City with the measuring of Ezekiel's city-temple (Ezek 40:1–49).

31. Recall that the 144,000 and the Great Multitude in 7:1–17 both reflect the totality of the people of God.

John, however, omits "tribes" from the formula in both 10:11 and 17:15. This is likely in order to keep the number of occurrences of "tribe(s)" at twenty-one. The other fourteen uses of "tribes" occur in the account of 144,000: "twelve tribes" (7:4, 5**, 6**, 7**, 8**, 9; 21:12). The significance for the present passage is twofold. First, John refers to the twelve tribes only in the account of the 144,000 in 7:3-8 and here in 21:12. Second, he only uses the expression "tribes of the sons of Israel" twice: once in 7:4 and here in 21:12. There is little doubt that the account of the Holy City alludes to the 144,000.

John also alludes to the 144,000 in his use of "144" to describe the walls (21:17). Although this may not seem like much of an argument, the fact that "144" occurs only four times in the book of Revelation and the other three occurrences all appear in the description of the 144,000 (7:4; 14:1, 3) continues John's consistent habit of linking passages by use of key terms or expressions. The fact that the Holy City is the eternal dwelling place of all God's people and that John's description of it alludes to the 144,000 reinforces my earlier argument that 144,000 represent all of God's people and not just ethnic Israelites.

In addition to this, as I will note below, the measuring of the Holy City (21:16-17) also alludes to the measuring in the account of the Two Witnesses (11:1-13).

The Angel Measures the Holy City and Its Wall 21:15-16

John continues his description of the Holy City by noting, "The one who was speaking with me had a gold measuring rod" (21:15). The purpose of the measuring rod was, "to measure the city and its gates and its wall." As I noted in the account of the Two Witnesses, the act of measuring represents a prophetic act that signifies the divine protection of what is measured.[32] The fact that John uses "measure" only five times

---

32. One might inquire as to why the Holy City is in need of divine protection. In response, I would simply note that it is not in need of divine protection. Since, however, it is the place where God dwells, divine protection is a natural part of its existence. Furthermore, we must continue to be reminded that John uses terms to connect various parts of the Apocalypse. Thus, it may have been more important in his eyes that we recognize the connection between the account of the Two Witnesses (11:1-13) and the

(11:1, 2; 21:15, 16, 17) and that these five occurrences are limited to these two accounts—the introduction to the account of the Two Witnesses and the present account of the Holy City—presents a formidable link between the account of the Two Witnesses and the description of the Bride/Holy City. In addition, the fact that John uses "measuring rod" only three times (11:1; 21:15, 16) and these three occurrences are limited to the account of the Two Witnesses and the Holy City further establishes the link between the two.[33]

The angel measures the city and John notes that the length, width, and height of the city are all, "12,000 stadia" (21:16).[34] The stadia was a Roman measure of distance which was approximately the length of a modern furlong.[35] In terms of miles, "12,000 stadia" is roughly 1,400 to 1,500 miles.[36] Of course, translating the text into modern numbers tends to obscure the fact that John wrote, "12,000"; which is the product of 12 x 1000 (10 x 10 x 10). As Barr comments, "The English translation misses the point, for the number is clearly chosen for its symbolic significance, not its realism."[37]

Two factors stand out with respect to the angel's measurements. First, it has been proposed that 12,000 stadia corresponds to the approximate size of the Hellenistic world.[38] This affirms, as I argued in the introduction to the new creation (21:1–8), that the Holy City constitutes the entirety of the new creation.[39] Second, the fact that "its length and the width and the height are equal" (21:16) indicates that it is a perfect

---

Holy City (21:9—22:9), than it was that the Holy City is measured.

33. This also confirms the argument that the measuring of the temple in 11:1–2 is a vital part of the account of the Two Witnesses proper (11:3–13). After all, if the measuring of the temple in 11:1–2 corresponds with the measuring of the Holy City in 21:15–17, and if the Holy City is a depiction of the people of God (the Bride) as a temple, then it stands to reason that the measuring of the temple in 11:1–2 similarly describes the measuring of the people of God.

34. Because John is describing the New Jerusalem as a temple, it is more likely that the city is a cube than a pyramid. After all, the Holy of Holies was a cube (see 1 Kgs 6:20).

35. Hence, the NKJ translation of "twelve thousand furlongs."

36. Hence, the NAU and NRS use "fifteen hundred miles"; and the NET and the NLT use "fourteen hundred miles."

37. Barr, *Tales*, loc. 4465–66.

38. See Kraybill, *Allegiance*, 176–77, 212–13.

39. This conclusion corresponds with the biblical mandate to "fill the earth" (Gen 1:28).

cube.[40] That it is a cube, however, suggests that it is not just the temple, but that it is the Holy of Holies within the temple.[41]

The importance of this cannot be overstated. The description of the Holy City appears to encompass the entirety of the new creation—after all, nothing else is described. But John does not actually describe a city. Instead, the dimensions of the City correspond only to the temple, and even then, only to the Holy of Holies within the temple. We might conclude, therefore, that the Holy of Holies encompasses the entirety of the new creation.[42] Of course, this makes perfect sense in that the Holy of Holies was where the presence of God dwelt. Since, as we were told in the introduction to the Holy City, "Behold the dwelling place of God is with mankind, and He will dwell with them, and they themselves will be His people, and God Himself with be with them" (21:3), and, as we will see even more so as we proceed, the entirety of the new creation is the dwelling place of God among His people. Hence, the Bride is the Holy City; and the Holy City is the Holy of Holies.

The Bejeweled City 21:18–21

John continues his description of the Holy City by listing the material components of the city (21:19–20). He next adds, "And the material of the wall itself was jasper" (21:18). The presence of "jasper" occurs again in 21:19: "The foundation *stones* of the city wall were adorned with every precious stone. The first foundation stone was jasper. As noted above, the prominence of jasper is evident in that it is the only stone used to depict the One who sits on the throne (4:3).

---

40. See Ezek 45:1–5; esp. 45:2 "square." See Howard-Brook and Gwyther, who note that "Herodotus described Babylon built as a square (History 1.178). To the Greek mind, a square was a symbol of order" (Howard-Brook and Gwyther, *Unveiling Empire*, loc. 4822).

41. Exod 26:31–33; 1 Kgs 6:20–28.

42. See Heb 9:7. The Holy of Holies represents the place where God dwelt and it is the place where the High Priest was permitted to enter the presence of God once per year. If indeed John's description of the Holy City is meant to be understood in terms of the Holy of Holies, then it comes as no surprise to learn that all those who enter the city will experience the glorious presence of God and, "will see His face" (22:4).

The importance of the list of twelve jewels (21:19–20) should not be overlooked.[43] It is of particular significance that the list of twelve stones recalls the twelve stones of the High Priest's breastplate.[44]

John also lists "gold" twice. First, he states, "and the city was pure gold" (21:18). Then he adds that "the street of the city was pure gold" (21:21). It is likely that the reference to gold alludes to the gold of the Garden of Eden (Gen 2:11–12).[45] This will become more evident in the description of the Holy City in 22:1–5. That the prophet Ezekiel combines the jewels of the High Priest's garments and those that adorned Eden (Ezek 28:13) lends credence to this conclusion.

No Temple in It 21:22

John's statement, "And I saw no temple in it. . . ." (21:22), may, at first glance, come as a surprise. After all, all ancient capital cities had temples. In fact, a city's status in the ancient world was often measured by the number and quality of temples. Furthermore, we have already seen numerous indications that the Holy City is not just a temple, but the Holy of Holies. The absence of a temple in the Holy City, therefore, is striking.

We realize fairly quickly, however, that John does not see a temple in the City because, as has already been established, the whole city is the temple. John affirms this when he adds, "because[46] the Lord God the Almighty and the Lamb are its temple" (21:22). DeSilva affirms, "John, however, has a clear rationale for this difference (21:22): the full presence of God and the Lamb in this city eliminate the need for a temple."[47] That the entire city is a temple derives from the fact that the key feature of the

---

43. That John lists the twelve stones suggests that they have some role to play in the narrative.

44. See Exod 28:17–20 LXX; 39:8–14. The list in Rev 21:19–20 is identical to the first 9 of 12 jewels on the High Priest's breastplate. See Caird, *Revelation*, 274–77. Caird contends that John's list does not derive from Exodus but from his knowledge of astrology. Caird notes, "he then deliberately reversed it to indicate his total disavowal of astrological interest" (Caird, *Revelation*, 277).

45. Jewish interpreters claimed that the jewels for the High Priest's breastplate came from Eden. See Beale, *Revelation*, 1085–88. There may also be an allusion to the gold of Solomon's temple. See 1 Kgs 6:20–22.

46. The Greek here (*gar*) often indicates "the reason why." Thus, though it is commonly translated as "for," it seems best here to use the more explicit "because." Compare the NET. All other major English versions use "for."

47. DeSilva, *Unholy Allegiances*, loc. 1896.

biblical temple is that it represents the place where God dwells. Since both God and the Lamb dwell throughout the entirety of the Holy City, the whole city has become the Holy of Holies.

Its Lamp Is the Lamb 21:23–24

John also notes, "And the city does not have need of the sun nor of the moon to give it light, for the glory of God gives it light and its lamp is the Lamb" (21:23). The result is, "The nations will walk by its light and the kings of the earth will bring their glory into it . . . and they will bring the glory and honor of the nations into it" (21:24, 26).

Its Gates Will Never Be Shut 21:25–27

John concludes this first unit by noting, "there will never be a time when its gates will ever be shut, for there will be no night there" (21:25; 22:5).[48] Nighttime, of course, was when an ancient city would be most prone to an attack. For this Holy City, however, there will be no fear of attack. After all, the nations and the kings of the earth are already inside it!

In the epilogue, John adds to this description, we he says, "Outside are the dogs and the sorcerers and the sexually immoral and the murderers and the idolaters and everyone who loves and practices lying" (22:15). Even though they are "outside" the Holy City, there is, of course, no concern that anything "outside" will come in. After all, they cannot: "And all the unclean things and the one who does what is detestable and lying will certainly not enter it" (21:27). The only ones who are, in fact, permitted to enter into it are, "the ones whose names have been written in the book of Life of the Lamb" (21:27).

---

48. This is a clumsy attempt to bring out the Greek. John says, "Its gates will never be shut *day*, for (*gar*) there will be no night there." The implication is, "There will never come a time at the end of a day when you will need to shut the gates before nightfall. After all, there will not be any night!"

Revelation 22:1–5
The Holy City: The New Eden

Introduction

JOHN'S REITERATION OF, "AND he showed me" in 22:1 marks the beginning of the second unit within this section (21:9—22:9. It is my contention, as I noted above, that this second unit highlights the Holy City as the restored or redeemed Eden. As such, John brings the biblical story to its fitting consummation.

River of Life: 22:1

John begins this unit with, "And he showed me the River[1] of the water of life bright as crystal coming from the throne of God and the Lamb" (22:1). Since Jesus sits on the Father's throne (3:21), it is not surprising that the River in the Holy City comes, "from the throne of God and the Lamb." That the River comes from the throne of God and the Lamb increases the likelihood that the River represents the Holy Spirit.[2]

That the River was as "bright as crystal" links the description of the Holy City to the throne room scene (4:1—5:14) where there was, "a sea of glass, like crystal" (4:6). That 22:1 and 4:6 are the only two uses of "crystal" in the book of Revelation strengthens the link.

---

1. The NAU, NLT, and NKJ all translate this as "a river." I think that this is not an ordinary river since it is associated with the "water of life" and it is "coming from the throne." Thus, it is "the" River.

2. See Ezek 47:1–12; Joel 3:18; Zech 14:8. Depicting the Holy Spirit as a river of water corresponds with John 7:37–39.

That the Holy City has a river strengthens the correlation of the Holy City with Eden: "Now a river flowed out of Eden to water the garden."

The Tree of Life: 22:2

The relationship between the Holy City and Eden continues as John notes that the "Tree of Life" (22:2) was also present.[3] John adds that the Tree of Life produced "twelve fruits" (22:2)[4] and, "the leaves of the Tree are for the healing of the nations" (22:2). The fact that its leaves bring healing "to the nations" affirms the conviction that at the heart of Revelation's narrative is God's love for the nations. DeSilva affirms, "A truly new society is founded—the New Jerusalem—which exists for the healing of the nations rather than for the conquest and exploitation of the same."[5] Barbara Rossing takes this conclusion one step further by suggesting, "Revelation's New Jerusalem is not merely a reward for the individual Christian . . . It is an alternative city, an entire political economy."[6]

Excursus: John and Ezekiel's City-Temples[7]

John's description of the Holy City corresponds closely with Ezekiel's vision of the eschatological city/temple in Ezekiel 40–48.[8]

First, in both Revelation and Ezekiel an angelic figure with "a measuring rod" measures the city and its gates (Ezek 40:3–49; Rev 21:15–17). In both accounts, there are three gates on each of its sides (Ezek 48:31–34; Rev 21:13). And, in

---

3. John is most certainly building off Ezekiel here. Eden references appear in Ezek 28:13; 31:16.

4. Gen 3:22, 24.

5. DeSilva, *Unholy Allegiances*, loc. 1040–41.

6. Rossing, *Two Cities*, 157–58.

7. Ezekiel, of course, is not the only text that plays a prominent role in the closing sections of the book of Revelation. As has been the case for much of the book of Revelation, the book of Daniel, especially the vision of Dan 7:1–28, plays a key role in Revelation's final chapters. Both the book of Revelation and the book of Daniel depict "thrones" (20:4; Dan 7:9). In both, we learn that "books were opened (20:12; Dan 7:10). Finally, both describe the destruction of the beast(s) (19:20–21; Dan 7:26), and the transferring of the kingdom to the people of God (20:4; Dan 7:22).

8. Robinson correctly observes, "In Revelation 20–22, John drew upon material from the last twelve chapters of Ezekiel" (Robinson, *Temple*, loc. 3911).

both accounts, the names of the twelve tribes are on the gates (Ezek 48:31–34; Rev 21:12).

Second, Ezekiel's eschatological city/temple corresponds with John's description of the Holy City as a temple. Ezekiel notes that he was taken "to the door of the house" (47:1)—which surely represents the temple.[9] Ezekiel then describes a river coming from "under the threshold of the house" (Ezek 47:1). Since the "threshold" is where "the Glory of the Lord" was when it departed the temple in Ezek 10:18, there is little question that Ezekiel's river flowed from the throne within the temple.

Third, the presence of a river in Ezekiel's vision (47:1–12) corresponds with John's River of the water of life (22:1). That Ezekiel's river comes from the "threshold" indicates that, like John's, the river comes from the place of God's presence. Furthermore, in Ezekiel, the river continues to deepen as it travels eastward and it makes everything it touches alive: "for these waters go there and the others become fresh; so everything will live where the river goes" (Ezek 47:9). This likely accounts for why John refers to the river as "the River of the water of life" (22:1).

Fourth, Ezekiel's account, like John's, includes trees that bring healing: "By the river on its bank, on one side and on the other, will grow all kinds of trees for food. Their leaves will not wither and their fruit will not fail. They will bear every month because their water flows from the sanctuary, and their fruit will be for food and their leaves for healing" (Ezek 47:12). The presence of "trees" that bring healing surely links with John's "Tree of Life" (22:2).

Although John's account corresponds significantly with Ezekiel's, he does present three modifications from Ezekiel's description. First, while Ezekiel's account has, "all kinds of trees" (Ezek 47:12), John has only one tree (22:2). This emendation most certainly derives from John's intention to depict the Holy City as the renewed Eden. That is, John's tree is the Tree of Life. Second, the trees in Ezekiel's eschatological

---

9. Everything about Ezekiel's vision has been about the temple. The fact that this "house" faces "east" (47:1)—as all temples do—and that it has an "altar" (47:1) surely indicates that the "house" is the temple.

temple are "for food and their leaves for healing" (Ezek 47:12). Third, John specifies, "the leaves of the Tree are for the healing of the nations" (22:2).

That John's portrait of the Holy City in 22:1–5 builds off the vision of Ezekiel 40–48 also reinforces a number of the convictions relating to John's account of the Holy City. First, John's description of the Holy City, like Ezekiel, depicts the city as a temple. Second, John's emendations so that there is only one tree affirm my contention that John's description of the Holy City is in terms of a renewed Eden. Finally, John's addition that "the leaves of the Tree are for the healing of the nations" (22:2) affirms my understanding of the centrality of God's love for the nations in Revelation's larger narrative.

There Will No Longer Be Any Curse 22:3

John continues his description of the Holy City by noting that there "will no longer be any curse" (22:3). This statement has a measure of redundancy to it. After all, we already know that nothing "unclean" will enter it (21:27). Furthermore, the presence of a curse would be superfluous since the Tree of Life is in it and it leaves "are for the healing of the nations" (22:2). That there "will no longer be any curse" (22:3) provides another unambiguous link with the Genesis account. In the Holy City, the Edenic curse has been reversed.

Throne of God and the Lamb 22:3

John then states emphatically, "And the throne of God and of the Lamb will be in it" (22:3).[10] The throne of God is one of the more prominent items in the book of Revelation.[11] As I noted earlier, the opening throne room scene (4:1—5:14) served as an emphatic affirmation that the world's true King was the One on the throne and not Caesar. As the narrative proceeded into 5:1–14, John explicitly declares that Jesus

---

10. See 21:3–4. It cannot be overemphasized that the essential feature of the Holy City, New Jerusalem is that it depicts the gloriousness of the people of God dwelling in the presence of God.

11. In 4:2–3, the heavenly throne-room vision began with the Father on the throne.

was enthroned with the Father—just as He indicated to the Laodiceans (3:21)—because He was the Lamb that was slain.

I argued in the opening discussion of the throne room scene that, in accord with a narratival reading of the book of Revelation, John's narrative centers on the question, "What is needed for the throne of God to come down to the creation?" The answer to this, as I have argued at length, included both the redemption of the nations and the restoration of the creation.

It is central then, to John's account of the Holy City to recognize that this has come to fruition. Thus, John's description of the Holy City has affirmed that the nations have not merely entered into the Holy City (21:24, 26), but that the leaves of the Tree of Life are for their healing (22:2). God's Edenic creation has been restored (22:1–3). That "the throne of God and of the Lamb will be in it," therefore, brings the entire narrative of the book of Revelation to its consummation.

They Shall See His Face 22:4

The result of the presence of God among His people is perhaps no more explicit than the declaration, "and they shall see His face" (22:4).[12] Not only will humanity be restored to God's Edenic presence, but we will experience the fullness of God's presence and power. Thus, what Moses was unable to do, "You cannot see My face, for no man can see Me and live" (Exod 33:20), we will do!

His Name Will Be on Their Foreheads 22:4

In addition, "His name will be on their foreheads" (22:4). I noted earlier that the Name of God on the foreheads of the people of God likely connotes a sign of ownership. In addition, it also serves as a contrast with "the name of the Beast," which was on the right hand or forehead of those who dwell on the earth.[13]

This raises the question as to why we might need God's name on our foreheads in the new creation. After all, there is no need to distinguish between the people of God and "those who inhabit the earth."

---

12. See Ps 30:7; Isa 59:2.
13. See 13:16, 17; 14:9, 11; 16:2; 19:20; 20:4.

The answer is likely that the name now signifies that the people of God display God's character.[14]

No More Night 22:5

John continues by noting, "And there will not be night any longer" (22:5). The absence of night surely derives from the fact that the Holy City is the place of God's presence. As a result, there is not only no night but "they will not have need for the light of a lamp and the light of the sun,[15] because the Lord God will give light to them" (22:5).

Although, in the present world, the sun provides light and heat, both of which are necessary for life, its absence will not be missed. After all, the sun can also be a source of searing heat, as it was in the Fourth Bowl (16:8). The absence of the sun correlates with the promise for those who come out of the Great Tribulation: "the sun [will not] beat down on them" (7:16). Now, in 22:5, we learn that the reason why the sun will not beat on them anymore is that the sun is no more!

They Will Reign 22:5

Finally, John notes, "they [His servants] will reign forever and ever" (22:5). The reigning of the people of God is an important theme throughout the Apocalypse. As I noted earlier, the people of God are already said to be "a kingdom" (1:6) and are those that "reign upon the earth" (5:10). They are also those who "reign with Him for a thousand years" (20:6). Now, they will reign with Him "forever and ever" (22:5).

In the Genesis narrative, humanity was created to bear God's image—"Let Us make man in Our image," (Gen 1:26)—in order that they may rule over His creation—"and let them rule" (Gen 1:26). That humanity now reigns alongside God and the Lamb (22:5) serves as another indication of the fulfillment of the Edenic ideal.

---

14. As the promise to the church in Philadelphia indicated (see 3:12).

15. The sun has been something that "beat(s) down on them" (7:16) and "scorch(es) people with fire" (16:8), and it is struck (6:12; 8:12; 16:8). It is also used to signify the glory of Christ (1:16) and the angel who stood on the sea and the land (10:1).

John Falls to Worship 22:6-9

Although 22:6-9 functions as the conclusion to the account of the Bride/Holy City, these verses, as I noted in the opening chapters on the structure, also mark the beginning of the prologue. Therefore, I have elected to discuss them in the following chapter.[16]

Excursus: The Contrast Between the Bride and the Great Prostitute

Of course, John's description of the Bride/Holy City (21:9—22:9) stands in marked contrast with the account of the Great Prostitute (17:1—19:10). Barr sums up the significance of this when he notes that the story has gone, "from a world controlled by evil to a world ruled by God."[17] The contrasts between the Great Prostitute (17:1—19:10) and the Bride (21:9—22:9) are evident. They serve as parallel and contrasting accounts of women/cities. That they are parallel is evident from the fact that the introduction to the Bride is virtually identical to the introduction to the Great Prostitute:

> And one of the seven angels who had the seven bowls came and spoke with me, saying, "Come, I will show you the judgment of the Great Prostitute" (17:1).

> And one of the seven angels who had the seven bowls full of the seven last plagues spoke with me, saying, "Come, and I will show you the Bride, the wife of the Lamb"(21:9).[18]

The descriptions of the two women/cities confirm that they stand in marked contrast to one another. The Prostitute represents Rome and its excessive wealth and materialism that has come at the expense of "bodies and souls of people" (18:13). The Bride represents the place where the people of God dwell eternally in the presence of God and they eat from the Tree of Life and "the leaves of the Tree are for the healing of the nations" (22:2). The Bride's clothing of "bright, pure, fine linen" (19:8) surely contrasts the unclean things in Babylon's cup

---

16. See Bauckham, *Climax*, 4–5.
17. Barr, *Tales*, loc. 4503.
18. Interestingly, the word "Lamb" occurs seven times within this section: see 21:9, 14, 22, 23, 27; 22:1, 3.

(17:4). As Rossing notes, "Revelation underscores the urgent contrast between the radiant bridal good-woman figure and her evil Babylon counterpart."[19] Furthermore, that the Bride's clothes represent "the righteous deeds of the saints" (19:8) juxtapose the Great Prostitutes, "crimes" (18:5).

The Bride's "fine linen" (19:8, 14) contrasts with the goods that previously flowed through Babylon but have now been taken away from her (18:12, 16). As Rossing observes, "The bride not only supplants the prostitute but also takes her garments and radiant splendor."[20] Consequently, as Tabb affirms, "The Apocalypse discloses to embattled believers that while it appears to be 'the best of times' for Babylon and 'the worst of times' for God's people, a great reversal is coming."[21]

Therefore, as Justo Gonzales observes, "Significantly, the Book of Revelation is in a sense a tale of two cities: the city of Rome and the new city that John sees coming down from heaven. These cities are not just urban centers; they represent entirely different ways of organizing life or, as we would say today, conflicting world orders."[22]

Conclusion

The descent of the Holy City brings to the consummation of John's narrative. At the same time, of course, John's narrative must be viewed in terms of the entire biblical story. As humanity was expelled from God's Edenic presence (Gen 3:22–24), they, at last, are restored, "and they will reign forever and ever" (22:5). By way of conclusion, several points are worthy of being noted here—each of which is worthy of a full-length treatise.

First, John's description of the Holy City serves as the ultimate offer of hope for the people of God and as an encouragement to overcome. DeSilva notes:

> John offers his vision of such a homeland as an incentive to his hearers to maintain a response of faithful obedience to God in the midst of their particular challenges, both laying out the

---

19. Rossing, *Two Cities*, 143.
20. Rossing, *Two Cities*, 144.
21. Tabb, *All Things New*, loc. 2936.
22. Gonzales, *Every People*, loc. 883–84.

conditions for entry into the new Jerusalem and the causes for exclusion therefrom (21.7–8, 27; 22.14–15). By means of such passages, the vision as a whole keeps before John's audiences the question of what kind of witness and practice they will adopt so that they might attain the desired ends and avoid the undesired consequences.[23]

Second, it is also important for contemporary readers to recognize that the Holy City and the restoration of all creation to God's presence is not something wholly future. Too often Christians look solely to the future and neglect the fact that the divine presence among the people of God is already, though only in part, a present reality. That the Holy Spirit already dwells within His people serves to declare that the people of God are already the place of the temple presence of God.[24]

Third, since the new creation has already begun in Christ, this means that working and living in accord with the new creation is something to which we are called to do in the present. We must not look at the New Jerusalem as something wholly future. We are to be the people of God who aim to implement in the present the key features of the new creation.

Finally, the new heavens and new earth are not the destruction of the cosmos, but their restoration. Rossing suggests that 22:2 is the most important verse for an ecological reading: "This pivotal verse underscores that God's will is to heal the world, not to destroy it. Notice that healing comes not directly from God or the Lamb, but through the created world through the leaves of a living tree."[25] Richard Bauckham adds:

> The contrast between 'the first heaven and the first earth,' on the one hand, and 'the new heaven and the new earth,' on the other, refers to the eschatological renewal of this creation, not its replacement by another, is further confirmed by the observation that Jewish and Christian writers could speak rather similarly of the earth that perished in the Flood and the new world that emerged from the Flood (2 Pet. 3:6), understanding the Flood as a reversion of creation to the chaos from which it was first created.[26]

---

23. DeSilva, *Discovering*, 284.
24. See Eph 2:18–20; 1 Cor 6:19; 2 Cor 6:14—7:1.
25. Rossing, "Ecology" loc. 2825–27.
26. Bauckham, *Theology*, 49–50.

Revelation 22:6–21
Epilogue

Revelation 22:6–21
Epilogue

Christians who keep on talking about "going to heaven"—as if that were their last great hope—seem to have missed the whole point of the way the Bible ends.[1]

If we look at the Apocalypse in terms of its action (understood as a series of causally connected events) a reasonably clear pattern emerges. First, there is a strong correlation between the beginning and the ending—as we expect in a good story.[2]

Introduction

THE EPILOGUE (22:6–21) BRINGS the book of Revelation to a fitting climax. In fact, in light of the connections between the Holy City and Eden noted in the previous chapter, we might even suggest that the epilogue serves not merely as the conclusion to the book of Revelation, but as the conclusion of the entire biblical story.

John Falls to Worship the Angel 22:6–9

Richard Bauckham is likely the most ardent proponent of the dual role of 22:6–9. Bauckham convincingly argues that 22:6–9 functions in a dual role as both the conclusion to the account of the Holy City (21:9—22:9) and as the beginning of the epilogue (22:6–21).

---

1. Wright, *God I Don't Understand,* loc. 194.
2. Barr, *Tales,* loc. 392.

Bauckham's argument that 22:6-9 marks the close of the narrative of the Bride derives from the clear parallels between 22:6-9, which he argues marks the end of the narrative of the Bride/Holy City, and 19:7-10 and the ending of the account of the Great Prostitute. As I noted earlier, both the account of the Great Prostitute and the account of the Bride/Holy City conclude with an angelic being affirming that the words are either "true" (19:9) or "faithful and true" (22:6). Then in each account, John mistakenly attempts to worship the angelic messenger only to be rebuked (19:10; 22:8-9). Bauckham asserts, "These structural markers delimiting two parallel sections—17:1—19:10 and 21:9—22:9—are so clear that it is astonishing that so many attempts to discern the structure of Revelation have ignored them."[3]

At the same time, Bauckham contends that 22:6-9 functions as the opening of the epilogue as well. He notes, "Those parts of 22:6-9 which are not verbally parallel to 19:9b-10 are verbally parallel to 1:1-3."[4] The fact that 1:1 and 22:6 form an inclusio also makes for a compelling argument.[5]

Bauckham's proposal gains further support from John's use of "to show" in 22:6, as I noted above. The fact that John not only repeats "to show" in both verses but that his use of "to show" in 1:1 and 22:6 are identical in form, reinforces the conclusion that 1:1 and 22:6 serve to mark the opening of the prologue and the epilogue respectively.

And He Said to Me 22:6

John opens the epilogue with, "And he said to me." This raises the question, "Who is the speaker?"[6] The fact that no new speaker is introduced in 22:6 suggests that the speaker is "one of the seven angels who had the seven bowls" (21:9) who told John, "Come, and I will show you" (21:9). That the speaker is an angel seems clear from the fact that the angel identifies himself, "the Lord, the God of the spirits of the prophets, sent His angel to show His servants what must take place soon" (22:6). This

---

3. Bauckham, *Climax*, 4.
4. Bauckham, *Climax*, 5.
5. See the opening chapter on "Inclusios."
6. Schüssler Fiorenza observes the conundrum, "Interpreters generally assume that the one who speaks in v. 6 ("and he said to me") is the bowl angel who has shown John the New Jerusalem; however, in 22:7, the speaker is clearly Christ himself" (Schüssler Fiorenza, *Revelation*, loc. 1785-86).

conclusion finds further support from the fact that John introduces his inappropriate act of worship with, "I fell down to worship before the feet of the angel who showed me these things" (22:8), and, as noted above, his effort is rebuffed with, "See that you do not do that. I am a fellow-servant of yours . . . ." (22:9).

What makes the identification of the speaker more complex, however, is the fact that the speaker continues with, "And behold, I am coming soon" (22:7). The expression, "I am coming" occurs seven times in the book of Revelation. The fact that in most, if not every, instance the speaker is clearly Christ leads to the obvious conviction that it is Christ here also.[7] That "I am coming soon" in 22:20 is immediately followed by the affirmation, "Amen. Come, Lord Jesus" (22:20) strengthens this conviction.

It is my conviction that the speaker throughout 22:6–8 is the angel, whom John attempts to worship in 22:8. At the same time, it is evident that the words in 22:7 are the words of Christ. Although we might conclude that 22:7 is simply an interjection by Christ, it is my conviction that we must simply recall that the source of transmission is from the Father, through Christ, through an angel, and to John (see 1:1).

These Words Are Faithful and True 22:6

The epilogue opens with a promise of blessing to the one who keeps the words of "this book." An angel then reiterates to John that what he has said is, "faithful and true" (22:6). The words spoken in 22:6 are identical to the words of the One on the throne in 21:5.[8]

"Faithful and true" are important adjectives in the book of Revelation. The expression occurs four times (3:14; 19:11; 21:5; 22:6). In 1:5, Jesus was introduced in the prologue as the One who was "the Faithful Witness." The title was then expanded in the message to Laodicea so that Jesus is, "the Faithful and True Witness" (3:14). In the account of the Second Coming (19:11–16), Jesus was identified as the One who is "Faithful and True" (19:11). Finally, in 21:5, the One sitting on the

---

7. For example, in 2:16, the One who is "coming soon" refers to the "sword of My mouth" which certainly alludes to the sword in the mouth of Christ (1:16; 2:12, 16; 19:15, 21).

8. The only difference is that in 22:6 the verb is absent. But this is of no significance. This does not have to mean that the speaker is the same, only that the two passages are linked.

throne commands John, "Write, because these words are faithful and true." In light of John's use of "faithful and true," it is my conclusion that because Jesus is the One who is "Faithful and True" (19:11), the reader/hearers may trust that the words of the book of Revelation are also, "faithful and true" (22:6).

What Must Take Place Soon 22:6

The expression "what must take place soon" (22:6;), which only occurs here and in the opening verse of the Apocalypse (1:1) serves to frame the book of Revelation. As noted previously, John seemingly modifies the Danielic expression in light of the Jesus event. Thus, what was according to Daniel going to occur, "in the latter days" (Dan 2:28) or "in the future" (Dan 2:29, 45), has become for John, "what must take place soon" (1:1; 22:6). As I argued previously, there is little doubt that John understood the Christ event as the key to everything. Daniel's "latter days/future" (Dan 2:28, 29, 45) has become the present because of Jesus's death and resurrection. The expression "what must take place soon" (22:6) conveys a realized imminence and, consequently, provides a sense of urgency for John's reader/hearers. John, in fact, immediately follows it with, "And behold I am coming soon" (22:7).

Blessed 22:7

The angel iterates the promise of blessing for, "the one who keeps the words of the prophecy of this book" (22:7). Seven times in the Apocalypse we learn of those who are or will be blessed.[9] The promises of blessings cannot be divorced from "hearing." Two of the seven promises of blessing relate directly to those who "hear" (1:3; 22:7). At the same time, hearing cannot be divorced from doing. On three occasions (14:13; 16:15; 22:14) those who are blessed are the ones who put into action what they have heard and suffer the consequences for doing so. The other two occurrences of blessing (19:19; 20:6) relate to the eschatological blessing—reserved, of course, for those who "hear" and "keep" it (1:3).

---

9. See 1:3; 14:13; 16:15; 19:9; 20:6; 22:7, 14.

REVELATION 22:6–21

John Attempts to Worship The Angel 22:8–9

John's response to the vision of the Holy City is to fall down and worship: "I fell down to worship before the feet of the angel who showed me these things" (22:8). On the surface, John's actions appear odd. After all, John was rebuked the last time that he attempted to worship an angel (19:10). Perhaps, we might suggest, he was unaware that it was an angel. The problem here is that he states explicitly that he fell down, "before the feet of the angel" (22:8). If he knows that it is an angel, then why is he falling down to worship it? Perhaps we might conclude that John was so overwhelmed by what he saw and heard that he instinctively fell down to worship. The problem here again resides with the fact that John seemingly knows that it is an angel. Perhaps we might suppose that John was unsure of who was before him. After all, there have been several occasions in the Apocalypse in which it is unclear if the one speaking was an angel or Jesus. This was certainly the case with the "strong angel" in 10:1. Furthermore, it is worth repeating that the lines of transmission in the book of Revelation are: from the Father, to Christ, to an angel, to John (1:1). Perhaps then, John mistook the angelic mediator for Christ Himself.

What if, however, our efforts to acquit John are unnecessary? After all, as we have observed, John's "actions" appear to function as a literary device by which he marks the end of the section.[10] John repeats the account of his attempt to worship an angel not because he was replicating his earlier mistake, but as a literary device that functions as a means of identifying the conclusion to the account of the Bride (21:9—22:9).

Do Not Seal Up These Words 22:10

After John's inappropriate effort to worship the angel (22:8–9), the angel continues his exhortations to John with, "Do not seal up the words of the prophecy of this Book" (22:10).[11] The reason why John is not to seal up the words is "because the time is near" (22:10; 1:3).[12] The exhortation to not seal up the Book stands in marked contrast with the exhortation in

---

10. See Bauckham, *Climax*, 133–40.
11. Note that Daniel was told to seal up his book (Dan 10:4).
12. "For" (*gar*) indicates the reason why.

Daniel, "But as for you, Daniel, conceal these words and seal up the book until the end of time" (Dan 12:4).

In light of the consistent use of Daniel, it may well be that the scroll which Daniel was to seal up is the one that Christ has opened. If so, then one of John's purposes in the book of Revelation is to confirm that Christ has fulfilled the words of Daniel and to indicate to the people of God what it means for them. Consequently, John is not to seal up these words because what for Daniel pertained to the "end of time" (Dan 12:4) now refers to the present.

Let Them Be 22:11

After being commanded not to seal up the book, John is then given a command that appears troubling. The angel says, "The one who does wrong let him still do wrong, the one who is unclean let him still be unclean, the one who is righteous let him still do righteousness, and let the one who is holy let him still be holy" (22:11). The conundrum is lessened, if not eliminated, if we recognize it as an application of Dan 12:10. In Daniel, a similar saying occurs. In Daniel, however, the statement appears as a fact: "the wicked will act wickedly, . . . etc." In John, however, it is a command—which is where the problem lies.[13] Why would God seemingly want the one who does wrong to still do wrong? Beale argues, and I think he is correct, that the answer is found in that John is reading Daniel as being fulfilled. The idea then, is that since Daniel prophesied that the "wicked will act wickedly" (Dan 12:10), John is encouraging it to happen in that it represents a fulfillment of prophesy.[14] Beale concludes, "Though this conclusion is theologically difficult, it correlates admirably with the prophetic nature of Daniel and with the notion that each person's identification with Christ or the beast has been determined."[15]

---

13. Hence, Longman's assertion, "There comes a time when it is too late to change" (Longman, *Revelation* 441) makes sense as the text in Daniel reads, but it does not account for why it is issued as a command in Revelation.

14. Beale, *Revelation*, 1131–36.

15. Beale, *Revelation*, 1133.

Exhortation and Promise of Blessing 22:12–14

As the narrative comes to a close, John adds a series of exhortations for his reader/hearers. The first exhortation begins with Jesus's assurance, "My reward is with Me" (22:12). He then adds, "Blessed are the ones who wash their robes, so that they will have the right to the tree of life and may enter through the gates into the city" (22:14). Those who trust in Christ are not only blessed, they are promised that they, "will have the right to the Tree of Life and may enter through the gates into the city" (22:14; see 2:7; 22:2*, 19). This final promise of blessing serves as the conclusion to the biblical narrative, which began in a garden in Eden (Gen 2:8) and now returns to a glorified Edenic garden.

The Alpha and the Omega 22:13

Jesus then declares that He is, "the Alpha and the Omega" (22:13). This is the third occurrence of this divine title (see 1:8; 21:6). In each of the first two occurrences, the title was applied to the Father.[16] In this occurrence, "the Alpha and the Omega" (22:13) is most certainly applied to Christ. That the speaker is Christ is evident first in that the speaker also affirms, "I am coming soon" (22:12), which, as I noted earlier, is best understood as applied to Christ.

In addition, that the title in 22:13 appears alongside, "the First and the Last" also suggests that the speaker is Christ. The title "The First and the Last" also appears three times in the book of Revelation (see 1:17; 2:8) and in both of the previous two other occurrences (1:17; 2:8), the speaker is Jesus. In fact, in both 1:17 and 2:8, the title, "The First and the Last" is closely associated with Jesus's death and resurrection.

Blessed Are the Ones Who Wash Their Robes 22:14

With the last of the seven promises of blessing, John again aims to encourage his reader/hearers with the assurance that the "ones who wash their robes" are blessed and "they will have the right to the Tree of Life and may enter through the gates into the city" (22:14). John uses "washed" only twice in the book of Revelation. The previous occurrence was in the account of the Great Multitude who were said to "have

---

16. Although the identity of the speaker in 1:8 could be either Jesus or the Father.

washed their robes and made them white by means of the blood of the Lamb" (7:14). For John, washing one's robes has to do with faithfulness to Christ. DeSilva suggests that John's imagery is based on the "necessity of washing one's clothes before coming into God's presence at the Sinai theophany (Exod. 19:10, 14)."[17]

Outside 22:15

While John encourages his reader/hearers to remain faithful, he also reminds them of the consequences for those who fail to do so. Thus, while those, "who wash their robes" are "blessed" and able to eat from the Tree of Life and enter the city (22:14), those who fail to do so remain "outside" (22:15).

I, Jesus 22:16

As the Apocalypse comes to a close, Jesus assures John that He is indeed the One who has spoken to him. In doing so, Jesus reiterates that the channel of communication, as we were told in 1:1, is through His angel (22:16).

Jesus's self-identification is important. He begins by stating, "I am[18] the root and the descendant of David" (22:16). The identification of Jesus as the "root of David" first appeared in the throne room scene, where John heard that "the Lion, the one from the tribe of Judah, the root of David, has overcome" (5:5). That "root" appears only here and in 5:5 strengthens the link with the throne room scene. It is interesting that Jesus does not identify Himself to John in a manner that corresponds to the opening scene on Patmos: such as the "one like a Son of Man" (1:12). Or that Jesus does identify Himself as "the Faithful Witness" (1:5), which is the first title applied to Jesus in the Apocalypse. Instead, Jesus identifies Himself with the One whom John heard about in the throne room scene. Perhaps, the identification of Jesus, as "the Lion, the one from the tribe of Judah, the root of David" (5:5) is reiterated here because Jesus is the One who "has overcome" (5:5).

Jesus also declares that He is "the bright morning star" (22:16). That Jesus is the "morning star" affirms what we have seen throughout our

---

17. DeSilva, *Seeing*, 288n3.
18. Note: that the "I am" is emphatic.

study. Namely, that the description of the people of God corresponds to Christ. Thus, the people of God are defined as those who follow the Lamb (14:4). They do so, however, by imitating Jesus. As a result, their voice, which was "like the voice of many waters" (14:2; 19:6) sounds like Jesus's voice (1:15). The implication, as I have noted throughout, is that just as Jesus is "the Faithful Witness" (1:5), we are to be as well. The only prior occurrence of "morning star" was in 2:28, where the promise to those in Thyatira who overcome included, "I will give that person the morning star." This supports my supposition that the people of God are depicted in a manner that corresponds to Jesus.

Come 22:17

The narrative of the book of Revelation nears completion in 22:17 with a series of four commands/exhortations, three of which center on "Come" or "to say, 'Come'" (22:17). First, "The Spirit and the Bride" say, "Come." Then "the one who hears" is exhorted to say, "Come." This is followed by an encouragement for "the one who is thirsty" to "come" (22:17).[19] Finally, the fourth does not employ "come" but instead focuses on what it is they are to come for: namely, "the one who wishes" is exhorted, "let them take freely the gift of the water of life" (22:17).

Exhortation and Warning 22:18–19

A final exhortation and warning sound forth. The angel[20] exhorts, "everyone who hears the words of the prophecy of this book" (22:18). The exhortation consists of two warnings. First, "If anyone adds to them [the words of the book], God will add to them the plagues that are written in this book" (22:18). Second, "and if anyone takes away from the words of the book of this prophecy, God will take away their part in the Tree of Life and from the Holy City that are written in this book" (22:19). Again, we must recognize that, as with the entirety of the book of Revelation, these closing exhortations are addressed to the people of God/the seven churches.

---

19. See Isa 55:1.

20. We may also dispute who is the speaker in 22:18. Since, even if the speaker is Jesus, He is speaking through the angel, I have chosen to indicate that it is the angel here.

This closing exhortation and warning has all the earmarks of a covenant formula. As Nicklas notes, "Revelation 22:18–19 uses a 'canon formula' (or better, integrity formula) similar to what is found in Deuteronomy."[21] Beale refers to it as, "a new law code for a new Israel."[22] The implication is clear that one of the primary threats to the people of God is false teaching that corrupts the message of God by either adding or taking away from what has been revealed.

Closing Words 22:20

John closes the book with a note from, "the one who testifies to these things" (22:20)—which likely refers to Jesus, though it may be the angelic mediator—who declares, "I am coming soon" (22:20). This prompts the only proper response: "Amen. Come, Lord Jesus" (22:20).

Benediction 22:21

The Apocalypse comes to a close with a benediction: "The grace of the Lord Jesus be with all" (22:21). Somewhat surprisingly, "grace" occurs only two times in the entire book of Revelation: here and in 1:4.

---

21. Nicklas, "Apocalypse," loc. 3248. See Deut 4:1–2; 12:32; 29:19–20; Prov 30:6.
22. Beale, *Revelation*, 1150.

Conclusion

The book of Revelation's condemnation of empire and insistence on resistance to its pressures and demands poses a timely counterpoint to the distinctive blend of patriotism and religiosity that came to the fore in the United States in the last several years.[1]

Rather, it calls readers to do, in their present contexts, precisely what John sought to do in his own: to discern what is Babylonish about the domination systems in the midst of which they live and of which they themselves may be a part; and then to discover the ways in which they can both divest themselves of participating in and bear prophetic witness against the same.[2]

Something beastly is at work, for example, in a world where people starve to death or die of preventable disease while nations spend billions on weapons and leisure. Jesus reassured believers who pray for divine intervention: "Will not God grant justice to his chosen ones who cry out to him day and night? Will he delay long in helping them? I tell you, he will quickly grant justice to them."[3]

I HOPE THAT I have shown that the book of Revelation tells a different story than what many have come to believe. The story begins and ends with the affirmation that God is the world's true Lord, not Caesar. In telling this story, John lays out for us the fact that Christ's kingdom is not like the kingdoms of the world. The kingdoms of the world rule by force and at the expense of the masses and for the benefit of those in power. Jesus's kingdom, however, comes through love. In Christ's kingdom,

1. Carey, "Shadow," 2286–87.
2. DeSilva, *Discovering*, 253.
3. DeSilva, *Discovering*, 299.

power is demonstrated by laying down one's life for one's enemies. Jesus, of course, demonstrated this kind of love on the cross. In the pages of the book of Revelation, John explains that Jesus calls us to do the same. Of course, we have nothing to fear. After all, Jesus was dead and now He is alive and He has the keys to Death and Hades.

Unfortunately, or shall I say "tragically," many contemporary interpreters of the book of Revelation have proposed that the devastation and destruction depicted in the book of Revelation—in particular, in the accounts of the Seven Seals and the Seven Bowls—are God's end times wrath. I wonder, however, why we don't consider the possibility that the portrait of God as the agent of wrath trying to convince the nations to repent before He brings further harm is fundamentally at odds with the Gospel.

Some may ask: "What are we to do with the plagues and death that John so vividly describes?" As I have argued throughout this study, this is what happens when the nations are left in power.

"But," someone may inquire: "Why hasn't God done anything about all the suffering that the nations bring about?" Well, He has, He is, and He will. He has in that He sent His Son who told us what it means to rule well. Then He demonstrated it on the Cross. He is in that He has sent us, His people, to carry forth what He has told us and shown us. We are called to "follow the Lamb" in sacrificial love. And He will. There will come a day when time shall be no more. On that day, wars will cease. Death, crying, and pain will be no more.

The book of Revelation is a love story. In this story, God lovingly allows the nations to persist in order that His people might faithfully, lovingly, and sacrificially lay down their lives for the nations so that the nations might also enjoy life in His Edenic city.

It is here that I want to cry out to the contemporary, Western church, "What are we doing?" It seems that we in the Western Church have not only partaken of the wealth and power that empire offers, but we have become good at justifying it. This leads to the question: "Have we gone to bed with the Beast?" I wonder if John's cry, "Come out of her My people," is not needed more today than it was when John penned the Apocalypse.

We cannot take lightly the fact that those to whom John wrote did not realize the gravity of it all until John explained it to them. Now, they may have conceded that Rome was corrupt and that they must tread lightly. But did they really understand that Rome and the Great Prostitute were empowered by Satan? Had they truly contemplated the millions of lives that Rome exploited and then discarded in order to build and maintain its power? Or did they just go about their duty trying to get by?

Maybe this is why John was so graphic. He was trying desperately to warn them. "No! The empire is drunk on the blood of the saints and all who have been slain. The gods have not placed Rome in power. Rome is in power because it has killed, raped, and enslaved millions. Therefore, 'Come out!'"

I would love to know what John's reader/hearers did with his message. Did they say, "You know what?; John's right. We need to come out of Babylon and get about doing the Lord's work by laying down our lives for our enemies"? Or did they say, "John's a crazy man; don't know what got into him, but whatever he's drinking, I don't need any"? I suspect that more Christians than we would like to admit said something along the lines of the latter.

The book of Revelation is in part a prophecy. And as much as we get excited to learn about the books of Isaiah and the prophets, we ought to admit that we don't really like prophets. Oh, we like Isaiah. But only because we read Isaiah as if he were speaking to "them." We like Jesus too. Especially the part where he told the religious leaders that they were "sons of hell!" You tell them, Jesus! But do we like Jesus when He says that if we want to follow Him, we must take up our crosses as he did?

I hope this study has made you long to follow the Lamb more passionately. I hope that it has given you a greater conviction for the Gospel and the kingdom. I hope it has instilled a righteous longing for what might well happen when we choose to follow the Lamb.

I also know that we live in a broken world. We suffer. And we see millions of people suffering every day; longing for food and clean water. And we suffer the loss of loved ones. I hope that the book of Revelation instills you with hope. Hope that there is something better. Hope that someday our suffering will end. And Hope that we will live forever with our loved ones. For it is then, that we will see His face!

Resources for Recommended Next Steps

There are a plethora of blogs on the book of Revelation and related topics on my website determinetruth.com (click on the "Blog" tab, then scroll down to the bottom of the page and search "Revelation").

The **determinetruth** podcast has an entire series of episodes on the book of Revelation beginning Mar 13, 2023 (The podcast is also accessible on the determinetruth.com website under the "Podcast" tab, or on ITunes, Spotify, and wherever you get your podcasts).

Books

My, *Follow the Lamb: a Guide to Reading, Understanding, and Applying the Book of Revelation* is designed for those who want to understand the basics of reading the book of Revelation. The questions at the end of each chapter are intended for individual and small group study.

Next, I recommend, in order:

Michael Gorman. *Reading Revelation Responsibly: Uncivil Worship and Witness: Following the Lamb into the New Creation.* Eugene, OR: Cascade Books, 2011.
David deSilva. *Unholy Allegiances: Heeding Revelation's Warning.* Peabody, MA: Hendrickson, 2013
Scot McKnight and Cody Matchett. *Revelation for the Rest of Us: A Prophetic Call to Follow Jesus as a Dissident Disciple.* Grand Rapids: Zondervan, 2023.
J. Nelson Kraybill. *Apocalypse and Allegiance.* Grand Rapids: Brazos, 2010.

For serious students:

David Barr. *Tales of the End: A Narrative Commentary on the Book of Revelation.* Storytellers Bible 1. Salem, OR: Polebridge, 2012. This is one of the finest commentaries available.
Wes Howard-Brook and Anthony Gwyther. *Unveiling Empire: Reading Revelation Then and Now.* The Bible and Liberation Series. Maryknoll, NY: Orbis, 1999. The last chapter, titled, "Coming Out of Empire Today," (chapter 9) is one of the finest works exposing how global capitalism and the international financial systems are the modern Beasts of Revelation 13.
James Resseguie. *The Revelation of John: A Narrative Commentary.* Grand Rapids: Baker, 2009. This is also one of the best commentaries available.

Bibliography

Aune, David E. "The Influence of Roman Imperial Court Ceremonial on the Apocalypse of John." *Biblical Review* 28 (1983) 5–26.
———. *Revelation.* 3 vols. Word Biblical Commentary 52. Dallas: Word, 1997–1998.
Bandy, Alan S. "The Prophetic Lawsuit in the Book of Revelation: An Analysis of the Lawsuit Motif in Revelation with Reference to the Use of the Old Testament." PhD diss., Southeastern Baptist Theological Seminary, 2007.
Barnett, Paul. *Second Epistle to the Corinthians.* New International Commentary on the New Testament. Grand Rapids: Eerdmans, 1997
Barr, David, ed. *Reading the Book of Revelation: A Resource for Students.* Resources for Biblical Study 44. Atlanta: Society of Biblical Literature, 2003.
———. *The Reality of the Apocalypse: Rhetoric and Politics in the Book of Revelation.* SBL Symposium Series 39. Atlanta: Society of Biblical Literature, 2006.
———. *Tales of the End: A Narrative Commentary on the Book of Revelation.* Salem, OR: Polebridge, 2012.
Bauckham, Richard. *The Climax of Prophecy: Studies on the Book of Revelation.* Edinburgh: T. & T. Clark, 1993.
———. *The Theology of the Book of Revelation.* Cambridge: Cambridge University Press, 1993.
Beale, Gregory K. *The Book of Revelation: A Commentary on the Greek Text.* New International Greek Testament Commentary. Grand Rapids: Eerdmans, 1999.
———. *John's Use of the Old Testament in Revelation.* JSNT Supplements 166. Sheffield: Sheffield Academic, 1998.
———. *The Temple and the Church's Mission: A Biblical Theology of the Dwelling Place of God.* New Studies in Biblical Theology. Downers Grove, IL: IVP Academic, 2004.
———. *The Use of Daniel in Jewish Apocalyptic Literature and in the Revelation of St. John.* Lanham, MD: University Press of America, 1984.
Beale, Gregory K., and D. A. Carson, eds. *Commentary on the New Testament Use of the Old Testament.* Grand Rapids: Baker, 2007.
Beasley-Murray, George Raymond. *Revelation.* New Century Bible Commentary. Greenwood, SC: Attic, 1974.
Blount, Brian K. *Can I Get a Witness?: Reading Revelation through African American Culture.* Louisville: Westminster John Knox, 2005.

BIBLIOGRAPHY

Borgen, Peder. "Polemic in the Book of Revelation." In *Anti-Semitism and Early Christianity*, edited by C. A. Evans and D. A. Hagner, 199–211. Minneapolis: Fortress, 1993.

Boring, M. Eugene. *Revelation*. Interpretation. Louisville: Westminster John Knox, 1989.

Boxall, Ian. *The Revelation of Saint John*. Black New Testament Commentary. Peabody, MA: Hendrickson, 2006.

Boyd, Greg A. *The Crucifixion of the Warrior God: Interpreting the Old Testament's Violent Portraits of God in the Light of the Cross*: Minneapolis: Fortress, 2017.

Boyer, Paul. *When Time Shall Be No More: Prophecy Belief in Modern American Culture*: Cambridge: Harvard University Press, 1992.

Caird, George Bradford. *A Commentary on the Revelation of St. John the Divine*. Holman New Testament Commentary. New York: Harper, 1966.

Carter, Warren. *Jesus and the Empire of God: Reading the Gospel in the Empire*. Eugene, OR: Cascade, 2021.

———. *The Roman Empire and the New Testament: An Essential Guide*. Nashville: Abingdon, 2006.

———. *What Does Revelation Reveal?: Unlocking the Mystery*. Nashville: Abingdon, 2011.

Charles, Robert Henry. *A Critical and Exegetical Commentary on the Revelation of St. John with Introduction. Notes and Indices*. 2 vols. International Critical Commentary. Edinburgh: T. & T. Clark, 1920.

Chilton, David. *The Days of Vengeance: An Exposition of the Book of Revelation*. Fort Worth: Dominion, 1986.

Clouse, Robert G., ed. *The Meaning of the Millennium: Four Views*. Downers Grove, IL: InterVarsity, 1977.

Colclasure, Chuck. *The Overcomers: The Unveiling of Hope, Comfort, and Encouragement in the Book of Revelation*. Nashville: Nelson, 1981.

Collins, Adela Yarbro. *The Combat Myth in the Book of Revelation*. Harvard Dissertations in Religion 9. Missoula, MT: Scholars, 1976.

Coloe, Mary L. *God Dwells with Us: Temple Symbolism in the Fourth Gospel*. Wilmington, DE: Glazier, 2001.

Coloe, Mary L., and Sandra M. Schneiders. *Dwelling in the Household of God: Johannine Ecclesiology and Spirituality*. Nashville: Liturgical, 2017.

Dalrymple, Rob. *Follow the Lamb: A Guide to Reading, Understanding, and Applying the Book of Revelation*. Bellingham, WA: Lexham, 2018.

———. *Revelation and the Two Witnesses*. Eugene, OR: Wipf & Stock, 2011.

———. "These Are the Ones . . . (Rev 7)." *Biblica* 86 (2005) 396–406.

———. "The Use of *kai*, in Revelation 11,1 and the Implications for the Identification of the Temple, the Altar, and the Worshippers." *Biblica* 87 (2006) 387–94.

Dempster, Stephen G. *Dominion and Dynasty: A Theology of the Hebrew Bible*: 15 (New Studies in Biblical Theology. Downers Grove, IL: InterVarsity, 2003.

deSilva, David. *Discovering Revelation: Content, Interpretation, Reception*. Grand Rapids: Eerdmans, 2021.

———. *Seeing Things John's Way: The Rhetoric of the Book of Revelation*. Louisville: Westminster John Knox, 2009.

———. *Unholy Allegiances: Heeding Revelation's Warning*. Peabody, MA: Hendrickson, 2013.

BIBLIOGRAPHY

Dixon, Sarah. *The Testimony of the Exalted Jesus in the Book of Revelation.* London: T. & T. Clark, 2018.

Fee, Gordon. *Revelation.* New Covenant Commentary. Eugene, OR: Cascade, 2010.

Giblin, Charles H. "Structural and Thematic Correlations in the Theology of Revelation 16–22." *Biblica* 55 (1974) 487–504.

Gladd, Benjamin L., and Matthew S. Harmon. *Making All Things New: Inaugurated Eschatology for the Life of the Church*: Grand Rapids: Baker, 2016.

Gorman, Michael. *Reading Revelation Responsibly: Uncivil Worship and Witness: Following the Lamb into the New Creation.* Eugene, OR: Cascade Books, 2011.

Harrington, Wilfred J. *Revelation.* Sacra Pagina 16. Wilmington, DE: Glazier, 2008.

Hays, Richard B. *The Moral Vision of the New Testament: Community, Cross, New Creation; a Contemporary Introduction to New Testament Ethics.* San Francisco: Harper, 1996.

———. *Revelation and the Politics of Apocalyptic Interpretation.* Waco, TX: Baylor University Press, 2012.

Hays, Richard B., and Stefan Alkier, eds. *Revelation and the Politics of Apocalyptic Interpretation.* Waco, TX: Baylor University Press, 2015.

Heiser, Michael S. *The Unseen Realm: Recovering the Supernatural Worldview of the Bible.* Bellingham, WA: Lexham, 2015.

Hemer, Colin J. *The Letters to the Seven Churches of Asia in Their Local Setting.* Biblical Resources Series. Grand Rapids: Eerdmans, 2001.

Hendriksen, William. *More than Conquerors: An Interpretation of the Book of Revelation.* Grand Rapids: Baker, 1961.

Hoeksema, Herman. *Behold, He Cometh! An Exposition of the Book of Revelation.* Grand Rapids: Reformed Free Publishing Association, 1969.

Horsley, Richard. *Jesus and Empire: The Kingdom of God and the New World Disorder.* Minneapolis: Fortress, 2003.

———, ed. *Paul and Politics: Ekklesia, Israel, Imperium.* Philadelphia: Trinity, 2000.

———, ed. *The Shadow of Empire: Reclaiming the Bible as a History of Faithful Resistance.* Louisville: Westminster John Knox, 2008.

Howard-Brook, Wes, and Anthony Gwyther. *Unveiling Empire: Reading Revelation Then and Now.* The Bible and Liberation Series. Maryknoll, NY: Orbis, 1999.

Hughes, Philip Edgcumbe. *The Book of Revelation: A Commentary.* Grand Rapids: Eerdmans, 1990.

Keener, Craig S. *Revelation.* NIV Application Commentary. Grand Rapids: Zondervan, 2000.

Kline, Meredith G. *Images of the Spirit.* Grand Rapids: Baker, 1980.

Koester, Craig R., ed. *Oxford Handbook of the Book of Revelation.* Oxford Handbooks. Oxford: Oxford University Press, 2020.

———. *Revelation: A New Translation with Introduction and Commentary.* Anchor Bible 38A. New Haven: Yale University Press, 2014.

———. "Revelation's Visionary Challenge to Ordinary Empire." *Interpretation* 63 (2009) 5–18.

Kraybill, J. Nelson. *Apocalypse and Allegiance: Worship, Politics, and Devotion in the Book of Revelation.* Grand Rapids: Brazos, 2010.

———. *Imperial Cult and Commerce in John's Apocalypse.* JSNT Supplements 132. Sheffield: Sheffield Academic, 1996.

BIBLIOGRAPHY

Ladd, George Eldon. *A Commentary on the Revelation of John.* Grand Rapids: Eerdmans, 1972.

LaHaye, Tim. *Revelation: Illustrated and Made Plain.* Grand Rapids: Zondervan, 1980.

Lakoff, George. *The Metaphors We Live by.* Chicago: University Press, 2003.

Lindsay, Hal. *There's a New World Coming.* New York: Bantam, 1975.

Longman, Tremper, III. *Daniel.* NIV Application Commentary; Grand Rapids: Zondervan, 1999.

———. "The Divine Warrior: The New Testament Use of an Old Testament Motif." *Westminster Theological Journal* 44 (1982) 290–307.

———. *Revelation Through Old Testament Eyes.* Grand Rapids: Kregel, 2022.

Lucas, Ernst C. *Daniel.* Apollos Old Testament Commentary, Downers Grove, IL: IVP, 2002.

Mazzaferri, F. D. *The Genre of the Book of Revelation from a Source Critical Perspective.* Beiheft zur Zeitschrift für die neutestamentliche Wissenschaft 54. Berlin: de Gruyter, 1989.

McKnight, Scot, and Cody Matchett. *Revelation for the Rest of Us: A Prophetic Call to Follow Jesus as a Dissident Disciple.* Grand Rapids: Zondervan, 2023.

Metzger, Bruce M. *Breaking the Code: Understanding the Book of Revelation.* Nashville: Abingdon, 1993.

Michaels, J. Ramsey. *Revelation.* IVP New Testament Commentary Series. Downers Grove, IL: InterVarsity, 1997.

Minear, Paul S. *I Saw a New Earth: An Introduction to the Visions of the Apocalypse.* Eugene, OR: Wipf & Stock, 2003.

Morris, Leon. *The Revelation of St. John: An Introduction and Commentary.* Tyndale New Testament Commentary. London: Tyndale, 1969.

Mounce, Robert H. *The Book of Revelation.* New International Commentary on the New Testament. Grand Rapids: Eerdmans, 1977.

Moyise, Steve. *The Old Testament in the Book of Revelation.* JSNTSup 115. Sheffield: Sheffield Academic, 1995.

Mouw, Richard J. *When the Kings Come Marching In: Isaiah and the New Jerusalem.* Grand Rapids: Eerdmans, 2002.

Osborne, Grant. *Revelation.* Baker Exegetical Commentary on the New Testament. Grand Rapids: Baker, 2002.

Paul, Ian. *Revelation: An Introduction.* Tyndale New Testament Commentary. Downers Grove, IL: InterVarsity Press, 2018.

Peterson, Eugene H. *Reversed Thunder: The Revelation of John and the Praying Imagination.* San Francisco: Harper & Row, 1988.

Pippin, Tina. *Death and Desire: The Rhetoric of Gender in the Apocalypse of John.* Literary Currents in Biblical Interpretation. Louisville: Westminster John Knox, 1992.

Ramsay, William. *The Letters of the Seven Churches of Asia.* New York: Armstrong, 1905.

Ryken, Leland, et al., eds. *Dictionary of Biblical Imagery.* Downers Grove, IL: InterVarsity, 1998.

Resseguie, James. *The Revelation of John: A Narrative Commentary.* Grand Rapids: Baker, 2009.

Rhoads, David, ed. *From Every People and Nation: The Book of Revelation in Intercultural Perspectives.* Minneapolis: Fortress, 2005.

Robinson, Andrea L. *Temple of Presence: The Christological Fulfillment of Ezekiel 40–48 in Revelation 21:1—22:5*. Eugene, OR: Wipf & Stock, 2019.

Rossing, Barbara. *The Choice between Two Cities: Whore, Bride, and Empire in the Apocalypse*. Harrisburg, PA: Trinity, 1999.

———. *The Rapture Exposed: The Message of Hope in the Book of Revelation*. New York: Basic, 2009.

Rowe, C. Kavin. *Christianity's Surprise*. Nashville: Abingdon, 2020.

Resseguie, James. *The Revelation of John: A Narrative Commentary*. Grand Rapids: Baker Academic, 2009.

Schnabel, Eckhard J. "Jewish Opposition to Christians in Asia Minor in the First Century." *Bulletin for Biblical Research* 18 (2008) 233–70.

Schüssler Fiorenza, Elisabeth. *The Book of Revelation: Justice and Judgment*. Minneapolis: Fortress, 1998.

———. "Composition and Structure of the Book of Revelation." *Catholic Biblical Quarterly* 39 (1977) 344–66.

———. *Revelation: Vision of a Just World*. Proclamation Commentaries. Minneapolis: Fortress, 1991.

Seiss, J. A. *The Apocalypse*. 3 vols. New York: Cook, 1917.

Slater, Thomas B. *Christ and Community: A Socio-historical Study of the Christology of Revelation*. Journal for the Study of the New Testament Supplements 178. Sheffield: Sheffield Academic, 1999.

Smalley, Stephen S. *The Revelation to John: A Commentary on the Greek Text of the Apocalypse*. Downers Grove, IL: InterVarsity, 2012.

Smith, Christopher R. "The Structure of the Book of Revelation in Light of Apocalyptic Literary Conventions." *Novum Testamentum* 36 (1994) 384–92.

Smith, Ralph L. *Micah–Malachi*. Word Biblical Commentary 32. Nashville: Abingdon, 1998.

Stephens, Mark B. *Annihilation or Renewal? The Meaning and Function of New Creation in the Book of Revelation*. WUNT 2/307. Tübingen: Mohr Siebeck, 2011.

Stewart, Alexander, and Alan Bandy, eds. *The Apocalypse of John among His Critics*. Bellingham, WA: Lexham, 2023.

Swete, Henry Barclay. *The Apocalypse of St. John: The Greek Text with Introduction, Notes and Indices*. 3rd ed. Grand Rapids: Eerdmans, 1968.

Sweet, J. P. M. *Revelation*. London: SCM, 1979.

Tabb, Brian. *All Things New: Revelation as Canonical Capstone*. New Studies in Biblical Theology. Downers Grove, IL: 2019.

Tellbe, Mikael. *Christ-Believers in Ephesus: A Textual Analysis of Early Christian Identity Formation in a Local Perspective*. WUNT 242. Tübingen: Mohr Siebeck, 2009.

Thomas, John Christopher, and Frank D. Macchia. *Revelation*. Two Horizons New Testament Commentary. Grand Rapids. Eerdmans. 2016.

Thomas, Robert L. *Revelation 1–7. An Exegetical Commentary*. Chicago: Moody, 1992.

Thompson, Leonard L. *Revelation*. Abingdon New Testament Commentaries. Nashville: Abingdon, 1998.

Trites, Allison. *The New Testament Concept of Witness*. Society for New Testament Studies Monograph 31. Cambridge: Cambridge, 2004.

Walvoord, John F. *The Revelation of Jesus Christ*. Chicago: Moody, 2011.

Timothy B. Weber. *On the Road to Armageddon: How Evangelicals Became Israel's Best Friend*. Grand Rapids: Baker Academic, 2004.

Weima, Jeffrey. *The Sermons to the Seven Churches of Revelation: A Commentary and Guide*. Grand Rapids: Baker, 2021.

Wilcock, Michael. *I Saw Heaven Opened: The Message of Revelation*. Downers Grove, IL: InterVarsity, 1975.

Wilson, Mark. *Revelation*. Zondervan Illustrated Bible Backgrounds Commentary. Grand Rapids: Zondervan, 2002.

———. "The Spirit in Revelation: Explorations in Imagery and Metaphor." *Criswell Theological Review* 17 (2019) 83–96.

———. "The Water of Life: Three Explorations into Water Imagery in Revelation and the Fourth Gospel." *Scriptura* 118 (2019) 1–17.

Wright, Christopher J. H. *The God I Don't Understand: Reflections on Tough Question of Faith*. Grand Rapids: Zondervan, 2009.

———. *Here Are Your Gods: Faithful Discipleship in Idolatrous Times*. Grand Rapids: Eerdmans, 2018.

———. *The Mission of God: Unlocking the Bible's Grand Narrative*. Downers Grove, IL: InterVarsity, 2018.

Wright, N. T. *Revelation for Everyone*. The New Testament for Everyone Series. Louisville: Westminster John Knox, 2011.

Appendix: Repetition of Key Terms and Phrases

Note an asterisk (*) indicates that the selected word/phrase occurs an additional time in the verse; one for each asterisk.

The words are listed in accord with my translation of the text

This list is a select list of words/phrases; it does not contain every word

1,260 (2x), 11:3; 12:6
144 (4x), 7:4; 14:1, 3; 21:17 (total 4x)
144,000 (3x), 7:4; 14:1, 3

Abominations (see "detestable things")
About to (12x), 1:19; 2:10; 3:2, 10, 16; 6:11; 8:13; 10:4, 7; 12:4, 5; 17:8
Abyss (7x), 9:1, 2, 11; 11:7; 17:8; 20:1, 3
Adorned, 21:2, 19
After these things (9x), 1:19; 4:1*; 7:9; 9:12; 15:5; 18:1; 19:1; 20:3
After this, 7:1
Alive (see "life")
Almighty (9x), 1:8; 4:8; 11:17; 15:3; 16:7, 14; 19:6, 15; 21:22
    Lord God Almighty (7x) 1:8; 4:8; 11:17; 15:3; 16:7; 19:6; 21:22
    God Almighty: 16:14; 19:15
Alpha and Omega (3x), 1:8; 21:6; 22:13
    1:8, Alpha and Omega
    21:6, Alpha and Omega, the Beginning and the End
    22:13, Alpha and Omega, the First and the Last, the Beginning and the End
Altar (8x), 6:; 8:3*, 5; 9:13; 11:1; 14:18; 16:7
    Golden altar, 8:3; 9:13
    Prayers of the saints, 6:9; 8:3 (5:8)
    Fire, 8:5, 14:8
    Souls under it "saying," 6:9
    Voice "saying," 16:7
Amazed (4x), 13:3; 17:6, 7, 8
Amen (8x), 1:6, 7; 3:14; 5:14; 7:12*; 19:4; 22:20.
Angel(s) (70x), 1:1, 20; 2:1, 8, 12, 18; 3:1, 5, 7, 14; 5:2, 11; 7:1, 2*, 11; 8:2, 3, 4, 5, 6, 8, 10, 12, 13; 9:1, 11, 13, 14*, 15; 10:1, 5, 8, 9, 10; 11:15; 12:7*, 9; 14:6, 8, 9, 10, 15, 17, 18, 19; 15:1, 6, 7, 8; 16:1, 2, 3, 4, 5, 8, 10, 12; 17:1, 7; 18:1, 21; 19:7; 20:1; 21:9, 12; 22:6, 16
    Seven angels with seven last plagues, (7x: 15:1, 6, 7, 8; 16:1; 17:1; 21:9)

APPENDIX: REPETITION OF KEY TERMS AND PHRASES

Angel(s) *(continued)*
  Twelve angels, 21:12
  Strong angel (7x), 5:2; 10:1, 5, 8, 9, 10; 18:21
  Many angels around the throne, 5:11
  4 angels, 7:1, 2
  4 angels bound Euphrates, 9:14, 15
  All angels standing around the throne, 7:11
  Angel of the abyss, 9:11
  Michael's angels, 12:7
  Dragon's angels, 12:7, 9
  Another angel (10x), 7:2; 8:3; 10:1; 14:6, 8, 9, 15, 17, 18; 18:1
  Angel standing in the sun, 19:17
  Angel coming down from heaven, 20:1
Another (18x), 2:24; 6:4; 7:2; 8:3; 10:1; 12:3; 13:11; 14:6, 8, 9, 15, 17, 18; 15:1; 17:10; 18:1, 4; 20:12
Apostles (3x), 2:2; 18:20; 21:14
Appearance (4x), 4:3**: vision 9:17
Ark, 11:19
Army(ies) (3x), 9:16; 19:14, 19
Authority (power) (21x), 2:26; 6:8; 9:3*, 10, 19; 11:6*; 12:10; 13:2, 4, 5, 7, 12; 14:18; 16:9; 17:12, 13; 18:1; 20:6; 22:14
Avenge, 6:10; 19:2

Babylon the Great (6x) 14:8; 16:19; 17:5; 18:2, 10, 21
Beast(s) (38x), 6:8; 11:7; 13:1, 2, 3, 4**, 11, 12*, 14*, 15**, 17, 18; 14:9, 11; 15:2; 16:2, 10, 13; 17:3, 7, 8*, 11, 12, 13, 16, 17; 18:2; 19:19, 20; 20:4, 10
  Throne, (13:2; 16:10)
Beginning (3x), 3:14; 21:6; 22:13
Beginning and the End 21:6; 22:13
Blasphemy/blasphemed (4x) 13:6; 16:9, 11, 21
Blessed (7x) 1:3; 14:13; 16:15; 19:9; 20:6; 22:7, 14
Blood (19x) 1:5; 5:9; 6:10, 12; 7:14; 8:7, 8; 11:6; 12:11; 14:20; 16:3, 4, 6*; 17:6*; 18:24; 19:2, 13

His blood: 1:5; 5:9; (lamb: 7:14; 12:11)
Moon became like blood: 6:12
Our blood: 6:10; 16:6; 17:6; 18:24; 19:2
Sea became blood, 8:8; 11:6; 16:3, 4
Robe dipped in blood, 19:13
Body 11:8, 9
Bondservant (See servant)
Book (see scroll)
Bound 9:14; 20:2
Bowls (12x) 5:8; 15:7; 16:1, 2, 3, 4, 8, 10, 12, 17; 17:1; 21:9
  (4) Seven bowls 15:7; 16:1; 17:1; 21:9
Breath/spirit (24x) 1:4, 10; 2:7, 11, 17, 29; 3:1, 6, 13, 22; 4:2, 5; 5:6; 11:11; 13:15; 14:13; 16:13, 14; 17:3; 18:1; 19:10; 20:10; 21:6; 22:17
Bride (4x) 19:7; 21:2, 9; 22:17 (also used generically in 18:23)
Bridle 14:20
Bright (5x) 15:6; 18:14; 19:8; 22:1, 16
Burned (5x) 8:7**; 17:16; 18:8
Burning 18:9, 18
Buy/purchase (6x) 3:18; 5:9; 13:17; 14:3, 4; 18:11

Called out 14:18
Captured 19:20
Carnelian 4:3; 21:20
Carried 17:3; 21:10
Celebrate (3x) 11:10; 12:12; 18:20
Christ (7x) 1:1, 2, 5; 11:15; 12:10; 20:4, 6
  3x with Jesus (1:1, 2, 5)
Churches (20x) 1:4, 11, 20*; 2:1, 7, 8, 11, 12, 17, 18, 23, 29; 3:1, 6, 7, 13, 14, 22; 22:16.
  7 Churches (4x) 1:4, 11, 20*
City (27x) 3:12; 11:2, 8, 13; 14:20; 16:19*; 17:18; 18:10*, 16, 18, 19, 21; 20:9; 21:2, 10, 14, 15, 16*, 18, 19, 21, 23; 22:14, 19
  Holy City (4x) 11:2; 21:2 (NJ), 10 (Jerusalem), 22:19
  City of my God: 3:12
  Beloved city: 20:9

424

APPENDIX: REPETITION OF KEY TERMS AND PHRASES

Great city (10x) 11:8; 16:19*; 17:18; 18:10*, 16, 18, 19, 21
Clean (5x) 15:6; 19:8, 14; 21:18, 21
Clothed (12x): 3:5, 18; 4:4; 7:9, 13; 10:1; 11:3; 12:1; 17:4; 18:16; 19:8, 13
Clothes:
    Washed their robes 7:14; 22:14
    White clothes (7x): using 3 variants (see below): 3:5, 18; 4:4; 6:11; 7:9, 13; 19:14
    Robe 6:11; 7:9, 13
    White garments: 3:5, 18; 4:4
    White fine linen 19:14
    Fine linen (5x) 18:12, 16; 19:8*, 14
    Clothed (3x)
        1:13—Christ
        15:6—Angels
        19:14—Armies of heaven
    Garments (7x) 3:4, 5, 18; 4:4; 16:15; 19:13, 16
    White garments: 3:5, 18; 4:4
    Garments: 16:15; 19:13, 16;
    Long robe 1:13
    Robe (5x) 6:11; 7:9, 13, 14; 22:14
Clouds (7x) 1:7; 10:1; 11:12; 14:14*, 15, 16
Come here 19:15
Come (36x) 1:4, 7, 8; 2:5, 16; 3:10, 11; 4:8; 5:7; 6:1, 3, 5, 7, 17; 7:13, 14; 8:3; 9:12; 11:14, 18; 14:7, 15; 16:15; 17:1, 10*; 18:10; 19:7; 21:9; 22:7, 12, 17**, 20*
    I am coming: (7x) 2:5, 16; 3:11; 16:15; 22:7, 12, 20
    Come (7x) 6:1, 3, 5, 7; 22:17*, 20 (4 x 3)
    The One who is to come (3x) 1:4, 8; 4:8
    Coming used with "repent" 2:5*, 16
    Behold, He/it is coming (3x) 1:7; 9:12; 11:14
Coming down (10x) 3:12; 10:1; 12:12; 13:13; 16:21; 18:1; 20:1, 9; 21:2, 10
    Out of heaven 3:12; 10:1; 13:13; 16:21; 18:1; 20:1, 9; 21:2, 10
Corners (2x) 7:1; 20:8

Crown (8x) 2:10; 3:11; 4:4, 10; 6:2; 9:7; 12:1; 14:14
    2:10 Crown of life
    4:4; 14:14 Gold crown
    9:7 Like gold
    12:1 crown of stars
Cried out (11x) 6:10; 7:2, 10; 10:3*; 12:2; 14:15; 18:2; 18:18, 19; 19:17
Crystal 4:6; 22:1
Cup (4x) 14:10; 16:19; 17:4; 18:6; the wine of his wrath:
    14:8; 17:4 Harlot makes the nations drink of her cup
Curse 22:3

David (3x) 3:7; 5:5; 22:16
Dead (11x) 1:5, 17, 18; 2:8; 3:1; 11:18; 14:13; 16:3; 20:5, 12, 13
    Christ: firstborn from the dead 1:5; was dead 1:18; 2:8
    John fell like a dead man 1:17
    Those in Sardis are dead 3:1
    Dead are judged 11:18
    Dead who die in the Lord 14:13
Death (17x) 1:18; 2:10, 11, 23; 6:8*; 9:6; 12:11; 13:3, 12; 18:8; 20:6, 13, 14*; 21:4, 8
    Second death 2:11; 20:6, 14; 21:8
Deceives/deception (8x) 2:20; 12:9; 13:14; 18:23; 19:20; 20:3, 8, 10
    2:20 Jezebel deceives
    12:9 Satan is the deceiver
    13:14; 19:20 FP deceives earth-dwellers
    18:23 Babylon: all nations were deceived by your sorcery
    20:3 Satan bound so that he cannot deceive
    20:8 Satan will deceive the nations
    20:10 the devil, who deceived them, . . .
Deeds/works (20x) 2:2, 5, 6, 19*, 22, 23, 26; 3:1, 2, 8, 15; 9:20; 14:13; 15:3; 16:11; 18:6; 20:12, 13; 22:12 (12x in 7 messages)
Descendant 22:16
Desolate (3x) 17:16; 18:17, 19
Destroy 8:9; 11:18*

APPENDIX: REPETITION OF KEY TERMS AND PHRASES

Detestable things (3x) 17:4, 5; 21:27
Devil (5x) 2:10; 12:9, 12; 20:2, 10
Devour (5x) 10:9, 10; 11:5; 12:4; 20:9
Diadems (3x) 12:3; 13:1; 19:12
Done ("It is done") 16:17; 21:6
Door (3x) 3:8, 20: 4:1
Dragon (13x) 12:3, 4, 7*, 9, 13, 16, 17; 13:2, 4, 11; 16:13; 20:2
Dwelling place/Tabernacle (3x) 13:6; 15:5; 21:3

Eagle (3x) 4:7; 8:13; 12:14
Earth: (82x) 1:5, 7; 3:10; 5:3*, 6, 10, 13*; 6:4, 8*, 10, 13, 15; 7:1**, 2, 3; 8:5, 7*, 13; 9:1, 3*, 4; 10:2, 5, 6, 8; 11:4, 6, 10*, 18; 12:4, 9, 12, 13, 16*; 13:3, 8, 11, 12; 13:13, 14*; 14:3, 6, 7, 15, 16*, 18, 19*; 16:1, 2, 18; 17:2*, 5, 8, 18; 18:1, 3*, 9, 11, 23, 24; 19:2, 19; 20:8, 9, 11; 21:1*, 24
Earth-dwellers: See "those who inhabit the earth"
Earthquake (7x) 6:12; 8:5; 11:13*, 19; 16:18*
  Great earthquake 8:5; 11:19; 16:18
Egypt 11:8
24 Elders (12x) 4:4, 10; 5:5, 6, 8, 11, 14; 7:11, 13; 11:16; 14:3; 19:4
  The elders and living creatures are paired together (7x) 5:6, 8, 11, 14; 7:11; 14:3; 19:4: never described in the same way twice
End (3x) 2:26; 21:6; 22:13
  Beginning and the end (2x) 21:6; 22:13
Euphrates 9:14; 16:12
Eyes (10x) 1:7, 14; 2:18; 3:18; 4:6, 8; 5:6; 7:17; 19:12; 21:4

Face (10x) 4:7; 6:16; 7:11; 9:7*; 10:1; 11:16; 12:14; 20:11; 22:4
Faithful (8x) 1:5; 2:10, 13; 3:14; 17:14; 19:11; 21:5; 22:6
  Faithful and true 3:14; 19:11; 21:5; 22:6

Faithful witness (3x) 1:5; 2:13; 3:14
Fallen (see Fell/fallen)
False Prophet (3x) 16:13; 19:20; 20:10
Famine 6:8; 18:8
Far away (3x) 18:10, 15, 17
Feast 19:9, 17
Feet: burnished bronze 1:15; 2:18
Fell/fallen (24x) 1:17; 2:5; 4:10; 5:8, 14; 6:13, 16; 7:11, 16; 8:10*; 9:1; 11:13, 16; 14:8*; 16:19; 17:10; 18:2*, 3; 19:4, 10; 22:8
  At his feet to worship
  Jesus 1:17
  Angel 19:10; 22:8
  Before the throne 4:10; 7:11; 11:16
  24 elders 4:10; 5:14; 11:16
  24 elders and 4 living creatures 5:8; 19:4
  Angels fell 7:11
  Before the Lamb 5:8
Fellow partaker 1:9
Fine linen (see clothing)
Finished (8x) 10:7; 11:7; 15:1, 8; 17:17; 20:3, 5, 7
Fire (25x) 1:14; 2:18; 3:18; 4:5; 8:5, 7, 8; 9:17, 18; 10:1; 11:5; 13:13; 14:10, 18; 15:2; 16:8; 17:16; 18:8; 19:12, 20; 20:9, 10, 14, 15; 21:8
  Lake (of fire) 19:20; 20:10, 14*, 15; 21:8
  Fire and brimstone (sulphur): 14:10; 19:20; 20:10; 21:8;
  Sulphur also occurs in 9:17, 18
  Fire from the altar: 8:5; 14:18
First (18x) 1:17; 2:4, 5, 8, 19; 4:1, 7; 8:7; 13:12*; 16:2; 20:5, 6; 21:1*, 4, 19; 22:13
First and last (3x) 1:17; 2:8; 22:13
First fruits 14:4
Five (3x) 9:5, 10; 17:10
Firstborn 1:5
Flee (fled) (4x) 9:6; 12:6; 16:20; 20:11
Foot/Feet (11x) 1:15, 17; 2:18; 3:9; 10:1, 2; 11:11; 12:1; 13:2; 19:10; 22:8
Forehead(s) (8x) 7:3; 9:4; 13:16; 14:1, 9; 17:5; 20:4; 22:4 (always the place of a name)

APPENDIX: REPETITION OF KEY TERMS AND PHRASES

Form/appearance 9:7
Forty (5x) 7:4; 11:2; 13:5; 14:1, 3; 21:17
  Forty-two months 11:2; 13:5
  144,000 7:4; 14:1, 3
  144 21:17
Found (13x) 2:2; 3:2; 5:4; 9:6; 12:8; 14:5; 16:20; 18:14, 21, 22, 24; 20:11, 15
Foundation of the world 13:8; 17:8
Four (28x) 4:4*, 6, 8, 10; 5:6, 8*, 14; 6:1, 6; 7:1**, 2, 4, 11; 9:14, 15; 11:16; 14:1, 3*; 15:7; 19:4*; 20:8; 21:7
Fourth (7x) 4:7; 6:7, 8; 8:12; 16:8; 21:19
Freely (2x) 1:6; 22:17
Fruit 22:2*
Full (7x) 4:6, 8; 5:8; 15:7; 17:3, 4; 21:9

Garments (see clothes)
Gates (11x) 21:12*, 13***, 15, 21*, 25; 22:14
Gather (5x) 16:14, 16; 19:17, 19; 20:8
Give (52x) 1:1; 2:7, 10, 17*, 21, 23, 26, 28; 3:8, 9, 21; 4:9; 6:2, 4, 8, 11; 7:2; 8:2, 3; 9:1, 3, 5; 10:9; 11:1, 2, 3, 13, 18; 12:14; 13:2, 4, 5, 7, 14, 15, 16; 14:7; 15:7; 16:6, 8, 9, 19; 17:13, 17; 18:7; 19:7, 8; 20:4, 13*; 21:6
Glass (n) 21:18, 21
Glassy (Adj) (3x) 4:6; 15:2*
Glorify 15:4; 18:7
Glory (17x) 1:6; 4:9, 11; 5:12, 13; 7:12; 11:13; 14:7; 15:8; 16:9; 18:1; 19:1, 7; 21:11, 23, 24, 26
Glory of God
  15:8 Temple filled with smoke from * of God
  21:11 NJ has * of God
  21:23 * of God illumines the city
  21:24, 26 Glory of the nations
Gold (5x) 3:18; 17:4; 18:16; 21:18, 21
  Adorned with gold 17:4; 18:16
  Pure gold 21:18, 21
Golden (15x) 1:12, 13, 20; 2:1; 4:4; 5:8; 8:3*; 9:13, 20; 14:14; 15:6, 7; 17:4; 21:15
  Golden altar 8:3; 9:13
  Bowls 5:8; 15:7

Crowns 4:4; 14:14 (like gold: 9:7)
Lampstands 1:12, 20; 2:1
Sashes 1:13; 15:6
Grace 1:4; 22:21
Great (80x) 1:10; 2:22; 5:2, 12; 6:4, 10, 12, 14, 17; 7:2, 10, 14 ; 8:8, 10, 13; 9:2, 14; 10:3; 11:8, 11, 12, 13, 15, 17, 18, 19; 12:1, 3, 9, 10, 12, 14; 13:2, 5, 13, 16; 14:2, 7, 8, 9, 15, 18, 19; 15:1, 3; 16:1, 9, 12, 14, 17, 18*, 19*, 21*; 17:1, 5, 6, 18; 18:1, 2, 10, 16, 18, 19, 21*; 19:1, 2, 5, 17*, 18; 20:1, 11, 12; 21:3, 10, 12
Great (loud) voice 5:2, 12; 6:10; 7:2, 10; 8:13; 10:3; 11:12, 15; 12:10; 14:7, 9, 15, 18; 16:17; 19:1, 17; 21:3. (total 18x)
Great city (8x) 11:8; 16:19; 17:18; 18:10, 16, 18, 19, 21 (Babylon 16:19; 18:21)
  Babylon the great 17:5; 18:2, 21
  Great Prostitute 17:1; 19:2
Great multitude (3x) 7:9; 19:1, 6

Hail (4x) 8:7; 11:19; 16:21*
Hand (16x) 1:16; 6:5; 7:9; 8:4; 9:20; 10:2, 5, 8, 10; 13:16; 14:9, 14; 17:4; 19:2; 20:1, 4
  Right hand: 1:16, 17, 20; 2:1; 5:1, 7; 13:16? 10:2, 5??
Harm (11x) 2:11; 6:6; 7:2, 3; 9:4, 10, 19; 11:5*; 22:11*
Harps (4x) 5:8; 14:2; 15:2; 18:22
Harpists 14:2
Playing the harp 14:2
He (And He Himself) (7x) 3:20; 14:10, 17; 17:11; 19:15*; 21:3
  Of Christ: He Himself 19:15*; God: 21:3
  They themselves 6:11; 12:11; 21:3
Heads-seven (5x) 12:3; 13:1; 17:3, 7, 9
Hear (44x) 1:3, 10; 2:7, 11, 17, 29; 3:3, 6, 13, 20, 22; 4:1; 5:11, 13; 6:1, 3, 5, 6, 7; 7:4; 8:13; 9:13, 16, 20; 10:4, 8; 11:12; 12:10; 13:9; 14:2*, 13; 16:1, 5, 7; 18:4, 22, 23; 19:1, 6; 21:3; 22:8, 17, 18.

427

APPENDIX: REPETITION OF KEY TERMS AND PHRASES

Heard (22x) 1:10; 4:1; 5:11, 13; 6:1, 3; 7:4; 8:13; 9:13, 16; 10:4, 8; 12:10; 14:2*, 13; 16:1; 18:4; 19:1, 6; 21:3; 22:8

Heat 7:16; 16:9

Heaven (49x) 3:12; 4:1, 2; 5:3, 13; 6:13, 14; 8:1, 10; 9:1; 10:1, 4, 5, 6; 11:6, 12, 13, 15, 19; 12:1, 3, 4, 7, 8, 10, 12; 13:6, 13; 14:2, 7, 13, 17; 15:1, 5; 16:11, 21; 18:1, 4, 5, 20; 19:1, 11, 14; 20:1, 9, 11; 21:1, 2, 10

    Heavens, earth, under the earth, sea, things in it (5:13)

    Heaven, earth, sea, spring/rivers (14:7; see 8:7–12; 16:2–9)

Here (6x) 4:1; 11:12; 13:10, 18; 14:12; 17:9

High (and great) 21:10, 12

Holds (8x) 2:1, 13, 14, 15, 25; 3:11; 7:1; 20:2

Holy (25x) 3:7; 4:8**; 5:8; 6:10; 8:3, 4; 11:2, 18; 13:7, 10; 14:10, 12; 16:6; 17:6; 18:20, 24; 19:8; 20:6, 9; 21:2, 10; 22:11, 19

    Referring to Jesus/God: 3:7; 4:8**; 6:10

    Holy city: 11:2; 21:2, 10; 22:19

Horns (10x) 5:6; 9:13; 12:3; 13:1*, 11; 17:3, 7, 12, 16

Horse(s) (15x) 6:2, 4, 5, 8; 9:7, 9, 17, 19; 14:20; 18:13; 19:11, 14, 18, 19, 21

Hour (10x) 3:3, 10; 9:15; 11:13; 14:7, 15; 17:12; 18:10, 17, 19

Humanity/man (24x) 1:13; 4:7; 8:11; 9:4, 5, 6, 7, 10, 15, 18, 20; 11:13; 13:13, 18; 14:4, 14; 16:2, 8, 9, 18, 21; 18:13; 21:3, 17

I am coming (7x) 2:5, 16; 3:11; 16:15; 22:7, 12, 20—all of these appear in contexts that address the people of God

Immorality/prostitute (verb) (5x) 2:14, 20; 17:2; 18:3, 9

    Noun (7x) 2:21; 9:21; 14:8; 17:2, 4; 18:3; 19:2

Incense (4x) 5:8; 8:3, 4; 18:13

Inhabit: see: those who inhabit the earth

Inherit 21:7

Iron (4x) 2:27; 9:9; 12:5; 19:15

    Rod of iron (3x) 2:27; 12:5; 19:15

Islands (3x) 1:9; 6:14; 16:20

Israel (3x) 2:14; 7:4; 21:22

"It is done" (2x) 16:17; 21:6

Jasper (4x) 4:3; 21:11, 18, 19

Jesus (14x) 1:1, 2, 5, 9*; 12:17; 14:12; 17:6; 19:10*; 20:4; 22:16, 20, 21

    7x in accord with the designation 'witness' 1:2, 9; 12:17; 17:6; 19:10*; 20:4

    Jesus Christ (3x) 1:1, 2, 5

Jerusalem (3x): 3:12 (new); 21:2 (new), 21:10

Jezebel 2:20

John (4x) 1:1, 4, 9; 22:8

Judgment (7x) 14:7; 16:7; 17:1; 18:10, 20; 19:2; 20:4

Just/righteous (5x) 15:3; 16:5, 7; 19:2; 22:11

Keeps (10x) 1:3; 2:26; 3:3, 8, 10; 12:17; 14:12; 16:15; 22:7, 9

Key(s) (4x) 1:18; 3:7; 9:1; 20:1

Kingdom (9x) 1:6, 9; 5:10; 11:15; 12:10; 16:10; 17:12; 17:17, 18

Kings/Kings of the Earth (21x) 1:5; 6:15; 9:11; 10:11; 15:3; 16:12, 14; 17:2, 9, 12*, 14*, 18; 18:3, 9; 19:16*, 18, 19; 21:24

Know (12x) 2:2, 9 13, 17, 19; 3:1, 8, 15, 17; 7:14; 12:12; 19:12

    I know (seven messages: 7x) 2:2, 9, 13, 19; 3:1, 8, 15

Lake (of fire) (6x) 19:20; 20:10, 14*, 15; 21:8

Lamb (28x) 5:6, 8, 12, 13; 6:1, 16; 7:9, 10, 14, 17; 12:11; 13:8, 11; 14:1, 4, 10; 15:3; 17:14*; 19:7, 9; 21:9, 14, 22, 23, 27; 22:1, 3

Lament/Mourn 1:7; 18:9

Lamp (3x) 18:23; 21:23: 22:5

Lamps of fire (Seven): 4:5; 8:10

APPENDIX: REPETITION OF KEY TERMS AND PHRASES

Lampstands (Seven) (7x) 1:12, 13, 20*; 2:1, 5; 11:4
    7 Lampstands (4x): 1:12, 20*, 2:1
    2 Lampstands 11:4
Leads astray (8x) (deceives): 2:20 Jezebel; 12:9 Satan/Dragon; 13:14 False Prophet; 18:23 Harlot Babylon; 19:20 False Prophet; 20:3, 8, 10 Satan
Liars 2:2; 21:8
Lie (3x) 14:5; 21:27; 22:15
Came to life/Alive/living one (13x) 1:18*; 2:8; 3:1; 4:9, 10: 7:2; 10:6; 13:14; 15:7; 19:20; 20:4, 5
Light (4x) 18:23; 21:24; 22:5*
Lightning (4x) 4:5; 8:5; 11:19; 16:18
Linen: see clothing (5x) 18:12, 16; 19:8*, 14
Lion (6x) 4:7; 5:5; 9:8, 17; 10:3; 13:2
Little/small (8x) 3:8; 6:11; 11:18; 13:16; 19:5, 18; 20:3, 12
Living creatures (20x) 4:6, 7***, 8, 9; 5:6, 8, 11, 14; 6:1, 3, 5, 6, 7; 7:11; 14:3; 15:7; 19:4
    (11x) Four Living Creatures: 4:6, 8; 5:6, 8, 14; 6:1, 6; 7:11; 14:3; 15:7; 19:4
Locusts 9:3, 7
Lord 6:10
Lord God Almighty (7x) 1:8; 4:8; 11:17; 15:3; 16:7; 19:6; 21:22
God Almighty: 16:14; 19:15
Love (noun) 2:4, 19
Love *agape* (4x) 1:5; 3:9; 12:11; 20:9
    God/Christ loved us 1:5; 3:9
    People of God did not love their life 12:11
    Beloved city 20:9
Love: *phileo* verb: 3:19; 22:15
Loud (see great voice)

Make/do (26) x1:6; 2:5; 3:9, 12; 5:10; 11:7; 12:15, 17; 13:5, 7, 12, 13, 14, 15, 16; 14:7; 16:14; 17:16, 17; 19:19, 20; 21:5, 27; 22:2, 11, 15
    Make war: 11:7; 12:17; 13:7; 19:19
Man: see humanity

Many waters (4x) 1:15; 14:2; 17:1; 19:6 (3x with "voice")
Mark—of the Beast: (7x) 13:16, 17; 14:9, 11; 16:2; 19:20; 20:4
Marvelous 15:1, 3
Marveled (see "amazed")
Measure (v) (5x) 11:1, 2; 21:15, 16, 17
    Measuring reed 11:1; 21:15, 16
Might (strength) 5:12; 7:12
Mighty: see strong
Millstone 18:21 (see stone)
Misleads (8x) 2:20; 12:9; 13:14; 18:23; 19:20; 20:3, 8, 10
Morning star 2:28; 22:16
Mountains (8x) 6:14, 15, 16; 8:8; 14:1; 16:20; 17:9; 21:10
Mounted troops 9:16
Mourn (3x) 18:11, 15, 19
Mouth (18x) 1:16; 2:16; 3:16; 9:17, 18, 19; 10:9, 10; 11:5; 12:15, 16; 13:2, 5, 6; 14:5; 16:13; 19:15, 21
Multitude, Great (3x) 7:9; 19:1, 6
Myriads (4x) 5:11*; 9:16*
Mystery 1:20; 10:7; 17:5, 7

Naked (3x) 3:17; 16:15; 17:16
Name (37x) 2:3, 13, 17; 3:1, 4, 5*, 8, 12**, 6:8; 8:11; 9:11*; 11:13, 18; 13:1, 6, 8, 17*, 14:1*, 11; 15:2, 4; 16:9; 17:3, 5, 8; 19:12, 13, 16; 21:12, 14; 22:4
    Name of My God; Name of the city of My God, My new name (12; 14:1; 22:4) fear your name 11:18): Beast has a name on his forehead (13:1); Beast blasphemes His name (13:6); Those who have the name of the beast (13:17; 14:11); People of God overcome the name of the beast (15:2); Harlot full of names (17:3, 5); no one knows His name (19:12, 13, 16)
    Christ's name (7x) 2:13; 3:8, 12; 13:6; 15:4; 16:9; 19:12
Nations (22x) 2:26; 5:9; 7:9; 10:11; 11:2, 9, 18; 12:5; 13:7; 14:6, 8; 15:4;

APPENDIX: REPETITION OF KEY TERMS AND PHRASES

16:19; 17:15; 18:3, 23; 19:15;
20:3, 8; 21:24, 26; 22:2
Every tribe (kings, multitudes),
tongue, people, and nation (7x)
5:9; 7:9; 10:11; 11:9; 13:7; 14:6;
17:15—"tribes" omitted in 10:11
replace by "kings"; "tribes"
omitted in 17:15 replace by
"multitudes"
they have:
They have drunk Babylon's wine
(14:8; 18:3)
Deceived by Babylon's sorcery
(18:23)
And by Satan (20:3)
They trample the Holy City (11:2)
They rage against God (11:18)
Object of Christ's judgment at the
Parousia (12:5; 19:15)
They worship God (15:4; 21:24, 26;
22:2))
Near 1:3; 22:10
New (8x) 2:17; 3:12; 5:9; 14:3; 21:1*, 2, 5
New song 5:9; 14:3
New name 2:17; 3:12
New Jerusalem 3:12; 21:2
New heaven 21:1; and new earth
21:1
Night (8x) 4:8; 7:15; 8:12; 12:10; 14:11;
20:10; 21:25; 22:5
Nourished 12:6, 14
Number (7x) 5:11; 7:4; 9:16; 13:17, 18;
15:2; 20:8

One who lives forever and ever (4x) 4:9,
10; 10:6; 15:7
One who is and who was 11:17; 16:5
One who is and who was and who is to
come 1:4, 8; 4:8
1,260 days (see time) 11:2; 13:5
Offspring (See descendant) 22:16
Open(ed) (26x) 3:7*, 8, 20; 4:1; 5:2, 3,
4, 5, 9; 6:1, 3, 5, 7, 9, 12; 8:1; 9:2;
10:2, 8; 11:19; 12:16; 13:6; 15:5;
19:11; 20:12*
Temple opened 11:19; 15:5
Heaven opened 4:1; 19:11

Other (18x) 2:4; 6:4; 7:2; 8:3; 10:1; 12:3;
13:11; 14:6, 8, 9, 15, 17, 18; 15:1;
17:10; 18:1, 4, 20:12
Outside 5x
(3x longer form) 11:2*; 14:20—both
with "trample"
(2x shorter form) 3:12; 22:15—
outside the temple (3:12) and
outside the city (22:15)
Overcome (16x) 2:7, 11, 17, 26; 3:5, 12,
21; 5:5; 6:2*; 11:7; 12:11; 13:7;
15:2; 17:14; 21:7
People of God exhorted to overcome
2:7, 11, 17, 26; 3:5, 12, 21
People of God as those who
overcame 12:11; 15:2
Jesus as the One who overcame 5:5;
17:14
Enemies as overcoming 6:2; 11:7;
13:7
The one who overcomes (15x): 2:7,
11, 17, 26; 3:5, 12, 21; 5:5; 6:2;
11:7; 12:11; 13:7; 15:2; 17:14;
21:7

People (9x) 5:9; 7:9; 10:11; 11:9; 13:7;
14:6; 17:15; 18:4; 21:3
every tribe (kings, multitudes),
tongue, people, and nation (7x)
5:9; 7:9; 10:11; 11:9; 13:7; 14:6;
17:15
Patient endurance (7x) 1:9; 2:2, 3, 19;
3:10; 13:10; 14:12 (4x in the
seven messages)
Pillar 3:12; 10:1
Pit (4x) 9:1, 2**
Place (8x) 2:5; 6:14; 12:6, 8, 14; 16:16;
18:17; 20:11
Plague (wound) (16x) 9:18, 20; 11:6;
13:3, 12, 14; 15:1, 6, 8; 16:9, 21*;
18:4, 8; 21:9; 22:18
Plagues (Seven) (4x) 15:1, 6, 8; 21:9
(see below)
Poor 3:17; 13:16
Pour out (9x) 16:1, 2, 3, 4, 6, 8, 10, 12,
17
Poverty 2:9

430

APPENDIX: REPETITION OF KEY TERMS AND PHRASES

Power (12x) 1:16; 3:8; 4:11; 5:12; 7:12; 11:17; 12:10; 13:2; 15:8; 17:13; 18:3; 19:1
Prayer (3x) 5:8; 8:3, 4 (prayer of the saints)
Precious (see stones/precious)
Priests (3x) 1:6; 5:10; 20:6
Proclaiming 5:2
Prophecy (7x) 1:3; 11:6; 19:10; 22:7, 10, 18, 19
Prophesy (v) 10:11; 11:3
Prophets (8x) 10:7; 11:10, 18; 16:6; 18:20, 24; 22:6, 9
    False prophet 93x) 16:13; 19:20; 20:10
Prostitute (5x) 17:1, 5, 15, 16; 19:2 (see great)
Purple 17:14; 18:16
Purchase: see buy

Quickly see "soon"

Rainbow 4:3; 10:1
Red 6:4; 12:3
Reed (3x) 11:1; 21:15, 16
Reign (7x) 5:10; 11:15, 17; 19:6; 20:4, 6; 22:5
    3x for God 11:15 (future), 17 (aorist); 19:6 (aorist)
    4x people of God 5:10; 20:4 (aorist), 6 (future); 22:5 (future)
Rejoice (3x) 11:10; 12:12; 18:20
Released/break (6x) 1:5; 5:2; 9:14, 15; 20:3, 7
    Christ released us 1:5
    "break" seals 5:2
    9:14, 15 release 4 angels
    20:3, 7 Satan will be/released
Remaining ones: (see Rest)
Repent (12x) 2:5*, 16, 21*, 22; 3:3, 19; 9:20, 21; 16:9, 11
Rest (noun) 4:8; 14:11
Rest (verb) 6:11; 14:13
Rest/remaining ones/people (6x) 2:24; 9:20; 11:13; 12:17; 19:21; 20:5
    People of God 2:24; 12:17
    Repentant nations 11:13

Unrepentant/nations 9:20; 19:21; 20:5
Things: 2x: Used of trumpets: 8:13; Things 3:2; neuter pl.
Resurrection (first) 20:5, 6
Revelation/Apocalypse 1:1
Reward 11:18; 22:12
Rich (5x) 3:17, 18; 18:3, 15, 19
Right (see hand)
Righteous/just (5x) 15:3; 16:5, 7; 19:2; 22:11
Righteous deeds 15:4; 19:8
River (8x) 8:10; 9:14; 12:15, 16; 16:4, 12: 22:1, 2
Robe: see clothing
Rod (4x) 2:27; 11:1; 12:5; 19:15
    All but 11:1 associated with shepherd
Root (of David) 5:5; 22:16
Rule see "shepherd"
Ruler Archon (m) 1:1:5
    Arche (f) (3x) 3:14; 21:6; 22:13

Sackcloth 6:12; 11:3
Saints (13x) 5:8; 8:3, 4; 11:18; 13:7, 10; 14:12; 16:6; 17:6; 18:20, 24; 19:8; 20:9
    Saints and prophets 11:18; 16:6; 18:24
    Prayers of the saints 5:8; 8:3, 4
    War against the saints 13:7
Salvation (3x) 7:10; 12:10; 19:1
Sardius 4:3; 21:20
Sash (see golden)
Satan (8x) 2:9, 13*, 24; 3:9; 12:9; 20:2, 7
Saw (56x) 1:2, 12, 17, 19, 20; 4:1; 5:1, 2, 6, 11; 6:1, 2, 5, 8, 9, 12; 7:1, 2, 9; 8:2, 13; 9:1, 17; 10:1, 5; 12:13; 13:1, 2, 11; 14:1, 6, 14; 15:1, 2, 5; 16:13; 17:3, 6,* 8, 12, 15, 16, 18; 18:1, 7; 19:11, 17, 19; 20:1, 4, 11, 12; 21:1, 2, 22
    "And I saw" (33x) 5:1, 2, 6, 11; 6:1, 2, 5, 8, 12; 7:2; 8:2, 13; 9:1; 10:1; 13:1, 11; 14:1, 6, 14; 15:1, 2, 5; 16:13; 17:3, 6; 18:7; 19:11, 17, 19; 20:1, 4, 11, 12; 21:1
Scarlet (4x) 17:3, 4; 18:12, 16

APPENDIX: REPETITION OF KEY TERMS AND PHRASES

Scorched 16:8, 9
Scorpions (3x) 9:3, 5, 10
Scroll/book: (28x) 1:11; 3:5; 5:1, 2, 3, 4, 5, 8, 9; 6:14; 10:2, 8, 9, 10; 13:8; 17:8; 20:12**, 15; 21:27; 22:7, 9, 10, 18*, 19* (Note 3:5; 20:15—masc with fem article)
1. 11x Scroll in the Father's hand (7x) 5:1, 2, 3, 4, 5, 8, 9; 10:8; Scroll-little: 10:2, 9, 10
2. 2x Scrolls/books—judgment day 20:12*
3. 6x Scroll/book of life: 3:5; 13:8; 17:8; 20:12, 15; 21:27
4. 8x Book of Revelation (this): 7x: 22:7, 9, 10; 18*, 19*; also 1:11
5. 1x Sky rolled up like a scroll 6:14

Sea: (26x) 4:6; 5:13; 7:1, 2, 3; 8:8*, 9; 10:2, 5, 6, 8; 12:12, 18; 13:1; 14:7; 15:2*; 16:3*; 18:17, 19, 21; 20:8, 13; 21:1
  Sea of glass before the throne 4:6; 15:2*
  Sea as people 12:18? waters 17:15
  Place of the dead 20:13
Seal (13x) 5:1, 2, 5, 9; 6:1, 3, 5, 7, 9, 12; 7:2; 8:1; 9:4
  Seal of God 7:2; 9:4
Sealed: verb (8x) 7:3, 4*, 5, 8; 10:4; 20:3; 22:10
Second death (4x) 2:14; 20:6, 14; 21:8
Sensuously/Luxuriously (lived) 18:7, 9
Servant (14x) 1:1*; 2:20; 6:15; 7:3; 10:7; 11:18; 13:16; 15:3; 19:2, 5, 18; 22:3, 6
Serpent (5x) 9:19; 12:9, 14, 15; 20:2
Service 2:19
Seven (54x) 1:4*, 11, 12, 16, 20*****; 2:1*; 3:1*; 4:5*; 5:1, 5, 6**; 6:1; 8:2, 6; 10:3, 4*; 11:13; 12:3*; 13:1; 15:1*, 6*, 7*, 8*; 16:1*; 17:1*, 3, 7, 9***, 11; 21:9**
  Angels of the 7 churches 1:20
  Angels with trumpets 8:2, 6 (same as 7 angels of the churches?)
  Angels with last plagues (7x) 15:1, 6, 7, 8; 16:1; (17:1; 21:9—one of them)
  Churches 1:4, 11, 20* (see "churches" above)
  Diadems 12:3
  Eyes 5:6
  Golden bowls 15:7; 16:1; 17:1; 21:9
  Golden lampstands 1:12, 20*; 2:1
  Heads 12:3; 13:1; 17:3, 7, 9
  Horns 5:6
  Kings 17:9 (11)
  Lamps 4:5
  Mountains/hills 17:9
  People 7,000 11:13
  Plagues 15:1, 6, 8; 21:9
  Seals 5:1, 5; 6:1
  Spirits 1:4; 3:1; 4:5; 5:6
  Stars 1:16, 20*; 2:1; 3:1
  Thunders 10:3, 4*
  Trumpets 8:2, 6
Sexual immortality (5x) 2:14, 20; 17:2; 18:3, 9
Sharp (7x) 1:16; 2:12; 14:14, 17, 18*, 19:15 (1:16; 19:15 inclusio?)
Shepherd (4x) 2:27; 7:17; 12:5; 19:15
Ship(s) 8:9; 18:19
Show (7x) + Participle 1:1; 4:1; 17:1; 21:9, 10; 22:1, 6
Sickle (7x) 14:14, 15, 16, 17, 18*, 19
Sign (7x) 12:1, 3; 13:13, 14; 15:1; 16:14; 19:20
  2x with another 12:3; 15:1
  2x with great 12:1; 15:1 (see 13:13); note 12:3 great dragon
  3x "in heaven" 12:1, 3; 15:1
  4x with doing: 13:13, 14; 16:14; 19:20 (always of the FP)
Sin (3x) 1:5; 18:4, 5
Sitting: (33x) 4:2, 3, 4, 9, 10; 5:1, 7, 13; 6:2, 4, 5, 8, 16; 7:10, 15; 9:17; 11:16; 14:6, 14, 15, 16; 17:1, 3, 9, 15; 18:7; 19:4, 11, 18, 19, 21; 20:11; 21:5
  The one who is sitting on the Throne (13x) 4:2, 3, 9, 10; 5:1, 7, 13; 6:16; 7:10, 15; 19:4; 20:11; 21:5

APPENDIX: REPETITION OF KEY TERMS AND PHRASES

To the one sitting on the cloud (3x) 14:14, 15, 16
Jesus on the white horse (3x)19:11, 19, 21
24 Elders sitting on thrones 4:4; 11:16
Sitting on the "x" horse (3x) 6:2, 4, 5, 8
(those) sitting on horses 19:19
Those (pl) sitting on them 9:17
Those (pl) sitting (dwell) on the earth 14:6
Great Prostitute sitting on the Beast 17:3
Great Prostitute sits on the 7 heads 17:9
Great Prostitute sitting on many waters 17:1, 15
Great Prostitute "I sit as a queen" 18:7
Slay/slain (8x) 5:6, 9, 12; 6:4, 9; 13:3, 8; 18:24
Small (see little)
Smoke (12x) 8:4; 9:2**, 3, 17, 18; 14:11; 15:8; 18:9, 18; 19:3 (7x in 8:1–9:21)
  "went up" (4x): 8:4—prayers: to God; 9:2—from the abyss; 14:11—of their torment; 19:3—her smoke went up forever and ever
  8:4 prayers of the saints
  9:2**, 3 from the abyss
  9:17, 18 proceeds from the mouths of the demonic horde
  14:11 smoke of torment
  15:8 Glory of God
  18:9, 18; 19:3 smoke of her burning
Sodom 11:8
Son (8x) 1:13; 2:14, 18; 7:4; 12:5; 14:14; 21:7, 12
  Son of God 2:18
  Son of Man 1:13; 14:14
  Sons of Israel 2:14; 7:4; 21:12
Song (5x) 5:9; 14:3*; 15:3*
  New song 5:9; 14:3
  Song of Moses (15:3) and the Lamb (15:3)

Soon/quickly (noun) 1:1; 22:6
Soon (6x) 2:16; 3:11; 11:14; 22:7, 12, 20
  I am coming soon (5x) 2:16; 3:11; 22:7, 12, 20
Sorcery 18:23
Sore 16:2, 11
Soul(s) (7x) 6:9; 8:9; 12:11; 16:3; 18:13, 14; 20:4
Sounds: see voice
Spirit/breath (24x) 1:4, 10; 2:7, 11, 17, 29; 3:1, 6, 13, 22; 4:2, 5; 5:6; 11:11; 13:15; 14:13; 16:13, 14; 17:3; 18:1; 19:10; 20:10; 21:6; 22:17
  In the spirit (4x) 1:10; 4:2; 17:2; 21:10
  The Spirit (10x) 2:7, 11, 17, 29; 3:6, 13, 22; 14:13; 19:10; 22:17
  Spirits (Seven) (4x) 1:4; 3:1; 4:5; 5:6
  Breath 11:11; 13:15
Spring (5x) 7:17; 8:10; 14:7; 16:4; 21:6
Stand (21x) 3:20; 5:6; 6:17; 7:1, 9, 11; 8:2, 3; 10:5, 8; 11:4, 11; 12:4, 18; 14:1; 15:2; 18:10, 15, 17; 19:17; 20:12
Star(s) (14x) 1:16, 20*; 2:1, 28; 3:1; 6:13; 8:10, 11, 12; 9:1; 12:1, 4; 22:16
Stone (7x) 4:3; 17:4; 18:12, 16, 21; 21:11, 19
Stones/precious (5x) 17:4; 18:12, 16; 21:11, 19
Strike 11:6; 19:15
Strong angel (7x) 5:2; 10:1, 5, 8, 9, 10; 18:21:
Strong/mighty (9x) 5:2; 6:15; 10:1; 18:2, 8, 10, 21; 19:6, 18
Sulphur (6x) 9:17, 18; 14:10; 19:20; 20:10; 21:8
Sun (13x) 1:16; 6:12; 7:2, 16; 8:12; 9:2; 10:1; 12:1; 16:8, 12; 19:17; 21:23; 22:5
Sword (10x)
  Romphaia (6x) 1:16; 2:12, 16; 6:8; 19:15, 21 (always Christ's except 6:8)
  Maxaira (4x) 6:4; 13:10*, 14

APPENDIX: REPETITION OF KEY TERMS AND PHRASES

Tabernacle: (see "dwelling place")
Tails (5x) 9:10*, 19*; 12:4
Temple: (15x) naos 3:12; 7:15; 11:1, 2, 19*; 14:15, 17; 15:5, 6, 8; 16:1, 17; 21:22*
    Temple of God 11:1, 19
    Temple which is in heaven 14:17
    His temple 3:12; 7:15; 11:1, 19
    Temple was opened 11:19; 15:5
    Temple of tabernacle of testimony in heaven 15:5
Ten (9x): 2:10; 12:3; 13:1*; 17:3, 7, 12*, 16
"Ten thousands" 5:11*; 9:16*
Testimony (9x) (f) 1:2, 9; 6:9; 11:7; 12:11, 17; 19:10*; 20:4
    Testimony of Jesus (6x) 1:2, 9; 12:17; 19:10*; 20:4
    "Their testimony" (3x) 6:9; 11:7; 12:11
    Commandments of God and testimony of Jesus 12:17
    Word (of God) and testimony (of Jesus [Christ]) (5x) 1:2, 9; 6:9; 12:11; 20:4
    Word of God and the testimony of Jesus Christ 1:2
    Word of God and the testimony of Jesus 1:9
    Word of God and the testimony which they had 6:9
    The word of their testimony 12:11
    Testimony of Jesus and the Word of God 20:4 (reverse order)
    Word(s) of God (7x): 1:2, 9; 6:9; 17:17; 19:9 (true words), 13 (Name of Jesus); 20:4
    Their testimony 11:7; 12:11
    The commandments of God and their testimony of Jesus 12:17
    testimony of Jesus 19:10*
Terrified (see fear)
Thief 3:3; 16:15
Third: 4:7; 6:5; 8:7*, 8, 9*, 10, 11, 12****; 9:15, 18; 11:14; 12:4; 14:9; 21:19
    third living creation 4:7; third angel 14:9

angel with the third Seal 6:5; third Trumpet 8:10; third Bowl 16:4
Thirst 7:16; 21:7; 22:16
Those who inhabit the earth; see "dwell" (10x11x?) 3:10; 6:10; 8:13; 11:10*; 13:8; 13:12; 13:14*; 17:2, 8
    3:10 hour of testing comes on . . .
    6:10 avenge our blood on . . .
    8:13 woe, woe, woe on . . .
    11:10 (follows four-fold reference) . . . rejoice over them
    11:10 these two prophets tormented . . .
    13:8 (follows four-fold reference) all . . . will worship him (Beast)
    13:14 (the Beast) deceives . . .
    13:14 telling . . . to make
    17:2 . . . were made drunk from the wine of her immorality
    17:8 . . . whose name has not been written in the book of life
Those who inhabit the earth are:
    guilty of the blood of the people of God (6:10)
    Under judgment (8:13)
    Enemies of the Two Witnesses (11:10)
    Deceived by the False Prophet and worship the Beast (13:8, 14; 17:8)
Thousand (9x) 11:3; 12:6; 14:20; 20:2, 3, 4, 5, 6, 7
Three/third (29x) 6:5*, 6; 8:7*, 8, 9*, 10*, 11, 12****; 9:15, 18; 11:9, 11, 14; 12:4; 14:9; 16:4, 13; 21:13***, 19
    Angel 8:10, 13; 14:9; 16:4
    (Quarts) Barley 6:6
    Creatures 8:9
    Days (3½) 11:9, 11
    Earth 8:7
    Gates 21:13***
    Living creature 6:5
    People (1/3) 9:15, 18
    Plagues 9:18
    Rivers & springs 8:10
    Sea 8:8

APPENDIX: REPETITION OF KEY TERMS AND PHRASES

Seal 6:5
Ships 8:9
Spirits (unclean) 16:13
Stars 12:4
Sun, moon, stars 8:12
Waters 8:11
Woe 11:14
Throne (46x) 1:4; 3:21*; 4:2*, 3, 4, 5*, 6*, 9, 10*; 5:1, 6, 7, 11*,13; 6:16; 7:9, 10, 11, 15*, 17; 8:3; 12:5; 14:3; 16:17; 19:4, 5; 20:11, 12; 21:3, 5; 22:1, 3 (2:13—Satan's) (3:21: Jesus') (4:4*; 11:16—(pl) elders) (13:2; 16:10—beast's) (20:4 (pl)—souls)
  In heaven (4:2)
  In the NJ (22:3)
  (12x) One sitting on it (4:2, 3, 9; 5:1, 7, 13; 6:16; 7:10, 15; 19:4; 20:11; 21:5)
    Was like a jasper stone and a sardius (4:3)
    Book right hand (5:1)
  River comes from it (22:1); Sea of glass (4:6)
  Before it: 7 Spirits (1:4)
  Around it 24 thrones (4:4); sitting (11:16)
  Center & around 4 living creatures (4:6)
  Great Multitude (7:15)
  Lamb standing in front of it (5:6; 7:17)
  Many angels around it (5:11; 7:11)
  Great multitude standing before it and the Lamb (7:9)
  Child taken to the throne (12:5)
  From it: Lightning, sounds, thunder (4:5)
  Golden altar (8:3)
  Worship
    4 living creatures: give glory, honor, thanks—to One on the throne (4:9)
    24 elders: fall down, worship, cast crowns (4:10)
    Every created thing: "blessing, honor, glory, dominion" (5:13)
    Great Multitude: "salvation" (7:10)
    24 elders fall on their faces and worship (11:16)
    144,000 sing before it (14:3)
    24 Elders & 4 living creatures fell down and worshiped (19:4)
  Great White Throne (20:11)
  Dead were standing in front of it (20:12)
  The one who sits on the Throne' (7x) 4:9; 5:1, 7, 13; 6:16; 7:10; 21:5
  Voice from the throne:
    16:17 "It is done"
    19:5 "praise to our God"
    21:3 "dwelling of God is with men"
  One sitting said: (21:5–6; cp 1:8)
    "I am making all things new"
    "Write, for these words are faithful and true"
    "It is done: I am the Alpha and the Omega, the Beginning and the End"
Throne of the beast (13:2; 16:10)
Throw/spew/swung (28) 2:10, 12, 14, 24; 4:10; 6:13; 8:5, 7, 8; 12:4, 9**, 10, 13, 15, 16; 14:16, 19*; 18:19, 21*; 19:20; 20:3, 10, 14, 15
Thunder (10x) 4:5; 6:1; 8:5; 10:3, 4*; 11:19; 14:2; 16:18; 19:6 (3x Seven Thunders; 7x: thunder in the singular)
Seven thunders (3x) 10:3, 4*
Time (4x) *chronos* 2:21; 6:11; 10:6; 20:3
Time (7x) *kairos* 1:3; 11:18; 12:12, 14**; 22:10
Time, time, and ½ time 12:14
Tongues (8x) 5:9; 7:9; 10:11; 11:9; 13:7; 14:6; 16:10; 17:15
Every tribe (kings, multitudes), tongue, people, and nation occurs (7x) 5:9; 7:9; 10:11; 11:9; 13:7; 14:6; 17:15

435

APPENDIX: REPETITION OF KEY TERMS AND PHRASES

Torment (n) (6x) 9:5*; 14:11; 18:7, 10, 15
Torment (v) (5x) 9:5; 11:10; 12:2; 14:10; 20:10
Trample (3x) 11:2; 14:20; 19:15
Tree(s) *dendron* (4x) 7:1, 3; 8:7; 9:4
Tree: *ksulo* (7x) 2:7; 18:12*; 22:2*, 14, 19
    Tree of life (5x) 2:7; 22:2*, 14, 19
Tribe (21x) 1:7; 5:5, 9; 7:4, 5**, 6**, 7**, 8**, 9; 11:9; 13:7; 14:6; 21:12
    12 tribes (14x) 7:4, 5**, 6**, 7**, 8**, 9; 21:12
    Tribe of Judah (1x) 5:5
    "all the tribes of the earth (1x) 1:7
        5:9 tribe and tongue and people and nation: Jesus purchased them
        7:9 nation, tribes, peoples, and tongues: Great multitude from them
        10:11 peoples and nations and tongues and kings: John is prophesy to them
        11:9 peoples, tribes, tongues, and nations: refuse to bury TW
            11:10 those who dwell upon the earth
        13:7 tribe, people, tongue, and nation: Beast has authority over them
            13:8 those who dwell upon the earth
        14:6 nation, tribe, tongue, and people: Gospel proclaimed to them
        17:15 peoples, multitudes, nations, tongues: Harlot sits on them
Tribulation (5x) 1:9; 2:9, 10, 22; 7:14
    Great tribulation 2:22; 7:14
Trodden (3x) 11:2; 14:20; 19:15.
True (10x) 3:7, 14; 6:10; 15:3; 16:7; 19:2, 9, 11; 21:5; 22:6
Trumpet (6x) 1:10; 4:1; 8:2, 6, 13, 9:14
Twelve (23x) 7:5**, 6**, 7**, 8**; 12:1; 21:12**, 14**, 16, 21*; 22:2

Twenty-four (6x) 4:4*, 10; 5:8; 11:16; 19:4
    24 elders (5x) 4:4, 10; 5:8; 11:16; 19:4
Two: (8x) 9:12; 11:2, 3, 4, 10; 12:14; 13:5, 11; 19:20
    11:2; 13:5: 42 months

Under the earth 5:3, 13

Virgins 14:4
Vision/appearance (4x) 4:3**; 9:17
Voice (55x) 1:10, 12, 15*; 3:20; 4:1, 5; 5:2; 5:11, 12; 6:1, 6, 7, 10; 7:2, 10; 8:5, 13*; 9:9*, 13; 10:3*, 4, 7, 8; 11:12, 15, 19; 12:10; 14:2***, 7, 9, 13, 15, 18; 16:1, 17, 18; 18:2, 4, 22*, 23; 19:1, 5, 6**, 17; 21:3
    Great (loud) voice (20x) 1:10; 5:2; 5:12; 6:10; 7:2, 10; 8:13; 10:3; 11:12, 15; 12:10; 14:7, 9, 15, 18; 16:1, 17; 19:1, 17; 21:3
    Voice from heaven (3x) 10:4, 8; 11:12; in heaven (4x) 12:10; 14:2, 13; 18:4
    Voice from the throne (3x) 16:17; 19:5; 21:3 (God is addressed in the 3rd person in latter two instances)
        16:17 & 21:6 both say, "It is done"
    Voice from the temple 16:1, 17
    Voice like thunder: 6:1
    Voice of the 4 living creatures 6:7
    Voice of a great multitude 19:6
    One sitting on the throne: 21:5
    Voice like many waters 1:15 (Christ); 14:2 (144,000? from heaven like loud thunder-they sang); 19:6 Great Multitude like loud thunder (in heaven 19:1)
    Sound (10x) 4:5; 8:5, 13; 9:9*; 10:7; 11:19; 14:2**, 5

Walk (5x) 2:1; 3:4; 9:20; 16:15; 21:24
War (verb) (6x): 2:16; 12:7*; 13:4; 17:14; 19:11

APPENDIX: REPETITION OF KEY TERMS AND PHRASES

War (noun) (9x) 9:7, 9; 11:7; 12:7, 17; 13:7; 16:14; 19:19; 20:8
   (7x) 11:7; 12:7, 17; 13:7; 16:14; 19:19; 20:8 war led by Dragon or his agents v people of God/Angels
   "To make war"
      2:16; 19:11 Christ makes war
      11:7 "with them"
      12:17 "with the rest of her offspring"
      13:7 "with the saints"
      19:19 "the One sitting upon the horse and with His army"
   (3x) 16:14; 19:19; 20:8 "to gather them for the war"; or having been gathered to make war

Was given (22x) 6:2, 4*, 8, 11; 7:2; 8:2, 3; 9:1, 3, 5; 11:1, 2; 13:5*, 7*, 14, 15; 16:8; 19:8; 20:4

Washed 7:14; 22:14 (see clothes)

Waters (18x) 1:15; 7:17; 8:10, 11*; 11:6; 12:15; 14:2, 7; 16:4, 5, 12; 17:1, 15; 19:6; 21:6; 22:1, 17
   Many waters (4x; 3x as a voice 1:15; 14:2; 19:6; 17:1 (woman sitting on)
   See also:
      Sea: (26x) 4:6; 5:13; 7:1, 2, 3; 8:8*, 9; 10:2, 5, 6, 8; 12:12, 18; 13:1; 14:7; 15:2*; 16:3*; 18:17, 19, 21; 20:8, 13; 21:1
      Lake (of fire) (6x) 19:20; 20:10, 14*, 15; 21:8
      River (8x) 8:10; 9:14; 12:15, 16; 16:4, 12; 22:1, 2
      Spring (5x) 7:17; 8:10; 14:7; 16:4; 21:6
      Water of life: 22:1, 17

Wealth 18:19

Weep (6x) 5:4, 5; 18:9, 11, 15, 19

Went up (12x) 4:1; 7:2; 8:4; 9:2; 11:7, 12; 13:1, 11; 14:11; 17:8; 19:3; 20:9

Where (8x) 2:13*; 11:8; 12:6, 14; 14:4; 17:9; 20:10

White (16x) 1:14*; 2:17; 3:4, 5, 18; 4:4; 6:2, 11; 7:9, 13, 14; 14:14; 19:11, 14*; 20:11

Wilderness (3x) 12:6, 14; 17:3: cognate "lay waste/desolate"3x: 17:16; 18:17, 19

Wine (8x) 6:6; 14:8, 10, 19, 20; 16:19; 17:2; 18:3, 13; 19:15
   Related to wrath (5x) 14:10, 19; 20; 16:19; 19:15

Wine press (4x) 14:19, 20*; 19:15

Witness (4x)(verb) 1:2; 22:16, 18, 20

Witness (noun) (5x) 1:5; 2:13; 3:14; 11:3; 17:6
   1st 3 times refers to Christ (always includes faithful)
   4th Two Witnesses
   5th blood of the saints who bore witness to Jesus

Woe (14x) 8:13**; 9:12*; 11:14*; 12:12; 18:10*, 16*, 19*

Woman/women (19x) 2:20; 9:8; 12:1, 4, 6, 13, 14, 15, 16, 17; 14:4; 17:3, 4, 6, 7, 9, 18; 19:7; 21:9

Word (18x) 1:2, 3, 9; 3:8, 10; 6:9; 12:11; 17:17; 19:9, 13; 20:4; 21:5; 22:6, 7, 9, 10, 18, 19
   Word of God and testimony of Jesus (See: Testimony)
   Word(s) of God (7x): 1:2, 9; 6:9; 17:17; 19:9 (true words), 13 (Name of Jesus); 20:4
   Word of God and the testimony of Jesus Christ (1:2)
   Word of God and the testimony of Jesus (1:9)
   Word of God and their testimony (6:9)
   Words of God (17:17)
   (true) Words of God (19:9)
   Testimony of Jesus (19:10)
   Word of God (19:13)
   Testimony of Jesus and the Word of God (20:4)
   8th: These words are faithful and true (22:6): not "word of God" to keep it at 7?

Word of my perseverance 3:10

Word of their testimony 12:11

Words of this book 22:9

Words of the prophecy of this book 22:9

APPENDIX: REPETITION OF KEY TERMS AND PHRASES

Works/Deeds: (20x) 2:2, 5, 6, 19*, 22, 23, 26; 3:1, 2, 8, 15; 9:20; 14:13; 15:3; 16:11; 18:6; 20:12, 13; 22:12 (12x in 7 messages)

Worship (24x) 3:9; 4:10; 5:14; 7:11; 9:20; 11:1, 16; 13:4*, 8, 12, 15; 14:7, 9, 11; 15:4; 16:2; 19:4, 10*, 20; 20:4; 22:8, 9
  Elders worship (4x) 4:10; 5:14; 11:16; 19:4
  Angels worship 7:11

Worthy (7x) 3:4; 4:11; 5:2, 4, 9, 12; 16:6
  4:11 Worthy are You, our Lord and our God, to receive glory and honor and power
  5:12 Worthy is the Lamb that was slain to receive power and riches and wisdom and strength and honor and glory and blessing

Wound (See Plague)

Wrath/passion (10x) 12:12; 14:8, 10, 19; 15:1, 7; 16:1, 19; 18:3; 19:15
  Anger/Wrath of God (7x) 14:10, 19; 15:1, 7; 16:1, 19; 19:15

Write/written: (29x) 1:3, 11, 19; 2:1, 8, 12, 17, 18; 3:1, 7, 12, 14; 5:1; 10:4*; 13:8; 14:1, 13; 17:5, 8; 19:9, 12, 16; 20:12, 15; 21:5, 27; 22:18, 19
  "Write"—command (12x) 1:11, 19; 2:1, 8, 12, 18; 3:1, 7, 14; 14:13; 19:9; 21:5

Zion 14:1

Scripture Index

Old Testament

Genesis

1:2	235
1:11–12	160
1:20–23	160
1:26–28	343n22
1:26–27	98, 160
1:26	243n40, 395
1:28	243n40, 386n39
2:8	407
2:11–12	388
3:1–5	169n30, 224n51
3:22–24	397
3:22	391n4
3:24	382n25, 391n4
12	151
12:2	151
12:3	110n23, 151
13:16	151n44
15	151
16:6	151n44
17:5	151n45
19:1–29	205n62
22:17–18	151n45
26:4	151n44, 151n45
37	217
37:4	362n29
37:9	217, 217n11
48:19	151n45
49:9–10	43, 106, 106n3
51:2	151n45

Exodus

2:15	221n31
2:23–25	178, 204
2:23	178
2:25	204
3–4	204
3:1–4:17	381n16
7:14–25	203n54
7:14–21	285n5
7:14	179n56
8:1–15	287n9
8:10	240n31
13:20–22	182n8
13:21–22	222n38
14:8–10	229n59
14:13–25	287n8
14:19–20	353n16
14:20	182n8
14:24	182n6, 182n8
15	277, 278
15:1–18	108n17, 109n18
15:1–17	277n7
15:2–4	278
15:3–4	278n8
15:4	278
15:11	240n31, 278n8
15:12	230n63
15:14–16	278
15:22	221n32
16:4–35	221n33
16:10	182n6, 182n8
16:13	353n16

Exodus (continued)

17:7	221n29
19–20	381n17
19:3–23	381n18
19:4–6	112
19:4	230
19:5–6	113
19:6	52
19:9	182n8
19:10	408
19:14–15	143n15
19:14	408
19:16–18	279n14
19:16	60, 182n8
19:18	134n54, 135
23:20	222n41
24:6	273n7
24:15–16	182n8
24:18	182n8
25:29	273n7
25:33	61
26:31–33	387n41
27:3	273n7
27:20–21	61n19
28:3	273n7
28:4–8	63n31
28:17–20	388n44
32:13	151n44
33:20	394
37:16	273n7
39:8–14	388n44
40:34–37	182n8
40:34–35	279n14
40:35	382n23
40:36–38	182n6

Leviticus

16:2	182n6
24:4	61n19
26:11–12	370
26:26	128n31

Numbers

1:3	142n14
1:18	142n14
1:20	142n14
11:25	182n6
12:5	182n6
14:14	182n6, 182n8
26:1–65	142n14
31:19–20	146n29, 147n35
31:24	146n29

Deuteronomy

1:10	151n44
1:30	221n26
1:33	182n8
2:7	222n37
4:1–2	410n21
4:11	182n8
5:2	182n8
8:3	221n33, 221n35, 222n39
8:14–16	221n28, 222
10:17	344n22
10:22	151n44, 152n49
12:32	410n21
17:6	200n39, 207n68
17:14–17	251n13
19:15	200n39, 207n68
23:9–14	257n8
28:62	151n44
29:18	165n11
29:19–20	410n21
29:19	165
31:15	182n6
31:30–43	277n7
32:10–12	230n61
32:10	221n33, 221n35
32:32	205n62
33:17	108n14, 236n16
34:1–4	381n18

Joshua

1:11	353n16
3:5	143n15
6	163n5
6:20	60

SCRIPTURE INDEX

Judges

3:27–29	163n5
7:16–22	163n5
5:1	277
5:2–31	277

1 Samuel

2:9	162
7:10	124n16
21:5	257n8

2 Samuel

11	143n15
11:9–13	257n8
17:11	151n44
24:1–9	142n14

1 Kings

1:34	163n5
1:39	163n5
3:8	151n44
4:20	151n44
6:20–28	387n41
6:20–22	388n45
6:20	386n34
7:15–22	90n62
7:23–26	100
8:10	382n23
10:14	250n13
17:1	203n53
17:2–6	221n33, 221n35
17:2–3	221n30
18:1	208
19:3–8	221n33, 221n35
19:3–4	221n30
19:14–18	209n74
22:11	108n14, 236n16
22:19	97n11; 98n12

2 Kings

1:8	201n41, 201n42
7:1	128n31
9:13	163n5
9:22	170n36

1 Chronicles

27:23	142n14

2 Chronicles

9:13	250n13

Ezra

2:13	250n13

Nehemiah

4:20	163n5
9:12	182n6, 182n8
9:19–21	222n39
9:19	182n6, 182n8
9:21	222
9:23	151n44
11:1	197n29
11:18	197n29

Job

9:13	218n14
26:12–13	218n14
37:2–5	124n16
41:1–34	218n14

Psalms

1:4	266n11
2	217, 217n12, 255n2
2:6	255n2, 256n3
2:7	217
2:9	217, 342
9:9	58n8
13:1–2	131n41
17:8	230n61
18:2	108n14
18:7–9	279n14
18:7	135n55
23	148n39
29:3–4	124n16
29:3	369n6
29:10	369n6
30:7	394n12

SCRIPTURE INDEX

Psalms (continued)

33:3	108n17		
35:10	240n31		
36:7–8	230n61		
40:3	108n17		
46:9	126n22		
63:1–2	230n61		
63:7	230n61		
68:7–8	134n50		
69:24	274n14		
71:19	240n31		
74:10	131n41		
74:12	369n6		
74:13–14	229n59, 369		
74:13	219n17		
74:14	219n17		
77:16–19	369n6		
78:14	182n6, 182n8		
79:5	131n41		
86:8–10	278n8		
89:10	219n17, 369		
84:11	69n49		
89:17	108n14, 236n16		
91:4	230n61		
91:11–13	230n61		
95:8–11	221n29		
96:1–3	108n17		
96:1	108n17		
98:1–2	278n8		
98:1	108n17		
104:28	369n6		
104:32	279n14		
105:39	182n6		
110:1	63		
136:16	221n30		
144:9	108n17		
149:1	108n17		

Proverbs

1–9	317
1:7	xviii
5:4	165
8:29	369n6
30:6	410n21
30:27	168n25

Isaiah

1:16–20	47
1:16	203n50
1:21	305n22, 316n30
2:12	203n50
2:16	203n50
4:5	182n6
6	110
6:1–6	279n14
6:1–4	97n11, 98n12
6:1	381, 381n19
6:2–3	101n29
8:14	224n50
10:22	151n44
11:1–10	106n3
11:1	106
11:2	49
11:4	66, 67, 203n50
11:10	106
11:14	342
12:1–6	277n7
13:10–13	133n48, 134
14:2	220n23
14:12–21	224n50
19:15	203n50
19:21	203n50
20:2	201n42
21:5	126n22
23–24	306n25
23:16–17	300n3, 316n30
24:1–6	133n48, 134n50
24:17–23	133n48
24:18–20	134n54
24:19–23	134n50
24:21–23	134n51
25:6–9	327
25:8	370n12
27	306n25
27:1	369, 369n6
28:16	224n50
29:6	134n54
30:7	219n17
34:4–5	134n51
34:4	133n48
40–66	382n23
40:3	222n41, 230n61
40:18	240

40:25	240n31	\multicolumn{2}{c}{Jeremiah}
40:31	230n61		
41:1	164n8	1:11–12	147n34
42:6	82n26	2:2	327n22
42:10	108n17	2:20–28	305n22
43:10	46	3:6–10	316n30
43:18–19	370n12	3:20	306
44:2	70	4:5–21	163n5
44:7	240n31	4:23–28	134n50, 134n51
45:16	164n8	4:23–26	135n55
46:5	240n31	5:14	203
47:5	162n1	5:21	76
47:9–10	170n36	6:1	163n5
48:2	197n29	6:13	209n74
48:5	170n36	6:17	163n5
48:19	151n44	7:5–11	170n36
48:20	321n7	9:15	165, 165n11
49:1	164n8	10:6–7	278n8
49:2	66	10:25	274n14
49:6	82n26	13:27	305n22
49:10	149n41, 370n12	23:15	165, 165n11
49:18	327n22	23:16–17	305n23
49:22	164n8	31:2	222
50:1	369n9	38:10	164n8
51:2	151n44	49:36	140n6
51:3	380n11	50–51	302n8, 306n25
51:5	164n8	50:8	321n7
51:9–10	229n59	50:42	126n22
51:9	219n17	51:6	321n7
52:1	197n29	51:13	307n1
52:11	321n7	51:25–26	163n6
52:13–53:12	43, 44n23	51:25	164n8
52:13	381n19	51:33	266n11
53	107n13	51:45	321n7
53:7	62n22, 107n13		
54:5–6	327n22	\multicolumn{2}{c}{Lamentations}
54:10	135n55		
55:1	409n19	2:10–11	162n1
58:8	382n23	3:15	165
59:2	394n12	3:19	165
60:1–2	382n23		
60:5	383n26	\multicolumn{2}{c}{Ezekiel}
60:9	164n8		
60:11	383n26	1	110
60:19	382n23	1:3	188n27
61:10–62:5	327n24	1:1—3:11	97n11
62:5	327n22	1:4	182n6, 182n8
63:3	339, 340	1:5–21	101n28

Ezekiel (continued)

1:6	101n30
1:10	101
1:13	97
1:22–28	188
1:22	100
1:26–28	97n11, 98n12
1:27–28	98
1:27	97
1:28	70
2:1	62
2:3	188
2:8—3:3	13n5, 180, 184, 188
2:8—3:1	188
2:9–10	188
2:10	184
3:3	185, 188
3:4	185, 188
3:27	76
4:10	128n31
4:16	128n31
6:8	141
9	141, 145n24, 191n5
9:4	141
9:5–6	141
10:1	97n11, 98n12
10:12–15	101n28
10:12	100n24
10:18	392
10:20–22	101n28
14:19	274n14
16:8–14	369n9
16:15–63	327n22
16:15–52	306n25
16:15–22	316n30
16:15	305n22, 306
16:16	306
16:17	306
23:1–49	316n30
26–28	302n8, 306n25
26:18	135n55, 164n8
27:32	162n1
28:13	388, 391n3
29:3	219, 221n26, 229n59
31:16	391n3
32:2–3	219n17
32:6–8	133n48, 134n50
34	342n20
34:11–16	148n39
34:25	221n36
36:20–21	82
36:35	380n11
37–48	335
37:26–28	148
37:26–27	370
38–39	289n17, 353
38:2	335, 353n13
38:3	335
38:14	335
38:16	335
38:18	335
38:19–22	293n25
39	345n2
39:1	335, 353n13
39:4	136n57, 356n22
39:6	335, 353n13
39:11	335
39:17–20	136n57, 335, 356n22
39:23	81
40–48	147n33, 191, 191n5, 192n6, 195n19, 391, 393
40:1–9	384n30
40:3–49	391
40:2	381, 381n16
40:5	192n7
40:6	192n7
40:8	192n7
40:9	192n7
40:11	192n7
40:13	192n7
40:19	192n7
40:20	192n7
40:23	192n7
40:24	192n7
40:27	192n7
40:28	192n7
41:1	192n7

41:2	192n7	7:4–7	236n15
41:4	192n7	7:4–6	238
41:5	192n7	7:6	219n20, 236n15, 240n32
41:13	192n7		
41:15	192n7	7:7—8:24	108n14
42:15	192n7	7:7	237
42:16	192n7	7:8	240n32
42:17	192n7	7:9–28	97n11
42:18	192n7	7:9	64, 65, 65n36, 65n37, 97n11, 98n12, 391n7
42:19	192n7		
42:20	192n7		
43:2	66	7:10	341n14, 391n7
43:10	192n7	7:11	240n32
45:1–5	387n40	7:13	53, 63, 265n7, 266n13
45:2	387n40		
45:3	192n7	7:17	238, 243
47:1–12	390n2, 392	7:18	113n29
47:1–7	380n11	7:20	240n32
47:1	392, 392n9	7:21	208
47:3	192n7	7:22	391n7
47:4	192n7	7:25	199n35, 200n36, 240n32
47:5	192n7		
47:9	392	7:26	391n7
47:12	392, 393	8:8	140n6
47:18	192n7	8:10	220n21
48:31–34	392	8:11–13	223n48, 223n49
		8:11	223n49, 240n30
Daniel		8:13	223n47
		8:25	240n30
2:28–29	41n16	9:24	197n29
2:28	41, 42, 42n17, 404	10:4	405n11
2:29	42, 42n17, 404	10:10–18	70
2:33	65	10:10	70
2:34–35	41	10:12	70
2:35	41, 164n8, 266n11	11:4	140n6
		11:7	208
2:36–43	41	11:30–39	147n34
2:41–43	65	11:36–37	240n30
2:44	41	11:36	240n32
2:45	41n16, 42, 42n17, 164n8, 404	11:44	147n34
		12:1	147n34
7–12	147n33	12:4	406
7–8	237	12:7	199n34, 200n36
7	235, 236, 238, 243	12:10	147n34, 250n11, 406
7:1–28	391n7		
7:1–8	219n20, 238		
7:3–7	253		

SCRIPTURE INDEX

Hosea

1:10	151n44
2:5	305n22
2:14–23	327n22
2:14–20	327n24
2:14	221n33
2:18	126n22
3:1–4:2	170n36
4:5	369n9
4:12–13	316n30
4:17–18	305n24
5:3	316n30
10:8	133n48

Joel

1:10–11	128n32
2:1	163n5
2:10	133n48, 134n50, 134n54
2:15	163n5
2:30–31	133n48, 134n50
2:28–32	40
3:13	266n12
3:15–16	133n48, 134n50
3:16	134n54
3:18	390n2
3:19	205n61

Amos

3:8	106n4
3:13	341n14
5:3	209n74
7:1–9	294
8:2–3	162n1
8:8–9	134n50

Jonah

3:4–10	201n41

Micah

1:4	135n55
4:12	266n11
5:12–6:8	170n36

Nahum

1:4	369n6
1:14	170n36
3:1–4	170n36
3:4	300n3, 316n30

Habakkuk

3:6–11	133n48, 134n50
3:6	135n55
3:8–15	219n17

Zephaniah

1:17	162n1
1:11	162n1
2:11	135n55
3:8	274n14

Zechariah

1–6	147n33
1:18–21	108n14
2:13—3:2	162n1
2:1–5	191n5
2:2	192n8
3:1–5	131n43
4	202, 202n46
4:1–14	202n45
4:2–10	62
4:2–6	72n57, 100
4:2–3	202, 202n44
4:2	62, 99n18
4:3	62, 99n18
4:6	62, 71n55, 72, 99n18, 100
4:10	99n18
4:11	202n44
4:14	202
6	140
6:1–8	140
6:2–3	140
6:4	140
6:5	140
12:11	289n14
14:4	135n55
14:5	341n14
14:8	390n2

SCRIPTURE INDEX

Malachi

3:1	222n41
3:2	133n47

New Testament

Matthew

2:15	222n42
2:16	220n25
3:3	222n41
3:12	266n11
3:13–17	226n55
3:17	217n12
4:1–11	215n2, 222n44
4:1	222n43
4:5	197n29
4:8	380n15
5–7	381n18
5:1	381n16, 381n18
5:4	32
5:6	32
5:9	291
5:10	45n28
5:14–16	61n22, 72n57, 72n58
5:17	204n55
6:10	214
6:24	260
7:12	204n55
7:14	58n6
8:20	62n26
9:37–38	265n11
11:17	76n9
11:21	201n41
12:8	62n26
13	215n4
13:9	76n9
13:18	40
13:40–42	341n14
17:2	69
17:6	70
18:11	71n54
22:40	204n55
24:1–14	122n11
24:4	248n9
24:24	122n12
24:31	140n6, 163n5
24:43	288n11
25:31–32	341n14
26:45	62n26, 63
26:61	192n10, 192n11
26:64	53n48, 266n13
26:65	63n29
27:53	197n29
28:18–20	364
28:19	49n37

Mark

1:3	222
1:6	201n41, 201n42
1:9–11	226n55
1:11	217n12
1:12–13	215n2, 222n44
1:24	338n6
3:20–30	360
3:23–30	215n5
2:28	62n26
3:27	215n3, 360
4:1–11	215n4
4:3–9	76n10, 360
4:4	215n4
4:9	40, 76n9
4:10	76n10
4:11	71n54
4:14	215n4
4:15	360
4:21–22	72n58
4:21	61, 61n21
4:23	40, 76n9
4:29	265n11
4:33–34	77n10
5:9	338n6
8:33	360
8:38	341n14
9:2–9	381n16
9:2–8	381n18
9:3	69n50
9:7	217n12
10:42–45	171n39
10:42–44	19
13	122–23, 125
13:2	122

SCRIPTURE INDEX

Mark (continued)

13:4	122
13:5–13	122
13:6–13	122n11
13:6	122, 125
13:7–8	122
13:8	122, 122n13
13:9–10	123
13:12	123
13:13	123
13:14–20	223n49
13:14	250n11
13:22	122n12
13:24–26	133n48
13:24–25	134n50
13:26	266n13
14:62	53n48

Luke

3:4	222n41
3:17	266n11
3:21–22	226n55
3:22	217n12
4:1–13	222n44
4:13	201n41
4:28–30	220n25
4:29	196n25, 197n27
8:8	76n9
8:10	71n54
8:16–17	72n58
9:29	69n50
10:18–20	168
10:18	226
10:19	269n24
12:39–40	288n11
14:35	76n9
15:1—17:10	7n7
15:1–2	7n7
15:3–32	7n7
15:3	7n7
15:11	7n7
16:1	7n7
16:14	7n7
17:1	7n7
17:11–12	7n7
17:22	62n26
20:17	224n50
21:9–19	122n11
21:11	122n13
21:20–24	223n49
21:24	269n24
21:27	53n48, 266n13
21:51	67
22:3	360
22:25–26	52
22:29	52
24:27	204n55

John

1:1–3	340
1:24–29	226n55
3:13	62n26
3:16	2
4:10	148n40
4:14	371
4:35–38	265n11
5:35	72n57
6:35	149n41
7:37–39	148n40, 390n2
8:44	215n5
9:34–35	197n27
10:1–30	342n20
12:21	197n27
12:31	226
12:32	226
13:2	215n5
13:27	215n5, 360
14:3	223n46
16:33	58, 147n34
18:11	67

Acts

1:8	72
1:15–26	98n14
2:19–20	40, 133n48, 134n50
4:25–27	217n12
7:10	58n7
7:11	58n7
7:39–43	222n40
7:48	382n25

448

7:58	197n27	**2 Corinthians**	
8:25–40	108n13	1:2	47n33
8:35	44n23	1:21–22	141
11:19	58	3:17	62n25
13:15	204n55	4:4	215n4
13:33	217n12	4:8	58n6
14:22	58, 147n34	6:4	58n6
15:20	170n36	6:14–7:1	398n24
19:23–41	85n38	6:16	192n10, 192n12, 193
20:23	58	7:5	58n6
24:14	204n55	11:2	327n24
		11:3	224n51
Romans		11:13–14	125
1:1	51n42	11:14	224n51
1:7	47n33	13:14	49n37
1:18–32	120n6		
1:18	81	**Galatians**	
1:21	81	1:1	51n42
1:24–29	170n36	1:3	47n33
1:24	81, 120	3:28	57n2
1:26	81, 120	5:20	170n36
2:4	2, 209		
3:21	204n55	**Ephesians**	
5–8	222n40	1:2	47n33
5:3	147n34	1:9	71n54
5:8	2	1:13	141
8:14–17	57n2	1:14	141
8:35–36	147n34	2:18–20	398n24
11:25	71n54	3:3	71n54
16:20	224n51	4:4–6	49n37
16:25	71n54	5:5	170n36
1 Corinthians		**Philippians**	
1:3	47n33	1:1	51n42
3:16	192n10, 192n12, 193	1:2	47n33
3:17	192n10, 192n12, 193	1:10	136n59
5:5	136n59	2:16	136n59
6:19	398n24	2:19–22	193n16
8:4–6	86n46	4:14	58n6
8:4	84n36		
10:1–13	222n40		
12:4–5	49n37		
12:12–27	57n2		
15:51–52	163n5		
15:51	71n54		

SCRIPTURE INDEX

Colossians

1:2	47n33
1:24	58n6
1:26	71n54
1:27	71n54
2:2	71, 71n54
3:5	170n36

1 Thessalonians

1:1	47n33
1:6	58n6
3:3	58n6
3:4	58n6
4:16–17	341n14
4:16	163n5
5:2	136n59, 288n11
5:4	288n11

2 Thessalonians

1:2	47n33
1:4	58n6
1:7	65, 341n14
2:2–3	136n59
2:4	192n10, 192n12
2:9	248n9

1 Timothy

5:10	58n6
6:15	344n22

2 Timothy

3:12	147n34

Titus

1:1	51n42

Philemon

1:3	47n33

Hebrews

1:5	217n12
2:14	226
3:7—4:7	222n40, 222n45
3:8–11	221n29
4:12	68–69
9:7	387n42
10:33	58n6
11:37	58n6
11:38	222n40
12:26–27	293n26

James

1:1	51n42

1 Peter

1:2	49n37
2:4–10	193n16
2:9	52
2:23	62n22
5:8	228
5:13	264n5, 305n20, 309

2 Peter

1:1	51n42
2:2	47n33
3:6	398
3:9	31
3:10	136n59, 288n11

1 John

3:8	226

2 John

1:3	47n33

Jude

1:1	51n42, 51n43
1:2	47n33, 51n43
1:14–15	341n14

Revelation

Reference	Pages
1:1–8	5, 24n14, 37–54, 379
1:1–3	37–47, 402
1:1	17, 25, 37–45, 47, 51n43, 52n44, 187, 379n8, 379n9, 402, 403, 404, 405, 408
1:2	25, 45, 45n26, 131n39, 131n40, 340, 351, 351n7
1:3	5, 5n12, 45–47, 404; 404n9, 405
1:4–8	47–54
1:4–5	48–51, 99
1:4	5, 18, 23, 24, 25, 44, 47–49, 53, 99, 210, 302n9, 366n1, 410
1:5–6	49–52
1:5	18, 19, 25, 49–51, 403, 408, 409
1:6	18, 51, 58n3, 71, 99, 112, 117, 195n24, 202, 352, 395
1:7–8	53–54
1:7	53, 182, 182n9, 266n13, 384
1:8	23, 24, 49, 53, 54, 210, 343, 371n13, 407, 407n16
1:9—22:9	6
1:9—3:22	4, 6–10, 12–13, 41, 57–91, 206, 284, 299, 333n3, 379n7
1:9–11	57–60
1:9–10	6, 8, 380n12
1:9	7, 12, 25, 44, 45n26, 47, 51n43, 57–60, 123, 131n39, 131n40, 147n34, 216, 228, 340, 351, 351n7, 379n7
1:10	6, 8, 12, 60, 380n13
1:10–11	12, 60
1:11	9, 25, 47, 60
1:12–20	9, 41, 51
1:12–16	49, 60–70
1:12	25n17, 60, 61–62, 201, 379n7, 408
1:13–18	220
1:13–16	60
1:13	53, 62–63, 64n32, 72, 202, 265n7, 266n15, 279
1:14–16	64–70
1:14	64–65, 277n6, 337, 337n4
1:15	65–66, 256, 409
1:16	66–70, 126, 182, 230, 230n62, 341, 395n15, 403n7
1:17–20	70–72
1:17–18	51
1:17	23, 51, 53, 60, 70, 407
1:18	18, 19, 42, 64, 71, 73, 208, 361, 361n28
1:19	60, 96n2
1:20	22, 25, 43, 61, 66, 71–72, 162n3, 202, 362n29
2:1—3:22	9, 25, 40, 41, 48, 59, 74–91
2:1	9n23. 25n17, 63, 75, 162n3, 202
2:2	59, 59n9
2:3	59, 59n9
2:5	18, 26, 78, 79n16, 80, 80n22, 202
26	78, 87
2:7	4n9, 38, 40n13, 48, 76, 77, 78, 79, 99, 115n38, 407
2:8	9n23, 23, 53, 75, 162n3, 407
2:9–10	147n34
2:9	58n4, 58n6, 78, 89

SCRIPTURE INDEX

Revelation (continued)

2:10	58n4, 58n6, 84, 208
2:11	4n9, 38, 40n13, 48, 76, 77, 78, 79, 99, 115n38, 352n12
2:12	9n23, 66n40, 69, 75, 126, 162n3, 403n7
2:13	18n6, 50, 87, 87n47, 89, 104, 366n1
2:14–15	84
2:15	87
2:16	18, 26, 79, 79n16, 80, 80n22, 126, 230n62, 290, 290n21, 403n7
2:17	4n9, 38, 40n13, 48, 76, 77, 78, 79, 99, 115n38
2:18–29	79
2:18	9n23, 75, 79n17, 162n3, 277n6, 337n4
2:19	59, 59n9
2:20–23	86, 318
2:20	27, 51n43, 52n44, 244, 347n7
2:21	26, 79, 79n16, 80n22, 81
2:22	147n34
2:22–23	80, 80n23
2:22	26, 58n4, 79, 79n16, 80n22
2:23	77, 80n20, 337n4
2:24	89
2:26	79, 115n38
2:27	342
2:28	409
2:29	4n9, 38, 40n13, 48, 76, 77, 78, 99
3:1	9n23, 24, 49, 75, 162n3
3:3	26, 79, 79n16, 80, 80n22, 288, 288n13
3:4	288, 288n13, 289
3:5	78, 99, 115n38, 131n43, 162n3, 186n20, 288, 288n13, 341
3:6	4n9, 38, 40n13, 48, 76, 77, 78, 99
3:7	9n23, 75, 162n3, 169n30, 230, 361
3:8	361n28
3:9	78, 89
3:10	59, 59n9, 110n24, 165n14, 241n35
3:11	18
3:12	23, 78, 90, 115n38, 192n10, 192n13, 193, 269n26, 269n28, 330, 369n8, 395n14
3:13	4n9, 38, 40n13, 48, 76, 77, 78, 99
3:14	9n23, 75, 162n3, 230, 337n 371n14, 403
3:16	230n62
3:18	99, 131n43, 277n6, 341
3:19	26, 79, 79n16, 80, 80n22, 82
3:21	13n3, 18, 38, 50, 51, 53n50, 54n51, 78, 90, 90n61, 91, 115n38, 148n38, 221, 225, 227, 302n9, 314, 366n1, 390, 394
3:22	4n9, 38, 40n13, 48, 76, 77, 78, 99
4:1—16:21	4, 6–10, 12, 13–14, 41, 75, 90, 96, 103, 114, 116, 119, 170, 176n50, 189, 211, 270, 284, 292, 295,

SCRIPTURE INDEX

	299, 333n3, 378, 379	4:9	102, 104, 302n9, 366n1
4:1—5:14	95–118, 119, 155, 155n14, 209, 257, 390, 393	4:10	26, 98n15, 102, 144n20, 211n2, 302n9, 366n1
4–10	97n11	4:11	100, 102, 103, 113, 113n42
4–5	97n11		
4:1–11	95–104, 383	5	180, 187, 363n31
4:1–3	216n6	5:1–14	182, 183–87, 325, 325n17
4:1–2	7, 8, 9, 13, 90, 96, 216, 231n64, 310	5:1–6	103n35
4:1	5n10, 8, 8n22, 90, 96, 96n2, 279n12, 282, 373, 378n5, 379n8, 379n9, 380n12	5:1–4	105
		5:1	9, 13, 103n35, 105, 138, 182, 302n9, 366n1
		5:2	105, 181, 182, 182n5, 292n22, 325n17
4:2–3	38, 90n61, 96–98, 393n11		
4:2	6, 8, 9, 13, 14, 96, 97, 302n9, 366n1, 373, 378, 378n6, 380n13	5:3–4	9, 114
		5:3	13, 105
		5:4	13, 105, 114
		5:5–7	90n61
4:3	97, 182, 302n9, 366n1, 382, 383, 387	5:5–6	9, 13, 115, 106–8, 150
		5:5	25n19, 26, 43, 50, 98n15, 106, 115, 169, 183, 225, 339, 384, 408
4:4–8	98–102		
4:6–8	274		
4:4	23, 26, 98–99, 103, 131n43, 144n20, 211n2, 302n9, 366n1	5:6	24, 25, 26, 43, 49, 65, 98n15, 102, 106–8, 107n11, 127, 127n28, 171, 236n16, 239, 240, 302n9, 366n1
4:5	24, 49, 71n55, 99, 108, 155, 277n6, 292, 302n9, 366n1		
		5:7–9	108–11
4:6–8	100–102, 274	5:7	13, 54n50, 108, 302n9, 325n17, 366n1
4:6	23, 100, 258, 272n6, 277, 302n9, 366n1, 368n2, 390		
		5:8	25, 26, 98n15, 102, 108, 108n16, 144n20, 159, 159n22, 160, 160n22, 160n23, 176, 176n50, 181, 195n22, 204, 211n2, 267, 272, 273, 273n8, 273n9, 274
4:7	101, 182n7		
4:8–11	97, 102–4		
4:8	23, 24, 49, 54, 54n53, 100, 102, 103, 108n15, 113n42, 210, 343		
4:9–10	211n3		

453

SCRIPTURE INDEX

Revelation (*continued*)

5:9–10	206, 214, 321
5:9	108, 109, 111, 220, 227, 239, 240, 258, 338, 384
5:10–14	112–114
5:10	18, 71, 99n17, 112, 112n28, 195n24, 352n10
5:11–12	146
5:11	26, 98n15, 102, 113, 144n20, 302n9, 366n1
5:12	25, 113, 116, 127, 127n28, 146, 146n32, 292n22
5:13	25, 113, 302n9, 366n1, 368n2
5:14	23, 26, 98n15, 102, 114
6	187
6:1–17	13, 119–37, 140, 154n5, 174
6:1–8	119–30, 140, 174
6:1–2	122, 124–26, 174
6:1	23, 25, 29n5, 123, 124, 124n15, 131, 157
6:2	123n14, 124, 124n17, 124n18, 125, 126, 126n24, 157, 337
6:3–4	126–27, 141n11, 174
6:3	123, 131, 157
6:4	124, 126, 126n24, 127, 127n28, 157, 219n18
6:5–6	127–29, 128n33, 174
6:5	123, 124, 124n14, 124n17, 127, 131, 157
6:6	23, 127, 128
6:7–8	130, 174
6:7	123, 131
6:8	79n17, 123, 124, 124n14, 124n17, 126n24, 130, 154n8, 335
6:9–17	130–37
6:9–11	131–33, 174, 195, 227, 350, 350n4, 350n5
6:9	45n26, 124, 127, 127n28, 131, 157, 195, 195n22, 227, 231, 340, 350, 351, 351n7
6:10	1n4, 15, 31, 110n24, 123, 131, 136, 137, 165n14, 174, 204, 216, 241n35, 267, 268, 268n21, 292n22, 326, 350
6:11	15, 20, 31, 126n24, 131, 131n43, 132, 147, 177, 188, 213, 341
6:12–17	133–37, 138, 139n5, 153, 162, 174
6:12–14	134
6:12–13	39
6:12	124n15, 293, 395n15
6:13	362n29
6:14–16	164n7
6:14	135, 164n8
6:15	51n43, 52n44, 135, 136, 164n8
6:16	25, 135, 136, 137, 164n8, 302n9, 366n1
6:17	133, 135, 136, 150, 163n4, 174, 277n5, 345n1
7:1–17	110n23, 138–52, 153, 154, 180, 181, 191, 217, 384n31
7:1–8	139–45, 158, 180
7:1–3	368n2

7:1–2	139–40		146n32, 147, 149,
7:1	23, 139, 140, 150,		152, 286, 341,
	368n2		342, 408
7:2	23, 126n24, 140,	7:15–17	148, 149, 384
	150, 181n4,	7:15	148, 149, 152,
	292n22, 368n2		302n9, 366n1
7:3	51n43, 52n44,	7:16	70n52, 148, 149,
	140, 141–42, 154,		152, 286, 371,
	259n12, 309n6,		395, 395n15
	368n2	7:17	25, 148, 149, 342,
7:3–8	152, 384, 385		366n1
7:4–8	139n5, 142–45,	8:1—9:21	162–79, 181,
	145		268n21
7:4	23, 142, 143, 150,	8:1–6	162–63, 271n3
	259n12, 385	8:1	13, 123, 139n5,
7:5–8	143, 144		154, 154n5, 157,
7:5	259n12, 385		159, 162, 174
7:6	385	8:2	162, 176, 212,
7:7	143, 144, 385		271n3
7:8	144, 259n12, 385	8:2–4	108n16
7:9–17	132, 139, 139n5,	8:2	13, 126n24, 154,
	145–52, 154, 158,		157, 159, 180n2,
	180, 326, 326n18,		271n3, 276
	384	8:3–5	163, 176, 195n22,
7:9–10	145–46		268, 325
7:9	15n9, 24, 25,	8:3–4	159, 159n20, 163,
	96n2, 109n22,	8:3	108n16, 126n24,
	111, 131n43, 138,		159, 159n20,
	145, 150, 152,		159n22, 160, 163,
	302n9, 326n18,		168n27, 176,
	341, 366n1, 384,		176n49, 181,
	385		181n4, 195n22,
7:10	25, 146, 150,		204, 267, 268,
	292n22, 302n9,		271n3, 272,
	326, 366n1		302n9, 321, 326,
7:11–12	146		366n1
7:11	23, 26, 98n15,	8:4	108n16, 159,
	102, 146, 146n32,		159n20, 159n22,
	182n7, 302n9,		160, 176, 176n49,
	366n1		178, 181, 204,
7:12	146		267, 268, 271n3,
7:13–15	327n23		272, 321, 326
7:13–14	147	8:5—11:19	212
7:13	26, 98n15, 147,	8:5	123, 154n5, 155,
	341		156, 157, 159,
7:14–17	370		174, 195n22,
7:14	25, 58n4, 131n43,		271n3, 277n6,
	132, 146, 147–48,		292n23, 293

Revelation (*continued*)

Reference	Pages
8:6—9:21	154
8:6	157, 159, 162, 176, 180n2, 271n3, 276
8:7—9:21	180
8:7–12	163–65, 173
8:7	155n10, 158, 160, 163, 180n2, 277n6
8:8–11	283
8:8–9	158, 164, 368n2
8:8	155n10, 164n8, 164, 180n2, 277n6, 368n2
8:9	155n10, 160, 164, 164n9, 351, 368n2
8:10–11	158, 165
8:10	155n10, 165, 180n2, 220n23
8:11	155n10, 160, 165
8:12	155n10, 158, 160, 165, 180n2, 362n29, 395n15
8:13	110n24, 157, 165–67, 165, 170, 241n35, 292n22
9:1–19	167–79
9:1–12	141n11, 167–68
9:1–11	158, 360
9:1–10	360
9:1–3	167, 363
9:1–2	167
9:1	126n24, 159, 167n21, 180n2, 361, 361n28, 362, 362n29
9:2	167, 167n21, 363, 364
9:3	126n24, 168
9:4	309n6
9:5–6	158
9:5	126n24, 167
9:7	159n19, 182n7, 290, 346n5, 361, 362, 364
9:9	159n19, 167, 290, 346n5, 361, 362
9:10	168, 219, 219n19
9:11–19	361
9:11	167, 167n21, 168, 246
9:12	96n2, 157
9:13–21	158
9:13–19	168–69, 360
9:13	159, 168, 180n2, 195n22
9:14	23, 168, 180n2, 287, 361
9:15	23, 155n10, 168, 361
9:16	144n20, 168
9:17	168n28, 169, 203, 203n51, 230n62
9:18	155n10, 158, 203, 203n51, 230n62
9:19	169, 219, 219n19, 225n53, 230n62, 361, 362
9:20–21	14, 169–70, 177
9:20	26, 79n16, 80n22, 170, 177
9:21	26, 79n16, 80n22
10	180, 363n31
10:1—11:14	180
10:1—11:13	139n5, 154n4, 171, 179, 180–209, 210, 217
10:1–11	13, 13n4, 158, 171, 181, 182, 183–87, 325, 325n17
10:1–2	180, 181–87
10:1	13, 180, 181–83, 184, 262n1, 277n6, 325n17, 395n15, 405
10:2	13, 182, 183, 184, 185, 186, 187, 189, 368n2
10:3–4	155n11, 183, 187
10:3	183, 184, 187, 292n22
10:4	187

SCRIPTURE INDEX

10:5–7	187–88	11:4	201–2, 206
10:5	182n5, 325n17, 368n2	11:5	203, 207, 277n6, 343
10:6	181, 187, 189, 216, 368n2	11:6	46n30, 203–4, 248, 248n10
10:7	51n43, 52n44, 188, 210, 214, 274	11:7	14, 45n26, 131n40, 167, 196, 201, 204–5, 207, 212, 214, 215, 216, 224, 226, 232, 235, 242, 242n37, 246, 270, 290, 307, 312, 346n5, 361
10:8–11	188–89		
10:8	13, 182n5, 185, 186, 187, 189, 325n17, 368n2		
10:9–10	189		
10:9	13, 182n5, 184, 185, 186, 188, 230n62, 325n17		
		11:8–10	205–7
10:10	120n3, 182n5, 184, 185, 186, 188, 230n62, 325n17	11:8	18, 205–6, 207, 256, 263n4, 264n4, 269n27, 293, 310n9
10:11	13, 24, 109n22, 111, 120n3, 189, 185, 188, 189, 190, 192, 200, 385	11:9	24, 25, 109n22, 110, 207–8, 384
		11:10	110, 110n24, 241n35
11:1–19	23n11, 62n23, 171, 172n43	11:11–13	272
		11:11–12	208
11:1–13	14n6, 111, 120n3, 139n5, 158, 181, 189, 190, 193, 213, 215, 270, 275, 343, 385, 385n32	11:11	14, 207–8, 248, 263
		11:12	182n9, 208, 279, 292n22
		11:13	114, 209, 210, 214, 269n27, 270, 279, 287n7, 293
11:1–2	14, 190–94, 200, 223, 269, 386n33	11:14–19	154, 158, 175, 210–14, 270, 292n23
11:1	126n24, 190, 191–96, 197, 386		
11:2	126n24, 193, 194, 196–200, 242, 268n23, 269, 269n24, 269n26, 269n28, 339, 354n17, 386	11:14	157, 181n3, 209, 210
		11:15–19	102n32, 136n56, 274
		11:15	25, 181n3, 230n62, 292n22
11:3–13	14, 191, 194, 194n17, 200–209, 386n33	11:16	23, 26, 43, 98n15, 102, 144n20, 182n7, 211, 211n2, 366n1
11:3–6	200		
11:3–4	191	11:17	23, 24, 48, 54n53, 343
11:3	198, 199, 200, 201, 241		

SCRIPTURE INDEX

Revelation *(continued)*

11:18	51n43, 52n44, 108n16, 161, 175, 211–12, 294
11:19	9n24, 156, 192n10, 212, 216, 271, 293
12–22	9n24
12:1—16:21	212, 215, 216
12–15	216,
12–14	215, 270
12:1—14:20	216, 217, 228, 270
12:1—14:5	216n7
12:1—13:8	212
12:1–18	199, 199n33, 215–33, 342
12:1–17	270, 335, 362, 363
12	89, 214, 215, 218
12:1–2	217, 232n66
12:1	9n24, 169n30, 215, 216, 217, 217n9, 217n11, 218, 362n29
12:2	217
12:3–4	169n30, 218–20, 235
12:3	22, 26, 27, 43n21, 126n23, 217n9, 218, 219, 224, 236, 237, 337, 337n5
12:4	27, 43n21, 219, 219n19, 220, 220n22, 227, 231, 232
12:5–17	232n66
12:5	217, 220, 226, 227, 232, 302n9, 342, 366n1
12:6	199, 199n34, 221–23, 223n49, 224, 226, 227, 241, 305n23
12:7–9	223–24, 227
12:7	27, 43n21, 220, 224, 229, 290, 346, 346n5, 361
12:8–9	224
12:9	27, 43, 43n21, 169n30, 219, 224, 230, 231, 347n7, 349, 362
12:10–12	225–28
12:10	25, 224, 225, 292n22
12:11	25, 45n26, 74, 131n40, 225, 227, 350n5, 351
12:12	166n17, 228, 368n2
12:13–18	229–32
12:13–17	218n13. 227
12:13	27, 43n21, 223, 229, 231, 232
12:14–16	230
12:14	198, 199, 199n34, 229–30, 305n23, 362
12:15	223, 230, 230n62, 232, 362
12:16	27, 43n21, 230, 230n62
12:17	25, 27, 43n21, 45n26, 51n43, 131n40, 230–31, 232, 290, 361
12:18	229n57, 231–32, 368n2
13	89
13:113	89
13:1—14:5	234–61, 271
13:1–18	27n21, 83n33, 229, 231, 253, 304
13:1–10	234
13:1–8	20, 169, 219n20, 235, 236, 237, 256, 288, 307, 335
13:1–2	235–38, 253,
13:1	22, 26, 126n23, 164, 229n57, 235, 236, 237, 240, 337, 337n5, 368n2, 369, 369n4

458

SCRIPTURE INDEX

13:2	27, 43n21, 104, 107n11, 169, 169n33, 229n60, 230n62, 237–38, 366n1	13:14	27, 68–69, 110n24, 126n24, 126n27, 165n14, 203, 217n9, 239, 239n24, 241, 247, 248, 288, 347, 347n7
13:3	125, 127, 127n28, 238–39, 253, 309		
13:4–6	240–42	13:15–17	249–50
13:4	27, 43n21, 244, 253, 290	13:15	30, 126n24, 248, 249–50, 311n16
13:5	126n24, 198, 199, 230n62, 240, 241–42	13:16–17	240
		13:16	51n43, 52n44, 249, 258n11, 309n6, 394n12
13:6	110n24, 230n62, 240, 241	13:17	84, 250, 251, 251n17, 257, 258n11, 259, 311n16, 394n12
13:7–8	242		
13:7	24, 108n16, 109n22, 110, 126n24, 204, 204n57, 224, 240, 241, 242, 244, 253, 271, 290, 346n5, 361, 384	13:18	244, 250, 251, 259, 312
		14:1–5	143, 255–61. 351, 384
		14:1	23, 25, 164n8, 240, 255–56, 258, 259, 309n6, 336
13:8	25, 110, 110n24, 127, 127n28, 165n14, 185, 186n20, 241, 241n35, 242	14:2–3	256
		14:2	124n16, 256, 258, 409
13:9–10	242–43	14:3–4	256–58
13:9	242	14:3	23, 26, 98n15, 102, 108n17, 143, 146n28, 243n39, 256, 257, 258, 259, 302n9, 366n1
13:10	59, 59n9, 68–69, 108n16, 126n27, 242, 243, 260, 264		
13:11–18	20, 235, 240n32, 246, 247–53, 264, 288, 335		
		14:4	25, 143, 256, 257–58, 259, 409
13:11–12	247–48	14:5	230n62, 258, 373n22
13:11	25, 26, 27, 43n21, 231, 247		
13:12–15	248	14:6–20	53n49, 79n17, 262–69, 276, 327n21
13:12	165n14, 239n24, 247–48, 311, 311n16		
		14:6–11	111n27, 165n14, 263–64
13:13–15	248		
13:13–14	288, 354n18	14:6–7	263
13:13	217n9, 248, 277n6, 288		

459

SCRIPTURE INDEX

Revelation (*continued*)

14:6	24, 79n17, 109n22, 111, 181n4, 262, 262n1, 263, 384
14:7	111, 262, 262n2, 263, 264, 292n22, 368n2
14:8	27, 79n17, 181n4, 262, 262n1, 262n2, 263, 264–65, 267, 300, 321
14:9–11	262, 264
14:9–10	264
14:9	79n17, 181n4, 258n11, 262n1, 262, 262n2, 263, 292n22, 309n6, 394n12
14:10	25, 264n6, 277n6
14:11	258n11, 327n21, 351n8, 394n12
14:12–13	50n40 233, 264–65
14:12	25, 51n43, 59, 59n9, 108n16, 264, 265
14:13	45n28, 99, 263, 404, 404n9
14:14–20	136n56, 263, 265–69, 279n13
14:14–16	265, 265n9, 266, 267
14:14	53, 66n40, 99, 182, 182n9, 263, 263n3, 265, 265n8, 266
14:15	79n17, 181n4, 182n9, 262, 263, 263n3, 265, 265n8, 266, 267, 276, 276n1, 279n13, 284, 292n22
14:16	182n9, 263n3, 265n8
14:17–20	265, 265n9, 266–67, 279
14:17	66n40, 79n17, 181n4, 262, 263, 263n3, 265, 265n8, 266, 267, 276, 276n1, 279n13, 284
14:18	66n40, 79n17, 181n4, 195n22, 262, 263n3, 265, 265n8, 267, 268, 276, 276n1, 277n6, 284, 292n22, 310
14:19	263n3, 264n6, 265n8, 266, 268
14:20	198, 267, 268, 269, 269n24, 269n28, 339, 343
15:1—16:21	24n15, 270–95
15:1–8	281–82
15:1	216, 217n9, 264n6, 271, 276, 276n2, 277
15:2–4	275, 277–79
15:2–3	271, 272, 282
15:2	251n17, 271, 272, 272n6, 277, 277n6, 368n2
15:3–4	271, 272, 277
15:3	18, 24, 25, 51n43, 52n44, 54n53, 277, 281, 281n1, 294, 326n20, 343
15:4	275
15:5–8	279–80, 271, 281, 281n1
15:5	96n2, 212, 272, 272n5, 279
15:6	276, 276n2, 279, 284
15:7	23, 264n6, 273, 273n8, 273n9, 274, 276, 276n2
15:8	276, 276n2, 279
16–19	305

16:1–21	136n56, 154n5, 172n43, 187n26, 281–95	16:12–16	24, 287, 356, 357, 358, 361
16:1	264n6, 273n8, 273n10, 274, 274n15, 275, 276, 276n2, 281, 284	16:12–14	287–88
		16:12	155n11, 273n8, 273n10, 274, 274n15, 284, 287, 361
16:2	155n11, 258n11, 273n8, 273n10, 274, 274n15, 284–85, 351n8, 394n12	16:13–17	166
		16:13–16	169n31, 358
		16:13	27, 43n21, 230n62, 247, 247n5, 287, 294, 341n16, 357, 361
16:3	155n11, 158n18, 273n8, 273n10, 274, 274n15, 284, 285, 351, 368n2	16:14	14n7, 24, 24n15, 54n53, 136n59, 217n9, 248, 287, 288, 289, 290, 292, 294, 294n28, 314, 343, 346n5, 353, 356, 357, 358, 361
16:4	155n11, 158n18, 273n8, 273n10, 274, 274n15, 284, 285		
16:5–7	282, 286		
16:5–6	303n13	16:15	18, 288–89, 291, 292, 357, 404, 404n9
16:5	23, 48, 284, 286, 294		
16:6	108n16, 273n10, 275n15	16:16	14n7, 166n19, 289–90, 292, 353, 356, 357
16:7	23, 54n53, 195n22, 281, 281n1, 284, 294, 326n20, 343	16:17–21	156, 292–94
		16:17	273n8, 273n10, 274, 274n15, 284, 292, 292n22, 302n9, 366n1, 370n10, 371
16:8–9	158n18, 286		
16:8	126n24, 155n11, 273n8, 273n10, 274, 274n15, 277n6, 284, 286, 395, 395n15	16:18	156, 292, 293
		16:19	27, 134n53, 263, 264n4, 264n6, 269n27, 293, 294, 310
16:9	26, 70n52, 79n16, 80n22, 148n37, 237, 282, 286		
		16:20	155n11, 164n8, 294
16:10–11	286–87	16:21	156, 237, 282, 292, 293, 294
16:10	104, 155n11, 273n8, 273n10, 274, 274n15, 284, 286, 366n1		
		17	299
16:11	26, 79n16, 80n22, 170n34, 237, 286, 287n7		

SCRIPTURE INDEX

Revelation (*continued*)

17:1—19:10	4, 6–10, 20, 160n23, 164, 164n9, 182, 285, 293, 293n27, 299, 300, 302, 304, 306, 328, 333n3, 334, 373, 378, 379, 396, 402
17:1–17	299–318
17:1–5	301
17:1–3	7, 216, 216n6, 307
17:1	5n10, 8, 8n21, 8n22, 9, 273n8, 276, 276n2, 276n3, 299, 300, 307, 313, 314, 320, 369, 378n5, 379n8, 379n9, 380n12, 396
17:2	110n24, 165n14, 241n35, 307
17:3–7	307–312
17:3	6, 7, 8, 26, 164, 199n34, 216, 219n18, 237n17, 300, 305n23, 307, 310, 338, 378, 378n6
17:4	219n18, 301, 307, 308–9, 397
17:5	10, 27, 263, 300, 301, 309, 309n6, 310
17:6	25, 51n43, 74, 108n16, 308, 309, 312, 320
17:7	26, 307, 309, 310
17:8–13	312–13
17:8	110n24, 165n14, 167n21, 186n20, 241n35, 309, 312, 380n14
17:9–10	
17:9	26, 135, 164, 164n8, 250n11, 307, 312, 312n17, 313
17:10	313
17:11	313
17:12	307, 313
17:14	25, 67, 290, 291, 313–14
17:15–18	314–15
17:15	24, 109n22, 111, 307n1, 369, 385
17:16–17	315
17:16	277n6, 307, 310n11, 314, 315, 318, 320, 327
17:17	45n26, 314, 340
17:18	264n4, 269n27, 293n27, 300, 305n23, 310, 316
18	167, 328, 363n31
18:1—19:10	319–30
18:1–24	136n56, 320, 321n7
18:1–8	321
18:1–3	321
18:1	96n2, 181n4, 321
18:2	27, 263, 285n6, 301, 310, 321
18:3	321
18:4	20, 301, 302, 305n23, 321, 324, 328, 330
18:5	397
18:6	302, 320
18:7	307n2, 310, 322
18:8	277n6
18:9–19	164, 285n6, 321–
18:9–10	321, 322
18:9	164, 321
18:10	27, 166, 166n18, 263, 264n4, 269, 269n27, 293n27, 310n12, 322, 326
18:11–17	321, 322, 323
18:11	321, 322
18:12–13	323, 323n11
18:12	219n18
18:13	160, 160n23, 321, 351, 396
18:14	351
18:15	321, 322

SCRIPTURE INDEX

18:16	166, 166n18, 219n18, 264n4, 269n27, 293n27, 322, 326	19:7	24, 25, 218n13, 327
18:17–19	321, 322	19:8	108n16, 126n24, 279, 301, 327, 341, 396, 397
18:17	322, 368n2	19:9–10	328
18:18	264n4, 269n27, 293n27, 322	19:9	25, 327, 328, 340, 345, 373, 402
18:19	164, 166, 166n18, 264n4, 269n27, 293n27, 322, 326, 368n2	19:10	10, 10n27, 25, 45n26, 46n30, 51n43, 131n40, 231, 301, 328, 402, 405
18:20	108n16, 302, 325		
18:21—19:10	325	19:11—21:8	4n5, 6, 10–11, 333–73
18:21–24	182, 325	19:11–21	24, 345n1
18:21–23	370n12	19:11–16	11, 65, 124, 124n18, 136, 265n10, 334, 335, 336–44, 355, 364, 373, 403
18:21	27, 182, 182n5, 263, 264n4, 269, 269n27, 293n27, 301, 310, 320, 325n17, 368n2		
18:22–23	162n2, 325	19:11	10, 11, 50, 124, 124n18, 125, 290, 334, 334n5, 335, 336, 337, 373, 373n22, 379n7, 403, 404
18:23	24n12, 27, 287, 312, 347n7		
18:24	108n16, 127, 127n28, 302, 312, 320, 324, 350		
		19:12	65, 125, 126n23, 237, 277n6, 337–38
19:1–6	256n4, 326–27, 384	19:13	338–40
19:1	96n2. 292n22, 326, 326n18	19:14	131n43, 290n20, 340–41, 346n5, 397
19:2	51n43, 52n44, 320, 326, 328, 350	19:15	24, 24n15, 54n53, 66n40, 68–69, 126, 198, 217, 230, 230n62, 264n6, 268n23, 269n24, 336, 339, 340–43, 403n7
19:3	326, 327		
19:4	23, 26, 98n15, 102, 144n20, 211n2, 302, 302n9, 326n19, 366n1		
19:5	51n43, 52n44, 302n9, 366n1, 370n10	19:16	33, 49, 50, 67, 124n18, 309n6, 344
19:6	24, 54n53, 124n16, 256n4, 326, 326n18, 327, 343, 409	19:17–21	11, 334, 335, 345–47, 356, 356n22, 357, 361, 367
19:7–10	402	19:17–20	355
19:7–9	327	19:17–19	136, 335

SCRIPTURE INDEX

Revelation (*continued*)

19:17–18	345–46, 356n22
19:17	10, 11, 136, 292n22, 334n5, 335n7, 345, 356
19:18	51n43, 52n44, 136, 345
19:19–21	346–47
19:19	10, 11, 14n7, 169n31, 290, 290n20, 292, 334n5, 335, 335n7, 345, 346, 346n4, 346n5, 353, 356, 356n21, 357, 358, 361, 404
19:20–21	136n56, 391n7
19:20	11, 27, 104, 217n9, 247n5, 258n11, 277n6, 288, 335, 346, 347, 347n7, 347n8, 351n8, 357, 394n12
19:21	68–69, 126, 230n62, 336, 341, 347, 352n9, 356n22, 403n7
20–22	391n8
20:1–10	11, 159n19, 289n14, 290, 292, 334, 335, 348–65, 367
20:1–5	169n31
20:1–3	224n52, 348, 349, 355, 359, 360, 362, 363
20:1	10, 11, 167n21, 334n5, 335n7, 348, 349, 361, 361n28, 363, 369n4
20:2–3	43, 349
20:2	27, 43n21, 349, 359, 362, 369n7, 369n8
20:3	27, 96n2, 167n21, 224n51, 347n7, 348, 349, 353, 359, 359n26, 363, 364, 365
20:4–6	6n16, 335, 350–53, 348, 350, 350n4, 350n5, 359, 364, 367
20:4	10, 11, 18, 25, 51n43, 74, 126n24, 131n40, 231, 258n11, 309n6, 334n5, 335n7, 340, 350, 351, 359, 365, 366n1, 391n7, 394n12
20:5	29n5, 351, 352, 352n11, 359, 359n26
20:6	18, 25, 112n28, 195n24, 352–53, 395, 404
20:7–10	353–54, 356, 357, 358, 359, 360, 361, 362
20:7	349, 353, 354, 358, 359, 359n26
20:8–10	356n22
20:8–9	349, 356n22
20:8	14n7, 23, 27, 169n31, 224n51, 290, 292, 335, 346n5, 347n7, 349, 353, 354, 356, 358, 361, 364, 368n2
20:9	108n16, 269n26, 277n6, 335, 353, 354
20:10	11, 27, 104, 224n51, 247n5, 277n6, 335, 347, 354, 347n8, 349, 354, 358, 369n8

20:11–15	6n16, 11, 31n9, 136n56, 334, 335, 353, 366–67	21:7	23, 370, 372, 372n21
20:11	10, 11, 302n9, 334n5, 335n7, 366, 366n1	21:8	16n13, 104, 277n6, 347, 352, 372, 372n22
20:12	10, 11, 186n20, 302n9, 334n5, 335n7, 366, 366n1, 367, 391n7	21:9–22:9	4, 5n11, 6–10, 14, 25, 25n20, 90, 104, 144n19, 149, 175, 193n15, 194, 194n18, 194n19, 198, 218n13, 300, 304, 333n3, 334, 335, 335n6, 369, 373, 377–98, 401, 402, 405
20:13–14	130n37		
20:13	368n2, 369		
20:14–15	367		
20:14	11, 277n6, 335, 347, 347n8, 347n9, 352	21:9–10	7, 198, 216, 216n6, 379, 380–81
20:15	11, 16n13, 186n20, 277n6, 347n8	21:9	5n10, 8, 8n21, 8n22, 9, 10, 24, 25, 218n13, 273n8, 276, 276n2, 276n3, 300, 301, 336, 378, 379n8, 379n9, 380, 381, 396, 396n18
21:1–8	334, 335, 368–73, 378, 382, 386		
21:1–2	368–69, 370, 373		
21:1	10, 11, 100n21, 302n9, 334n5, 335, 368n2, 369, 373	21:10–27	380
21:2	23, 24, 24n13, 91, 193, 193n14, 194, 197n29, 198, 218n13, 269, 269n26, 369, 373, 382	21:10	6, 7, 8, 14, 23, 24n13, 91, 164n8, 193, 193n14, 194, 197n29, 216, 269n26, 300, 381, 378, 379, 379n8, 379n9, 380, 381
21:3–4	370, 373, 393n10		
21:3	23, 70n52, 292n22, 301, 302n9, 366n1, 370, 378, 387	21:11	382–83
		21:12–14	383
		21:12	383, 384, 385, 392
		21:13	391
21:4	149, 370	21:14	25, 269n26, 383, 384, 396n18
21:5–8	371–73		
21:5	4n9, 366n1, 371, 371n13, 403	21:15–17	386n33, 391
		21:15–16	385–87
21:6	23, 53, 54, 149, 149n41, 371, 372, 372n19, 407	21:15	194, 269n26, 385, 386
		21:16–17	385
21:7–8	398	21:16	194, 269n26, 383, 386

465

Revelation (*continued*)

21:17	194, 384, 385	22:5	18, 99n17, 112n28, 301, 389, 395, 397
21:18–21	387–88		
21:18–19	377	22:6–21	5, 5n11, 379, 380n10, 401–6n14, 380n10, 396, 401–
21:18	269n26, 382, 387, 388	22:6–9	
21:19–20	387, 388, 388n44	22:6–8	5n11, 403
21:19	193, 269n26, 382, 387	22:6–7	53n46
21:21	269n26, 378, 384, 388	22:6	4n9, 42, 51n43, 52n44, 379n8, 379n9, 401–4
21:22–23	148n38, 149	22:7	5, 18, 46, 46n30, 402n6, 403, 404
21:22	24, 25, 54, 54n53, 336, 343, 388–89, 396n18	22:8–9	402, 405
		22:8	10, 10n27, 44, 301, 403, 405
21:23–25	33		
21:23–24	389	22:9	5n11, 10? 301, 403
21:23	25, 61, 104, 149, 287, 389, 396n18	22:10–16	53n46
21:24	15, 209, 383, 389, 394	22:10	46, 46n30, 405–6
		22:11	406
21:25–27	389	22:12–14	407–8
21:25	383, 383n27, 389	22:12	18, 407
21:26	389, 394	22:13	18, 23, 53, 407
21:27	25, 186n20, 301, 372, 372n22, 389, 393, 396n18, 398	22:14–15	398
		22:14	5, 149, 182n7, 301, 330, 404, 404n9, 407–8
22:1–5	380, 390–95		
22:1–3	394	22:15	269n28, 372, 372n22, 389, 408
22:1–2	377, 388		
22:1	25, 38, 148n38, 149, 149n41, 366n1, 379, 379n8, 379n9, 390–91, 392, 396n18	22:16	25, 47, 51n43, 408–9
		22:17	99, 149, 149n41, 218n13, 372, 372n19, 409
		22:18–19	409–10
22:2	384, 391, 392, 393, 396, 398	22:18	46, 46n30, 409
22:3	18, 25, 51n43, 52n44, 148n38, 149, 301, 366n1, 393–94, 396n18	22:19	24, 46, 46n30, 194, 197n29, 330, 407, 409
		22:20	5, 18, 25, 51n43, 403, 410
22:4	97, 135, 309n6, 387n42, 394–95	22:21	5, 25, 47, 51n43, 410

www.ingramcontent.com/pod-product-compliance
Lightning Source LLC
Chambersburg PA
CBHW050934300426
44108CB00011BA/735